HANDGUNS '97

9th Annual Edition

EDITED BY RAY ORDORICA

DBI BOOKS
a division of Krause Publications, Inc.

TABLE OF CONTENTS

FEATURES

STAFF

EDITOR
Ray Ordorica
SENIOR STAFF EDITOR
Harold A. Murtz
ASSOCIATE EDITOR
Robert S.L. Anderson
PRODUCTION MANAGER
John L. Duoba
EDITORIAL/PRODUCTION ASSOCIATE
Laura M. Mielzynski
ASSISTANT TO THE EDITOR
Lilo Anderson
ELECTRONIC PUBLISHING DIRECTOR
Sheldon L. Factor
ELECTRONIC PUBLISHING MANAGER
Nancy J. Mellem
ELECTRONIC PUBLISHING ASSOCIATE
Larry Levine
GRAPHIC DESIGN
John L. Duoba
Bill Limbaugh
MANAGING EDITOR
Pamela J. Johnson
PUBLISHER
Charles T. Hartigan

ABOUT OUR COVERS

For years, the semi-auto handgun has held sway when it comes to ammunition capacity, but these days the revolver is coming into its own and is on nearly equal ground. With some revolvers now holding as many shots as some autos, many shooters are again turning to the ultra-reliable double-action revolver, like the two stainless steel Smith & Wessons on our covers.

Shown at the top is Smith & Wesson's new Model 617, a *ten-shot* 22-caliber wheelgun that matches the magazine capacity of most semi-automatic pistols on the market today. This gun has a 6-inch full-lug barrel for tack-driving accuracy, reduced recoil and steady holding on target. The grip is Hogue's pebble-grained rubber Monogrip with comfortable finger grooves.

A descendant of the legendary K-22, the Model 617 has the smooth double-action mechanism and crisp single-action trigger that sets Smith & Wesson revolvers apart from all the others. It sports a Patridge front sight and fully adjustable rear, and like all medium- and large-frame adjustable-sight revolvers from S&W, it's drilled and tapped for easy installation of your favorite optics.

Also shown is the new Model 686 Magnum Plus 357 Magnum revolver with 6-inch barrel. What sets off this revolver from most other 357s is its *seven-shot* cylinder. This, too, rivals the capacity of many semi-automatic pistols, but it has more power.

The heavy full-lug barrel holds a red ramp front sight, and in back there's a micrometer click-adjustable white-outline blade for quick target acquisition. Should you wish to mount optics, the gun is drilled and tapped to make the job easier. The excellent Hogue premium synthetic grips round out this powerful package to make it more comfortable to shoot effectively.

Smith & Wesson is a leader in this technologically complex firearms industry, and with finely developed revolvers like these they will remain one of the benchmark names in the world of quality firearms long preferred by professionals.

Photo by John Hanusin.

HANDGUNS 97

Handgun Trends

Knox previews election year, page 8.

The latest one-hand guns, page 11.

Making your new gun your own, page 16.

INDUSTRY NEWS

by RAY ORDORICA

WE CONTINUE IN HANDGUNS '97 to attempt to give you the latest and best information available in the world of handguns. By the time you read this, you will already have seen favorable press on firearms during the Summer Olympics, and in this book Gary Anderson, director of all Olympic shooting, tells us about the handguns used at Atlanta. Unfortunately, we must report the general state of the firearms industry as of mid-July 1996 is that not many folks are buying guns.

The industry is still feeling the effects of the panic buying that followed the passage of the Brady Law and the ban on firearms that utilize magazines holding more than ten shots. Apparently everyone bought all the guns they thought they'd need, and, with the coming of the Republican congress two years ago, panic diminished and demand dried up. Manufacturers had been making guns hand over fist and didn't stop quickly enough when demand dropped off, a fact that is currently causing most of them heartaches in the form of layoffs and excess inventories.

Add to that the relaxing of trade barriers with other countries and the resultant good prices and some outstanding bargains on imported new and used guns, and the picture gets a bit darker.

This problem has hit overseas companies as well, with major movers such as FN suffering severely. My man in England, Jan Stevenson, tells us ("European Scene") that things are really dismal on the Continent, with several gunmakers having gone under and more to follow.

Some U.S. gunmakers have attempted to win back their share of the market through the introduction of revolvers that hold more than the usual six shots. Smith & Wesson brought out a seven-shooter 357 and a ten-shot K22, and Taurus now has a new eight-shot 357. Novices are best served with revolvers, but they weren't happy giving up all that "firepower" to the autos. With a ten-shot limit on magazines, the differences between the types is now diminished.

It may be hard for some folks to make a decision on what handgun to buy because there are almost too many choices. You can get essentially anything you want in firearms today, including things no one dreamed there'd ever be any demand for, like Le Mats and Schofields (from two makers, no less), any configuration or caliber of Colt SAA or 1911 clone including a great variety that bear the Colt name. More new guns or new configurations are being offered every month. Take the H&K USP, for example. There are three calibers with nine variants, and two color combinations. That's fifty-four versions of one handgun. With so many options, buyers are undoubtedly confused, hence their unwillingness to make a choice.

Formerly rare imports like the Makarovs, inexpensive Lugers and broomhandle Mausers and hosts of others are selling for bargain prices, so there's more choices, and some stunning bargains. The Chinese Norinco copy of the Colt 1911 sold for as little as $240 during 1996, and they are pretty

good firearms. Compare that to the suggested selling price of a genuine Colt Government Model at over $700 and you see why it's hard for gunmakers to stay in business. Early this year prices for new stainless Rugers were under $250, off $150 from normal retail, and Beretta 92s were selling for about $100 under dealer cost. The big winner right now is you, the gun-buying public, but we don't know how long that'll last.

The industry has already realigned itself to the biggest current need: concealable powerful handguns. This "need" exists because of the national push for concealed carry, which has spawned a desire that undoubtedly is larger than the numbers of recently issued licenses would indicate.

The new small guns are generally in powerful calibers, because if you can only carry ten shots, they might as well be big 'uns. Typifying the current trend is the new Glock G27. Nearly as small as a Chiefs Special, the Glock holds double the number of rounds. The Glock, in spite of its plastic construction, sells for more than the all-steel Smith Centennial, with its state-of-the-art CNC machining. Which do you think has the higher profit margin? Why do you think S&W is coming out with plastic pistols?

I'd say that if you want a good all-steel pistol made much as they were a century ago, buy it now. The makers won't be making them at affordable prices for long, despite investment casting and CNC machining.

On a happy note, Ruger is selling a lot of firearms. Latest figures indicate

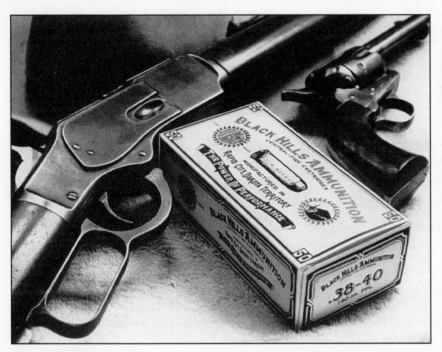

New from Black Hills is their Old-West-packaged 38-40 load, designed for modern cowboys. Editor's 1884-vintage '73 Winchester and 1901 SA Colt both like this new fodder. The Stetson is an original, too.

Hot Nine

The brand-new **9x23** is from the combined efforts of **Colt** and **Winchester.** Winchester makes the 125-grain ammo and Colt chambers their Government Model for it. Performance is akin to that of similar-weight bullets from a 357 Magnum revolver, only now you have ten shots available. The 9x23 autos need a redesigned magazine and receiver, as well as a new barrel. Claimed velocity is 1450 fps with a 125-grain bullet.

Super New 40

Peter Pi's new **400 Cor-Bon** is basically the 45 ACP necked down to hold 40-caliber bullets, and they are loaded to very high velocity. Current ballistics are: 135-grain at 1450 fps, 155 at 1330, and 165 at 1200 fps. To convert your 45 Auto to handle the 400 Cor-Bon, all you need is a new barrel. Barrels are currently available from **BarSto, Jarvis, Olympic, Auto-Ordnance, Les Baer,** and **AccuMatch.** Starline makes the brass and almost everybody makes suitable bullets. The cartridge is now under consideration by Glock, SIG, Colt, S&W, and one or two others. ●

that Ruger's first-quarter earnings are up from a year ago, which was a boom year for the market. In spite of all the industry sluggishness, Sturm, Ruger stock climbed steadily higher throughout the first half of 1996, so at least one company is continuing to do well.

Some items of interest came to us too late for in-depth evaluation, but we didn't want to wait a year to tell you about them. Here are a few of them.

38-40 Loads

The ammo makers are catering to Cowboy Action Shooting by offering loaded rounds particularly suited to the low-velocity, cast-bullet demands of the game. **Black Hills** is now loading 38-40 ammo, the first maker other than Winchester to offer that round since the mid-1930s. The 38-40 was first offered for the 1873 Winchester lever-action rifle in 1884, and Colt chambered their SAA for it immediately. It was popular then, and more so now for Cowboy Action Shooters who like its somewhat reduced recoil over the 44-40. The new Black Hills loads are boxed in period packaging (see photo), with the indication it comes from "Dakota Territory." **Starline** makes the brass for

the new loads, and it's also available from that company as a component.

Cowboys Move East

Bull-X, one of the prominent cast bullet makers who also offer reloaded pistol ammo, sponsored their first Cowboy Action event in June 1996, and it was an unqualified success. The company is based in Illinois, so the new wild West is spreading east nicely. They got good, positive press coverage, too.

Wave of the Future

Smith & Wesson is following the success of their polymer 380 Sigma with the compact **SW9M,** which they claim is the smallest 9mm they've ever offered. Like the 380 it has the simplest controls, with essentially nothing on the outside. It holds seven plus one, and is "affordably priced."

Another new gun we've yet to see is the **CZ100,** a plastic-frame handgun from **Magnum Research,** out of Czechoslovakia. Add to that the as-yet-unseen polymer **P-99 Walther,** and you can see the future of handgunning is clearly with plastic pistols. I dread seeing a polymer-frame single-action Colt clone as much as you do.

GUN LAW REPORT

by NEAL KNOX

WITH DEMOCRAT BILL Clinton in charge of the 1996 White House, pro-gunners holding a strong majority in the House of Representatives since 1994, and the Republican-controlled Senate split down the middle on the gun issue, one word describes the last two years in Congress:

Stalemate.

As frustrating as these two years have been for those of us trying to repeal the bans on military-look semi-autos and new over-ten-shot magazines, it was infinitely preferable to the prior two years, where the combination of the most anti-gun President in history and an anti-gun Congress saddled us with the magazine and ugly-gun bans, the Brady Act, higher fees for Federal Firearms Licenses and numerous other provisions that damaged, dented and destroyed gun rights.

The frustrations of 1994-96 will be fondly remembered if President Clinton is reelected and the anti-gun crowd again takes control of both houses of Congress—which appears quite possible as this review is concluded on the 220th anniversary of U.S. Independence Day.

The President is making guns, "gun control," and the hated National Rifle Association a centerpiece of his 1996 campaign, bringing those issues to a prominence never before seen in U.S. politics. He is still smarting from the defeats of the 1994 election, which he largely blamed on NRA—telling the *Cleveland Plain Dealer* in January 1995 that gunowners caused the Republican Congress.

By equating "gun control" with "crime control," as Mr. Clinton seems to have done with an incredibly high percentage of the public, and making it such a major campaign issue,

if elected he will claim a mandate to enact the most sweeping gun laws the nation has ever seen—never mind the Second Amendment (which his Supreme Court appointments will say doesn't mean anything).

Since the outcome of this fall's election will be such a determining factor, I can only make "What if" guesstimates about the future of the gun-law fight. But before we get into that, let's review the last couple of years.

We've lived long enough under the so-called "assault weapons" ban that we're feeling and seeing its effects:

1) Near-zero impact on military-look guns, which continue to be made and marketed under new names, but without such "evil" features as bayonet lugs or "protruding pistol grips."

2) Lessened availability and higher cost of replacement and backup high-capacity magazines for modern pistols.

3) *More-concealable, higher-powered handguns* built to the specifications of the 1994 gun ban—the very opposite of what the supporters of the law intended.

The ink was barely dry on the 1994 gun ban when its principal sponsor, Sen. Dianne Feinstein (D-Calif.), was sniffling that the gun manufacturers weren't following "the spirit of the law." No madam, they weren't—which was that they should close down their manufacturing plants.

In following the letter of the law, the makers merely got rid of the offending features—like those bayonet lugs which have allowed so many bayonet charges between drug gangs.

Because the primary controlling factor in handgun size is its capacity, the makers have begun producing smaller, lighter, high-powered ten-shot guns that are marvels of efficiency. These guns came along, thanks to Sen. Feinstein and Rep. Charles Schumer (D-N.Y.), just in time to meet the needs of the swarms of newly licensed carriers of concealed firearms. (The progress of those right-to-carry laws is detailed on page 116 of this issue.)

Such unintended consequences are quite common in law, but particularly in firearms law and its promotion, mainly because the advocates make it a point of pride to know nothing about the guns and lawful gunowners whom they regulate.

The gun-banners have the truly astounding faith that if, for instance, they ban small, cheap, low-powered handguns, as they have tried to do for the past third of a century, that the crimes being committed with what they call "Saturday Night Specials" will simply cease to occur.

In fact, as anyone with two brain cells to rub together could have told them, the criminals would simply substitute that which was available for that which was not available. Because most small, cheap guns were banned from importation by the 1968 Gun Control Act, and have been the targets of numerous state laws, police frequently complain that they no longer see "Saturday Night Specials;" now they see high-quality, powerful 9mms and 40s.

Yet once the anti-gun mind gets fixated on something, it never gives up. This past year Sen. Barbara Boxer (D-Calif.) and Rep. Jack Reed (D-R.I.) introduced—and were expected to attempt to force defining votes prior to the 1996 election—what they now call a "junk gun" ban. It would ban domestic manufacture of the undefinable "non-sporting" "Saturday Night Specials" which were prohibited from importation by GCA '68, presumably using the same arbitrary point system.

That point system has never been either law nor regulation; it was cooked up in a series of meetings between importers of high-quality pistols and then-Alcohol, Tobacco and Firearms Division of the IRS. They drew up the point systems—different systems for revolvers and pistols—to allow the importation of guns they had decided to "approve," and to keep out those which they didn't like. It was an *artificially objective* method of "defining" a *totally subjective* list of disapproved guns. This is precisely the same thing that appears to have been done in "defining" so-called "assault weapons," by looking through the pages of *Gun Digest* to see which guns they didn't like.

No U.S. pistol that I can think of has ever had a point-gaining loaded-chamber indicator; and many could not meet the size, weight or trigger-blocking safety requirements of that arbitrary system. If the point system on imports were extended to domestic production, it would prohibit the manufacture of the classic Colt Single Action Army-style cocking system that has been almost continuously made for 150 years.

Applying the point system to U.S. handguns would result in precisely the same kind of handgun redesign that we've seen as a result of the ten-shot magazine limit. It would eliminate the smaller guns, none of which qualify for the term "junk," but it wouldn't have any slight impact on the crime rate.

Prof. James D. Wright, now of Tulane, then of the University of Massachusetts, estimated in his second massive Justice Department-funded study ("Armed and Considered Dangerous," 1985) that if handguns were banned and criminals couldn't obtain them (a far-fetched assumption), *the murder rate would remain unchanged* if just 20 percent substituted more-lethal sawed-off shotguns and rifles. But he found that the homicide rate would actually *increase* because "a majority of the gun(-using) criminals—and more than three-quarters of the predators—said they would respond by carrying sawed-off shoulder weapons," and many of the convicted felons surveyed said they had done so.

While Congress has been limited to vigorous skirmishing, the Supreme Court has agreed to consider the constitutionality of the Brady Act—not on Second Amendment grounds, but Tenth Amendment, which reserves to the people and states, respectively, those powers not specifically delegated to Congress. At issue is whether Congress can require non-federal law enforcement officers to perform criminal records checks. Four of five district courts agreed with NRA-backed complaining sheriffs, then two circuit courts of appeal reached opposite conclusions, causing the Supreme Court to agree to hear the issue.

After years of paying no more attention to the Tenth Amendment than the Second, in 1992 the Supreme Court ruled Congress couldn't demand that states enforce its environmental laws. And in 1995, the Court struck down the "Gun-Free Schools Act," saying it was outside Congress' authority and had nothing to do with interstate commerce (the claimed power for *almost all* federal gun laws).

If even part of the Brady Law is stricken, it may expose the thread that will allow federal gun laws to be unraveled—even if the Court never accepts a Second Amendment case (which they've repeatedly refused to consider for almost sixty years).

Challenging Brady in the courts, and repealing the eleven-shot magazine ban and the prohibition on the military-look rifles that use them, have been NRA's major focuses ever since Congress passed those laws.

In January 1995 I was one of the participants in a meeting between NRA and the five House Republican leaders, including Speaker Newt Gingrich and Majority Leader Dick Armey. The Speaker and GOP leadership agreed to hearings on Waco and Ruby Ridge, and a vote on repealing the gun and magazine ban. The repeal vote was scheduled for May 16, but on April 19, the horrendous bombing at Oklahoma City changed the political climate.

Only the night before that bombing, President Clinton plaintively declared that he was "relevant"—an amazing admission of just how insignificant he and his Administration had become. Oklahoma City changed that, for the President does a masterful job as "chief mourner."

The Oklahoma City bombing also cast a pall over the Congressional investigations into the devastating BATF and FBI abuses of the Randy Weaver family at Ruby Ridge, Idaho, and at the Branch Davidian church near Waco, Texas. Both of those horrors—which disturbed civil libertarians of all political stripes—started out as enforcements of federal gun laws.

Although the press reports of the Waco hearings focused on salacious child sexual abuse charges—which is not within BATF's jurisdiction, or even a federal offense—a considerable record was built up against both BATF and FBI. That may be why, more than a year after the hearing, the investigating committees had refused to issue a report that could only damage federal agencies, and their methods of enforcing federal gun laws. Had such conduct involved enforcement of anything other than gun laws, the press would never have allowed such a whitewash.

Similarly, the law-and-order Republicans in the Senate—this time with the full support of gun-hating Senate Democrats—generally soft-pedaled the Ruby Ridge investigation. But the most telling evidence of official (though never-admitted) wrong-doing was the $3.1 million settlement the Justice Department gave the Randy Weaver family, plus the suspension of six senior FBI officials in an investigation of an official cover-up of Ruby Ridge misbehavior.

The chairman of the subcommittee which investigated Ruby Ridge, Sen. Arlen Specter (R-Pa.), who is anything but an NRA lackey, was so angry with BATF's performance that he called for their abolition. His subcommittee held hearings on BATF's future in early 1996, but no concrete plans or decisions have been made.

Despite the *de facto* $3.1 million apology to the Weaver family, in March the Marshal Service honored the six Deputy U.S. Marshals involved in the killing of 14-year-old Sammy Weaver "for exceptional courage, their sound judgment in the face of attack, and their high degree of professional competence during this incident."

Almost a year after suspension of the six FBI officials, including the former Deputy FBI Director who supervised both the Waco and Ruby Ridge fiascoes, only one had been given a clean bill of health. The other five were still facing possible criminal charges.

While the FBI obviously hopes that nothing will come of these matters, more trouble is boiling for them. A British newspaperman who has probed various issues that the Clinton Administration would sooner keep hidden, and most of the U.S. press has ignored, claims that aerial infrared video tapes made immediately before the Waco fire "clearly show" federal agents firing into the building. Several Congressmen have seen those tapes, as I have; if they are what they appear to be, they will blow the lid off Waco.

In any event, both Waco and Ruby Ridge are far from resolved, and will certainly play a role in future firearms law debates.

Those tragedies were brought up—by both sides—when the magazine and semi-auto repeal vote finally came to a vote in the House March 22, 1996. By then, due to repeated veto promises by President Clinton and Sen. Dianne Feinstein's pledge of "the mother of all filibusters" to block it in the Senate, there was no question that the bill would not become law.

But you would never have known it from the furious, emotional, invective-loaded debate on the House floor. By 239-173 the House endorsed the repeal, with 183 Republicans and 56 Democrats voting to restore the Second Amendment, knowing they would be slandered by the press and their opponents this fall. The winning margin was not much different from the spread that I predicted in last year's issue. But as I also predicted then, it wasn't going anywhere in the Senate, for we didn't have the votes. When then-Majority Leader Bob Dole said the same thing immediately after the House action, he was castigated by some firearms groups—a classic case of shooting the messenger.

Dole has been hammered by the press in the Presidential election campaign because he has called for repealing the semi-auto and magazine ban, which I am confident that he would sign if he were President. But he may not get the chance, judging from Bill Clinton's early lead.

As I said earlier, the outcome of that election will determine what we'll be facing next year. If Clinton is reelected, but pro-gunners—not necessarily just Republicans—maintain control of both houses of Congress, we'll see the same stalemate on gun bills that we've seen for the last two years.

If we lose our margin in the House (and I'm fairly certain we'll lose much of it), the next two years will be dicey, particularly if the new Senate is as divided on guns as is this one. But if Clinton wins heavily while campaigning on an anti-gun platform and is even close to controlling both branches of Congress, we'll see a reverse of the pro-gun sweep in state legislatures in 1994.

And we're going to be in deep trouble in Congress.

In that case, we're going to see the Handgun Control, Inc., agenda moving in Congress like the Johnson Administration's Gun Control Act swept through in 1968.

The HCI dream bill, introduced as H.R.3932/S.1886 on Feb. 29, 1994, has every provision on the anti-gunners' wish list short of a total handgun ban, and in fact would ban many handguns. It would create the total registration system necessary to make an eventual confiscation law work and would require handgun owners to be licensed, after police safety training. Handguns couldn't be privately transferred, and could only be manufactured if they met the same undefined "sporting purposes" required by the Boxer-Reed bill.

Handgun ammo would have a 50-percent tax, and that with armor-piercing or radically expanding bullets would be taxed at 1,000 percent. All handgun ammo with over 1200 foot pounds of energy would be classed as "prohibited weapons," prohibited from manufacture—*including handloading*—and guns like my beloved single-action Colts or those small new Colts, Glocks and SIGs would be transferable by present owners only under the same restrictions as machineguns.

Its most far-reaching provision—that which should wake up even the hunter and Skeet or trap shooter who doesn't get too excited about handgun restrictions—is a requirement for a $300 federal "arsenal license" for anyone who has more than 20 *firearms* and/or more than 1000 rounds of ammo or primers. Local law enforcement would have to give permission for such "arsenals," and *BATF could inspect those homes three times per year* to verify all records and security requirements were being met.

Instead of getting rid of the present ban on magazines holding over ten rounds, HCI's proposal would ban magazines that held over *six* rounds.

There's much more on that huge wish list, but you get the idea. You'll become intimately familiar with its provisions if Clinton's forces make the election sweep they're already tasting.

Never before has a single election represented such a clear fork in the road, with one path leading to significantly fewer restrictions, the other pointing toward the most sweeping gun laws this nation has ever seen. ●

How DO YOU make a handgun? The traditional—and still sensible—way is by forging, where a massive hammer strikes a red-hot billet of steel in a forging die. It's essentially the technique of the blacksmith, automated in modern factories, but retaining the virtues of traditional forging. This method of working steel to build a major part of a gun—receiver, barrel, etc.—tends to realign the molecular structure of the metal to make it stronger. This is not the only way to do it, however.

Bill Ruger brought the lost wax

Compact CZ 75s are growing in popularity; from Magnum Research.

NEW HANDGUNS

by WILEY CLAPP

method of casting gun components into the 20th century and nothing, as the cliche holds, has been the same since. The technology that makes the 20th century so full of wonderful wizardry has come to the gun industry with such innovations as plasma welding, EDM (electronic discharge machining) rifling and MIM'ed (metal injection moulding) small parts. However, across all techniques for gunmaking lies the shadow of the CNC (computer numeric control) mill, the robot that finishes virtually every gun part to dimensions so tight no human machinist could economically compete.

Perhaps even more significant than the robotic mill is the development of moulded polymers of various types, used to make major components of the gun. The point is simply this—we are at a point in the history of firearms production where we can make anything

we want. If there's a demand, there can be a product.

Consumer demand drives the firearms industry, as it does all other industries. At this point, you have to kind of figuratively step back and look at what people seem to be asking for. In other words, what kinds of guns are the most consistently demanded? What are gun buyers using their guns for? And, most important from a business point of view, what are folks willing to pay for them? The answers to these questions make up the competitive framework of an active, progressive handgun industry.

Deviant members of our flawed society still present criminal threat to many citizens every year. Therefore, it's not surprising to see politicians willing to concede what the Second Amendment guaranteed in the first place—the right to go armed. In the practical sense, that means continuing and in-

creasing need for a small carryable handgun. We now have a miniaturization frenzy in place in the case of both revolvers and automatics. Some of the major makers have introduced completely new models; others have found ways to shrink (abbreviate might be a better word) existing guns. The result is a marketplace full of miniature 357 revolvers and watch-pocket, locked-breech 9mm and even 40 S&W autos. Most of them are great little guns. In the case of the autos, I wonder how long we would have had to wait for them if the magazine capacity ban had not been a part of the Brady Bill.

We are also seeing a pronounced interest in nostalgia shooting. The official name is Cowboy Action Shooting, but the fun these men and women are having reminds me an awful lot of the early days of IHMSA. Their costumes and leather receive great attention, but these folks are also crazy for authenticity in the guns. For years, the handgun of choice was a replica of the revered Colt Peacemaker. While a Remington replica occasionally crept in, the SAA had the inside track. Now, there are two different companies bringing in replica S&W Schofields and the Cowboy Action Shooters are snapping them up. I wouldn't be at all surprised to see other frontier-era handguns replicated, including some of the other S&W models. Shooting cowboy-style must surely be popular, because everywhere I went at this year's SHOT Show in Dallas I saw western-style guns. And happily enough, that includes the Colt booth. Other forms of competition, from Bullseye to IPSC and IHMSA, are alive and well, as is the growing practice of handgun hunting.

As much as shooters seem to be looking back, they are also looking forward. Polymer receivers for autos are very much alive and one waggish critic even ventured the opinion that a polymer-receiver pistol is one with a plastic receiver that costs over 200 bucks. That bit of whimsy oversimplifies the situation a little, but polymer is really synonymous with plastic, no matter how you alloy the stuff with glass, nylon or the like. What Glock started, just about everybody now follows, and Colt and Ruger will join Glock, Kel-Tec, S&W, Heckler & Koch, Star and others with new polymer guns in the near future.

Looking to the 21st century, gun design also includes new breech-locking systems and high-tech features like integral lights (good idea) and lasers (bad idea), as well as pistols that are essentially ambidextrous. On the wall of the Walther booth at the SHOT Show there was a poster depicting a new pistol which the German designer was not talking about, but which appeared to epitomize high-tech gun design. We'll have to wait and see on this one.

We have some new automatic pistols to check out this year. Some of them were introduced in 1995, too late to include in HANDGUNS '96, but others are new. There's always plenty of interest in fresh pistol design, but I am surprised at the amount of attention the venerable old wheelgun is getting. You might even regard this trend as the "Revolver Revisited" or some such colorful moniker. Smith & Wesson, for example, is working their way through a major redesign of the revolver line. When the blue and silver team gets done, the S&W revolvers will look pretty much the

same, but they'll be a lot different—and better—on the inside. Further, we are seeing more interest in revolvers that extend the wheelgun performance envelope farther. That includes more power in a small revolver, as well as more capacity in the medium and large ones.

With the foregoing discussion as a background, let's take a look at the range of new handgun products introduced since the last issue of this book. We'll also stop along the way to comment on some classics and the continuing health of some standards. First, let's take the major companies, both domestic producers and major importers. Then we'll move to the smaller outfits and see what they are up to. In alphabetical order that means we start with....

Beretta USA, which is enjoying considerable success with their M9 service pistol (aka Model 92F, in civilian guise) and 8000-series, rotary-barrel Cougar models. The company currently sells lots of guns to law enforcement agencies, as well as to civilians. But one of their bread-and-butter pistols is still the little tip-up barrel Bobcat in 22 LR and 25 ACP, and this year the gun will be available in 32 ACP. This is arguably a somewhat better defensive cartridge, but is by no means an entirely adequate one. Still, the little Tomcat 32 is very small and conceals very easily, both solid selling points.

Another American company that imports large numbers of quality handguns is **Browning.** I am astonished to count up the finish and feature options of the basic Buck Mark 22 pistol—there are seventeen different versions of this gun, four of them new this year. One of the bet-

Browning's new Buckmark Bullseye 22 auto.

The CZ 75/85-type pistol with gracefully updated lines and new features is Magnum Research's Baby Eagle.

A silhouette version of the High Standard 22 for IHMSA shooters.

ter ideas would have to be the Buck Mark Bullseye models, which have a special barrel for top-notch accuracy and a fully click-adjustable rear sight. The classic Hi-Power is still in the catalog in both 9mm and 40 S&W, again in multiple variations. The most unusual pistol in the Browning line is not in the catalog and will not bear a Browning label. It's the FN BDA, a double-action (and optional DAO) version of the Hi-Power which was in the catalog for a few years in the 1980s, but never materialized in the U.S.

I am going to list **Cimarron Arms** here, as they seem to be the major player in the great cowboy-revolver import game. In addition to the replica single-action Remington and Colt revolvers, Cimarron will have a Schofield S&W, chambered for the original 45 S&W (45 Schofield or 45 Short Colt) cartridge. The gun is authentic in every dimension and contour. Their main product will nevertheless continue to be really good-looking copies of the great one, the Peacemaker.

In the old days, Peacemakers were made in a plant in Hartford, Connecticut, and they still are. **Colt's Manufacturing Co.,** through their Custom Shop, makes several variations of the Peacemaker. Many of these guns get varying degrees of embellishment, just as they did in days gone by. Colt still makes most of their money via variations of the Colt Government Model (Gold Cups, Officers ACPs, Commanders, etc.). They will almost certainly have the long-awaited polymer-frame Law Enforcement Pistol out this year.

European American Armory is one of the newer import firms on the handgun scene, but they've snared several outstanding lines: Spanish Astras, Italian Tanfoglios, German Weihrauchs and Italian Benellis. The Tanfoglio guns are still popular with the IPSC crowd and both Tanfoglio and Astra pistols may be had with second-caliber conversion units in some calibers.

If anybody has cut a special and unchallenged niche for themselves, it has to be **Freedom Arms.** Their big single-action stainless steel revolvers come in just a few calibers—22 LR, 22 WMR, 357 Mag., 44 Mag., 454 Casull and 50 AE—but they are extremely well-made guns that are the choice of serious handgun hunters and the IHMSA shooters. I've worked with a couple of them and I believe they're the most accurate wheelguns ever made.

Across the Atlantic in Austria and also in the U.S. headquarters in Georgia, the **Glock** salespeople just smile benignly. Their innovative handguns, less than ten years in the U.S. marketplace, continue to impress civilian and law enforcement handgunners. I was able to attend both the Glock armorer's course and the instructor's workshop last summer and my respect for the gun is greater because of it. Naturally, the hottest Glock pistols right now are the Models 26 and 27 (9mm and 40 S&W), the subcompacts introduced in the middle of last year.

One of Glock's major competitors is **Heckler & Koch,** which got the order for several thousand SOCOM pistols for our Special Operations people. Limited numbers of those guns, called the Mark 23, Mod O, will be available for civilian sale this year. I shot one recently for a story in *HandGunning* magazine and found it to be a solid performer, if somewhat large and heavy. A more practical gun for law enforcement and civilian defense use is the USP, which is now available in stainless steel with black polymer receiver. The compact version of the USP will be available soon.

Yet another import company of great renown is **Interarms** of Alexandria, Virginia. They import three lines of handguns—Spanish Star autos, Brazilian Rossi revolvers and German Walther autos. They also make licensed copies of the smaller Walther autos in America. The magazine capacity ban nudged some of their better autos off the market (Model 31 and Megastar Stars), but the majority of the guns (Firestar, Ultrastar, Firestar Plus) are there. For this year, Interarms is offering a great little Rossi 2-incher called the Model 877, the smallest six-shot 357 snubbie ever made. They also have a ported-barrel version of the adjustable-sighted 977 357 revolver.

H&K developed this pistol for our Special Operations forces. It's the Mark 23 SOCOM 45 ACP. It may be available to civilians soon. Also new from H&K is a compact USP.

The new Baby Eagle FS in 9mm offers a frame-mounted safety and a shorter barrel than the standard Baby Eagle Pistol. The FS is available in standard black (as shown), matte hard chrome or brushed hard chrome.

The Lone Eagle is a switch-barrel single shot from Magnum Research. Lone Eagles are specialty pistols and very accurate ones.

Magnum Research imports automatic pistols from several places in Europe, as well as building some in American plants. Their massive Desert Eagle autos, which fire big revolver cartridges, are now scheduled to be built here, as are the polymer-frame 22s called Mountain Eagles. This company's most generally useful line of guns is, in this writer's opinion, the CZ series from the Czech Republic. I had the opportunity to wring out a CZ85 9mm pistol this year and it's superbly accurate. **Navy Arms** is one of the oldest importers of quality firearms from abroad and their lineup is mostly black-powder stuff. They are still bringing in the magnificent Schofield replicas in two barrel lengths and two calibers, 45 Colt and 44-40.

Para-Ordnance set off a wave of copying with their double-wide 45s several years ago. The designers found a way to take the basic and oh-so-popular 1911 pistol and widen the receiver to accept a double-stack magazine. They're still at it, but the magazine capacity ban isn't helping much with their larger models. Look for a new and smaller 45 from these innovators in 1997.

Sigarms came out with their own proprietary cartridge, the 357 SIG, two years back and it is starting to really take off. This year, you'll see plenty of options, such as their flagship P226 pistol chambered for the 357 SIG, as well as extra barrels to convert existing SIG pistols in 40 S&W to the new caliber. Biggest news from Sigarms is their new sub-compact P239, available in 9mm and 357 SIG.

Smith & Wesson...how on earth do they keep track of all those different models? In their 1996 catalog S&W lists no fewer than ten different new models and a number of special editions. In the revolver line we have new editions of the five-shot J-frame 357s, including Chiefs, Bodyguards and Centennials. The stainless-and-alloy J-frame 38s will now all be built on a frame with the same dimensions as the 357s. One that got our Editor's attention is the 3-inch M60 with adjustable sights, which he tests in this book. He also tests a talked-about gun of several years ago, which is now a reality: the ten-shot K22. I just finished wringing out another new S&W Model, the 686 Plus, which is an L-frame, seven-shot 357 Magnum. It's every bit as much of a performer as the regular L frames. In autos, look for simplified blue steel and alloy versions

Everyday 45—the Ultra Compact from Springfield with Bi-Tone finish.

A couple of nice 1911-pattern shorties from Springfield Armory show the porting system of the ultra-compact V10 45 ACP (top), and the same gun without porting, called the Ultra Compact.

This is Ruger's all-new P95 pistol in 9mm.

of the mini 9mm, 40 S&W and compact 45. The latter gun, called the M457, is a sure bet for big-numbers popularity. It, too, is tested herein, this one by Jerry Burke.

Naturally, the S&W Performance Center has not been idle, and they have several new specials. I think the best of that crop would have to be the Shorty Forty-Five, a compact 45 auto with the accuracy of a match pistol. I doubt if I'll be alone in the belief that a Stocking Dealer special may turn out to be the sleeper of the year for S&W. It's a 4-inch, tapered-barrel Mountain Gun in 45 Colt. Mine cuts tight cloverleafs with the right ammunition.

Springfield Armory continues to be a great choice in M1911-style pistols. They have more variety than anybody in size and options. Their V-10 is

a subcompact carrying gun with hard-to-believe dimensions and modest recoil, thanks to an innovative integral muzzlebrake. At the Illinois plant, the custom shop continues to produce top-of-the-line Carry and Competition pistols.

Sturm, Ruger & Co. is one of the unquestioned giants of the handgun business and they have a couple of new designs to go into that big catalog. One of them is a shorter version of the ageless 22 Auto. Called the Mk-4B, this little 22 has a 4-inch bull barrel and is a natural choice for rambling around in the woods. But Ruger also announced a gun better suited for carrying in urban environments. It's their polymer-frame 9mm pistol called the P95. Made in either DA/SA or DAO versions, the new pistol has pleasing lines, 10+1 capacity

If you look close at the cylinder flutes, you will quickly realize that the new Taurus is an eight-shot. The M608 is in 357 Magnum.

Nostalgia gun for today's handgunners—the slim-barreled S&W Mountain Gun in 45 Colt.

and weighs only 27 ounces. Massad Ayoob wrings it out in these pages.

Thompson/Center concentrated more on their rifles this year, but they still made plenty of those superb Contender single shots and blackpowder guns. Their custom operation also continues to build one-of-a-kind Contenders at very reasonable prices.

No handgun manufacturer ever made as much progress so fast as did the Brazilian giant, **Taurus International.** The lineup for this Miami-based importer includes a full line of autos and revolvers. In both handgun types, you can choose from the smallest 22s to the big 44 and 45 cartridges. For Taurus fans, the best news would have to be the return of the Model 85, the company's snubbie 38 Special. For handgunners everywhere, there's even

more good news in the announcement of a completely new revolver which the Taurus folks refer to as the Ultimate. It's really called the Model 608, a large-frame 357 Magnum with eight precision-drilled chambers in that big cylinder. How's that for one-upmanship?

That winds up a discussion of the bigger names in the trade and their new products for this year. Smaller and often influential firms abound, and one of the more interesting asides to this small-gunmaker business is the unusual situation of Gun Valley—California. Did you know that the combined production of three firms—**Davis, Lorcin,** and **Phoenix**—located in the Chino Valley, make this region the largest handgun producing area in the world? The products are mostly inexpensive small semi-

autos, but they sell in the hundreds of thousands every year. For a shooter on a budget some of these little guns make a lot of sense. So do the guns from the late Harry Sanford's **AMT, Inc.,** which is in Irwindale, California. Most of the familiar designs—Hardballers, Automags, etc.—are still in the catalog, but the best seller is unquestionably the little 45 ACP DAO Back Up gun.

American Arms, out of Kansas City, Missouri, spends a lot of time and effort bringing in a variety of good shotguns, but there's also some fine handguns in their line. Many of their guns are Uberti-made SAA and blackpowder replicas, but there's also a new single action in stainless steel. It's heavily reinforced for the 454 cartridge and has a transfer-bar action. This company also sells the Escort, an ultra-thin (13/16-inch) DAO 380 semi-auto weighing but 19 ounces.

American Derringer Corp. offers a bunch of different stackbarrel two-shooters roughly based on the Remington Double Derringer design, but their best bet is the DA Double series. These are little DAO over/unders in 38 Special up to 40 S&W.

American Frontier Firearms is a new company that has done something truly different. In the early cartridge revolver period just after the Civil War, many gunsmiths altered Colt and Remington revolvers from the caplock style to accept cartridges. This company imports replicas of these conversions from Italy and they are very handsome revolvers indeed.

Auto Ordnance is heir to the Tommy Gun line and even makes a version of the famous gun as a semi-automatic pistol. But they are still long-standing members of the replica M1911 pistol wars. They have a number of variations of the Government Model in several calibers. One of their newest competitors would have to be **Brolin Arms,** a company with a line of 1911-style pistols in a variety of sizes and features. Their little P45C Carry-Comp is particularly ingenious in the way they work a barrel compensator into John Browning's classic design without enlarging the overall gun size.

Century Arms imports a bunch of good stuff from abroad. Sometimes they have small batches of exotics like Finnish Lugers, etc., but they always seem to have plenty of good Makarovs and Nagants.

EMF (Early and Modern Firearms) is another player in the cowboy-gun race. They have replica Colts and Remingtons aplenty, but their Hartford Model Colt is an absolute dead ringer for the original gun. Another kind of appreciation for old-time quality may be seen in the guns of the new **High Standard** **Corp.** This Texas firm makes the famous High Standard 22 pistol in most of the gun's original variations, plus some new ones like the special Silhouette model, intended for knocking down the little critters in IHMSA matches.

H&R 1871, aka **Harrington & Richardson** is an old-time New England gunmaker with a good selection of economy-priced revolvers in their catalog. I

CUSTOMIZING YOUR NEW GUN

ON THE AVERAGE, a new handgun costs several hundred dollars. There are some surprisingly good deals out there in the form of quality handguns of different types for as little as $300 or so. You can spend a lot more on a box-stock handgun, as much as a couple of grand for a top-of-the-line SIG-Hämmerli target pistol, slightly less for a Freedom Arms single action. Both are examples of highest-quality handguns that deliver performance right out of the shipping carton. Performance is, however, a relative term and lots of handgunners have specific non-standard features they'd like to have on their own guns. It might be an improved sighting arrangement for reduced-light shooting or an upgraded accuracy level via a premium barrel. Trigger pull, the shooter's means of rapidly and accurately delivering a shot, gets a lot of attention as does the shape and handling quality of the pistol. Defense, competition, hunting or just plain plinking all have their specific requirements. For this complex of reasons, a big segment of the handgun industry is now oriented toward the custom handgun. It is an explosion, of sorts.

It's amazingly varied, when you get to thinking about it. Screwing an after-market pair of grips onto a favorite gun is customizing of a sort. On the other end of the scale, let's consider a custom 45 pistol King's Gun Works just completed for me. I gave them a Colt Officer's ACP and carte blanche to do their thing. In the fullness of time, they returned a large bag of original parts and a magnificent custom pistol. On this gun, the pistolsmiths in the King shop didn't use much more than the receiver and slide, giving me a complete rebuild of the pistol. Between the two extremes, a lot of money changes hands all across this country for varying degrees of custom work. The world of custom, upgraded, or special-purpose pistols and revolvers has a lot of facets that we need to consider.

Surprisingly, a lot of this stuff happens right at the factory. When the gun companies began to realize the size of the custom market, some of them took positive steps to get a piece of the action. Long years ago, when Colonel Sam was building his company's reputation, **Colt Firearms** had what amounted to a custom shop. Most of the effort went to embellishing with classy engraving and gold inlay, but they often built special guns. In the 1930s, the Colt custom operation was largely a big Irishman named John Henry Fitz-Gerald, who built unusual "Fitz Specials" for special clients. The current Colt Custom Shop does a lot of special-finish guns, but they also build small runs of IPSC and defense pistols, as well as unusual-barrel-length SAAs in different calibers. One-of-a-kind handguns of various types are still available from Colt.

Thompson/Center hit paydirt with the Contender pistol and its switch-barrel design. For a while it seemed like they were getting their cartridge list from *Cartridges of the World*. When the demand stabilized on a couple of dozen chamberings, everything else logical went over to the T/C Custom Shop. That's now in the hands of an associated firm called Fox Ridge Outfitters, right next door. Not only do they make special calibers, but they also offer extra features like positive ejectors and special barrel contours.

European American Armory (EAA) has a special operation to make full-race competition guns for IPSC shooters, as well as more realistic handguns for the Limited matches. It's not widely known, but they will still make up mix-and-match Tanfoglio Witness pistols for defensive use. A similar situation exists with the **Taurus Custom Shop.** Here the effort runs to slick action jobs for defense guns and a special barrel porting arrangement. Pistolsmith Jack Wiegand does precision installation of a form of the Hybrid comp on Taurus pistols and revolvers.

Since its very inception, I have followed the progress of the **Smith & Wesson Performance Center** with enthusiastic interest. It is literally a factory within a factory, making runs of a few hundred S&W pistols and revolvers at a time. Their most famous guns are the fine little Shorty Forty pistol and several revolvers with the unique carry-comp porting system. This year, the Center introduced a compact 45 ACP auto called the Shorty Forty-Five, which is sold through Lew Horton Distributing Co. I'm betting it will earn as many fans as the Shorty Forty already has. In discussing the Performance Center guns, you have to understand that these pistols and revolvers are not modified versions of stock handguns, but rather completely different guns, built from the ground up for enhanced performance.

Many custom pistolsmiths in small shops across the nation stay hard at work building custom handguns.

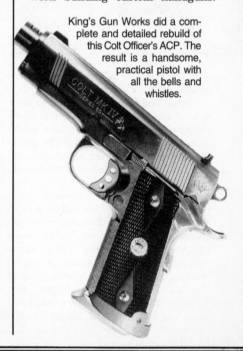

King's Gun Works did a complete and detailed rebuild of this Colt Officer's ACP. The result is a handsome, practical pistol with all the bells and whistles.

did an in-depth piece with one of their classic break-top 999s this year for another publication and found it to be quite an accurate and shootable little gun.

J.O. Arms imports several distinctive handguns from Europe. I reported on the Golan 40 S&W in this book last year and I am looking forward to shooting one of their Kareens, a Hi-Power copy, soon.

KBI has a bunch of interesting imports in their catalog, including 9mm and 45 ACP pistols from Hungary with strong S&W and Browning design influences. They also have new Makarov pistols from Russia.

Look in this year's *Guns Illustrated* for my detailed comparative review of the miniature 9mm pistols from **Kahr Arms** and **Kel-Tec, Inc.** Both are completely original designs. The slightly

---

Much of the time, they begin with a standard handgun and make different modifications to it. Sometimes, however, they approach a custom handgun in the same manner as the race-car builders approach their craft. They buy both major and minor components and assemble them with care. No pistol style is so popular as the M1911 Colt and several firms make basic receivers and slides for the grand old gun. **Caspian Arms Ltd.** is one of the leading suppliers of these parts, as well as barrels and other smaller parts. I am having a special 9x23mm widebody built and the basis is a Caspian receiver.

Other chassis builders are **Strayer-Voight, Para-Ordnance, Les Baer, Springfield, Essex** and probably several others. Most of the folks who build 1911 receivers also build slides. Every gun needs a barrel and there are even more precision machinists at work on this aspect of parts supplying. The Brownells catalog lists barrels from **Nowlin's, King's, Ed Brown, Clark, Briley, EAA, D&J Custom, Storm Lake, Wilson** and **Volquartsen.**

This custom or enhanced performance handgun business has created a number of well-known custom handgun shops. They are really small factories that produce special models in quantity and with plenty of custom options, as well as-one-of-a kind specials for discerning customers. Some of these operations employ multiple pistolsmiths and turn out thousands of handguns annually. Further, some of them make special parts for their own and other's guns. Safeties, sights, 1911 beavertails, hammers, triggers, sears, grips, screws, compensators and many other whoozizes and whatchamacallits all are made in one place or another. Let's take a quick look at some of the better-known of the big shops.

Ed Brown Products is a midwestern operation that is best known for several innovative products for the 1911 pistol. Brown was the first to design a high-sweep beavertail and produce it in quantity. He has branched out into a wide variety of other parts for the Colt, S&W and Browning handguns. Ed Brown was so busy designing and producing parts that he got out of the custom gun building end of the business for a time. Happily, he has now returned to crafting limited numbers of tactical pistols.

Clark Custom Guns probably has seniority in the full custom handgun field. Jim Clark is a past national pistol champion and runs a really large custom operation from his shop in Louisiana. He builds just about everything from custom Ruger 22s for Bullseye shooting to PPC revolvers. Clark made the very first conversions of Colt 38 Supers to 38 Special for the centerfire stage of NRA 2700 matches. He presently offers a wide variety of choices in both revolvers and pistols for many different handgunning needs.

King's Gun Works designs and builds many custom parts for handguns, as well as building up the guns themselves. In a recent trip to Arnold "Al" Capone's shop I handled a completely reconstructed black-powder Colt revolver, a nifty Ruger fixed-sight single-action conversion, a super Hi-Power and about a dozen different Colt 1911s with a variety of different features. This is beautiful work, done with meticulous attention to detail. The latest part from Capone's imagination is a magazine floorplate that fits perfectly into the inner curve of his bolt-on magazine well.

Cylinder & Slide, Inc., is the formal name for Bill Laughridge's gun-part and custom-gun operation in Nebraska. He specializes in package guns with a predetermined range of features on each. C&S can also do the work on your gun and offers a range of parts and features for whatever might tickle your fancy. It's one of the few shops that specialize in Hi-Powers.

Wilson's Gun Shop, Inc. Bill Wilson's motto for the business is "The Choice of Champions," and it's almost an understatement. Most of the great action shooters of recent times either use, have used, or are about to use Wilson race guns. But the company also offers a diverse assortment of other types of pistols and revolvers, suitably customized to your budget and the gun's use. Wilson also designs and manufactures many innovative parts.

The **Robar Companies, Inc.,** is a specialized custom shop in Phoenix run by transplanted South African Robbie Barrkman. This outfit makes a lot of SWAT rifles and shotguns, but they specialize in exotic metal finishes like NP3 and Roguard, both of which are eminently practical in the field. Robar also makes some of the more sensible 1911-pattern autos you'll ever find. He's also building 45 Supers, the ultra-hot 45 wildcat developed by the late Ace Hindman. Gary Sitton tested one for HANDGUNS '97 and you can find his report in the test section of this book.

Gunsite Training Center Custom Shop. People shoot a lot at the nation's premier shooting school and that means on-site pistol-smithing with rapid turnaround time. Ted Yost, one of the great unsung craftsmen in the pistol-smithing field, directs several gunsmiths in a well-equipped shop. In the past few years, the Custom Shop has branched out into one of the better full custom pistolsmithing operations in the country. I have a Yost Signature Series M1911 that is an absolute gem.

Novak's Inc. Wayne Novak designed the fine automatic pistol sight that bears his name and finds its way onto most of the high-quality defense pistols made in the country. Novak-trained craftsmen are utterly pragmatic and build the most reliable pistols you can possibly find. The motto is "real guns for real people," and the firm seldom touches competition handguns for anything but Limited class shooting. Novak is a Hi-Power devotee and builds the best of these I have ever seen. Personally, I would not care to go armed with an automatic pistol that had not been on Novak's bench.

larger and heavier Kahr K9 is an all-steel pistol with striker-fired DAO action and seven-plus-one capacity. Kel-Tec's P11 is a double-column hammer-and-firing pin DAO with ten-plus-one capacity. The Kahr gun is more expensive, but it's of very high quality and is on its way to cult-favorite status. I was deeply impressed with the gun's performance in every way. Legendary shooter Chip McCormick collaborated with **Kimber of America** in the design of a high-quality pistol of the M1911 pattern. The result is a real gem of a gun, built to the highest standards of quality and with virtually every part designed to optimize its functional reliability and shooter-friendliness. The slide and receiver are milled forgings.

Les Baer Custom builds 1911-style pistols by starting out with a raw forging for slide and frame. He then mills them to shape in his own shop and finishes them up with small parts of his own design and production. There are a number of custom shops around the country that can build you as good a 45 as Baer makes, but they usually want at least a grand more to do it. New from Baer this year are a Commander-sized 22 LR and a six-inch long-slide 45.

Mitchell Arms has a widely diversified line of pistols, including accurate 22s of the High Standard design, Gold series 45s in several Government Model types, the Guardian Angel derringer, and a Jeff Cooper-approved 45 pistol.

Fort Worth Firearms has a series of stainless, custom-finished 22 LR autos built on lines similar to the High Standard target pistols, but with some significant additions. These include ears on the rear of the slide to ease cocking with a scope mounted; full-length scope-attach rails; and custom trigger pulls to write home about. These guns are targeted toward those who would shoot the Team Challenge events. In the test section of these pages, Don Fisher wrings out one that is fitted with the hot new Bushnell HOLOsight.

Really unique guns? Take a look at the line of mini (better make that mini-mini) revolvers from **North American Arms.** Tiny little five-shooters in 22 Long Rifle and 22 WMR, these guns have no rivals. They showed me a caplock blackpowder gun this year.

The unique gun of the show came from **Phillips & Rodgers.** It's called the Medusa, after the mythological lady with the reptilian hairdo. The revolver is a six-shot DA/SA type with swing-out

Kahr K9s are now available with a teflon/nickel finish.

This is the Kareen in compact form, from J.O. Arms.

(Below) The Medusa Model 47 from Phillips & Rodgers is the world's only patented multi-caliber revolver. Its patented extractor allows it to chamber, fire and extract many different cartridges in the 9mm to 357 Magnum range, with no half-moon clips, extra cylinders, barrels or any other adjusting devices needed.

Multi-Cal cylinders from Phillips & Rodgers allow gun enthusiasts to chamber, fire and extract over twenty-five cartridges from the same cylinder in their own handguns. Retro-fit cylinders are currently available for New Model Ruger Blackhawks and the Smith & Wesson.

cylinder. By dint of an unusual segmented extractor and carefully shaped chambers, the gun will accept and fire something like twenty-five different cartridges, running from 380 Auto to 357 Magnum. The company also has a replacement cylinder for Ruger single actions and S&W L-Frames that does the same thing. How's that for different? To find out how well they work, see Finn Aagaard's writeup in the test section of this book.

Another gunmaker producing Colt SAA clones is **United States Patent Fire Arms Mfg. Co.,** and they are actually located in the old Colt digs in Hartford, Connecticut. They custom-assemble and finish parts made by Uberti in Italy, and do the job extremely well. They offer many options, including different grades of engraving and genuine ivory grips. Sheriff Jim Wilson tests three versions in his report elsewhere in this book. ●

Handgun Tests

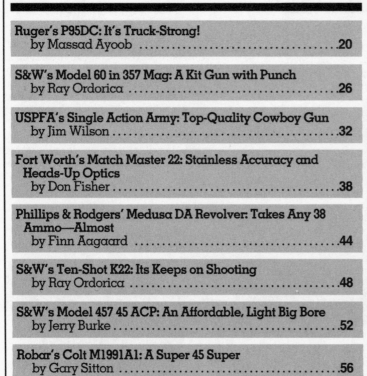

Ayoob gives it a tough workout, page 20.

A top-notch gun and new sight, page 38.

Burke breaks in this bad boy, page 52.

HANDLING RUGER'S NEW P95 auto at the 1996 SHOT Show in Dallas, my mind flashed back to a couple of different conversations with Bill Ruger, Sr. One had been well over a decade earlier, when he'd sworn me to secrecy and shown me the drawings and early frame castings of his proposed centerfire 9mm autoloader. He wanted it to be to defensive handguns what his classic 22 Standard had been to sporting pistols. "A 9mm for Everyman" was the phrase he used, a gun that a work-

RUGER's

P95DC
It's Truck-Strong!

by MASSAD AYOOB

ing stiff could afford to buy to defend his family that would have all the "wondernine" features of pricier hardware.

The second conversation, like the first, took place in Bill's office at the Newport, New Hampshire plant, but several years later. We were looking at plastic castings of Ruger auto frames. Two of them were cracked after extensive torture testing. "Haven't got the damn polymer composition right yet," Bill growled in the voice that tells people who know him that he has accepted a challenge. "But we will. We will."

Now, turning a P95 over in my hands, it occurred to me that he had fulfilled both promises.

P95 Heritage

That original "9mm for Everyman" turned out to be the P85, a designation that bore its year of official introduction despite the fact that they didn't really hit the commercial market until around '87. The first of these guns were flawed in several ways. They felt blocky in the hand, their vestigial safety/decock levers were awkward to reach, and they shot horrible groups. Worse, some examples would experience feed stoppages.

Ruger P95	
Action:	DA Semi-auto (optional DAO)
Caliber:	9mm
Others:	N/A
Finish:	Stainless/black polymer; or black/black
Barrel:	3.75″
Capacity:	10 + 1
Sights:	Fixed
Weight:	29.4 oz. empty
Height:	5.25″ overall (with mag)
Length:	6.88″ overall
Width:	1.4″ overall
Price:	$351

The latest from Ruger is their 9mm polymer-frame P95, which author Ayoob calls an affordable 9mm for Everyman. It's available in two variants and two color combinations.

A jam-amatic Ruger had never happened before. Bill froze production until the necessary changes could be made, knowingly sacrificing millions of dollars in guaranteed sales to save a hard-won reputation for a brand name that meant rugged reliability. Soon the P85 Mark II was on the market, to be superseded by the P-89 of today. Ergonomics were vastly improved, reliability was back up to the usual Ruger standard, and the gun now grouped as well as most of the other big-name 9mm service autos.

The P90 came next, its barrel design comparable to a BarSto in its exquisite accuracy. This 45 ACP remains the most accurate of the Ruger centerfire autos and one of the most accurate available from any maker, consistently delivering 1- to 1.5-inch groups from a rest at 25 yards. Utterly reliable, it is probably the best value in a 45 auto today.

The P91 came along next, in caliber 40 S&W, but the next real milestone was the P93 compact 9mm. Perform a word association test with a Ruger aficionado; if you say "P93" he'll probably answer, "Ergonomics." Grooves went up and over the rounded edges of the no-longer-boxy slide. The grip fit your hand instead of your hand having to fit

it. The improved accuracy of the 9mm P89 remained intact.

The grip size was identical on the P94 9mm introduced a year later, though this gun was "service length" with a barrel 4 1/8 inches in length to the P93's 3 3/4 inches. The P93 had been made without manual safety, in either a DC (decocker only, double-action first shot) or DAO (double action only with a long trigger stroke for every shot) format. Neither gun, of course, requires a manual safety catch to be "drop safe." The P94 has those options, plus the standard safety/decock lever mounted on the slide.

The P95 was the next step in the evolution of the 9mm Ruger auto.

Polymer Pistol from Prescott

Bill Ruger does not give up on things he wants. Design geniuses appreciate the genius of their peers, and Ruger admired both the ingenuity of Gaston Glock and the advantages the Austrian manufacturer had perceived in polymer-frame handgun technology. Chief among these, to Ruger, were light weight, and cost reduction that could be passed on to the consumer. It was with this in mind that he began the quest for a plasticene pistol frame that culminated in the P95. Like all other Ruger centerfire autos, the

gun is produced at Ruger's state-of-the-art factory in Prescott, Arizona.

Ruger had found his particular formula of "drastic plastic" at last. It's a Ruger exclusive, so proprietary that the company won't divulge even to stockholders anything more than this: it begins as Dow Chemical's Isoplast, and is then sent to a compounder who adds something proprietary to the formula. The result is an extremely high-tensile-strength polymer that is reinforced with long glass fibers.

This may well be "the mother of all handgun polymers." It is hard yet resilient, and it withstands the spectrum of what the military calls "hostile environments," having been torture tested in temperatures ranging from Arctic cold to literally boiling, 212 degrees Fahrenheit, shooting all the way through without logging any malfunctions or breakages.

Like the P93, it is not available in the classic format in which the slide-mounted lever serves as both a manual safety and a decocker. There are four models available, all priced identically. You can get the P95DC (DA first shot, with the lever functioning as a dedicated decocker only) or a slick-slide P95DAO with no slide-mounted lever at all.

These pistols span a decade of Ruger 9mm auto design (from left): original P85, P94 and P95DC.

You can buy either version with a stainless "upper," giving a nice two-tone contrast to the black polymer frame, or in blue for a businesslike "all-black" look. It's not a catalogful, but it's three more choices than Henry Ford gave your great-grandfather.

This is interesting in that the standard safety/decocker model is not represented in the polymer line, and there is no plan at this time to introduce it, yet that has historically been Ruger's best-selling centerfire autopistol format. It could be that they've extrapolated police sales trends, which have been influenced of late by a KISS ("keep it simple, stupid") philosophy. My spies tell me that for the last two years, Ruger centerfire auto sales have broken down as follows:

Ruger Semiauto Sales

Design Style	% of Sales in All Calibers	
	1994	1995
Classic safety/decock	65.7	56.7
Decock only	31.0	37.1
Double action only	3.2	6.1

Yeah, I know, the figures don't add up to exactly 100.0 percent in either case. Blame it on my spies, OK? Suffice to say that they're close enough to gather trends from, and the trends seem to be the following:

- DAO sales are almost entirely to police because of department policies mandating guns that have a long, heavy trigger stroke for every shot for civil liability reasons. The DAO guns, though available to the public, are a minuscule amount of Ruger sales to that segment of the handgun market.
- Guns with the option of a manual safety still have the lion's share of sales, despite the fact that such popular models as the P93 don't even have that option.
- There is nonetheless a trend toward "draw and fire" pistols that don't have a "remove safety" step in between.

It is worth noting that Ruger has not announced immediate plans to chamber this gun in 40 S&W, though that would be the next logical progression. Ever since the embarrassment of announcing his first 9mm auto in 1985 and not being able to deliver it to his loyal customers until two years later, Bill Ruger has played his cards close to the vest and does not showcase new models until they're perfected and

ready to be shipped. It is also worth noting that with some 1.4 million Ruger centerfire autos manufactured as of April 1996, some 70 percent have been chambered for the 9mm Parabellum cartridge. Since 1988, BATF has listed Sturm, Ruger as the largest volume manufacturer of semiautomatic pistols in the United States.

With the fact in mind that most readers would be opting for the double-action first shot version (single action for followup shots), I requested a P95DC in stainless for my test sample. P95DC # 311-02083, its serial number on a metal strip embedded in the polymer frame on the side opposite the warning to not handle the gun before reading the owner's manual, showed me that I was indeed holding "a handgun of the Nineties."

Getting the Feel of the P95

Until now, the P93 had been the best-feeling Ruger "service automatic" I'd held in my hand. The P95 exceeded it in this regard. Unlike an aluminum alloy frame, the polymer with its big horizontal grooves in the side manages to be smooth without being slippery. Its grip angle is 15 degrees on the frontstrap and 20.5 on the backstrap.

The pistol weighs a feathery 29.37 ounces unloaded. The ten 9mm rounds in its politically correct magazine, and the eleventh in the chamber, don't add much weight. Fortunately, the gun will take the older model P85 and P89 pre-ban magazines, and it was these that I carried in the pistol during the test period. With a load like the Black Hills +P 115-grain hollowpoint, I didn't feel undergunned carrying it, but with sixteen rounds instead of eleven in the gun, I felt a whole lot better about it. (The spare mag at my other hip, however, was the new one. The sharp edges of the old style dug into my side. The new ones have rounded edges on their plastic bottoms and are comfortable to carry, even inside the waistband.)

The gun fits comfortably in the hand. To me, I think, the big enhancement of the P95 over the P93 in terms of feel is the "warmth" of the polymer gripframe in the hand and tight against the body in the holster. (My primary carry leather was an LFI Concealment Rig by

P90 45, top, is not so ergonomic or streamlined as the newer P95 9mm, below, but remains the most accurate of Ruger service pistols.

Unlike other P-series Rugers, the slide stop comes completely out of the frame during routine field stripping.

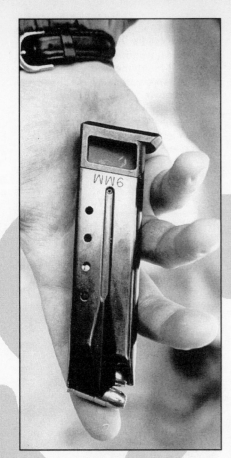

Two ten-round magazines like this one come with the gun. Full-time law enforcement officers are eligible for fifteen-round magazines under Clinton law.

Dedicated decocking lever on P95DC is slide mounted and easily manipulated.

Ted Blocker, worn inside the waistband.) By warm feel, I mean it's like Micarta on a knife handle or pistol grip...it's a pleasant, subjective feel common to all polymer-frame handguns, a user-friendly feature that most reviewers haven't picked up on, which comes with this breed of sidearm.

With the frame so feathery light, the barrel and slide mass give a pleasing forward weight that results in an excellent balance in the hand, enhancing the natural pointability of the well-thought-out grip angle. It's comfortable to carry, and comfortable to grasp.

The P95 is easy to take down: you follow the usual Ruger formula, with the exception that instead of Bill's trademark captive slide stop that stays in the frame, this one comes out of the gun during disassembly à la the Colt, Browning, or S&W duty auto. This is part and parcel of the single major design change that differentiates the P95 from the other defensively-oriented Ruger semiautomatics that came before it.

The earlier designs could be characterized as "recoil operated, tilting barrel, link actuated" pistols, explains Ruger executive Bob Stutler, but the P95 meets only the first two of those three design paradigms. Instead of being link actuated, the P95 is cam-lock actuated. The cam-lock system simply takes better advantage of the natural resilience and shock absorption of the polymer frame.

Ten days of all-day, every-day carry proved to me that the P95 had but one sharp edge that could cause a comfort problem: it was located on the forward edge of the ambidextrous decocking lever. This is one of the few things an amateur like me can fix with a Dremel Moto-Tool without screwing up a perfectly good handgun, but I'd like to see it corrected at the factory.

What I did see in the human engineering side of this gun were several small, subtle points that were disproportionately advantageous to the user Bill Ruger had in mind: the armed citizen, cop, or security professional who

might one day have to defend his or her life with this product. Consider:

1. The backstrap is smooth, flowing into horizontal grooves that go downward as the pistol is carried in the holster. Purists look at this and wonder, "Why not checkering, or at least, a grenade grip like on a plastic police baton?"

I discovered the answer working at speed. The unique grip design glided my hand immediately into a proper drawing grasp when working with the gun tight against my torso in an inside-the-waistband holster. It allowed me to outdraw three seasoned shooters at the same skill level as me, two of them drawing from theoretically faster speed scabbards. Two had custom Colt Government Models, the third, a Beretta 9mm.

2. The smoothly tapered slide may very slightly enhance drawing speed, though it more noticeably enhances a clean one-handed reholstering of the gun by feel, which is one of the marks of the true handgun professional.

3. The P95 has an ambidextrous magazine release, which operates with pressure on a slight forward-and-inward angle that is different from what you get used to with other autoloaders, but which is quickly learned. This allows the shooter to use the tip of the trigger finger to press in on the strong side, instead of having to slow down during a speed reload to shift the gun in the hand so the thumb can get a proper release angle on the opposite side. For short-fingered folks, this is a blessing. Unlike some other ambidextrous mag release concepts, this one won't unintentionally release the magazine when you and your holstered pistol bump into something at that point. I couldn't make that happen even when I tried.

Magazine changes were lightning fast, not something you can say about all polymer-frame handguns. The empty mags all dropped cleanly and instantly when they were supposed to, and never dropped when they weren't.

Shooting the P95

The bad news is, the P95 doesn't have the exquisite match-grade accura-

cy of the 45-caliber Ruger P90. The good news is, neither does any other out-of-the-box service automatic you can buy until you hit close to twice the P95's price, though S&W's new Model 457 comes awfully close.

High-quality, low-cost ammo seemed logical fodder for a high-quality, low-cost pistol; I shot Black Hills brand almost exclusively through the test gun. Shooting from the 25-yard bench for accuracy at the Wolf Indoor Range in Manchester, New Hampshire, I used what has become my standard protocol. The first round from an auto, chambered by hand, is likely to go to a different point of impact than subsequent shots. This is because the pistol's own mechanism cycles itself into a subtly different battery, or alignment of the parts. Therefore, I blow away the first shot and fire four more seriously, then factor out the worst and measure the best three to allow for human error. This generally comes remarkably close to a machine-rest five-shot group at the same distance and is much quicker and more convenient, a short-form accuracy test if you will.

I began with the load I carried for personal protection in this gun during the test period, Black Hills' 115-grain +P jacketed hollowpoint at a nominal

1250 fps. It put its best three shots (which I consider to be representative of mechanical accuracy potential) into a very good group measuring 1³/₈ inches. The human error shot blew the group size out to 3¹/₄ inches. Gelatin tests aside, the autopsy and after-action reports I see indicate that this weight JHP bullet running at this speed or better is the most dynamic "stopper" avail-

The sights proved easy to see. Though not a slim pistol, as photo illustrates, the P95 sits comfortably in the hand.

P95 is placed under the tire of a Jeep Grand Cherokee weighing 5500 pounds. Note tape on muzzle to keep dirt out of the barrel.

The Jeep rolls forward...and the Ruger disappears under its tire...

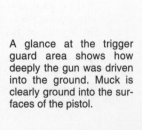

...to be pressed flat into the ground.

A glance at the trigger guard area shows how deeply the gun was driven into the ground. Muck is clearly ground into the surfaces of the pistol.

able in conventional ammo for this caliber.

A standard-velocity (a little over 1100 fps) Black Hills 124-grain JHP gave me a "best three" group of 2⅝ inches, with the human error shot extending the group to 4¼.

Finally, Black Hills' inexpensive "blue box" remanufactured 115-grain ball gave a mediocre 5-inch group. However, most 9mm pistols don't do their best with ball ammo. It's just not an inherently match-grade round. That said, a helluva lot of my students shoot 300 out of 300-point 100 percent qualifications with Black Hills 9mm ball. Personally, I shot a 299 with it on the tough IPSC target at an LFI-I course hosted by attorney Tim Noe in North Carolina, and the one hit dropped into the "4" ring was entirely my fault, not the gun's; I simply lost focus on the first double-action shot from the Weaver stance at 15 yards.

In summary, accuracy was average with two types of ammo and better-than-average with another. Hey, you can't get great human engineering and a National Match-grade pistol for 350 bucks, OK?

The test gun shot low with its fixed, three-white-dot sights. Recoil was extremely mild despite the light weight; I suspect that, as with the Glock pistol, subtle flexion in the polymer frame is absorbing some of the kick. One person suffering acute arthritis in the hand fired this P95, and experienced no recoil discomfort even with the hot Black Hills +P.

The double-action first-shot stroke is good to very good, but not great as it is in the metal-framed P-90, and some "stack" or increasing pressure is palpable just before you complete the trigger pull. On the other hand, the approximately 5.5-pound subsequent single-action releases are consistent and crisp, making for good shooting at high speed without undue civil liability problems of the "hair trigger" kind. Shooting at high speed, the double-action shots went into an only slightly larger group than those fired single action.

The factory reportedly ran these guns through 20,000-round torture tests with +P+ ammo, that is generally around 37,000 CUP pressure levels instead of the usual domestic standard of about 31,000. There were no malfunctions. A colleague I respect who writes for one of the monthly gun magazines and has won many pistol matches, Layne Simpson, put 1200 assorted 9mm rounds through his P95DC stainless with no malfunctions, either. I put some 700 through mine, and same story: no malfs, no breakages.

After driving over the gun, Ayoob then chambered a round, and the pistol fired its entire ten rounds without a hitch and put every round into a 2-inch group in 7-yard rapid fire.

Ruger P95 Test Results

Cartridge	—Bullet— Wgt. Grs.	Type	MV (fps)	Group (ins.)	Comments
Black Hills	115	JHP	1250	1.4	Plus P
Black Hills	124	JHP	1100	2.6	
Black Hills	115	Reload	1050	5.0	
Remington	147	HP	1000	2.5	Subsonic load
Winchester	115	Ball	1150	2.0	
Federal	115	JHP	1250	1.4	Consistent

Jeep Tough

Is this pistol indestructible? Could be. I deliberately laid it on the thawing frozen ground of the Pioneer Sportsman outdoor range in Dunbarton, New Hampshire, and had my assistant Mike Rippett run over it with a Jeep Grand Cherokee. I then picked it up, chambered a round, and emptied a ten-shot magazine rapid fire into a target seven yards away. All ten Black Hills +P rounds hit where aimed in about a 2-inch group, without a stutter. Disassembly showed no breakage. Gross vehicle weight of the Cherokee is 5500 pounds.

Bottom Line

I saved the best for last. Price on this handgun is an incredibly low $351 suggested retail! One hundred percent reliability, light weight, great human engineering, average accuracy for guns of its kind, and it comes up shooting after you run over it with a truck. What the hell more could you ask for at this price!

The P95 actually fulfills three promises from Bill Ruger. An affordable 9mm for Everyman...a super-tough polymer Ruger auto...and the continuation of the tradition of extraordinary firearms value for the dollar that the Ruger name has come to exemplify. ●

Handguns for the trail or woods ought to be small yet powerful, in my estimation, if they are to serve their function properly. A handgun ought to be unnoticed while it is being packed, yet be able to provide the needed punch for whatever task it might have to perform when you grab it. The nature of that task might range from small game hunting to self-defense, or from plinking to bear-stopping. While most of us will have precious little need to stop a bear with a handgun in our lifetimes, those

other tasks just mentioned might someday become the order of our day. When that happens, I know of very few handguns more suited for the trail than the new 357 Magnum Smith & Wesson Model 60 with 3-inch barrel.

This lovely little gat comes with fully underlugged barrel and fully adjustable, clearly visible sights, one of the necessities for any serious handgun designed to utilize a variety of loads. It is of stainless steel, and is equipped with Uncle Mike's Combat finger-grooved rubber wraparound stocks that give a good grip to damp hands, and help cushion recoil in the bargain.

The gun is made by Smith's new computer-controlled machining processes, and is as precise a piece of goods as was the Model 640 Centennial 357 Magnum I tested on these pages last year. Like 'em or not, the new Smiths take a back seat to no one when it comes to finely machined and finished handguns—notwithstanding a little problem that cropped up with this one.

After I had wrung out the Centennial last year, I told Ken Jorgensen, PR man for Smith & Wesson, that I suspected they would soon come out with the M60 in 357 with a 3-inch barrel, and he admitted that I was right. I asked for

S&W's
MODEL 60 IN 357 MAG
A Kit Gun with Punch

by RAY ORDORICA

Smith & Wesson Model 60

Action:	DA revolver
Caliber:	357 Magnum
Others:	N/A
Finish:	Stainless
Barrel:	3.0″
Capacity:	5 shots
Sights:	Adjustable
Weight:	24.5 oz. empty
Height:	4.75″ overall
Length:	7.75″ overall
Width:	1.3″ overall
Price:	$466

Smith & Wesson's latest 357 Magnum is the 3-inch M60 with full-length underlug, adjustable sights, and Uncle Mike's Combat grips. Black sights make for a good sight picture, and the new shape on the cylinder latch keeps it off the thumb in recoil.

one of the first copies off the production line, and Ken delivered.

First Impressions

The gun weighs 24.5 ounces and comes in a lockable blue plastic container which is also a handy carrying case. The gun's finish is semi-matte stainless, and one of the first things I noticed is the new shape of the cylinder latch, now common to all S&W revolvers. This is triangular in shape, and has more of its material above its centerline than previously. This gives more room for the thumb in recoil, and makes it unnecessary to grind off the bottom half, as many of us did in times past.

I'm not sure why they went to the shape they did, and I'm just as unsure that I like it. However, I found that this latch does not hit my thumb in recoil; and yes, it immediately identifies the gun as having been made in 1996 or later, and that will help historians or students of the marque in times to come. We conservatives simply must have a gripe or two.

The 3-inch barrel features a full underlug, which protects the ejector rod from dings and bumps that can bend it. This lug also adds much-needed weight to what amounts to a very powerful but light handgun. The ejector rod is longer than what you're used to on J-frame Smiths, and does a fine job of ejecting spent cases.

The single-action trigger pull of this gun is astonishingly good. I was extremely eager to shoot the gun when I found it had that target-grade SA pull. The double-action pull was very good, and the smooth front of the trigger made it better, but there was a problem. I was occasionally able to tie up the gun while cycling it double action. Something internal was not quite coming back to where it ought to, and it was intermittent. I suspected the problem would disappear with use, but I wanted to know more about the problem before I went any further. Accordingly, I delayed my shooting tests until I could look inside. Oiling the gun from the outside didn't help, so it was time to pop off the sideplate.

The first thing I noticed was the completely redesigned hammer. It appears to be a very precise investment casting, with lots of air space in its design to make it lighter and, therefore, faster falling, which will cut lock time and theoretically aid accuracy. The firing pin is no longer the dangling bit on the front of the hammer that Smith fans have come to expect, but is captured in the frame. The rest of the internals looked very familiar.

Concerning the cylinder locking problem, I found that something was preventing the trigger arm (called the hook) from going fully into the bolt recess as the trigger went forward, after having fired the gun. Therefore, when I attempted to pull the trigger again in double action, the bolt was not being retracted to free the cylinder. If the cylinder can't turn, the trigger can't move. I oiled the two parts directly, and while this helped, it didn't cure the problem completely, as I later discovered.

Ammo Choices

With the problem alleviated, I collected an assortment of loads from Black Hills, Federal, Winchester, Cor-Bon and CCI. I had asked for relatively heavy bullets, knowing that short-barrel 357s put out some bad muzzle blast, and heavy bullets cut that down. However, I knew many of my readers would be unhappy if I didn't tell them how well the hottest 125-grain loads performed, so I asked for them as well.

From Winchester I got some 145-grain Silvertips and some of their 125-grain 38 Special Plus P Silvertip loads. Speer/CCI

The perfect gun for the trail, the 3-inch S&W M60 in 357 Mag. fits easily into author Ordorica's Samsonite daypack, but he thinks it is a bit much for novices. The stainless finish does nicely in the out-of-doors.

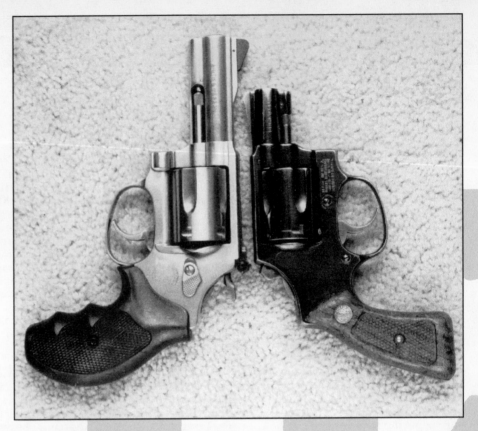

The full-power 357 Mag. M60 is only a bit bigger than this older square-butt M36 with bobbed hammer. The frame of the M60 is slightly longer, and also a bit deeper behind the cylinder. Internals are a bit different; the new gun is very well machined.

S&W

sent me some of their fine 125- and 158-grain Gold Dot JHPs. Federal sent along some 125-grain Hi-Shok loads and some of the latest version of their Premium 158-grain Hydra-Shoks. Federal also sent along some light practice loads in the form of their fine Gold Medal Match 148-grain 38 Special wadcutters. I have found that target loads work well in these small revolvers, and serve many useful purposes. I had some Cor-Bon 125-grainers on hand. Finally, Black Hills sent some ammo that I thought would be just about the most practical all-around ammo for the gun, their 158-grain cast semi-wadcutter load. I took this selection to the range.

First Shots

The first round I fired through this little cannon made me rethink my conviction that I had found the perfect gun for the trail. I chose the 180-grain Federal Hi-Shok 357 Magnum load, and it sailed over my Oehler P35 screens at about 1050 fps. The first round felt OK to my hand, and the blast was tolerable, so I fired four more.

Speer's Allan Jones warned me about heavy bullets in hot loads in this gun. "Ray," said Allan, "I've been there, done that, read the book and bought the tee-shirt. You don't want to put heavy bullets through that gun!" Did I

listen? Certainly not bwana Editor! I ended up feeling the effects of those 180-grain bruisers in my shooting hand for three days.

Next up were the Winchester 145-grain 357 Magnum Silvertips and they averaged 1185 fps. Digging back into my ammo box I next shot some Winchester 38 Special loads, their 125-grain Silvertips giving 810 fps average, and they felt like balm to my savaged hand.

Back into the fray, I thought, grabbing the Federal 158-grain Hydra-Shoks. These gave me 1175 fps out of the Model 60, and muzzle blast was stout, but still reasonable. These didn't hurt my hand as much as the 180s, yet my calculations indicate about the same recoil energy (8.7, versus 8.8 foot pounds for the 180), and nearly the same Taylor KO value (9.5 vs. 9.6).

Along came Peter Pi's Plus-P-Plus Cor-Bon 125-grain ammo. These JHPs whistled over the screens at 1405 fps. The blast nearly tore my hat off. Whew! This was as much fun as I could stand out of this gun for one day, so I called a halt to the session.

Problems

With most loads, the gun spit bits of powder and jacket fragments out to the side. These missiles bounced off the walls of the shooting enclosure at my local range and hit me in the face. I didn't like that. Besides, the gun still occa-

sionally bound up in double-action shooting, so I decided it was time to pull it apart again.

This time I took out the offending parts and cleaned them up with a hard Arkansas stone and then burnished them with good steel to give glass-smooth rubbing surfaces. Then I lubed them with moly-disulfide grease thinned with Shooter's Choice oil, reassembled the gun and tried it. It still didn't work.

I needed to remove metal from the bottom of the hammer hook (the part of the hammer that "hooks" the bolt to drag it down, out of engagement with the cylinder, freeing the cylinder to rotate under the influence of the hand) in order to permit it to drop into the notch of the bolt freely. This accomplished, and the above polishing and lubricating redone, the gun now functions perfectly.

The M60's spitting problem led me to expect to see problems with the forcing cone, but I was disappointed. Most spitting problems come from misalignment between the cylinder and the barrel; or with a new gun, the absence of sufficient diameter of forcing cone. If the cone isn't big enough, the bullets simply hit the edge of the funnel as they pass from the cylinder into the barrel, and bits of their surface are shaved off and find their way out the gap...and, in this case, into my face.

The cone looked okay. I traced the spitting problem to the fact that the ejector rod didn't fit all that snugly into its hole in the front of the yoke. This allowed the yoke to wobble a bit more than it should when the gun was closed, permitting the cylinder to slightly misalign itself with the bore. It doesn't take much misalignment for bullet and powder particles to spray out to the side. To fix the problem I could have staked the metal of the yoke to tighten the fit of the ejector rod, but instead I chose to slightly enlarge the forcing cone.

I recently acquired a forcing-cone cutter from Brownells, one of the simplest and handiest tools I have encountered. The tool consists of a threaded rod that passes through a mandrel which centers it at the muzzle, thence through the bore of the gun to screw into a cone-shaped cutting head. The outer end of the rod accepts a handle. To cut a new forcing cone, or enlarge the existing one, you assemble the tool into the barrel of your handgun, put some cutting oil onto the head, and turn the handle slowly and carefully by hand while pulling on the rod, keeping the tool centered at the muzzle with the mandrel. The tool cuts very quickly and cleanly, and you must use care not to cut too much. My tool cuts an 11-degree cone, and I found that to be very close to what the Smith already had.

Following Brownells' clear instructions I recut the forcing cone on the Smith & Wesson M60 357 Mag. revolver. I'm sure this voided my warranty, but I thought it to be a good tradeoff for not getting shot by my own gun any more. And, of course, it worked.

Now I had a gun that was fully functional. I figured I had the worst kickers already chronographed, so I would be

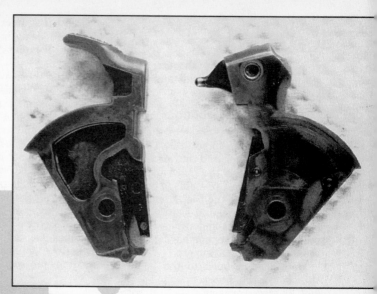

Smith's newest hammer, a masterpiece of investment casting, is at the left. Older model from ancient M36 with bobbed hammer shows mottled case coloring and lots more costly handwork, unacceptable in the 1990s. The new hammer has no firing pin because that's in the frame now.

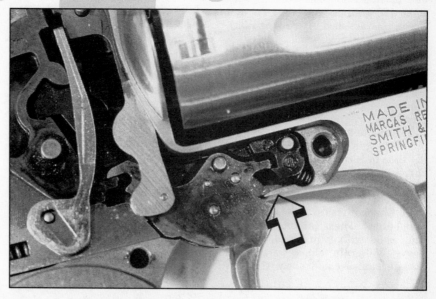

Author Ordorica found that the gun tied up in double action, so he took the gun apart. He found that the bolt didn't always snap into place over the trigger hook. Here the two parts are not in their proper position (arrow), and the gun is bound up. The cylinder won't turn with DA trigger pressure unless the bolt is first pulled down by the hook. Nothing was touching the gun when this photo was taken. See text for the solution.

There's a bit of rubber behind the backstrap of the frame, which helps cushion the recoil of hottest loads. If you need more concealment, you can install smaller grips. These Uncle Mike's Combat grips came on the gun, and are a good compromise. Smith shows clean work throughout.

able to complete my shooting tests without busting my hands any more. Back to the range I went.

More Shooting

This time I fired some of the outstanding Federal 148-grain Gold Medal Match wadcutters, and they put me to the test. I'm sure the gun will shoot them better than I was able to demonstrate. They gave the best grouping of all ammo I tested, and were a joy to shoot as well. This Federal load really must be tried by anyone having one of these guns—it's that superb.

Then I went back to the torture chamber of the dungeon, so to speak, and blasted everyone's ears off with some 125-grainers from Federal and Speer, then finished up with the Black Hills 158-grain SWCs and Speer's 158-grain Gold Dot load. These last two loads proved my theory to me again that light bullets have no place in short-barrel guns. These heavier numbers didn't produce a fraction of the blast of any of the 125-grainers.

Big bullets are slow enough getting out of the gun that they give the powder time to burn within the barrel and chamber, not in the air in front of the gun. I found this out long ago with my 45 Linebaugh Colt, trying hot loads with Elmer Keith's 260-grain SWC cast bullets. These produced a stunning blast with a full load; yet the heavy 350-grain slugs were quiet enough that I could shoot the gun without ear protection, as I often did when wandering in the Alaska bush. The heavier bullets give better performance, too.

In spite of the heavier bullets, the 158-grain 357 Mag. loads didn't seem to kick anywhere as much as did the hot 125-grainers. I went to my computer to see if this could be, and got the following:

125/1350 = 9.8 ft-lb recoil energy
158/1120 = 8.8 ft-lb recoil energy

The Taylor KO value for the 125-grain load, 8.6, lags behind the 9.0 of the 158-grainer. Believing, as I do, in the relevance of the application of Pondoro Taylor's formula to handguns, I'd rather use the heavier bullets for any serious application, and save my ears in the process.

General Utility

I thought this gun would be the ideal trail companion, and it might be. However, I think the gun is not for the novice, not with full 357 loads. The recoil and blast are beyond what most shooters would be happy with. If you are a seasoned handgunner and are willing to work with the gun, then you will be able to make it sing for you. If you're not sure about all the blast and how well you would shoot this gun, stick with 38 Special loads.

Within that realm there is a great variety of loads available for target or self defense. My choice for self-defense use in 38 Special guns that can handle it is the Federal 140-grain Plus-P-Plus Hydra-Shok. Those will come out of the M60 at about 900 fps. A bit softer load is the Winchester 125-grain Silvertip, which gives 810 fps to a lighter bullet. There is some blast, but recoil is very light.

The 3-inch M60 is unquestionably light and handy, and should pack well on the trail in a good leather holster like the superb PMK rig by Milt Sparks, or in one of the Nytek holsters from Michaels of Oregon. The grips on this little gun are an ideal compromise between concealment and comfort. A shooting buddy of mine has a 22 Kit Gun equipped with rubber grips that are a good deal larger than these by Uncle Mike's, and he likes them a lot. He suggested they might make the Model 60 into a better trail gun if you want to shoot hot loads a lot and handle them easier.

Also, one can put on a smaller grip, such as the Boot Grips by Uncle Mike's as found on the 640 S&W, to aid in concealing the gun. They cut down the grip length, but are about the same width. The smaller grip won't give any cushion to the web of the hand.

The 3-inch M60 can be an effective self-defense handgun, provided it gets enough action slicking and reliability checking to satisfy this most demanding of all handgun tasks. In spite of what I already said about muzzle blast of the 125-grain loads, they might be a most effective way of neutralizing a potential threat without having to kill anyone. One shot in the bad guy's direction and the blast ought to scare just about anybody off, never mind if you hit 'em or not. If you shoot and miss, and the other guy runs away, you save yourself lots of paperwork, loss of the gun, and possible jail time. Also, the offender

Author likes these loads best of those tested. His choices run from light target loads to the latest and hottest hi-tech 158-grain JHPs. The M60 shot them all well.

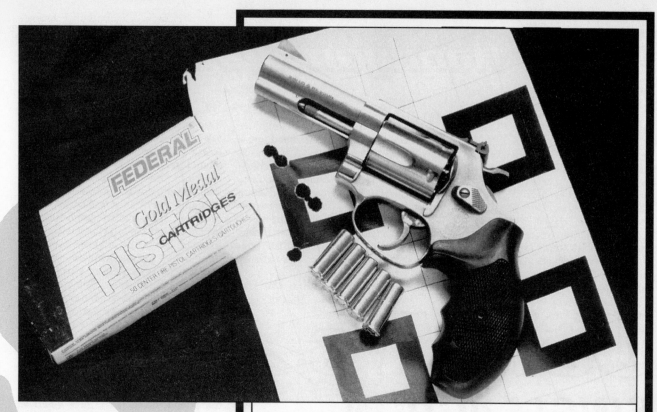

Author's choice for fun shooting is the superb premium Federal Gold Medal wadcutter load. They easily cut this group and you can shoot 'em all day without busting your hand.

can be easily rounded up later. Just send the cops to the nearest ear specialist to look for the guy suffering from terminal tinnitus.

Seriously, with good loads the 3-inch Model 60 ought to be one of the very best concealable revolvers on the market. Yes, the hammer and the rubber grips can catch on clothing, and you may have to deal with those things. However, the stainless construction means you don't have to worry about rust if you sweat onto the gun. It is slim enough to hide well in a good concealment holster, even one worn under the arm. It will fit easily into a purse or fanny pack. The great variety of loads available for 357s and 38 Specials will make practice easy, and any load you might choose to use for self-defense should be easy to find.

There are lots of different kinds of ammo you can drop into this handgun and make it work. This could be one of the best teaching guns available. The grip is small and comfortable enough that women or youngsters should have no trouble hanging on to it, and it has all the accuracy anyone would want. The adjustable sights are right at home here, too.

The barrel is long enough to permit a decent sight radius and give good velocity to reasonable loads, yet not so long as to be a hindrance to concealment or carrying. The 3-inch Model 60 is a good compromise for what I consider to be a compromise cartridge. If I want a big-

Chronograph Results S&W M60 3″ 357 Magnum				
Cartridge	—Bullet— Wgt. Grs.	Type	MV (fps)	Accuracy Comments
Federal (38)	148	GMM WC*	700	Phenomenal accuracy
Federal	125	Hi-Shok JHP	1370	
Federal	180	Hi-Shok JHP	1045	Hand-buster
Federal	158	Hydra-shok	1175	Outstanding load
Winchester	145	Silvertip	1185	Good accuracy
Winchester (38)	125	Silvertip	810	Good novice load
Cor-Bon	125	JHP	1405	Tremendous blast, but great accuracy
Speer	125	Gold Dot	1230	Blast; good group
Speer	158	Gold Dot	1115	Superb; min. blast
Black Hills	158	SWC lead	1050	Great all-around

*Gold Medal Match Wadcutters

ger gun I'll choose it in a bigger cartridge. I can't imagine wanting a much smaller gun for the trail. This is a kit gun with punch.

For home defense I think there are better choices. A larger gun (in the same caliber) would be more intimidating and easier to shoot well. However, the bright stainless finish makes any gun look bigger at night.

All said and done, I'd pick this gun for trail use above many other choices because of the relative lightness of the cartridges, plus the effectiveness of some of the heavier loads. I could pack along a box or two of wadcutters or light handloads for target-shooting fun in camp and have a handful of hot loads (my choices are the 158-grain Federal Hydra-Shok, the 158 Speer Gold Dot, or the Black Hills 158 SWC) in a couple of speedloaders to pack in the gun for self-defense along the trail. That is the use to which I will put this fine little gun, because Smith & Wesson isn't getting this one back. ●

THE UNITED STATES Patent Fire Arms Co. (USPFA) was founded just a few years ago and is housed in the east entrance of Colt's Old Armoury, in Hartford, Connecticut. The company contracts with Uberti of Italy for its single-action component parts. These parts are shipped in the white to Connecticut, where employees of United States Patent Firearms Co. assemble and fit them according to the high standards required by American shooters.

In keeping with early American tra-

ditions, the single actions of USPFA are called Single Action, Central Fire, Army Pistols. They are currently offered in 22 LR/WMR, 38 Special, 357 Magnum, 38-40, 44 Special (and Russian), 44-40, 45 ACP and 45 Colt. The company also offers a broad selection of finishes. They feature hand-finished bone case-hardened frames with what they call Dome Blued barrels and grip straps. They are also available with full nickel-plate or the entire gun done in full Dome Blue finish. One-piece walnut grips are standard, but ivory, stag, or pearl can be specified at extra cost. The guns are available with several grades of engraving. Best of all, they carry a lifetime warranty to the original retail purchaser.

In preparation for this test, I asked USPFA to send me two standard-production guns. One of the guns would be a 7½-incher in 44 Special, the other with 4¾-inch barrel in 45 Colt. I then found out that my friend Thad Rybka had a USPFA sixgun with a 3-inch barrel, in 45 Colt. I managed to get him to contribute that little gun for the tests, too, along with a couple of his good custom holsters.

All three test guns had barrels and gripstraps of a beautiful deep blue. The frames and hammers displayed tasteful

USPFA's
SINGLE ACTION ARMY
Top-Quality Cowboy Gun

by JIM WILSON

Single Action, Central Fire, Army Revolver

Action:	Single-action revolver
Caliber:	44 Special & 45 Colt
Others:	22 LR/WMR, 38 Special, 357 Mag., 38-40, 44-40, 45 ACP.
Finishes:	Blue & case hardened, nickel, blue
Barrel:	4¾", 5½", 7½" (3" & 4" bbls. without ejector)
Capacity:	6 shots (5 recommended)
Sights:	Fixed
Weight:	37 ounces (7½" bbl.)
Height:	5" overall
Length:	13" overall (7½" bbl.)
Width:	1¾" overall
Price:	$737.00 (3"), $745.00 (4¾"), $750.00 (7½")

The 4¾-inch USPFA Single Action Army in 45 Colt.

case coloring that they call the Old Armoury Bone Case. Grip straps, frame and barrel were mated to each other very smoothly and tightly. There was no overlapping. The same is true of the one-piece walnut grips, which are fitted to the frames perfectly.

The actions of all three guns were properly timed and tight. There was no slop or end play in the cylinders, and in each case the cylinder pin was a tight fit in the cylinder bushing. Proper fit and finish are all indications of quality firearms. So far, so good.

The single-action revolver is one of the greatest enigmas in the world of firearms. It is one of our oldest handgun designs, harking back to the days when Sam Colt whittled out a wooden revolver while on board a sailing ship. Single-action percussion revolvers were much sought after by our men who fought in the Mexican War. They were also the weapon of choice of numerous Civil War cavalry units. Countless settlers stuffed the old sixgun in their belts before starting out to do their own little part in settling the frontier.

To the western history buff, the single action is also a tangible piece of frontier lore. After all, it was the weapon favored by Bat Masterson, Wyatt Earp, and countless other lawmen who tamed the Kansas cowtowns. Single actions rode on the hips of the 7th Cavalry as they swung north into the valley of the Little Big Horn. They were found in the hands of most of the frontier Texas Rangers as they battled renegade Indians, bandit gangs, and hired killers. From Pat Garrett to Gen. George Patton, the single-action sixgun has been the choice of most savvy fighting men.

Still, the single-action revolver didn't die out with the American frontier. Just the other day, a rancher flagged me down at the feed store and asked for some help. He'd locked his keys in his pickup. We had the truck open in short order and turned to visiting, as Southwesterners do. Knowing my interest in handguns, the rancher asked if I'd like to see his sixgun. Digging around under the truck seat, he produced a 7½-inch Single Action Army stuffed with 45 Colt handloads. Not a piece of nostalgic art, this old-timer was a working gun and had the scratches and marks to prove it.

Reflecting on our visit, I realized that he is one of hundreds of ranchers, cowboys and outdoorsmen that I know personally who still pack a single action. Like most of the rest, he carries it without regard for history or tradition. He packs it because it is a tough, dependable handgun that is equally at home on horseback, in a pickup, or in a wilderness camp. He packs a single action because they still get the job done.

Like many other shooters, my first handgun was a single action. To be honest, I acquired it because of my love of all things Western and the desire to own a piece of history. However, if that were the only thing to recommend single actions, I would only own that original gun. As it is, some sixty percent of my present handgun collection is made up of good SA sixguns.

Along the way, I've learned a few things about the old single action. Critics will tell you that the old guns are prone to breakage. They suggest that the bolt and trigger spring are not strong enough, or that the hand-spring and locking bolt can break. I suppose that all of this might have been true during the fast-draw craze of the 1950s, but my personal experience does not bear it out. I've replaced no more parts on my single actions than I have on my various double-action revolvers and autos. With a minimum of care the old single action is plenty tough.

Another feature that endeared the single action to me was its ability to redirect the felt recoil. Double-action handguns, with that hump at the top of

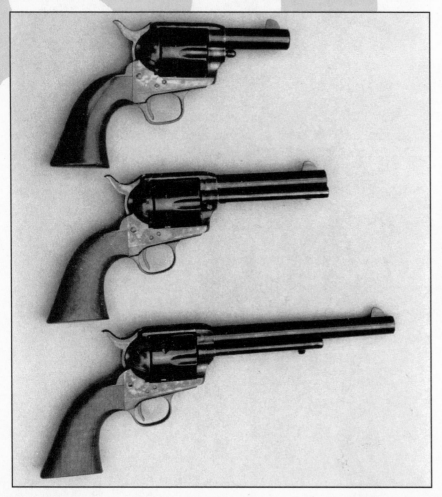

The 3-inch-barrel Sheriff's Model in 45 Colt (top), 4³/₄-inch-barrel Army in 45 Colt (middle), 7¹/₂-inch-barrel Army in 44 Russian & Special (bottom).

the grip, tend to send the recoil directly back into the hand and on into the shooting wrist. However, the curved grip of the single action allows the gun to roll in your hand and dissipate a good bit of that recoil. Just about all of my heavy-caliber hunting handguns are single actions for just that reason.

Single actions also have a place of honor in the fastest-growing shooting sport that any of us has ever seen, Cowboy Action Shooting. This sport started on the West Coast and has quickly spread all across America. Since the emphasis is on fun instead of competition, the entire family is encouraged to participate. I believe Cowboy Action Shooting is responsible for bringing more non-shooters into wholesome contact with firearms than any other shooting activity to date.

Participants arm themselves with sixguns, rifles and shotguns to compete in shooting scenarios that are right out of the pages of the old West, and the weapons must be faithful to the period. Scores are derived from combining the shooter's hits with his elapsed time to complete the particular scenario.

On a second front, Cowboy Action Shooting clubs require their members to take on a Western alias of a historical, or fictional, nature. Members are encouraged to research their character and make an effort to dress the part. Men and women alike compete to see who can come up with the most authentic outfit. Most matches award a separate set of trophies for the most authentic frontier dress. A whole new industry of cowboy clothes and gear has sprung up as a result of this exciting new sport.

As a result of all this modern popularity, single-action sixguns are in high demand, and United States Patent Fire Arms Co. is helping to fill that demand.

All of the USPFA single actions come with a hammer-block device, located on the hammer just beneath the firing pin. The U.S. government requires some sort of safety device on all imported revolvers to keep the weapon from firing if it is accidentally dropped. While I have no doubt that such devices work, years ago I adopted a much better plan of action.

Early single actions allowed the firing pin to rest on the primer of the cartridge beneath the hammer, so it was not a good idea to load one with a full six rounds. The old-timers simply loaded their sixguns with only five cartridges and let the hammer down on the empty chamber. The old method was called "five beans in the wheel," and is easy to learn. Placing the hammer on half-cock, we load one, skip one, and load four more. The hammer is pulled to full cock and then eased down on the empty chamber, which will come up beneath it. With a little practice, the single action can be safely loaded without ever having to look at it. Since I own all kinds of single actions, this is the practice that I personally follow and recommend to all other shooters.

The 7½-inch test gun from USPFA is marked "44 Russian and S&W Special." It is chambered for the modern 44 Special cartridge but, of course, will fire the shorter 44 Russian cartridge. This particular single action was tricked out in the "blackpowder" motif with a screw in the front of the frame, directly

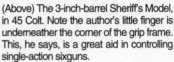

(Above) The 3-inch-barrel Sheriff's Model, in 45 Colt. Note the author's little finger is underneath the corner of the grip frame. This, he says, is a great aid in controlling single-action sixguns.

(Left) The 7½-inch Single Action Army in 44 Russian & Special (left), 3-inch Sheriff's Model in 45 Colt (center), 4¾-inch Single Action Army in 45 Colt (right). Cartridge belt is by Galco International.

beneath the cylinder pin, to retain the base pin. It also has the old "bullseye" thumbpiece on the ejector rod.

These parts are characteristic of the Colt sixguns manufactured during the blackpowder era. The style was discontinued about the time that the guns were strengthened for smokeless powder. However, all USPFA sixguns are built for use with modern smokeless powder and the use of these parts is strictly for nostalgia's sake.

[Editor's note: Some early Colt SAAs have the spring-loaded cross pin to retain the base pin, but they are still blackpowder guns. Single-action Colts with serial numbers below 192,000 are warranted for blackpowder only, in spite of their frame design. Thanks to Mike Venturino for this info.]

The USPFA 4³/₄-inch 45 Colt is indicative of the sixguns made after the advent of smokeless powder. The spring-loaded cylinder-pin release is located in the side of the frame, just in front of the cylinder. The ejector-rod thumbpiece is also the smaller variety. The 45 Army is 10 inches in overall length and weighs approximately 39 ounces. The front edge of the cylinder is slightly beveled in the old style. Altogether, it is an attractive sixgun.

Thad Rybka's contribution to my test was a USPFA Army with a 3-inch barrel. Unlike the other two revolvers, this little gun has no ejector-rod housing, nor is the right side of the frame milled to hold such a part. On the frontier, these snub-nose single actions were called the Storekeeper's Model. In later years, they have come to be called the Sheriff's Model.

Lawmen, detectives and armed citizens liked the style and barrel length because these guns could be more easily concealed. Border lawman Jeff Milton was one of the many officers who favored the short-barrel single actions. Milton regularly carried one in a shoulder holster, under his shirt, to augment the big sixgun on his hip.

Checking my ammunition supply, I collected the various factory loads that I happened to have on hand. I found representative selections from Winchester, Black Hills and CCI/Blazer. I also tested the 45 sixguns with two loads from the 4W Ammunition Company.

The handloads tested were some that I have used with a good deal of success. The 45 Colt load features a 250-grain semi-wadcutter from the Mount Baldy Bullet Co. loaded over 8.0 grains of W231. This load was suggested to me by John Linebaugh and has proven to be quite accurate. It about duplicates the power of the old 45 Colt blackpowder factory load.

My 44 Special handloads were built using bullets cast from the RCBS 250K mould. This is the most faithful duplication of Elmer Keith's original bullet design that we have today, and it has proven an excellent choice. Besides the old standby, Unique, I also used Hodgdon's new Universal Clays powder. This powder has given me very good accuracy and it is very clean burning.

I did my test firing on bullseye and silhouette targets at 25 yards. I used sandbags and also the new Millett Bench Master shooting rest. Velocity data was obtained from the PACT Professional chronograph.

As I suspected, the hand-fitted and tight actions of the USPFA guns paid off in good accuracy. A quality revolver, using good ammunition, ought to deliver five shots into 2 inches or less at 25 yards. The single-action revolvers from USPFA are clearly capable of that level of performance. Had I taken the time to have a gunsmith tune the triggers a bit, many of the groups would have been closer to one inch.

You will also notice that I made no attempt to craft really heavy handloads in either caliber. While this can safely be done in the larger Ruger single actions, it is not a good practice in the Colt-size guns. Pressure in the Colt-size single actions, including the USPFA sixguns, should be kept to around 15,000-16,000 CUP. Loads at that pressure level with most popular handgun powders give about 900 fps to a 250-grain bullet, which is plenty of power and well within the safety zone of these fine handguns.

Once the serious work was over, it was time to play a bit. Setting up silhouette targets, tin cans, and other targets of opportunity, I tried the guns at hip shooting. No handgun lends itself to instinctive shooting as does a good sin-

(Above) USPFA Single Action Army showing the hammer block safety in the face of the hammer just under the firing pin. Below is a Colt Single Action Army for comparison.

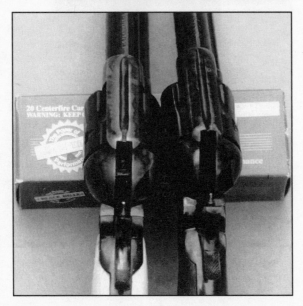

At left is the Colt Single Action Army showing the modern rear sight that has a broader opening. The USPFA Single Action Army shows the traditional "pinched" rear sight.

gle-action sixgun. The balance is just about perfect for that sort of work, even the 3-inch-barrel Sheriff's Model.

For good positive work, the shooter should cock the sixgun with the first joint of his shooting thumb. Hollywood fast-draw artists often used just the tip of the thumb, but the thumb tip can easily slip off without bringing the pistol to full cock. All of the old-timers that I ever watched laid their thumb over the top of the hammer and cocked the weapon with the first joint of the thumb. When shooting from a two-hand hold, it is quite fast to simply cock the weapon with the thumb of the weak hand.

While hip-shooting these USPFA single actions, I used the technique of slipping my little finger under the front corner of the pistol's grip. This simple technique gives much more control over the recoiling weapon. As the single action climbs in recoil, the shooter recocks the hammer and tightens the grip of his little finger to bring the pistol back on target. This method may feel awkward at first, but actually gives the shooter much more control. I was able to hit pretty well from the hip, and this type of shooting reminded me of some old movies.

Some time back, European manufacturers began to produce copies of the single-action Colt for American shooters. This was in the days of the "spaghetti Westerns," and, in fact, those foreign copies were used in most of those films. The guns were generally less costly than their American counterparts, but did not always meet the quality-control standards that American shooters demanded. Frankly, I didn't like the spaghetti Westerns and liked the spaghetti sixguns even less.

Most of them featured brass grip frames that bore only a distant resemblance to the real thing. In addition, the parts used were rarely of the sort of quality that American shooters have come to expect in their handguns. In short, they broke a lot. The fit and finish of these early guns suffered, too. Grip straps and frames did not always meet in smooth, graceful lines, and there were always a lot of rough sharp edges. Generally, when you saw a fellow packing one of those dogs, you just couldn't help but feel sorry for him and wish he could afford a real sixgun.

But my, my, my, how times have changed! American importers have realized that there is an excellent market for European single actions, if they are properly made.

The next step, of course, is the one that United States Patent Fire Arms has taken: Import the basic components and let American gunsmiths assemble them. The second verse of that song is to stay in tune with the folks who use the sixguns. For that reason, USPFA has taken every opportunity to spend time with Cowboy Action Shooters, and other single-action fans, to find out just what their customers want.

An important part of the United States Patent Fire Arms Co. is their Old Armoury Custom Shop. The Custom Shop offers a full array of special features to dress up the Single Action Army to the specific customer's taste. In addition to ivory, pearl and

stag grips, the company offers scroll engraving in four stages of coverage. Also, gold wire inlay, silver and gold plating, scrimshawed grips or your name down the backstrap are all services rendered on the guns. Plus, the company offers presentation cases and hand-tooled gun rigs.

In my field test of three randomly selected single actions from United States Patent Fire Arms, I found them to be well-fitted, well-made sixguns that compare favorably to anything that is being manufactured anywhere. My accuracy tests showed that these guns deliver the sort of accuracy that I have come to expect from good fixed-sighted revolvers. The suggested retail prices of the guns are reasonable and

Well-dressed Sheriff Jim Wilson packs the 4³/₄-inch 45 in Trailblazer rig and 3-inch 45 in Rybka's cross-draw rig. Cowboy Action Shooters will need two single actions to compete in most scenarios. Both sixguns are positioned for use by the shooter's strong hand.

Two-handed aimed fire at silhouette target. Author is shooting 3-inch Sheriff's Model in 45 Colt.

The 4³/₄-inch-barrel Single Action Army, in 45 Colt, did well in hip-shooting. Author Wilson shot this group at 15 yards. Ammo was author's handload using a 250 SWC cast bullet over 8 grains of W231.

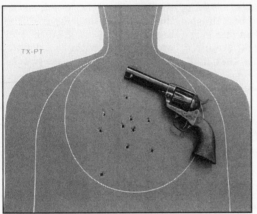

Performance Test of USPFA 44 Special With 7½″ bbl.

Make	—Bullet— Wgt. Grs.	Type	MV (fps)	ES* (fps)	Group (ins.)
Black Hills	240	SWC	819	18.3	1.8
Black Hills	200	JHP	898	43.9	2.2
CCI-Blazer	200	JHP	892	13.3	1.7
RCBS Cast 250K	7.5	Unique	1014	26.8	2.3
RCBS Cast 250K	6.5	Univ. Clays	926	15.8	1.5

*ES = Extreme Velocity Spread

Performance Test of USPFA 45 Colt With 4³/₄″ bbl.

Make	—Bullet— Wgt. Grs.	Type	MV (fps)	ES* (fps)	Group (ins.)
Black Hills	250	FN	822	18.5	1.7
CCI-Blazer	255	RNL	837	36.5	2.8
CCI-Blazer	200	JHP	909	35.6	2.1
WW	225	JHP	803	49.3	2.6
4-W	230	RNL	800	32.1	2.6
4-W	250	FNL	823	30.2	2.3
250 SWC	8.0	W231	868	33.3	1.6

*ES = Extreme Velocity Spread

The 7½-inch Single Action Army in 44 Russian & Special shot this group from a rest at 25 yards. Ammunition is Black Hills 44 Special factory load, using a 240-grain SWC bullet.

Performance Test of USPFA 45 Colt With 3″ bbl.

Make	—Bullet— Wgt. Grs.	Type	MV (fps)	ES* (fps)	Group (ins.)
Black Hills	250	FNL	720	19.3	2.2
CCI-Blazer	255	FNL	742	39.0	3.3
CCI-Blazer	200	JHP	794	18.0	2.6
4-W	230	RNL	752	42.1	2.9
4-W	250	FNL	746	23.9	2.7
255 SWC	8.0	W231	818	15.0	1.9

*ES = Extreme Velocity Spread

In all three cases, five-shot groups were fired at 25 yards from a rest. Velocities were obtained using PACT Professional chronograph set 15 feet from the muzzle. Temperature was 88 degrees, Fahrenheit.

well under the money that one would expect to give for a new Colt. By careful shopping, I suspect that the shooter will be able to shave the retail prices even a bit more.

All of the above encourages me. The single-action sixgun is a useful part of our tradition, as well as our everyday lives. It is still around because it meets the needs of a whole raft of American handgunners. These are folks who don't follow the latest fads but, rather, stick to something that they know and can depend on.

As a shooter, I am pleased to see the great interest in Cowboy Action Shooting. It is good, clean family fun that reminds us of our heritage and our search for liberty. Cowboy Action Shooting is also a very positive method to get the joy of the shooting sports over to non-shooters and, incidentally, the anti-gun crowd. As long as there are cowboys and people who love their freedom, there will be privately owned handguns, and many of them will be good single actions. It is good to see that United States Patent Fire Arms Co. is doing its part to uphold that tradition. ●

THE MATCH MASTER Deluxe pistol from Fort Worth Firearms, Inc., is a stainless steel clone of the High Standard Victor, right down to its gold-plated trigger. To my eye it's an almost exact copy, though with a few nice changes. It's nice to see this handgun return to the market, and my first impression was very favorable.

The entire pistol has the best finish I've seen on a production gun in a long time. The sides of the barrel are nice and flat with no flaws of any kind, and the top and bottom are bead-blasted to a fine-looking sheen. The entire rib is also bead-blasted to provide a non-glare sight picture. The frame is polished to a high shine as is the slide. All the flat surfaces are free from ripples or other marks of poor workmanship. The fit of all of the parts is excellent. The walnut stocks are well checkered, and there's a thumb rest on the left panel. The wood-to-metal fit is as good as you could want. This is, without a doubt, a very well-made and attractive pistol.

FORT WORTH's
MATCH MASTER 22
Stainless Accuracy and Heads-Up Optics

by DON FISHER

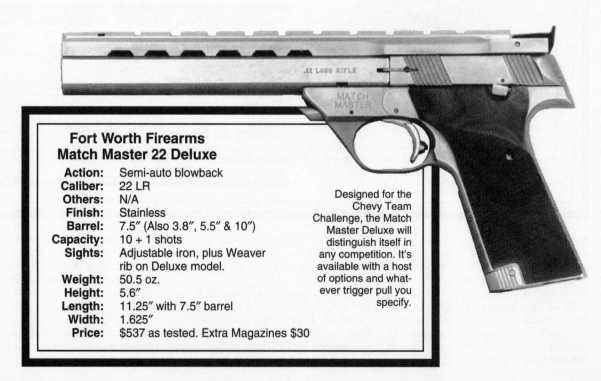

Fort Worth Firearms
Match Master 22 Deluxe

Action:	Semi-auto blowback
Caliber:	22 LR
Others:	N/A
Finish:	Stainless
Barrel:	7.5″ (Also 3.8″, 5.5″ & 10″)
Capacity:	10 + 1 shots
Sights:	Adjustable iron, plus Weaver rib on Deluxe model.
Weight:	50.5 oz.
Height:	5.6″
Length:	11.25″ with 7.5″ barrel
Width:	1.625″
Price:	$537 as tested. Extra Magazines $30

Designed for the Chevy Team Challenge, the Match Master Deluxe will distinguish itself in any competition. It's available with a host of options and whatever trigger pull you specify.

One of the changes from the Victor is that the sight rib is made of aluminum rather than steel, and it has been machined to be a Weaver-style scope mount base. The iron sights can be used as is, or any optical sight that fits the Weaver-style base will fit over the iron sights.

For this test I was able to secure the use of one of the new Bushnell HOLO-sights, and mounted it onto the sight rib. More on that sight in a moment.

Three small holes are drilled and tapped into the bottom of the 7¼-inch barrel, and they have plug screws installed. They are for mounting extra weights.

A few other minor changes in the pistol are a beveled magazine well, dual extractors for positive extraction, a quick-release lever for the magazine on the right side of the gun, and the addition of small bumps at the back of the slide to provide a better purchase when you want to open the slide.

Those bumps come in mighty handy. There is very little room to get your fingers on the slide, and it is very hard to pull the slide back even with the added purchase provided by the bumps. The problem gets worse with a scope in the way. When the gun is cocked, it's not a problem, but when the hammer is forward, it will take all your strength to rack the slide. In fact, I'd like the bumps to be a little bigger, assuming that it wouldn't ruin the appearance of the gun.

In case you're wondering why the gun has a quick-release magazine and a beveled mag well, it is because the Fort Worth Firearms people are building these for use in the Chevy Team Challenge match. That's also why it has the scope base on the sight rib. An optical sight is just about a must for the Team Challenge match, and this gun makes it easy to add optics.

In that match, it's important to be able to reload in a hurry, hence the quick mag release. The lever is on the right side of the frame right behind and slightly below the trigger. For the right-handed shooter, the release fits between the trigger finger and the middle finger. It takes only a small movement back from the trigger to the lever to drop the empty magazine, and the gun is ready for a fresh one. The original magazine release from the Victor design is still there and can be used, but it is way too slow for competition such as the Chevy Team Challenge.

At first, I was afraid that the lever might be too close to the trigger finger and might get in the way, but it never did. That brings me to the one complaint about the gun. The slide release is also on the right side of the gun, an inch above the mag release lever. When I try to release the slide after a magazine change, I often hit the magazine release instead. Actually, the knuckle of my middle finger hits the lever, not my index finger. The solution to the problem would be to move the slide release to the left side of the gun, but that's not an easy design change.

What I think would be an easy fix, in the meantime, would be to increase the spring tension on the magazine release so that just touching the lever will not release the magazine. This should be an easy change, and one that I will suggest to the company. The force needed to release the magazine is very light, and doubling or tripling the tension of the spring shouldn't cause trouble for any shooter with enough strength to pull a trigger.

That brings up another interesting point about this gun. The trigger pull on the factory gun is set to a maximum of 3 pounds, with the normal trigger pull between 2 and 2½ pounds. That's the trigger pull as the gun normally comes from the factory. Here comes the fun part: if you request it, the factory

Disassembly into these components is accomplished by pressing the button in front of the trigger guard.

will set your gun up with a lighter pull for you, and the cost is *zero dollars*.

When I talked to Dennis Fewell at Fort Worth Firearms about getting a gun for this report, he asked me what weight trigger pull I wanted. I asked for a real light pull. The gun showed up with a trigger pull of 20 ounces. That's a pound and a quarter, folks, which is not bad for a factory trigger, and you can't beat the price. The trigger pull on my Smith & Wesson Model 41 is only 28 ounces, but it feels heavy to me now.

When I took the Match Master apart to inspect the inner workings of the thing, I found exactly what Mr. Fewell said I would. The machining of the parts is as nice on the inside as it is on the parts that show. The top of the frame where the barrel seats against it is so smooth it looks like the surface was polished, not just machined. One look down the barrel and I knew that if this gun didn't shoot nice small groups it wouldn't be the fault of the barrel. The inside of this barrel is as nice as any I have ever seen.

All the sliding surfaces are extremely smooth. Mr. Fewell assured me that this test gun has nothing extra done to it other than adjusting the trigger pull to my request. This is the way all of their guns look when they leave the factory.

The Sight

As I noted, I mounted the Bushnell HOLOsight onto the Match Master for shooting tests. At first, I hated the sight. It has a reticle, actually a hologram, that I can only describe as coming from a jet fighter. It took me back to my time as a radar technician in Southeast Asia working on F105 fighters. There is a large red circle with a small dot in the center, and there are four small lines around the edge of the circle at 3, 6, 9, and 12 o'clock. The circle is not clear and smooth, but appears to have whiskers along the outside of the ring. It looked like it needed a shave. There was no way I was going to be able to shoot well with that reticle. It was *blurry*.

Yet, as I looked at it in the sunlight at the range, I noticed that the dot was in clear focus. The circle surrounding it still looked not unlike Don Johnson on Miami Vice a few years back, but that didn't matter. I wasn't looking at the ring anyway. As my shooting partner pointed out to me, if the ring is covered with whiskers, that might force me to look at the dot in the middle. It was a simple matter of the unconscious mind making my eye do what I should have been smart enough to do in the first place: look at the dot.

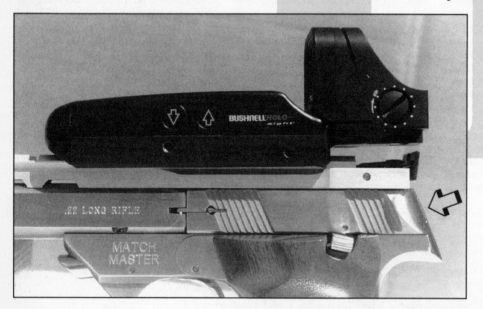

Bushnell's HOLOsight mounted easily enough to the Match Master's rib. Note the wide gripping knobs at the back of the slide (arrow). Author Fisher liked the gun's fit and machining, and came to like the sight a lot.

Bushnell HOLOsight	
Optics:	Holographic
Magnification:	1x
Weight:	9.5 oz. as tested
Length:	6″
Eye Relief:	1/2-inch to 10 feet
Batteries:	Two type N, 1.5 v. Lithium (included)
Battery life:	30-100 hours
Adjustment:	.25 MOA
Brightness:	20 levels
Price:	$549 suggested retail
Extra reticles:	$99 each.

Bushnell's HOLOsight is a natural for competition such as the Team Challenge. Offering variable brightness and different reticle images, it mated well to the Match Master.

A second reason I didn't initially like the sight is that the spacing of the cross bolts that hold the sight onto the scope base didn't match the notches machined into the rib. But again I was fooled. Only one of the bolts goes into a notch in the rib. The other bolt is raised an eighth of an inch and crosses above the notches, so notch spacing doesn't matter.

A small center dot for precision shooting at long range, a bright circle for fast shooting up close and personal—that's a hard combination to beat in an optical sight. I think with time I could really get used to this sight, and my shooting with it would improve.

In the end, the only complaint I had about the sight that held any water is that at about 9½ ounces, the thing is heavy. However, that's a personal opinion based on my preference for light guns for IPSC-style shooting, which is mostly what I have been doing the last twenty years. I do admit that for precision shoot-

ing, NRA Bullseye, the Bianchi Cup, or the Chevy Team Challenge, a heavy gun does hold steadier if you are strong enough to support the extra weight without shaking. The Chevy Team Challenge being the event this gun was built for, this sight seems like a good choice for testing with this pistol.

The sight has a stepping switch to control the intensity of the reticle. There are twenty settings to choose from. The intensity is automatically set to #15 when the sight is turned on. You can have the intensity come on at full power (#20) if you want, just by holding the Up intensity button when you turn the sight on. Or you can have it come on at #1 if you hold the Down button when you turn it on. Both of these choices are nice, but I would rather have the reticle stay at the setting I had chosen before I turned it off. Why waste time adjusting it at the beginning of every stage of a match?

The sight has a battery test mode

that will come in handy for anyone who uses this sight. Just press a button and if the reticle blinks at you, the batteries are at less than 20 percent of their full strength. I've had the battery in my ProPoint go dead on me in the middle of a Bianchi match once or twice over the years. Not a good feeling.

All the switches are flush with the sight body. There are no knobs sticking out that might get bumped while drawing, or while shooting around a barricade. Another nice touch is that the sight doesn't get in the way of the field of view. I can see the target better than I can with other optics. There are no adjustment knobs in the way. And if you don't like the standard reticle, there are three more to choose from, with no need to readjust the point of impact if you change the reticle. So, after a misjudged first impression, I can say that I like this sight rather a lot. Good job, Bushnell!

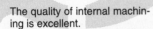
The quality of internal machining is excellent.

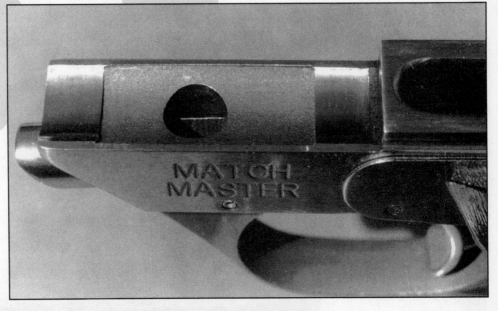

The slide release is just above Fisher's trigger finger here, and the quick-release magazine button is just under it. Their locations led to a problem when tripping the slide release.

Test Plans

In order to get what I consider to be a good test of the Match Master pistol, I decided to shoot it alongside my personal Smith & Wesson Model 41, which has a 7³/₈-inch barrel. The sight radius of my Model 41 is 9¹/₄ inches compared to 9³/₄ inches for the Match Master, so things were about even with iron sights.

I figured shooting the one gun with both sights, iron and dot, would give me a good idea of how well the HOLOsight works. With the HOLOsight mounted directly on the barrel, as are the iron sights, the accuracy should be the same if I can maintain the same degree of sight alignment precision. This would be a much better test of the HOLOsight than if it were mounted on the frame, as it would be with most centerfire semi-automatic pistols. On the Match Master, there would be no misalignment between the barrel and the sights due to a sloppy slide-to-frame fit.

The S&W Model 41 is extremely accurate so it would give the Fort Worth gun

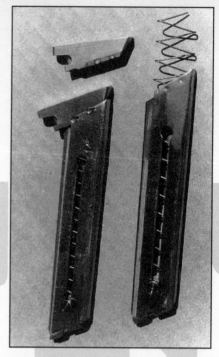

One of the magazines had its bottom plate come off, the result of improper spot-welding, says author. Factory immediately sent a replacement.

a good run for its money. Twenty years ago, when my eyes were younger and my hand was steady, I could shoot ³/₈-inch groups with my 41 at 25 yards with cheap ammo. With the match-quality ammo I had available for this test, I expected some great groups. It was time to head to the range and find out how these two guns compared with match ammo—and my 49-year-old eyes.

Range Results

First the bad news. One of the magazines that came with the gun fell apart. The floorplate was spot welded on, and it looks like the welding machine was not properly adjusted. The good news is that two replacement magazines arrived immediately after I called the factory to complain, yelling and screaming as usual. Actually they were very nice and I didn't have to resort to yelling at all; which ruined half my fun.

The shooting session wasn't as rewarding as I had hoped. I got some good groups, but not every time. I shot my best groups with RWS ammunition,

(Above) Fisher's index finger is about to trip the slide release, but his second finger's knuckle is bearing against the lightly sprung magazine release, and it occasionally dropped the mag.

(Right) The quick magazine release is just behind the trigger. Fisher says one fix is to increase its spring tension.

(Above) Feeding failures like this were traced to insufficient internal magazine length. Some ammo drags inside the magazine, then disrupts things.

something called FP50. Not being able to read German, I don't know what the stuff is designed for. All I know is it shot well in this pistol, better than the most expensive ammo I tried.

Some of the groups were a lot worse than I would have expected from the gun. Even when I had the sights right on the center of the target and I called the shot "perfect" for all five shots, I had some groups that measured over an inch. Some of it could have been me, but not that much, so at first I didn't know what the problem was.

There were a few failures to feed, after about 150 rounds. The nose of the bullet ended up at the top of the barrel, above the mouth of the chamber. It may have been because of the magazine, not a design problem with the gun. Magazines generally cause more feeding problems than any other aspect of the whole design package: gun, magazine, and ammo. With any new gun, even a clone of an old design, I'd bet magazine problems are the cause of most troubles, and I'm sure that Fort Worth Firearms will solve any feeding disorders when they fix the floorplate spot-welding problem.

After receiving two new magazines I retested the Match Master and I had only one failure to feed. The problem seems to be that the magazines are a little too small front-to-back, and the nose of the bullets drag on the inside of the magazines. This causes the bullet to hang up in the magazine just enough to cause a problem. The Winchester Power Point rounds are a little longer than the rest of the ammo and were hard to load into the magazine. They gave the worst feeding problems. All rounds that loaded into the magazine with enough room to move a little, front to back, fed with no failures of any kind. A slight change in the magazine forming should solve the problem with the longer ammo.

I discovered that the HOLOsight's dot has to be centered for best results. I could see the dot move on the target as I moved my head from side to side (parallax). I don't know how much this movement affects the size of the groups, but I did better after I made sure I had the dot centered in the field of view.

By comparison, the ProPoint people claim their dot doesn't have to be centered. As long as you can see the dot on the target, the bullet will hit what you aim at. I couldn't detect any movement of my ProPoint's dot on a target at 25 yards as I moved my head from side to side, so it seems that ProPoint's claims are true.

I tested the Match Master with the factory iron sights, and I found the groups were bigger without the aid of the HOLOsight. Its dot covers an area of

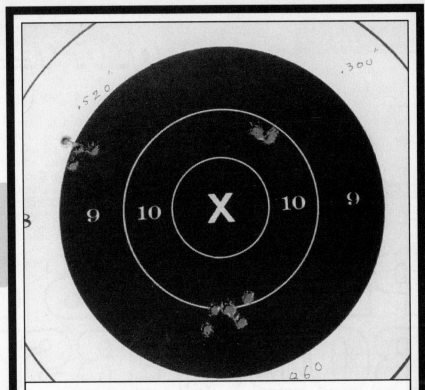

Groups fired with RWS FP50 ammo were the best, says Fisher. These three measure .30-, .52-, and .86-inch diameter, at a full 25 yards. The gun *shoots*.

Fort Worth Firearms Match Master Deluxe 22 Test Results

Cartridge	MV (fps)	Group Size (ins.)		
		Smallest	Largest	Average
Remington Thunderbolt	1129	.890	1.350	1.093
Remington Target	1030	.775	.950	.875
Federal Power Flite	1113	.750	1.225	.945
Federal Gold Medal Target	1014	.660	1.110	.870
Federal Gold Medal Match	1053	.440	.835	.678
Federal Gold Medal Ultra Match	1023	.480	1.280	.980
Winchester T22 Target	1036	.755	1.005	.880
Winchester Power Point	1145	.680	1.240	.965
Winchester Super Silhouette	1089	.650	.810	.733
CCI Green Tag Competition	947	.650	1.020	.810
CCI Pistol Match	928	.800	.870	.841
CCI Standard Velocity	954	.565	.950	.801
Dynamit Nobel RWS FP50	982	.305	.860	.560
RWS FP50 using iron sights		.725	1.225	.875
RWS FP50 shot in S&W 41	1011	.560	.890	.690

All firing was done from sandbags at 25 yards. Three five-shot groups were fired and all shots were chronographed over a PACT timer. Air temperature, 75 degrees F.

only about 1/4-inch at 25 yards, so I was able to hold a very precise sight picture. I doubt the sight moved more than 1/8-inch on the target from shot to shot. It's hard to hold that well with iron sights.

The targets I got using iron sights with both my Model 41 and the Match Master were proof of the quality of the Bushnell HOLOsight. They also showed the difficulty of aligning iron sights exactly the same way for every

shot. Both my S&W 41 and the Match Master shot about the same size groups with iron sights, while the Match Master with the HOLOsight shot groups about half as big.

The Match Master and the HOLOsight are both fine pieces of equipment. I don't think you would go wrong to invest your money in either one. Together, they make an excellent package. •

WOULDN'T IT BE neat to have a handgun that would shoot any ammo one could lay his hands on? Impossible? In the broadest sense, yes. But the firm of Phillips & Rodgers, Inc., in Conroe, Texas, does offer a revolver that they claim will function with a wide variety of straight-walled 35-caliber pistol rounds, from the 357 Mag. through most of the 9mm clan, and down to the 380 Auto. They call it the Medusa. Why one would name a pistol for a jellyfish, or for the snake-haired Gorgon whose head Perseus lopped off, with a little aid from nymphs and gods, escapes me; but there it is.

The Medusa received for testing is your basic S&W K-frame-style 4-inch

PHILLIPS & RODGERS'
MEDUSA DA REVOLVER
Takes Any 38 Ammo—Almost

by FINN AAGAARD

Phillips & Rodgers Medusa

Action:	DA Revolver
Caliber:	Any 38/357/380/9mm
Finish:	Matte blue
Barrel:	4" (2½", 3", 5" or 6" available)
Capacity:	6 shots
Sights:	Adjustable
Weight:	34 oz. empty
Height:	5.6" overall
Length:	9.5" overall
Width:	1.5" overall
Price:	$899 suggested retail

The Medusa features an un-fluted cylinder, decent grips, a blocky-looking barrel and unparalleled versatility.

revolver with an unfluted six-shot swing-out cylinder, a blocky, rectangular barrel, and adjustable sights. It is fitted with Uncle Mike's rubber stocks marked for, "S&W K and L, Sq. Butt." The internal mechanism is strictly Smith & Wesson, including the hammer block. Whether the parts would actually interchange I cannot say, but they look identical. The firing pin floats in the frame, instead of being pinned to the hammer. An obvious difference is that the extractor's return spring is on the outside of the rod, rather than being internal. The reason becomes apparent when the rod is pushed in. In place of the normal star-shaped extractor, six long flat springs ride the side of the rod, their hooked ends protruding into the heads of the chambers to engage cartridge rims or extractor grooves.

The chambers have recesses to accept and support the .440-inch diameter rims of 357 Mag./38 Special cartridges. The entrance diameters of the chambers run about .393-inch, greater than the actual rim diameter of most 9mm Parabellum (Luger) cartridges, which are then supported against the firing pin blow mostly by the springy extractor. The 9mmP's rim is supposed to protrude .001-inch beyond the head of the case. The Medusa's extractor pushes the cartridge against the outside of the chamber, so that this minuscule rim protrusion may offer some support. Or,

it seems, sometimes it may not. The 38 Super Auto (and the original 38 Auto version) is a semi-rimmed round. Its .405-inch diameter rim is quite well supported in the Medusa.

The 380 Auto, on the other hand, with its .374-inch nominal rim diameter, is a loose fit and receives little support from the chamber. It is supposed to have .001-inch rim protrusion, but in a batch I have been measuring, rim and head diameters were exactly the same, .371. The 380 Auto's rim is a little thinner than that of the Parabellum, and it seats deeper into the chamber, creating a condition of slightly excessive headspace.

The Medusa's charge holes taper to a diameter of about .360-inch at their mouths. A .358-inch diameter cast lead bullet drops through them of its own weight, but only just. It is a pretty good fit, though the chamber mouths of both a S&W 357 Mag. and a S&W 38 Special in my possession are tighter. The Medusa's chambers and chamber mouths would appear to allow the .355-inch diameter bullets of the 9mm cartridges and the 380 Auto more "windage" than is ideal.

Despite its massive slab-sided barrel, the Medusa weighs only a couple of ounces more than my 4-inch S&W M19 Combat Magnum, and fits into my old Bianchi holster for the latter quite well. It has a wide, grooved "target" trigger, as does the M19. Given my preference, I

would opt for a smooth, narrower trigger on both guns, but it is no big matter. The front sight, with its integral base, is inletted into the top of the barrel and secured with a hex-head screw. It has a red plastic insert. Unfortunately it is inserted so far down on the sight blade that a broad black band of metal is visible above it, which could be confusing, especially in poor light. The adjustable rear sight works in a similar fashion to that of the S&W, but looks cruder. I had to move it left as far as it would go to get the piece to shoot where I was looking. The finish is a matte blue. It is not quite as smooth as on most Smiths, but is still pretty good.

In single-action mode the trigger lets off at a crisp 3 pounds. Double-action requires perhaps a 12-pound pull (my RCBS trigger gauge goes only to 10 pounds). There is, however, a hitch in the middle of the stroke that makes precise double-action work difficult. I'm sure a gunsmith could easily cure it, and a lot of dry-firing might alleviate it.

Phillips & Rodgers lists twenty-five cartridges for which the revolver is said to be suitable. However, several of them are just the same round by a different name, as, for example, the 380 Auto and the 9mm Kurz. Eliminating the duplications, we are left with eighteen recommended cartridges, to wit: 380 ACP, 380 Revolver, 9mm Browning Long, 9mm Ultra, 9mm Glisenti, 9mm Bayard Long

The Medusa is quite comparable to a 4-inch S&W M19, including the internal lockwork. Medusa's cylinder is unfluted

PHILLIPS & RODGERS

(or Largo), 9mm Steyr, 9mm Mauser, 9mm Parabellum (or Luger, or 9x19mm), 9mm Federal Rimmed, 9mm Winchester Magnum, 38 Auto, 38 Super Auto, 38 Short Colt, 38 Long Colt, 38 S&W, 38 Special (including Plus-P and Plus-P-Plus), 357 Magnum. I would add the 9x21 mm. The 9mm Makarov is specifically *not* recommended, presumably because its .363-inch diameter bullet is oversize for the Medusa's nominal .357-inch groove-diameter barrel, while the 357 Maximum is over-length for the 1.70-inch-long cylinder. Bottleneck 9mm cartridges, such as the 357 SIG, will, obviously, not go into the Medusa's charge holes.

It will accept the 38 S&W, which with its nominal case diameter of .386-inch is not supposed to be usable in regular 38

Special and 357 Mag. guns. I borrowed a box of Remington 38 S&W ammo from our local dealer. It fitted nicely in the Medusa, but when I tried it, it fitted the chambers of the 357 Mag. M19 as well. The calipers revealed an actual case diameter of .380-.381, close enough to the nominal .379-inch case diameter of the 357 Mag. to work. I did not fire any of it, else I would have had to pay for the whole box, and I have no use at all for the puny cartridge.

Almost any cartridge based on necked-down 357 Mag. brass—such as the 22 Jet—will enter the chamber and should fire. The same appears true of the 218 Bee, the 25-20 and the 32-20. Of course, the bullets would rattle down the bore, accuracy would be non-existent, and velocity greatly reduced.

Cases could split, too. But at very close range these rounds might do the business if nothing else was available. A 35 Winchester Self-Loading cartridge in my collection also entered the chamber. Its .405-inch rim should support it firmly enough to ensure reliable ignition, though its .351-inch diameter bullet would still be undersize. It will fit a regular 357 Mag. chamber too, but as the cartridge was discontinued in 1920, who cares? Neither I, nor, most emphatically, Phillips & Rodgers or DBI Books, recommend firing any of these cartridges, or any others not specifically listed as suitable by Phillips & Rodgers, in the Medusa revolver.

I tried the gun with six different loads that I had on hand: PMC 150-grain Starfire JHP 357 Mag., WCC (Winchester) generic 150-grain lead RN 38 Special, old (maybe twenty years old) Remington 130-grain metal case 38

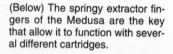

Ammo tried in the Medusa. From left, 380 Auto, 9mmP, 38 Super Auto, 357 Mag., 38 Special, 38 S&W.

(Below) The springy extractor fingers of the Medusa are the key that allow it to function with several different cartridges.

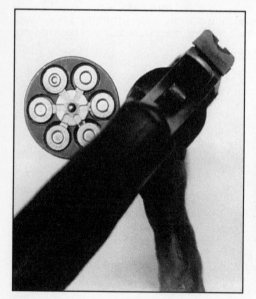

(Above) The Medusa's cylinder is filled with 380 Auto ammo, and it's a very loose fit. The case at 11 o'clock has been fired. The one at 9 o'clock shows imprint of light firing pin strike. It misfired. (The problem was traced to an improperly heat-treated firing pin.)

Super Auto, Speer Lawman 115-grain TMJ 9mm Luger, Speer Lawman 147-grain TMJ 9mm Luger, and Speer 90-grain Gold Dot HP 380 Auto. Chronograph velocities (Oehler M35P) at 12 feet are shown in the nearby table.

The differences in velocities obtained with 357 Mag. and 38 Special ammo in the Medusa and the M19 are no more than one could expect from any two similar guns. The performance of the 38 Super in the Medusa was quite fair, as the listed velocity is from a 5-inch barrel, and was probably optimistic in the first place. The 9mm cartridges yielded significantly lower velocities in the Medusa, compared to the 4-inch S&W M39-2 autoloader. A little of this may have been caused by gas loss at the revolver's flash gap, which measured a minimal .003-inch, but most I would attribute to gas blowing by the bullets in the chambers, and possibly in the bore. Marginal ignition may have contributed also. The greatest velocity loss came with the 380 Auto. Its 90-grain bullet lost 284 fps in the Medusa, compared to the Colt Mustang pocket pistol with its 2³/₄-inch barrel.

I fired three shots with each load on the same target, from a rest at 25 yards and from offhand at 10 yards. At the longer range all eighteen shots—six different loads—formed a group of 6³/₄ inches, widest spread. At 10 yards all the shots clustered into just under 4 inches. At 5 yards a cylinderful, one round of each load, cut a slot less than an inch long. Thus all these different loads shot close enough to the point of aim, with the same sight setting, for most defensive purposes.

Reliability was another matter. In my limited amount of shooting, the Medusa functioned perfectly with the 357 Magnum, 38 Special and 38 Super ammunition. They are what I would choose for any serious business, in that order of preference. (The 38 Super ammo will not normally seat in 357 Mag./38 Special chambers, by the way. It is too fat-headed as is the 9mmP.) There were three or four misfires—light firing pin strikes—with the Lawman 9mm Luger ammo, due, I expect, to inadequate support against the firing pin blow. (There were no misfires in the M39 autoloader, where cartridges headspace on the case mouth, as they are meant to do.) One 9mm case slipped under the extractor, and had to be poked out.

The 380 Auto rounds are such a loose fit in the chamber that one can see light all around them. If they fire, though the cases come out badly bulged, none split in my shooting of them. Close to 50 percent of the time they didn't fire, how-

Author with target shot at 25, 10 and 5 yards with six different loads in the Medusa. The rule is 7 inches long. Even at 25 yards all shots would have landed in a vital area.

Chronograph Results						
Caliber	—Bullet— Wgt. Grs.	Type	Gun	MV (fps)	Medusa MV (fps)	Loss (fps)
357 Mag	150	PMC	S&W M19	1117	1055	62
38 Spec	150	LRN	S&W M19	756	748	8
38 Super	140	MC	Claimed	1280	1091	n/a
9mmP	115	S&W	M39 (4")	1131	918	213
9mmP	147	S&W	M39	1002	884	118
380 Auto	90	GDHP	Colt Mustang Pocketlite (2³/₄")	914	630	284

ever, and one double-action string gave five misfires out of a cylinderful. Phillips & Rodgers says they got better results with Federal 380 Auto ammunition; nevertheless, it is not to be relied on in this gun, and I would not employ it for self-defense unless I had nothing else. Even so, I would be prepared to have to use the revolver as a club. A 90-grain slug at 630 fps seems somewhat trifling, to boot. If it could be arranged, greater firing pin protrusion, approaching that of the typical auto pistol, might make ignition more reliable with rimless cartridges.

[Rodger Hunziker, head of Phillips & Rodgers, told me they got a supply of firing pins that were out-of-spec too soft, one of which was in Finn's test gun. The heads peened to where they wouldn't let the pin fly foward properly to contact the primer. This problem is now fixed. Ed.]

The Medusa concept is interesting and ingenious. It is fun, but is it of any practical value? In some third-world or European countries where ammo resupply may be a problem, the ability to utilize several different cartridges could be extremely worthwhile. In this country, right now, it is much less so, unless one happens on, say, a lot of surplus 9mm at a give-away price. If we permit our noble politicians to start banning all sorts of ammo, purely for our own good, naturally, the Medusa's adaptability could come to matter a great deal. May the Lord—with our help—forfend.

For now, I regard the Medusa as a good medium-frame 357 Magnum that, incidently, can fire some other cartridges as well. Presently, for U.S. residents, it offers no great advantages over conventional 357 revolvers of like size and quality, nor any apparent disadvantages. But, under some circumstances, the Medusa could be the only way to go.

●

S MITH & WESSON'S NEW Model 17 is a black-finished ten-shot K22 revolver, and it's a real winner. While they still offer the six-shot Model 617 in stainless, the new ten-shot is ideal for several sorts of competition, handgun hunting, plinking, training, or just about whatever you might want to do with a 22 handgun. However, you first might have to convince yourself, as I did long ago, that you really need a rather heavy revolver chambered for the 22 LR. In my case it took a while, but in retrospect, buying a K22 was one of my better moves.

A very long time ago and quite far away I was engaged in the hardest work of my life, running a trapline in darkest Alaska. Every morning I'd get up, curse the bitter cold, and build a fire in my barrel stove to warm up the cabin a bit. Then I'd put on some coffee and, while it cooked, get dressed with layer after layer of clothes. In spite of the layers, I dreaded strapping on the deadly cold lump of steel under my left arm, where it would hang for the next twelve hours.

It seemed like it took a good hour or more to warm up that 6-inch K22 Masterpiece until it would stop chilling me to the bone. The endless night of subarctic Alaska took the temperature outside my little trapping cabin down to anywhere from 20 to 40 below zero, sometimes colder and very rarely warmer, and the cold would get deep into the heart of the gun and freeze its every molecule, no matter where I hung it for the night. As I rode along the trail in that weather the gun would get cold again; packing it was not much fun.

I carried it in a Bianchi X-15 Large shoulder holster to protect it from the harsh Alaskan environment. The 100-mile trapline kept me outdoors for about twelve hours every day all winter, and I'd be falling off my snowmobile into four-foot-deep snowdrifts all along the way. Besides the fact that I needed that sixgun, I happened to like it very much. We had been down many a trail

S&W's
TEN-SHOT K22
It Keeps On Shooting...

by RAY ORDORICA

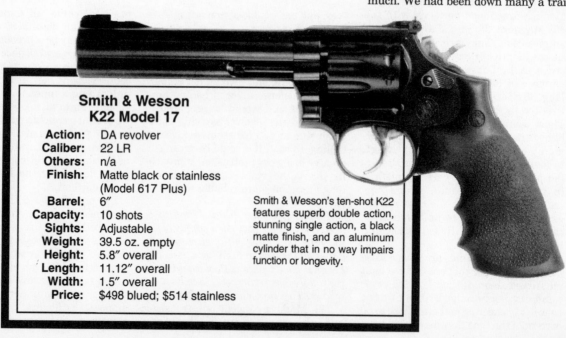

**Smith & Wesson
K22 Model 17**

Action:	DA revolver
Caliber:	22 LR
Others:	n/a
Finish:	Matte black or stainless (Model 617 Plus)
Barrel:	6″
Capacity:	10 shots
Sights:	Adjustable
Weight:	39.5 oz. empty
Height:	5.8″ overall
Length:	11.12″ overall
Width:	1.5″ overall
Price:	$498 blued; $514 stainless

Smith & Wesson's ten-shot K22 features superb double action, stunning single action, a black matte finish, and an aluminum cylinder that in no way impairs function or longevity.

together before I moved to Alaska, and I didn't want to lose that fine revolver. That's why I packed it in the protective and snug shoulder holster. When I wanted it, there it was, ready to go to work. It never failed me, and I grew even more attached to it over the years I trapped with it. My K22 is one of my all-time favorite handguns.

In spite of my fondness for the K22 and the fact that I've shot mine so much—I've put well over 9000 rounds through it—I fought buying it for a long time. I thought the Kit Gun with 4-inch barrel was the ideal 22, but couldn't find one. I must add that I hadn't fired either type of revolver at that time. I was going on presumption.

Someone told me the K22 was an outstanding handgun, but I couldn't see it. Too big. Not enough rounds for that much gun. Clumsy and unattractive. Yet I couldn't condemn it for its lack of accuracy, because I knew enough about K22s to know they were used at Camp Perry for Bullseye competition, and guns of its ilk had done quite well there before the advent of semi-autos.

As so often happens, I fell into the ownership of a K22 when someone offered me a deal I couldn't refuse. The gun came into my life in May 1973. I acquired it from a man who had bought it new in the mid-'60s and had fired it but little. The gun was in like-new condition. I did a quicky action job on it, just enough to remove the rough spots, which were mighty few on Smith & Wesson handguns back then. It had the target hammer and trigger, but instead of target stocks it had the standard checkered wood Magna stocks that hug the profile of the backstrap and extend to its top. This setup proved ideal for my purposes, and though I experimented with different grips, including some monstrous thumb-rest target stocks, nothing suited me as well as what came on the gun.

Shortly after I bought it I moved to Las Cruces, New Mexico, and had ample opportunity to shoot my new gun. I shot the heck out of it for about two years. Out in the desert where no one could get hurt, I was able to practice on hand-thrown aerial targets, shooting double action. The relatively small Magna grips came into their own for DA shooting, I found. I also practiced offhand at NRA targets, shot at extreme long range, practiced hip-shooting with each hand, and did a lot of double-action shooting as fast as I could empty the gun.

I burned up well over 6000 rounds out in the desert. One day, my friend Ken Dallmeyer watched me put five of six shots out of that K22 from the hip into the standard black six-inch bull at 25 yards, shooting as fast as I could. It was nice to have something to show for all that practice shooting.

What does all of this have to do with the new ten-shot K22? In spite of my great love for my personal six-shot version, I'm sorely tempted to add the ten-shot to my battery. I like the addition of four extra shots, but that's not all. Though S&W still sells the six-shot stainless edition as of this writing, I suspect the ten-shooter (black or stainless) will outsell it ultimately. There are some sound reasons for that prediction.

The K22s, all of them I've seen including the latest, have a superb double-action stroke. These big revolvers are at their absolute best, in my opinion, as trainers, particularly for double-action shooting. The latest ten-shot K22 will be even better, for reasons we'll explore in a moment.

The ten-shot K22 utilizes a somewhat heavy barrel that makes hits come easier than with my old gun. The weight of the barrel with its full-length top rib and full-length underlug steadies the gun for offhand shooting, and particularly so for fast double-action work.

This gun would be perfect for the hunter who likes revolvers, and if he were to put a scope on it...Wow! Putting optics on the new K22 is made easier by the fact that S&W has drilled and tapped the top strap under the excellent adjustable rear sight that comes on the gun. The

Author's early six-shot K22 has slimmer barrel, full-length top rib, target hammer and trigger, and Magna grips. The new ten-shot version at left has a larger-diameter barrel and a full-length underlug, smooth case-hardened trigger and hammer, and matte black instead of glossy finish. It's also available in stainless.

removal of one screw exposes the drilled holes for the scope mount. Although I scoffed at scopes for many a year, I find that if I use my reading glasses these days with iron-sighted guns, I can shoot smaller groups. The only problem is in seeing the target well enough, and a scoped K22 revolver would make plinking a whole lot more productive.

The new gun has all the match accuracy of the old version, either one capable of shooting far better than most can hold. Only a Ransom Rest would be able to determine their ultimate accuracy. With the new K22, grouping on the order of about an inch at 25 yards is possible with a variety of ammo, including CCI Stingers.

If you can hit easier, and there are more shots in the gun, why not go for the higher capacity? This new gun is especially attractive when one consid-ers it will do all the old one will, and then some.

Next we have double-action shooting, the big sleeper with this gun. I have already told you how much fun DA shooting is with the six-shot K22, and the ten-shooter can be even slicker. Because a ten-shot cylinder doesn't have to turn as far as a six-shot with each full-length double-action pull, there is less friction with each trigger pull. The double-action pull—all else being equal—will be smoother than that of a six-shot version. The new K22 has one of the finest out-of-the-box double-action pulls I've felt. I'd like to try a version that's been tuned by one of our best custom revolver men. It'd be a stunningly smooth DA handgun.

As long as you haven't made any dumb mistakes like leaving oil under the extractor star so it picks up unburned powder and binds up the gun, the new K22 is slick and fast for double-action shooting. Shots go where you want, and the weight of the barrel helps steady things down. The trigger is smooth on its front face, which helps DA shooting. In my testing, I put six shots double-action into about an inch at fifteen yards. The other four went wide because I left too much oil on the gun, so the DA pull bound up. That was my mistake, not the gun's. The hammer is sharply checkered for ease of cocking for single-action shots.

This gun would be ideal for NRA Bullseye shooting. One problem I had with my six-shot K22 is that the barrel was just a bit whippy, compared to my Smith 41 autoloader. That was one reason I shot the 41 in matches, but I was actually able to score better with the K22 in slow-fire stages. I shot timed fire by cocking the revolver for each shot, but I shot rapid fire in double-action mode. That whippy barrel, combined with my lack of skill, caused me problems. The ten-shot version stays on target better, double action, and I'd not hesitate to shoot it in Bullseye competition.

The near-bull barrel dimensions of the new K22 make author's early six-shooter seem whippy. The extra weight makes for steadier holding in single- or double-action shooting.

Author's six-shot K22 is very experienced, but he says the four extra shots might come in handy. The ten-shot cylinder is of aluminum, but the star is steel.

The ten-shot K22 has a dead-flat black finish that I like, and that'd be perfect for hunting. One of the reasons for this finish is that the cylinder is made of aluminum. This is, apparently, a manufacturing necessity stemming from all those holes in the cylinder. This material is entirely adequate for rimfire pressures. The gun is fitted with the Hogue Monogrip with its finger grooves, a grip I usually don't like, but it's just fine on this gun. Under the grip the gun has a rounded butt, and a variety of different stocks will fit, giving you whatever type grip you might want.

This gun is ideal for the 22 LR pin shooters who prefer a revolver to a semi-auto, but don't like the limited number of shots with the six-shooter. The five-shot stages give them only one spare shot with the old gun, but five spares with the ten-shot.

I'd make sure I did some testing to find out what brand and type of ammo burned the cleanest and left the least amount of unburned powder granules and crud behind, so there would be the fewest problems shooting double action. Don't oil the gun too much. Smith personnel say that this revolver is designed to operate rather dry. It doesn't need any surface oil.

Any 22 revolver, and centerfires too, for that matter, can get tied up from too much oil, especially when you use ammo loaded with powders that tend to burn incompletely in revolvers. Some 22 LR ammo is designed to operate best in rifles, and while it will work OK in handguns, there is usually some unburned powder left in the case, the chambers and, of course, the barrel. When you eject the empties, any oil under the ejector star will collect that unburned powder and it'll stick there. In the worst case, you won't be able to close the gun. Imagine my surprise when that happened to me after firing just ten shots out of this brand-new gun!

The first ten shots went out OK, then I ejected them and dropped the next ten into the chambers and found that I couldn't close the bloody gun. I jiggled it around here and there, but to no avail. Something seemed stuck. The cylinder seemed to have grown in length, and wouldn't go back into place, but finally it did. The problem was cured by wiping all surplus oil off from under the extractor star.

With the problem fixed I proceeded with my testing, and it proved to be somewhat boring. I couldn't find any ammo the gun really didn't like. I could only discover trends in accuracy. Like the cowboys of old, if I had this gun in my holster and was also packing my favorite rimfire rifle, I'd use exactly the

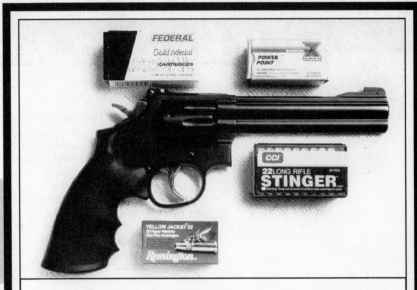

Author Ordorica preferred these types of ammo in the K22. In his tests, nothing beat Federal's Gold Medal Match for accuracy, but Winchester's Power Point was pretty good, at much higher speed. CCI's Stingers are his first choice for general use, but Remington's Yellow Jacket were close behind. No ammo shot poorly. He found exactly nothing wrong with this gun.

CHRONOGRAPH RESULTS
S&W M17 6" 22 LR

Bullet Maker	Weight (grs)	Type	MV (fps)	Comments
Speer/CCI Mini-Mag	40	Solid	995	
Speer/CCI Mini-Mag	36	HP	1031	
Speer/CCI Mini-Mag +V	36	WC	1185	Exc. for hunting
Speer/CCI Green Tag	40	Solid	869	Very accurate
Speer/CCI Pistol Match	40	Solid	845	Superb accuracy
Speer/CCI SGB*	38	WC	991	Good hunting choice
Speer/CCI Stingers	32	HC	1251	3/4" First choice!
Remington Viper	36	HP	1086	
Remington Yellow Jkt	33	HP	1100	
Federal Classic	40	Solid	1012	
Federal Classic	38	HP	1076	Good all-around
Federal Gold Medal	40	Solid	968	Top target ammo
Winchester Power Point	40	HP	1038	Fast, heavy bullet.

*Small Game Bullet

same ammo for both, and pack only the one type in my kit bag. My favorite 22 rifle uses nothing but CCI Stingers, and the K22 shoots them quite well. They gave 1250 fps out of the K22.

This K22 would be an ideal companion on a serious pack-horse hunting trip. A fine plinking or small game hunting handgun, it would be able to fill the pot with grouse or rabbits along the trail where you don't want to spook bigger game. It would be ideal on canoe or raft trips for all of the above reasons. On the water, however, you might opt to pack the stainless M617 or M617 Plus instead.

Right around home you can train anyone well in the fine art of handgunning with a good 22 revolver, and the

heavier the better for novices. This gun will be nearly impossible to wear out, in my estimation. Buy one today and shoot it as much as you like, care for it as it deserves, and your great-great-grandchildren can still shoot the heck out of it a hundred years from now. I sure wish my dad had bought a K22 long, long ago. What a fine legacy it would have been.

To this day I have nothing but extreme respect for the K22 in any version, and I doubt that any handgun in the world could beat it for training in fast double-action shooting. You'll never regret the purchase of a Smith & Wesson ten-shot K22. By the way, what would the politicians do if this were an eleven-shot? ●

My OPPONENT LOOMED tall, dark and not more than 5 yards to my front. Backing me up was a veteran of WWI and two others who had helped rid the planet Earth of the despicable Axis powers during the 1940s. I used two hands to hold the heavy handgun, cocking back the hammer as I struggled to align the sights. Under pressure, I did my best to squeeze the trigger. The big horse pistol barked, and I was rewarded with a satisfying "thud" as the heavy jacketed bullet connected with the thick corner post of a 500-acre south Texas pasture.

I was probably fifteen years of age at the time; that would have made it 1958. I was armed with my most recently acquired piece of ordnance, a Smith & Wesson Model 1917 in 45 ACP, a U.S. Army combat veteran just like the three relatives who solemnly stood behind me that day. They'd each been issued one of the double-action 1917s early in their war years. The Smith, along with a similar offering by Colt, went into production as the U.S. entered WWI because we didn't have enough capacity to manufacture the Army's official sidearm, the Colt 45 M1911 semi-automatic pistol.

In any case, that one hit on the corner post was all it took for the men towering behind me to voice their approval—by making no comment at all. Perhaps they were reflecting on their own war years...or what might be in store for my generation. Having been previously instructed on how to use the stiff half-moon clips and properly manipulate the swing-out cylinder on the gun, I was left to enjoy my prize and the limited supply of steel-cased ammunition I had stuffed in the front pockets of my Levis, with the admonition to "be careful with that thing."

S&W's
MODEL 457 45 ACP
An Affordable, Light Big Bore
by JERRY BURKE

Smith & Wesson Model 457

Action:	Double-action/single-action semi-automatic
Caliber:	45 ACP
Finish:	Non-reflective, glass-bead matte blue
Barrel:	3³⁄₄″
Capacity:	7 shots
Sights:	Fixed, low-profile, drift-adjustable front & 2-dot rear
Weight:	29 oz. unloaded
Height:	5.5″ overall
Length:	7.25 overall
Width:	1.25″ overall
Price:	$490 suggested retail

Smith & Wesson's new "Value Series" compact 45 ACP, the Model 457, has an aluminum alloy frame and abbreviated dimensions that make it easy to pack. Priced right, the 457 comes with two stainless steel 7-round magazines.

I was recently reminded of that long-ago day as I took my first look at Smith & Wesson's newest handgun chambered for the battle-proven 45 ACP, the lightweight, compact semi-auto designated the Model 457. A member of what S&W calls their Value Series, the 457 was designed as a concealed-carry self-defense weapon or "house gun." At 29 ounces, the 457 is a full 5 ounces lighter than the popular Model 4516, a similarly configured S&W compact 45 ACP crafted from stainless steel.

Handgun packaging has definitely come a long way since I purchased my first new Smith & Wesson decades ago. Although quite serviceable and today even collectible, that famous blue cardboard box with stapled corners was rather primitive compared to the modern version. These days, Smith & Wesson provides a nearly indestructible snaplock plastic box fitted with foam liners to protect their handguns from damage. An integral carrying handle is included, as well as mated holes in lid and base to accommodate a lock to discourage unauthorized use of the firearm, especially by children.

A sticker inside the box alerts the shooter to retrieve the Owner's Manual from inside the lid. No matter how many new handguns pass through my hands, I

always read the manual before getting seriously acquainted with any firearm. These guidelines not only vary from manufacturer to manufacturer, but from model to model as well. In addition, firearms companies continue to work on improving their products even after production has begun; that Owner's Manual might contain important information on features not found on the last similar-but-different handgun you've handled. In this instance, I was reminded that Smith & Wesson semi-autos feature a magazine disconnector, rendering the weapon inoperable if the magazine is not fully seated, whether or not a round is in the chamber. While this feature has both its champions and detractors, on average, it's a definite "plus" in avoiding "I didn't know the gun was loaded" accidents.

On examining the 457, my first impression was how incredibly "clean" it is. The compact 457 is extremely snag resistant. There's little to catch on clothing or equipment that would impede a clean draw, even from under a suitcoat. The 457's sights feature a white dot up front and two at the rear, which allow for an excellent sight picture. They're positioned as low as practical atop the carbon steel slide. The ejection port is seriously relieved, giving

empty shell casings plenty of room to successfully exit the pistol during the firing cycle. The slide, as with all other exterior surfaces on the 457, is covered with a non-reflective bead-blasted blue finish, just the thing for a serious hideout gun.

The 457's slide-mounted, left-side-only decocker doubles as a manual safety. As the decocker lever is fully depressed, the cocked hammer is dropped only after the firing pin is beyond its reach. The decocker/manual safety lever then stays put in the "down" or "safe" position. A deliberate swing of the lever to a position parallel with the slide is required to place the 457 in fire-ready condition. Once again, Smith & Wesson has incorporated this as an added safety feature.

Although absent from the front of the grip frame and trigger guard, there is checkering on all three sides of the one-piece, wraparound grip. This grip is only slightly angled and has a straight backstrap, and blends perfectly with the exterior finish of all metal parts. The single-side (left) button magazine release is located just behind the trigger guard, and provides for very positive securing and release of the seven-shot magazine. Happily, the S&W Model 457 comes complete with two magazines, both constructed of stainless steel and with finger extensions.

The 457's hammer is bobbed, placing it flush with the back of the slide when in the full-forward position. Besides deactivating the trigger, another check on the manual safety is the hammer, which protrudes slightly from the back of the slide when the safety is "on." Although not a recommended way of cocking the hammer when it's in the full-forward position for safety reasons, it is quite possible to pull the trigger slightly to begin moving the hammer to the rear, and catch the hammer with the thumb of the non-shooting hand. The hammer can then be drawn back to the full-cock position. This allows for a single-action shot from the pistol after a round has already been chambered in this double-action pistol. While I don't recommend the practice, I have the option of making that first shot a single-action one in a real-life situation. To make this as easy and secure to accomplish as possible, I plan to have the top of my 457's hammer checkered or

S&W's Model 457 quickly field-strips into easy-cleaning major components. Dual recoil springs put the brakes on rearward slide movement. The grip frame assembly is feather light, thanks to aluminum alloy construction.

Author Burke tested the new S&W 45 in ways that it would be used in an actual encounter, including one- and two-hand point-shooting, plus traditional aimed fire. Traditional target practice alone will *not* prepare the concealed handgun licensee to successfully resolve real-life encounters. Here he engages a gunfight-distance target, point-shooting from the hip.

Author found the new S&W 457 easy to put into action, even from under a suitcoat. The smooth double-action trigger pull permitted accurate first-shot placement. Excellent, inexpensive holster is Uncle Mike's Sidekick Professional, inside-pants, open top model. The easily constructed assailant target adds an element of realism.

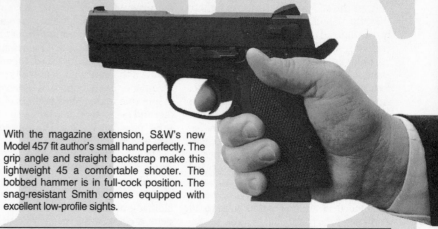

With the magazine extension, S&W's new Model 457 fit author's small hand perfectly. The grip angle and straight backstrap make this lightweight 45 a comfortable shooter. The bobbed hammer is in full-cock position. The snag-resistant Smith comes equipped with excellent low-profile sights.

The S&W M457 digested this variety of 45 ACP ammo with no problems, except for target ammo (third from right), which fed well but didn't cycle the slide every time.

S&W

grooved for a positive grip.

The alloy-frame gun weighs just 29 ounces with unloaded magazine, sports a 3³/₄-inch barrel, and has an overall length of just 7¹/₄ inches. The body of the gun is just an inch wide, or add a bit more to include the slightly protruding slide stop and decocker/manual safety lever. Height of the compact S&W from base of the magazine extension to the top of the rear sight is 5¹/₂ inches. In summary, this is a truly compact lightweight, and a 45 ACP to boot!

The new model 457 is quick and easy to field strip for cleaning, breaking down into frame, slide, barrel, slide stop and recoil spring assembly. For my money, in the unlikely event any fur-

ther disassembly is required, I want the Smith & Wesson *factory* to do the job; I'm real picky when it comes to a gun I might have to bet my life on. A quick look inside the 457 confirmed what I expected, that while the exterior may have an economical but practical finish, there's nothing "budget" about the inner workings of this mighty little pistol. The craftsmanship, fit and finish are what Smith & Wesson has provided its customers worldwide since 1852, first rate, and nothing less.

My next step was to select a variety of 45 ACP ammunition to run through the exciting new 457. I picked only what I consider top-quality factory ammunition, products from companies with whom I've had decades of prior success. In the nearly forty years I've enjoyed reloading, I never have reloaded ammunition for semi-autos, and I never will. Single shot handguns as well as single- and double-action revolvers do not require absolutely unwavering perfection in the ammunition they're fed; the

S&W Semi-Auto "Firsts"

Yrs/Mfg.	Model	Caliber	Action	Size	Remarks
1913-22	35 Auto	35 S&W	SA	Pocket	First S&W semi-auto
1983-89	469	9mm	DA/SA	Compact	First modern S&W compact semi-auto
1985-89	645	45ACP	DA/SA	Full	First S&W 45 ACP semi-auto
1996	457	45ACP	DA/SA	Compact	First aluminum-frame S&W 45 semi-auto

semi-auto is much less forgiving. Besides, the S&W 457 is designed to save your hide under the most grave circumstances. I don't even want to *practice* with ammunition that might cause my combat gun to malfunction!

On that note, I selected Federal, Remington, CCI/Speer and Winchester ammo, but that's not to say there aren't a number of other firms cranking out quality cartridges. From Federal's lineup I went with the 230-grain Hydra-Shok jacketed hollowpoint and a full-metal-jacketed version in the same bullet weight. The first of these, with its tapered center post visible inside the tip of the projectile, provides efficient transfer of energy to the target and produces very effective mushrooming; the second is a more traditional but effective GI-style load which maximizes feeding reliability and proper functioning.

From Remington, I chose their metal-clad, match-grade wadcutter, which was never intended for use in a compact defensive combat handgun, but is a very accurate round I enjoy shooting through my full-size 45 semi-autos. A more practical choice for the test was Remington's 185-grain jacketed hollowpoint, which combines controlled bullet expansion and good penetration for its intended use.

CCI/Speer, another industry front-runner, offers a number of great 45 Auto loadings, including Gold Dot jacketed hollowpoints in 185- and 230-grain bullet weights. I also included CCI/Speer Lawman ammunition, which is virtually identical to that firm's popular budget-priced Blazer brand, except reloadable brass cases are utilized. The Gold Dot HPs include a jacket which wraps over the bullet tip and deep into the hollow point. The on-target result is at least 150 percent bullet expansion from its original diameter.

Three Winchester 45 ACP loads were on hand for test firing: the 185-grain Silvertip jacketed hollowpoint plus 230-grain versions in both Winchester's Subsonic and SXT configurations. Winchester's Silvertip ammunition delivers excellent penetration and uniform bullet expansion. The Subsonic cartridge was originally developed for the U.S. military, and in addition to excellent performance, provides limited recoil and muzzle flash. Winchester's SXT (Supreme Expansion Technology) ammunition includes a unique two-stage hollowpoint cavity, and delivers excellent accuracy, expansion and weight retention.

I tried, then eliminated the Remington metalclad wadcutters, even though they turned in the best accuracy. The remaining nine cartridges tested in the new S&W 457 cycled through the com-

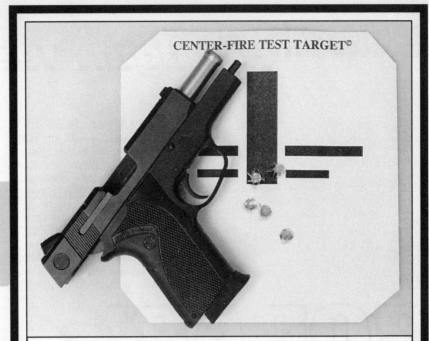

CENTER-FIRE TEST TARGET©

The only limit to accuracy with the Model 457 is the ability of the shooter. Controlled "timed fire" from a standing, two-hand position produced groups like this at 15 yards. The author developed this inverted "T" target long ago for accuracy testing; aim point is the base of the vertical bar.

Test Results

Brand	Wgt. Grs.	Type	Avg. Vel.* (fps)	Avg. Group** (ins.)
Federal	230	Hydra-Shok HP	830	1.62
Federal (Match)	230	FMJ	820	1.83
Remington	185	JHP	930	1.82
Remington (Match)	185	JWC	707	1.32
Speer Gold Dot	185	HP	994	1.94
Speer Gold Dot	230	HP	820	1.77
Speer Lawman	230	TMJ	830	1.59
Winchester Silvertip	185	JHP	986	1.90
Winchester SXT	230	JHP	852	1.50
Winchester Subsonic	230	JHP	840	1.78

*Shooting Chrony chronograph used to determine velocity; equipment placed 6 feet from gun muzzle.
**Results average best five-shot group fired at 15 yards from a rest. Group sizes measured center-to-center of two widest shots.

pact 45 flawlessly. At 15 yards, each proved itself worthy of top-flight accuracy for a handgun of this type. Five-shot groups ranged from 1.5 to just under 2 inches. Frankly, part of the grouping difference was a function of wind conditions on the test day, coupled with a pause or two for intermittent rain showers. All in all, the test-firing session, which included more than 250 rounds, confirmed the accuracy and reliability of Smith & Wesson's new Model 457, as well as the consistent quality of the ammunition available to today's shooter.

A great deal of thought went into the design of this new gun. The result is a triple threat, should the pistol need to be called to action. First, the Model 457 offers the battle-proven power of the 45 ACP cartridge; second, that power is offered in a highly-refined, compact and lightweight configuration making it ideal for daily concealed wear; and finally, Smith & Wesson's new 457 is backed by a tradition of quality dating back to 1852. At a suggested retail price of $490, the 457 is an excellent value, combining all the refinements handgunners have come to expect from this company at a price that's affordable in today's marketplace. When Smith & Wesson announced that the 457 was to be an addition to their Value Series, they certainly meant what they said. ●

THEY SAY APPEARANCES can be deceiving, and so it is with the pistol and cartridge that are the subjects of this report. At first glance, the pistol appears to be a cleanly customized 1911-type autoloader; the cartridge looks for all the world like the 45 ACP. On closer examination, however, profound differences are evident, differences born of the restless urge to improve upon the Government Model and its prototypical ammunition.

Some might insist that the big Colt auto and its better replicas, given certain modifications, already constitute the highest attainment of combat-handgun design. Similarly, a strong case can be made for the preeminence of modern factory loadings for the 45 ACP among defensive handgun cartridges. I could not argue with much conviction against either of these assertions. Nevertheless, humans in general, and gunnies in particular, never have been able to leave well enough alone. The result, sometimes, is called progress.

The Pistol

The Robar Companies are probably most often associated in the minds of shooters with advanced plating and coating technologies. In fact, Robbie Barrkman's outfit does a highly diversified business in customized, high-performance firearms—concealed carry packages, fighting shotguns, stopping rifles for dangerous game, sniper rigs and more. All of the work from the Robar shops that I have examined has been nicely executed. More important, perhaps, Robar's custom guns reflect Barrkman's extensive practical experience as a combat veteran, IPSC competitor and teacher of the shooting arts.

ROBAR's
COLT M1991A1
A Super 45 Super

by GARY SITTON

Robar 45 Super

Action:	SA Auto
Caliber:	45 Super/ 45 ACP interchangeably
Finish:	Roguard/NP3
Barrel:	5″
Capacity:	7 +1 shots
Sights:	Fixed
Weight:	36 oz. empty
Height:	5.4″ overall
Length:	8.5″ overall
Width:	1.35″ overall
Price:	$1600 package price (1991A1). Conversion: $325 for your gun

The slide finish is Roguard and the frame is coated with NP3. These are specialties of The Robar Companies, as is their superb functional stippling. Note the low lever on the safety, made by Robar. The forward slide serrations are for safer press-checking.

The pistol Barrkman loaned me for use in developing this report started life as a Colt M1991A1. After thorough modification by Robar, its mother would scarcely recognize it. Barrkman has a strong penchant for two-tone pistols, so the test pistol has his preferred finishes. The slide is coated with black Roguard, which is durable and quite resistant to corrosion and abrasion. The frame and its associated small parts, as well as the barrel bushing and recoil spring plug, are plated with NP$_3$. This latter finish combines electroless nickel and micro-particles of a polymer to protect the steel. NP$_3$ is slightly slick to the touch and tends to smooth the movements of working parts; it also lightens trigger-pull weights somewhat.

To expedite reloads, the Colt's magazine well was given a gentle bevel. The front of the grip frame was given the rather coarse stippling that Barrkman prefers to checkering on gripping surfaces. He says stippling is easier on cover garments. I am inclined to believe it is less likely to gnaw on the shooter's flesh than sharply pointed checkering. At any rate, the stippling provides plenty of purchase for the fingers of the strong hand. The mainspring housing

is Wilson's flat, checkered unit. The grip safety is also from Wilson, the High Ride Beavertail, incorporating a speed bump (Wilson calls it a Posi-Release Tab) to ensure grip safety disengagement with the highest possible shooting grip.

Other aftermarket parts on the pistol include a skeletonized Videki trigger, a skeletonized burr hammer by Ed Brown, and Robar's own low-mount thumb safety. Having learned to shoot the Government Model back when "gay" still meant happy and carefree, I don't operate with my thumb up and riding on the safety-lever. If I were to make the transition, though, all of my 1911-type pistols would have this Robar thumb safety. The modestly extended and gently curved lever is positioned lower on the safety than normal, so the thumb can rest on it comfortably and without danger of dragging on the slide.

Grips are of the classic double-diamond pattern by Kim Ahrends. From the color and contrast of the wood, I would guess them to be cocobolo.

Novak sights were dovetailed into the slide, front and rear. Tritium inserts—a green dot fore and two yellow dots aft—are a great aid to low-light shooting. I

have the same combination of dots and colors on a Springfield Stainless Government Model, albeit from Wilson, and they have made me a missionary for such sighting equipment. The tritium tubes are surrounded by white rings, which creates a sight picture quite like that of the conventional arrangement of three white dots in good light. The general configuration of the Novak sights is, of course, almost universally admired among students of combat pistolcraft.

All of the pistol's corners and edges have been melted, broken, dehorned or whatever you choose to call dulling the sharp, potentially painful angles on a handgun. The ejection port is lowered and faired back. In addition, the surface of the slide's top, between the sights, has been lightly stippled, creating a false rib some 3/8-inch wide. Finally, vertical serrations are cut into the front of the slide. The forward serrations are supposed to facilitate press-checking the pistol with the weak hand positioned under the slide and dust cover. This operation is easier written than done for reasons to be explained momentarily.

So far, so normal for a neat, no-nonsense carry gun. This brings us to the

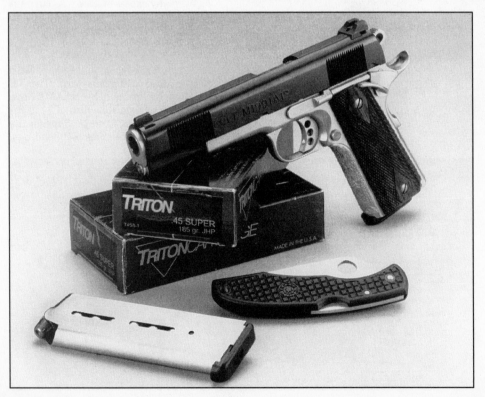

No ordinary 1911, Robar's two-tone 45 Super shoots 45-caliber missiles at much higher velocities than possible with 45 ACPs, but it'll handle those, too.

ROBAR

good parts, if you will forgive the pun, and the real substance of this essay.

The slide bears the usual factory markings—"COLT M1991A1™" and "SERIES 80." Between the ejection port and the front slide serrations, it is also stamped with this identifier: ".45 SUPER." Immediately behind the "-COLT 45 AUTO-" marking on the barrel, the characters "4S5" are stamped. Obviously, ".45 SUPER" and "4S5" are meant to communicate the fact that this is more than another customized Government Model.

The message of those unusual stampings is communicated nonverbally when you rack the pistol's slide. Based on the effort required, it is clear that you are working against something altogether different from the typical 18-pound recoil spring. Even with the improved purchase afforded by the front slide serrations, press-checking the pistol requires considerable hand strength. Field-stripping the pistol reveals the reasons behind this extreme stiffness.

With the magazine removed and the chamber double-checked to make certain the pistol is unloaded, retract the

slide and lock it in its rearmost position. This exposes almost two inches of the full-length recoil-spring guide rod. Just forward of the dust cover, a vertical hole has been drilled through the guide rod; it is the secret to controlled disassembly. A pin of some sort has to be placed in this hole. The pin should not protrude appreciably above the top surface of the guide rod, but it must extend below the bottom far enough to bear against the recoil spring plug. Cutting an L-shaped section from a heavy paper clip to size worked for me. With the pin in the hole and held snugly against the guide rod by a rubber band, the slide can be released carefully and eased forward until the recoil spring plug bears against the pin. The slide is thus freed from tension and the slide release pin can be removed from the pistol. The slide, barrel and recoil spring assembly are then removed from the frame in the usual fashion. The remainder of the disassembly procedure goes according to the program for a conventional 1911-type pistol. Reassembly is accomplished by reversing the order of disassembly.

In the 45 Super pistol, you want desperately to keep the recoil spring, one-piece guide rod and recoil spring together as a unit. If the retaining pin slips out of position, the double-wound

32-pound spring will send the plug across the room at high velocity. This extra-stout spring is central to the pistol's operating system, but once apart, you will not get the recoil spring assembly back together without resorting to a vise and strong language. Believe me, I know about this. In addition to the big spring, the recoil forces generated by the 45 Super cartridge are moderated by a special buffer that is permanently held between two plates at the aft end of the guide rod.

About the only other discernible difference I could find between a standard Government Model and the Robar pistol had to do with the firing pin. Because the 45 Super runs at pressures in the neighborhood of 32,000 psi, as compared to 21,000 psi for standard-pressure 45 ACP loads, a stock firing pin is apt to pierce primers. To eliminate this potential problem, the firing pin was ground off to a length of 2.240 inches, and the edge of the tip was beveled at a 45-degree angle. The remaining flat on the tip of the pin is equal in diameter to half the diameter of the firing pin.

The Ammunition

A number of factors contribute to the terminal efficiency of a pistol cartridge. Beyond the design and construction of bullets, the elements of most common concern are caliber, bullet weight and velocity. The 45 ACP surely has ample bullet diameter and weight for its intended applications, but it never has enjoyed any excess of speed. As currently loaded by the factories, the 45 ACP in standard-pressure form is supposed to deliver muzzle velocities of 1000 fps with 185-grain bullets, 975 fps with 200-grain projectiles, and 880 fps with the original 230-grain load. The +P loadings sanctioned by SAAMI have published muzzle velocities of 1140 fps for 185-grain slugs and 1055 fps for the 200-grain bullets. The +P loadings,

(Above) Dimensionally identical to 45 ACP ammo (right) the Triton 45 Super loads are distinguished by "TRITON 45 SUPER" headstamp and the NP3 coating on the cases.

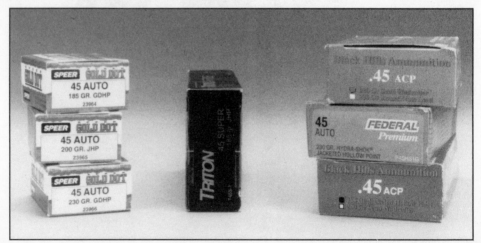

Author Sitton shot this variety of loads, and the gun handled them all perfectly. Change of ownership of Triton Co. made ammo procurement difficult.

58 HANDGUNS '97

then, are notably faster than standard-pressure ammo, but they hardly elevate the 45 ACP's performance into that of an entirely different cartridge.

Efforts to pump up this cartridge have heretofore been limited by the design of the 1911-type pistol and conventional brass for same. In the 45 ACP Government Model, a section of the case is unsupported in the chamber. Over this unsupported area, firing pressure is contained by the web of the case alone. Raising pressures much beyond the maximum permitted by industry standards will bulge or bust the case. This is a bad thing.

Dean Grennell, perhaps the most knowledgeable and inventive of living writers on handgun matters, reasoned that brass for the defunct 451 Detonics Magnum might be adapted to the 45 ACP chamber. The shortened 451 cases provided significant margins of strength and safety due to their thicker walls and web sections. The resulting cartridge, externally identical in all dimensions to the 45 ACP, was dubbed the 45 Super. Properly shortened and reamed, 45 Winchester Magnum and 308 Winchester brass can be used in loading the 45 Super as well.

Ace Hindman, the late pistolsmith of Kerrville, Texas, worked with Mr. Grennell in modifying pistols to contain the Super. The recoil spring assembly, buffer and firing pin alterations described above were Mr. Hindman's contributions to the project.

At that point, they had a wildcat cartridge and a fully functional pistol to shoot it. As a bonus, the Hindman-converted 1911s also handled standard and +P ammo for the 45 ACP with complete equanimity.

Factory ammunition for the 45 Super became available in 1995 from the Triton Cartridge Company. A fair variety of loads was cataloged, including a 185-grain JHP at 1300 fps, a 200-grain JHP at 1200 fps, a 230-grain JHP at

1100 fps, and reduced loads for tactical purposes (185/1200fps and 200/1150 fps). A 230-grain FMJ load with a starting speed of 1100 fps was also listed for applications demanding maximum penetration. The Triton ammo features cases plated with the same Robar NP_3 as protects the frame of our test gun.

Cases for the Triton ammunition are manufactured by Starline. Triton will reportedly make unprimed 45 Super brass available to handloaders at a later date. Meanwhile, those wanting to reload for the hot new number will need to shoot factory ammo first.

Range Note

Actually shooting the Robar 45 Super was interesting, informative and among the most memorably frustrating experiences of my twenty-five-year career as a writer. Make no mistake, there is nothing wrong with the pistol. It performed flawlessly. Ammo was another story, and a long, sad story at that.

I requested test quantities of representative 45 Super ammunition from Triton early in 1996. None arrived. As the deadline for this article approached in April, I began calling the company. My calls were not returned. Eventually, I did connect with Mr. Barry Portnoy, Triton's new CEO. He explained that the company has experienced growing pains. Changes in management had occurred. The manufacturing operation was being moved from upstate New York to Pennsylvania. As soon as they resumed operations, he would have the requested ammo shipped. As this is written in mid-June, said ammo has not yet arrived.

You do not drive down to the local bait shop/gun store/gas station and casually pick up a few boxes of 45 Super. I did manage to beg 100 rounds of the 185-grain JHP load from Robbie Barrkman. That, I regret to say, was the extent of the 45 Super ammunition

on hand for testing. In the end, I had to make the best of a bad situation.

Triton's 185-grain 45 Super load, at least, is the real deal. It averaged 1320 fps over my PACT Professional chronograph. By comparison, Speer's 185-grain Gold Dot hollowpoint 45 ACP load registered 994 fps, and the 185-grain JHP load from Black Hills clocked 989 fps. Not only did instrumental velocities exceed published claims for the Triton load, but the kinetic energy over the skyscreens was a thumping 716 foot pounds. That is an increase of some 75 percent over the standard-pressure 45 ACP loads.

Recoil, muzzle jump and torque might be fairly compared to the 10mm Auto in a Government Model. Put another way, my subjective read on recoil and shot-to-shot recovery with the 45 Super would make comparison with full-power 357 Magnum loads in a medium-frame revolver appropriate. The 45 Super's setback is brisk, decidedly more vigorous than that of the 45 ACP, but certainly not punishing.

Accuracy was about what you would expect from a custom Colt set up for reliability, not precision. Five-shot groups at 25 yards spanned from 2.5 to 4 inches, on centers, depending on the

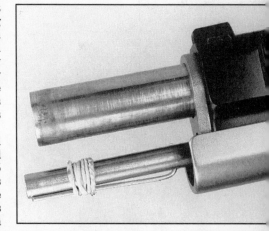

(Above) Disassembly requires capturing the recoil spring assembly to relieve tension. Author Sitton made the high-tech pin from a large paper clip. It's held in place with a rubber band. If the pin slips out after disassembly, he says, bad things happen at great speed.

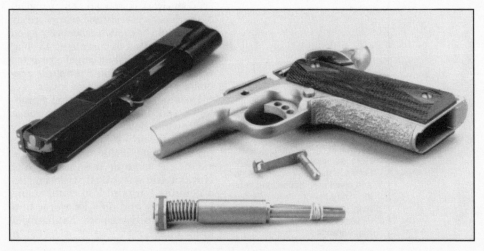

Here are the major parts groups. Note the Delrin buffer between steel plates at the left rear of the recoil spring assembly.

load. Groups with the 185-grain Triton load varied from 3.5 to 4 inches. Functional reliability with all ammunition, including the three loads mentioned earlier, plus four other 45 ACP factory loads, was perfect. I am told 45 ACP softball loads will not cycle the pistol, but since I did not try any of the low-pressure target ammo, I have no judgment to offer.

Final Thoughts

If Triton's 200- and 230-grain ammunition for the 45 Super makes claimed muzzle velocities (and credible sources say it does), the cartridge is ballistically equal to the 10mm Auto, given bullets of comparable sectional density. The option of 10mm performance in a pistol that will also shoot the milder and relatively inexpensive 45 ACP is surely no bad deal.

When Triton Cartridge Co. gets up and running again, and particularly if they offer unprimed 45 Super cases, the

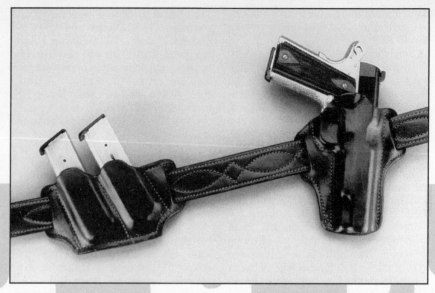

Robar's 45 Super in carry leather from Insearch, Ltd. Whether loaded with ACP or Super ammo, this is a formidable defensive rig.

cartridge may create for itself a specialized niche among those who admire the Government Model and the 45 ACP but want more power on call. Were I to

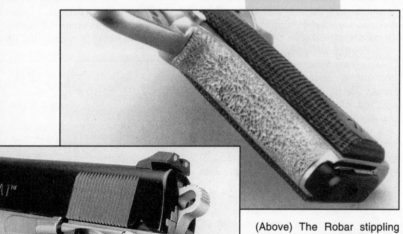

(Above) The Robar stippling must be experienced. Even the Editor says it's really good stuff.

Here we see the Videki trigger, Brown hammer, Wilson beavertail and checkered mainspring housing, eight-shot Wilson/Rogers mag, and Robbie Barrkman's low tactical safety. The stocks are by Kim Ahrends.

have Robar convert one of my pistols to 45 Super, I would lay in a goodly supply of the special Starline brass. Investing in a gun with capabilities that depend entirely on a single source of ammunition makes me very nervous.

It is easy enough to envision practical justifications for the Robar 45 Super. It would make a decent hunting pistol for deer and other medium game, though I believe I would limit my shots to 50 yards or less. I would also want good adjustable sights on the gun. Sights that make standard 45 ACP loads shoot to point of aim at 25 yards are likely to be off for the 45 Super at twice that range. And I would ask for a bit of accurizing work. Twenty-five-yard groups in the 3- to 4-inch range are acceptable in a service or combat handgun, but that translates to 6- or 8-inch groups at 50 yards, and that is not good enough for game.

Some citizens will like the added authority of the 45 Super for defensive uses, just as some swear by the muscular 10mm Auto. Law enforcement officers who work remote areas may find all of the Super's velocity and energy attractive. I would be cautious about relying on bullets designed to operate at 45 ACP speeds, though. They might prove too soft to hold together and penetrate adequately at the 45 Super's velocities.

Despite present ammo supply problems, the 45 Super seems to me a worthwhile development. I definitely like the Robar pistol. With a package price of $1600, including the gun and excluding some of the niceties like Novak/tritium sights, it strikes me as a genuine bargain. You could spend more money and do a lot worse in a flexible, multi-purpose handgun. I know I have. ●

HANDGUNS 97

Self-Defense Scene

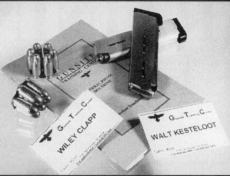

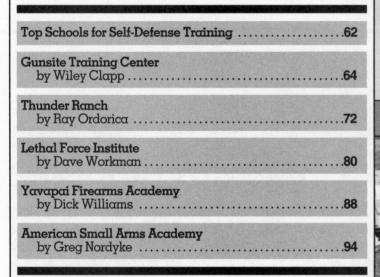

Clapp tests Gunsite's training, page 64.

Workman stressfires at LFI, page 80.

An outline of Taylor's ASAA, page 94.

TOP SCHOOLS FOR SELF-DEFENSE TRAINING

A COMPLETE OVERVIEW

Gunsite Training Center

"Possibly the most rewarding aspect of the whole experience is witnessing the development of a positive and confident attitude within everyone in the class, particularly in the case of really inexperienced shooters."

—*Wiley Clapp*

Thunder Ranch

"Thunder Ranch is about gunfighting. It is about shooting. Most of all it is about logic... the pinnacle of logic (is) to avoid any kind of fight in the first place."

—*Ray Ordorica*

Last year on these pages we offered expert suggestions on what to buy for a home-defense handgun. Each of our five experts also suggested the need to get good training along with the new gun. We took our own advice and sent five writers to school to find out what's available in the way of top-notch instruction for beginners, and present their reports to you here.

All of what our writers learned is applicable to home defense and is also appropriate for—even geared toward—concealed carry. That is a logical extension of home defense, of course, because once you're used to the idea of defending yourself, it does not make a lot of sense to leave your protection at home.

There are now at least a million folks in thirty-one states who have licenses to carry a concealed weapon. We guess that fewer than ten percent of them have any significant training. Training means more than simply learning how to shoot. It also means how to avoid a fight, how to recognize the specific conditions that must be met before you shoot, and what to do afterward.

We report here on entry-level courses taken at five top training schools, and by comparing their differences and similarities, you can find out what to expect from them. There are other good schools. Ray Chapman's, John Farnham's, and Dr. Piazza's new Front Sight Institute come to mind. Any one school's specialized training might make you want to start with them so you can move on to advanced courses under the same instructor.

Two of our five, Gunsite and Thunder Ranch, are on permanent (and rather extensive) facilities. The others are roving courses that come to a shooting range near you. Each type has advantages. They all offer at least several chances per year to attend and have advanced courses for graduates.

Good training can cost as much as a good handgun. However, knowing how to react to a gunfight can save you millions of dollars in lawsuits, maybe even your life.

Concealed-carry laws come from the desire of people to be able to defend themselves. It makes good sense to first find out how to shoot, instead of practicing mistakes that could cost you dearly. Your choice.

Lethal Force Institute

"Ayoob's classroom segment is not for the squeamish. An LFI entry-level course on the judicious use of lethal force takes a student through the dynamics of a self-defense shooting, and much more."

—*Dave Workman*

Yavapai Firearms Academy

"It was the "tactical thinking" that really hit me. At no time during the three-day course were you allowed to stop thinking about the situation you were in, and how you chose how to handle it."

—*Dick Williams*

American Small Arms Academy

"One of the points Chuck (Taylor) consistently emphasizes is that *you are the weapon*, the gun is only a tool. How you use that tool is your responsibility."

—*Greg Nordyke*

"Push-Pull"—the basic Weaver stance involves pushing forward with the gun hand and pulling to the rear with the support hand.

GUNSITE TRAINING CENTER

by WILEY CLAPP

TENS OF THOUSANDS of neophytes take up the handgun as a defensive tool every year. Particularly in the light of newly liberalized laws regarding concealed carry, we are seeing more and more responsible citizens arming themselves against the very real possibility of criminal attack on the street, at home or in business settings. Carrying a handgun is serious business, and I would hope that those who choose to exercise their right to go armed do so with sound training behind them. In my view, one of the best possible places to take your combat handgun training is Gunsite.

The legendary Gunsite Training Center is located in the rolling, juniper-covered hills north of Prescott, Arizona. Many hundreds of students attend a variety of combat shooting courses there every year. In addition to several levels of handgun training courses, the school also teaches the use of the combat shotgun, carbine, long-range rifle and submachine gun. Specialized courses for women only are available, as are ones that are required for Arizona CCW permits. When students are in attendance, the clear, high desert air at Gunsite fairly crackles with the rattle of gunfire. This might be intimidating to the tyro, but there are a number of good reasons why this school has the most positive atmosphere

imaginable. After the first few hours of a course, students begin to pull together and enjoy the learning experience very much.

So how do they create such a positive atmosphere? I have been to Gunsite a number of times, and it seems to me that several things go into the equation. For one thing, there's a clearly defined doctrine that is routinely taught and understood by all of the instructors. It's also true that the instructors have positive attitudes about their work and the patience of Job.

Shooters come to the school from diverse backgrounds and with varying levels of experience. It's common to find one or more students in every class who have exactly zero experience with a handgun and with do-it-this-way training systems. The instructors move patiently from one point to the next, and pretty soon, those beginners have darned well learned something. The facilities—ranges, classrooms and tactical simulators—are excellent for the subject matter.

When Editor Ray Ordorica and I discussed a section on handgun training for HANDGUNS '97, I pressed for an opportunity to go back to Gunsite for another course. The logical thing for me to do would have been to go on to a #350 Tactical

Side-by-side on the firing line, Gunsite #250 students practice the basics.

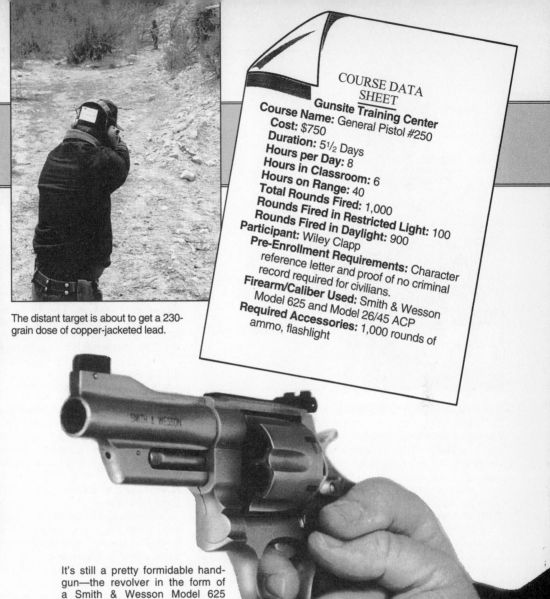

The distant target is about to get a 230-grain dose of copper-jacketed lead.

COURSE DATA SHEET
Gunsite Training Center
Course Name: General Pistol #250
Cost: $750
Duration: 5½ Days
Hours per Day: 8
Hours in Classroom: 6
Hours on Range: 40
Total Rounds Fired: 1,000
Rounds Fired in Restricted Light: 100
Rounds Fired in Daylight: 900
Participant: Wiley Clapp
Pre-Enrollment Requirements: Character reference letter and proof of no criminal record required for civilians.
Firearm/Caliber Used: Smith & Wesson Model 625 and Model 26/45 ACP
Required Accessories: 1,000 rounds of ammo, flashlight

It's still a pretty formidable handgun—the revolver in the form of a Smith & Wesson Model 625 Mountain Gun with 4-inch tapered barrel in 45 ACP.

Pistol course, which would build on the experience of the #250 General Pistol I had taken in 1993. But we also wanted to get a part of the training section of the book dealing with the revolver as a defensive firearm. For that reason, I agreed to go back and take the same course again, this time with a wheelgun.

The most valuable part of a repeated experience such as this is simply the opportunity for comparison. And that's not just a comparison of the two types of guns, but also a comparison of one handgunner's ability to manage them under the same rough field circumstances.

My partner for the second course was a local handgunner of no small skill named Walt Kesteloot, who used a Colt 45 semi-auto with a few custom touches and Novak sights.

On my first trip to Gunsite in '93, I used a handsome Colt M1911A1 45 ACP semi-auto, completely worked over by Wayne Novak's shop. The gun was fitted with a Bar-Sto barrel and Novak's own patented fixed sight system. The basic pistol is an American classic, and this customized specimen is an absolutely first-rate example of what a sensible, shootable fighting pistol ought to be.

On my second trip to Gunsite and to keep the semi-

auto/revolver comparison on a level playing field, I used a Smith & Wesson Model 625 and a Model 26, both of them 45 ACP revolvers. The Model 625 was a lightly customized version of the Springfield Arsenal Commemorative, essentially a Mountain Revolver in 45 ACP. The main distinguishing feature of the Mountain Gun is the slim, tapered barrel which has the same light, graceful shape and weight as the guns of yesteryear. The Model 26 is also known as the Model of 1950 Target. It was S&W's first attempt to satisfy the demand for a target grade revolver in 45 ACP. I bought this gun used several years ago and had the barrel shortened to 4 inches.

Both revolvers had top-notch action jobs, because I went with the belief that most of my shooting would be in the double-action trigger mode. Also, I used full-power 230-grain ball ammunition with the autoloader in '93 and the same type of ammo in the revolvers this year. Using a 45 ACP revolver means using the little full-moon clips of sheet steel. More on them in a few minutes.

Before we go any further into a description of the training course, let's spend a minute or two on the subject of guns for Gunsite. One of the keystones of the Gunsite doctrine involves the use of a major-caliber handgun. Despite the oft-

"YOU DIE
T YOUR GEAR"

(Above) Walt waiting for a bout in the final shootoff. He'll take the two far targets down, change magazines and drop the near target. Another shooter is to his right, facing an identical setup. Whoever drops the near target first wins the bout.

Stovepipe! Dave Starin is all set to practice a malfunction clearance drill.

repeated allegation that Gunsite is a M1911A1 school, the staff does not particularly care what type of pistol or revolver you use. They stand ready, willing and able to train you on anything that's a truly serious defensive handgun. Guns that are slow to reload, such as single-action revolvers of any caliber, are assuredly not recommended, nor are cheap little semi-autos of inadequate power.

Some two dozen students attended my class. The M1911A1 was well represented, with about a third of the class carrying one version or another of the grand old gun, but the remainder was almost equally divided between Glocks, Berettas, and SIGs. There was one shooter (who performed very well) using a Magnum Research Baby Eagle 9mm. I was the only shooter with a revolver. It's interesting to note that one woman shooter was using a SIG P229 in the new 357 SIG caliber. This is an unusual bottlenecked cartridge which some would have you believe is a problem feeder. She encountered not one single malfunction of any kind in the entire week. Hmmm....

As flexible as the instructors are when it comes to dealing with individual shooter's preferences and problems, they are completely rigid and inflexible where safety is concerned. Students get an initial safety lecture at the beginning of training, and the four principles of safety are on everything from wallet cards to "Burma-Shave"-type sequential road signs on the way to the ranges. They might let one inadvertent screw-up slide by, but repeated bad gunhandling is cause for termination of training. The plus side of this grim situation is simply that you learn how to handle your gun safely if you are a beginner and have long-standing principles reinforced if you are not.

The essence of the Gunsite doctrine of defensive shooting is summed up in a triad of mutually supporting principles. Mindset is the psychological aspect of resolving a personal attack. Gunhandling sums up the essential skills required to manage your weapon of choice—various methods of carrying the gun, loading and unloading, malfunction clearance drills, etc. Marksmanship is the developed skill necessary to quickly deliver shots to the target under varied conditions— Weaver stance, flash sight picture, compressed surprise trigger break. Teaching is systematic, proceeding from the simple to complex, basic to advanced. Take the draw stroke,

for example. Gunsite instructors teach this by the numbers in a five-count system. You spend a considerable amount of time learning how to get your handgun smoothly out of the holster and into a proper firing grip and stance.

The first couple of days at Gunsite are taken up with these sorts of step-by-step drills and shooting exercises at close range. The instructors also begin teaching alternate positions for longer-range shooting, such as braced kneeling and rollover prone. Most of the shooting is done at the 3-, 5- and 7-yard lines. These are short shooting distances by most standards, but they are completely consistent with the realities of most actual gunfight scenarios.

Very early in the program, the instructors begin to require a pair of shots rapidly delivered to the torso of the special Gunsite camouflage silhouette. By the end of the second day, shooters find themselves doing this in two distinctly different ways. One way, called the "controlled pair," occurs when the shooter uses a separate sight picture for each shot. The other technique is called a "hammer," and it's two shots fired with only the initial sight picture. Eventually the handgunner learns the "Mozambique" or "failure" drill. This is two to the torso, assess for effect, then one to the head. It's named for its place of origin and a realization that even the best of ammo sometimes fails to have the desired effect.

The main practical combat marksmanship techniques taught at Gunsite are a smooth presentation of the pistol from the holster into a solid Weaver stance, a flash sight picture, and the compressed surprise break. Assuming the shooter is equipped with a major-caliber pistol (typically 45 ACP) and ammo of serious power, these elements combine to fulfill the requirements of the familiar combat shooter's motto: *Diligentia, Vis, Celeritas*—Accuracy, Power, Speed.

To master all of it requires many repetitions of the drawing, aiming and firing cycle. The by-rote training system used in those first few days on the school range at close distances begins to develop the muscle memory required to come out of the holster and deliver accurate shots very quickly. But a Gunsite #250-level class is only the beginning of a combat/defensive handgunner's education. He needs a lot of practice on his home range, as well as possibly returning to Gunsite for other intermediate and advanced courses, such as #350, #499, ATP 1 & 2, etc. However, Gunsite #250 is

Braced kneeling is a steady position for longer shots.

A variant kneeling position puts both knees on the deck. It's called the California kneeling.

about the best possible beginning you could find in the sense that it does develop the very basic skills almost indelibly.

In the last two full days of the #250 week, shooters work out on the tactical simulators, both indoor and outdoor. These are simulated tactical situations in which the student traverses either an outdoor trail or a multi-roomed house. All of the shooting here is with live ammo. Naturally, there are many bad-guy targets along the way, each of which requires an appropriate response. In the indoor simulators, there are also a few "don't shoot" targets.

Students don't get to shoot any of the simulated tactical exercise courses until an instructor reviews a number of sound tactical principles for the class. I have now had this particular course from two different instructors. As conducted by either Bill Murphy or Larry Landers, this short lecture is an excellent piece of realistic instruction.

Interspersed with the simulator training, the class continues to polish the basic skills and begins to practice exercises conducted at close range in which multiple targets are engaged at extreme speed. There are also both Dozier and *El Presidente* drills. Particularly in the case of the *El Presidente*, movement is involved. Facing away from the targets with a holstered gun, the shooter executes a 180-degree turn, then engages a trio of targets spaced widely apart and some 10 yards downrange. There's a mandatory reload and a second sweep across the targets, delivering two more shots to each. It's not hard at all—that is, until you consider the speed required. Ten seconds is maximum time.

On the final half-day of the course, the shooters run through a review of the exercises for score and class ranking, then go on to an enthusiastic man-on-man shoot-off to determine who is the best shooter in the class. It's a lot of fun, and the day ends in the classroom with a presentation of diplomas. Possibly the most rewarding aspect of the whole experience is witnessing the development of a positive and confident attitude within everyone in the class. Particularly in the case of really inexperienced shooters, the training produces an air of self-reliance that you don't often see.

In this light, let's take a look at what happened to my partner, Walt Kesteloot. He went to Gunsite with the basic marksmanship training of a reserve deputy with the local sheriff's department. Walt is an avid hunter and shooter whose childhood training was with a very good NRA basic smallbore rifle program. Admittedly apprehensive about training at the legendary school, Walt was about as open-minded and diligent a student as you could possibly imagine. When the instructors directed the class to do so many repetitions of the five-count draw stroke in our quarters at night, Walt did twice that number. He was determined to get the most from the experience. By the end of the second day, the confidence level of this shooter was just beginning to blossom. By the end of the week, he had an air of self-assured poise as he went about the various drills and exercises. If you apply yourself, Gunsite will teach you more than just gunhandling skills.

That pretty well covers the generalities of what they do at Gunsite and why they do it. Many of the twenty-four students in my class (three instructors) were police officers or active-duty military personnel, but there were also quite a few civilians. Six students were women. Some shooters were far more experienced than others, and some, as we have already noted, were complete tyros. I'd estimate that about half the class were novices, a quarter were somewhat experienced, and the other quarter consisted of pretty good shooters. Everybody learned and everybody gained.

For me, bringing a revolver to a course that I had earlier attended with a semi-automatic pistol taught me a few things for which I was totally unprepared. I can summarize all of the experience by saying that I now believe—and I did not before—that a shooter who chooses a revolver is at a disadvantage to the semi-automatic shooter, although not a critical one. To put it another way, the adept revolverman is hardly ill-armed, but he's not as well off as the skilled guy with the autoloader.

For the better part of twenty years, I carried a revolver as a police officer. I witnessed the development and acceptance of the various types of speed-loading devices in the course of shooting countless PPC matches. When I went to Gunsite this time, I was pretty confident in my ability to handle the gun well. Nothing taught at Gunsite about revolver management is inconsistent with any of my earlier training or experience. The reloading technique I used as a cop is essentially the same as what I was taught at Gunsite.

In reloading a revolver, speed is important for two reasons.

(Left) Speed reload. The shooter makes sure he has the reload magazine in hand before he drops the partially empty one from the gun.

NOT DOOR

A tactical reload is fast, and it can save a partially loaded magazine for later use.

Flat to flat. Shooter matches the flat on the back of the magazine to the flat on the back of the magazine well.

GUNSITE AFTER DARK

ONE OF THE more interesting blocks of instruction at Gunsite is the session conducted just after dark. We fired about 100 rounds (of the recommended 1000 we brought along) in limited light. We got a chance to see how hard it is to shoot well in conditions of reduced visibility. The session includes a commentary on the use of tritium inserts (night sights), which are surprisingly effective. You can achieve perfect sight alignment with good night sights, which enables you to shoot well as long as you can see the target.

Another very effective technique involves the use of a flashlight. For many years, the Harries flashlight technique (developed by Michael Harries long ago in California) was the best way to shoot by flashlight. The Harries method involves crossing the wrists so the

backs of the hands are pressed together to achieve stability. The result is something like the Weaver stance. The thumb of the non-shooting hand activates the flashlight button.

In recent times, the light of choice has been the 6P Sure-Fire lithium-battery light from Laser Products of Fountain Valley, California. It's a compact, very bright flashlight made of aluminum, with the activating button in the tailcap.

The same company's new Model 6Z is a decided improvement, and it has spawned a new shooting technique called the "Rogers Sure-Fire" method. By reducing the diameter of the flashlight barrel and wrapping it with a couple of tough rubber grommets, Laser Products has built a light the shooter grasps in the manner of a syringe. The light is activated by pressing it back against the heel of the hand. This technique avoids the awkward and uncomfortable crossed hands of the earlier method. It's a quick, easy grip and stance to assume. The new Laser Products 6Z or the longer three-battery 9Z are definitely state of the art.

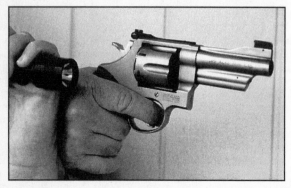

The Harries technique still works very well.

Laser Products' 6Z works beautifully with the Rogers Sure-Fire technique.

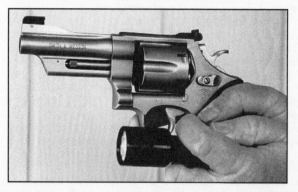

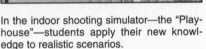
In the indoor shooting simulator—the "Play-house"—students apply their new knowl-edge to realistic scenarios.

Wrong! Walt is too close to that deadly corner.

Much better. Take the corner in segments and stay away from it.

First, the gun is out of action while you are reloading (unlike a semi-auto). Second, if you happen to be engaged in a really hot fight, the six-round capacity of a wheelgun means you will be reloading somewhat more often than you would with a self-loader.

The system of six 45 ACPs clipped into a full-moon clip is, I believe, superior to typical rimmed revolver cartridges and speedloaders. It is fast because the clip and cartridges go into the cylinder as a unit. It's also better in unloading because the clip and empty brass come out of the gun as a unit. Since 45 ACPs are much shorter than the magnum rounds for which the cylinder dimensions were intended, the stroke of the extractor rod can be much shorter. But whatever you do, don't bend the clips! A bent full-moon clip can completely tie up the gun.

WHAT YOU'LL NEED

GUNSITE RECOMMENDS ANY modern revolver or semi-auto pistol, but no single actions or miniature handguns. Some other items of equipment that prospective students should consider include a hat with visor to shield the eyes, and sunblock and ChapStick for sun protection. Eye and ear protection are mandatory. Good glasses (prescription, if necessary) should be part of every shooter's kit, but any good impact-resistant sunglasses will do. Ear muffs, particularly the electronic variety, are very nice, but the little foam plugs still work very well. After the gun, the most important pieces of equipment are the belt and holster. Many different holsters are available on the market, but I would recommend the higher-quality rigs if you are going to use leather.

Happily enough, the store at Gunsite carries a wide variety of this stuff along with vests, jackets, tee-shirts, pins, etc. If you are in doubt about your gear, wait until you get there and pick from their selection with the help of their professional staff. As a matter of fact, the Custom Shop will sell you a gun of your choice from their diverse stock. That includes the shop's own custom guns, built with the features most handgunners want, all sighted-in and ready to go. Don't even think about showing up without several spare magazines that work in your gun and a carrier for them as well.

Colt 45 semi-auto; Galco belt, holster and pouches; Dillon electronic ear muffs; Laser Products 9Z tactical light; Wilson magazines.

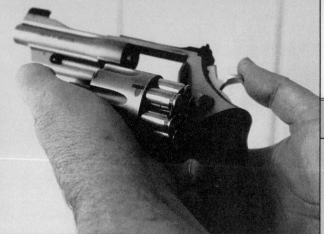

Starting the revolver reload: Shift the gun to the left hand and thumb the latch and cylinder open.

Reloading with the full-moon clips is at least as fast as using a speedloader.

There are several ways to speed-reload a wheelgun. I think this is the best way: When you need to reload, punch the cylinder latch with the thumb of the shooting hand and swing out the cylinder with the fingers of the support hand. Transfer the gun smoothly to the support hand. As the shooting hand drops to the clip (or speedloader) pouch on the belt, the non-shooting hand pivots the revolver muzzle upward and vigorously strokes the ejector rod with the thumb. This clears all empty cases from the cylinder. The gun is then brought in closer to the body and turned muzzle down to accept the reload, which the shooting hand has pulled from the belt carrier. When the rounds are in the cylinder, the shooting hand goes back to a firing grip as the support hand wipes the cylinder closed.

This is the technique I have always used and which seems to be as sure and speedy as any. At the beginning of the course, I was able to do this reload a trifle faster than most of the pistol-armed students in the class could execute a speed magazine change. By the end of the course, most of them had caught up with me.

Early on, I discovered a problem with my revolvers I had not anticipated. For all the years I had used the wheelgun as a duty and PPC tool, I was using a K-frame S&W, which has its barrel axis not much higher than the top of the shooting hand. The 38 Special ammo, whether duty or match, produced modest recoil. When I used an N-frame S&W 41 Magnum for IHMSA matches, I fired the gun slowly and deliberately. Muzzle rise was not a particular problem. However, with full-power Black Hills 45 ACP ammunition in my rather light S&W revolver, I found that the muzzle was going all over the place. Fast, accurate pairs presented a distinct problem. I hate to admit it, but it was bothering me. I was neither as fast nor as accurate with the revolver as I had been with the semi-automatic pistol.

I also discovered the need for proper grips. My 1950s-vintage Model 26 had a nice pair of Herrett's Jordan Troopers made to fit my hand. I found myself shooting a lot better with this gun, because the superb grip shape spread the recoil force into the palm of my hand and left me in far better control of the gun. It sure looks to me that old-time handgunner Bill Jordan well knew what he was doing when he designed that grip. However, disaster struck when the forcing cone of that grand old revolver gave up the ghost and started throwing key-holed shots on target. I was forced to use another gun of the same general characteristics, but it had a round butt, and therefore I couldn't swap grips.

In spite of that problem, I still had some of the traditional advantages of the revolver in my favor. Getting the gun out of the holster and on target is probably a trifle easier with a revolver, because the butt of the gun is more amenable to acquiring a fast grip. Getting off the first shot seems to be about as fast as with the single-action semi-auto in the hands of a Gunsite-trained shooter (who carries it cocked-and-locked and makes depressing the safety part of the presentation). The revolver is well ahead of the DA semi-auto for that first shot.

HOW TO SIGN UP

Gunsite Training Center's #250 is a 5½-day course running from Monday through Saturday noon. The cost is $750, which includes the instructional materials and training in the classroom and on the range. You'll spend about six hours in class and forty on the range.

Ammunition (1000 rounds) must be provided by the student, and it's available at the school at attractive prices. Accommodations in local hotels and motels are available in Prescott or Chino Valley at a variety of prices. The daily noon meal is catered, or the student can bring his own.

The class is offered twenty-one times a year, and you have to have a character reference letter or proof of no criminal record from your local police to get acceptance.

More information may be had from: Gunsite Training Center in Paulden, Arizona.

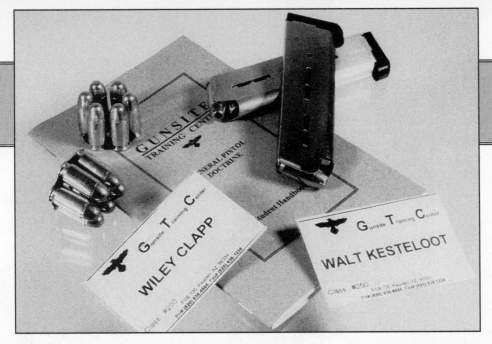

Revolver vs. automatic, cylinder vs. slide, moon clip vs. magazine. Take your pick.

The DA trigger pulls on my two S&Ws were smooth and easy to manage through a long arc, with some 10 to 11 pounds of pressure. And when the semi-automatic shooters spent hours learning malfunction drills of three different types, I just pulled that smooth trigger one more time and brought up another cartridge.

Any revolver loses to the semi-auto in a capacity comparison. Six rounds versus seven, eight, nine, ten, or even more shots in the magazine plus the one in the chamber makes the semi-auto a better choice for protracted battle. In reality, though, I believe the six rounds in the cylinder of a revolver are probably enough for almost any confrontation.

There's another effect of the reduced capacity of a revolver. Part of the field-simulator training at Gunsite involves multiple targets and some degree of anxiety. The instructors don't coach you, and ammunition management is your responsibility. The classic boo-boo is running your gun dry and hearing the dreaded "click" instead of a satisfying "boom." If you enter one of those simulators with a six-shot revolver, you are acutely aware that "click" is just a few shots away. At least with me, this had the twin beneficial effects of forcing me to be sure of my sight alignment before I dropped the hammer and of being sure to reload when I could, and not when I had to.

At one point in the indoor simulator, I was about to enter a wide room with 180 degrees of possible target locations. I had four rounds left in the revolver and was in a position of reasonable safety. I quickly reloaded with a clip of six, dropping four live rounds on the floor. It's a good thing I did, because there were no fewer than three hostile targets in the next room, one of whom was armed with a submachine gun.

I wouldn't want to place undue emphasis on this aspect of the Gunsite revolver-versus-semi-auto comparison, because it's obvious you can waste shots with anything if you don't pay attention to what you are doing. But you do tend to be more careful when you're on-tap ammo supply is limited. Having more shots available in your gun is never a mistake, but the misuse of high-capacity handguns is a common phenomenon. If you give up power in order to increase capacity (i.e. a greater number of lesser-powered cartridges), you are playing with fire.

Nevertheless, one other aspect of the revolver-versus-semi-auto comparison became obvious in the course of my second trip through Course #250 at Gunsite. I fired most of the up-close and furious exercises during the week in double action. Both of my revolvers were as good as you can get, as both had superior action jobs. But on several occasions when I was shooting at greater distances or when I knew a shot was coming up, I thumb-cocked that big S&W hammer. The trigger pull of a tuned S&W revolver in single action is a pure delight, about 3 pounds of pressure with a clean, crisp break. You can't safely carry a cocked revolver to get that crisp single-action pull for every shot, but when you pay attention to what you are doing and can make use of it, it greatly enhances your chances of a hit.

However, you *can* have that superb, crisp trigger pull for every shot with a M1911A1-style single-action pistol. In the fast, close-quarters shooting exercises that make up training at Gunsite—and which closely mirror actual shooting situations—it's the trigger pull of the single-action semi-auto that makes it the weapon of choice for the shooter who wants the best.

The key to using the big Colt well is training. I would never recommend a shooter arm himself with a M1911-style handgun unless he is willing to expend the time, effort and money to learn to use it properly. I believe the revolver in a major caliber is an entirely acceptable substitute. In the final analysis, the trigger action of any handgun is what determines its utility.

For a shooter who wants to develop his defensive shooting skills, I heartily recommend the training courses at Gunsite Training Center. My revolver training was better than anything I experienced as a police officer and had the beneficial effect of focusing my attention on the real differences between revolver and semi-auto. I doubt if I end up selling all my wheelguns, but I am sure I will be more kindly disposed towards future good deals on any M1911A1 pistol in 45 ACP, 10mm or even the new 9x23mm Winchester.

The combat shooting mavens at Gunsite build knowledge and skill, from which grows poise and confidence. No matter what ordnance you've chosen for your own personal defense, they'll teach you to use it well. In the process of doing so, they contribute to your overall sense of security in a turbulent and sometimes hostile world. They teach you to deal with the criminal, lethal confrontation that nobody wants, but too many have to face. They teach living without fear. ●

The Editor is caught in the middle of a tactical reload. The fresh magazine is held between the first and second fingers while the partially used mag is withdrawn and pocketed, for possible later use. (Robbie Barrkman photo)

Gunfights take place at close range, sometimes within touching distance of your adversary. The idea is to avoid a fight if possible.

THUNDER RANCH

by RAY ORDORICA

"**D**ROP THE GUN! Do it now!" Bangbang ...bangbangbangbang!

"Cover! Watch 'em!" Bangbang! "Come back! Keep coming back!" You holler at your "partner" to make sure he retreats as fast as you do.

"Stop, Puleese!" Bangbangbang!

The stress is terrific. Your heart is pounding, adrenaline rushing; your legs and back hurt from the constant strain; your breathing is shallow and rapid...when you remember to breathe. Your hands are sore from gripping the gun as hard as you can, and your arms ache from the constant pushpulling to control the recoil of the 45 semi-auto in machinegun rapid fire. Just when your ammo runs low, your partner hollers "Cover!" and you've gotta watch his side, too. You're moving back out of danger and feeling for cover with your back foot, all the while keeping your gun pointed right at the target.

The "bad" guy pops up again and your gun runs dry after one shot, so you snatch a quick reload and shoot and shoot again, and keep on shooting until the problem goes away.

This time, you're down on the ground, your head toward the target, lying on your face. You're spitting distance away from the target image of a guy standing over you with a gun. You've still got your gun and you have to shoot, so you bring it up...but you can't see the sights, and the strain on your back hurts like the dickens. So you roll onto your side and up comes the gun, you focus on the front sight and squeeeze...BangBang! Easy, when you know how.

Now it's night, and the felons are there in the dark and you can't even see your gun, much less the front sight. You've got it pointed somewhere in their direction, but you don't know if they're armed. Are they a threat to your life? If not, you can't shoot. A car turns a corner somewhere behind you and its headlights briefly throw dim light onto your suspects, and you see a subgun in one guy's hand, a shorty shotgun in the other. In the brief burst of light they saw your gun, too, and they're starting to raise their weapons. The light goes away, but the threat is still there, and you have to shoot, so you imagine the front sight, see a picture of it in your mind's eye, centered in the rear notch, and the sight picture centered on target. You shoot, hoping for the best.... Post mortem indicates dead-center hits. Something is going right.

Although the targets are paper, and they jump to electronic signals given maliciously by the superb instructors, the

Operations Officer Terry Kenney instructs students on the line at Thunder. The microphone goes to a public-address system that is audible to ear-protected students.

COURSE DATA SHEET
Thunder Ranch
Course Name: Defensive Handgun I
Cost: $850
Duration: 5 Days
Hours per Day: 7½
Hours in Classroom: 4
Hours on Range: 35 (5-day)
Total Rounds Fired: 1,150
Rounds Fired in Restricted Light: 150
Rounds Fired in Daylight: 1,000
Participant: Ray Ordorica
Pre-Enrollment Requirements: 50% deposit in advance (refundable with 60-day prior notice); local police no-crime clearance in writing.
Firearm/Caliber Used: Robar 1991 Colt/45 ACP
Required Accessories: 1000 rounds of ammo, top-quality belt holster, spare mag holder (speedloader & pouch for revolvers).

Thunder Ranch is located in midwestern Texas, near the town of Mountain Home, about 100 miles northwest of San Antonio.

stress at Thunder Ranch is real. The class, Defensive Handgun I, forces you—like it or not—to deal with stress as you go, making you analyze what you're doing before you shoot, if you shoot.

Thunder Ranch forces you to deal with what is, in most cases, an entirely new experience. The idea is to put you, the student, into as real a scenario as is possible without actually endangering your life. I doubt there is a better way to prepare for a situation we all hope never happens, the need to defend our life through the use of deadly force. In today's violent society, the chance of a problematic encounter is with us on a daily basis. If it happens, as Director Clint Smith puts it, you've got the rest of your life to solve the problem. How long you live depends on how well you solve it.

In mid-February, I left frozen Chicago and flew to San Antonio, Texas, hired a car and drove northwest out of town. As the city disappeared behind me and the air got cleaner, the gentle roll of the hills became more pronounced. As I drove along, I quickly became accustomed to the wide open spaces of Texas so reminiscent of my beloved Alaska, where you can drive for hours and see not much of anything except the countryside. I like that. After an hour or so of rather

pleasant driving, I found the cutoff and turned left toward what was to be my home on the range for five Thundering class days, Y.O. Ranch. I found the entrance to the Y.O. with no trouble, drove their long driveway past hordes of exotic game, and made it in time for an excellent home-cooked dinner at their family-style restaurant. Then I repaired to my room.

Ensconced in the very comfortable room (early Western decor with, thankfully, no TV), I unpacked, dug out my Robar-tuned 1991 Colt, the Milt Sparks Executive Special holster and my ancient Bianchi mag pouch, and made sure everything was ready to go. I had time to consider my "combat" shooting history.

I never had any formal training in combat-style shooting, though I had competed in many IPSC events twenty years prior to my matriculation at Thunder. Back then in Colorado I had some good competition: Ross Seyfried, Chuck Taylor, Ken Hackathorn, Don Fisher, and one or two others. I spent lots of time training and shooting with those guys, and even met The Guru, Jeff Cooper, but never went through any shooting classes prior to Thunder. Back then, I shot well enough to have made the state team, but instead of going to

Editor Ordorica, second from right in checkered shirt, engages a target while back-pedaling and hollering for the "bad guy" to drop the gun.

The Editor shot from concealed carry as part of the training. The target shows good hits on the "computer" portion of the head. (Robbie Barrkman photos)

the Nationals I moved to Alaska. My rapid-fire 45 shooting languished, unused for two decades.

In the Alaska bush, one hardly needs to pack anti-personnel weaponry, but when chance caused me to move nearer to the more "civilized" big cities where you really ought to pack a self-defense handgun, it seemed like a good idea to learn something about how it should be done. But where to go? I heard about Thunder Ranch one gentle night near the ocean in Dar es Salaam, Tanzania, from my hunting partner Robbie Barrkman.

In his South African-accented perfect enunciation, Robbie told me, "Ray, you really need to go to Thunder Ranch."

"Why?" I asked.

"Because it's the best...and I'm one of the assistant instructors."

In between bouts of chasing Cape buff and other assorted African beasties, I told Robbie I'd go to Thunder and would try to arrange things so that he would be there when I attended. And that is what we did.

Breakfast at the Y.O. was at 7 a.m., and Bertie the cook also had a bag lunch for me to pack along, part of the deal of staying at the Y.O.

After about a half-hour drive, I arrived at Thunder Ranch, and met Clint and his three assistants, Robbie, Terry Kenney and Ginny Lyford.

A course of instruction is no better than its instructors, and Thunder Ranch has top personnel. Clint Smith is a Marine Corps vet with two tours in Vietnam. He has been a cop and senior SWAT team member, was Jeff Cooper's operations officer at American Pistol Institute (API), and was training services director of H&K, Inc.

For ten of his twenty years as a cop, Terry Kenney was chief instructor with the Criminal Investigation Bureau of Coconino County Sheriff's office and was an instructor for Cooper's API at Gunsite for seven years. He has been operations officer of Thunder Ranch since January 1993.

Robbie Barrkman was, of course, armorer to API, which led to his very successful Robar Companies, Inc. He has won state and national IPSC matches, and has lots of practical field experience gained during his time with the South African army.

Ginny Lyford teaches self-defense shooting in her own Personal Safety Institute in Washington state and is NRA and USPSA certified.

Our class began with a lecture about gunfighting. Headman Clint Smith gave us a four-hour machinegun delivery of street-fighting facts loaded with logic that set the pace for the remainder of the week. Clint is a gifted teacher with the knack of getting the class's attention and keeping it. Yes, we twenty students were there because we were vitally interested in what he had to say, but when was the last time you spent four solid hours listing to a lecture about anything?

Clint's classroom concerns what we should do if we ever have the need to shoot at someone who is trying his or her best to kill us. Most of what he says is pure common sense, yet most of us never think about these sorts of things. Most of us think in familiar grooves, and that can work against us. Once you have been exposed to the presentation of some of life's realities in class, you will at least be prepared to think a bit differently and, most likely, more defensively.

The key, Clint says, is to train yourself to be alert to what's happening around you all the time. People who are unaware of their surroundings and the people and events interacting in their vicinity are prone to becoming victims. They don't notice the guy casually leaning on the lamppost half a block ahead on the dark street until the guy relieves them of their wallets at gunpoint. "If you look like lunch, you're going to get eaten," says Clint.

General unawareness is called Condition White, one of five military terms regarding stages of readiness. The others are Yellow (always alert), Orange (potential fight situation), Red (fight imminent), and Black (fight in progress). To avoid fights in the first place, it is your responsibility to possess a perpetual Condition Yellow thought process. This vital step is the basis of the combat mindset.

My personal observation is that people generally don't want to be in Condition Yellow, because they can't accept the reality that bad things can happen to them. Therefore, the next step in developing the combat mindset is to accept the fact that a fight can come to you at any time. All that Thunder Ranch can do to teach you that fact is to give you some things to think about and make you aware of some of the potential problems.

The average citizen never thinks about what he'd do if, for

Night shooting is part of the training during the five-day Defensive Handgun I course. Editor Ordorica's gun (center) shows two flashes from his double tap in this timed exposure shot. Note the line of fire pointing rearward from the gun at the right, indicating the ejection port opened a bit too soon. That gun was firing hot ammo without the benefit of a heavy recoil spring. (Robbie Barrkman photo)

instance, someone pulls a knife and starts running toward them. The common thought is, "It'll never happen to me!" Yet it happens.

One of Clint's examples: Two men are running toward you. One is dressed in a three-piece suit and is clean cut, the other in a grubby leather motorcycle jacket and sporting a beard. Which one is the greater threat? Most folks naturally would say the motorcycler, yet in today's world he might be an undercover cop. The other guy could be a serial murderer. "Not good, not bad, just real," says Clint Smith.

Another: You get the drop on a robber at a convenience store, and someone comes in the door in a police uniform and says, "Drop the gun!" You start to say "It's all right, I'm the good guy," but because you don't drop your gun, the cop blows you away. Or he might not be a cop at all, but the crook's accomplice in a stolen uniform.... Not good, not bad, just real.

Clint emphasizes that the worst can happen at any time, and we won't be able to predict what it will look like. It used to be the national average that one in three of us will have a violent encounter sometime in our lives. Today's statistic, I'm told, is one in two. The trick is to avoid a fight if at all possible, but if a fight happens, as Thunder Ranch emphasizes, the purpose of fighting is to win.

After the first day's lecture we never sat in class again, but the information was always coming our way. Some of it came in high-powered doses on the firing line, some in quiet conversation during lunch breaks. Storehouses of experience and information, Clint and his team interacted well with all members of the class. We learned little, but important, things. I learned that I've been reloading my 45 wrong for more than twenty years. I always had those leather pads under my magazines and, as often as not, pinched my hand when jamming in the fresh mag. Robbie showed me a slight alteration of my hand angle that not only made the job easier, less painful and more positive, but I no longer need those leather pads. A little thing, you say? Why didn't I pick up on it myself?

We were taught tactical reloading, which means recharging the gun before it runs dry and retaining the partially used magazine. I never had to perform this simple exercise at any IPSC match, yet it is vital to survival and is dictated by

common sense. The need for a tac reload can arise often. Say, for instance, you have shot at a bad guy and he ducks behind a car. You fired three or four rounds and have a few seconds to regroup before things might get hot again. Now is the time to recharge your gun, but you ought not to drop the old magazine on the ground. The trick is to return the partially used magazine to your pocket. Makes sense to me. You might need those few rounds left in that magazine. Why drop 'em on the ground?

My hands and arms got incredibly sore the first two days. We were told to assume the ready position with gun up, push-pull pressure in our arms, and to hold that position until told to shoot. By day three, I was able to hold the pose as long as necessary...almost! This is something one must work at to keep in shape, and that is made obvious on the range.

We were told we had to use hardball in the "Terminator," Clint's hermaphroditic clearing-house, because of the special targets in there. I used hardball all the time.

We did a lot of shooting. In five days I burned up 1150 rounds of Black Hills' 45 ACP hardball reloads, and it functioned perfectly in my Robar-tuned Colt 1991 (see sidebar). The muzzle flash of the Black Hills ammo was minimal in the dark, and the loads were very uniform.

For most of our shooting we were moving. Moving? Yes, retreating, taking cover, moving right or left, shooting all the while, reloading on the move, tactically reloading while your partner covers you, moving back away from the target and moving to take cover.

The idea is to maximize the distance from you to the threat for the simple, logical reason that most "bad" guys can't shoot, so the farther from them you are, the less chance of their hitting you. This retreating is not simply backpedaling. It's more of a karate shuffle. We moved a giant step rearward with the rearward leg, feeling for a place to put the foot, then retreating with the leg closest to the target, all the while keeping a solid platform with our bodies.

All of this makes perfect sense to me. You're getting away from the threat, bouncing around so you're not an easy target, hollering at the bad guy to drop the gun, and shooting until the threat is eliminated.

Moving sideways makes it harder for the bad guy to hit

(Left) Robbie Barrkman, one of the instructors, shows the class how to clear a stovepipe jam. All twenty students in this class session used autoloaders.

Shooting from odd positions such as this gives students confidence to handle many scenarios. With the head toward the target, it's hard to see the gun, much less shoot. (Robbie Barrkman photo)

you as well. Clint holds his hands up, one moving and one still. "Which one is easier to hit?" he asks. We move. I told former women's national IPSC champion Jo Anne Hall about retreating while firing, and she said that she had done lots of shooting while running, but never while retreating from the target as fast as possible. Seems to me like some practicality has been left out of "practical" shooting competition.

One of the more compelling lessons we got was in house-clearing. If you suspect someone is in your house and you have to make a search of the premises, the idea is to maximize your distance from the potential target and minimize yourself as a target to whomever might be inside, while searching for him. The technique we were shown is to slice off sections of each room a bit at a time, continuously clearing the dwelling room by room. To teach this art, Clint has a

MY ROBAR SELF-DEFENSE PISTOL

"**T**HERE ARE THREE things a self-defense gun *must* do," said my friend and African hunting partner Robbie Barrkman. "First, above all, the gun absolutely *must* work when you need it. Second, and this is *vital*, the gun needs to function correctly every time you pull the trigger. Third, equally important, is that every time you press the trigger, the gun goes *'Bang!'*"

Robbie is a master gunsmith who runs The Robar Companies, Inc., and before that he was the armorer at Gunsite when Jeff Cooper ran it, so he knows his way around 45 semi-autos. Robbie did the modifications to my 1991 Colt 45 to turn it into a reliable fighting machine, and I used it at Thunder Ranch.

During the five-day course, I shot 1150 rounds of the excellent Black Hills 230-grain hardball and put an additional 350 rounds of Black Hills and other brands of hollowpoints of varying weights and nose configurations through the gun before I went. True to Robbie's above tongue-in-cheek mandate, the gun went "bang" every time I asked it to.

How does one select what ought to be done to a personal self-defense handgun? I shipped off the new gun to Robar with very few instructions. I chose to let Robbie use his discretion and vast experience to outfit my gun properly. However, I had some preferences.

I knew I had to have a long trigger. I didn't want an ambidextrous safety, but did want an extension on the standard unit. I wanted fixed sights with tritium inserts.

I used the outstanding combat-design grips of Kim

Ahrends, which have checkering on only the lower front portion of their surfaces. I have to flip the gun to get at the mag release and in the past have used smooth grips so the gun wouldn't stick to my hand. I found that the smooth upper portion of the Ahrends "Tactical" grips makes reloading fast and easy. They're good looking, too.

I have had checkered frontstraps and mainspring housings on all my 45 semi-autos and thought I wanted them here as well. Robbie told me his version of stippling was better than checkering if I planned to shoot the gun a lot.

"Our brand of stippling is easier on your hand."

"But I don't like stippling," said I.

"Then you will get checkering," he replied.

At the 1996 SHOT show, I saw one of Robbie's 45 Supers with a stippled frontstrap, and it looked better than all other stippling I have seen. As soon as I wrapped my mitt around that handle, I told Robbie, "You were right. This is what I must have on my gun."

Now it's the evening after the third day of unceasing shooting and blasting at Thunder Ranch. In my room I took out my spare 45, a tried-and-true M1911 made in 1914. It has my checkering on the frontstrap and mainspring housing. Grasping my familiar old gun hurt my overworked hand so much that I was almost unable to hold onto it, much less take a firm grip. I silently thanked Robbie.

In fact, everything Barrkman has told me about guns and gunfighting has proven to be exactly right. I could

At the range command, students "verbally request compliance," which means hollering for him to drop the gun. If that doesn't work, you've gotta shoot.

Here students engage the enemy while continuing to retreat.

facility that he calls the Terminator. It is a concrete block building that has movable walls, so the interior can be modified at will. There is no roof, mostly for ventilation, but also so someone can be upstairs, watching.

Each room may or may not contain one or more "bad guys," and you have to find them and engage them. For this operation, we donned a bulletproof vest and went in one at a time, with the instructor right behind us. There were some tricky

bits to this, and we all learned a lot. I put this information to use the night I returned from the school.

My watchdog was not yet back from the kennel the night I returned home, so when I awakened in the middle of the night to a strange noise, I had to go look. The folks at Thunder would have been mighty proud to have seen the way I waltzed through my house. It sure wasn't the way I did it in the past! Happily, the noise was only the house creaking from the cold.

have argued with him about adjustable sights, longer life of very tightly fitted guns, match-grade accuracy, etc., on into the night. The plain fact is, I just don't have the experience to know these things, and you probably don't either. I haven't worn out dozens of 45s in competition (just one, in fact) nor have I had the chance to experiment with hundreds of guns to see what works, like he has. What Robbie said about accuracy is true: My 1991 Colt, as modified by Robar, shoots with far more accuracy than I can possibly utilize.

Specifics

The gun has front cocking serrations in the slide, the use of which is made quite clear at Thunder Ranch: You must not press-check your 1911 to see if it's loaded. Use the serrations. They work.

The gun also has a Videki match trigger with the overtravel screw removed; Robar's special low-lever safety; Robar stippling on the frontstrap and on the flat steel (replacement) mainspring housing; highly visible sights (made by Robar) with the windage adjustable by means of drifting and lockable with a set screw. (I filed the front blade for correct elevation with Black Hills' hardball). The ejection port is lowered and flared; there is a Commander-style extended ejector, and the extractor is "tuned."

The beavertail is a Wilson High Grip with palm swell, and the hammer and sear are by Brown, adjusted for a very crisp 4½-pound letoff.

Robbie replaced the recoil spring with a 20-pound Wolff and installed a matching firing-pin spring. The standard Colt barrel is throated and polished, and Robar test-fired the gun to make sure everything worked properly.

The Robar-tuned gun that went "bang" every time, with engraving by the Editor. The holster is a Milt Sparks Executive Special.

I wanted Robar's NP-3 finish on the entire gun, but before they put that on, I had them ship me the gun so I could engrave it. I did that, then shot Thunder Ranch with the gun in the white. After the school I added the Thunder Ranch logo to the top of the slide along with the names of the director and his three assistants. I also put the Y.O. Ranch brand onto the top of the slide, because they were a significant part of the whole experience. I then shipped the gun back to Robar for plating.

The completed gun is a joy. I have long had the simple philosophy, "Always have at least one 45 semi-auto." This one is it.

Thunder Ranch Director Clint Smith shows students how to enter a dwelling (the Terminator) with the least chance of getting shot in the process.

Here Robbie (left) shows students how to slice the pie in a house-clearing exercise. He's keeping his M&M intact. See text for details.

We went through the basics: grip, stance, sight picture, sight alignment, trigger control, etc. We did only a little shooting from the holster. We were told to make it a smooth draw, not a fast draw. Throughout the week, emphasis was placed on focusing on the front sight, squeezing the trigger, scanning to see if other threats were there, and lots of other things to do after the gun is in your hand. One or two of the students were relative novices and not up to fast gun handling, and the class accommodated those folks as well.

This class was for pure beginners, though even the most experienced shooters got a lot out of it. In Defensive Handgun II and III, more emphasis is placed on presenting the gun from concealment. By the way, you must take Handgun I before you take more advanced courses, no matter your training or background.

My nineteen classmates were all men, ages about 25 to 65. All of us used semi-automatic handguns of one or another sort. About half were M1911s, there were a couple of Glocks, a SIG, one Beretta 92, a S&W 9mm, one Hi-Power in 40 S&W, an H&K USP in 40, and one or two others that I didn't check out.

There was one cop in the class, a firearms instructor, a paramedic, an editor (me), a gun writer, a gun shop owner and his uncle, a detective, a rancher, and assorted others. The students came from as far away as Virginia. About 10 percent of them were novices, 75 percent had some shooting experience, and 15 percent knew their way around a combat handgun pretty well.

We were at the ranch over eight hours a day, and most of that was spent on the range. There was a short break for lunch, with other very short breaks during the day.

Our class was a five-day event, and these are held about three times a year. There is an optional three-day class held about six times a year. There is currently a waiting period of about six months to get into Thunder Ranch. To enroll, you must first get the written approval of your local police, then pay half the fee in advance (refundable with sixty days' notice). The current fee for the five-day class is $850. That does not include lodging, meals or ammo.

The minimum gun requirement is 9mm or 38 Special. This must be carried in a good belt holster, and a spare mag holder (or speedloader pouch for revolvers) is also needed. For the night shooting, a push-button-type flashlight is recommended, but you can buy a Sure Fire light—they are state of the art—in the store at the Ranch. Of course, you need eye and ear protection, and a cap of some sort. In spite of my hat I got hot brass down my shirt. It's tough to keep shooting when that happens.

There is a well-equipped gun-stuff store at the ranch where you can buy sweatshirts, hats, ammo, flashlights, holsters, things like that. There are lodgings available on Thunder Ranch, but no domestic service. You cook your own meals from food you bring with you, clean up after yourself, etc. These cabins have one of the most dramatic views in Texas. You can opt to stay at the Y.O. Ranch, as I did, or drive to Kerrville, some 46 miles away, or to Junction about 33 miles north. Tent camping facilities are available with prior notice.

I spent some time with one of the novices and watched his progress through the week. I asked him about his past experience, and though he said he had rather a lot of time with revolvers, he had decided to shoot a semi-auto this time around. At first, he had the common problem of many, the inability to shoot quickly at a large target. Plinkers and target shooters want to shoot with deliberation, and that can get you killed.

You say you can shoot the eyes off a gnat at 50 meters? Fine, how good are you at hitting a basketball at five feet in less than a second? That's more like gunfighting. Most encounters take place at handshake distances. Speed counts.

By the end of the week, with lots of prodding from the instructors, this gentleman was a creditable pistol shooter. He had trouble carrying his M1911 cocked-and-locked at first, another problem common to those who shoot revolvers a lot, but by mid-week this was second nature to him. He was not entirely comfortable with his autoloader, but he had learned a lot. He was capable of shooting rather fast, and also while moving rearward as well, something that I found quite hostile to my nature when I first tried it.

In his opinion, the course was well worth while, money well spent. He said he learned that the semi-automatic was a far better fighting tool than the best revolver. In fact, he liked the course well enough that he signed up for the Handgun II course, which I thought was a pretty good endorsement.

In addition to time on the range and in class, we were

Thunder Ranch's instructors while the Editor was there were (from left): Terry Kenney, Clint Smith, Ginny Lyford and Robbie Barrkman. All are eminently qualified.

given home exercises, not all of which involve shooting. The draw, or presentation from the holster, for instance, is something you can practice as often as you like with an empty gun, the more the better. For concealed carry, I doubt you can over-practice drawing the gun. These exercises should be carried out regularly, to keep you in touch with gun management long after the memories of Thunder Ranch fade.

Day four, Thursday, we broke at noon and came back at dinner time. We had a group dinner and then did some shooting after dark. That was very instructive, and I feel the need for lots more of that type of practice. After all, most real-life shootings take place in weak light or in the dark, yet most of us never practice it.

On the last of the five days, we had a qualification drill, in which we had to perform several gun-clearing operations and do some fast shooting under the eye of the instructors. Our week's partner graded and evaluated us. We also had a chance to evaluate the instructors and the class.

Oddly, some students complained about the stress. One guy said to his partner that he didn't like to feel so uncomfortable on the range, that it wasn't natural, and of course he missed the whole point. The idea at Thunder Ranch is to give you a glimpse of how it will be on the street if you are ever in a gunfight, and some students just never get the message. They can't relate the stress on the firing line to how they will feel on the street when someone is trying to cut out their heart or knock their head for a home run.

After all, this is supposed to be as close to the nightmare of an actual street shootout as it can be. The hectic atmosphere is intentional, brought on by the instructor hollering in your ear for you to keep shooting until the threat goes away, reload as necessary, continually keep moving, cover your partner as he reloads—you might suddenly have to engage as many as four targets, two of them moving—reload while he covers you, scan for other targets, move to any available cover, keep moving, look at the front sight, control the trigger and shoot, shoot, SHOOT!

Thunder Ranch is about gunfighting. It is about shooting. Most of all, it is about logic.

It is, for example, the pinnacle of logic to avoid any kind of fight in the first place. As director Clint Smith says, "I can go down to the road right now, stop the first car that comes by, and get into a fight with the driver." As he points out, that's not very smart. What is smart is to avoid the fight altogether, which is even more important if you're carrying a gun.

On the range, the first time I fired whilst moving rearward away from the target, it seemed very strange. Yet after a very short time, it felt most natural, and that feeling has stayed with me ever since. Now, even during dry drills at home, the natural tendency is to retreat quickly and take cover. It's logical.

One time on the range I ran the gun dry, stuffed in a full magazine, brought my hand over the top of the gun and tugged the slide rearward, letting it fly forward to chamber a new round. No sooner had I done that when Robbie hollered in my ear, "Use the slide release, it's faster!" Logic prevails.

Thunder Ranch does not turn out finished gunfighters. It does make you aware of what it is you don't know about gunfighting, and what you might want to think about if you carry a gun. It also makes it obvious what it is you need to practice. You can't get enough practice in a week to become proficient in the management of a concealed-carry gun, or any handgun for that matter, but you can learn lots about what you don't know.

One common misconception is that, yes, I'm going to Thunder Ranch in a few weeks. Therefore, I ought to practice a lot. "Wrong!" says Clint. "Take the class first, learn how to do it right, and then practice a lot. Otherwise you're only practicing mistakes."

Is the course worth the $850 fee, the time off work, and the cost of well over a thousand rounds of ammo, not forgetting wear and tear on your sidearm? I think so. Ultimately, the individual must decide how much time and money he feels like spending to learn how to do something that might never be needed. If these skills are needed...well, what's your life worth?

Thunder Ranch is not for everyone. If you truly believe that you might someday have to use what is taught here, then you're well on the way to surviving a gunfight. If it seems like a dream, or you expect fun and games, stay home.

My week at Thunder Ranch opened my eyes to just a few of the potential problems facing those who would go armed. I'm going back...I have a lot more to learn. ●

Massad Ayoob takes his LFI course on the road. Here, he drills students in shooting tactics at a Seattle range.

LETHAL FORCE INSTITUTE

by DAVE WORKMAN

DRAWING A GUN on someone is a very intense experience. Having to shoot them is definitely much worse. Killing them can be downright awful. But face it, in a life or death confrontation, the alternative to any or all of the above is a nightmare from which you and your loved ones may never awaken.

This presents no small dilemma to the average citizen. Nobody wants to be a crime victim, and no rational person wants to take the life of another. Likewise, nobody wants to be the poor guy who survives a lethal encounter only to be crucified at the courthouse.

Watch enough television, listen to enough bad advice, read some misinformed hokum in a gun magazine and you might forget there was ever a Bernie Goetz. Also, you may even believe that shooting some intruder who showed up in your front room at 3 a.m. will earn you a medal from the cops, the adoration of your neighbors and a pat on the back from the prosecutor's office. There's just one little fly in the ointment. Murphy made up most of the rules, and he's a very unforgiving guy.

Enter Massad Ayoob and his Lethal Force Institute. Spend forty hours with him and you'll learn that it's not only the bad guys you have to worry about. There's a legal system just waiting to eat you alive, both in the criminal courts and in civil proceedings if you do something that is even the least bit questionable.

Bernie Goetz knows what I mean. In December 1984 Goetz shot four people during a subway encounter in what was determined to be self-defense. Goetz was acquitted on all assault and attempted murder charges at his criminal trial. However, Goetz lost a civil trial last year and was ordered by a New York jury to pay $43 million to one of the survivors.

Investing in the basic LFI-1 course may be the best insurance against post-shooting problems the armed citizen can buy. When you're all alone in what is commonly referred to by LFI grads as "the dark place," what Ayoob has taught you can bring you back into the sunshine.

LFI students learn, in sometimes graphic detail, what a lethal-force encounter is all about. For example, Ayoob talks about these concepts:

● The "Reasonable Man Doctrine," which is a cornerstone of self-defense. You acted in a manner that any reasonable man would have, under similar circumstances, knowing what you knew at the time.

You will shoot about 500 rounds in two intense days on the range, says the author. Reliable guns are a good idea.

COURSE DATA SHEET
Lethal Force Institute
Course Name: LFI-1/LFI-1 Completion
Cost: $600/$300
Duration: 40 hrs/16 hrs
Hours per Day: 5/2
Hours in Classroom: 24
Hours on Range: 16
Total Rounds Fired: 500
Rounds Fired in Restricted Light: None
Rounds Fired in Daylight: All
Participant: Dave Workman
Pre-Enrollment Requirements: Student must possess valid concealed carry license (CPL/CCW) or provide a letter attesting to his/her character from attorney or local police chief.
Firearm/Caliber Used: Springfield Model 1911-A1/45 ACP
Required Accessories: 500 rounds of ammo, at least 2 spare magazines or speed loaders, eye and ear protection, baseball-style cap, pouch for mags/speedloaders, jacket.

This target shows the results of two days of shooting with Ayoob's LFI. Students are required to shoot a qualification course at the conclusion of the class that becomes part of their permanent LFI record. This student couldn't do this well before LFI training.

- "Disparity of Force," which translates to the difference between the physically strong and physically weak, or a lone individual against multiple attackers, such as in the well-publicized Goetz incident. (Goetz's problem was not so much what he did, but his conduct during police interrogation and in cross-examination on the witness stand.)
- Never shoot to kill, or to wound. You only shoot to stop.
- Always load your personal defense gun with factory ammunition to avoid being portrayed in court as some sort of gun nut who sits at home concocting ammunition specifically designed to brutally maim someone.
- The correct methods of holding suspects at gunpoint.

The Man

Since 1981, Ayoob has been instructing police officers and private citizens from every corner of the nation about the intricacies of preparation for, engagement in, and the aftermath of a gunfight. He gives it to you down and frequently dirty, but he drives home the point that self-defense is not nearly so simple as black and white, nor does it fall into the realm of polite society. Gunfighting is, of course, a serious item, and when Ayoob lectures on the subject, he is all business.

About 60 percent of the LFI-1 course is given to classroom time, and 40 percent to the range. Taking this course is also a non-negotiable prerequisite for more advanced LFI courses. Most of his courses are open to private citizens. One, Lethal Threat Management for Police (LTM), is open only to peace officers and bonafide security personnel with arrest powers, and to police training personnel.

What Ayoob teaches may drive some politically motivated prosecutors crazy. It most assuredly gives ulcers to those who preach total acquiescence in the face of potentially lethal danger and counsel their fellow citizens to never resort to firearms for self-protection. However, those whose lives have depended upon what they learned at LFI just love this guy.

Massad Ayoob is the genuine article. A sworn police officer having achieved the rank of captain, his credentials as firearms instructor are well established. He has, for example, been a special instructor at the Chapman Academy. He was international director of police firearms training at the Defensive Tactics Institute, 1980-82. He has lectured at the Smith & Wesson Academy and Florida's Metro-Dade Police Academy. He is the national chairman of the committee on

Ayoob demonstrates the correct trigger finger placement on a pistol frame; finger is kept straight and off the trigger until you're ready to shoot.

police firearms training for the American Society of Law Enforcement Trainers.

He was first in his class at the Smith & Wesson Academy's course for Advanced Combat Shooting, and the same school's Instructor course, Combat Match course and Officer Survival course.

He has studied hostage negotiation for supervisors, post-shooting tactics, house-clearing techniques, off-duty confrontation tactics and other subjects offered by the New York City police department.

Mas Ayoob has a very analytical mind. He can pick apart a shooting and tell what someone did, right or wrong, and when he or she did it. This is why he is frequently called as an expert witness and is recognized as such across the nation.

Ayoob has also studied the martial arts, and out of that involvement he developed a shooting technique he calls StressFire, adopted by many professional gun-carriers. Ayoob wrote a book on the subject, aptly name *StressFire,* and he teaches a 16-hour course on the technique.

Mas also writes columns for several gun periodicals, and perhaps the most popular is "The Ayoob Files," a feature of *American Handgunner* magazine. This column offers detailed analyses of shootings involving police and private citizens. Earlier this year, a paperback compilation of the best of that column appeared on bookshelves.

LFI students get all the benefits of Ayoob's vast experience and talent. They also get something else: The assurance that what they're learning from Ayoob is not offered to everybody who comes knocking at the LFI gate.

LFI

The Lethal Force Institute accepts only those students who can provide evidence that they are licensed to carry a concealed firearm or provide letters of reference from a judge or police chief. Anyone who meets the admissions criteria is welcome, and people from all walks of life have been in the classroom. Doctors, lawyers, school teachers, journalists,

housewives, nurses, secretaries, public employees, business executives—you name the occupation, Ayoob probably has at least one in his student files.

Better still, LFI students don't have to hop an airplane to New Hampshire. Mas Ayoob takes his course on the road. In a society where crime may be an epidemic, Ayoob might best be called the "personal-defense doctor," and he makes house calls. He travels the country to most population centers in a predermined schedule of classes, and you can find out if he's coming to your area with a call or note to LFI. However, if you'd like to visit the New England countryside, the LFI range facility is at Dunbarton, near Concord.

My acquaintance with Ayoob dates back some sixteen years. I read the serialized version of his landmark *In the Gravest Extreme* in the pages of a magazine and was captivated. I've still got the much-worn copy he sent to me for review when I was a regional editor at *Fishing & Hunting News* in Seattle. Over the years, I've talked with him via telephone and in person about personal defense. I'm also a firearms instructor, and I've understood for years that it is possible for even teachers to learn something new.

One reason I took his course is that I've "been there." I have experienced the unpleasantness of drawing guns in self-defense and in defense of others, and once assisted the police in an arrest. My dad taught me how to shoot. Personal experience gave me the judgement about when and when not to shoot. Ayoob's LFI curriculum put it all into proper perspective for me. The course covers all these bases for the novice.

The Class

Ayoob's classroom segment is not for the squeamish. An LFI entry-level course on the judicious use of lethal force takes a student through the dynamics of a self-defense shooting, and much more.

Ayoob developed this course not only to help his students defend themselves from criminal attack, but also to prevent them from becoming victims of the judicial system. At LFI,

Author Workman (with M1911 and bare arm) and his classmates go through the StressFire exercise, an Ayoob invention to help keep you alive in a shootout.

the self-defense mindset encompasses much more than gunfight survival. It might best be defined thus: Hope for the best but plan for the worst, be prepared to meet it head-on, and overcome.

He details the circumstances under which a person may resort to lethal force, specifically when you are in "...imminent and unavoidable danger of grave bodily harm or death." He also tells when such force is not permitted.

Students also learn how to issue the proper challenge to a suspect, hold that suspect at gunpoint, and how to avoid being mistakenly shot by responding police officers. In a face-to-face, for example, Ayoob counsels his students to hold the gun at low-ready so the muzzle is aimed below the beltline. Why? Several good reasons. With the gun so positioned, you can observe any hand movement by your opponent and act accordingly. Also, if you have to shoot in an emergency, the bullet will be angled downward and strike the pelvis bone structure, thus causing the suspect to collapse. Finally, as Ayoob wryly observes, "It intimidates the hell out of 'em."

The correct procedure to hold a suspect is to order him to lie on the ground facedown with his arms and legs spread, the palms turned upward and the face turned away. When he is thus positioned, you can reholster your gun so that when responding officers arrive, they will not see you standing over a prone body with a gun in your hand. Honest citizens have been mistakenly shot in such situations.

Ayoob offers advice on proper firearms, ammunition and holsters, tactics for home defense, the difference between cover and concealment, street gunfighting tactics ("Jump behind that big steel mailbox!") and more. Ayoob uses both lecture and video, brings students into the conversation, and challenges them to seriously think about their actions and what to say to the investigating officers, detectives and prosecutors to justify their actions.

A typical LFI graduate would never make the mistakes that Bernie Goetz made on the now-famous videotaped confession and on the witness stand. These lessons are ham-

mered home with a clear message about what can happen to a private citizen who fouls up. Even a citizen who acts according to the law can wind up in a world of hurt in the aftermath of a shooting, and this applies to more than just the legal aspects of a shooting investigation.

Say you escape criminal prosecution. You can still be the victim of a civil lawsuit in which you can lose big-time. An LFI student's ace in the hole is that Ayoob can be called to testify in your behalf, as he has testified many times on behalf of cops and private citizens who have had to take a human life.

But say you battle successfully through this legal nightmare. There are emotional aspects of a shooting that can scar you for life. Ayoob details the various proven, documented symptoms of post-shooting trauma, and he pulls no punches. These symptoms can (and often do) include social ostracism, loss of appetite, sleep disorder and sexual dysfunction. Add all of this on top of potential loss of job and income, home and other property, your family, your reputation and your freedom, and it's easy to understand why LFI students come out of class with a new appreciation of the term "personal responsibility."

A few years ago, I sat through LFI's intense 16-hour "Introduction to Lethal Force" course, but because of time constraints and conflicting schedules I had to wait until recently to go through the shooting segment of Ayoob's course. When Mas and I shared a bus ride at the Dallas SHOT Show, he mentioned that an LFI completion course was scheduled to be held at Marty Hayes' Firearms Academy of Seattle, not too far from my home. It was scheduled for an April weekend. I easily decided that firewood cutting and home improvements could wait.

Guns & Gear

The LFI course requires you to have a gun and at least two speedloaders or two spare magazines for the reloading exercises. You also need a baseball-type cap to keep hot brass from getting caught between your shooting glasses and your eye.

The author's gear: D&D Gun-leather T-Bar/IWB holster (made by author); two-tone Springfield 1911 45ACP with fixed sights, short trigger and modest beavertail; Uncle Mike's Mirage dual mag pouch made of Nytek; and his Spyderco knife, which he used to cut his way out of numerous jams.

I brought two handguns, a Springfield 45 ACP Model 1911-A1 and a backup 9mm TZ-75 that never left the gun box, ten spare mags for the Springfield and four spares for the 9mm, plus about 600 rounds for each.

I carried the 45 in a strong-side D&D Gunleather T-Bar inside-the-waistband holster of my own design. (A flattering moment came when Ayoob strolled over and asked; "That's an interesting holster you've got there. Where'd you get it?" I replied, "Well, Mas, I built it.") Slicked up with a couple of drops of Leather Lightning from the superb Mitch Rosen Extraordinary Gunleather, it performed flawlessly. Sorry to admit this, the gun didn't. More about that in a moment.

I started off wearing a pair of Uncle Mike's terrific new leather shooting gloves, but abandoned them soon. After all,

LFI COURSE DESCRIPTIONS

LETHAL FORCE INSTITUTE has a full schedule of class offerings, eighteen different learning options at this time, and there is more than one level of training for some of those. While some may question the need for so many course offerings and levels, bear in mind that nobody learns everything they need to know in first grade. Here is a brief overview:

- **Judicious use of Deadly Force:** A two-day, lecture-only session that details prevention, intervention and aftermath management. This is an intense 16-hour course that explains when a citizen can and cannot use a firearm in self-defense, plus tactics for home defense, street gunfighting tactics, how to take a criminal suspect at gunpoint, psychological preparation for violent encounters and justifying your actions in court.
- **LFI-1/Judicious Use of Deadly Force:** All of the above, plus two full days on the firing line. This course goes well beyond law school and the police academy in terms of decision-making, and is the class I took and reported on here.
- **LFI-2/Threat Management for Civilians:** This picks up where LFI-1 left off. Students learn combat shooting skills and survivability in violent encounters. The course includes return-fire techniques when wounded, mastering the combat shotgun, maintain-

ing weapon control in a struggle, retrieval of partners taken hostage, search tactics for buildings, and more. There's even a man-on-man role-playing session using dummy weapons or paintball guns.
- **LFI-3/Advanced Threat Management for Civilians:** This was the most advanced course until recently. The course includes "outer limits" exercises of advanced combat handgun and combat shotgun. There is also an introduction to assault rifle and submachine gun, ambidextrous shooting skills and shooting under extreme pressure.
- **LFI-4/Highly Advanced Course:** This is Ayoob's new, experimental seven-day course that is strictly limited to LFI-3 grads. It involves intensive role play with dummy guns in street fighting and building-search scenarios, which will all be videotaped. Weapon retention progresses to instructor level. The students undergo rigorous cross-examination by lawyers and law students or police prosecutors.
- **LTM/Lethal Threat Management for Police:** This cops-only course is designed for the police instructor in firearms, officer survival and SWAT tactics.
- **StressFire:** This is an intense 16-hour course for the person already grounded in deadly force training and who wants to improve his/her combat-shooting potential.

LFI students are also required to pass a comprehensive written exam before they graduate. Test results are kept in the student's file. Here, Ayoob discusses the answers to some very tough legal questions.

how many people do you see walking around wearing shooting gloves, just waiting for a gunfight? Just didn't seem practical.

While Ayoob handles his classroom sessions virtually solo and delivers all lectures personally, on the range there is ample help from line coaches and assistant instructors. Our class of thirty-six students (nine of them women) was backed by a staff of eight, plus Ayoob and Hayes. That's a very good coach-to-student ratio, and it makes for a good learning environment, especially for the less-experienced student. More than a dozen of our class were relative novices, about half had some experience with handguns, and four or five of us had burned a bunch of powder in our time. Rather than criticize, these LFI coaches encourage, offer suggestions and give

- **Introduction to the Combat Handgun:** This is a one-day shooting program that includes safe speed draw and holstering, shooting with the double-action revolver and double- or single-action semi-auto, and speed reloading. Students also learn the Weaver, Chapman and isosceles two-hand techniques, and StressFire positions.
- **Advanced Combat Shotgun:** A good course for newcomers or veterans, this "immersion course" focuses on safe and effective operation of the shotgun from close range to 100 yards. Students use defensive shotguns from 10- through 20-gauge with emphasis on the 12-gauge.
- **Handgun Retention:** A one-day course on disarming techniques, and how to defeat them from all angles.
- **Defensive Tactics:** How to restrain violent individuals without weapons. The majority of techniques are aikido-based.
- **Kubotan/Persuader:** Students learn how to use this universally legal self-defense tool and become certified at the end of the course. It covers all the bases.
- **Kubotan/Persuader Instructor:** Taught under the auspices of the Monadnock Persuader program, successful graduates are certified as instructors with the Persuader mini-baton.
- **Weapon Retention Instructor:** Here's a course for people who wish to become certified instructors of the Lindell method of handgun retention and disarming. This is a 16-hour course.
- **Emergency Auto Rifle:** Developed by LFI for the

Michigan Department of Corrections, this course covers the use of the 223- or 308-caliber semi-auto rifle, or the pistol-caliber carbine. All firearms, whether selective fire or semi-auto, will be fired on semi-auto. Course covers standing, kneeling, prone and cover position shooting.
- **Hell Week:** Don't let the title scare you. This course is for competent shooters whose background is lacking in unarmed self-defense, but do not have the time to commit to conventional martial arts training. This course includes aikido and striking instruction, blocking punches, kicks, releasing all types of chokes, head locks, bearhugs and other grabs.
- **Refresher Programs:** LFI offers students the opportunity to take refresher courses, for half the listed tuition price.

If you're interested in attending the Lethal Force Institute, call or write to them in Concord, New Hampshire, to request course information. You will be sent a class schedule showing when and where LFI courses will be held, up to a year in advance.

Actually, my recommended first step is to take a basic firearms safety course, such as those offered by the National Rifle Association, as a prerequisite. This will get the firearms safety basics ingrained before spending hundreds of dollars at LFI.

Between the time you apply for entry into an LFI course and actual participation, be sure to get your copies of *In the Gravest Extreme* and *StressFire*. They're good preparation for any LFI course.

Ayoob runs a cold range. Guns are not loaded until he says so. The pictured students are in the ready position.

advice. Judging from the improvements in the shooting accuracy of just about everyone over the two-day shooting segment, the instructors got the proper results.

Ayoob encourages students to wear strong-side holsters rather than shoulder rigs, cross-draws or fanny packs. This prevents students from crossing an adjacent shooter with the gun muzzle during one of the many shooting exercises. However, Ayoob will accommodate students if they must use such rigs on duty, or if they have determined that there is absolutely no other way for them to carry a gun. He'll put them on the end of the line, or wherever he has to, and instruct them in the proper draw.

Whatever else he may be, Ayoob is a stickler for safety. He is an excellent firearms instructor, from the basic level to the most advanced techniques. The novice shooter can expect a firm but gentle learning experience and will come out of the LFI-1 shooting segment fully competent with a handgun. The experienced shooter will pick up new knowledge and improve on skills already developed.

Ayoob runs a cold range, guns unloaded unless you're otherwise instructed. Violators of his safety requirements are pulled off the line for the day for a first offense and ejected from the course for a second—with no refund. (Would you want to be shooting next to some jerk for two days? Neither would I.)

The shooting course spans two very intensive days, during which the LFI student can expect to:

a) Easily go through 500 rounds of ammunition.

b) Be introduced to several shooting techniques, including the famous Weaver stance, Ray Chapman's modified Weaver, the isosceles stance, the cover crouch (a high-speed replacement for kneeling), high and low kneeling, and individual weak- and strong-hand shooting, plus a way of gripping the pistol with two hands called "The Wedge." Ayoob's reasoning for offering so many shooting techniques is simple. In his own words, "A boxer with only one punch doesn't have a chance."

c) Take a written test on their newly acquired knowledge of the judicious use of lethal force.

d) Shoot a police-level qualification course, the results of which become part of your permanent LFI student record.

Throughout the shooting exercises, Ayoob or one of his assistants frequently reminds each student to keep shooting. If a gun jams, clear it as quickly and safely as possible, and get back into the fight. Stopping in the middle of a string, he suggests, can ingrain the wrong instinct to give up the fight if your gun runs dry or jams (or you are shot) during a real gunfight. That can get you killed and may cost the lives of innocents you are trying to protect. At LFI, that is simply unacceptable.

On The Range

On the morning of Day One of the shooting session, Ayoob and his staff went through the safety lecture in detail: muzzle pointed in a safe direction at all times; finger off the trigger until ready to shoot; thumb firmly on the hammer when reholstering; in short, every fundamental aspect of safe gun handling. Then it was up to the line.

First, every student went through basic drills while dry-firing. We practiced the Weaver, the modified Weaver and the isosceles. Only when Ayoob was satisfied that everyone knew where to point the muzzle did we load up.

Every shooting exercise in the LFI course is based on the use of a six-round sidearm, to accommodate people who show up with wheelguns. In our class, everybody carried a semiauto, and just about every popular brand and type was represented. No matter how many rounds a gun is designed to carry, we always loaded just six, with six rounds in each backup magazine.

The class went from the basics through rapid reloading, drawing and firing, weak-hand shooting and, on the second day, the StressFire method. To get the full appreciation of StressFire, you've got to take Ayoob's course and also read his

After the class, author Dave Workman (center) shares a moment with LFI Director Massad Ayoob (left) and range host Marty Hayes.

book. Here's a tidbit: StressFire involves shooting one-handed with the opposite hand clenched in a fist and held against the chest at about heart level. This dynamic allows shooters to get a more solid grip on the gun, and it does improve marksmanship. Students learn about biomechanics, stress control, and how to use stress as an advantage.

Over two long days, we learned to shoot from a crouch, high kneeling and then low kneeling positions. The class went through reloading exercises from these positions, too. Alas, there was no low-light shooting. That comes in an advanced LFI course.

We used muscles that evidently needed to be used, and this from a guy who hikes and hunts up and down Pacific Northwest ridgetops, runs up and down stairs at the office, lifts weights regularly and splits cordwood to relax.

Ayoob drilled us in the "power" shooting forms, everything from the proper grip on the gun to foot placement and which knee to bend. The class went from close-range shooting to 10- and 15-yard ranges. Those of us who were pretty good when they got there were even better when we left.

It was midway on Day Two that my beloved Springfield began giving me fits. Failures to feed and extract were the main bugaboo, which my friend and fellow instructor Norm Aubin eventually traced to a faulty extractor. We replaced it and thought the problem was solved, but the pistol continued to malfunction throughout the class. Despite these malfunctions, I didn't stop shooting. Years of competing against a clock teaches you that, but at LFI, the instinct takes on a far more serious intent. I have now installed a Wilson extractor that, so far, seems to be working just fine.

Amid the malfunctions, it was Ayoob to the rescue...sort of. He just happened to be packing a Government Model and graciously swapped guns. He indicated that his had a 4-pound trigger as opposed to my gun's stiffer factory job. I immediately "threw" the first two shots out of his gun to bust my chances of qualifying with a perfect 300. Then I settled down to that light trigger and cruised through the rest of the

qualification, finishing two points down and third in the class behind a couple of perfect scores.

The entire class gathered for a postmortem and going-away visit, and I could tell from observing all those faces that they had learned plenty, all of which we will carry through whatever years we've got left.

Some might consider Ayoob diabolical. From my own perspective as a firearms instructor, my opinion is that he's a good and thorough teacher, a guy who wants to make sure that if anybody is going to be standing after the shooting stops, it will be the LFI graduate.

In short, an LFI student needn't fear about wasting his or her money. You will get every penny's worth, and then some, in terms of excellent classroom material and shooting instruction. For the amount of time one invests, an LFI course is a bargain. The current cost of LFI-1 is $600 for the full five-day, forty-hour course, and it is offered about twenty times a year in various locations.

When you take the class, be prepared for an experience that may give you a couple of restless nights when you begin thinking about everything you've learned, mistakes you might have made, misconceptions you may have had. What this simply means is that you learned what Ayoob wanted you to learn, and it sank in. However, over the long haul, you, the LFI graduate, will sleep a lot more soundly. You'll know that everything Ayoob has taught you is directed at your survival, both in a gunfight and in the legal nightmare that could follow. ●

About the Author

Dave Workman is the Guns and Shooting Editor for Fishing & Hunting News *and Senior Staff Editor for Outdoor Empire Publishing in Seattle. He is a certified firearms instructor.*

Protecting the gun in a close-quarters draw-and-shoot situation.

YAVAPAI FIREARMS ACADEMY

by DICK WILLIAMS

IT'S A RATHER sad fact that the majority of today's attention to handguns is focused on their use against our own species. Civilian carry licenses, stopping power, concealability, magazine capacity, incapacitation capability; the antipersonnel-oriented list goes on. Man is a combative animal, and the simple fact is that the only serious threat to us on the planet is us.

Having acknowledged that while the current situation is sad, it is historically not at all unusual. Most of the progress in weaponry, at least since the Clan of the Cave Bear, has been motivated by the simple desire to get an edge on some other man or men rather than on improving our hunting techniques or making a more exciting game. There have been a few improvements prompted by specific sports-oriented objectives, e.g. accurized autoloaders for Bullseye shooting, dot scopes and compensators for IPSC, and long-range cartridges for IHMSA. For the most part, handgun improvements in both hardware and technique have been prompted by the threat of man against man.

The reason for this focus on handguns in *mano a mano* situations is that a small segment of society has determined that it can make a living preying on its fellow citizens. The

hardware most used in the pursuit of that "trade" is the handgun. You have a choice. You can lament the situation and pray that the establishment will protect you, which seems pointless, since the establishment has repeatedly acknowledged that it cannot protect its citizens. Or you can acknowledge the situation as it realistically is and prepare to protect yourself as best you can. Situational awareness and avoidance should be a large part of anyone's self-protection plan. But if you are unable to avoid a situation, the ability to retaliate with a response at least the equivalent of the threat becomes the only viable solution. Realistically, for most of us, we are talking about handguns.

It is possible to achieve a credible level of competence in protecting yourself through the process of self-education. However, if you were selecting a brain surgeon to remove a tumor from your head, would your first choice be a guy with a few correspondence classes under his belt and some practice time in his garage?

Applying the wisdom that comes only with the achievement of advanced journalistic status, our Editor assigned a few of us writers to attend some of the various training programs available around the country. I was very fortunate and

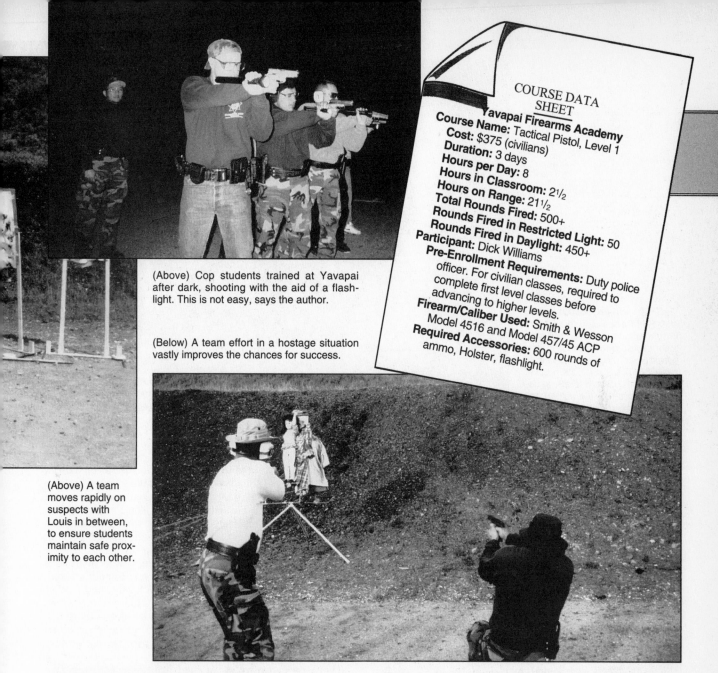

(Above) Cop students trained at Yavapai after dark, shooting with the aid of a flashlight. This is not easy, says the author.

(Below) A team effort in a hostage situation vastly improves the chances for success.

(Above) A team moves rapidly on suspects with Louis in between, to ensure students maintain safe proximity to each other.

COURSE DATA SHEET
Yavapai Firearms Academy
Course Name: Tactical Pistol, Level 1
Cost: $375 (civilians)
Duration: 3 days
Hours per Day: 8
Hours in Classroom: 2½
Hours on Range: 21½
Total Rounds Fired: 500+
Rounds Fired in Restricted Light: 50
Rounds Fired in Daylight: 450+
Participant: Dick Williams
Pre-Enrollment Requirements: Duty police officer. For civilian classes, required to complete first level classes before advancing to higher levels.
Firearm/Caliber Used: Smith & Wesson Model 4516 and Model 457/45 ACP
Required Accessories: 600 rounds of ammo, Holster, flashlight.

drew Louis Awerbuck of the Yavapai Firearms Academy in Prescott, Arizona. Louis is from South Africa, one of my favorite places, and it should be sufficient introduction to state that he was brought to America by Jeff Cooper to run Gunsite when Jeff first started his famous training center. Louis established permanent residence in Arizona and has been teaching ever since.

In comparing Louis's schedule of training classes with my availability, the only class I could attend in time to make the deadline of HANDGUNS '97 was in San Jose, California, in March 1996. This was to be a police-only session. The original intent of this exercise was to review classes available to civilians. Cops are civilians whose job doesn't give them the luxury of avoiding life-threatening situations; they are required to enter exactly that kind of arena and resolve the situation. What better way to get a taste of how to handle the worst possible situations?

I sent Louis a brief resumé of my shooting experience (omitting how creative I am at the word processor) and convinced him that, although I had never served in law enforcement, my handgun abilities and background would hopefully not hinder the progress of the class.

Let me jump ahead and share with you the two most significant conclusions I formed during the three-day training session: 1) I'm not nearly the hot-shot *pistolero* I thought I was, and 2) I don't know if I could qualify to be a police officer. The demands we place on them are too high, the salary we pay them is too low, and the level of gratitude we offer them for what they do isn't nearly up to the level of "stroking" that most of us require in our daily lives.

The course was called "Tactical Pistol, Level 1," and it is designed to "...develop the fundamentals of gunfighting: marksmanship, gunhandling and tactical thinking." Louis acknowledged that he hasn't determined the dividing line between a Level 1 gunfight versus a Level 2 gunfight; when you're being shot at, it won't matter.

It was the "tactical thinking" that really hit me. At no time during the three-day course were you allowed to stop thinking about the situation you were in and how you chose to handle it. The brochure said the course encompassed "...shooting from a ready position; the drawstroke and shooting from the holster; shooting from various tactical positions; loading, unloading and reloading drills; shooting on the move; dim light and flashlight shooting techniques; and weapons retention." The

The Phillips kneeling position (named after Ron Phillips of Colorado) provides maximum protection and minimum exposure while shooting from behind cover. This is an effective technique if you can get into the position. About half the class was able to use it. Older guys (like the author) and those with injuries had difficulty.

objective was, and is, to learn all of these skills and perform them without conscious thought while devoting your brain to resolving your situation.

There were fourteen students in the class. Twelve were active-duty police officers from Northern California communities with from eighteen months to twenty-five years of experience.

During the three days, we fired at least 500 rounds per person. The exact number was not dictated; you handled each and every situation until it was satisfactorily resolved, using whatever number of rounds you thought it required. No one left the firing line until he had brought a situation fully under control. If someone was having difficulty with a particular skill, he stayed on the line until he mastered both the skill and the tactical situation. I didn't count the exact number, but I fired about fifty shots during the restricted-light and flashlight exercises.

The recommended firearm for the cops was their duty gun—no point in training with one thing and venturing onto the mean streets with something else. All the cops fired their respective department's duty ammo. Weapons included Glocks, SIGs, S&Ws and one Colt M1911. Calibers included 9mm, 40 S&W and 45 ACP. Holsters and belts were also duty rigs, with most of the holsters being one of the Safariland multiple-safety types. These rigs were a bit slower than unrestrained holsters, but not much. I was using two different open-top holsters, and while I usually cleared leather a little faster, I rarely got off the first shot.

In conjunction with a couple of other assignments (and my personal desire to try the Smith & Wesson compact 45s), I had checked with Louis about switching between the S&W Model 4516 and their new lightweight Model 457. I used a variety of Black Hills' ammo, including their 230-grain Hornady XTP-bullet load, the 200 LSWC, and the 230 LRN reloaded ammo. In roughly 500 rounds fired, I had exactly one malfunction with one reloaded LRN in the Model 457. It was during a "team" situation. I immediately cleared and slapped in a new mag without checking the malfunction, since there are no timeouts in a gunfight.

Checking after the exercise was over, I found that the round nose of the lead bullet had an indented line across it, like it had jammed into the edge of the loading ramp. There

were no problems with the Model 4516, and I fired more rounds through it than through the Model 457. Despite Louis's suggestion, I did not clean either gun during the three days, because I wanted to see how the guns performed dirty. This is, of course, not a good idea in real life.

I used two holsters interchangeably. One was the Bianchi Avenger; the other, Safariland's Open Top Paddle holster. The Avenger is completely open on top, giving easy access both for the draw and return. I was pleased I chose it because the training sessions required returning the gun to leather without taking your eyes away from the threat in front of you. I would have had a tough time with an unfamiliar retention-type holster. The Safariland paddle holster had leather ears that covered the rear sides of the slide, protecting the wearer and clothes from the ambidextrous safeties. Both holsters were extremely comfortable and quick, even when reaching under the sweatshirt I wore during the cooler days and for the evening session.

There were no overnight or meal facilities on the range. We broke for lunch each day, and we had to arrange for rides to and from class because there wasn't any commercial transportation other than cabs. Hotels were nearby, and there was a Holiday Inn within 5 miles.

Attending officers were asked to bring their "duty" flashlights for the evening session. I was the only attendee who had never received any training shooting by flashlight, but it didn't seem to slow things down. Several of the cops had been taught different techniques, and Louis went through all of them along with a couple that some students had not tried. The idea was not to establish the best system for everyone, but rather for each individual to be aware of the different techniques (and flashlights) available and use whatever worked best for him.

I had a great deal of difficulty in controlling both gun and flashlight together, but after some experimentation with a borrowed rear-button light and by locking my hands back-to-back, I was able to keep both gun and light beam under a degree of control. It was the only time I remember noticing a big difference in recoil between the light alloy-frame Model 457 and the all-steel Model 4516. With only one hand actually gripping the gun, the 457 was more difficult to recover.

(Above) Louis makes the dolls dance as one of his students waits for a shot opportunity. Patience is the key here, says the author.

(Left) The author was responsible for the ugly black hole in the kneecap of the doll, which was a moving "hostage." Williams says this made him glad he's not a cop.

At the beginning of the three-day class, we spent the first couple of hours indoors. The first phase was the completion of administrative paperwork. As expected, the first subject on the lecture agenda was safety, and it was considered of paramount importance over the next three days.

The subject came up frequently:

"Keep fingers off triggers until actually looking through the sights."

"Keep muzzles pointing downrange when not in holsters."

"Don't draw the guns behind the line."

With a group of experienced police officers, firearms safety didn't require as much classroom time as it would have with a group of new shooters, but it received no less emphasis. Louis carried a functioning "non-gun" throughout the training program that did everything but shoot. For the next three days, it was the only "gun" that Louis ever touched, and it was the only "gun" that was ever pointed at anyone or used in any of the contact demonstrations. It was an excellent training aid for just about everything from demonstrating gun clearing techniques to disarming maneuvers.

Other than basic safety rules, there was only one rule for the three days. *You have to hit the target.* Anything offered by Louis during the training was to be taken as his personal opinion. It was up to each student to think about what was said and either accept or reject it. Whatever you decided, you didn't leave the line without hitting the target and ending the threat.

One of the most interesting things that Louis said was, "If you lose a gunfight, you probably beat yourself." For three days, I practiced different ways of doing different things, trying to minimize the probability of beating myself if I ever get into a shooting encounter. I think I got better, but I'm absolutely certain I became much more aware of how fatal a mistake can be and the importance of not making any.

If you were confused on how to handle something, his message was simple: "Always come back to basics." If you had trouble with the execution of a particular technique, even basic marksmanship, group action stopped while Louis focused on the individual student's need and performance. We did not progress to the next exercise until everyone had successfully resolved the current problem.

During the classroom session, Louis said that we would be using sighted fire throughout the class. It was not an order, nor did it evolve into a discussion on point-shooting versus the use of the sights. You simply had to hit the target. If you could do that fast at 6 feet with something other than a classic bullseye sight picture, but required an extra second to use the sights at 10 yards, you did whatever was required to hit the target. There were no time-clocks, no mandatory double-taps, or "two to the body, one to the head" drills. You shot until you resolved the problem with as many hits on target as you thought appropriate. I think the analysis was like driving a car. If the max speed at which you can take a corner is 45 mph, you need to find that out in the classroom (driving school) rather than attempting 48 mph on the street and crashing.

We were told in the initial classroom session that the shooting would be at close range, 10 to 12 yards, since this was not a special tactics or SWAT training session. However, about midway through the three days when we were getting pretty good at our close range "hosing" technique, there was an exercise where we had to draw, fire one round and hit a man-size steel plate at about 60 yards. Then we had to draw, fire one round and hit a head-size steel plate at about 30 yards. The action slowed dramatically, and while everyone hit the required target in one shot, we did not all do it on the first try!

There was no mandatory firing position or stance required. Louis made the explanation as simple as I've heard. The Weaver stance works for most people because it's like shooting a rifle except you move your gun hand forward to hold the handgun grip. It's the way most of us started out with our first 22 rifle, and it enabled us to shoot in a naturally balanced position. The overriding message is that training for a gunfight must be oriented toward results. Who cares how you do it, as long as it works.

After the first day in class, other than for a 20-minute session prior to the night-shooting session, we did not see the inside of the classroom again. As we filed out onto the range, I didn't see how we would productively fill three days of range time based on Louis's classroom inputs. Of course, good theories are usually grasped much quicker than good practices.

Gaining access to concealed guns requires practice. On the first try (left), the student clears his clothing in a smooth draw. Later, the gun catches in his baggy sweater as it comes out of the holster.

To build confidence, and so we all knew we could shoot small groups—even if we hadn't lately—we started by shooting very slowly, gripping the gun with only the thumb and middle finger of the firing hand. When everyone's groups were small and centered, the other fingers and weak hand were brought into use without changing group size or location. Then we moved on to more serious exercises.

We shot in two shifts, with seven people on the line at a time. Shooting distances varied from a few feet to about 12 yards. We moved and shot. We moved forward, backward and sideways, always keeping track of the other six men around us while engaging the target in front of us, and watching the targets on each side of our target. If the firing line wavered to where it might become dangerous, Louis was there to straighten it or halt the action. We learned to move sideways and backward by feeling and clearing the way with our feet while keeping our eyes and guns on the threat.

At a given command, we were all able to fire immediately because we were properly balanced and had kept our sights on the target. We learned to move forward rapidly without bouncing our heads, eyes or guns, so that we were again able to fire instantly on command. Again, not everyone did this on the first try, but before we moved on to the next exercise, everyone did it successfully.

It wasn't intuitively obvious to me why I might need to move forward rapidly, though I could see that a cop might need this skill. However, don't all the books tell us that a civilian threatened in his own home should retreat with his family to the most defendable room in the house? When you hear that first scary bump in the night, where are your kids? In your room? In most homes, they're as far away from mom and dad's room as we can put them. So step one involves going to get them just as rapidly as you can while being prepared to deal with any threat you might encounter. This is a good exercise for civilians as well as for cops.

An odd thing happened as we moved laterally around the range. The targets changed shape. Louis got tricky and put some contour-type bulges in the targets and set them deliberately at various angles, even when they were directly in front of us. Suddenly the classic center chest shot wasn't any good as a probable stopper. You might simply graze the

threat or, worse, miss entirely if either of you twitched. We went through several sessions dealing with this new, more lifelike, three-dimensional threat that required you to aim where you had never been trained to aim before.

A viable, new anatomical stopping shot presented itself. The hip area, which isn't usually as wide as the shoulder area of a man, now offers the widest/largest area of skeletal structure to the student. A shot in that area may not totally stop all activity, but it will break down the supporting structure and immobilize the threat. It's not a "new" target, it just becomes a more realistic target as angles change. The head also presents a larger area than before as it turns toward profile, but the aiming point is drastically different. As Louis stated in the classroom, learning these variations is done in training so that you're not surprised—and beaten—on the street.

About the time we adjusted to the anatomical differences of targets at varying angles, we were introduced to the Yavapai moving target. The target was secured to a pivot point at the base, but the torso could be rotated and moved left and right about the pivot point. Movement of the target was controlled and directed by means of ropes on each side of the target running to Louis's hands. The movement was not totally random. Louis watched the shooter, just as the bad guy would, and timed his moves in accordance with anticipated fire.

We learned patience. The basic premise (you *must* make the shot) was now tempered by having to wait until you were *sure* you could make the shot. It was not an easily learned lesson, and there were many misses before everyone did it right. Then things got seriously difficult. We went to the hostage dolls, and I learned why I wasn't sure I could be a cop.

The bad-guy doll was wearing an ugly, stained plaid shirt, and your inclination was to shoot him if only as a favor to the fashion police. Unfortunately, he was holding a little-girl doll in tights and a pink dress as a hostage in front of his chest, and he moved in an agitated fashion. Even worse, for part of the exercise, he had another person immediately behind him that could get in the line of fire.

For two days, I had been shooting well and basically doing things right. One of the shooters ahead of me had even nicked the girl doll's arm, so the pressure seemed to

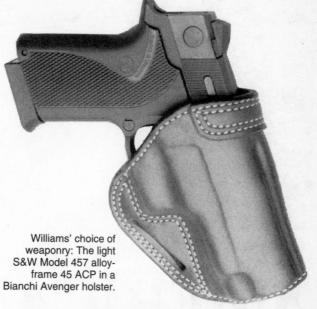

Williams' choice of weaponry: The light S&W Model 457 alloy-frame 45 ACP in a Bianchi Avenger holster.

be off in terms of not being the first student to make a mistake. I forgot all about follow-through and blew it big time. Letting the gun come up in recoil, I lost my concentration on the target and heard a faint groan before recovering. I felt sick looking at the 45-caliber hole I had put in the doll's kneecap.

How does a police officer ever learn when he or she should take a shot in a hostage situation? I think there are two answers. I saw one of them demonstrated by my classmates that day on the firing line: patience. You *must* wait for a shot you're certain you can make. The second answer is repeated training in how to handle a hostage situation. Not everyone in the class was a better shot than I, but they all showed more patience and experience than I did.

My heart wasn't in it, but Louis made me stay on the line until I got it right. I suspect he was much gentler in moving the target on my repeat efforts, just as I was considerably more patient. This is not a situation for the untrained, nor is it a situation I ever want to face in real life. That blackened hole in the kneecap will stay in my mind forever.

Following my fiasco, we went through the same hostage situation with two-man teams. A two-man team, particularly one that has worked and trained together, has a substantial advantage over a single officer. Doubling the officers more than doubles their probability of success; I suspect it's more like an order of magnitude improvement. You can spread your resources (and the bad guy's attention) with one officer providing distraction and the other looking for the shot opportunity. Even with a team, I still don't want to face a hostage scenario, but the class did provide us with better ways of handling this ugly possibility.

On the last day, as desired by the individual students, Louis covered the utilization of concealment holsters and fanny packs. Students brought whatever they used, and the training included discussions on the pros and cons of different systems, followed by the opportunity to practice the suggested techniques. Same philosophy: You choose what works best for you from the different possibilities. I only watched this part of the program because I don't currently have a concealed-carry permit. However, I fully intend to get one when California sees the light.

The fanny-pack-type holster may not be much of an advantage for a cop, but they work well for civilians. Once the off-duty officer confronts a bad situation—and he will because that's his job—he is now operating as a cop with his weapon accessibility seriously restricted. Also, he's probably not had much training or practice getting the gun into play from this kind of carry. Additionally, the bad guy knows the gun is zipped securely into that fanny pack, and his attention is riveted on any move toward it. The second you move, he's on you.

Rather than trying to save a fraction of a second by using both hands to get the gun, consider learning to draw from the pack with one hand while fending off a possible attack with the other. With a few minutes' practice, three students who tried it got pretty proficient. What will they use on the streets? Like everything else learned at Yavapai, it's their choice.

I'd like to express my sincere thanks to Louis Awerbuck and all the Northern California law enforcement officers in the class for allowing me to attend the session. Even though I'm not a police officer, the class was extremely informative and useful. In addition to the individual skills and techniques I learned, my respect for the skills and judgement required of our street cops is enormously enhanced. I'm proud that they permitted me to participate.

For those readers who don't have the opportunity to attend a law enforcement training session but who want to know more about defending themselves and their family with a handgun, I seriously recommend they take some kind of civilian training course like this. At $375, Yavapai Firearms Academy costs less than a good gun and could be even more instrumental than a gun in saving lives. ●

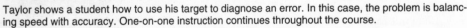

Taylor shows a student how to use his target to diagnose an error. In this case, the problem is balancing speed with accuracy. One-on-one instruction continues throughout the course.

AMERICAN SMALL ARMS ACADEMY

by GREG NORDYKE

I AM NO STRANGER to firearms, having been around them most of my life. While not an avid hunter during my growing-up years, it was fun to go to the local dump and plink at a tin can or two. After I matured, it became obvious that the world around me was not a happy place and some people were not happy people. I decided to take self-defense shooting a little more seriously.

But where could I go to learn how to shoot to defend myself? I checked with the local gun club, read some magazine articles and talked with some friends, but they all led me to the same thing: "Ready on the right. Ready on the left. Ready on the firing line!" Then a whistle would blow and people would start shooting. To me, this seemed unreal. I wondered if the Range Master giving those commands would be standing on a street corner waiting to give me directions if I got into a gunfight. Somehow I didn't think so.

Then I checked with the police. After all, they carry a sidearm and they *must* train with it, right? So, I talked with the local chief and, ultimately, his departmental firearms instructor, but the results were less than encouraging. I found out that most police departments are, at best—because of budget problems—only adequately trained. I also discov-

ered that their training is usually limited to a short qualification course with little time for serious instruction and that they shot at larger-than-life-size silhouette targets. Officers were expected to step up to the firing line and shoot a specified number of shots at a target in a specified amount of time.

I received permission to attend a departmental qualification and, guess what? "Ready on the right, Ready on the left, Ready on the firing line!" Sound familiar? From 3 yards, they had three seconds to fire two rounds, drawing from the holster, into an irrelevantly placed X-ring on the target. Then, from 7 yards, they had twelve full seconds to fire twelve shots! So, after the start whistle, there was a volley of fire followed by many seconds of silence, then sporadic fire as the officers reloaded and tried to fire all the required number of shots in the allowed time. Most of them shot pretty well, and I noticed that the better shooters placed most, if not all, of their hits in the X-ring. Seeing this made me feel better, but something still nagged at me.

I remembered that the FBI said most gunfights occurred at 7 yards or less, with the majority occurring at 7 feet. I also remembered that the gunfight times were *very* fast—two to three seconds—with fewer than three shots fired. Something

In the classroom, Chuck conducts extremely informative lectures covering a wide range of topics. Questions are encouraged. His lectures, with an accompanying slide presentation, are always eye-openers.

Chuck Taylor, founder and director of ASAA, has authored numerous articles on a variety of subjects from self-defense to hunting. He is a Combat Handgun Master with eight different handguns and the first Four Weapon Master. Chuck has devoted a lifetime to his work and is a leader in the weaponcraft field.

wasn't right. At 7 yards, the police had *twelve seconds* to fire twelve shots. Based on the FBI data, after the first three seconds and the first two shots, it would be over! It all sounded like the local gun club and looked almost the same.

Disappointed, I went back to the local gun club and subsequently became a spectator at some "combat" matches. Wow, these guys were in *good* shape, running all over the place, jumping over obstacles, shooting at targets, running back again. There was a long course of fire, with the shooter being required to reload on the run, and it took about thirty seconds or so. The fastest runner with the most hits won. Hmm...7 feet...two seconds...two shots...nobody shooting back at you...life or death? A fellow spectator leaned over to me and said, "This is great...It's *practical*." It didn't seem so to me.

One day a friend showed me some letters that got my attention. Here are some excerpts: " ...I just wanted you to know that your training served me well in a fatal shooting encounter... "

"The professional manner and expertise in which the classes were given are truly state of the art."

"Even though I am just now recovered from all the cuts, scratches and bruises, I feel (the class) was worth every one, I even surprised myself with things I did not think I could do."

Starting to get interested? So was I. I read on.

"In my opinion the combination of your personal background in both military and police affairs makes you one of the finest if not the finest instructor I have ever met."

"Your techniques were logical, easy to learn and retainable in conflict, and have already resulted in at least one "save" in our most recent conflict in Panama."

OK just one more.

"A gun magazine with Chuck Taylor's byline is considered to have a voice of authority."

These letters had been sent to Chuck by some of his graduates, and I got to see them through a mutual friend.

But who was Chuck Taylor? I went back to the gun magazines, made a few phone calls, and with some research, I started to get the picture.

The American Small Arms Academy (ASAA) was founded by Chuck Taylor in 1980 and is a unique school of combat weaponcraft. It uses nothing fancy, no gimmicks, no games, has no false motives. ASAA's driving force is to *win*. Others have tried to copy Chuck's techniques, with varying degrees of success, but with ASAA you get your money's worth.

(Above) Taylor's instructors are hand-picked and highly trained. Years of preparation are devoted to training the trainers. ASAA instructors are more interested in saving lives and advancing the state of the art than in making money.

Weapon-handling drills are an important part of the ASAA Basic course. To be able to shoot is one thing; however, if you don't know how to properly handle your weapon, you're more dangerous to yourself and others than to the bad guy! Checking the weapon's condition and loading/unloading are just a few of the procedures with which the student becomes highly familiar.

What makes Chuck Taylor and ASAA unique?

First, he has a no-nonsense, hands-on, *realistic* approach to self-defense. Leave your ego behind, be prepared to think, to learn, to work. In fact, you'll learn more in one day than you ever thought possible. Forget your preconceived notions, what you see on TV or what your friends tell you. Want to learn about stress? Time? Speed? Anatomy? Shooting basics that will last you a lifetime? Want to have fun at the same time? Then ASAA is for you. But a warning—if you're not serious about life or death, don't bother. ASAA doesn't play games.

Second, Chuck's background and experience is unique. He served in the U.S. Army, achieving the rank of captain. He lived through Ranger School, Airborne training and two tours in Vietnam. While in the military, he earned Expert ratings with the M1911 45 pistol; M-1, M-14, M-16 rifles; M-1 carbine; M-14A1 squad auto rifle; M-60 machine gun; and M-79 40mm grenade launcher. He holds NRA Expert ratings in Light and High-Power rifle. He is an NRA certified rifle/pistol instructor, a former World-class IPSC competitor and U.S. Team member. He's the first of only four men to achieve the title of "Four Weapons Master" and the first "Handgun Master," of which there are only twelve in the world.

He's trained SWAT teams and military special operations units. His training methods and techniques have been officially adopted by the Swiss army. He has consulted and trained members of the FBI, DEA and Secret Service. He's trained police officers in the U.S. and Europe. (There is even a European branch of ASAA.)

Chuck has written over 1100 feature articles in publications such as HANDGUNS '96 and HANDGUNS '97, *Combat Handguns, SWAT, Shootist, Special Weapons, Glockster Pistol Magazine* (USA), *Aim and Fire!* (Belgium), *Deutches Waffen Journal* (Germany), *Action Guns & Le Cible* (France), *The Swiss Army Journal*, and others. There have been numerous newspaper articles written about him. Chuck's ASAA has been rated by virtually all of the gun magazines as one of the four best training schools in the world.

Taylor has been described as totally professional, outspoken, brutally honest and controversial, but remember this:

Chuck has been shot at and missed and *shot at and hit*. His experience comes from real-world situations, not out of a magazine or second-hand, from some armchair expert. He has a unique combination of experience and ability.

So, what does the ASAA Basic Defensive Handgun course entail?

Any good entry-level course begins in the classroom, but ASAA's basic course goes much further. There are eight full hours of lecture, covering a multitude of subjects. Chuck not only teaches you how to defend yourself, but also gives you a perspective on anatomy, firepower, ammunition, the firing-range mindset, holsters, the law, home-defense tactics, crisis management and shooting aftermath. Just how powerful is a handgun? He talks about types of handguns, calibers, stocks, sights, weapon modifications and the different finishes that are available; in short he discusses almost every subject that pertains to the self-defense handgun.

Most of all, Taylor wants his students to *think*. One of the first questions he asks is, "What do you want to do with your handgun?" Is it a status symbol for target shooting or for serious defense? He says there is no perfect handgun, although some will tell you otherwise. He has gone to amazing lengths to bring usable information to his classroom about what works. He gives the student the data and then lets him make his own choice.

The "firing-range mindset" was discussed in detail. Taylor points out that we do a lot of things by rote. We drive a vehicle without thinking. We eat at specified times. We have that cup of coffee first thing every morning. If anything disrupts our routine, we're uncomfortable, but don't really know why. It's called conditioned response.

Want to know *why* we are uncomfortable with change? Change upsets our daily routine; change means something new and unfamiliar. Shooting is no different. We get so accustomed to doing things a certain way that we forget to think. We program ourselves to do the same thing over and over until it becomes second nature, even if it's wrong. The danger with having a firing-range-conditioned response is that we wait to shoot until someone tells us to.

ASAA won't be there in a gunfight to tell you what to do, so

In a four-day Basic course, students are given the chance to utilize all they have learned. A course is laid out and the student must walk a predetermined path, identify situations, make the proper choice of field positions, and decide whether or not to shoot.

you'll have to think on your own. Over and over again, you'll see how the firing-range-mindset can get you killed in a real encounter. One of the points Chuck consistently emphasizes is that *you are the weapon*, the gun is only a tool. How you use that tool is your responsibility.

There is yet another bonus in taking an ASAA course—how to save money. Listen carefully to what Taylor has to say and you'll be able to walk into a gunshop knowing exactly what you want and don't want. Don't worry gals, all this pertains to you, too. In fact, women often end up doing better in ASAA courses than the guys.

After the morning classroom session, there is a break for lunch, then the students meet at the range. Range safety is the first order of business, then students get their weapons and equipment checked. Range commands are explained, as is an overview of each afternoon's program.

One of the first topics discussed is the target used. Chuck designed a target that would represent an average-size human and that could be used in multiple training scenarios. He wanted a target that would break the norm of the bulls-eye and too-large silhouette types that have been around for years. In essence, he wanted a target that gave a more realistic representation of human vital areas and would require the proper balance of speed and accuracy. It's not a bowling pin nor a small steel circle—it's practical.

Loading and unloading drills are then discussed and demonstrated, then practiced by the students. There are many different ways to load and unload a handgun, but over the years, Chuck has developed a technique for each type of gun that is simple and effective, and works efficiently under stress. Some of the movements learned in these drills will be used in other weapon-handling drills, the idea being to have to learn as little to solve as many different problems as possible. Keep it simple, remember?

For example, Chuck invented the tactical reload, which incorporates some of the same hand movements as his loading, unloading and malfunction clearance procedures. Remember stress? The simpler the technique, the quicker it can be learned and the better it can be performed. Chuck's tactical reload incorporates all relevant factors.

No one has been able to find any documentation in which a speed reload has changed the outcome of a gunfight. Yet, some instructors spend a vast amount of time and energy teaching it. Chuck explains that there are only two reasons why you would need to speed reload: 1) The situation has developed beyond your best efforts to control it. 2) You're missing too much! So, while he teaches the speed reload, like all his other methods, it is kept in its proper perspective.

Stances are next. Two are taught, the isosceles and the Weaver. After an explanation and demonstration, students are encouraged to try both. In general, if higher skill levels are the student's goal, he will select the Weaver.

Once stances are established, the student is shown the "ready" position, which has the weapon in the shooter's hands pointed down at 45 degrees below horizontal. This enables him to have total target visibility and a fast presentation. Some instructors erroneously teach what is referred to as the "contact ready," which places the gun almost directly in front of the shooter's face, obstructing the target both before and after shooting. Once again, too many things to remember under stress. Considering that most gunfights occur in dim light and that there is a growing number of encounters involving multiple assailants, the more target visibility you have, the better. Taylor's ready position handles all situations.

Then, shooting fundamentals are reviewed. There are three shooting fundamentals, which Chuck refers to as "the three secrets." While in actuality they are not secrets at all, many instructors forget their importance or assume that the student already knows them. They are 1) sight alignment; 2) sight picture; 3) trigger control. Each is explained, and through a series of dry-practice drills, the student becomes familiar with them and learns their importance.

Once the student is comfortable with the basics, live-fire drills begin. Starting with one shot on the target from ready, the student engages targets at 3, 5, 7, 10, and 15 meters. After several times through those drills, Taylor explains the importance of placing two shots on a single assailant. The student then repeats the drills, firing twice at a single target at the various ranges. Chuck's assistant instructors move up

Students are drilled well in the basics. Taylor says that gives them a sound foundation to fall back on during times of great stress.

and down the line, paying constant attention and giving suggestions to the students as needed. Even the good shooter is watched closely with an extra eye for detail to help him improve.

Toward the end of the first day, the element of urgency is introduced. Taylor gives an explanation of time as it pertains to deadly encounters and how you will react to it under stress. Then, Taylor gives a demonstration of what can be done in a specified amount of time. Many students can't believe their eyes when Chuck or one of his instructors steps up to the 3-meter line and fires two shots, drawing from a holster, in one second, with good center chest hits. While the basic student is not expected to perform this task, students usually are astonished that, within in a very short period of time, they, too, can shoot quickly and accurately.

In turn, this leads into a discussion of balancing speed and accuracy. If you shoot too slowly, you give your opponent too much time to get you. On the other hand, if you shoot too fast, you'll miss. More practice is done under time pressure, with the student continually being coached on a one-on-one basis.

By the end of the first day, the student is both mentally and physically tired. Whether they realize it or not, a great deal of information has been given to them in eight hours. Taylor's teaching system allows for this, and while most students are wanting more, it is time to stop.

The morning session of the second day concludes the classroom lecture portion of the curriculum. The afternoon and all of the following days are spent on the range further developing skills. Everything previously mastered is a basis for what follows: more dry-practice work, presentations from the holster, malfunction clearance drills, responses left and right, and reloading drills.

The entire program is kept simple, but provides the student with a unique sense of enjoyment. At the end of the course, the student is tested. Time limits are used not only for the shooting portion, but also during the weapon-handling sections of the evaluation. The student leaves the course with a tremendous amount of knowledge and a solid repertoire of handgun skills. A 60-year-old businessman in Chuck's recent class was somewhat apprehensive when he stepped into the classroom. However, the informal atmosphere, Chuck's lec-

ture style, his willingness to answer any question and the effectiveness of his instruction during the shooting portion of the course gave the businessman confidence. By the end of the first day, he was all smiles and commented several times that he had never believed that he would ever shoot as well as he did.

Is the ASAA Basic Defensive Handgun Course worth the time and money spent? In my opinion, yes. Can you effectively defend yourself with a handgun after completing Chuck's basic course? Yes, the basic level skills are there, and a vast amount of information has been given to the student. More than that, the student has also been given a complete understanding of the inner workings of a deadly encounter, based on Taylor's twenty-five years of research, training and experience. Can the individual apply what he/she has learned? That is up to you. Chuck gives you the tools and knowledge needed to handle a deadly encounter. He gives you something to think about. He wants to break you of the firing-range mentality or competition mindset and get you into a "tactical mindset." The type of training you get from ASAA is not gamesmanship but real training for real situations in the real world.

Chuck is usually accompanied by one or more of his staff, who are specially selected and trained by Chuck himself. Each is highly skilled and capable of effective one-on-one instruction. His instructors must have years of experience, not only in weaponcraft skills but in instruction as well, before he will allow them to assist in any of his classes. It is important to him that each student gets as much attention as possible.

In conclusion, Taylor brings to his classes superb shooting skills, a certain gift of instructional ability, and real gunfighting experience. Perhaps the best evaluation are the comments made by his students during and at the end of the course. To watch a police officer come up to Chuck, shake his hand and thank him for the potentially life-saving instruction is a wonderful sight to see. Over and over, comments like, "I thought I knew how to shoot, but you really taught me something," are made via letter, phone or in person.

What better testimony as to the effectiveness of the course can there be?

●

HANDGUNS 97

Law Enforcement And Military Scene

What's the best used by the best, page 100.

A tool barely seen and not heard, page 113.

This old gun tells an old story, page 121.

HANDGUNS OF THE U.S. ELITE

by KEN HACKATHORN

IN RECENT YEARS, a great deal of interest has been expressed about the small arms used by U.S. Special Operations Command (USSOCOM). Many manufacturers of arms and related gear like to allude to the use of their arms or related equipment by the Spec Ops community. In fact, the list of weapons is much shorter than many may think.

Due to the nature of special operations, units of these elite forces are generally smaller military organizations staffed with highly trained and professional soldiers. Quick response to a crisis situation, whether a terrorist incident or the hostile actions of an unfriendly nation, requires the absolute best caliber of soldiers available.

As a result of the up-close and personal job that elite forces "operators" must do, the handgun has become a key item of their issue equipment. Most regular soldiers do not require a handgun. The issue service rifle will more than serve the typical infantry scenario. With Spec Ops personnel, the handgun is considered necessary for close-quarters battle (CQB) skills. The CQB requirement has placed the handgun in a position of great importance, and training is extensive in order to maintain skill at arms with the handgun.

Within the U. S. Special Operations community there are at present three handgun designs being used. For most Army, Air Force, and Marine units, the

standard pistol issued is the Beretta 9x19 NATO. Navy SEAL teams use the SIG P226 9x19 NATO pistol. The top Spec Ops unit in the world, the U. S. Army's Delta Force, still carries custom-modified M1911 45 ACP pistols, as do the elite Marine Force Recon companies. The big news in the Joint Special Operations Command (JSOC) is the adoption of the new 45 ACP pistol, the Heckler & Koch Mark 23. This new H&K 45 is designed to replace all pistols within USSOCOM. While the Mk 23 has many good features, it is still untested in combat, and I would be very surprised to see it replace the M9, P226, and M1911 pistols in the hands of *all* Spec Ops forces.

After ten years of issue, the M9 Beretta has been well received by the U.S. military. Because of its widespread distribution within the entire military, the M9 has become the pistol most commonly issued to special operators. Among the exclusive units using the Beretta M9 are U.S. Army Special Forces and Rangers, Air Force Special Operations Squadron, Combat Control Teams (CCT), and Para Rescue. Marine FAST Companies and some Force Recon units also rely on the M9 as their sidearm.

Navy SEAL teams were the first to be issued the M92F Beretta, but their experience with the early M9 pistols included slide fractures and parts failures. The SEALs chose to use another

If the Spec Ops "shooter" runs out of ammo or his weapon suffers a stoppage, he must transition to his secondary weapon—the handgun.

All three commonly used Spec Ops sidearms will fire standard ball ammo for 99 percent of their use.

pistol, the SIG P226, and standardized it as the Mk 24. Extensive field testing has proven it to be ideal for their needs.

U.S. Army 1st Special Forces Operational Detachment Delta *[The full name of the Army's "Delta Force". Ed.]* issues the same pistol that it began with when Col. Charles Beckwith first started the elite counter-terrorist unit. Beckwith chose the M1911 45 ACP pistol in National Match form. These M1911 NM pistols have been refined continuously to make them serve better in the hands of the Delta operators. Despite blurbs in the gun press stating that Delta issues the M9 or some other 9x19mm pistol, the custom-modified M1911 45 is the standard-issue arm. A semi-custom M1911 is provided to special Marine units. These MEUSOC 45 pistols are popular sidearms with the Spec Ops Marines who carry them.

Every Special Operations unit trains their operators extensively. Spec Ops personnel are referred to as "shooters," a title that is earned and worn by the troops with pride. Each shooter shoots his pistol endlessly to achieve top-level skills, carries it in a unique holster, and modifies it to meet his specifications. The amount of ammunition fired by Spec Ops shooters in one month is greater than the average infantry soldier will fire in his entire military career. As a result of this high round consumption, the majority of the Spec

Ops pistols will see more wear and tear than most handguns were designed for. Many units issue two pistols per man to ensure that if a pistol is down for repair or replacement, the operator will have a backup pistol available. Depending on the pistol, parts wear, breakage, and replacement of magazines and springs will be impacted heavily by the volume

of rounds fired. While the M9, Mk 24 and M1911 pistols all have proven to be very rugged and reliable, they all break parts and wear out. A key factor with the handguns used by the elite forces is that the operators must be able to closely monitor their sidearms for signs of excessive wear or damage.

The means by which the handgun will be carried is now fairly standard. Nearly all Spec Ops units rely upon some form of the basic "assault holster." These rigs are worn lower on the leg than conventional belt holsters and are held in place by a leg strap. This design places the pistol below the body armor or assault vest, making for easier access. Most commonly issued are the ballistic nylon models made by Eagle Industries, Ltd., (SAS III series) or the Blackhawk equivalent. Safariland's Model 3004 or 3005 are the latest favorites and offer better weapon retention and security. The standard M12 Bianchi holster for the Beretta is rarely worn, except where protection is the primary factor.

Other items used to enhance the pistol as a close-quarters combat weapon include extended high-capacity magazines, white-light mounts for target identification in low-light scenarios, and tritium insert night sights. For some missions, a suppressed pistol may

The pistol is a secondary weapon. The primary Spec Ops arm is a long gun, typically the M4 CAR or H&K MP5.

Two Beretta pistols: the standard-issue M9 and the M9 with Sure-Fire M612 light mount installed and with twenty-round extended magazine. These two pistols are typical for Marine FAST teams.

M9 Beretta pistols are typically carried in either the Safariland M3004 or 3005, which is a Kydex plastic holster. The M9 fitted with its light mount is carried in an Eagle Industries, Ltd., SAS III assault holster. The design of the Eagle rig allows for the extra bulk of the light mount.

U.S. ELITE

be required. Specialty gun finishes that protect against harsh environments are used by those units that must operate in tropic or saltwater areas.

The M9 Beretta

After a decade of use in places like Panama, Kuwait, and Somalia, the M9 Beretta has demonstrated its rugged, reliable performance. It is easy to shoot and has proven itself to be highly accurate. Hard lessons have been learned concerning its strengths and weaknesses; it remains a popular choice. Marine FAST, Security Force, and some Force Recon personnel have praised the Beretta's well-established record of performance as a CQB pistol. Army Special Forces, Rangers, and TF 160 crews like the Beretta. Special Forces "Charlie Company" operators have vast experience with the M9 and find it very reliable and accurate, even when shooting on the move. Elite Air Force units like the 20th Operations Squadron, Combat Control Teams, and Para Rescue troopers all have great respect for the M9. Any of these guys can quickly find themselves in a real hot spot where the pistol is a key survival tool.

One of the most common G.I. fixes on the M9 pistol is to replace the hammer mainspring with one from a standard M1911, which provides a lighter and smoother double-action trigger pull. Some units have their M9 pistols fitted with tritium night sights, which vastly improves low-light shooting performance. The Laser Products Model 612

Sure-Fire 6-volt light mount is commonly installed on the M9. These lights will often be permanently mounted on the pistol, or kept handy in an equipment bag. If the mission has a night or low-light requirement, the M612 can be quickly installed. Both Eagle and Blackhawk offer holsters designed to work with the light mount attached to the pistol. Knight's Mfg. Co. of Florida made a conversion of the M9 with a special extended barrel to accept their suppressor and modified slide-lock assembly. With the suppressor fitted, and with subsonic ammo, the result is a very quiet close-quarters pistol. Normally, the suppressed M9 is a dedicated handgun set up for this use only. While suppressed handguns sound like a good idea, most Spec Ops units rely upon a H&K MP5-SD with electronic dot sight, for dedicated suppressed work. If the operational plan states that suppressed pistols are a requirement, then the Army, Navy, Air Force, and Marines have the Knight's-equipped suppressed pistol available.

When the M92F Beretta was first issued, it went to the Navy SEALs. They were quite fond of the twenty-round extended magazine offered by Beretta. With it, the SEALs were ready to clear even the most confining corners of a ship, knowing that the twenty rounds available were more than enough firepower to solve any CQB scenario.

M9 pistols received a great deal of negative publicity concerning the dramatic failure of some of their slides. Slide fractures resulted in injury to some personnel and were widely noted in the gun press. Since the SEALs were the first troops to be issued the Beretta,

they were the first to suffer injuries. Because of other parts breakage problems with the M9, the SEALs dropped the pistol from their inventory and replaced them with the SIG P226. Today, slide failures of the M9 still occur, but at a far reduced level. The breakage of the locking block remains the great weak link of the M9. Beretta designed a new locking block to solve the fracture problem. Most shooters carry a small package of spare parts that includes the locking block. Close scrutiny of the pistol each time it is given preventative maintenance is critical to insure that all parts are sound and free of damage.

Certainly two of the best virtues of the M9 are that it is easy to maintain and remains very reliable even when dirty and low on lubrication. I have always been impressed that the M9 pistol is the *most* reliable service pistol I have ever used. Nearly all malfunctions can be traced to dirty or damaged magazines. The magazines of the M9 are strong, easy to disassemble for cleaning, and not overly difficult to load. Sand seems to be the only thing that

Special Forces troopers train with an H&K MP5 PDW with a standard-issue M9 Beretta in a leg assault holster for backup. Note that the drop-loop leg assault holster places the pistol well below the body armor, for easy access in an emergency. These guys don't like their faces shown.

sageways. For many applications, even if the primary weapon is a H&K MP5 or CAR-15/M-4 carbine, the handgun is much easier to use in really confined spaces.

Since the SEALs often have to operate in a saltwater environment, corrosion and rust are constant problems. P226 pistols coated with the Sigarms' "K-Kote" polymer finish are well protected against rust. The most popular speciality finish used by Spec Ops units for their weapons is the outstanding Birdsong "Black-T" polymer coating. Whether applied to the M9, Mk 24, or M1911, Black-T from Walter Birdsong has proven to be in a class by itself. This finish is also available in a NATO green. The factory matte-blue finish that is standard on the P226 rusts terribly in any humid or salt air environment. Efforts have been made to have future Mk 24 pistols equipped with stainless steel slides like those of the P229, and then coated to match the black matte finish of the P226/Mk 24. With the pending adoption of the Mk 23 H&K 45 ACP pistol, the updated Mk 24 variant may not come to pass.

Replacement of the pin that holds the breechblock in the slide is recommended at least every 10,000 rounds. Many operators carry a spare trigger-bar spring and decocking-lever spring, both of which often break. As with the M1911 pistol, it is unwise to load the pistol by dropping a round into the chamber, then releasing the slide to

snap the extractor over the cartridge rim. This can damage the extractor and even cause it to break if done constantly. The welds that hold the magazine body together sometimes split at the top rear of the magazine, especially if the mag is dropped often onto a hard surface like pavement or ship decks. Wise maintenance of the Mk 24 requires inspection of the magazine for failures of the weld.

A nylon holster was original issue, but most SEAL teams are now carrying their Mk 24s in the new Safariland M3004 Kydex assault holster. For a better grip when the hands are wet or cold, operators use bicycle

SIG P226/Mk 24 pistol is often packed in Eagle Industries' SAS III assault holster. If extra firepower is needed, spare twenty-round magazines are the choice of most Mk 24 "operators."

will compromise the function of any double-column magazine. Many a soldier learned in the Middle East desert that if downloaded to only eight or nine rounds, the M9 magazine will still work well in spite of the presence of fine sand.

The Mk 24 SIG

In the original M9 pistol trials, both the Beretta M92 and SIG-Sauer P226 were selected as the final choices. In the price bidding for the M9 contract, Beretta won out over SIG. As previously mentioned, when the Navy SEAL team "shooters" began to suffer from the M92 Beretta slide and locking block failures, they replaced their Berettas with SIGs. Adopted and standardized by the SEALs as the Mk 24 pistol, the SIG has proven to be a very fine pistol. Again, like the M9 Beretta, the Mk 24 is regularly fitted with a Laser Products Sure-Fire light mount for use in searching and clearing the dark confines of a ship. With a twenty-round magazine in place in his Mk 24, the SEAL is well equipped to search air ducts, storage compartments and pas-

SIG P226 9x19mm NATO pistol is adapted and used by the Navy SEALs as the Mk 24. Both standard fifteen-round and longer twenty-round magazines are used. For anti-terrorist use, hollowpoint expanding ammo is permitted. However, most of the time standard ball ammo is used by Spec Ops units.

U.S. ELITE

innertube slipped over the grip frame for a better gripping surface. Also, the pressure switch of the Sure-Fire light can be held in place via the innertube, allowing the operator to position the switch where it will work best for him.

The smooth double-action trigger pull of the SIG P226 is considered one of its best features, highly conducive to promoting fast and accurate shooting. Extreme reliability in harsh environments combined with simple operation has made the P226/Mk 24 a superb pistol for the SEALs.

The M1911 Colt

The M1911 pistol, supposedly obsolete and outdated, remains in use by both the top Marine Spec Ops shooters and the U. S. Army Delta operators. Both groups use modified custom pistols, and have chosen to remain with the M1911 pistol because they are convinced that it is the top handgun for close-quarters combat. The MEUSOC 45 pistol used by the Marines is custom assembled by the MTU shop at Quantico. Using select standard-issue M1911A1 frames as a base, a new aftermarket slide is fitted to the frame. A Bar-Sto drop-in match-grade stainless steel barrel is installed, and recoil springs and mainsprings are replaced with Bar-Sto stainless springs. A ramp front sight of higher profile is silver soldered in place, and a new high, no-snag rear sight is made and fitted by the armorers at Quantico. The ejection port is lowered and the magazine well is beveled. A Commander-style hammer is fitted and the trigger pull is adjusted to 4.5 pounds. The top-notch Videki long trigger and a Wilson beavertail grip safety are also fitted. Add an ambidextrous safety and Pachmayr stocks, and the picture is complete. Wilson/Rogers seven-round magazines are standard. Most of these MEUSOC M1911 Marine Corps pistols are Parkerized, but some have had Birdsong's Black-T applied. The normal issue holster is of the Eagle SAS series. One of the key reasons for the continued use of these tuned M1911 pistols is that despite the many thousands of rounds each operator fires annually, these pistols continue to perform reliably with minimum repair.

The other M1911 45 pistol popular with the elite forces is the custom 45 issued to Delta operatives. Considered to be the best of the best, Delta troopers have proven themselves to be the top shooters in the world of the elite.

Mid-generation Delta M1911 45 pistol. Based upon a modified National Match gun, it has been improved with beavertail grip safety, extended manual safety, S&A mag well, Novak tritium insert sights, and Wilson/Rogers magazines.

The Sure-Fire Light mount on the M1911 45 pistol. The "white light" mount is critical to allow target identification in low light CQB scenarios.

They could have any pistol they desire...and the M1911, tuned to their specifications, remains their first choice.

The Delta Force 45 has undergone quite an evolution. Standard M1911 National Match pistols were used initially. Later, these guns were equipped with lower sights more suitable for holster carry. Commander-style hammers, beavertail grip safeties, speed or ambidextrous thumb safeties, Smith and Alexander mag wells, and Novak tritium sights became standard. Current pistols are assembled on Caspian slides and frames since stocks of G.I. National Match pistols are depleted. Fitted with match-grade bar-

rels, 4- to 4.5-pound triggers, and using Wilson magazines, these pistols have proven to be superb tools in the hands of the Big D. At this time, custom pistolsmith Bill Wilson offers a pistol nearly identical to the issue Delta handgun. It is called the "Spec Ops CQB." It features a Parkerized finish (as does the G.I. original), but may also be had with Birdsong's Black-T, a finish found on many of the Delta operators' guns.

Within the ranks of elite special operations groups is the FBI's Hostage Rescue Team (HRT). These select FBI agents have, since their formation, used the P-35 9x19 Browning Hi-Power. Sporting Novak tritium sights, these pistols have served well. Recently, the HRT has switched over to the custom Les Baer M1911 45 ACP pistol built on the P14 Para-Ordnance frame. These HRT 45 Para pistols are accurized and tuned to FBI specs. Each pistol has most of the custom touches an IPSC Limited pistol would wear. With checkered grip strap, Novak night sights, beavertail grip safety and Birdsong Black-T finish, these are serious sidearms. Loaded with 230-grain Federal Hydra-Shoks or Remington 230-grain JHP Golden Sabers, these pistols offer fifteen rounds of potent medicine. Latest news from the FBI is that all their SWAT teams will be issued custom 45 pistols similar to the HRT pistols, but they will have the more conventional single-stack magazines.

Whether the Army's best or the federal government's best—Delta or HRT—these M1911 45 pistols are carried in Safariland M3004 assault holsters. Each operator can fit his pistol with a Sure-Fire light mount, and if desired, Wilson provides Delta with ten-round extended magazines for those who wish to use them.

Case histories have shown that the pistol, when used in special operations, is a secondary weapon. The primary arm will be the H&K MP5, CAR-15/M4, or a shotgun. If this weapon fails or runs dry, then the handgun is put into action. If extremely close quarters like small rooms, closets, or air shafts must be searched, the handgun may be the better primary weapon. The key point is that the standard pistol with an eight- or nine-shot capacity has proven to be fine for this kind of work. The old adage that high-capacity pistols are only an advantage if you miss a lot remains true. These elite guys are not paid to miss, so high magazine capacity is not all that important.

There are times that these operators must carry their handgun concealed, on missions like protection details, target reconnaissance and when on surveillance. A good concealment holster that allows for carrying the M9, Mk 24, or M1911 undercover is critical. Inside-the-pants holsters like the Sparks Summer Special or Executive Companion are top choices.

Despite all the rumors about specialty ammo, Spec Ops shooters in the U.S. military normally rely on ball ammo. There are some missions that allow hollowpoint ammo for anti-terrorist use, but standard M882 9x19mm NATO ball and 230-grain 45 are basic issue for Army, Navy, Air Force and Marine personnel. FBI HRT and SWAT "shooters" have a law enforcement mission that allows the use of JHP ammunition. Currently, Federal 147-grain JHP Hydra-Shok in 9mm and Federal 230-grain JHP 45 Hydra-Shok is standard ammo for them. Magic bullets are not the answer—shot placement is.

Mk 23 H&K

The big news in the Special Operations community is the addition of the Mk 23 45-caliber pistol, manufactured by Heckler & Koch, to the SOCOM armory. H&K is not a new name to the world of Spec Ops. Their excellent MP5 submachine gun has become the world standard. Decades ago, when the SEALs wanted a suppressed pistol, the H&K P9S was used because it offered a roller-locked recoil system with a barrel that would accept a suppressor, yet remain reliable. Other popular service pistols use a tilting barrel that will not function reliably with a heavy suppressor attached. The P9S was very much ahead of its time with its polymer frame and frame-mounted cocking lever on a double-action pistol. H&K worked closely with the Navy on this P9S pistol project. While quantities procured were small, the P9 was successfully used by early SEAL teams.

When the U. S. Special Operations Command first set the criteria for their new "offensive" pistol, the specifications seemed nearly impossible to meet, but H&K met the challenge, and their pistol was selected as the Mk 23. It is an extremely impressive pistol. It's rugged, reliable, accurate and functional. An option is a new suppressor manufactured by Knight's Mfg. Co. Also specified in the accessory package is a laser aiming module (LAM) that attaches to the frame forward of the

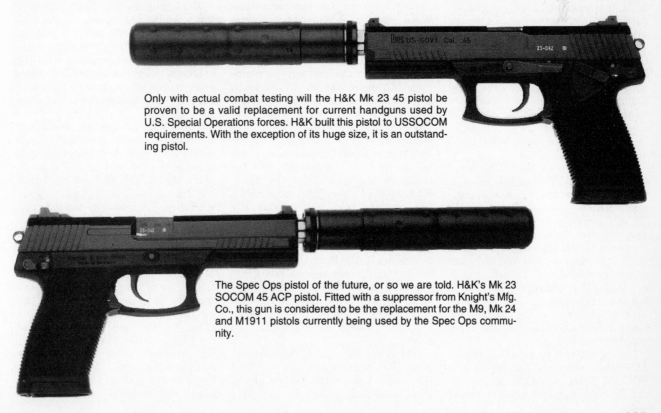

Only with actual combat testing will the H&K Mk 23 45 pistol be proven to be a valid replacement for current handguns used by U.S. Special Operations forces. H&K built this pistol to USSOCOM requirements. With the exception of its huge size, it is an outstanding pistol.

The Spec Ops pistol of the future, or so we are told. H&K's Mk 23 SOCOM 45 ACP pistol. Fitted with a suppressor from Knight's Mfg. Co., this gun is considered to be the replacement for the M9, Mk 24 and M1911 pistols currently being used by the Spec Ops community.

Elite units require that skill at arms with both primary and secondary weapons be maintained through extensive practice and training.

U.S. ELITE

trigger guard. When fitted with an infrared filter, and used in conjunction with night-vision goggles, the IF laser has some merit.

The Mk 23 pistol is a large handgun, and when fitted with suppressor and LAM, it is ungainly, hardly the handy combat weapon that we would normally expect the Spec Ops shooter to prefer. The Mk 23 is over an inch longer than the M9 Beretta, and weighs, when loaded, nearly 3¼ pounds. For shooters with small hands, the Mk 23 is a real handful. The sidearm is a secondary weapon, and thus while the step up to 45 ACP is wise, the size of the Mk 23 seems a bit more than most users would care to pack around.

In early troop tests, the Mk 23 proved to be typical H&K—rugged, reliable, accurate, and resistant to hostile environments. The first troops to get the Mk 23 will probably be the SEALs and Special Forces, then Ranger Battalions, Air Force Special Operations units, and finally the Marines. It would be logical to assume that the Mk 23 pistol will do everything that it is required to do. I do not see it replacing the M9, Mk 24, or M1911 pistols now in the hands of the current Spec Ops shooters, but being supplemental to those.

It is of interest to note that the 45 ACP round was mandated for the new SOCOM pistol. A decade ago, everyone from the wonder boys of the DOD to the sheep-like gun writers were jumping on the 9mm bandwagon, and some authorities hinted at secret tests that "proved" the 9x19 was equal to or better than the 45 ACP. Yet the specifications for the new SOCOM pistol require 45 ACP.... Studies of handgun wound capabilities finally indicated what has been suspected for most of this century: 9x19mm ball ammo has a pitiful record for incapacitation. Word from those shooters now testing the Mk 23 pistol is that, while exceptionally large, it is the most reliable 45 ACP pistol they have ever used, superbly accurate, and easy to maintain. The pistol has an easy-to-learn manual of arms, and the twelve-round magazine is faster to speedload than any other handgun these guys have used. Negative features include the long trigger reach for those with small hands, its bulk and weight, and the height of the bore above the hand. H&K adopted a very good recoil reduction system that helps tame the cycling of the Mk 23, but recoil is a relative thing to most shooters. It is far too early to predict the success of the new pistol in the Spec Ops community. It would seem that it has great potential, and whether it is widely accepted will have little to do with H&K, because this pistol was made to U.S. government specifications, not H&K's.

Nearly all elite units use sidearms other than those which are standard issue. Check the arms room of any of these units and you will find a variety of small arms. Many are just tested and forgotten. Other handguns are used for special missions such as undercover operations or missions that require "sterile" weapons that will not be recognized as obvious U.S. military weapons. Also, suppressed 22 LR pistols are common in most arms rooms. The Ruger 22 semi-auto fitted with a suppressor is a favorite.

The handguns that do 99 percent of the work in the hands of the elite forces are the M9, Mk 24, and the tuned M1911. Often fitted with a Sure-Fire Light mount, occasionally with extended magazines installed...these guns do the job. Ask any of the elite shooters what is most important about the handgun they carry, and the answer will always be reliability. Everything else is secondary. Laser sights are the tools of gun-shop commandos, not the real guys. The future of the Mk 23 H&K 45 pistol looks good, but I doubt that it will see any use with the LAM, and only limited application with the suppressor. Since the handgun plays only a limited role in even Spec Ops scenarios, little will change in their overall use. If the M1911 45 semi-auto pistol remains the choice of the best Special Operations forces in the world, I doubt that anything new will have a dramatic effect on the use of the handgun for CQB. Unlike the image of Spec Ops warriors using high-tech laser-equipped weapons, the truth is that these guys count on skill and performance over gadgets. ●

A NEW SEVEN-SHOT SERVICE REVOLVER?

by WILEY CLAPP

JUST WHEN A lot of pundits were dismissing the revolver as a relic of our frontier past, the world's largest revolver maker has come up with a new wrinkle. Smith & Wesson now offers a classy new version of their mainline 357 Magnum revolver, the Model 686. It's called the 686 Plus and the plus is for an extra shot. That's right, the gun is a seven-shooter, and it sure seems to me that those police officers who choose the revolver as a sidearm (or have it mandated for them) would be better armed with this revolver than any other. There's no compromise in the quality or strength of the gun, and it's no larger than the parent six-shot Model 686. In some ways, as we shall presently see, the 686 Plus is actually stronger than the original.

If this were December 1, 1983, (my last working day as a deputy sheriff) and I took my L-frame S&W from the top shelf of my locker to go to work, I would do what I always did—swing the cylinder open to check for ready status. Having carried S&W six-shot wheel-guns for the better part of two decades, I would have been shocked to see what I saw just a minute ago when I picked up a 686 Plus and checked it. Dammit, that cylinder seems lopsided or something...there are seven chambers bored into the thing. But when I check the action of the unloaded gun, everything seems to be just as I—and tens of thousands of other police and civilian shooters—have come to expect. Untuned, it's a smooth, slightly heavy arc requiring

Smith & Wesson makes the new seven-shot 686 Plus in three barrel lengths—2½, 4 and 6 inches.

about twelve pounds of trigger pressure. The single-action pull is a clean-breaking press of about three pounds. Pistolsmiths who have examined the 686 Plus tell me that a half hour or so inside the gun will deliver the same sensuous trigger action that has made S&W the professional's choice in revolvers. The point is simply that nothing of importance was lost in the reengineering of the revolver to make it a seven-shooter.

Unquestionably, something was gained. The 357 cartridge has been developed to a high degree of versatility and power. Most cartridge authorities rate it very highly as a service-pistol round, right alongside the 45 ACP. The limitation of the 357 caliber was never ballistic performance but, rather, gun capacity. Increasing the cylinder capacity by one round means stepping up the firepower by almost 17 percent. It moves it closer to that of the semi-auto, al-

The regular L-frame cylinder is large enough to accept seven charge holes—this is really the essence of the gun. Also note the placement of cylinder stop notches *between* chambers.

HKS is the only maker of speedloaders for the 686 Plus. Author used these extensively and they worked perfectly.

SERVICE REVOLVER?

though modern pistols in big-bore fighting calibers (40 and above) still have a considerable capacity edge. Modern jacketed bullets and high-speed loads have advanced the 357 Magnum revolver to performance levels never envisioned by the cartridge designers of the 1930s.

In those long-ago days, police and sportsmen alike were concerned with handgun power. It was the era of the gangster, a time when policemen were beginning to look at their revolver as something more than a badge of office. Most police revolvers of that time fired low-velocity 38-caliber ammo (38 S&W, 38 Colt New Police, some 38 Specials) and 32s were far from uncommon. The need for more powerful guns and ammo had a number of interesting consequences.

Over at Colt, J.H. FitzGerald lobbied for a more powerful loading of the obsolescent 41 Long Colt. This was a midbore round that easily went into Colt's Official Police frame. An updated police version of the 41 Long Colt (it was closer to 40 than 41) reminds us of the debates that resulted in the 41 Magnum police load of thirty years later. The idea never caught on, and Colt's attempt to get the semi-automatic pistol into police use didn't, either. That effort resulted in the fine 38 Super cartridge, which went into a version of the Colt Government Model pistol. Although a few departments tried the 38 Super, it never really took off as a law enforcement cartridge, partially at least because the law enforcement community of the 1930s was not ready for beat cops packing cocked-and-locked automatics.

Those who were really interested in more powerful guns were willing to carry a little weight. Smith's big N-frame had been used for 44 Special revolvers since 1907 and was pressed into wartime service as a 45 ACP during WWI. It was sufficiently strong to accept hot-loaded 38 Special ammo, and S&W introduced the 38-44 Heavy Duty revolver in 1930. There was a lot more potential to the N-frame revolver, but it took several more years to fully develop a longer 38 Special, which the company called the 357 Magnum. The cartridge and its high-velocity ammunition were instantaneous successes, even though the original N-frame revolvers were priced beyond most cops' budgets in the late 1930s. When S&W went over to wartime production at the beginning of the Big One, the first Magnum was still doing well. In the postwar period, it really took off.

The flossy original 357 Magnum went back into production soon after the war. In 1954, S&W took pity on a lot of highway patrolmen (and other working cops) by bringing out the Highway Patrolman, a less expensive, service-finished version of the fancy 357 gun. Still, the biggest boost the Magnum ever got came in late 1955 when they introduced the Combat Magnum or Model 19. While the police of this country once thought the smashing power of the magnum just had to go into a big revolver, Smith's engineers managed to craft a perfectly sound gun for '50s-vintage 357 Magnum ammo and do it on the much smaller K frame. In time, stainless steel and fixed-sight versions of the Combat Magnum came along and filled interesting niches in the product line, particularly where policemen were concerned.

But the ammo used in these guns began to evolve toward higher-velocity loads with ever-lighter bullets driven by powders with higher flame temperatures. Departments wedded to the 357 Magnum revolver usually went to one of the screaming-hot 125-grain JHP loads. They are undeniably effective, but in the long run, the ammo was evolving beyond the ability of the K-frame Magnums to handle it and still deliver an extended service life. The answer to the problem was a completely new gun, sized intermediately between the smaller K frames and the big beefy N frames. It was called the L frame and was first produced in 1980. This is the same basic frame as is used for the Models 581 and 681 fixed-sight revolvers and Models 586 and 686 adjustable-sight ones. It's the basis for the revolver at hand, the new Model 686 Plus seven-shot.

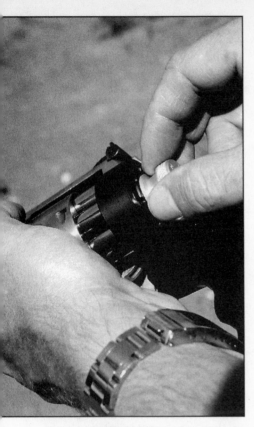

Using the HKS Speedloader. Insert seven in the cylinder and turn the knob to release them from the loader.

A seven-shooter? Sure, why not? When you thumb the hammer of a conventional six-shot revolver, the hand reaches through the standing breech, engages the ratchet and causes the cylinder to turn exactly 60 degrees. In a five-shot revolver, the same thing happens, except the turn is slightly more, 72 degrees. My hat is off to the engineer who made the 686 Plus work, because when you divide the 360 degrees of a circle by seven for that number of chambers, you get a gawd-awful figure. Let's see....360 divided by 7 equals 51.428571428571..... How would you like to set up the tooling for that one?

Somebody did it and maintained that critical cylinder-to-barrel alignment that makes a revolver work. I have now fired three different specimens of the Model 686 and have experienced nothing in the way of excessive spitting or flash at the barrel-cylinder gap. Accuracy is excellent overall and absolutely outstanding in one gun.

L-frame S&Ws are guns specifically intended for the 357 Magnum cartridge and soundly engineered to handle everything from the 110-grain loads all the way up to 180-grain JHPs intended for hunting deer and other medium game. The system used in S&W six-shot revolvers places a cylinder-stop notch directly over each chamber. This system is common to most other makes of revolvers as well. It can't be changed without a complete redesign of the entire gun system. When S&W engineers went about building the five-shot 357 Magnum on the trim little J frame a couple of years ago, they did it knowing that the odd number of chambers would work to their advantage in the cylinder strength department. The same is true of the 686 Plus.

It works like this. All revolvers have notches into which the bolt locks to align the cylinder; they're placed directly over the chamber wall in six-shooters. That's the thinnest part of the cylinder. If you happen to get a carelessly loaded handload or other defective cartridge with higher-than-standard pressure and it ruptures the brass case, the pressure will follow the path of least resistance. That means a probable blowing out of the relatively thin steel in the bottom of the stop notch. In the rare cases of total failure of a revolver cylinder, the splitting and breaking of the cylinder almost always begins at this critical point. In a seven-shooter, those notches are cut into the thickest part of the cylinder, between the individual chambers. This is no indictment of any six-shooter, which function with great reliability on normal ammo. I make the commentary solely because some readers might

JUDGING COMBAT ACCURACY

I HAVE AN interesting theory about accuracy in combat handguns. In view of the size of the targets you are likely to encounter, as well as the ranges from which you will most commonly find yourself engaging those targets, you don't need an accurate handgun. Accuracy is a relative thing and a handgun—revolver or semi-auto—that will consistently shoot inside a 3- to 4-inch circle at 25 yards with serious fighting ammunition is accurate enough. Gunfight statistics show that most fights occur at much closer ranges and sometimes at contact distance, so why do you need a gun that wads them into a tight cluster at 9 feet? Most handguns from major makers will easily make the 3- to 4-inch, 25-yard standard.

But I *like* more accuracy than that, and I have a reason that makes perfect good sense to me. It's not an objective reason; in fact, it's completely subjective. I most strongly believe I approach shooting a handgun under any circumstances a lot

more confidently when I know that gun will cluster its shots into one hole when the need arises and I do my part. It just plain makes me feel better, and since I am doing the shooting (and in this case, the writing), I tend to prize the more accurate guns. And that brings us to the performance of the Model 686 Plus.

As is my custom, I fired the 686 Plus (three different barrel lengths) by going twice around the cylinder, fourteen rounds, from the Ransom Rest at 25 yards. That's a cruel standard for judging any gun, but here's what happened:

If there's anything to be learned from this exercise, I guess it's how accurate modern ammunition can be when you give it a proper launching platform. Both of the two longer-barreled guns were superb shooters, averaging well under 2 inches for fourteen shots at 25 yards. The 4-incher ran 1.87 inches average group size, the 6-incher went 1.64. The snubby 686 Plus didn't do as well

The barrel ports on the short 686 Plus help defeat recoil, but degrade accuracy in the process.

and I am prepared to believe it would have turned in far better performance if it were not for the porting system, which is clearly having an adverse effect on the stability of the bullet in the barrel. That's the down side to improved recoil control.

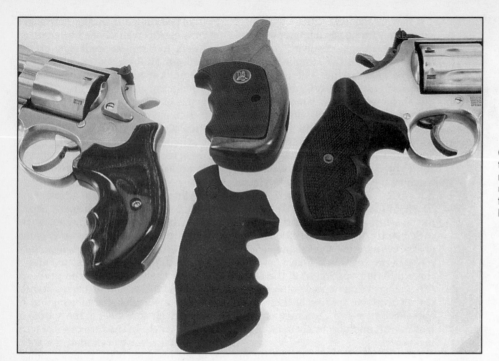

One of the major advantages of the revolver is its adaptability to many sizes of hands through the use of different grips (clockwise from the top): Pachmayr, Uncle Mike's, Hogue and Ace Grips.

SERVICE REVOLVER?

think a cylinder of the same size with an additional chamber might be weaker. Not true—it's actually a little stronger.

In the fifteen or so years the L-frame 357 Magnum revolvers have been in active service with policeman all over the country, they have earned a reputation for rugged reliability and accuracy. Compared to the earlier K-frame Models 19 and 66, the 686s are about the same overall length in comparable barrel lengths, but the weight is about 5 ounces heavier. Most of the reason for the increased weight is the barrel contour. It features a full underlug running all the way to the muzzle. This not only makes the gun a little heavier, it also shifts the weight forward. Most shooters prefer this for ease of pointing when firing the gun in instinctive point-shooting style. The overall size of the L frame is a little larger than the K, since the cylinder is of a larger diameter and sits a trifle higher above the hand. Many of the action parts—triggers, for example—interchange between the two guns. Hammers do not.

In the course of preparing this report, I had an opportunity to examine and fire three specimens of the seven-shot 686 Plus. I did so with a view to their use as police service guns and with somewhat of a retrospect on my personal use of the L-frame-style revolver as a duty weapon. The last revolver I used in law enforcement was a now-discontinued Model 581, the blue steel, fixed sight, six-shot 357.

For most police work, I believe that fixed sights are entirely adequate and have the added advantage of a reduced possibility of snagging on clothing and gear. That has to be a minority opinion, because the Models 581 and 681 are not currently produced. The most popular gun in the L-frame series is probably the Model 686 with a 4-inch barrel. The same style revolver is now done up as the seven-shot Model 686 Plus.

If you like the revolver as an everyday carrying gun in uniformed circumstances, this is about as close to the ideal as you can get. At 41 ounces in weight and running to an overall length of 9.56 inches, the 686 Plus 4-incher is relatively compact, but still points and balances well. There's enough weight to partially absorb the recoil of hot ammunition and let you get back on target for a fast second shot. The gun is of such a size as to be readily usable from virtually every kind of holster—high-riding Tom Threepersons, Jordan Border Patrol, even today's whiz-bang security holsters. By overwhelming acclaim, the typical service revolver sports a 4-inch barrel, making this likely to be the most popular version of the 686 Plus among police officers.

Some policemen prefer the greater sight radius and more muzzle-heavy balance of the longer 6-inch barrel. They also get a little more from their ammunition. The accompanying chart shows some loads increasing by more than 100 fps when fired in the 6-inch

tube as compared to the shorter 4-incher. As a general rule in 357 Magnum ammo, recoil increases as the bullet weight increases. The 6-incher is heavier than the shorter length by about 5 ounces, so there is somewhat reduced recoil with the same ammunition. I tried a 6-inch revolver for a few weeks once and I could not get used to the awkward draw from any kind of holster. I even tried that staple of the motor officer, the long-shank swivel holster. I ended up feeling like a fugitive from the Mexican Revolution and quickly went back to my Hume Border Patrol and a 4-inch revolver. Probably the only answer for a uniformed officer who wants to pack a longer revolver is some form of front-break holster. Before someone beats me up for disparaging the 6-incher, let me say if there were no problem with carrying and drawing the gun, I would much prefer the longer barrel for ballistic performance and actual shooting. Sight radius for longer, deliberate shots is better and the pointability of the gun for up-close and personal work is much better.

S&W also offers the 686 Plus with a 2½-inch barrel. The specimen I had was a "stocking dealer" special edition made up by the Smith & Wesson Performance Center and bearing their logo. It differs from the same-barrel-length version from normal production by virtue of a pair of small ports machined into each side of the barrel, adjacent to the sighting rib. It also has a tuned action with modified hammer spur and a pair of laminated grips from the Ace Grip company. It's pretty rare

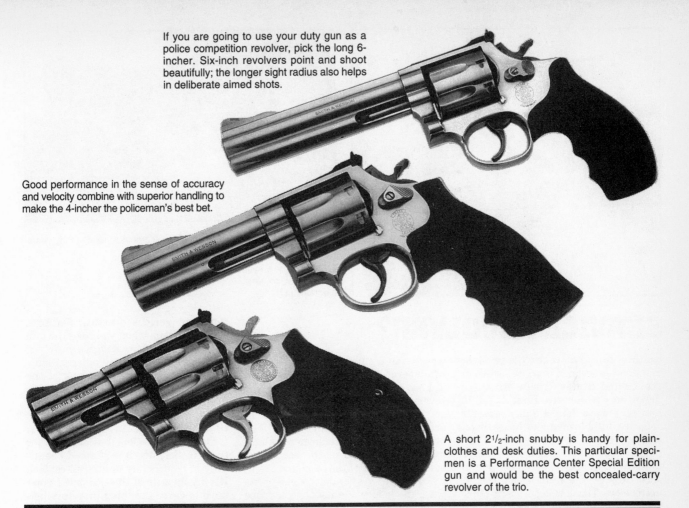

If you are going to use your duty gun as a police competition revolver, pick the long 6-inch. Six-inch revolvers point and shoot beautifully; the longer sight radius also helps in deliberate aimed shots.

Good performance in the sense of accuracy and velocity combine with superior handling to make the 4-incher the policeman's best bet.

A short 2½-inch snubby is handy for plainclothes and desk duties. This particular specimen is a Performance Center Special Edition gun and would be the best concealed-carry revolver of the trio.

S&W Model 686 Plus Performance Results

Ammo Used	Barrel Length (ins.)	Average Velocity (fps)	Standard Deviation (fps)	Group Size (ins.)	Ammo Used	Barrel Length (ins.)	Average Velocity (fps)	Standard Deviation (fps)	Group Size (ins.)
Pro Load 125-gr. JHP	6	1392	33	1.83	Pro Load 158-gr. JHP	6	1377	39	1.76
	4	1272	41	1.99		4	1281	37	1.99
	2.5	1301	46	2.98		2.5	1104	42	3.67
Speer 125-gr. JHP	6	1503	31	1.79	Hornady 158-gr. HP/XTP	6	1299	26	1.07
	4	1390	31	1.88		4	1201	22	1.52
	2.5	1149	32	4.77		2.5	1050	20	1.84
Federal 125-gr. JHP	6	1432	33	1.89	Black Hills 158 gr. JHP	6	1231	26	1.52
	4	1270	61	2.08		4	1141	29	1.77
	2.5	1183	22	3.25		2.5	1027	11	2.23
Winchester 125-gr. JHP	6	1498	40	1.90	Federal 180-gr. JHP	6	1159	29	1.77
	4	1423	40	2.14		4	1088	33	1.99
	2.5	1183	27	4.44		2.5	977	15	2.23
Remington 140-gr. JHP	6	1438	35	1.59	Remington 180-gr. JHP	6	1159	33	1.27
	4	1331	36	1.87		4	1068	31	1.44
	2.5	1152	25	1.86		2.5	939	29	1.92

Notes: Accuracy results are based on a 14-shot group fired from the Ransom Rest at 25 yards. Velocities measured with an Oehler Model 35P chronograph with skyscreens placed approximately 12 feet from the muzzle.

to see a uniformed police officer carrying a duty revolver with a barrel this short, but the shorties can be pretty convenient when you're working a desk job, prisoner transportation or other duties. Plainclothes officers have traditionally used shorter barrels for obvious reasons. With full-power ammunition, the snubbies are real bears to control. The porting system in this particular model makes it a better gun for fast shooting, but it remains a hard shooter. It also has a deficiency in that the stroke of the ejector rod is shorter than normal because of the barrel underlug length. This adds up to less than full case ejection. A 3-inch barrel would be a more practical length because it would allow a full-length ejector rod. A few years ago, S&W actually made a run of 3-inch 686s for the U.S. Customs Service. They were really slick little revolvers. I am told that the Performance Center is setting up to do a run of 3-inch 681 Plus guns with fixed sights. Those would just have to be superior concealed-carry revolvers.

Since the day the first magazine-fed automatic pistol was introduced to the market, the revolver has been taking a

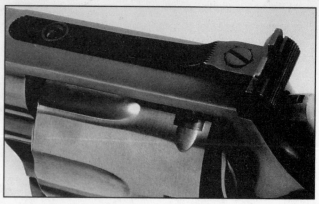

(Above) The same reliable rear sight we have used for so many years.

This is the new cylinder latch to be used on all S&W revolvers. It provides improved ejection clearance.

SERVICE REVOLVER?

beating. In recent years, the revolver has steadily declined in police service in the United States. There are three major reasons for this. First, the auto almost always has a much greater capacity, fully loaded and ready to go. Second, the modern auto, with its quickly replaceable magazine, is faster to reload if the beleaguered policeman goes through the initial loading and needs more. Third, when properly managed (i.e., when the shooter doesn't run the gun dry and leaves a round in the chamber), the automatic is not out of action during the reloading process. If the revolver is to respond to these major advantages of the auto, it would seem to be largely a matter of reloading speed.

As recently as the late 1960s, when I entered the law enforcement service, we loaded from dump boxes or belt loops and sometimes from a single, dedicated pocket of the trousers or jacket. Dark Ages stuff, right? While there were earlier speedloading devices, the real breakthrough came in the early 1970s when the modern speedloader burst onto the market. In those days there must have been a dozen different models out there, all of which had at least some merit. As far as I know, the only surviving speedloader makers are HKS and Safariland, which were always two of the best. For the new 686 Plus, HKS makes a seven-shot unit in their "A" series, which holds seven rounds firmly in place with no cartridge jiggle. I've been playing with this unit in the process of preparing this report and I am impressed.

It's called the HKS Model 587-A. I've filled them up and reloaded my sample revolvers over and over. The $8.50 unit

works like a charm, with no failures whatsoever. While I can't really prove it, I have the subjective impression the seven-shot loader is a hair quicker in getting an empty revolver back in action than the six-shot type. The problem with any speedloader is aligning the bullet end of the cartridges held in the unit with the chambers in the revolver's cylinder. Mostly, we place the loader against the rear face of the opened cylinder, turn the loader slightly until there's alignment, then insert and turn the release knob. When there are seven holes to align, the turning motion to get it done is reduced slightly. The difference is slight, but it appears this is an advantage for the 686 Plus.

There's another advantage to the new revolver. Smith & Wesson now produces all of their considerable line of revolvers (J, K, L and N frames) with round butts. I have always preferred this shape and not because my hands are small. When the somewhat trimmer round-butt style is part of the design of a particular revolver, it is simply more usable for a wider spectrum of handgunners. The 686s are not little guns, particularly the 6-incher, but the smallish round butt accepts an almost endless array of after-market grips. Indeed, S&W has ceased production of their wooden grips and provides composite material ones from Hogue, Pachmayr, or Uncle Mike's as original equipment. In the case of police officers with smaller hands, this feature of the gun means that careful choice of grips can fit the gun to almost any hand. You can't say this about any automatic pistol.

Almost all of the foregoing commentary on the 686 Plus deals with its ori-

gins and various practical features. What happens when you take the gun to the range and fire it with a variety of 357 ammunition? In an adjacent sidebar, you'll find a detailed look at the accuracy of the three sample guns as fired with different loads. In shooting the gun in various tactical exercises that emphasize in-the-hand performance, I developed a fondness for the 6-incher, which performed beautifully in pointability and recoil control. It's my favorite of the trio, but I don't have to carry the thing in a duty holster all day.

In the middle part of my career as a deputy sheriff, a new tactical shooting concept became common. In realization of the limited power of any handgun cartridge, we began to practice and use the idea of double-taps, wherein two shots went into the target, followed by a quick assessment of the effect. With a revolver, you had three of these pairs on tap. You can logically argue that if you hit what you are shooting at, you won't finish the first cylinderful. That is undeniably true—right up to the day when it isn't. Controlled pairs and hammers are sensible techniques, as is the Mozambique or failure drill, where the first pair is followed by a quick assessment, then a sighted shot to the head. With a conventional revolver, two Mozambiques of three shots each or three controlled pairs each produce the same effect, an empty gun that cries to be reloaded. With a 686 Plus, you have one more round in the cylinder that can be used if you need it as you move to cover or prepare to reload. The extra shot makes plenty of sense to me. Literally, it's sort of a "three pair, one spare" rationale and it makes this newest S&W the gun of choice for working policemen who favor the medium revolver.

●

THE WORLD'S SMALLEST SUPPRESSOR

by CHUCK KARWAN

FOR MANY YEARS the movies and television have shown tiny little attachments on the end of guns of all kinds that effectively silence the report of the gun being fired. Those of us who have had occasion to use the real thing generally just laugh and wish that there were such devices. The real thing is rarely so effective and never so small as the ones that grace the television and movie screens. Well, thanks to Gemini Technologies and their president, Dr. Philip Dater, that wish has been fulfilled...almost.

Called "silencers" by some, a more accurate name for such a device is "noise suppressor," since none actually silence anything. Noise suppressors for use on firearms have been around and in common use since just after the turn of the century. In general, they work in the same manner as the mufflers found on internal combustion engines used in cars, motorcycles, lawnmowers, etc.

The state of the art in noise suppressor technology has come a long way in the last thirty years. So far, in fact, that Gemini Technologies (Gemtech) has developed one that is nearly as small as the ones seen on TV and in the movies, even though it is not as quiet.

This little gem is called the Aurora. It is, to the best of my knowledge, the

World's smallest "silencer," the state-of-the-art Gemtech Aurora mini-suppressor is ideally mated to the mini-Glock G26 9mm. The G26 requires only a threaded barrel from a longer Glock. The wet-technology suppressor works for about two full magazines; pre-assembled wipe set makes refitting simple. This package is designed for Air Force use.

most compact 9mm pistol suppressor available anywhere in the world. It has an overall length of only 3.1 inches, a diameter of only 1.125 inches, and a weight of just 2.7 ounces. Folks, this is a *small* suppressor! While it will work on a wide variety of handguns if their bar-

rel has been threaded properly, the Aurora was designed specifically for use with the incredibly small and capable Glock G26 subcompact 9mm.

The original concept as it was described to me by Phil Dater was to come up with a gun and suppressor package

Julie Dater, daughter of the Aurora's designer and Gemtech president Phil Dater, shot the Glock with the Aurora mini-suppressor, and she didn't need ear protection. The device cuts the noise by 24 db, making the 9mm quiter than a 22 rimfire.

SUPPRESSOR

that is small enough to be easily carried by military pilots and aircrewmen for survival use if they have to bail out into a combat environment. Mission requirements dictated extreme compactness, high efficiency for the size, a reduction in sound level of at least 20 decibels, and an operational life (usefulness of the suppressor) of at least two magazines without service or maintenance.

The introduction of the G26 by Glock in the fall of 1995 took care of half the package. Here was a pistol the size of a 2-inch S&W Chiefs Special that weighs only 21 ounces, yet holds eleven rounds of 9mm ammunition. In spite of its small size it is easy to shoot well. It's also quite accurate. It also has the tremendous durability, reliability, simplicity, and corrosion resistance that have helped make the Glocks so popular. Gemtech took care of the other half of the package by designing the Aurora.

Through the use of a clever combination of technologies the Aurora actually surpasses the original design goals. Incredibly, this tiny little suppressor lowers the sound level of a subsonic 9mm load by at least 24 decibels. This is accomplished through the use of specially designed urethane "wipes" and what is known in the suppressor world as "wet technology." This consists of the presence of a liquid-type substance in the suppressor to help absorb heat and energy. The liquid can vary from water to a wide variety of different grease-like substances. The Aurora uses the latter approach.

The suppressor body consists of an easily disassembled aircraft-grade 2024-T6 aluminum can anodized black. All maintenance requirements can be performed with minimum tools. After about two full magazines have been run through the suppressor the sound suppression begins to drop off, and the wipe set needs to be replaced. Gemtech has designed a pre-assembled wipe cartridge that can be inserted into the Aurora as a unit once the used-up wipe assembly has been removed from the can. Unfortunately, because of federal regulations imposed on the shipment and possession of silencer parts, the Aurora is impractical for civilians who would have to file paperwork and return the suppressor to its manufacturer for rebuilding after every couple of magazines had been fired through it.

It is difficult to describe the effectiveness of the Aurora in sound suppression, but I will try. There is still a pop or mild bang when a shot is fired, but it's far less than when the gun is fired without the Aurora. The sound is less than that made by a 22 rimfire rifle, and the gun can be fired quite comfortably without wearing hearing protection. The noise level is low enough that it would easily be covered by the noise of a portable electric generator or diesel truck. It is low enough that if the gun were fired inside a typical house, the sound would not carry to the outside, and vice versa. In a wooded area the sound would not carry very far.

While it would be desirable to have more noise suppression, the only way it could be achieved to any significant degree would be to go to a much larger unit that would be impractical for a pilot or aircrew member to carry on his or her person.

Also, the small size and weight of the Aurora make it usable on virtually all pistols that use the Browning tipping-barrel locking system (such as the S&W, Glock, SIG, etc.) without resorting to cantankerous recoil-enhancing

Small enough to allow the use of issue sights, the Aurora also completely hides the muzzle flash. Nice for Special Ops or airmen downed in enemy territory.

accessories. Heavier and larger suppressors interfere with the dynamics of the barrel unlocking on such guns and generally reduce the pistol to being a manually operated repeater.

Naturally, to mount the Aurora the barrel of the pistol must stick out in front of the pistol enough to be threaded $1/2$ x 28 for a distance of $3/8$-inch. For the Glock G26, it is a simple task of using a slightly modified Glock G19 barrel with the end threaded appropriately.

All suppressors that use wipes have some restrictions as to how they are used, and that applies to the Aurora as well. First they must be used with fully jacketed bullets because softpoints or hollowpoints can be deformed or deflected while going through the wipes. Also, to avoid the sonic crack characteristic of supersonic ammunition, suppressors must be used with subsonic ammunition. Wipes also degrade the accuracy of the weapon to some degree, but a good combat level of accuracy is still easy to obtain with the Aurora.

One of the major advantages of the Aurora is that its small diameter does not block out the sights of most pistols like the typical suppressor does. Thus, sights that are higher than normal—or any supplementary sights—are not needed for shooting with the suppressor attached. When I tried out the Aurora on a Glock I found that the weapon's zero with the suppressor attached was close enough to its regular zero that I could hit where I wanted out to at least ten yards, and adequate combat accuracy was there at even longer range.

The idea behind the Glock G26 and Aurora suppressor combination is to have a gun and suppressor set that is small enough and light enough that a pilot or aircrew member could carry it on his person at all times so that it will be with them if they have to eject, parachute out, or crash-land in enemy territory. The Glock has the added advantage that it will fire and function even if it is full of water or even underwater, should the airman end up in the drink. Theoretically, a pilot floating in the ocean could even shoot a shark under water with his Glock if one got too close.

Once the downed pilot has his feet on the ground he could attach the Aurora to his Glock. If it became necessary to shoot an enemy sentry or other soldier, the Aurora will make it possible to do so without drawing attention to the pilot. Also the Aurora would allow a downed pilot to shoot a wild or domestic animal for food without drawing attention to himself. With the Aurora attached, there is absolutely no muzzle flash to give away the shooter, should the weapon be fired in the dark. There is no question that the Glock G26 and Aurora suppressor combination would increase the chances of survival of our military aviators if they are downed in enemy territory.

The Aurora suppressor is high in the "neat" factor because it is so much smaller than anything else on the market. It wouldn't surprise me to see the Glock G26 and Aurora suppressor also adopted by government intelligence operatives, military Special Operations personnel, and others that need a small yet powerful handgun that can be fired quietly without muzzle flash.

For more information on the Aurora and the many other suppressors offered by Gemtech, contact them in Boise, Idaho. Assuming that your state laws allow it, under federal law civilians may own firearm sound suppressors as long as they are registered with the feds and a $200 tax is paid when they change hands. ●

LAWFUL CONCEALED CARRY: ITS TIME HAS COME

by NEAL KNOX
with Mark Overstreet

IN AN AMAZING reversal of the trend toward ever-greater gun restrictions, laws guaranteeing honest citizens the ability to have and carry firearms for defense of self and family started as a trickle twenty years ago, became a stream a decade ago, and have become a flood since the 1994 elections.

Prior to 1976, when Georgia passed the first of the modern "shall-issue" concealed carry laws, citizens of only a few states could demand a carry license—which still might require extensive hearings or even a lawsuit.

Vermont residents alone had, and have, the right to put a self-defense gun under their jacket or skirt and then go about their lawful business—without getting the approval or blessing of anyone or any agency. The only restriction, other than that the person is not disqualified by criminal or mental history from possessing a gun, is that the gun cannot be carried for the purpose of committing a crime.

By 1986, law-abiding citizens in ten states, with 11 percent of the nation's population, were assured that they could carry a defense firearm concealed. By 1996, law-abiding citizens of thirty-one states—about half of the U.S. population—could obtain a license to carry a concealed firearm by meeting certain fairly reasonable standards and requirements, and paying a fee based somewhat on the cost to the state of processing the application. What is "reasonable" is always open to debate, but the residents of these states (outside of Vermont), if they are law-abiding and willing to jump

through bureaucratic and legislative hoops, can get their license even if the local sheriff, chief of police or newspaper editor doesn't like it.

That sudden change in the laws—half of it in just the past three years—reflects not just fear of crime but the growing public realization that police have neither the ability *nor the responsibility* to protect individual citizens, and are denying those citizens the ability to protect themselves.

But those changes wouldn't have happened if NRA hadn't made "right to carry" a high priority in both their political and legislative efforts. Though improving concealed carry laws—the antithesis of gun control laws—has usually been a major goal within NRA-ILA, not until their successes in the federal and state elections of 1994 did ILA have the luxury of not spending almost all its resources and energies defending against more restrictive laws.

At last, ILA has been able to do what NRA members always wanted: Go on the offense.

The best indication of just how much the public perception of armed self-defense has changed, and been changed by, concealed carry laws was a recent *New York Post* editorial about the woman who secretly tape-recorded her carjacker's threats and her own pleas for mercy before he killed her. The *Post* mused: "What if, instead of a tape recorder, Kathleen Weinstein had been carrying a gun?"

After South Carolina became the thirty-first state to pass mandatory concealed

carry last June, anti-gun Sen. Frank Lautenberg (D-NJ) went into hysterics: Those laws are "...spreading across our nation like a deadly cancer," Lautenberg said. "Now, they're trying to infect New Jersey as well. Well, the NRA may want to turn New Jersey into the wild, wild West, but we're not going to let it happen without a fight. I will be introducing legislation in the Senate that would ... generally make it a federal crime to carry a handgun in public." Everywhere in the country, even in New Jersey, the elite—people with money and/or political influence—have always been able to get official or tacit permission to own and carry a concealed gun, regardless of the severity of the local laws.

The states that did authorize permits generally allowed law enforcement authorities to issue them only to those who "needed" to carry a gun. "Need" was rarely defined and varied from state to state, county to county, or town to town. Depending on where you lived, and who was the issuing official at the time, a carry permit might require only a certain prosperity, or the right skin color, or a generous campaign contribution, or simply having a degree of respectability or political influence.

Most states whose laws required a demonstration of "need" gravitated toward a perverse system like Maryland's, where the law allows the use of deadly force only for protection of *life*, but carry permits are issued only for protection of *property*—a contradiction that worries the state police not a whit.

A few state laws limited law enforce-

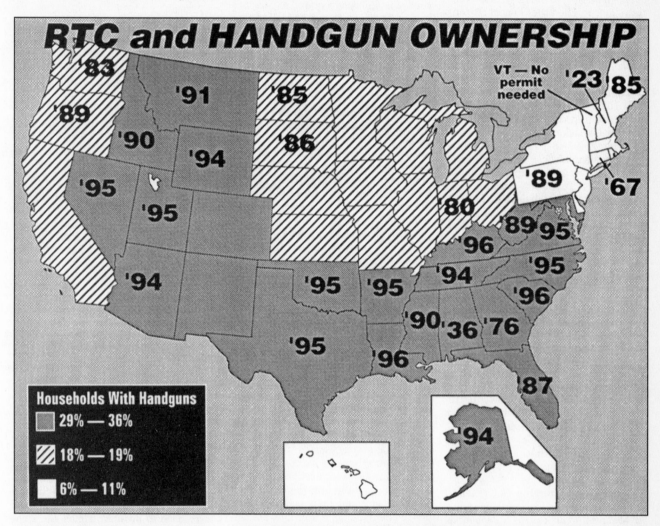

RTC and HANDGUN OWNERSHIP

VT — No permit needed

'83 '91 '85 '23 '85

'89 '90 '86 '89

'95 '94 '80 '67

'95 '89 '95

'94 '96 '95

'95 '95 '94 '95

'90 '36 '76 '96

'95 '96

'87

'94

Households With Handguns
29% — 36%
18% — 19%
6% — 11%

ment's discretion, but such restrictions were often ignored. Conversely, some local authorities might issue a carry permit with minimal hassle. I well remember my surprise when New Yorkers praised their state's laws, for many from rural areas had carry permits valid "until revoked" for anywhere except in New York City.

The first of the concealed carry reforms involved making it clear in the law, or through the courts, that such laws were to be obeyed by police agencies. As the 1960s came to a close, Connecticut gun-rights activist Dan Juliani and a few others in the Connecticut Sportsmen's Alliance, including now-NRA-ILA Executive Director Tanya Metaksa, pushed through a watershed law establishing a "handgun license review board" that put a stop to the arbitrary denial of permits. Dan was made the first chairman.

TABLE 1
The Concealed Carry March

Vermont (Never had a law against carrying concealed)
1923—New Hampshire, "shall issue."
1936—Alabama, some issuing discretion.
1961—Washington, some discretion, "shall issue" required 1983.
1969—Connecticut, Handgun Review Board created to reduce arbitrary denials.
1976—Georgia, "shall issue unless disqualified to own," no training requirement; applied statewide by Attorney General ruling in 1989; reciprocity approved 1996.
1980—Indiana
1985—Maine, North Dakota
1986—South Dakota
1987—Florida
1989—Oregon, Pennsylvania (except Philadelphia), West Virginia
1990—Idaho, Mississippi
1991—Montana
1994—Alaska, Arizona, Tennessee, Wyoming
1995—Arkansas, North Carolina, Oklahoma, Texas, Nevada, Utah, Virginia, Pennsylvania (Philadelphia brought under state's law).
1996—Kentucky, Louisiana, West Virginia (revised "shall issue" after state Supreme Court struck 1989 law), South Carolina.

CARRY LAWS

Just when the pendulum began to swing toward shall-issue carry licenses is debatable, particularly since some state laws implied that honest citizens should be granted carry permits. But such hints were often ignored, especially if the applicant were poor or black.

I consider the beginning of the mandatory issuance laws to be Georgia's 1976 legislation, drafted by that late, great red clay lobbyist and NRA Director Ed Topmiller, who talked now-Governor Zell Miller into introducing a bill with the most desirable elements of a mandatory-issuance-unless-disqualified wording. Topmiller, a retired U.S. border patrolman, considered it a conflict of interest for law enforcement to be the issuing authority. He wanted that authority to be elected so they would be responsive to voters, but with only enough ties to law enforcement to perform the required criminal background checks. Topmiller chose the elected county probate judges.

To make the licenses available to average people, the initial fee was only $20 for three years, and there was *no requirement* for any formal training. Though opponents succeeded in adding some ambiguous "may issue" language in one section of the bill, in most of the state—mainly outside Atlanta—the mandatory-issuance intent was followed. (In 1989, the Georgia attorney general removed that ambiguity by declaring "shall issue" meant just what it said.)

A few years after the Georgia law went into effect, the FBI began charging for background checks. At a legislative hearing concerning a fee increase (to $30 for five years), the president of the probate judges' association testified that there had been no known cases of licensed carriers committing crimes or other offenses with legally carried guns. The "Old West shootouts" which had been angrily predicted by the *Atlanta Constitution* (and by fanciful editorial writers wherever such laws have since been considered) simply didn't occur. (When Georgia further improved its law in 1996, adding provisions to recognize out-of-state licenses of states which recognize theirs, opponents attempted to add a training requirement. They could not give a reason why, because there had been no problems. Police have had far more gun accidents than licensees.)

In 1980, the late Maurice "Red" Latimer and the Indiana Sportsmen's Council—after many conversations with Topmiller, and help from NRA-ILA—

pushed a mandatory issuance law through their state legislature, then had to sue the state police to make them comply with the law. Later, in another NRA-ILA-supported lawsuit, Gary, Indiana, Mayor Richard Hatcher and his chief of police were required to personally pay damages to citizens after they flatly refused to issue carry licenses.

In 1983, Washington state passed an excellent shall-issue law, and similar laws were passed in Maine and North Dakota in 1985, and South Dakota in 1986.

Perhaps the greatest disadvantage of the Georgia law was that its deliberate decentralization made it difficult to determine how many licenses were issued, how many were revoked, and how many cases of lawful self-defense had occurred with licensed guns. Further, the law wasn't easily adapted as a model that would fit other states.

Those problems were boldly corrected by the shall-issue law that now-NRA President Marion Hammer pushed through in Florida in 1987. She followed the Topmiller pattern in having the secretary of state—an elected, non-law-enforcement agency—issue the licenses. And, with confidence that law-abiding citizens never presented a crime problem, a concept backed up by the experience in other states, the statute called for careful record keeping that would show how well the law was working.

The press had largely ignored the shall-issue laws that had passed in more-rural states; Florida was a different matter. It was a large-population state, the traditional vacation and retirement state for the anti-gun Northeast and Chicago, and their establishment press. The notion of requiring state officials to allow just any law-abiding citizen to carry a concealed firearm became national news, and Marion and her Unified Sportsmen of Florida had a ferocious fight on their hands.

Gun-control advocates had been sure that popular opinion would go their way in Florida. After all, the media and anti-gun politicians had repeated, over and over again, their predictions that right-to-carry would lead to gunfights on every street corner. A "pistol-packing citizenry will mean itchier trigger fingers...every mental snap in traffic could lead to the crack of gunfire," and the Sunshine State would become the "GunShine State," complete with "Wild West shootouts" in every neighborhood, the anti-gunners said.

But Marion pushed the law through, and again the dire predictions didn't happen. A year after the law went into effect, the chief of police of Jacksonville,

TABLE 2
Concealed Carry vs. Crime Rates*
(In effect over five years)

State	Year	Homicide	Robbery
Georgia	1976	13.9	142.4
[1]Atlanta	1989	12.7	271.1
	1994	10.0	222.6
Indiana	1980	8.9	141.4
	1994	7.9	130.2
Washington	1983	4.9	105.4
	1994	5.5	139.7
Maine	1985	2.4	24.4
	1994	2.3	22.4
North Dakota	1985	1.0	6.4
	1994	0.2	11.4
South Dakota	1986	4.0	16.2
	1994	1.4	18.7
Florida	1987	11.4	356.6
	1994	8.3	328.8
[2]With guns	1987	6.9	
	1994	4.6	
[2]W/ handguns	1987	5.0	
	1994	3.1	
Oregon	1989	4.8	151.8
	1994	4.9	138.2
Pennsylvania	1989	6.3	149.7
([3]Exc. Phil.)	1994	5.9	186.7
West Virginia	1989	6.5	42.7
	1994	5.4	42.4

*FBI Crime Rates per 100,000.
Notes: [1]Concealed carry licenses were not issued in Atlanta and some other urban areas until 1989 Attorney General ruling. [2] Florida Dept. of Law Enforcement figures detail homicides by type of gun. [3]Pennsylvania concealed carry law excluded Philadelphia until 1995 revision.

who had bitterly opposed the bill as president of the chief's association, was asked by a reporter if he had been keeping track of crimes committed by licensed carriers. Indeed he had, he said. "There aren't any."

But there soon were well-publicized cases in which lawfully carried guns were used to prevent crimes and save lives, like the Miami cab driver who killed a robber whose long rap sheet included a conviction for attempted first-degree murder of a police officer. The cabbie didn't draw and fire until the robber tried to shoot him because $90 wasn't enough loot.

As Metro Dade County Police Sgt. Green said, "This sends a major message to the rest of the robbers out there." Indeed it did. The crooks began looking for easier and safer victims, just as predicted by Prof. James D. Wright's Justice Department-funded study, "The Armed Criminal in America." It showed criminal predators are justifiably afraid of confronting an armed citizen.

There has been much national publicity about Florida's criminals deliberately targeting and often killing tourists, particularly foreign tourists. Who in Florida is least likely to be carrying a licensed firearm? A tourist.

Lower Violent Crime Rates In "Right to Carry" States

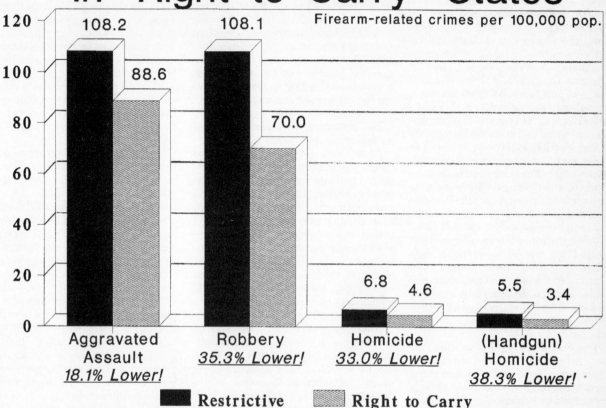

Firearm-related crimes per 100,000 pop.

- 108.2 / 88.6 — **Aggravated Assault** — *18.1% Lower!*
- 108.1 / 70.0 — **Robbery** — *35.3% Lower!*
- 6.8 / 4.6 — **Homicide** — *33.0% Lower!*
- 5.5 / 3.4 — **(Handgun) Homicide** — *38.3% Lower!*

■ Restrictive   ▨ Right to Carry

Data: FBI Uniform Crime Reports, 1994

Who *cannot* have a legal firearm? A *foreign* tourist.

Crooks are dumb, but they aren't stupid. Why pick on someone who might shoot back?

When a licensed carrier uses a gun for self-defense, the anti-gun crowd dismisses it as "merely anecdotal." However, there are no anecdotes about licensed carriers slaughtering innocent bystanders while trying to stop a mugging, dueling with other gun-toters at a traffic light, or any of the other wild scenarios that opponents dream up as arguments against carry laws.

Shortly after the Texas law went into effect, a licensed carrier shot and killed another motorist after their pickup mirrors brushed in Dallas. It seemed to exactly fit the warnings of the anti-gun crowd and was immediately on the national news. But a grand jury heard the rest of the story: the other motorist was a 6-foot-6, 250-pound man who followed, then brutally attacked the licensee when he was blocked in traffic, and who failed to back off even after being warned that the permit-holder was carrying a gun. The grand jury felt the shooting was justified, and refused to indict.

"We are appalled," a spokesman for a Texas anti-gun group fumed. If not for the carry law, the man's assailant "would still be alive today." Probably true, and the licensed gun owner might not be.

Anti-gunners virulently oppose right-to-carry laws because they contradict the essence of the gun-control argument: that more guns result in more crime. Those who want to "treat the illnesses" of criminals, who want to "eliminate the conditions that breed crime," and who abhor the notion of severe punishment—particularly the death penalty—are appalled by the thought of citizens being armed for self-defense and "self-appointed judge, jury and executioner."

There is no punishment which can equal the speed, certainty or severity of an armed woman defending herself or her daughters from a rapist.

Because there are so many variables that affect the crime and violence rates, it's simply not possible to "prove" that there is less crime where law-abiding citizens are armed. However, it can be proved that the predicted increases in crime simply have not occurred in states and cities which have had right-

to-carry laws long enough to measure the impact.

And it can unquestionably be proved that licensed citizens are not contributing to the crime problem, no matter how fervently editorial writers wish it were so.

The detailed Florida statistics are clear. Of the 339,433 concealed-carry licenses issued between the October 31, 1987, inception of the law and April 30, 1996, precisely sixty-two have been revoked because license holders committed gun offenses—that's .018 percent!

Between 1987 and 1994, the last year for which complete FBI crime data are available, the Florida murder rate declined from 11.4 per 100,000 residents to 8.3; murder with firearms declined from 6.9 to 4.6; and murder with a handgun dropped from 5.0 to 3.1. Perhaps more significantly, the robbery rate declined from 356.6 to 328.8. Nationally, both the murder and robbery rates increased.

How many of those saved lives can be attributed to the carry law is speculative, but some can be proved from newspaper clippings, and no one can claim

CARRY LAWS

that the law hurt the crime rates. Of course, the anti-gun crowd tried. In March 1995, a group of researchers from the University of Maryland released a "study," paid for with *taxpayers' money* from the federal Center for Disease Control and Prevention. It claimed gun homicide rates increased in Miami, Jacksonville and Tampa after Florida's carry law took effect, and the news media trumpeted the tale.

But Florida Department of Law Enforcement Commissioner James T. Moore told *Time* magazine that he doubted the findings. FBI crime data revealed that total homicide rates declined 10 percent, 18 percent and 20 percent, respectively, in the three Florida metropolitan areas from 1987 until 1993, the latest available data when the study was released. The University of Maryland team had created its misleading figures by carefully picking different starting years—up to *fifteen years* before Florida's law was enacted.

But even if Florida's homicide rate had increased, it would have been immaterial: Not one of those homicides, *except justifiable homicides,* had been committed by holders of carry licenses.

In shall-issue states for which data have been available for five years, the homicide rate has stayed the same or gone down (with one exception), and most have reported reduced robbery rates (see Table 2). In a recent, still unpublished study, "Right-to-Carry Concealed Guns and the Importance of Deterrence," Professors John R. Lott, Jr., and David B. M. Mustard of the University of Chicago, found that "...'shall issue' laws coincide with fewer murders, rapes and aggravated assaults" in the 3054 counties surveyed, from 1977 to 1992. After state concealed gun laws took effect, "murders fell by 11 percent, and rapes and aggravated assaults fell by 5 percent" in those counties. If all states and the District of Columbia had had right-to-carry concealed gun provisions in 1992, Lott and Mustard estimated, "murders in the United States would have declined by 1838" and "the number of rapes in states without 'shall issue' laws would have been fewer by 3041 and aggravated assaults by 37,148" annually.

How often firearms are used to prevent crimes and save lives has been most extensively explored by Florida State University criminology professor Gary Kleck. He is perhaps best known

for his 1991 book, *Point Blank: Guns and Violence in America,* for which he received the American Society of Criminology's award for the most significant work in several years. In a study published in the Fall 1995 volume of the Northwestern University School of Law's *Journal of Criminal Law and Criminology,* he and co-author Marc Gertz reported that civilians *use* guns for defense 2 to 2.5 million times annually. According to their massive survey, 80 percent are with handguns; in 59 percent of defensive gun uses, citizens protected themselves against assault, robbery or rape.

Kleck and Gertz concluded that "there seems little legitimate scholarly reason to doubt that defensive gun use is very common in the U.S., and that it probably is substantially more common than criminal gun use. This should not comes as a surprise, given that there are far more gun-owning crime victims than there are gun-owning criminals, and that victimization is spread out over many different victims, while offending is more concentrated among a relatively small number of offenders."

Anti-gun groups and their activist cronies go into a frenzy when confronted with Kleck's findings. But in an article in response to the Kleck-Gertz study, published in the same Northwestern volume, one of the world's leading criminologists, Marvin E. Wolfgang, admitted that he could find no flaws in either its methodology or its findings.

In his article, "A Tribute to a View I Have Opposed," Wolfgang says he is "as strong a gun-control advocate as can be found among the criminologists in this country." If he were able, he says, he "would eliminate all guns from the civilian population and maybe even from the police." Unfortunately, few anti-gunners are as honest about their views.

The anti-gun crowd has a fervent faith that privately owned firearms are bad, and that allowing those guns to be carried for protection is worse. The fact that close to a million people are now licensed to do just that, and haven't destroyed their neighbors, themselves or each other, can't shake their near-religious faith. In every state where right-to-carry laws are proposed, the same tired and disproved opposition arguments are made.

Because most of the "easier" states—those where handgun ownership is highest—have enacted shall-issue carry laws, the pace of new laws is slowing. The next step, already started in some states, is removing unnecessary restrictions as to where law-abiding citizens may carry their licensed guns, lowering

fees and excessive training requirements, and adding reciprocity provisions to honor licenses from states which honor their licenses.

Granted, we wouldn't have to be cleaning up those problems if we had passed an ideal Vermont-type no-restrictions-against-carrying law in the first place. But in today's political climate, it is simply not possible to enact legislation that doesn't provide for some kind of license, issued after a criminal records check and some evidence of firearms familiarity. Those who demand perfection or nothing will get nothing.

The advantage of fighting on offense is that our foes have to spend their time, money and energy defending against our efforts, instead of the other way around. And when you're fighting on offense you can make headway so long as you're moving in the direction you want to go, which is what the anti-gunners have been doing to us for years.

Though a lot of gun owners are calling for a national carry license, that would present major constitutional problems, plus the practical question of whether it is wise to give BATF or any other federal agency such authority.

A constitutionally sound approach, proposed in the 104th Congress by Rep. Cliff Stearns (R-FL) as H.R. 2634, would require states to recognize the carry licenses issued by other states, under the Constitution's requirement that states give "full faith and credit" to the official acts of other states. The NRA Board of Directors in early 1996 approved the concept, particularly if the bill were amended to allow carrying by those who are not required to have a license to carry in their states, such as Vermonters and police officers. No portion of such a bill will become law if it requires President Bill Clinton's signature, but ILA is working with Rep. Stearns in an effort to force action on the bill.

Despite the frequency with which citizens defend themselves with guns, despite the outstanding record achieved by citizens who carry firearms lawfully, despite the lower and declining crime rates in right-to-carry states, and despite the fact that 82 percent of Americans surveyed say they generally feel safer when ordinary citizens can legally carry concealed weapons, we can expect those who oppose the exercise of the right to arms to continue their war of fear, distrust and lies about the evils of guns and carrying them for defense.

It's their religion.

Meanwhile, the NRA and gun owners around the nation will be pushing for more and better carry laws. ●

THE GUN THAT SHOT SAM BASS

by JERRY BURKE

IT WAS THE 1950s, and Great Uncle Chester often hummed that old ballad about Texas outlaw Sam Bass as we headed into town, perched in the cab of his 1935 Chevy pickup truck. On occasion, he'd break into the words of the last stanza, apparently his favorite. He'd learned it as a boy, no doubt at the one-room schoolhouse he'd attended through the fourth grade. In his day, that was considered sufficient schooling for the sons of ranchers and farmers.

I knew there was more to that old ballad, but it would be many years before I learned the complete version. Even later came the truth surrounding the legend of Sam Bass, who caught the public fancy from the late 1870s until well into the 20th century. Sam was seen by many as a Western Robin Hood, taking from rich railroad barons and fat bankers, then doling out his plunder to citizens who helped him elude The Law.

Born in Indiana in 1851 and soon orphaned, Sam Bass grew up longing to be a cowboy. While still in his teens he headed West, finding work in Denton, Texas, with Sheriff "Old Dad" Eagan, who would later help hunt Bass down. In addition to learning to rope and ride, Sam became proficient in the use of Colt's 36-caliber 1851 Navy percussion revolver. Forerunner of the Single Action Army revolver (SAA), the Colt Navy was easy handling and quick on the draw, hurling a lead ball with power similar to that of today's standard 38 Special.

While roping, riding and free-ranging, Sam took to the sporting life in the form of fast horseflesh. He made good money trading in broomtails, and hit the jackpot when he acquired the Denton mare, so named after the small burg north of Dallas where Sam hung out. Sam sorely neglected his taxing chores as a cowboy,

$1,000 REWARD

WILL BE PAID FOR THE CAPTURE OF

SAM BASS

ONE OF THE ROBBERS of the Union Pacific Train, at big Springs, Nebraska, on September 18, 1877. He had about $10,000 in GOLD pieces of the stolen money in his possession, of the coinage of the San Francisco Mint of 1877. The above reward will be paid for his arrest and detention and 10% of all moneys recovered.

NOTIFY AUTHORITIES

A $60,000 Nebraska train robbery and the free spending which followed made Sam Bass both infamous and popular in his own time. Bass' criminal career, measured in months, ended abruptly in a shootout with Texas Rangers.

The actual Colt revolver used by Texas Ranger George Herold to end the brief criminal career of Sam Bass. Caliber is 45 Colt, with blackpowder frame and one-piece walnut stocks; at the time, the barrel was 7 1/2-inches long. Produced in 1876, it was first shipped to J.P. Moore's Sons, one of the original five "Colt Allies," wholesalers who all but cornered the market for SAAs in the first years of civilian production.

and Eagan gave him the boot, which suited the young man from Indiana just fine.

But soon, all of Texas was too familiar with the Denton mare for Sam's own good, and he was unable to get even the greenest of greenhorns to bet against his prize equine, so Sam turned to other endeavors for his livelihood. To fill the void, Bass and his pal Joel Collins rustled some cattle, and the pair looked at the south end of forty steers

all the way up to Kansas and points beyond. The neophyte cow thieves sold the stolen beeves for a handsome profit, no questions asked.

Not wanting to see Texas again just yet, the duo invested their money in a pleasure resort or two, and later a gold mine in the Black Hills. But it wasn't long until Sam and Joel were flat busted. They teamed up with some bushwhackers of their acquaintance and robbed a few stages, and soon graduated to train robbery.

On the night of September 19, 1877, the gang of six commandeered a Union Pacific train as it stopped to take on water in the middle of nowhere. One gang member kept an eye on the engineer; two more set about relieving passengers of their money, jewelry and firearms. The other three bad boys concentrated on the express car, which might contain major-league valuables in transit. The guard inside the car refused to open up; immediately thereafter, a withering barrage of 45 Colt and 44-40 WCF projectiles smashed into the car. As wood splinters settled on the dusty floor, the express car's door was quickly unlimbered for the unwelcome guests.

Once inside the car, the messenger was ordered to open the strongbox. When the guard claimed not to have the keys, Joel Collins pistol-whipped him for a lack of cooperation. The outlaws then commenced shooting at the big locks on the strongbox with their six-shooters, but ended up only dancing around each other's ricochets. Frantically looking around the car for anything of value, Bass noticed a few innocent-looking cloth bags casually sitting beside the strongbox. It was the gang's lucky day; inside the bags was $60,000 in brand-new U.S. $20 gold pieces, straight from the San Francisco Mint.

Sam and his men "lit a shuck" on their cow ponies, putting plenty of distance between themselves and the crime scene. When the coast was clear, they divided the gold equally—$10,000 apiece. The outlaws split up into three pairs, and went their separate ways to avoid detection. Four of the gang were soon cornered and either shot to pieces or captured; a good share of the $40,000 they took was recovered.

Jack Davis had teamed up with Bass himself, but when hot pursuit literally loomed on the horizon, even they split up. Davis made his way to South America and into the history books, possibly resurfacing in Arizona decades later, still plenty wary of star-packers (lawmen). Wily as a coyote, Bass altered his appearance and boldly drove a wagon back to Texas with his plunder. With nerves of steel, Bass even camped with a group of men out hunting for him. Soon back in the Denton area, he told friends and family he'd struck it rich by way of a gold mine in the Black Hills. He began spreading around plenty of money, always in the form of those highly traceable, newly-minted $20 gold pieces.

Quite the entrepreneur, Bass assembled a new robbery ring of seven, plus himself. This Bass Gang, Phase II, promptly got down to business, setting a record for the number of train robberies in the fewest number of days; they stayed within a 20-mile radius of Dallas. On one occasion, Bass confidant Seaborn Barnes received four lead balls from "blue whistlers" (12-gauge double-ought buckshot) fired by train guards and angry passengers; the wounds would later be used to identify his relatively worthless, definitely lifeless body.

It wasn't long until hiding out became a full-time job for Bass and his men, and Sam knew exactly how to fade after a little thievery. In those days, an area north of Denton, Texas—nearly the size of the state of Delaware—was a tangled mess of trees, *chaparral* (brush) and creek bottoms, where it didn't make full daylight until high noon. To Sam Bass, it was like a second home. As Sam's fame and the reward for his capture grew, so did the number of posses bent on serving the public interest and lining their own pockets. These part-time manhunters occasionally opened fire on one another when coming into mutual view. For the most part, Bass simply ventured out when he pleased, then got a jackrabbit start back to his thorny lair.

After fifty days and four train robberies within 20 miles of Dallas, then-Governor Richard Coke knew just how to spell relief: "R-a-n-g-e-r-s." Major John B. Jones, commander of the Texas Rangers, was ordered to rein in all this lawlessness. Jones headed for Dallas, where a gaggle of newspapermen fueled even the most outlandish of rumors, and a U.S. Marshal with up to twenty deputies set out from a fine hotel each day in search of Bass and his band. The Pinkerton men were there as well, and many self-appointed do-gooders were also combing Denton County. No regular Rangers were in the Dallas/Denton area at the time; they were needed for frontier defense. To fill the void, Major Jones selected a fine, local lawman by the name of June Peak to enlist a temporary company of Rangers for the sole purpose of snagging Sam Bass. Peak and his men provided a great service keeping Bass on the run, even managing to kill one of the gang and run off all their horses.

As public excitement grew, many a north Texan came into contact with Sam Bass...at least they claimed they did. Some unwittingly—others knowingly—helped the outlaws continue their criminal behavior unabated.

Sam was known among local folks as having a heart of gold, which was easier

for Sam than for most Texans—he hadn't exactly earned the gold the old fashioned way! The gang convinced at least one rancher they were Texas Rangers from June Peak's Company, while paying the rancher's wife the equivalent of four months' pay for a top hand, in gold...for a single meal! If fresh horses were needed, Sam's generosity also bought him quick results and tight-lipped silence. Many years after the fact, a man told of being sent as a boy to the river bottom outside Denton with instructions to deliver a side of beef to some men who were camped there. Excited about earning a little spending money, the lad strapped the beef behind his prize possession, a brand-new saddle fitted with saddlebags. He found the camp and promptly delivered the meat, but leaving wasn't so simple. The heavily armed bandit leader switched the boy's new saddle for his worn-out one. Enraged but powerless to object, the boy departed astride the old saddle and cried his way back to town. Disgusted at this loss, the youngster ripped the outlaw's reject from his horse and threw it on the ground. As he did, something jingled inside the saddlebags; it turned out to be four shiny $20 gold pieces!

On rare nighttime appearances in town, Bass' easygoing, friendly demeanor and his uncanny ability *not* to look like an outlaw provided him with needed intelligence. He'd have a drink or two with some of the itinerants relaxing after a long day of hunting for that scoundrel named Sam Bass. Sam kept informed on how the hunters planned to capture him as well as how they planned to spend the reward money.

But there was more to Major Jones' plan than just authorizing a temporary company of Texas Rangers. He decided to bring justice upon Bass' willing accomplices and smoke out some insider who would turn informant. Arrest warrants were issued; the guilty hauled in; court quickly convened. One pair targeted was Jim Murphy and his father Henderson of Denton, both known to have figured heavily in Bass' ability to dodge the law with impunity.

Jim Murphy not only helped his friend Bass stay on the lam, but was himself an occasional member of the gang. In exchange for immunity against prosecution for himself and his father, Jim Murphy agreed to become a snitch for the Texas Rangers. The younger Murphy was allowed to jump bail and rejoin Bass in the tangles north of Denton. Murphy told Bass he'd decided to embrace a full-time life of crime.

Sam had no problem allowing Mur-

Colt's Single Action Army revolver became a favorite of gun-totin' professionals upon its introduced in the early 1870s. Texas Rangers at the 1878 Round Rock fight with "Sam Bass & Company" were no exceptions. Many a horseback star-packer preferred the ol' thumb-buster's original 7½-inch barrel length.

(Above) Major John B. Jones of the Texas Rangers was wearing his Sunday gun when the shooting unexpectedly started in Round Rock. His double-action 41-caliber Thunderer was the very latest from Colt. Jones boldly fired on the fleeing Sam Bass gang, receiving a hail of gunfire in response. The intrepid commander's face was showered with stinging rock fragments. (From the Collection of Tom Burks)

Although sporting an 1851 Colt percussion Navy revolver in his early days, Sam Bass packed a 44-40 WCF, 4¾-inch Colt Single Action Army during his brief criminal career. Except for the pearl grip panels, this Colt is identical to Sam's. The gunbelt and holster, created by El Paso Saddlery Co. in the 1870s, is generally typical of the era, on both sides of the law. (Photo courtesy of John Bianchi.)

phy back into the group, but Seaborn Barnes wasn't buying the act. He moved to kill Murphy on the spot. The Rangers' informant came close to taking the "long dirt nap," except for the intervention of fellow gang member Frank Jackson. Jackson assured Bass and Barnes he'd known Murphy all his life, and that Jim was completely trustworthy. Barnes agreed to let matters ride, but let everyone present know he'd be on the lookout for Jim's slightest misstep.

All his friendly spending cost Sam Bass plenty, and it wasn't long until he'd parted with the last of these $20 gold pieces in a Waco saloon; it was time to replenish his bankroll. The gang ambled south toward the quiet town of Round Rock, bent on attacking a bank. On the way, Murphy slipped into a post office and dropped a letter to Major Jones in the box. Murphy's act was spotted by Bass, but Jim claimed it was a letter to his mother. Major Jones

received Murphy's letter at his headquarters in the Texas capitol building at Austin. The letter informed Jones the bandits were heading for Round Rock, where they would rest their horses for four or five days, and then rob a train or attack a bank. In the letter, Murphy begged Jones to prevent the theft "for God's sake," but it was his own hide Murphy was concerned about. Major Jones began preparing a trap for the elusive Mr. Bass at Round Rock.

The Texas capitol building had been financed by an English cattle consortium, which received what amounted to ten counties in West Texas in exchange for the elaborate structure. Adding to the unique history of this beautiful edifice, a contingent of Texas Rangers was continually camped on the capitol grounds in those days. There, in the shadow of the dome, a handful of Rangers cooked over an open fire, slept under the stars and stood ready to ride on the most arduous of journeys on

short notice. Rangers Dick Ware, Chris Connor and George Herold were selected by Jones to ride immediately to Round Rock, twenty-five miles to the north; he would follow by train with ex-Ranger, then Travis county deputy sheriff, Morris Moore. The men were to blend into the Round Rock woodwork until receiving further orders.

Major Jones instructed Cpl. Wilson, eating Mexican strawberries (pinto beans) on the expansive state house lawn at the time, to ride for Lt. Reynolds' Company off to the northwest. Ranger Wilson was to spare neither himself nor his mount in making the sixty-five-mile ride just to catch the morning stagecoach; in the process, he literally rode his gallant little gray mount to death. It was full dark on July 18, when Reynolds received the news to move on Round Rock. He picked eight men and the fastest horses in the Company for the mad dash. Lieutenant Reynolds' poor health made it neces-

Texas Ranger (later Captain) James B. Gillett on "Dusty," in a photo dating from the time of the Round Rock fight with Sam Bass and his gang (1878). Note Colt SAA, Winchester Model 1873 carbine and no-nonsense dagger, all typical of the era.

Close-up of Model '73 Winchester carbine Texas Ranger James B. Gillett carried during his action-packed, Indian- and outlaw-fighting career. Although used heavily, the quick-handling 44-40 WCF is still in perfect working order. Gillett had this lever-gun with him at the Round Rock fight with the Sam Bass gang.

BASS

sary for him to travel in a mule-drawn wagon, but his wiry team kept a fast, steady pace all through the night and long into the next day. For all this, they would arrive in Round Rock less than ten minutes *after* the battle with Sam Bass' crew on July 19; they missed Bass and Barnes in their flight from justice along the Chisholm Trail by less than five minutes!

But for the foreknowledge of the Rangers, Sam Bass' selection of Round Rock for what would become his final attempted robbery was a sound one. It was just far enough north of Austin to be isolated, with plenty of open countryside leading away from town in every direction. Sam thought they'd soon be in the chips again, and it wouldn't be the buffalo kind! While all this Ranger activity was in the works, Bass and his men had already been in town twice to look over the bank. They agreed on July 20th for the robbery, but Sam and his boys left their camp near Round Rock on the 19th for one last look around town before the heist.

As they traveled along, Jim Murphy was beginning to sweat everything but real bullets. For starters, he had no idea if Major Jones received his letter, much less if he had believed its contents. Murphy's next concern was how to act like part of a gang the decidedly lethal Texas Rangers were now hunting in earnest. "Judas Jim" had an excellent chance of becoming seriously dead in the imminent action. But Major Jones *did* get the letter, and he figured Murphy was serious about beating the charges against himself

and his father. The three Rangers from the capitol lawn arrived in Round Rock and were soon joined by Major Jones and Deputy Moore. Bass wasn't expected just yet and the Rangers went about blending in.

July 19, 1878, promised to be a hot one in Round Rock. No mortal could have guessed how hot it was about to get; no one, perhaps, except the informant Jim Murphy. Bass, Barnes, Jackson and Murphy passed the Old Round Rock cemetery where graves would soon be dug to hold the remains of two of them. An intrepid Texas lawman would be laid to rest there as well, but with honor and the gratitude of the state. The gang traveled along the historic Chisholm Trail, past the big round rock in Brushy Creek for which the area was named. Murphy slyly dropped

off at a feed store along the way, ostensibly to buy grain for the horses; the other outlaws continued on their ride. Barnes didn't object; after all, the big show wasn't scheduled until the following day.

The three outlaws tied their mounts in a mott (small stand) of trees behind Main Street (see accompanying diagram, "Anatomy Of A Gunfight"). As their broomtails commenced swatting away flies in the welcome shade, Bass, Barnes and Jackson moved up the street looking for all the world like typical Texas cowboys. As the trio crossed Main Street, Texas Ranger Lt. Reynolds and his men were fast closing on Round Rock, having traveled straight through the night and past midday of the 19th. The Rangers, like the outlaws, did not expect action on this day.

As Bass and his cohorts moved along the store fronts, they attracted the attention of Deputy Moore; the lawman thought one of the cowboys was packin' iron. Texas was a long way from being tamed in 1878, but the legislature had already seen fit to ban the carrying of concealed weapons in incorporated areas. But Moore was from Travis County, down in Austin. Checking out these innocent-looking strangers was the task of Williamson County Deputy Sheriff "High" Grimes. The two lawmen crossed the street together, following the range riders as they entered Kopperal's store next to the bank. The situation had all the signs of being the 1870s equivalent of a modern routine traffic stop. Both deputies, of course, knew the Rangers were on hand to handle the

Bass gang when they arrived. Besides, Bass' band of robbers were thought by some to number as many as sixty, with various members taking part in different robberies; these three drovers were probably in town for supplies.

When Bass, Barnes and Jackson entered Kopperal's, they asked clerk Simon Jude for tobacco; Sam was running low. As the clerk turned to get a pouch, Deputy Grimes entered alone and approached Sam, putting his hand on the outlaw's arm and asking if he were armed. Sam answered in the affirmative, and everyone present except the clerk went for the Colt SAA at their side; in the blink of an eye, life or death hung in the balance. In the shock and adrenaline rush, it's unlikely the combatants heard the deafening, disorient-

ing booms from those big-bore Colts or noticed the billowing clouds of acrid smoke that filled the little store from the blackpowder 45 Colt and 44-40 WCF loads. The outlaws' slight head start clearing leather proved critical; Deputy Grimes went down forevermore.

Jumping over Grimes' body to escape, the outlaws burst from Kopperal's store on a dead run for their horses. Standing just outside when the shooting started, Moore was clearing leather when Bass, Barnes and Jackson bolted into the middle of the street. Duty required Moore to be sure of his intended targets as well as avoiding any innocent bystanders before firing his weapon. Desperate and not compelled to wait for anything, the outlaws sent a volley of powder smoke and hot lead toward

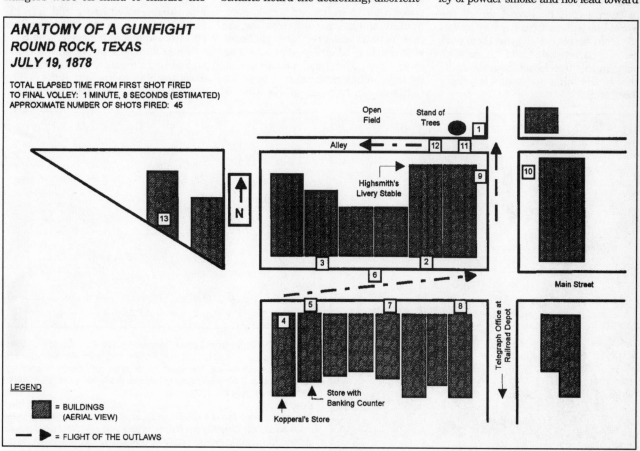

ANATOMY OF A GUNFIGHT
ROUND ROCK, TEXAS
JULY 19, 1878

TOTAL ELAPSED TIME FROM FIRST SHOT FIRED
TO FINAL VOLLEY: 1 MINUTE, 8 SECONDS (ESTIMATED)
APPROXIMATE NUMBER OF SHOTS FIRED: 45

Open Field
Stand of Trees
Alley
Highsmith's Livery Stable
Main Street
Telegraph Office at Railroad Depot
Store with Banking Counter
Kopperal's Store

LEGEND

= BUILDINGS (AERIAL VIEW)

= FLIGHT OF THE OUTLAWS

Anatomy of a Gunfight

1. Bent on casing the local bank for a robbery the following day, outlaws Sam Bass, Frank Jackson and Seaborn Barnes conceal their horses and proceed to Kopperal's store.
2. Deputy Sheriff and former Texas Ranger Morris Moore observes three "cowboys," one of whom he suspects is armed.
3. Deputy Moore links up with Deputy John "High" Grimes; the two lawmen follow the strangers to Kopperal's store.
4. Grimes enters the store; Moore remains outside. Deputy Grimes puts his hand on Bass, demanding to know if he's armed. Outlaw gunfire kills Grimes instantly. Bass and his men bolt from Kopperal's on a dead run.

5. Deputy Moore fires on the passing outlaws and goes down, shot through a lung.
6. Texas Rangers and plucky Round Rock citizens open fire on the fleeing outlaws. Bass is shot in the hand.
7. Lathered up for a shave, Ranger Dick Ware erupts from the barber shop and empties his 7$\frac{1}{2}$-inch, 45-caliber Colt Single Action Army revolver at the outlaws.
8. Rushing back from the telegraph office, Major John B. Jones (Texas Ranger commander) opens fire on the outlaw trio with his "Sunday gun" (the new double-action Colt Thunderer in 41 Long Colt caliber). Jones' fearless challenge is answered with a volley of near misses from the outlaw band's 44-40 WCF and 45 Colt-

chambered Colt SAA revolvers.
9. Ranger Dick Ware plunges after the outlaws, reloading and continuing to fire on the run.
10. Fellow Texas Ranger George Herold joins Ware in the fight, administering Sam Bass a devastating wound.
11. Outlaw Seaborn Barnes is killed by Ranger Ware with a head shot.
12. Frank Jackson, Bass' most loyal follower, ignores a hail of gunfire and helps severely wounded Bass mount his horse. Bass and Jackson ride off toward Old Round Rock and up the Chisolm Trail, passing fellow gang member and Texas Ranger informant Jim Murphy on the way.
13. Bass dies two agonizing days later. It was his 27th birthday.

Moore as they sprinted past; a 45 Colt slug cost the ex-Ranger a lung.

Only seconds had elapsed since the shots that killed Deputy Sheriff Grimes and wounded Moore, but Rangers Chris Connor and George Herold, along with a number of plucky armed citizens, emerged from various establishments along Main Street. Running at top speed and firing as they went, the outlaws ran the gauntlet that Main Street was quickly becoming. Next, Texas Ranger Dick Ware—all decked out for a shave in the barber shop—burst onto the street with a faceful of shaving cream and dressed in a flowing barber's cloth. Ware startled the fleeing outlaws; in their panic, he looked for all the world like a ghost from the very bowels of hell as he blazed away at them with his long-barreled, 45 Colt SAA. At some point in this free-for-all, Sam Bass was shot in the hand and began leaving a blood trail.

Major Jones had been off at the railroad telegraph office, sending a report to Governor Coke. Hearing gunshots, the diminutive Jones came tearing up the street and into the action. Not expecting a fight until a day later, he was armed with his "Sunday" gun—Colt's then-new double-action Thunderer revolver, in 41 Long Colt. Meant for concealment, this handy handgun included many of the treasured features of the SAA, but sported a bird's-head grip to improve packability. Although the mechanism on that first Colt DA was both intricate and delicate, it was quite popular among lawmen of the era.

The lightweight Thunderer was more difficult to shoot with accuracy than Colt's Single Action Army, but Jones opened up on the outlaws from an exposed position in front of a rock storefront. Running, firing and reloading, the three outlaws answered Jones' challenge with clouds of billowing gunsmoke from their Colts. The very embodiment of courage, Jones never moved until his Colt was empty. Some of the outlaws'

bullets struck so close, they splintered rock fragments into the Major's face. At this point, the outlaws rounded the last building on the block and made a mad dash for their horses. Ranger Dick Ware, now sans barber cloth but still trailing soapsuds, administered Seaborn Barnes a head shot that dropped him like a rock in the dusty alley.

Acrid blackpowder smoke was everywhere; in the background, mounting shouts and curses filled the air as more armed civilians came running to the fight. Texas Ranger George Herold, firing at the bandits at the same time as Ware, hit Bass, sending a red-hot 45 Colt bullet through the upper portion of Bass' holster and gunbelt, splitting two cartridges in their loops. The bullet entered Bass' right side just above the hip, mushroomed badly and tore his right kidney to shreds. In shock, Bass still tried to mount his horse.

When Sam was hit, outlaw Jackson was already mounted and heading off down the alley to freedom. But when he saw Bass go down, Jackson rode back into

(Above) This letter from Texas Ranger John R. Banister to his mother confirms the official Grand Jury finding that fellow Ranger George Herold gave Sam Bass his death blow. With corrections in spelling, punctuation and abbreviations extended, the letter reads as follows:
"Round Rock July 22, 1878
Dear Mother,
We are both well. The notorious Sam Bass died yesterday at 4:20 p.m. He made no request. Two minutes before his death, he said, 'This world is but a bubble, troubles wherever you go.' And after saying this, in two minutes his soul was launched into eternity. I have a relic which he gave me...his six-shooter, belt and scabbard. The shot that killed him passed through the top of the scabbard and through the belt. An awful excitement prevails over the little town of Round Rock. Dick Ware killed Barnes and George Herold killed Bass. Herold is one of our Company. The ex-Ranger [Morris Moore] is still alive. The wagon started with the body of Bass 20 minutes ago to the graveyard. I think we will return to San Saba soon. Well, I will close; write to San Antonio. From your dutiful son, J.R.B."

(Left) When the shooting started in Round Rock, plucky citizens joined the Texas Rangers in providing a deadly *bon voyage* party for Sam Bass and company. This solemn-but-solid citizen is armed with a Winchester Model 66 "Yellow Boy" carbine showing considerable use; and a Colt SAA, with 7$\frac{1}{2}$-inch barrel in a full-flap holster. Tintype images were laterally reversed, a fact of old-time photography which led to the widely held public misconception that Billy the Kid was left-handed. (Courtesy of the San Antonio Conservation Society.)

the revolver and carbine fire with Colt a-blazing to help his boss reach the saddle. During this selfless, courageous act that even the Rangers admired, Jackson never received so much as a scratch. Bass and Jackson rode off toward their camp beyond Old Round Rock, where they'd stashed their rifles. On the way, they galloped past Jim Murphy at May's store, who simply stood and stared. To this day, the cowardly "cowboy Judas" still holds the world's record for the longest time needed to buy a sack of corn.

Although Jackson protested, Bass realized he was done for; he instructed Jackson to leave him under a tree and make good his own escape. Jackson finally agreed, and literally rode off into obscurity; it's believed he made his way to New Orleans, and possibly on to South America. During the night of Jackson's reluctant departure, Bass suffered unimaginable pain. In the morning, he walked to a nearby house for water. Frightened at first, the woman eventually relented, and granted Bass' request. The Rangers—including the men from

Lt. Reynolds' Company who arrived just minutes after the brief but lively Round Rock fight—discovered Bass the next morning under a tree; he was too far gone to drink the water he so desperately craved. During that longest of nights, Sam had torn up his undershirt into more than a hundred pieces in an attempt to wipe up blood from his massive wound. Bass was gingerly returned to Round Rock by wagon, where Major Jones saw to it he had the best medical treatment available. Richard Hart, the enterprising citizen whose shack was used to house Bass for his final hours, would later bill the State of Texas for the cot, sheet and pillow soiled by Bass.

Major Jones asked Sam if he didn't want to do some good at this point, and provide the names and whereabouts of the other gang members. Bass, however, was steadfast in his conviction that such knowledge should go with him to the grave; and so it did. On July 21, 1878, Sam Bass died; it was his 27th birthday. His life of crime could be measured in months, not years. Bass and cohort

Seaborn Barnes were buried in the least desirable section of the Old Round Rock cemetery, way in the back, hard against the section reserved for slave burials. Williamson County Deputy Sheriff "High" Grimes, who dedicated his life to upholding the laws of Texas, was interred in a place of honor in the same cemetery—as far from the graves of Bass and Barnes as was possible. He left a wife and three young children.

And what of Jim Murphy, the informant, the "cowboy Judas"? He rushed into town as soon as Bass and Jackson passed him on their flight from disaster. Town was still buzzing with excitement when Murphy arrived, and he helped identify Barnes from those buckshot wounds received in an earlier robbery attempt. This aroused the suspicions of the milling crowd, but Major Jones corroborated Murphy's claim to have helped solve the Bass problem. Murphy even received a reward for his cooperation, but it didn't do him much good. Despised by everyone, receiving threats from some, Murphy lived a life of tor-

THE MAN WHO SHOT SAM BASS

Surrounded by considerable controversy at the time, official reports credited Texas Ranger George Herold with firing the bullet that mortally wounded the outlaw Sam Bass. Herold's colorful life was rather atypical for a Ranger, especially his multiple marriages.

For starters, the correct spelling of George's last name is uncertain, although "Herold" was used by his children and appears most often in official records. The problem was complicated by Herold's inability to read or write; he signed documents with an X. Born on May 9, 1840, near Richmond, Virginia, Herold found his way to Texas sometime before the war between the states. In 1861, he enlisted in what became the Second Texas Field Battery. He participated in numerous battles, settling in San Antonio after the War. Between 1867 and 1899, Herold married four Hispanic women in succession, the first two in San Antonio, followed by two more in El Paso.

He enlisted in the Rangers' Frontier Force in 1870, but by the mid-1870s, he was serving as city Marshal in the rough, tough border town of Laredo. However, when Herold again enlisted in the Rangers

during 1877, he was a blacksmith in the San Antonio area. Between May and August of 1878, Herold rode in Lt. N.O. Reynolds' Company E, which covered the time of the Round Rock fight with the Sam Bass gang. In 1879, Herold served with Lt. G.W. Baylor's Rangers near El Paso, and participated in action against the renegade Apache Victoria, whom the Texans chased into old Mexico. An accomplished scout, cool and fearless, he served in General Nelson A. Miles' campaign against Geronimo.

George Herold may have been a chief of police in Mexico prior to

1883; during that year, he joined the El Paso Police Department, not retiring until 1916. He held a special Texas Ranger commission from the time of his retirement from that organization until well into the 1890s. When Herold died in 1917, his body carried scars from at least three bullet wounds. He was buried with full honors, including a mounted escort, in the Confederate plot at El Paso's Evergreen cemetery. Considered a first-rate fighting man, Herold was the oldest lawman in Texas at the time of his death.

—*Jerry Burke*

Texas Ranger Herold's Colt SAA is now owned by Texas A&M Professor Dr. James H. Earle. Once sporting a 7½-inch barrel, the gun that killed Sam Bass was later altered to a more packable length for up-close and personal use—no front sight required!

ment in the year that followed. His biggest fear was that Frank Jackson would return to settle the score, "in spades." Murphy was so terrorized, he often asked the sheriff to lock him up in the local jail for the night. While lingering around the jail, Murphy developed a mild eye infection, and a local sawbones gave him a highly toxic remedy, to be administered only infrequently and highly diluted. Seeing this as a way out, Murphy drank it to the last drop, straight from the bottle. A few agonizing hours later, Murphy joined Bass and Barnes in hell.

A Coroner's Jury was convened to review the causes of deaths that day in Round Rock, but no Texas Ranger was interested in taking credit for killing anyone, infamous or not. It was officially determined that George Herold had fired the shot that resulted in the death of Sam Bass. A letter from Ranger John R. Banister to his mother on the day Bass was interred provides additional evidence to support the finding (see accompanying letter). In the confusion of the gunfight, there were some who felt certain Dick Ware administered the fatal blow, but Ware himself did not agree. Ware was an especially popular Ranger, known to be cool under fire as well as a crack shot; some present just naturally assumed Ware was the likely candidate for having gotten the job done.

Except for Major Jones' double-action 41-caliber Colt Thunderer revolver, the handgun of choice on both sides of the law in the Round Rock fight was the larger, more powerful Single Action Army revolver. Although the "handgun that won the west" had many competitors, the holsters of most "pistolians" (a term coined by Captain Will Wright, 41 years a Ranger, from 1898-1939) of the day were filled with Colt SAA six-shooters in 45- or 44-caliber. Nothing else was quicker on the draw; nothing more powerful.

More than thirty-five years ago at this writing, the Colt SAA used by Sam Bass during the Round Rock fight could be seen at the Buckhorn Trading Post in Dallas, Texas. It was in excellent working order, featuring a 4³/₄-inch barel and one-piece walnut stocks, but little in the way of its original blue-with-case-hardening finish. The caliber was 44-40 WCF, allowing Bass to carry one type of ammunition for both his Colt and Winchester rifle.

Ranger George Herold's 45-caliber Colt single action is owned by Dr. James H. Earle, Texas A&M University professor. It is on display at the incomparable Texas

Monument erected in 1990 at Sam Bass' grave site in the Old Round Rock cemetery. This is the fourth or fifth stone placed there since the outlaw's death in 1878; the base of the previous stone can be seen behind the new one. Relic hunters systematically chipped away earlier versions. The bottom inscription reads: "A brave man reposes in death here. Why was he not true?"

Ranger Museum, in Waco, Texas. Although Colt single actions predominated, more than one Winchester was unlimbered on that fateful day in Round Rock. Texas Ranger Captain Jim Gillett counted on his Model '73 carbine throughout his distinguished career; it is also in the Texas Ranger Museum collection.

The criminal career of Sam Bass lasted less than a year. During that time, only one robbery—that first Union Pacific train job in Nebraska—netted much more than pocket change. In spite of this, the legend of Sam Bass, "beloved bandit," grew quickly and well out of proportion. "The Ballad of Sam Bass," whose words and music date from soon after the shootout, has never quite died; at least, not in Texas. Consummate cowboy singer Michael Martin Murphey recorded the Bass ballad in recent years, true to the original (Cowboy Songs III, *Rhymes Of The Renegades*, Warner Bros. Records).

On a recent rip to the Texas capitol building, the same one where Rangers were camped on the lawn in Sam Bass' day, I stopped off at the Old Round Rock cemetery. Bass' grave is marked with a monument, erected in 1990. It is at least the fourth such marker put up since Bass' death; previous stones were

chipped away by souvenir hunters. Sam's grave was adorned with flowers and a fancy vase that day. Deputy Sheriff Grimes' final resting place looked like hundreds of other well-kept graves in the historic burial ground, where also rest the remains of citizens of the Republic of Texas, when Texas was Her own sovereign nation.

Relatives of Sam Bass' gang members still live in Round Rock. Adding rumor to legend, some folks believe descendants of Bass himself, now living in Dallas, are harboring a fortune, passed on from their errant progenitor. But the truth is, Sam spent his share of the loot, down to the last $20 gold piece. And despite the controversy at the time, Texas Ranger George Herold was officially credited with ending Bass' criminal activity with his standard 45-caliber Colt Single Action Army revolver. As another famous Captain of Texas Rangers, Bill McDonald, once said, "No man in the wrong can stand up against a fellow that's in the right and keeps on a-comin'." Texas Rangers always have, and still do, "keep on a-comin'." And it seems too, that Colts have always worked best on the right side of the law!

●

HANDGUNS 97

Custom Handguns

Pellet-firing conversion for plinking, page 130.

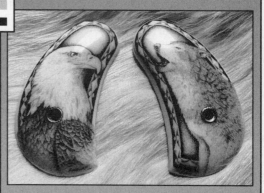

Super scrim sets the standard, page 135.

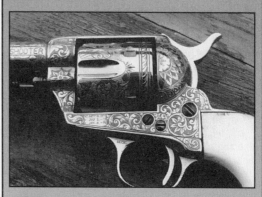

Elaborate and engaging engraving, page 137.

SENSIBLE ADD-ONS

by DAVE ANDERSON

ACCESSORIES THAT YOU can drop into your handgun may not make it into a custom piece, but they can go a long way to help you get the best service from your handgun. Holsters, grips and scopes are covered elsewhere in this issue, but here we'll look at some of the other items that are available.

We'll start with where to get some of these parts, and perhaps the best overview of the accessories industry may be seen by looking in a current edition of **Brownells'** catalog. Brownells is a major supplier to the gunsmithing trade, offering an incredible array of parts, accessories, and gunsmithing tools. The current 48th edition has 244 pages, and there is also a 14-page new products insert.

Other companies providing a broad range of accessories include Wilson Combat, Ed Brown Products, Chip McCormick Corp., Clark Custom Guns, Nowling Mfg., Cylinder & Slide, King's Gun Works, and Evolution Gun Works (EGW).

Subcaliber Devices

Many gun owners don't practice enough because of the noise, recoil, and expense of centerfire handgun ammunition. Caliber conversion units firing quiet, low-cost 22 ammunition are an effective means of becoming familiar with the handling of a centerfire pistol. The Colt conversion unit (not currently available) was well made but its floating chamber was a questionable design feature.

Jonathan Arthur Ciener makes 22 LR conversion units for various military-style rifles, as well as suppressors under contract for the armed forces. More recently he began making conversion units for handguns. The test sample was for a full-size Colt Model 1911-type handgun. Units are also offered for the Colt Commander and for some Beretta and Taurus pistols. A unit to fit Glock pistols is being developed.

Unlike the old Colt unit the Ciener operates as a straight blowback, just like most popular 22 automatics. The sample unit came packaged in a handy storage box with one ten-shot magazine (spares are available). The barrel of the Ciener unit is steel, the slide is machined from high-grade aluminum alloy.

The front sight is integral with the slide, and the rear sight fits in a dovetail slot and is adjustable for windage only. Accuracy, materials, parts fit, and overall workmanship of the Ciener unit indicate a high-quality product in every respect.

Jarvis Gunsmithing recently began manufacturing a conversion unit for 1911 autopistols. The unit was designed by Centaur Systems, a company which at one time offered a cleverly designed match barrel system for 1911 autos. It's a good design and workmanship is excellent.

The Jarvis unit also operates as a straight blowback. The front portion of the steel slide is open on top, rather like a Beretta. The unit comes ready to install on any full-size 1911 frame, e.g. Caspian, Colt, Norinco, Springfield. For use on Commander or Officer's ACP pistols a different ejector (supplied with all units) replaces the standard ejector.

Five-shot groups at 50 feet averaged 1.5- to 2 inches with Federal and Winchester high-speed ammunition, with groups centered and about 2 inches low. Remington Thunderbolt ammunition gave slightly larger groups, averaging 2.5 inches, but shot right to the point of aim.

Wilson Combat will be introducing a 22 conversion unit for 1911 pistols. My understanding is that it will be similar to the Ciener unit but with Wilson's fixed sights and with a Black-T satin polymer finish. Black-T is an attractive, very tough finish. Because of time constraints I wasn't able to get a test sample, but I have no doubt it will be up to Wilson's traditional high standards.

Convert-A-Pell from **Loch Leven Industries** is an ingenious device that converts most centerfire handguns to use 177 pellets. The basic unit consists of a rifled brass barrel liner that fits inside the handgun's barrel, centered and secured by several rubber O-rings. Machined brass "cartridge cases" are designed to accept 177-caliber pellets in the nose. Power is supplied by a standard pistol primer seated in the case's primer pocket. Six cases are included in the package.

The sample unit was for a 4-inch S&W 357 Mag. To install it I lubed the O-rings with a small amount of the supplied lube, slid the brass barrel liner into place and secured it by

Convert-A-Pell lets you shoot primer-powered pellets from most centerfire handguns. The brass barrel insert is mighty accurate, says author, and reasonably priced, too.

turning the knurled end-piece against the direction of the rifling. There is no metal-to-metal contact, so the unit cannot damage the handgun's bore.

To prepare the brass "cartridges," place a standard pistol primer on a flat surface, press the case against the primer to start it into the primer pocket, and tap the case with something like a plastic-headed mallet to fully seat the primer. The directions state that the primer pocket dimensions work best with Winchester primers. They also recommend the use of only Benjamin or Beeman Kodiak pellets. With a primer seated, start a pellet in the nose of the case, then seat it with the special tool supplied. The process takes just a few sec-

Subcaliber devices are "in," to help shooters get proficient with 22 ammo in their 45s. This one's from Ciener, Jarvis makes one, and Wilson Combat has one in the works.

onds. The brass cases are beautifully machined and evidently held to very close tolerances. I found that Winchester primers fit exactly as they should, snug but not overly tight.

Accuracy of the unit was quite good. I was able to get 1-inch groups at the recommended 20-foot range. At 20 feet, point of impact was about $2\frac{1}{2}$ inches low. My revolver has adjustable sights but there is not enough adjustment range to suit the pellets. Pellet velocity is around 500 fps. Fired at pine boards, the pellets would fully bury themselves in the lumber. Obviously the unit is not a toy, demanding the same care and attention as a cartridge arm.

The Convert-A-Pell is a very well made, useful and worthwhile accessory. The price, considering the quality of the product, is quite reasonable.

Magazines

An autopistol without a magazine is a rather useless device. I don't consider a pistol complete without at least one, preferably two, spare magazines. The current ten-round limit on new magazines has increased the value of the high-capacity magazines made prior to the ban. Although there are millions of them out there, the supply is finite unless the legislation can be changed.

Owners of pistols with high-capacity mags should consider purchasing a couple of ten-round magazines for use in routine practice sessions. Unlike the high-caps, they can be readily replaced if they wear out or get dropped and stepped on.

Ten shots doesn't always mean a reduction in capacity. For example, 1911-pattern and SIG-Sauer P220 pistols in 45 ACP usually come with seven-round magazines. Standard-length mags holding eight shots, and extension mags holding ten shots are available. With my 1911 pistols I get the best reliability with standard seven-shot and extended ten-shot mags. The ten-round models extend about $1\frac{1}{2}$ inches from the bottom of the grip, which may make them unsuitable for concealed carry. They can be carried as a spare, and are excellent for a home defense or competition handgun.

ProMag Industries makes magazines for most popular autopistols, over 100 variations in all. ProMags are offered in blued steel except those for the HK USP 9mm and 40 S&W, which are polymer. I tested ten-shot models for several guns including the TZ-75 9mm, Browning 40 S&W, and SIG P220 45 ACP. All showed excellent materials and workmanship. All the ProMags locked properly into place, functioned reliably, locked the slide back when empty and ejected freely. ProMag magazines appear to be quality products in every respect.

I first became aware of **Mec-Gar** magazines while testing a Taurus PT-100 pistol and found them to be very well made and reliable. For this article I obtained two more, for a Browning 40 S&W and a Colt 45. These likewise proved to be high quality, reliable magazines. They are made for most popular autopistols and have a corrosion-resistant black oxide finish. Most are also offered in high-luster nickel finish. High-capacity (over ten round) models are available to law enforcement agencies.

Pachmayr match-grade magazines for 1911-style pistols in 38 Super and 45 ACP have long been popular with IPSC competitors. These fine stainless steel magazines, heat-treated for maximum durability, are also available for several other popular pistols. Ten-shot models I tried for a Colt 45 and a Browning 40 S&W were both up to Pachmayr's usual high standards, providing flawless functioning. Pachmayr mags come with rubber base pads which help ensure positive locking and provide protection against impact when ejected.

Millett, best known for sights, also makes a full line of magazines. Most are offered in blued or stainless steel. HK USP and Glock mags, like the originals, are polymer. Two Millett ten-round 1911 mags functioned perfectly in both my full-house IPSC pistol and in two box-stock 1911s. A TZ-75 mag, which comes with a polymer baseplate, likewise functioned properly in both a TZ-75 and a Jericho 941.

Ram-Line magazines feature a patented constant-force spring that is actually part of the follower. It's an unusual design, but effective. I've used a Ram-Line ten-shot mag in a 1911 pistol for some time with no problems. TZ-75 9mm and Browning 40 S&W mags from Ram-Line also worked perfectly. They're made for most popular pistols in both blue and stainless steel.

In 1985 I bought six **Wilson/Rogers** magazines for my 1911 45 ACP match pistols. They've been in constant use since then, in matches, practice sessions and gun tests. How many rounds have gone through them I don't know, but the total would be probably into six figures. They still work perfectly today. They're made for 1911-style pistols in calibers 38 Super, 10mm, and 45 ACP. All are made from heat-treated stainless steel with polymer followers and base pads. I don't know of a better 1911 magazine.

Sights

Hamilton Bowen, **Bowen Classic Arms Corp.**, one of America's finest pistolsmiths, has a replacement adjustable sight for Ruger New Model single- and double-action (Redhawk/Super Redhawk/GP-100) revolvers. The Bowen sight is of all-steel construction with heat-treated adjustment screws providing approximately one MOA movement per click. The rear sight blade is serrated to reduce glare. Anyone demanding accurate, repeatable sight adjustments that will stand up to hard use will find the Bowen sight an attractive option. *[This is the sight I chose for my 500 Linebaugh. See Dick Williams' report on "The Big Fifties" elsewhere in this book. Ed.]*

Ed Brown Products now offers a set of compact high-visibility fixed sights for 1911 pistols. Installation is quite inexpensive since both front and rear sights require only a single dovetail cut. They can be installed by your favorite gunsmith or, if you prefer, Ed Brown can complete the installation for you. Sight picture options are plain black or three-dot, and the front sight profile can be either a post or a ramp. Night sight inserts are an option.

Richard Heinie offers a superior fixed rear sight for 1911s and Hi-Powers. Properly fitted, it looks like part of the slide. It offers a superb sight picture, with the rear sight blade flush with the slide. Heinie also makes an excellent set of replacement sights for Glocks, in black or with tritium inserts.

Chip McCormick Corp. offers a "Competition/Carry" low-mount fixed rear sight for 1911-style pistols. All edges and sharp corners have been smoothed and rounded to eliminate snagging, and the rear face of the sight is serrated to prevent reflections.

Millett adjustable sights have earned a fine reputation for quality construction, positive adjustments and an excellent sight picture. They're standard on S&W's Model 41 target pistol. Recently Millett has made them even more attractive by offering tritium inserts as an option. Millett uses a bar-dot-bar pattern so that in dim light the shooter will have no doubt about which is the front sight. The front sight dot is

Here's Wilson Combat's Nite-Eyes tritium non-adjustable sights. The front is bright green; the rear, subdued yellow. Wilson offers two-day installation if you're in a hurry.

Pro-Mag supplies mags for most popular autos, in blue or stainless, and the author likes them. This one's for the Beretta 950.

noticeably brighter. They fit the dovetail cuts that are standard in many popular service automatics, but 1911-style pistols will require machining.

Miniature Machine Corporation (MMC) has come up with one of the most practical fully adjustable sights I've ever seen, as tough, compact and snag free as fixed sights. Beautifully machined and finished, the MMC adjustable sight is currently available for Glocks, HK USPs, S&Ws, and 1911s. The 1911s require the machining of a dovetail slot for a proper mount. With the others, installation means drifting out the fixed sight and drifting in the MMC. Standard finish is black oxide; black teflon is optional, and the base can be ordered in stainless steel with a black teflon-coated sight blade. Blades are available in different widths, and in black, white outline, or white dot. Tritium night sights are optional in a choice of several colors and patterns.

The **Novak's, Inc.**, fixed rear sight for pistols has become extremely popular and in fact is standard equipment on many S&W pistols. Advantages are an excellent sight picture, smooth snag-resistant profile, and maximum durability. When properly low-mounted, it looks good as well. It's available for many popular service guns.

Wilson Combat's Nite-Eyes are a compact, fixed sight set with tritium inserts. For faster sight pickup, the front insert is a bright green dot, while the rear dots are a more subdued yellow. They're available for 1911, Glock, Browning, and most SIG pistols. Wilson's offers a two-day service for anyone needing prompt sight installation. Call 800-955-4856 for a confirmation number, ship your slide UPS, and Wilson's will install the sights within two working days.

Other Stuff

Not all accessories attach to the gun. Sometimes they are attached to the shooter. When shooting handguns with heavy recoil, or for long practice sessions with any handgun, a proper pair of shooting gloves can increase comfort and control.

PAST Corp. makes a variety of shooting apparel including vests and recoil absorption pads. PAST shooting gloves are very well made and very comfortable. When you order

(Left) Millett made these sights for the Glock, and they glow in the dark with a bar-dot-bar pattern, to make finding the front sight easy. The fully adjustable rear fits standard slots on many guns.

Hamilton Bowen makes this gorgeous all-steel replacement sight for Ruger revolvers; the Editor has one on his 500 Linebaugh.

Pistol rests make checking your loads easier. Here are a trio from (left to right) Hoppe's, MTM, and Millett.

them it's necessary to specify hand size and let them know which hand does the shooting. The palm of the shooting-hand glove is soft leather, well padded in the palm and in the area over the web of the hand. The other glove is covered with a tough, rather sticky synthetic to provide both protection and a secure grip. Backs of both gloves are open mesh for air circulation. An adjustable wrist band provides a snug, comfortable fit.

Some shooters go a step further, putting a few wraps of tape around the knuckle of the second finger when shooting really powerful handguns. PAST has this angle covered too. They make little padded rings to slip over the knuckle so you can concentrate on shooting without fear of knuckle damage.

Michaels of Oregon, who makes an amazing array of useful products under the **Uncle Mike's** brand name, recently added shooting gloves to their line. Very handsomely made of soft leather, Uncle Mike's gloves have panels of stretchy Lycra and an adjustable wrist strap for a snug fit. The palm and web areas are heavily padded. The glove's second finger is considerably longer than the others and is padded over the knuckle.

For accuracy testing of guns and ammunition a pistol rest is a highly desirable accessory. If money is no object, nothing beats the superb **Ransom Rest** to really see how well your handgun shoots. There are also some less expensive alternatives.

MTM, makers of all those useful ammunition and storage boxes, makes a cleverly designed and versatile pistol rest. The gun-supporting fork can be adjusted to twenty different positions. The fork is heavily padded with rubber to prevent any marring of the handgun. Rubber feet help keep it in place. For storage and transport the fork stores inside the base. The MTM rest readily adapted to handguns ranging in size from a Contender to a little Browning 380. It is inexpensive but well made and does the job for which it was designed.

Millett offers the BenchMaster pistol rest made from some sort of tough synthetic that won't damage gun finishes. Unlike the MTM system, the BenchMaster has a fixed front pedestal with a sliding wedge-shaped rear portion that adjusts for gun size and elevation. The synthetic material has a soft, tacky surface that provides stability on the bench. Powder burns wipe right off, leaving the unit looking like new.

Hoppe's, makers of the famous line of gun cleaning products, also makes a host of useful accessories ranging from shooting glasses and muffs to gun cases. The Hoppe's Pistol Rest combines the popular mini-benchrest with a padded steel base. Three wood screws are included to mount the unit. The threaded post on the pedestal provides an adequate range of adjustment for most sizes of handguns. Because it is infinitely adjustable it is easy to get the sights aligned on target. Compact and moderately priced, the Hoppe's pistol (or rifle) rest works very well.

The Hoppe's Shooter's Screwdriver Set has a tough polymer handle that holds fourteen screwdriver bits. Bits are contained in four clearly marked tubes. The Hoppe's screwdriver is top quality with premium grade steel bits and stainless steel shaft.

Biggest, most expensive, and most sophisticated of the pistol rests tested is the **Outers** Pistol Perch. This well-made unit has a heavy steel base with rubber feet. The gun butt rests on an adjustable sheepskin-padded platform while the barrel rests on an adjustable rubber-covered fork. The entire upper unit swivels on the base, and a large knurled knob adjusts the angle. The shooter quickly and easily gets the handgun aligned right on target. It is not necessarily more precise than sandbags, but is more convenient.

Because I travel a lot I'm always on the lookout for compact gun-cleaning and maintenance accessories. One of the neatest little cleaning kits is the **Pachmayr** pocket kit. Not much bigger than a deck of cards, it's a tough plastic case that contains a two-piece brass rod, wire and bristle brushes, bore mop, jag and adapter, and an oil vial with an O-ring-sealed cap. I found space beneath the interior compartment for a few cloth patches. This handy little kit takes up hardly any room in my gear bag.

Outers makes a couple of compact cleaning kits. The Field Kit contains a jointed rod for both handguns and long guns, solvent and oil, brushes and jags, patches and a silicone cloth. Even better for handgun owners is the Outers Police Pro-Pack kit. The zippered nylon storage case contains a cleaning rod, solvent and gun lube, a utility brush, bore brush, jag, patches and silicone cloth. I made my Pro-Pack even more useful by packing the Hoppe's Screwdriver Set in it. With that and a few pin punches, I have everything I need for routine maintenance.

Kleen-Bore makes a full line of gun care products. I particularly like their Field Pack cleaning kits. The rifle/handgun kit contains a jointed rod, bronze and bristle brushes, Formula 3 conditioner, jag, patches and silicone cloth, all packed in a compact nylon pouch. The Kleen-Bore PocKit handgun cleaning rod consists of a plastic handle in which the rod sections, brush, mop, jag and muzzle guard are stored. It's for calibers from 22 to 45 and will handle barrel lengths up to 8³/₈ inches.

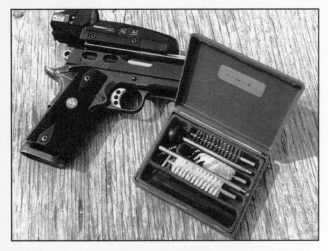

Pachmayr's pocket cleaning kit is not much bigger than a deck of cards, yet everything is there. Patches go under the tray.

How to avoid the nightmare of unauthorized access to your shootin' iron: the Mini-Vault opens to your individual touch on the programmable buttons. From Gun Vault, Inc.

Security

Handgun ownership carries with it a responsibility to prevent access by children or unauthorized adults. Some states have passed, or are considering, legislation to require safe storage. Gun safes provide the best security but the slowest access. Many owners of defensive firearms are looking to trigger locks or bedside gun chests to combine security with accessibility. In fact there are so many new security items I don't have space to do more than give examples of what's available.

Trigger locks are generally either key or combination activated. For those needing locks for several guns, the key-locked models are more convenient. They can be purchased keyed alike so that the owner needs just one key. Quality examples are the **Master** gun locks and the new **Outers** models.

Those wanting a lock on a single home defense arm will likely prefer combination locks so there will be no need to hunt for a key, nor can the key be inadvertently left where a child might find it. Two good examples are the Gun Blok from **Security Products**, and the Protector from the **Securecase Co.** An interesting variation is the electronic Speed Release from **Trigger Block, Inc.** Powered by a long-life battery, it unlocks with a four- or five-digit code. The control panel can be backlit for easy operation in the dark.

Trigger locks help prevent unauthorized use but are little deterrent against theft. A burglar who finds your handgun on a nightstand is likely to take it, lock or no lock. Even if he's unable to pry the lock off, he's not likely to bring the gun back. Gun chests offer a higher level of security. **Palmer Security Products** offers a range of chests and wall safes, most of which use a combination push-button lock for fast access. The Model 5500B is a single-gun model that can be used with optional extra mounting plates. For example, you could have one plate bolted down at home, another at your store. The chest is placed on the plate and locks in place as the drawer is closed.

Gun Vault, Inc., makes the rapid-access battery-powered Mini-Vault. The chest can be bolted to any flat surface, retaining the gun in a heavily padded interior. Grooves guide the fingers into position over the combination buttons, and when the proper combination is entered the spring-loaded door snaps open. In the case of complete battery failure the chest can be opened with a key.

Necessary Concepts, Inc., offers two Insta-Guard locking units, the Model 1100 for a single handgun or long gun, and the Model 1200 which stores both a handgun and shotgun. It's designed to bolt to a wall; the handgun is fully contained while the long gun is secured around the receiver/trigger guard, much like the shotgun locks used in police cars. A mechanical push-button lock and spring-loaded door provide fast access.

Today's trends are toward concealed carry, and many would-be and actual carriers of handguns look toward certain kinds of competition, such as Limited IPSC, to get some meaningful practice. The trends in gadgetry and accessorizing are toward those kinds of self-defense thoughts and away from the outer-limit handguns seen at IPSC matches in the past few years. The trend is toward practicality. Many of the new add-ons mentioned here, particularly the sub-caliber devices for cheap and plentiful practice and home handgun security devices, are targeted toward those who would carry a gun, or at least keep one for self-defense. The small cleaning kits are becoming more popular as well, particularly for the traveling handgunner.

Well-chosen accessories can enhance the performance, durability, versatility and reliability of a handgun, which in turn can enhance the performance of the shooter. ●

Art *of the* SCRIMSHANDER

Scrimshaw by Susan

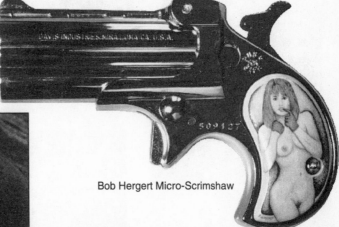

Vickie L. Hielscher

Bob Hergert Micro-Scrimshaw

Lynn L. Benade

Art of the SCRIMSHANDER

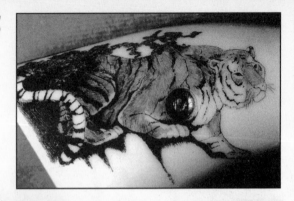
Star Harless/Arrow Forge
(Photo by Albert Cardwell)

Gaétan Beauchamp

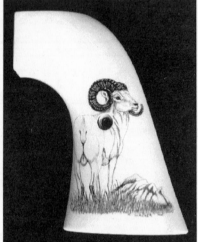

Karen L. Walker

Bob Hergert Micro-Scrimshaw

Scrim by Trena Polk
Engraving by Walter Shannon

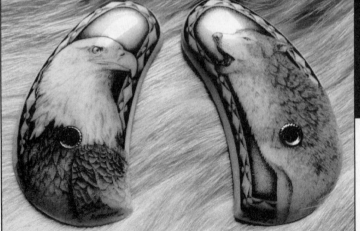

John Barraclough
(Photo by Walter Rickell)

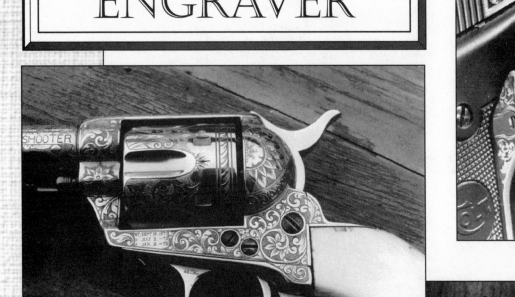

Art
of the
ENGRAVER

Ron Lutz

"Widowmaker's" gun
by Wayne Reno

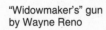

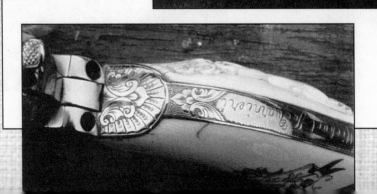

Art *of the*

ENGRAVER

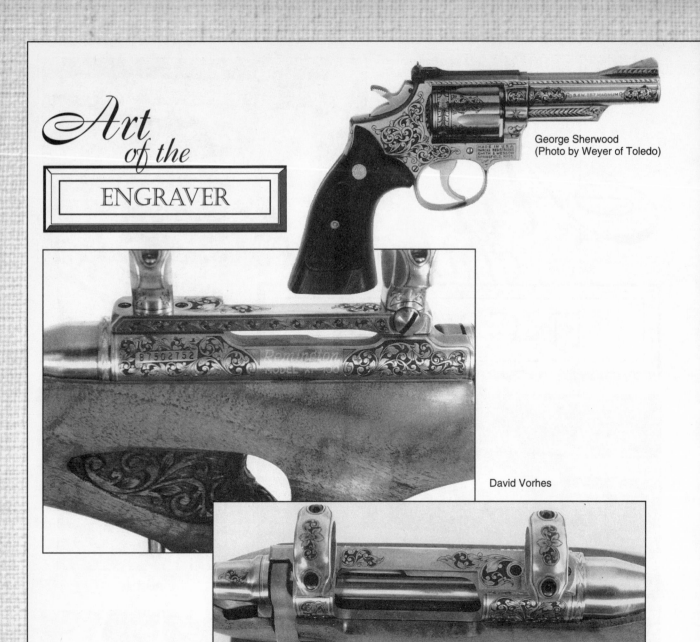

George Sherwood
(Photo by Weyer of Toledo)

David Vorhes

J.R. Blair Engraving (Photo by Becker)

Roger Sampson

Billy R. Bates

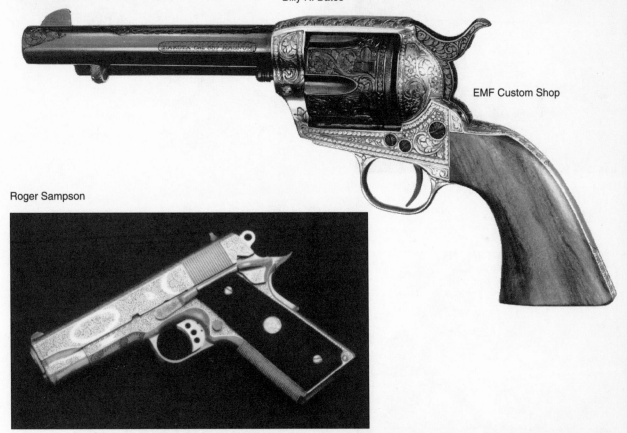

EMF Custom Shop

Roger Sampson

Jere Davidson

Art *of the* ENGRAVER

John J. Adams, Jr.

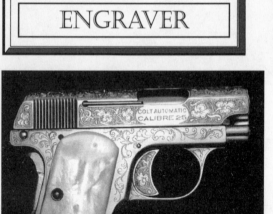

Scott Pilkington (Photo by Michael Smith)

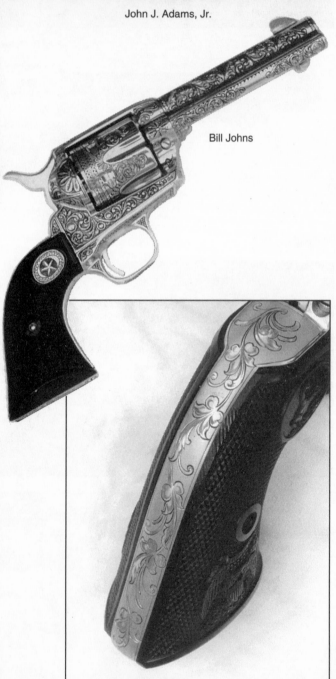

Bill Johns

Barry Lee Hands

HANDGUNS 97

Ammunition And Reloading Scene

Cold facts about hot new fodder, page 142.

Fisher goes long range, page 147.

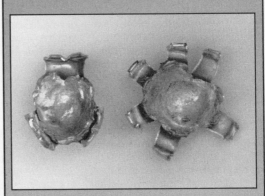

Some energy is lost on impact, page 153.

The author tested a good variety of new ammo.

FACTORY AMMUNITION TESTS

by FINN AAGAARD

IT IS QUITE remarkable, really, how recent a development is the availability of expanding bullets in standard production centerfire pistol ammunition. It used to be that in autopistols one shot full metal jacket (FMJ) "hardball," and in revolvers, lead. Even ten years ago, expansion with many factory-loaded jacketed hollowpoints and softpoints was decidedly "iffy," especially with heavy bullets and velocities below 1000 feet per second (fps). Nowadays, however, in measure due to the FBI's testing programs, we can rely on factory hol-

lowpoint bullets to open up under almost any circumstances, certainly within defensive-pistol ranges, even when their cavities are partially packed with dry material from penetrating clothing and the like.

The main revolution occurred a few years back, though, and this year's latest offerings consist for the most part of developments and refinements, rather than any startlingly new concepts. We asked the major domestic manufacturers for samples of what they had that was new, and tested them for velocity,

Eldorado Cartridge Corp's PMC 45 Colt ammo is ideal for today's cowboys.

functioning, and, where appropriate, for expansion and penetration. (I had to stipulate that I had no guns available chambered to 357 SIG, 356 TSW, 38 Super, 10mm, and some others.) The results are listed in the accompanying tables. Not all the manufacturers responded, and not all who did were able to supply every item requested. It sometimes takes several months before a newly-listed item actually gets into the supply pipeline—that is just the way it is.

I did not run a formal accuracy test, from a rest at 25 yards, with any of the ammunition. None of my centerfire handguns are target arms, they are all defensive pistols (except for a 6-inch M29 44 Magnum, which I suppose is a hunting gun). I shot all the test loads on paper at 50 feet, from an unsupported Weaver-type two-handed hold, except for the 380 Auto and the 25 Auto, which were tried at 21 feet. All the test ammo proved capable of making vital-area hits with every shot at those distances. Naturally, different loads often shoot to widely separated points of impact, but not always. My Springfield 1911-A1 45 ACP put twenty rounds, seven different loads with bullets

varying in weight from 145 grains (Glaser) to 230 grains, inside 4¹/₂ inches. The twenty-first shot, called a flier as the trigger broke, brought the group out to 5³/₄ inches. On the other hand, a 45 Colt put the lightweight Glasers 4 inches lower than its standard 250-grain lead bullet load. One simply must check the zero when switching loads.

All the hollowpoint bullets were tested for expansion and penetration in wet telephone books at 15 feet. Velocities were recorded by an Oehler M35P chronograph, with the skyscreens set 12 feet from the muzzles. Generally, five shots could be placed on each stack of books, without the "wound channels" interfering with each other. One of those shots was always with Remington's 357 Magnum 125-grain HP, which served as a reference load to compare the others against. The 125-grain HP 357 Magnum

is said to be the conventional pistol load most likely to immediately incapacitate an aggressor. If that is so, then its 6¹/₂ inches of penetration in wet paper ought to be ideal, and one should normally choose loads that penetrate in the 6- to 7-inch bracket. When complete penetration must absolutely be avoided, as in crowds, one might go with less, and in other circumstances more might be requisite. It is up to a responsible pistol-packer to learn what the different loads will do, and to choose accordingly. Note that this 125-grain HP typically fragments to the extent of losing more than a third of its original weight, yet it remains very effective. Fragmentation is not necessarily a fault, provided sufficient penetration is achieved to reach the vitals. Nor does the diameter of a recovered bullet necessarily indicate the greatest expansion it attained during its penetration.

From left, Speer Gold Dot HP (handload), Remington Golden Saber, PMC Starfire, Hornady XTP, all in 230-grain 45 ACP, with recovered bullets.

Here's how the lighter 45 Auto bullets performed, with the "standard" Remington 125-grain 357 JHP, second from left, for comparison. From left: 165-grain Cor-Bon; 357/125 control; 200-grain Hornady XTP; 185-grain Remington Golden Saber.

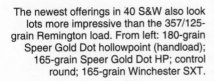

The newest offerings in 40 S&W also look lots more impressive than the 357/125-grain Remington load. From left: 180-grain Speer Gold Dot hollowpoint (handload); 165-grain Speer Gold Dot HP; control round; 165-grain Winchester SXT.

In 9mm there are some innovations like Federal's zinc-core BallistiClean bullet (left) that can't expand like the lead 90-grain slug from Cor-Bon can, at right. In the middle is the 357 Mag 125-grain "standard stopper" by Remington.

FACTORY AMMUNITION

Lead pollution has become a concern lately, particularly on indoor ranges. Conventional FMJ bullets are open at the base, leaving the lead core exposed. The heat of combustion turns some of the lead into gas, and gaseous lead in the air one is breathing does him no good. In addition, conventional primers contain lead and other toxic metals. Ammo manufacturers are addressing the problem. Speer/CCI's Clean-Fire Blazer and Lawman munitions use non-toxic primers and their Total Metal Jacket (TMJ) plated bullets that show no exposed lead. Winchester's Super Unleaded and Remington's Leadless offerings also utilize fully encapsulated bullets with no exposed lead, and lead-free primers. Federal goes the same route with their Premium Nyclad 9mm load, whose lead core is completely clad in nylon. A problem with lead-core bullets is that they tend to shatter when they impact steel targets, releasing airborne lead. Federal's answer is their new BallistiClean line, which in addition to their Toxic-Metal Free primers sports jacketed "softpoint" bullets with zinc, not lead, cores. They do not expand, but there is no way they can cause lead pollution.

Winchester designed their SXT (Supreme eXpansion Technology) bullets, which have reverse-taper hollow-point jackets, to replace the ill-fated Black Talon in their Supreme line. Latest additions are 130-grain 38 Special +P and 165-grain 40 S&W. The latter performed very well in my tests, giving almost ideal penetration combined with full expansion to chop a wide wound channel.

Remington's Golden Saber bullets are also quite innovative. Their brass jackets are reduced to bore diameter ahead of the rear-located driving band, leading to less barrel friction and improved accuracy, it is claimed. The nose cuts curl one edge of each "petal" under the next one, and go all the way through to the generous cavity, to ensure great expansion even at low

velocities. A recent addition is the Golden Saber 45 ACP +P 185-grain BJHP (Brass Jacketed Hollow Point) at a listed 1140 fps. It performed beautifully in the test medium, yielding the largest final frontal area, while penetrating more than adequately. The 230-grain Golden Saber, though not rated +P, gave over 900 fps, and expanded nicely. Its penetration equalled that of its 185-grain sibling. Outstanding bullets, both of them.

Hornady's Vector tracer ammunition has less than $1/20$-grain pyrotechnical material inserted along the bullet's central axis, resulting in good accuracy, short burn time, minimal heat generation, and no fire hazard. I had difficulty following the bright trace to the target, as the gun in recoil tended to obscure it, though a bystander or instructor would have had no problem. My chronograph certainly saw it, and was totally confused by it! First issued in 9mm, Vector ammo is now available in 40 S&W, and

other calibers are promised. Hornady's XTP (eXtreme Terminal Performance) bullets have been with us for some years, earning a reputation for deep penetration combined with reliable expansion. I included their Custom 45 ACP +P 200-grain and +P 230-grain XTP loads in the testing. Both achieved their listed velocities—950 fps ain't bad with a 230-grain bullet—and gave the deepest penetration of any of the tested expanding bullets, combined with worthwhile expansion.

Eldorado Cartridge Corp. is offering 45 Colt (they call it the "Long" Colt) ammo with the traditional flat-nose 250-grain lead bullet at a claimed 800 fps. It did not achieve that in my gun, but proved a nicely accurate, pleasant load that will be perfect for the Cowboy Action Shooting game, and will look exactly right in the loops of an old-timey gun belt. It should work a like a treat in carbines also. Eldorado's Starfire JHP bullets feature distinctive fluted cavities that are said to enhance expansion. They expand readily, even at standard 230-grain 45 ACP veloci-

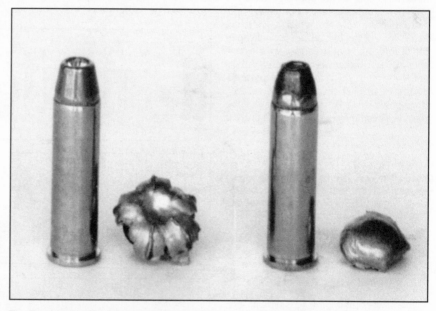

The Remington 125-grain stopper at the right looks like pretty small potatoes next to the 150-grain PMC Starfire load from Eldorado. Both are 357 Magnums.

Ammo makers have developed better loads for smaller guns. Here's a 90-grain Speer Gold Dot HP in 380 Auto (center) with one of its bullets (left) recovered from author's test box. At the right is a 380 Silvertip by Winchester. Pretty impressive stuff.

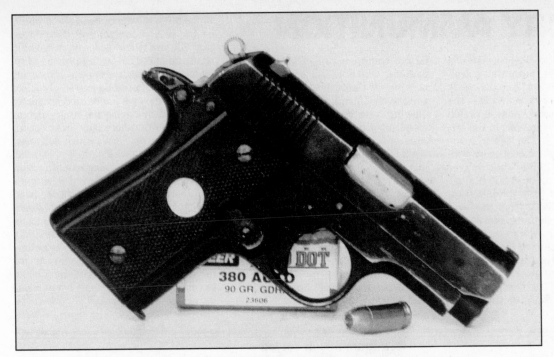

Author's diminutive Colt Mustang Pocketlite SA auto in 380 can be more effective with today's fine expanding ammo.

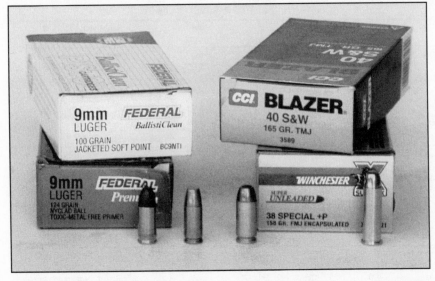

Lead-free ammo offerings are growing quickly. Federal's BallistiClean actually contains no lead whatsoever.

ties, to present five ribbed petals, reminiscent of some exotic flower. They, too, are great bullets.

Blount's Speer/CCI division introduced their Gold Dot HP bullets a year or two ago. They are made by plating lead cores with the jacket material, which means that cores and jackets are truly and firmly bonded. When the nose cavities are punched, a dot of yellow jacket material remains in the bottom of the hollow, hence their name. Besides making them available to handloaders, Speer offers Gold Dot bullets in loaded ammunition. They load their 165-grain Gold Dot to a rather modest 970 fps in the 40 S&W, apparently because FBI research indicated that produced the most effective combination of penetration, expansion and accuracy. Recoil is very tolerable, to boot. In my test its 6

inches of penetration came at the bottom end of the "ideal" range, while its expansion was excellent. On a whim, I included two handloads with heavyweight Gold Dot bullets, 45 ACP and 40 S&W, that I use in my guns. For the 380 I happened to have a couple of Winchester 85-grain Silvertip rounds, and I pitted them against the 90-grain Speer GDHP loads. The Silvertips expanded more, the Gold Dots dug deeper. Which to use would depend on circumstances, and personal preferences.

Cor-Bon's Peter Pi believes in *velocity*! His ammo won its reputation for producing instant stops by using frangible bullets at top-end velocities. The two new Cor-Bon offerings tested, 165-grain in 45 ACP and 90-grain in 9mm, both loaded to +P+ pressures, gave impressively high velocities, more or

less disintegrated after impact. They caused huge "wound cavities" at about the 2-inch depth in the test medium and had limited penetration. When deep penetration is not a requirement they should be awesomely effective, and are among the best choices when over-penetration cannot be tolerated. Peter Pi has introduced a cartridge that epitomizes his thinking. Called the 40 Cor-Bon, it uses the 45 ACP case necked down to 40-caliber, and will supposedly work in most 45 ACP pistols with merely a barrel change. It is said to be capable of driving a 135-grain JHP to 1450 fps, which ought to have a noticeable effect on anything that gets in its way.

Even less likely to over-penetrate are the Glaser Safety Slug, Inc., products. Introduced more than twenty years ago, the Glaser Safety Slug consists of a special bullet jacket containing a compressed load of either #12 or the newly introduced #6 shot. In the first case the bullet (shell? canister?) nose is sealed with a blue plastic cap, and in the latter with a silver cap. The "silver" loads are meant to give 50 percent more penetration than the "blue," but deliver only 30 pellets as against 200 (9mm). Glaser claims that Safety Slugs fragment only in soft tissue, that they will penetrate through clothing, boards and the like without opening up. On the other hand, when they strike hard surfaces at an angle, the thin jackets rupture, obviating dangerous ricochets. Nor are they likely to over-penetrate, hence the "Safety Slug" epithet. They did not fragment properly in my test medium, which is denser even than most muscle tissue, probably because it held the shot string together instead of allowing it to disperse. Those that I tested on a defunct goat, some time back, sprayed #12 pellets in a wide swath through the lungs. Glaser Safety Slug ammo has lately been given a softer nose cap to enhance fragmentation even at low impact velocities. It is available in most defensive pistol cartridges from 25 ACP to 45 Colt, and in some military rifle cartridges. (It functioned perfectly in my Astra 25 ACP auto. I am skeptical of expanding bullets in the 25, which lacks penetration under the best of circumstances; but then I am skeptical of the 25 as a lifesaver, period.

If one must rely on it, head shots would be the best recourse, and it could be that Glasers would prove more reliable than the standard round-nosed FMJs, which, by report, tend to glance off bone.) They should be extremely effective when they get inside, and are likely the optimum choice for many urban environments. Accuracy was good, except in my 40 S&W, which delivered them to the target side-on.

Incidentally, not a single malfunction of any sort was experienced during all this testing, which says a lot for both the guns and the ammo. Modern ammunition is *good stuff*. All the loads tested performed quite admirably, but far from identically. So much the better, but it does mean that today's *pistolero* must give some intelligent thought as to what loads will best suit his particular needs. Good shooting! ●

New Ammunition Tested

Cal.	Maker	Type	Wt. grs.	MV (fps)	Pene. (ins.)	RW (grs.)	Exp (ins.)	Comments
45 Colt	Glaser	Safety Slug	145	1180		not tested		Claimed 1350 fps
	PMC	Lead FP	250	720		not tested		
45 ACP	Glaser	Safety Slug	145	1430				+P Claimed 1350 fps
	Cor-Bon	JHP	165	1260	4.7	71	.62	+P Claimed 1250 fps
	Rem.	Golden Saber	185	1140	7.2	184	.71	+P Brass jacketed HP
	Hornady	XTP JHP	200	1030	7.5	191	.63	+P
	Hornady	XTP JHP	230	955	7.4	228	.67	+P
	Rem.	Golden Saber	230	900	7.2	230	.69	Brass jacketed HP
	PMC	Starfire JHP	230	850	6.6	230	.68	
	Speer	Gold Dot HP	230	895	7.0	229	.66	Handload
40 S&W	Glaser	Safety Slug	115	1335				Claimed 1650 fps
	Win.	SXT	165	1040	6.2	155	.62	
	CCI	Blazer TMJ	165	970				
	PMC	Target FMJ/FP	165	1030				
	Speer	Gold Dot HP	165	960	6.0	165	.62	
	Hornady	FMJ Vector	180	n/a				
	Speer	Lawman TMJ	180	978				
	Speer	Gold Dot HP	180	1000	7.3	180	.62	Handload
357 Magnum	Glaser	Safety Slug	80	1790	6.0			Blue. Claimed 1800 fps Not much spread.
	Glaser	Safety Slug	80	1720	6.0			Silver. Not much spread.
	Rem.	JHP	125	1440	6.6	73	.54	Reference/control load
	PMC	Starfire JHP	150	1100	7.1	144	.66	
38 Special	Glaser	Safety Slug	80	1385				Claimed 1500 fps
	Glaser	Safety Slug	80	1450	6.0			+P Claimed 1650 fps Little spread.
	Win.	Supreme FMJ	158	795				+P Encapsulated unleaded
9mm Parabellum	Glaser	Safety Slug	80	1610				+P Claimed 1650 fps
	Cor-Bon	JHP	90	1490	4.0	34	.50	+P Claimed 1475 fps
	Federal	BallistiClean	100	1240	16.8	100	none	No-lead primer; zinc core
	Hornady	Vector FMJ	115	n/a				
	Hornady	Vector FMJ	124	n/a				
	Federal	Premium ball	124	1160				Nyclad, lead-free primer
380 Auto	Glaser	Safety Slug	70	1104				Claimed 1350 fps
	Win.	Silvertip	85	938	3.7	85	.60	
	Speer	Gold Dot HP	90	910	5.0	89	.49	
25 Auto	Glaser	Safety Slug	35	1114				Claimed 1150 fps

Velocities measured with the Oehler M35P chronograph at 12 feet; ambient temperature 85-95° F.
Velocity claims are as stated on package.
Pene = penetration in wet phone books at 15 feet.
RW = retained weight of recovered bullet.
Exp = average expanded diameter of recovered bullet.

HALF-MILE HITS

by DON FISHER

HOW MANY PEOPLE have ever sat down and tried to figure out what all of the things are that affect accuracy? What is it that stops the second bullet fired downrange from hitting in the same hole as the first? After my first interview on the subject with my old friend Don Bower about his long-range handgun shooting, I thought about it all the way home. It was apparent to me that Mr. Bower had given the matter a lot of thought. In his shooting, he has eliminated as many of the variables as he could. What remains is a method of building and shooting handguns that works.

Don Bower claims to have built handguns that can shoot 3-inch groups at 500 meters. According to him, the hard part of the job is getting someone to believe that he can do it. I have known Mr. Bower for over twenty years and I know

better than to bet any money against him. Don Bower is one of the two people who taught me how to shoot about twenty-two years ago, and I competed against him for a lot of years, so I tend to listen to what he has to say. He showed me back then that it's possible to hit a 6-inch round plate with a 44 Magnum handgun from 100 yards—standing up, no less. When I heard about his claims of 3-inch groups at 500 meters, I had to find out what he was up to now.

One of the things Don taught me long ago that really helped me the most was that the bullet will go where the sights are aligned, if I don't screw up. The gun will get the job done as long as I do my part. Once I learned that simple lesson, the rest was easy. Just hold the sights aligned with the target, increase the pressure on the trigger until the gun

fires, and I can hit almost anything I aim at. Do it right and almost all guns are accurate. Do it wrong and we might as well go back to the bow-and-arrow days.

When I was first given this assignment, I sat down and tried to put together a list of what can go wrong with the flight of a bullet. The only thing I have to do to put two bullets though one hole is to eliminate all of the variables. The hard part is to come up with a list that includes all of them, and then find out the best way to eliminate them one by one. That list is rather long yet rather simple. I wanted to prepare myself before my first interview with Don Bower, who I hadn't seen in over ten years. In order to learn, I had to know what to ask—and be willing to listen.

Author Fisher fired this 1.02-inch 200-yard group with coaching from master long-range handgunner Don Bower. The T/C Contender is chambered for the 7mm Super Bower.

HALF-MILE HITS

What most people find hard to understand is how a handgun can shoot as well as a rifle at 500 meters. They seem to think that a rifle should be more accurate. If you think about it, there are two factors that have to be considered here. One is the accuracy of the gun, and the second is how well a shooter can shoot it. It's important to separate the two elements of the equation if we want to shoot small groups. Let's consider accuracy, then, in two parts, the mechanical and the human.

The mechanical aspect includes the quality of the barrel, the sighting system, the ammunition, and that's really about it. A good and light trigger pull is important to shooting small groups, but only in that it makes it easier to maintain the alignment of the sights and the target until after the bullet has left the barrel. If the barrel is fixed in a device that doesn't allow any movement, then a poor trigger doesn't hurt anything. But as we all know, a poor trigger makes it impossible to maintain sight alignment, and that's one of the variables that must be eliminated. Everything else that I can think of is really a matter of how well the gun can be shot—the human aspect.

The rifle has held an advantage over the handgun in the area of the sighting system for a long time, but the new scopes that have become available have changed that to a large degree. As long as we had open sights to work with, it was no contest. The longer sight radius of the rifle meant a higher degree of precision in aligning the sights. The scope sight doesn't care how long the barrel is, so sight alignment between the rifle and handgun is now equal in the equation.

The longer barrel no longer is an aid to accuracy. In fact, it can be a source of poor sight alignment. Remembering that it is the alignment of the barrel and the target *until the bullet exits the barrel* that matters. The longer the bullet remains in the barrel, the more time the shooter has to *screw up*. A shorter barrel means less barrel time and that means less screw-up time. The shorter barrel of the handgun should translate into better accuracy, all else being equal.

In Don Bower's search for the smallest groups possible, he has come up with what he feels is the best handgun for the job. Don starts with a Thompson/Center Contender pistol and fits a Burris 10x scope to it. With the scope mounted on the barrel and not to a receiver as on most bolt-action rifles, one source of error is eliminated. Not that mounting a scope on a receiver is bad, but what could be better than mounting the scope right on the barrel?

Next, he rechambers the barrel to a caliber of his own design. The barrel is chambered so that the gun headspaces on the rim of the case and not the shoulder. The brass is then resized so that the shoulder is set back about .002-inch from the shoulder of the chamber. This eliminates the chance of the round headspacing on the rim and the shoulder at the same time, or the shoulder one time and maybe the rim the next. That's one less variable to worry about.

Don likes to seat the bullets so that they extend into the rifling about .002- to .003-inch. This holds the case back against the breech face and gets the bullet aligned with the bore.

These are the only reloading steps he uses to load his ammo. He doesn't weigh his brass or turn the necks to uniform size or any of the other time-intensive things that most benchrest

This is full recoil of the Fisher-compensated 7mm Super Bower with the correct light one-hand grip on the gun. The right hand isn't touching it. Bower says consistency is the key.

This 7mm Super Bower is fitted with a small and efficient compensator designed and made by author Don Fisher.

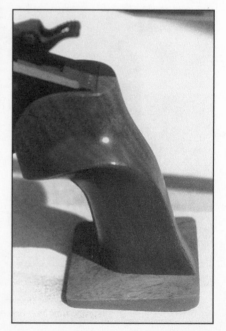

Bower adds a flat bottom to the T/C stock and then "beds" the gun in place on the sandpaper top of the shooting bench. Once the gun is on target it stays there without being touched.

shooters consider necessary. And he loads the ammo on a normal press that every shooter has available. Some of his equipment is over fifty years old, so the newest, and most expensive, tools are not needed.

While I know that fancy benchrest loading methods can reduce the variables in reloading match-grade ammo, I know from my own experience that I can build a match-grade AR-15 that will shoot $1/4$-inch groups at 100 yards with no fancy reloading tricks. As long as I use match bullets and brass of one headstamp, trimmed to length, that is all I need to get $1/4$-inch groups. If I

Don Bower uses the 307 Winchester case (left) for his line of wildcats, not the 225 Winchester that J.D. Jones uses. Bower's case holds more powder. This is the 223 Super Bower.

From left, here's the 22, 6mm, 6.5mm, 7mm, 300, factory 307 Winchester FP, 30 Alaskan, 358, 429 and 358 Shorty Bower wildcats.

wanted better groups than that, I might have to turn the necks and ream the flash holes and weigh cases, but I'm not talking about breaking records at benchrest shooting. A $1/4$-inch group at 100 yards is good enough for the type of shooting I do and I don't think it's worth the effort to get down to $1/8$-inch or so. Not to me it's not.

Don designed a line of calibers for his pistols to help get the most velocity possible from the relatively short barrels common to this type handgun. He has been accused of stealing his designs from other people who are in the business of building custom handguns for hunting. One of the people whose designs he is accused of stealing is J.D. Jones. When asked about this, Bower said that his designs are based on the 307 Winchester family of cases and not the 225 Winchester that Jones uses for

his designs. The 307 cases give his designs a 22-percent increase in volume, and can be loaded to higher velocities for that reason. As an example, his 30 Bower Alaskan is the 307 Winchester with the shoulder blown out by fire-forming factory ammunition in the rechambered barrel.

Don recommends using a Burris 10x scope for the best results. He says if Burris comes out with a new scope with more power, it would be even better, but for now, Bower considers this to be the best scope for the job.

For the highest velocity possible the 14-inch T/C Contender barrel is better than the 10-inch tubes. Bower is now using even longer barrels. Both 16.5- and 21-inch barrels are available from Bullberry Barrel Works, Ltd. The extra length raises the velocity enough to make hunting with the guns a lot easi-er. The flatter trajectory can make the difference between a miss or a one-shot kill when you are considering hunting antelope at over 300 yards.

While Bower does not sell barrels, he can rechamber your Thompson/Center Contender barrel to one of his designs. Rechambering and recrowning your barrel costs $120, and custom reloading dies, made from Redding dies, are available for $78. According to Don, the barrels are rechambered in a mill so that the reamer turns, rather than the barrel, and this results in a smoother chamber. I don't know how much smoother the chambers are because of this method, but it can't hurt.

The hardest part of the shooter's job is to maintain the alignment of the sights and the target until after the bullet has left the barrel. A steady hold is what is needed and this is what Don Bower has built into his guns. He builds a custom forend and matching grip for the Contender that are made to sit flat on the shooting bench. The forend is basically a 2 by 3-inch piece of wood

that is inletted to the barrel. The grip is machined square on the bottom to sit flat against the top of the bench. Between the two, the gun is much easier to hold steady. With that flat-bottom grip, it's also easy to hold the gun so that the crosshairs are never canted to one side or the other.

If that wasn't enough, he built a matching rest that works with the square forend and grip. The area of the rest that contacts the gun is covered with sandpaper so that the gun can be slid back and forth against the rest until the surfaces are lapped together to form a perfect joint. The forend is slightly tapered from front to back to allow for elevation adjustments by simply sliding the gun forward or back a little bit. Once you sand the wood to mate with the rest, you can align the sights on the target and let go of the gun. It stays put, right on target, waiting for you to press the trigger. Don sells the rest, new grip and forend as a set for $156.

Of all the things that Don Bower does to put together a gun that shoots well, I feel that it's the custom stocks and matching pistol rest that does the most to produce a tiny group. I was expecting to hear all about his new ways to load better ammo than anyone else, but as I mentioned, he doesn't even weigh his brass or the charge, nor spend time turning case necks or anything else that benchrest shooters swear by. Most match shooters would look at his reloading bench, see the old press and powder measure and call his reloading practices a joke. But all the tools and reloading skills in the world won't help you shoot small groups if the gun moves while you shoot.

And that reminds me of another reason for the sandpaper on the rest. The extra friction helps to stop the gun from moving due to the movement of the hammer. The gun no longer tends to slide forward when the hammer hits

HALF-MILE HITS

the firing pin, and that should help keep the sights aligned until the bullet is safely on its way.

If you can set the gun down on a pistol rest, move the gun around on a solid base until the sights are on the target, and let go of it and not have it move, do you think you could shoot a handgun better than you do now? A long time ago I was taught that I should not know when the gun is going to go off. It should be a surprise break when the trigger releases the hammer. Let the gun go off when it's ready, don't make it go off. Good advice, but it's hard to hold the gun on target until that happens, while you increase the trigger pressure as slowly as you can.

With the gun sitting rock-steady on the rest, it becomes a matter of having the patience to let the gun go off as if by itself. If you do that while holding the gun with just enough force to prevent it from jumping over your shoulder, and do it the same way every time, you will be amazed at how accurate a pistol can be. And it will work for your rifle shooting *almost* as well. After all, that long barrel increases barrel time, and that means more time for you to do something wrong before the bullet is safely on its way to the target.

For this article I was able to shoot three guns that Don is building for other shooters. The first two guns had 10x scopes, and I had a hard time with them. The eye relief for those scopes is hard to work with for someone not used to them. I couldn't get my head in the right place and still be comfortable. I had to work at it to keep the sights in alignment while at the same time keeping my head in the center of the tube so as to not have a problem with parallax. My arm had to be bent, rather than out straight, so I never felt comfortable with the setup. Even with the rest to help hold the gun steady, I couldn't shoot good groups.

I have the use of only a 200-yard range at the shooting club I belong to, so all shooting was done at that distance. The best I could do with the first two guns was 3- or 4-inch groups. One of the guns had left-handed stocks and I'm sure that didn't help, but the main problem was with the eye relief of the scopes.

Another problem with my shooting the guns is that I like to maintain a light hold on a handgun when I try to shoot for accuracy. With the power of these hunting handguns, that was a problem for me. The recoil of the 30 Bower Alaskan combined with the left-hand stock made it impossible for me to hold the gun the same way for each shot. I could see the gun recoil in a different way every time. If the gun recoils to the left one shot and the right the next, I know I'm doing a poor job of shooting. And one look at my first dozen targets was proof of just how poorly I was doing.

Luckily Don had a third gun with him that had a right-hand stock and was fitted with one of my own custom-made compensators and a 7x Burris scope. This scope was of the extended eye relief type rather than of intermediate eye relief, and I could hold it much

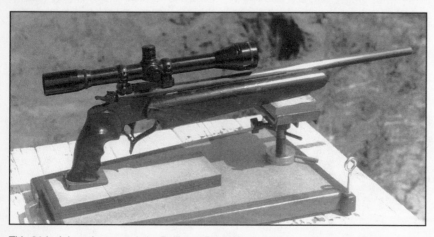

This 21-inch barrel was made by Bullberry Barrel Works, Ltd.

Impressive proof that Don Bower's ideas are right on target is this 2½-inch, five-shot group fired on a steel plate by Greg Childress at a measured 500 yards. Childress shot this in October 1995 using a T/C Contender chambered for the 30 Alaskan Bower.

How Accurate is Accurate?

by Don Bower

WHAT IS accuracy? How do we attain it? How is it that some shooters always seem to have better accuracy than others? Is accuracy a one-inch group with a 30-06 rifle at a hundred yards? Can a novice shooter easily attain consistent accuracy? Can one buy accuracy?

Questions such as these are asked hundreds of times every day by a multitude of shooters. In all reality, accuracy is 100 percent in the eyes of the beholder!

Man does not build accuracy into a gun. This is the big fallacy. Man builds concepts into a gun, and thru these concepts man can enhance his accuracy level through repeated practice.

The most misused method of determining accuracy is by the performance of one shooter against the performance of another. A typical example is my performance during the rapid-fire stage of a high power rifle match at Fort Riley, Kansas, in 1969. The temperature was a scorching 96 degrees, combined with 96 percent humidity. Sweat literally poured into my eyes as I tried to keep them locked onto the front sight while I slowly and deliberately pulled the trigger, as the post front sight was near the center of the bullseye. I knew my rifle was a sure-fire 1 MOA gun, so I just did the best I could, staring at the clouded front sight as I squeezed the trigger. I knew the accuracy of the rifle would prevail as long as I did my part. I blasted out a 400/8X for the two combined stages of rapid fire at 200 and 300 yards, and won the rapid-fire aggregate. The second-place finisher fired a score of 399/21X. Who had the most accurate rifle? Who had the most accurate score?

More often than not, the term "inaccuracy" is applied to the shooter's inability to shoot properly, using the basic fundamentals of marksmanship. Many shooters go out for the first time, sometimes with a $2000 rifle, without getting $5 worth of basic marksmanship instruction. Generally they will fare poorly. Until the shooter masters the techniques of precision bench shooting, he will not be tuned in, so to speak, with accuracy.

Another form of accuracy is called "inherent." This, simply put, means that every innovation possible is built into the rifle or handgun. Some of the more common innovations are glass-bedding the stock, a target trigger, installing bedding screws into the stock forend, lapped locking lugs, you name it. All of these concepts are built in to create an accuracy level that is acceptable to the shooter. The gun may shoot 1-inch groups all day at 200 yards, which is a fine performance indeed, yet you may not be satisfied. Knowing how to shoot properly could very well tighten that group into 3/4-inch.

It is more important to learn how to shoot properly than to trust the gun to do it.

Trying to buy accuracy is like having $10,000,000 worth of religion and only 10¢ worth of faith. The custom innovations are to ensure that the *gun* will perform the same functions flawlessly, every time it is shot, regardless of how good, or bad, the shooter is.

My particular shooting love is long-range handgun, benchrest shooting out to 800 meters, shooting at 1 MOA and smaller steel plates. Since the inception of this unique sport, the guns have become so accurate that we were pressured to reduce the overall size of all the plates just to make the sport more challenging.

Then came along the development of the Bower bench-gun rest, combined with the modified grip and forend for the Contender. This allows for zero gun movement during firing. Now with everything in perfect harmony we get 1.5-inch three-shot groups at 500 meters. I soon predicted that a 2-inch group wouldn't win a thing, and I was right!

What contributes the most to accuracy? Long-range handgun shooting has proven to me that *consistency* is the greatest contributing factor. This covers loading techniques, consistently gripping the gun in the same manner each time we shoot, even placing the finger on the trigger the same way. It also means to stare at the aiming dot consistently, rather than looking at the target. The list goes on and on until one ultimately performs like a finely tuned machine.

Never settle for any given accuracy level simply because of what you read or hear, or attempt to do. Rather, keep striving for the unknown. There is no telling what you might discover. Perhaps, just perhaps, it might be a 4-inch group at 850 meters—of course, fired from a handgun. That's accuracy!

Master shooter Don Bower takes handgun accuracy to the limits. His three-shot groups are smaller then 3 inches at 500 meters.

HALF-MILE HITS

better. My neck no longer hurt, and I could relax for a change. The compensator reduced the recoil so much that I didn't have to hold the gun as tightly as before and that helped a lot. Now I could get the sight on target and just press the trigger, and my grip became a constant factor instead of a variable. I was not *screwing up* any more!

The difference made an immediate improvement in my shooting. After

about six rounds to sight-in the gun at 200 yards (remember, Don Bower builds these guns for *500 meters*) I was able to shoot real nice groups. This gun was chambered in 7mm Super Bower, and we shot a half-dozen different loads that all performed well. My best group was fired with ammo loaded with a 140-grain Nosler Ballistic Tip bullet that goes out of the 14-inch barrel at 2560 fps. The 200-yard group measured

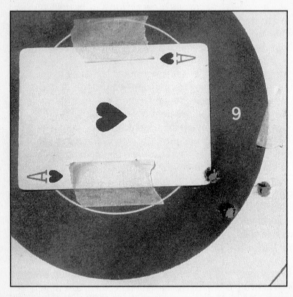

Here's a look at one of the author's 200-yard groups. The more he shot, the smaller the groups, says the author, as he got comfortable with the technique. It works.

(Below) Author Don Fisher with the 7mm Super Bower and a .970-inch group fired at 200 yards, the longest range he could find.

0.975-inch. A second group using a 120-grain bullet measured 1.050 inches. The more I shot, the better the group size.

It was apparent to Bower and me that my improvement came from being able to hold this gun better and getting comfortable with it. That, and learning how to shoot his guns. It takes practice and time to get used to his system of shooting, but if you have the patience and are willing to learn, it can be done. All I had to do was relax and let the gun do what it was built to do.

Here is exactly what I did to get those one-inch, 200-yard groups: I slid the gun into position until the sight was on the target. I then let go of the gun and checked to see if it stayed in place. If the sight was still on target, I placed my hand back onto the stock and pressed the trigger until it fired. If the sight moved off the target when I released my grip, that meant that I was forcing it on target, so I started over and tried again. By doing that for every shot, groups look good. It works. Once I stopped introducing errors, it was easy.

One last thing about shooting small groups at long range: Use the right kind of target. A square white target on a black background is much easier to hold on than a round black target any day. I had my best results when we used a white playing card on top of a standard black pistol target bull's-eye. It has been Don Bower's experience that shooters can fire smaller groups when using a square target rather then a round one. A two to one ratio is not uncommon. Try it.

Don Bower has spent over seventeen years developing his methods of building and shooting handguns. That's after spending thirty (30) years in the Air Force as both a shooter and a coach. His love for handgun hunting has led him to find a way to shoot small groups at long range. Being able to hunt with a handgun at ranges equal to those of the rifle is what he has worked at all those years.

His ideas make sense. Start with a short, stiff barrel, attach a good scope to it and build a stock and rest combination to hold the gun steady. Chamber the gun in a caliber that headspaces correctly and has enough capacity to load it to hunting velocities, and the rest is a matter of learning how to shoot.

For information on his guns contact Mr. Don Bower in Aurora, Colorado.

Available calibers: 22, 6mm, 6.5mm, 7mm, 300, 358, and 429 Super Bower plus the 30 Bower Alaskan and the Shorty 358. Loading dies are available for all calibers. ●

Winchester's 44-caliber 210-grain Silvertip after static impact of about 40 foot-pounds. The marble that transferred the impact energy is still in place in the bullet's deformed nose. Most of the bullets tested showed some degree of lopsided deformation, suggestive of imperfections in our testing setup.

EXPANSION REQUIRES ENERGY!

by M.L. McPHERSON

ALL SELF-DEFENSE HANDGUN loads share one fundamental property: limited impact energy. Under certain circumstances police officers and others have found even the most powerful 357 Magnum loads sorely lacking in *the* fundamental requisite, instant fight-stopping ability. My philosophy on this subject is very simple. If I should ever be so unfortunate as to have to shoot someone, I want to be all done after firing one reasonably well placed shot. *[While this is ideal, today's self-defense schools teach a different philosophy. Ed.]*

Until about ten years ago, handgun bullets came in two general varieties: Dependable non-expanding and undependable expanding. Many experts disdained early expanding jacketed hollowpoint (JHP) handgun bullets because expansion was neither consistent nor dependable. A generation ago, the most respected experts universally touted the non-expanding Keith-style semi-wadcutter (SWC) as a superior self-defense

EXPANSION

choice. There were two equally important bases for their argument.

First, the SWC design allowed the bullet to transfer its energy to the target comparatively fast. This characteristic limited penetration while maximizing wounding potential and "stopping power." Second, expanding self-defense bullets were not dependable.

Testing various types of 38 Special, 44 Special and 45 ACP loads demonstrates the huge difference in penetration and expansion. In saturated telephone books, 230-grain 45 ACP ball impacting at about 800 fps generally penetrates about 12 inches. The 246-grain round-nose (RN) lead 44 Special bullet impacting at about 700 fps typically achieves 13 inches of penetration. In any of these loads, substitution of a typical SWC bullet of similar weight

and velocity reduces penetration to about 9 inches. Lightweight SWC bullets generating muzzle energy comparable to the above loads typically penetrate about 6-7 inches.

The best modern JHP bullet can do even better, if one's only concern is limiting penetration. When loaded to the same velocity as similar-weight SWC bullets, modern JHP bullets typically penetrate about 25-40 percent less. The lightest typical SWC bullets, therefore, penetrate

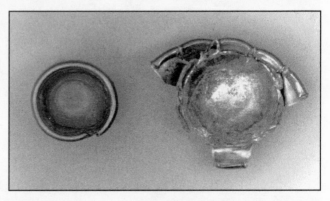

Comparison of two different types of older 185-grain 45-caliber JHPs after static impact of about 40 foot pounds of energy. Note the extreme variation in bullet response. Generally, obsolete JHP designs demonstrated extreme variation in response to this static test, even bullets from the same box.

Here is one half of the test apparatus. The hardened lead weight is suspended at a specified height by a loop of nylon twine. When the flame from the propane torch touches the twine, the loop releases the weight, which then freefalls until it impacts, centered on the marble, which sits atop the bullet. The only sophistication of this basic technique was filling the bullet nose with water, which helped appreciably in getting consistent results.

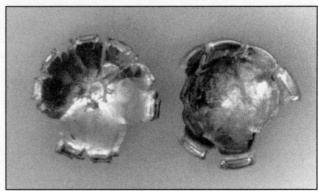

Comparison of new 185-grain 45-caliber JHPs shows how consistent modern bullets are. This is typical of the best modern JHP designs.

Here is the other half of the author's "sophisticated" testing apparatus. Yes, that is a marble atop Winchester's 210-grain 44-caliber Silvertip. In this test, the glass marble transferred and directed the impact from a dropped weight. The weight did not bounce or deform, so one can assume that most of the impact energy was absorbed by the bullet.

about the same distance as mid-weight JHP bullets (see Table 1). This approximation holds for other calibers and chamberings. As a specific example, a 178-grain SWC loaded to 1025 fps in the 45 ACP will usually penetrate about the same distance as a modern 200-grain JHP loaded to about 950 fps.

As shown in Table 1, compared to a typical non-expanding RN bullet, a similar SWC bullet will penetrate only about 60-75 percent as far. Since these are non-expanding bullets, performance is very consistent with both types. The best modern expanding bullets can *almost* match the consistency of these bullets in this test medium. However, that "almost" is important! In the real world, no expanding bullet can ever be thoroughly consistent—too many impact-related variables.

Several manufacturers have generally solved the problem of making dependable handgun bullets. The best current factory handgun loads from Black Hills, Hornady, PMC/Eldorado, Remington, Speer, Winchester, Zero and several other companies effectively eliminate any concerns about terminal bullet performance. Handloader bullets are available from Hornady (XTP), Speer (Gold Dot) and Winchester (Silvertip). *[Most legal experts advise against the use of handloaded ammo for self-defense. Ed.]* This would suggest that one should look first to the best modern JHP bullets for any self-defense handgun load. However, for a very fundamental reason this might not always be the best approach.

When the chips are down, we would hope to have a gun in our hand that used a cartridge which would instantly stop the fight. In reality, what most often happens is that any manageable cartridge used delivers so little power that its ability to instantly stop a fight depends upon either precise shot placement or pure luck.

Anything that reduces the energy the bullet can deliver to the target also reduces the potential for the bullet to do the required job. For this reason we should look for loads delivering the most energy to the target. Along with that, we want loads where the bullet consumes the least possible energy in self-deformation. Since non-expanding bullets do not consume *any* energy in self-deformation, these offer a distinct advantage for loads fired in guns delivering marginal energy for self-defense purposes.

Guns that deliver marginal energy might include anything less powerful than the 357 Magnum. In certain circumstances even that number has proven inadequate. One questions whether the 380 Automatic can do the job. Nevertheless, many individuals carry 380s for self-defense.

In this low-powered class of handguns the use of even the best of the modern JHP bullets might, therefore, be counterproductive. A lightweight SWC bullet might better serve the purpose. A lightweight SWC can deliver all of its energy to the target without consuming any of the available impact energy in the process of self-deformation. Is that deformation energy significant?

My son and I explored the question of how much energy various types of JHP bullets might consume in self-deformation.

In our tests we dropped a specially shaped weight from a known height onto sample bullets and measured the resulting deformation. We increased the drop height, and therefore kinetic energy, until bullet deformation was similar to that exhibited when we fired the same

Table 1

Penetration Results
Traditional handgun bullets fired into
water-saturated telephone books

Cartridge	Bullet type	Weight/MV (grs/fps)	Penetration (ins.)
38 Special	RN	158/800	12
	SWC	158/800	9
	JHP	158/800	6
	SWC	125/900	6
	JHP	125/900	4.5
44 Special	RN	240/700	13
	SWC	240/700	9
	JHP	240/700	6
	JHP	200/850	6
	SWC	180/900	6
45 Automatic	RN	230/800	12
	SWC	230/800	9
	JHP	230/800	6.5
	SWC	200/950	7
	JHP	200/950	5.5
	SWC	185/1000	6
	JHP	185/1000	5
	SWC	178/1025	5.5

Author McPherson fired the 185-grain 45-caliber Speer Gold Dot bullet at left into wet phone books at about 1100 fps. The object at right is the same type bullet after he dropped a weight onto it. Conclusion: a significant part of the bullet's kinetic energy is dissipated in the act of deforming itself, and can't be used on the target.

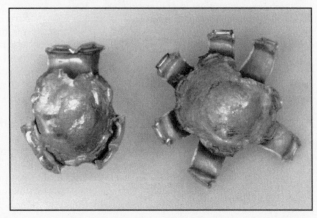

Comparison of 9mm Silvertip bullets: 115-grain (right) and 147-grain; static impact of about 25 foot pounds of energy. Evidently, the heavier bullet is designed for use in higher intensity loadings.

EXPANSION

type of bullet into wet telephone books. We knew the kinetic energy of the dropped weight so we knew how much energy it took to deform the bullet.

This study clearly demonstrated that the best modern JHP handgun bullets consume significantly less energy in self-deformation than do early JHP designs. These results also suggest that the amount of energy in self-deformation can be a considerable percentage of its impact energy. In some instances,

measured deformation energy exceeded 15 percent of the total available.

The actual mechanism of the expansion of a fired bullet creates more core deformation than our test method did. Examination of fired bullets shows that their cores have folded in a more convoluted manner than did our test bullet cores. If this is true, then actual deformational energy will be greater then our results.

Which bullet type is the better choice? This study suggests that by choosing any JHP one might be sacrificing 10-15 percent (or more) of the available

wounding potential of a load. However, since the JHP performs differently, it might still deliver a more incapacitating wound, despite this handicap—the jury is still out. JHP bullets can create superior wounding potential because these produce sharper cutting edges that intersect more material as the bullet penetrates. For these two reasons the JHP might produce more trauma. We certainly do not propose to have answered that question here!

Lest anyone misconstrue the information in Table 2, I must make the following points. First, XTP and Gold Dot bullets are not the only efficient expanding bullets on the market. As noted in the opening text, Winchester's new Silvertip is also an excellent performer. Although we did not obtain sample Silvertip bullets in time to test expansion characteristics for inclusion in Table 2, the testing we did suggests those are fully as efficient as either the Gold Dot or the XTP. Further, there are several factory-load-only expanding handgun bullets that are similarly efficient. Second, although our testing suggested that Gold Dot bullets were slightly more efficient in this one aspect, compared to XTP bullets, the XTPs have other advantages. (We believe this apparent XTP disadvantage was a consequence of the particular experimental setup and, therefore, illusory.) All numbers listed in Table 2 are averages of many drop tests using several types of JHP bullets. We make no claim to any hint of absolute accuracy.

Finally, the data shown represents typical top load performance for both factory ammunition and handloads for jacketed bullets. For the sake of comparison, we have shown the same impact energy for cast lead bullets in the same cartridge. For various reasons, when loaded to the same pressure, cast lead bullets typically generate 5-10 percent more muzzle energy, compared to similar jacketed bullets. In cartridges delivering limited impact energy this is no small consideration. When one factors in this effect, lightweight non-deforming bullets become particularly attractive for use in cartridges such as the 380 Automatic. We must note that the complete lack of flat-pointed lightweight non-expanding bullets limits the 380's potential performance in this regard. A 0.355-inch 90-grain truncated cone might be a good addition to someone's bullet line.

We do not intend this study to suggest any particular course of action. Both basic bullet types have advantages and both have potential disadvantages. Our purpose here is only to provide information about some of these factors. ●

Table 2

Approximate kinetic expansion energy results
Various JHP handgun bullets

Cartridge	—Bullet—		Deformation Energy (ft.-lbs.)	Typical Impact Energy	Available Impact Energy
	Wgt. Grs.	Type			
380 ACP	88	JHP	35	220	185
380 ACP	90	XTP	25	220	195
380 ACP	90	GD	20	220	200
380 ACP	90	RN	—	220	220
38 Spl +P	125	JHP	40	275	235
38 Spl +P	125	XTP	30	275	245
38 Spl +P	125	GD	25	275	250
38 SPl +P	110	SWC	—	275	275
44 Spl	180	JHP	55	325	270
44 Spl	180	XTP	40	325	285
44 Spl	200	GD	35	325	290
44 Spl	180	TC	—	325	325
45 ACP	185	JHP	55	410	355
45 ACP	185	XTP	40	410	370
45 ACP	185	GD	35	410	375
45 ACP	178	SWC	—	410	410

Two 185-grain 45-caliber JHP bullets after 40 foot pound impact. Left, old style; right, Hornady XTP. Note failure of bullet jacket on old style and contained swelling of XTP bullet shank. New bullets are tough.

Here's a side view of Winchester's 9mm 115-grain Silvertip after mashing. These bullets were extremely consistent in this test.

HANDGUNS 97

Handgunning Today

Some like to shoot with smoke, page 160.

They only *look* like powder-burners, page 162.

Fine guns need fine leather, page 170.

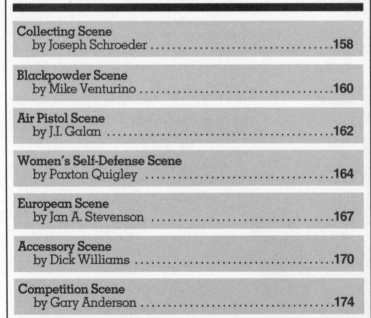

COLLECTING SCENE

by JOSEPH SCHROEDER

COLLECTOR-QUALITY HANDGUNS still remain a pretty good place for the knowledgeable gun buff to invest his money in 1996. Though prices haven't appreciated much in the past year, due at least in part to the current low inflation rate, prices of good and better-quality older handguns of almost all varieties have been moving upward at a respectable if not spectacular pace.

In this country the majority of handgun collectors seem to be interested in cartridge rather than muzzle-loading arms, perhaps as much because of availability as any lack of interest in the earlier eras. Colt and other Civil War-era percussions are not hard to find but are not cheap when in true collector-quality condition. They—along with U.S. and better-quality European flintlock handguns—sell in the low to mid-four-digit range, putting them out of the reach of many would-be collectors.

On the other hand, the majority of cartridge handguns—even many of those meeting the federal definition of "antique" (made in or before 1898)—are much more affordable. Many nice examples of small-caliber 19th century Colts, Smiths, Remingtons, Merwin and Hulberts and other U.S. handgun makers' products can be found in the $100 to $500 range, enabling a collector on even a modest budget to assemble a very presentable collection over a relatively short period of time.

However, handguns of the 20th century are the current collecting interest of more U.S. collectors than are earlier pistols and revolvers. U.S. martial handguns—particularly 1911 Colts—remains a hot field, with prices continuing to move up accordingly. Though serviceable 1911s or 1911A1s are readily available for a few hundred dollars, those of true collector quality—and that includes common variations in excellent original condition—are now usually priced at around $1000 or more.

Colt single actions have also continued to appreciate. Blackpowder-era examples—particularly U.S. martials—are hard to find in acceptable condition for less than a couple of thousand dollars, and almost any first-generation single action in decent shape will bring close to a thousand. Second-generation SAAs have also been appreciating, though unless they are "new in the box," only the rarest variations attract much collector interest.

Though other larger-caliber U.S. cartridge revolvers—Colt

New Services and the big-frame Smiths, for example—remain popular, interest in smaller U.S. revolvers of all makes has been relatively light. Foreign revolvers, particularly Webleys and the scarcer European militaries, continue to be popular, with most priced in the $300 to $500 range. Recent quantity imports of Russian Nagants, on the other

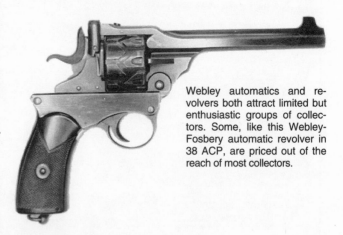

Webley automatics and revolvers both attract limited but enthusiastic groups of collectors. Some, like this Webley-Fosbery automatic revolver in 38 ACP, are priced out of the reach of most collectors.

Nambus of all kinds have been appreciating nicely. The scarcer variations like this nice "Baby" are in the $2000 range.

hand, have driven their prices down to below $100 except for some of the rarer early production examples.

Self-loading (automatic) pistols have also continued to attract an active following. Lugers still seem to remain number one in this field, and despite the recent importation of some reworked and largely mismatched Lugers, prices have either held their own or increased slightly. It's hard to find any collector-quality Luger—even the most common models—at under $500; those even a little bit scarce tend to bring over $1000. Walther P-38s have not done so well, thanks largely to the importation from Russia of quite a few—many of them scarce early variations—in fairly nice original or properly refinished condition. Walther PPs and PPKs, though still popular, have seen little appreciation; earlier Walthers, for the most part, have also been flat.

Though the flood of Mauser C96 "broomhandles"has been cut off for some time by the Clinton administration's ban on gun imports from China, there still seems to be an ample supply in the pipeline. Since most of these seem to be common variations in relatively sad shape, however, their influence on C96 prices seems to have waned and the prices of nice-condition, non-recent-import examples have been on the increase.

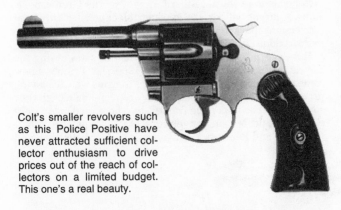

Colt's smaller revolvers such as this Police Positive have never attracted sufficient collector enthusiasm to drive prices out of the reach of collectors on a limited budget. This one's a real beauty.

WWII military automatics such as this Hungarian Model 37 made under German occupation in 1941 have a devoted collector following.

World War II-era European self-loaders have also been appreciating, particularly those that saw service with the Third Reich. Not only the native German products from Mauser, Walther and Sauer, but Czech, Hungarian, French, Belgian and Spanish automatics of that period, in particular those with German military or police markings, have been moving steadily upward. German-occupation Polish Radoms have also been appreciating, with top examples approaching the prices of low-end pre-war "eagle" Radoms. Webley autos of all sizes also continue to attract a following; on the other hand, with few exceptions earlier European pocket autos have not seen much appreciation.

Pre-war Belgian and Canadian-made Inglis Hi-Powers have remained very popular, despite pre-ban importation of a number of decent but well-used examples from China that depressed prices for a while. Japanese handguns, including the Type 26 revolver, the Model 94 pistol, and all the variations of Nambus, continue to attract significant collector interest, again despite the importation of a number of well-used common model Nambus from China. Nice Type 26s, Model 94s and common Nambus are now bringing $300 to $400; a nice "Papa" Nambu will bring $1000 or more; a "Baby," $1500-$2000; and the rare "Grandpa" starts at $3000.

Pre-WWI automatics have held their own or appreciated. Colt 1900s continue to be priced in the $2000 to $4000 range, while the more common 1902 and 1905 models bring about half that. Colt autos with U.S. military test history will, of course, bring a considerable premium. Prices of Savage, Remington, Smith & Wesson, Harrington & Richardson, and other lesser-known U.S. pocket pistols have been stagnant, but Hi-Standard 22s have been moving upward slightly. Among the more common pre-WWI European semi-autos, Browning 1900s and 1903s, Frommer Stops, Roth Steyrs and Steyr-Hahns have all seen appreciation when in nice shape.

The rarities in early self-loaders continue to bring high to very high prices. Borchardts, Bergmanns, most Mannlichers, six- and twenty-shot Mausers, and the other limited-production handguns of that era start in the thousands and go rapidly upward. This is not a field for the fainthearted or those on a limited budget.

What's ahead for handgun collectors? At least for the short term, that depends heavily on next November's elections. If Clinton gets back in, he and his cohorts will continue their push to make gun purchase and ownership more difficult. However, though this may discourage some more fainthearted would-be collectors, it will only be an irritant to those of us serious about our passion for guns. If, on the other hand, next November sees another Republican sweep we can expect not only to be left alone for a while but may even see some relaxation of some more onerous current restrictions.

Thus, by and large, handgun collecting is still alive and healthy in 1996 and not a bad place to invest your money, if you do it wisely. Follow the prices at gun shows, auctions, gun shops, in the various "Guns for Sale" publications, and the better price guides such as the all-new tenth edition of *Modern Gun Values* from DBI Books. Remember that, except for the rarest of guns, choice condition is paramount. You'll have lots of fun, meet a lot of great people, learn a lot of history, and should actually see your investment appreciate while you enjoy it. ●

BLACKPOWDER SCENE

by MIKE VENTURINO

IN THESE PAGES last year I predicted that one type of blackpowder handgun which would experience great growth was the cartridge conversion. Such were the cap 'n ball percussion sixguns which, during the 1870s, were converted by both the original factories and independent gunsmiths so they could utilize the new metallic cartridges. I was right.

Currently there are two gunsmiths specializing in such conversions, and they are both very busy. From Spokane, Washington, there is John Gren whose specialty is converting the cap 'n ball percussion revolver you send to him. Another company doing this work is R&D Gun Repair of Beloit, Wisconsin. Headman there is Kenny Howell, whose shooting passion for most of his life has been the various cartridge conversion handguns. R&D will either convert the cap 'n ball revolver you send to them, or they will sell you one already made up.

Original calibers for the Colt cartridge conversions were four: 44 rimfire and centerfire, and 38 rimfire and centerfire. These modern cartridge conversions are not so limited. First of all, both of the above gunsmithing firms are offering conversions by two methods. One is with the barrel left with full inside diameter, which is the authentic way. That means the reloader must use cartridges loaded with heel-base bullets.

For examples of that type of bullet just look at any 22 Long Rifle cartridge. The other method, which is the modern way of doing things, is to reline the barrel down to modern diameters of .357-inch for 38s and .429-inch for 44s. This allows the reloader to use inside-lubed bullets as is standard in all modern handgun ammunition. This way, the gunsmiths can offer other calibers. Some that I have heard of being chambered in modern conversions, besides the traditional 38 Long Colt and 44 Colt, are 32-20, 32 S&W Long, 38 S&W and 45 S&W (in five-shot cylinders).

Interestingly, the Gren conversions in 38 Long Colt and 38 S&W are rated by the maker as being safe with smokeless factory loads in those calibers. However, the Gren conversions of larger caliber are marked "blackpowder only." All conversions marketed by R&D Gun Repair are for blackpowder cartridge shooting only.

However, not only independent gunsmiths are eyeing the cartridge conversion market. At the 1996 SHOT Show, a new company named American Frontier Firearms was displaying prototypes of several types of factory conversions which they say they will be importing from Italy. Those on display were Richards and Mason conversions of Colt-type cap 'n ball revolvers, and Remington conversions of the Model 1858 and

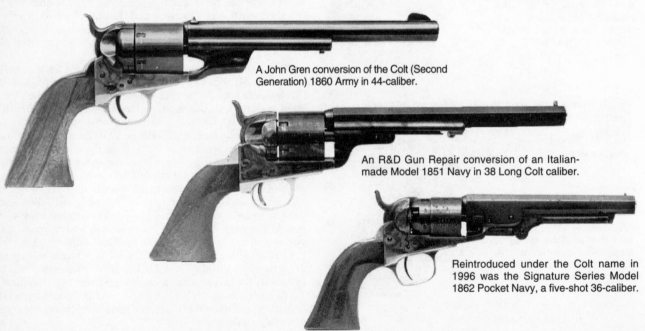

A John Gren conversion of the Colt (Second Generation) 1860 Army in 44-caliber.

An R&D Gun Repair conversion of an Italian-made Model 1851 Navy in 38 Long Colt caliber.

Reintroduced under the Colt name in 1996 was the Signature Series Model 1862 Pocket Navy, a five-shot 36-caliber.

The reason for the upswing in blackpowder handgun shooting is the great interest generated by Cowboy Action Shooting.

1863 44-caliber percussion revolvers. Calibers to be offered are 38 and 44 Specials.

A spinoff of the interest in cartridge-conversion revolvers is that both the American Frontier Firearms Co. and R&D Gun Repair have prototypes of the Colt Model 1871/1872 open-top revolver, and according to spokesmen for both companies, they will have guns to sell by late 1996 or early 1997. The Colt Model 1871/1872 Open Top was Colt's first revolver designed from the beginning to fire metallic cartridges. However, after testing, the U.S. military determined that they would prefer the revolver to have a topstrap for added strength. Colt offered the Model 1871/1872 only in 44 Henry rimfire caliber, and only a few thousand were produced. American Frontier Firearms will offer their Model 1871/1872 Open Tops in 38 and 44 Special calibers, while R&D plans for theirs to be chambered for 38 Special and for the 44 S&W American round, which is as close as a centerfire cartridge can get to the original 44 Henry caliber.

Another trend I see developing in the blackpowder handgun market is that of using both blackpowder and Pyrodex in reloading for cartridge-firing single-action revolvers. Spurred by the sport of Cowboy Action Shooting, interest in actually shooting revolvers (and copies thereof) from the late 1800s with ammunition close to that originally used is on the upswing.

Starline, the Missouri-based handgun brass manufacturer, in 1995 introduced cases for the long-discontinued 45 S&W (Schofield) cartridge. Naturally, much of this will be used for smokeless-powder reloading, but already Cowboy Action Shooters have realized that blackpowder loads put

into the 1.10-inch case of the 45 S&W cartridge (25 to 28 grains) are much milder than the 33 to 36 grains accommodated by the 1.29-inch case of the 45 Colt.

Also, it may be worthy to note that the first samples of Cimarron Arms' new Smith & Wesson Schofield replica have arrived on our shores and were on display at SHOT Show 1996. Differing from the Navy Arms version, which was made slightly longer in the frame to accommodate the 45 Colt case, the Cimarron Arms version has the same length frame as original S&W Schofields. However, their cylinders are as long as those of the Navy Arms and will also chamber 45 Colt cartridges. The way they managed this was to shorten the butt end of the barrel by about 1/8-inch. Cimarron Arms is also planning to make this revolver available in the original 45 S&W chambering, identical in every dimension to the original guns. With Starline's brass I'm sure many of these new Schofields will be fired with blackpowder or Pyrodex. I know mine will.

In the traditional cap 'n ball percussion-revolver arena, there is very little change. All basic models of Colt and Remington revolvers have been reproduced for many years and imported by many firms. Starting a couple of years back, Colt once again entered this market (if in name only) with their "Signature Series," called thusly because a fascimile of Sam Colt's signature is on the backstrap of every gun put out.

These "third generation" Colt cap 'n ball revolvers—as they are coming to be commonly called, to sort them from originals (first generation) and those made in the 1970s and '80s (second generation)—have been made in a wide variety of models and sub-versions from the huge Walker down to the 31-caliber Model 1849 Pocket. New for 1996 is a Whitneyville/Hartford Dragoon, which was a little-known transition between the Walker and the later 1st, 2nd, and 3rd Model Dragoons. Also in 1996 the five-shot, 36-caliber Model 1862 Pocket Navy was reintroduced, and also a stainless steel version of the 44-caliber Model 1860 Army, which should prove popular with shooters.

Aside from the new models introduced, standbys in the new Colt line are the Walker, Models 1851 and 1861 Navy 36s, the 3rd Model Dragoon, and the Model 1860 Army. Their accessory line now includes black leather holsters, belts, and cap boxes actually made by Bianchi, and a Stetson-made hat patterned after Civil War cavalry headgear.

Ruger is also eager for its share of the Cowboy Action Shooting market. Their long-produced Old Army with its adjustable sights was allowed only in Cowboy Action Shooting's modern class. Therefore, Ruger started equipping its Old Army with a traditional groove down the topstrap. This gun now qualifies for more of Cowboy Action Shooting's categories.

Interest in all the late-1800s revolvers is in a tremendous upswing, and I feel that part of the trend is a reaction to the synthetic modern autoloaders found so distasteful by many traditionalists. As things are shaping up in the handgun world, we will soon have a segment of ulta-modern autloading space-age handguns offset by just as large a trend toward traditionally styled single-action revolvers. Watching this happen is something I find extremely interesting. ●

AIR PISTOL SCENE

by J.I. GALAN

A LOT HAS been happening lately in the world of air pistols, most of it quite exciting. In fact, I cannot recall any other time when there were so many different air pistol models being produced by so many manufacturers. To illustrate the preceding, let me just mention that at the 1996 SHOT Show, for instance, I counted seventeen new air pistols being introduced by several companies, domestic and foreign. It seems as if everyone out there has suddenly discovered the potential of the air pistol market and is trying to claim a piece of the pie. Interestingly, while 1995 turned out to be a dismal year for sales of powder-burning handguns, air pistols enjoyed brisk sales at practically all levels, and the trend is, so far, continuing.

An increasing number of people are discovering how pleasurable it is to spend an afternoon plinking away in basement or backyard with an air pistol. Others have realized that some air pistols are ideal for training new shooters who might initially be intimidated by the loud bang and flash produced by most centerfire handguns. Air pistols generally allow for a more relaxed atmosphere when dealing with tyros, as I have personally experienced on many occasions. Even as a tool to help us stay sharp with personal defense handguns, air pistols have a great deal to offer, usually with a very modest cash outlay when compared with the cost of just a few boxes of centerfire handgun fodder.

The trend that I discussed in HANDGUNS '96 regarding the proliferation of air pistols that resemble specific firearms continues to grow. In recent months several new "firearm replica" air pistols have been unveiled by both domestic and foreign manufacturers. These new models join the already substantial variety of air- and CO_2-powered firearm clones available to consumers.

A bird's-eye view of these new air pistol models begins with, of all things, some *Russian* BB handguns imported by

Daisy's new Model 454 shoots BBs semi-automatically and has a blowback action powered by CO_2.

Walther sure surprised everyone with the introduction of the CP88 semi-auto pellet pistol, a replica of their own P88 combat "wondernine." The grips are in bright red, white and blue colors.

From Russia, with fun. Anics Firm, Inc., is marketing several interesting CO_2-powered BB handguns that appear to be very well made.

Anics Firm, Inc. This company displayed three basic models at the 1996 SHOT Show, each with a long-barreled version for those who would like a slightly more potent and more accurate BB handgun. Two models are semi-autos—one, a stunning copy of the S&W 6906 compact "wondernine"—with fifteen-shot BB magazines, while the third is a DA/SA wheelgun with capacity for thirty BBs in its cylinder. My initial impression of these CO_2-powered guns was that they are extremely well made, featuring mostly metal construction throughout. These pistols should be available by the time you read this.

Moving on to Germany, we find that the famous Walther company is now producing a CO_2-powered pellet semi-auto replica of their pricey P88 combat autoloader. As you might guess, this 177-caliber pistol is dubbed the CP88 and features an eight-shot rotary magazine—similar in many ways to that of the Crosman 1008 pistol—plus a choice of either a standard 4-inch barrel or a 6-inch barrel competition version. Either one looks and performs most impressively, indeed. The Walther CP88 is imported by Interarms.

The Spanish firm of Gamo (imported by Daisy Mfg. Co.) has also thrown its hat into the ring regarding cartridge-pistol look-alikes. Their first CO_2-powered model along those lines is the superb R-77 revolver. This compact 177-caliber pellet wheelgun has a $2^1/_2$-inch rifled barrel, swing-out cylinder and DA/SA operation. The sample I tested performed extremely well. There is no doubt that the Gamo R-77 is a first-class plinking gun, but its snubnose styling also makes it perfect for self-defense training applications.

Our home-grown air pistol makers have been busy, also. Crosman Airguns is introducing a pair of pure fun plinkers, called the Black Fang and Black Venom, that I predict will go over *big* with shooters of all ages. Although nearly identical in appearance and operation, these new spring-piston pistols have certain important differences. The Black Venom, for instance, is the more powerful of the two, producing a top muzzle velocity of 250 fps. It has a seventeen-shot BB magazine and the capability of shooting 177-caliber pellets as a single shot. The Black Fang produces muzzle velocity of 220

fps and works as a seventeen-shot BB repeater only. Both models are styled after the popular Colt 22 Target autoloader.

Crosman's direct competitor, the Daisy Mfg. Co., has also introduced two exciting new CO_2 semi-auto pistols under their Power Line logo, the Models 2003 and 454. The 2003 is fairly large and is Daisy's first handgun to employ that company's amazing thirty-five-shot helical pellet magazine. With a top muzzle velocity of around 400 fps and high-capacity magazine, the Daisy 2003 is a truly impressive performer. If you prefer shooting BBs instead, the new Daisy 454 is certain to please you. In addition to a twenty-shot magazine, this model features a most realistic blowback type of operation and a muzzle velocity of up to 420 fps. Although not "spittin' image" replicas of specific firearms, both of these pistols look entirely realistic in every way.

In the realm of more traditional-looking air pistols, there are a few recent entries out there. Walther, for instance, has the LP200 match pistol, a pre-charged pneumatic that can yield up to 500 shots from one filling of compressed air. Although expensive, this world-class 10-meter competition pistol is truly a "dream machine" capable of producing the hair-splitting accuracy required in international matches.

Hämmerli's 10-meter match air pistols are currently distributed by Sigarms, Inc. Following in the footsteps of their top-notch Model 480, Hämmerli has now introduced the Model 480K. The latter is a slightly lighter-weight version of the 480—a model that works with either compressed air or CO_2—designed to work with compressed air only. Both models come loaded with the features that Olympic-grade shooters want and appreciate.

Some long-popular models refuse to fade away and are, in fact, given a face lift of sorts in order to boost their appeal as the competition becomes stiffer. Such is the case with the Beeman Precision Airguns HW70. This traditional-style spring-piston air pistol has been a good seller since its introduction some twenty-one years ago. Beeman's "Midnight Series" version of this Weihrauch-made pistol is dubbed the HW70S and sports an attractive silver finish combined with a new, stylized black grip. In addition, the HW70S incorporates a snazzy silencer-like muzzle extension that doubles as a cocking handle. All in all, the Beeman HW70S earns top marks as a really sharp-looking air pistol in the best German tradition.

Not to be outdone by Beeman, Dynamit Nobel-RWS has given their ever-popular RWS Model 5G spring-piston pistol—made by Dianawerk in Germany—a similar treatment, with a matte nickel finish on the action contrasting beautifully with black grips. This new version is called the 5GN, and I suspect that it will enhance this basic model's already impressive track record with its elegant new look.

Space constraints, unfortunately, prevent a more detailed look at the entire picture of the contemporary air pistol. As things stand right now, I fully expect to see an ever-growing variety of air pistols making their debut in the near future. Even if we discount totally the ever-present threat of more restrictive legislation on firearms as a reason for air pistols to gain even more popularity in the long run, the many practical advantages offered by air pistols in this hectic, crowded world certainly paint a most optimistic picture. ●

WOMEN'S SELF-DEFENSE SCENE

by PAXTON QUIGLEY

"WHEN I MARRIED, my husband had a number of handguns in the house and I felt OK, but after we had our first child I was too afraid to have guns around. Now the children are older and with crime all around us, we decided to have a gun in the house for protection. I don't know if we should show them the gun or whether we should take them to the range so that they can see the damage a gunshot can do." Phyllis, one of those attending my "Personal Protection Strategies" seminar for Junior League members and their daughters, explained her indecision.

I've heard this so often that I've come to understand people's apprehensions about guns in the house where there are children or grandchildren. There is always a risk in owning a gun, just as there is a calculated danger in having sharp knives, cleaning fluids, and medicine on hand. As with all potentially harmful products, care must be taken in their storage, and instructions given as to their potential for injury.

Easy to say, I know. But for a mother, not so simple to do. Having a gun for personal protection and still keeping it safe from children is a big concern. The safer the gun is—that means an unloaded gun—the less ready it is for emergency use when you need it. Conversely, the quicker you can pull the trigger, the more chance for a mishap. An unloaded gun that is perfectly safe is perfectly useless. I told Phyllis that if she really wanted to have a gun available for that just-in-case situation, she and her husband needed to make some changes in their home and lifestyle.

Since 51 percent of all American households possess at least one firearm, it is not unreasonable to assume that many, many children in this country have been taught gun safety and are coexisting comfortably with the risks and benefits of gun ownership.

From the onset, make it clear to your youngsters that they are never to handle a real gun when you are not with them, and, of course, never to point even a toy gun at anyone. At the same time, tell them if they want to handle—not play—with a gun in your presence, they will be allowed to do so.

Teach your kids the rules of gun safety as early as possible. The most important are:
• Treat every gun as if it is loaded.

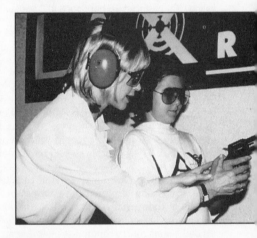

The author believes that gun-proofing your children is ultimately better than child-proofing your guns. Proper instruction at the right age can instill a sense of respect for firearms in youths that they will carry all their lives.

• Never point a gun at anything you don't intend to destroy.
• Keep your finger off the trigger until you're ready to shoot.
• Be sure of your target.

If you or a friend are thinking about having a gun in the house, there is a lot to consider. But if you've been fairly well organized in life and are a responsible adult, then the changes to be made are really not that difficult or time-consuming.

Loaded or Unloaded

The decision to keep a gun loaded and ready for use should only be made after a thorough appraisal of the risks and advantages involved. Here are some of the things that I've learned in years of considering the subject.

First, make no mistake, loading a gun in the face of danger, adrenaline pumping, is no easy task. According to all police authorities and shooting experts, fear and panic render your arms and legs a lot less dependable than they normally are.

You can experience some of the lack of motor coordination under stress yourself, at home, by doing the following exercise. Place an unloaded gun on a table, and put brass (for safety reasons, don't use live ammunition) on the other side of the table. Have a friend give you the signal to load and then time you. This will in no way simulate the stress of a real crisis, but you will clearly see how clumsy you can become from the mere pressure of being timed.

If you own a revolver, you may counter by saying that you use speed-loaders, which make loading far easier. Yes, but if you don't *practice* speed-loading, and practice *in the dark,* it can be difficult under extreme pressure.

Because of these adrenaline-induced constraints, I've come to the conclusion that if you can *safely secure* your gun (and more on that later), you're reasonably entitled to consider keeping it loaded. Years ago, while writing *Armed & Female,* I felt differently and said that ". . .your gun should be loaded only when you are at home, and if, for example, you come home at night and load your gun and then decide to leave, you should unload it and safely secure it again."

I've changed my position based on practical experience. I now realize that most people don't necessarily focus on their handguns during their normal comings and goings and simply won't take the time to unload and load their guns. However, I have still not altered my stance on unloading a gun and safely securing it if you're going away for an extended period of time and not taking it with you. You wouldn't want your gun in the hands of a burglar, who more than likely would sell it on the black market—to only God knows who.

Securing Your Gun

There are a plethora of trigger locks on the market, but frankly, the one I've found that works the best for most semi-automatics and revolvers is the Saf-T-Lok. It works without batteries or keys, can be installed with a screwdriver and becomes an integral part of your handgun. A child or thief can't remove it without doing serious damage to the gun.

Fitting the Saf-T-Lok is a matter of removing the grips and screwing on a mounting plate, lock and special rubber custom grips. The operating mechanism—three small tabs and a reset button—is positioned at the grip top where your thumb can brush the tabs downward to the correct number of clicks (your own combination) to release the lock. The 999 possible combinations go a long way toward preventing a child from accidentally firing your handgun, and render it useless to a thief. Saf-T-Lok prices range from $119 to $149 depending on the make of the gun.

Another tried-and-true lock for a revolver is the old stand-by padlock still used by many law enforcement officials. Just place it in the trigger guard behind the trigger and your gun is secure from most children. It will, of course, require your key before even you can use it.

Many people prefer to store their handguns in a portable safe. My favorites are the Fast-Access MiniVaults (for one gun) or the Fast-Access MultiVaults (two guns). These battery-operated durable safes are made of 16-gauge steel and look very presentable. To open, slide your fingers along the contoured grooves, locate the correct buttons using the Braille-like dots, and enter your private security code. If your child gives it a try, the built-in computer will block access after five wrong attempts. The unit mounts vertically or upside-down, so you can have it under your bed for easy access without the lid popping open and the gun falling out. The Fast-Access MiniVault retails for $159.95. The larger one costs $199.95.

Gun Vault Co.'s Fast-Access MiniVault lets you keep your gun out of the wrong hands, yet you can get at it quickly by punching your personal code into the buttons on top. The vault can be mounted in a variety of positions or carried with you.

Predetermining a Family Code System

If you have a loaded weapon in your home and family members are coming in at night while you're asleep, I strongly recommend that you set up a code system so that you will never, *ever* mistake your child or spouse for an intruder. Let's say that your teenager returns home at 1 a.m. Rather than be quiet when entering, he should be instructed to awaken you and yell out a code word or phrase that you've agreed upon in advance. Following this simple procedure can help avoid confusion when you're awakened by footsteps or noise.

Teaching Children About Guns

As Massad Ayoob says, instead of childproofing guns, you must gunproof children. Just how do you gunproof your children, and when? Although it may sound radical at first, the ideal strategy is to show your children how your gun operates while you're cleaning it, and then, later, to take them to a range and show them how to use it. Once a child understands how a gun operates, has heard the sound of a gunshot, and has witnessed the potential damage, he or she will have a much different view of a gun. They'll consider them with newfound respect and a sense of caution.

At what age should children be educated about guns? There is really no hard and fast rule, but most gun instructors say that a good barometer of responsibility is the care of the family pet. A child who is responsible enough to handle the feeding, medication and cleaning chores for cats or dogs is a child who will probably be trustworthy with guns. Of course, there are some children (as well as some adults) who are emotionally unstable and should never handle a gun.

Dr. Richard Blasband, a former member of the teaching staff of the Department of Psychiatry at Yale University and currently in private practice, says that the average, mentally and emotionally healthy child may be safely introduced to the operation of small firearms between the ages of seven and twelve. In most cases in our society, I'd say between ten and twelve is best.

"This is the time that the child acquires the ability to mentally transform information about the real world so that it can be organized and used selectively in the solution of problems. This means that the child has progressed from the ability to perform simple actions or goal-directed behavior to operations where certain actions are bound up with others in an integrated structure," explains Blasband. "By this age, the average, mentally healthy child will be able to readily differentiate between fantasy and reality and therefore know what a gun is, what it can do, and can integrate this knowledge with other internalized information and be responsible for it."

I recently introduced my nephew, age ten, to my handgun while I was cleaning it with a new, non-smelling environmentally safe cleaner, called MP-7. He happened to be at my home and I knew that he was interested in guns and knew that I taught handgun shooting. It was a perfect time to safely show him the gun, and also teach him how to clean one. Our next step will be to go to the range, but only after I've talked with his parents and received their approval.

When you feel that your children are mature enough to see what happens when a gun is fired, take them to an outdoor shooting range or other outdoor safe area and equip them with eye and ear protection. I recommend the following exercise, which is graphic and gets the point across. Place a cantaloupe or other type of melon on a box about seven yards away and have your kids watch you fire a round (preferably a hollowpoint, because it is more damaging) into it. If you're on target, the melon will be blown off the box and badly shattered, its juice and insides gushing out. With your children, examine the incredible destruction and locate where the bullet entered and exited. Since a melon is similar in size to a human head, you can easily explain what would really happen if a person were shot with just one bullet. This lesson is *critical*, because most children believe that a bullet only makes a small hole in the body, like in the thousand or more shootings they see every year on TV. You may frighten your youngsters with this exercise, but if it takes a little fear to gain respect for a gun, it is well worth doing it.

When your children want to shoot, your next step is some kind of proper instruction. You can, of course, do your own teaching. You might also consider contacting a local NRA club that offers a firearms familiarization program or Junior Rifle courses in which your kids can shoot with a team. For nonathletic kids, this is an excellent way to learn the meaning of teamwork and the excitement of competition.

But your kids don't have to be target shooters for you to gunproof them. What they need to know, through your own gun-safety practice and instruction, is that guns are dangerous and should be treated with great respect. If they are trained, your concern will not be that your children may take your gun, but, in a world where every second house contains a gun, that your son or daughter may be in another child's home and that child may irresponsibly take the family gun out of a drawer or a closet.

I strongly advise that you make absolutely clear to your children that, if they are visiting someone's home and see a firearm, short or long, they are to leave that house immediately and inform you of what happened. If I were you, I would also telephone the parents and tell them of your child's experience.

I have spoken to a number of children who know how to shoot. One such boy is Jonathan Spencer, who calls himself a cyberspace whiz. When he was ten, his parents signed him up for a computer course; today, at fifteen, he is developing his own programs.

Also when he was ten, his parents took him to a shooting

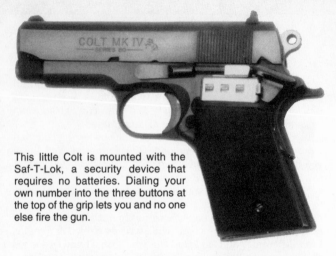

This little Colt is mounted with the Saf-T-Lok, a security device that requires no batteries. Dialing your own number into the three buttons at the top of the grip lets you and no one else fire the gun.

range to teach him gun safety. Not at all interested in guns, Jonathan didn't want to know about them, but his parents insisted on it after a series of robberies in their Dallas, Texas, neighborhood. The senior Spencers had just purchased a Smith & Wesson Model 686 and were practicing when they became concerned about Jonathan's safety with a loaded gun in the house.

Jonathan enrolled in a series of Saturday-afternoon gun safety classes especially designed for children. To this day, Jonathan recalls the first time he watched his instructor shooting at a filled half-gallon plastic Coca-Cola bottle, exploding it with one shot. That was lesson number one. "We all looked at this messed-up bottle and it was awesome! I knew that guns were incredible, because I've watched a lot of television, but I didn't know what one bullet could do. On TV or in the movies, the bad guy falls down, and then Arnold Schwarzenegger is on to the next shooting," said the exuberant teenager.

Before any of the students even touched a gun in the class, they were drilled in the rules of safety, which Jonathan still remembers today, repeating them to me as if he were reciting the Ten Commandments.

Months later during a tell-a-story assignment at school, Jonathan gave a twenty-minute talk on gun safety and his experience in learning how to shoot a gun. He used charts from the gun club that illustrated the various parts of a handgun, and ended by distributing gun-safety pamphlets. Afterward, a number of his classmates told him that their parents also had guns in their homes and they, too, wanted to sign up for the Saturday gun classes. For his work, Jonathan got an A+.

Finally, as responsible adults, wherever your guns are in the house, make absolutely certain that they are safely secured so your children and their friends will not handle them unless you want them to. As far as your children are concerned, gun safety is *your* responsibility! ●

About the Author

Best-selling author Paxton Quigley is a spokesperson for Smith & Wesson as well as an instructor of safety strategies, primarily for women. She has appeared on more than 300 radio and TV shows, including *60 Minutes*, and has been widely quoted in major newspapers.

EUROPEAN SCENE

by JAN STEVENSON

IT IS NOT the best of times for European gunmakers. With its primary export market, the United States, saturated from three years of panic buying, the home market asphyxiated by oppressive legislation, the defence market demobbed with the end of the Cold War, and in a world awash with surplus small arms, the European firearms industry could scarcely find itself in less propitious circumstances. The results are as you would expect: tens of thousands of gunmakers out of work in Oberndorf, two-thirds of the workforce in the Spanish handgun industry facing the ax, and the mighty Fabrique Nationale of Belgium reduced to a skeleton operation.

But adversity breeds inspiration, desperate times call for desperate measures, and the result is a profusion of new designs, as manufacturers dispute niche markets or, indeed, resort to novelty in the expectation that anything new will attract a few curiosity sales, and that a few sales beat no sales.

Competitive target shooting is a refuge from the vagaries of the defence market, and many firms try to maintain a presence there. Target shooting consists of a host of specialized niche markets, each of them tiny and hard to please but, on the other hand, steady, comparatively reliable and willing to pay a premium.

The most buoyant of these segments is Practical and Action Shooting where the past two years have seen a rush of new models to market. These consist on the one hand of service pistols gussied up for the target circuit and, on the other, of purebred match machines as the heavyweight names of Olympic or UIT shooting like Pardini, FAS and Walther venture into this new arena.

The problem is that equipment for these games—particularly Practical—is very much a matter of fashion and the fashions, for the most part, are set in the U.S. None of the European makers has devoted more time and resources to trying to buy a slice of fashion in this area than Tanfoglio, the Italian makers of IPSC-approved competition pistols based on the CZ75. At the 10th World Championships at Bisley in 1993, Doug Koenig took 2nd in Open class while Brian Enos was 2nd in Standard, each shooting a Tanfoglio. Tanfoglios still trail a perhaps outdated reputation for parts breakage,

Heckler & Koch's USP is the new Bundeswehr P8 and is distinguished in that guise by a hammer-trip thumblever that stays on "safe" and has to be clicked upward before it will fire. Of general Browning layout, with a polymer frame and a PetersStahl unlocking cam, it is a very tough and reliable pistol.

but they have had a lot of engineering attention lavished upon them and we have always been impressed by the level of workmanship. Thirteen permutations of their basic model are offered—out of the box—with everything allowed in the Stock, Standard and Open classes, with 9mm Parabellum, 40 S&W, 38 Super, 10mm and 45 ACP the calibres on offer. There is also an extensive selection of ex-factory "custom" replacement parts.

Pardini, the maker of world-class UIT pistols, created a stir last year when their PC series was announced in Stock and Open formats. Giampiero Pardini, the firm's founder and himself a top-ranking UIT shot, had plainly put a lot of expertise into these guns: they reeked points-grubbing sophistication. The one aspect that is likely to arouse a mixed

EUROPEAN

response is the grip angle of 25 degrees, which is quite a bit steeper than the 13 degrees of the 1911, which most Practical shooters are trained to. Now, at any rate, they have a choice.

Matching Pardini on the sophistication front is the Delta Top Gun from FAS (ex-IGI-Domino, of UIT fame) which offers all the fine adjustments to trigger pull of which practitioners of the Olympic disciplines are so fond. Versions are offered in both steel and aluminium frames, with single- or double-column magazines, in 9x21mm, 40 S&W or 45 ACP. Curiously, 9x19 is not offered, even in the defence model. The Top Gun is roller locked, with an action based on the Czech M1952 service pistol, and the manufacturer extols the virtues of straight-line recoil, with the barrel never deviating from its axis. The pistol we examined was a prototype, with deliveries expected by mid-year. This will definitely be one to watch.

Meanwhile, the famous FAS Standard Pistol, on which the firm's fame rests, was reengineered two years ago to a modular concept which has made it almost as much fun to take apart as it is to shoot. FAS fans will be relieved to know that the famous internal magazine, inserted through the ejection port, was undisturbed in the redesign. Joining the Model 607 22 LR and 603 32 Long to complete the UIT trilogy is the Model 608 in 22 Short for Rapid Fire, expected soon.

Back to Practical pistols, one of the most impressive, to our mind, is the Bernardelli Practical VB, the latest iteration of their service P1, best described as a double-action, double-column descendent of the SIG P210, with a cocked-and-locked safety right where it belongs. Machined from forgings and meticulously fitted, the P1 is a wonderful pistol. I bought serial number 3 when it was first introduced, and shall be tempted to do likewise with the new VB or P1 Sport, which comes in nine variations. Calibres are 9x19, 9x21 and 40 S&W.

Practically every manufacturer now has a competition version of the firm's service pistol: Walther with the P88 Competition, SIG-Sauer with comp versions of the P226, and Beretta with the Model 92, 98 and 96 Stock and Combat Competition models. When the original Model 92 was introduced in 1975, it carried a 1911-type cocked-and-locked safety and Beretta has incorporated an improved version on the new series. But one is obliged to wonder how interested some of the other manufacturers are in this particular market, which is going to warm neither to a hammer-trip (SIG-Sauer) which forces a double-action first shot, nor to a gun that is only available in 9x19mm (Walther).

Resolutely single action, of course, is the Llama derivative of the Colt-Browning pistol, of which the Basque gunmakers this year have introduced no fewer than eleven new versions, most targeted at one or another categories of Practical Pistol. None of them is likely to make much headway in the U.S. or, for that matter, the rest of Europe where, rightly or wrongly, Spanish gunmaking is still shaded by a cloud of distrust. Hopefully, they will find a better reception in the firm's traditional markets in Latin America, Africa and the East.

Nearby in Eibar, Star Bonifaccio Echeverria are staying well to the fore of handgun fashion and technology with their second polymer-framed model under development. The prototype I examined is easily described as a SIG-Sauer P226 with a polymer frame. At a glance, the fabricated slide seemed identical to that on the Swiss/German pistol and another glance revealed no conspicuous changes to the firing mechanism. I am sure it will be an excellent pistol, but it failed to enchant, particularly since Star already has a polymer 9mm in the line that I like a great deal. This is their 9mm Model 205 Ultrastar, the last design by Eduardo

Iraegui who recently retired as Star's chief designer after thirty years of service. A polymer consultant was brought in to make sure that the frame was right in every respect, but the guts and layout reflect Iraegui's decades of experience. It is a neat gun.

Any mention of neat plastic pistols conjures the new Walther P-99, scheduled for production in three months as this is written, with delivery early in 1997. It is the most recent of the polymer generation of battle pistols, and comes with an outstanding pedigree, having been designed by Horst Wesp and his assistant, Peter Dallhammer. Wesp was thirty-four years in the design bureau of Steyr-Daimler-Puch (later Steyr-Mannlicher) where he was largely responsible for the famous Steyr AUG—the polymer assault rifle—before moving to Glock in 1992 as senior engineer with responsibility, it was said, for "trouble shooting."

After a decade of whittling on the P-38 (P-38K, P-5, etc.) and another decade of toying with the P-88 before deciding that perhaps it really did not have much of a future, it was past time that Walther got organized if it intended staying in the military and police markets. Bringing in Wesp to head a small and tightly focused defence design team was the response and the P-99 is the result.

The P-99 was designed to German police parameters so as to be in position to replace the now aging generation of sidearms (Walther P-5, SIG-Sauer P-6 and Heckler & Koch P-7) adopted in 1978. It came too late for consideration for adoption by German special forces, but will make every effort to capture the 250,000-gun balance of the Bundeswehr contract when that comes up for tender in the near future.

Heckler & Koch of Oberndorf (now British owned) won the first tranche with the USP (adopted as the P-8), an excellent gun. Capitalizing on it, however, will require managerial direction which at present is lacking. H&K's newly appointed chief executive resigned after half a year and has not been replaced. The firm has been headless for months.

Scarcely headless, and keen to capitalize on the reputation earned for them in the West by their legendary CZ75, whose availability in Europe had American shooters clawing at the Iron Curtain for a decade, Ceskoslovenska Zbrojovka will be a contender in any market open to them. Their polymer-framed CZ100, of which I examined serial number 2, is expected to ship in two months; a reduced capacity version with a single-column magazine will be available six months later.

Three variations to the steel-framed classic—the CZ75BD with a decocking lever, the CZ75 Police with the decocker and a loaded-chamber indicator and the CZ75 DAO—reinforce the impression that the famous Czech gunmakers will henceforth be contesting Western administrative contracts. If so, the historic excellence of their products combined with a post-Communist, backs-to-the-wall ability to bid low will no doubt cause some anxiety in the trade. For competitive shooters, the sophisticated CZ75 Champion is also worth a close look. All except the compact versions of this extensive family of handguns are available in 9x19, 9x21 and 40 S&W.

Yet another firm to prosper on the backs of the Czechs (we have mentioned Tanfoglio's CZ75 clones, but have not yet mentioned John Slough of London, who makes the rock-solid Spitfire, nor Manurhin of Alsace, who makes the elegant Sphinx in Switzerland) is, as we were saying, Israeli Military Industries, whose Jericho series has achieved an extraordinary popularity in Great Britain, at least. There is nothing fancy about them—they just shoot extremely well and are keenly priced and, with the introduction of new compact models, now form an extensive range.

Steyr-Mannlicher could do with something like that, for their line is currently bereft of anything credibly definable as a service pistol, a remarkable lacuna for the makers of the immensely successful AUG. They do have Friedrich Aignev's

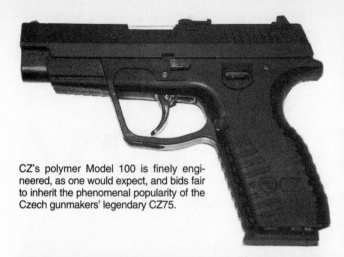

CZ's polymer Model 100 is finely engineered, as one would expect, and bids fair to inherit the phenomenal popularity of the Czech gunmakers' legendary CZ75.

Star's latest in the polymer stakes is the prototype M260 at top, based on the SIG-Sauer P220 series. Author prefers the M205 Ultrastar underneath it: a neat piece of gunmaking that reflects the designer's thirty years of experience.

SPP—a buttless SMG which may have an application in some operational rôles, but is furlongs from meeting *Pflichtenheft*—or anybody else's—dimensional maxima for a holster gun.

Doubtless, they will get to it. Meanwhile, the great Austrian arms maker is poised to make waves in UIT circles with their new Model FP free pistol. Designed by Emil Senfter, the FP is a tour de force on every front. It is visually striking, technically impeccable, incorporates a real competitive advantage and lends itself to economic manufacture (hence a worthwhile margin of profit).

The novelty, as will be immediately apparent, is the bore line, which is a prolongation of the forearm bone, eliminating pre-departure muzzle lift. Whether this advantage will be offset by enhanced canting error (due to the greater distance between the line of sight and the bore axis) remains to be seen. Suffice it that Free Pistol shooters will pay to find out.

Their willingness will be enhanced by the fact that Senfter's (hence Steyr's) UIT credentials are well established. It is hard to see that his Model LP1CP 10-metre air pistol is significantly better than, say, Hämmerli's or Walther's, but it wins and wins at the top levels of competition, recently and notably the gold medal at the Barcelona Olympics. Due for introduction soon is a five-shot semi-automatic repeating version, the LP5CP, a superlative Rapid Fire trainer for which dedicated competitions no doubt will follow. I have seen an East European prototype on similar principles which will give it a hard run commercially.

If Steyr-Mannlicher is known worldwide, another Austrian firm, Ultramatic, aspires to be. Their first product, a 45 Practical comp gun, is about to ship after eight traumatic years of development. The designers, Franz Gabriel and Max Vojta, went bankrupt after the tenth prototype, and the design was bought from the creditor banks by Monica Wolfe and Karl Rejlek, who risk a similar fate, having invested a reported $5 million in bringing the design to production.

The Ultramatic is nothing if not dedicated, and the gun intrigues. It looks like a beefy 1911 and functions like an MG42 machine gun on a delayed blowback, roller-retarded system. It operates on the billiard ball principle: the case head impacts the breech face, which does not move, but the knock-on effect impulses a floating bar inside the breechblock rearward, allowing the locking rollers to retract. The barrel is fixed and serves as the recoil spring guide. The spring is compressed by a collar which is coupled to the breechblock by a tie bar which lies above the barrel in a groove in the roof of the barrel housing.

The makers claim that, by virtue of the fixed barrel, very light breechblock, and weight distribution, the gun is extraordinarily fast cycling, reliable and scarcely lifts at all in recoil. The prototype we had in hand felt quite good, and may deliver on its promises. The Ultramatic will be available in the U.S. from Lew Horton distributors.

With the exception of Britain, as is well known, Europe pretty well dumped revolvers as soon as the self-loading pistol was perfected early in this century. In France, however, the wheelgun enjoyed a remarkable renaissance at the end of the 1960s when de Gaulle's head of personal protection returned from Quantico preaching the FBI gospel. The gun he selected for elite elements of the French National Police was later introduced by Smith & Wesson as the Model 13. Manurhin, with an expanding market clearly in view, soon introduced their MR73, which was then, and still is, one of the finest revolvers made. Next year will see the introduction of a new revolver by the same makers, latching at the crane, with a short action and a rather steeply raked grip. The object is to reduce manufacturing cost without sacrificing quality or performance. We have no fears on the latter points. ●

Note: Since this report was written, Britain has been traumatized by the Dunblane disaster, in which sixteen pupils and their teacher were massacred by an armed madman at a Scottish primary school on the 13th of March. A copycat incident in Tasmania shortly thereafter rocked Australia, and the shooting communities in both countries are now fighting for their very existence. In Britain, where firearms of all sorts have long been strictly controlled, the police are campaigning vigorously for a prohibition of all pistols (except for single shot 22-caliber free pistols), of all rifles (except for single shots) and of all magazine-fed shotguns.

In the wake of the disaster, the government set up a public inquiry under Lord Cullen, a leading Scottish jurist, and much will depend on the recommendations of his report, expected in September. The battle will then move to Westminster, when Parliament reconvenes the month following. All of the opposition political parties have made submissions to the Cullen inquiry supporting, or going beyond, the police agenda. The governing Conservative party has taken no position, but the Home Office submission was clearly calculated to bolster the police demands without actually saying so.

American shooters would do well to take note of the tide of authoritarianism sweeping many of the old democracies, and redouble their commitment to defend their Second Amendment liberties, along with all the others.

[*Editor's note: Mr. Stevenson personally wrote and submitted a 33,000-word body of evidence to Lord Cullen's Inquiry.*]

ACCESSORY SCENE
by DICK WILLIAMS

THE GOOD NEWS is also the bad news: there is a plethora (I love that word) of handgun accessories on the market today. You can outfit your shootin' iron with just about anything you can imagine, but you must choose from myriad offerings. Which means you need to weigh your needs and wants against the products available or you'll never be able to make a selection. To help make this part of the review process manageable, we will look at only three major categories of accessories on the market: holsters, scopes (not including beam projection devices) and grips. We'll focus on the major trends in these three areas and not cover every item listed in catalogs.

Holsters

Holsters are probably the easiest to start with because there's a clear and dominant trend. The CCW laws being passed in states across the nation have generated an interest and need for concealed-carry holsters in a whole new segment of society. Civilians who have never really examined the difficulties and discomforts of carrying a gun hidden on their person for hours on end are now facing the realities of keeping a weapon readily available for self-protection. Compounding the problem is the vast differences in body shapes of human beings. It isn't just the difference between men and women, it's differences in height, weight, and configuration of individuals of the same sex. Throw in the amount of clothing worn in differing climates, and the problem is anything but simple to solve.

You can start by asking questions of whomever teaches the qualification or training classes that allow you to obtain a CCW. He or she may not want to steer you toward a specific brand or model, but if they carry, they can certainly address some of the generalities and get you evaluating the right criteria for your needs. Many of the personnel who work in retail gun stores where you'll be shopping for a holster carry a handgun, at least for the eight hours they are in the store, and should be able to help. Meanwhile, let's look at some basics with pros and cons.

The simplest approach is the strong-side hip carry. This puts the gun as close to your dominant hand as you can get it. The holster can be worn either hanging outside your pants or slipped inside them. Some outside-the-pants holsters have a flare-shaped paddle that tucks inside; others can be slipped inside your pants and have a clip that goes over the belt to secure them.

Chris Endersby, president of *ON TARGET* indoor shooting range, with a Tasco Propoint on a Springfield 9x25 Dillon.

My favorite on-belt, outside-pants holster is Bianchi's leather Avenger. It rides high, allowing easy access to the gun without your snagging a handful of clothes on the draw. The holster is formed to the gun, which means it will retain the weapon without a safety strap and stay open for reholstering, a serious but often overlooked consideration. For me, it's a very comfortable rig to carry concealed, but I'm kind of an ectomorph with love handles and a bit of a beer gut. In addition to the basic wide, leather back through which the belt must be threaded, there is a slot at the rear of the holster. If the belt is also threaded through it, it causes the gun butt to pull in tight to the body. This minimizes the "print" of the gun through an outer garment, but you still have the bottom part of the holster exposed to view as you do with any external-carry rig.

For the same carry position using a paddle inside the pants, I'm very partial to the Safariland Open Top Paddle holster. It has a tension adjustment screw and a pair of leather "ears" that cover the rear sides of the slide to protect the clothes (and any body bulges) from abrasions or wear caused by things like ambidextrous safeties. It's also very quick for access and carries comfortably on me. I used both the Bianchi and Safariland holsters in a recent three-day class with Louis Awerbuck at the Yavapai Firearms Acad-

JoAnne Conn with Ruger 41 Magnum, Tasco scope, shoulder holster from Never-Summer Ranch and an almost-ready-to-eat javelina.

Galco's SOB (small of back) holster with Model 1911.

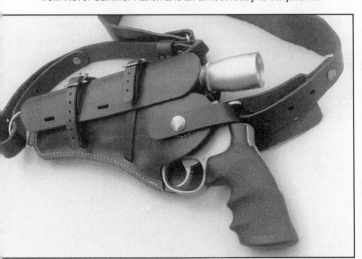

Hunter leather holster for scoped revolvers can be had in shoulder or belt-carry version.

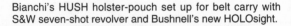
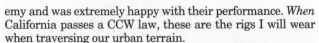

Bianchi's HUSH holster-pouch set up for belt carry with S&W seven-shot revolver and Bushnell's new HOLOsight.

emy and was extremely happy with their performance. *When California passes a CCW law, these are the rigs I will wear when traversing our urban terrain.*

I've also been trying one of Galco's inside the pants holsters, called the Royal Guard, to see how it works with full-size semi-autos, specifically the 1911 and Browning Hi-Power. Folks at Galco say this system works quite well for people with love handles (surely they weren't talking about me). Actually, the holster is quite gentle on love handles, carrying the entire gun quite low relative to the belt line with only the gun handle exposed for the draw. The advantage here is that the pants break up the outline of the lower gun and there is no leather exposed to view below the belt line. The rig is comfortable, offers good access to the gun's grip, and is stiff enough to keep the holster top open for an easy, no-look return to leather.

Galco also has a unique holster called the SOB which is worn on the rear of the belt in the small of the back. These are selling quite well, especially to women, since it takes the gun off the hip and avoids the difficulties that type of carry

ACCESSORY

can cause the female shape. It does bulge when the wearer is seated, but if there is a back to the chair in which you're seated, the bulge becomes more of a comfort than a concealability issue. Downside is the increased difficulty of access, particularly in a seated position in a car, but that may be an acceptable tradeoff.

Pancake holsters and abbreviated "slide"-type holsters are also offered for concealed carry. If the pancakes are stiff enough to maintain the holster opening when the gun is removed, the long distance between belt slots tends to straighten the belt for several inches, causing a bulge and some discomfort. If the pancake is soft enough that it can be pulled in close to the body by the belt, it is very comfortable, but the holster top will tend to close, making it difficult to reholster the gun using only one hand. Slide holsters provide a simple carry system with a minimum amount of leather, but they don't offer protection to clothes and body from any sharp edges, like the front sight, on the protruding muzzle end of the gun.

Many of the holster companies are heavily into the law enforcement market, and much of the police gear, including a number of concealed-carry rigs, is made from synthetic materials. Some materials in some applications, such as ballistic nylon in ankle holsters and fanny packs, may offer you advantages over leather. The only new holster material this year is Uncle Mike's Nytek, a leather look-alike made from bonded nylon fibers. I had a chance to "touchie-feelie" at the SHOT Show, but have not actually worked with it yet. The material looked extremely interesting, and I'm eager to try it later this year, both in concealed-carry applications and in the handgun hunting arena.

Speaking of handgun hunting, this is an area that seems to be growing in interest, but is extremely difficult to quantify. Other hunting sports have separate seasons or licenses that indicate the number of participants, like archery hunting tags. Handgun hunters have to hunt in the long-gun seasons,

so there is no breakdown from Fish & Game departments of who hunted with what weapons. This makes it difficult for the major holster companies to determine the value of using limited development dollars to pursue "niche" marketing items. Talking to marketing as well as R&D personnel indicated that several companies are "looking at the handgun [hunting] market," but aren't committing to specific efforts. Uncle Mike's has said they hope to have a belt holster for scoped handguns in the near future; perhaps made of the new Nytek?

As of today, Hunter makes a scoped-handgun holster in leather, for either over-the-shoulder or belt carry, but not interchangeable. Bianchi's HUSH nylon rig handles scoped handguns and can be carried over the shoulder or detached from the padded carry strap and worn on a belt for hip carry. I'm not a big believer in a "universal" anything, but I did use the Bianchi as a hip holster to carry two different S&W revolver/scope rigs for several days of javelina hunting, and was impressed with the holster's comfort and versatility.

Both Michaels' and Bianchi's over-the-shoulder holsters will work with various scoped handguns, but both are bulky and more cumbersome and padded than a shoulder holster needs to be. The best handgun hunting rig for large scoped single shots I've ever used was designed by fellow handgun hunter and writer Phil Briggs in the late 1980s, and is now being manufactured in limited quantities in Montana by Never-Summer Ranch Enterprises for a very reasonable price. Phil and I wore the holster/harness assemblies all day, every day, in total comfort for two weeks on an African hunt. It is made of ballistic nylon thick enough to offer adequate protection to gun and hunter, but thin enough to wear almost concealed by a tall person wearing a light jacket.

Optics

Two developments in optics have caught my attention over the last year. Brand-spanking new at the '96 SHOT Show was Bushnell's holographic sight. It won't give you a free-standing hologram of Princess Leia from *Star Wars*, but the HOLOsight does present interesting sight pictures on sever-

Weaver's Qwik-Point red-dot scope with variable dot-size selector.

Bushnell's new HOLOsight on seven-shot S&W 357 Magnum revolver.

Shown are various popular accessories (from left): Ruger's Redhawk 44 with Pachmayr rubber finger-groove grips and 2x Leupold pistol scope; Horton S&W Performance Center's 44 Magnum with Hogue rubber finger-groove, square-butt grips; and Freedom Arms' Field Grade 357 Magnum with rubber Pachmayr grips and 4x Leupold pistol scope.

(Below) Desert Eagle 44 Magnum with Hogue grips, interchangeable barrels, and Simmons dot scope.

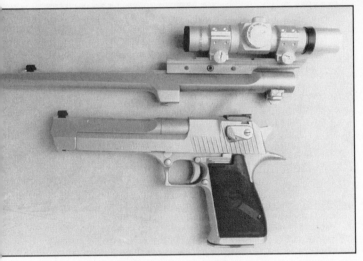

al different reticles that can be selected and installed in the unit by the user. You can choose between dots within circles for fast acquisition in action shooting events, small minute-of-angle dots for hunting, or dots in a line for a combination of action/hunting. The sight package is much more compact for holstering than scopes since the housing is flatter, allowing it to be mounted tight to the barrel with only the lens protruding upward. Brightness is controlled one push-click at a time rather than by the circular rheostat found on dot scopes, but the shooter can select a default intensity setting based upon ambient light conditions. This is important because some of the sight presentations contain a large number of elements which can obscure the target if they are too bright for early morning or dusk hunting conditions. It's not as complicated as I make it sound. The first time anyone looks through the sight, he or she immediately smiles and utters something profound like, "Wow!"

Now a reality are dot scopes that allow you to select different dot sizes. I've enjoyed hunting with Weaver's 33mm variable dot with size selections of 4, 8 and 12 MOA. A sliding lever located on top of the tube behind the elevation control knob can be moved easily left or right to the desired setting. On the opposite side of the tube from the windage elevation knob is the rheostat for instant brightness control. The Weaver variable is a bit bulkier than regular scopes, but kind to aging eyes with focal distance problems.

Regular scopes abound from the reputable manufacturers for all kinds of applications. Burris has the highest fixed- and variable-power pistol scopes for all kinds of hunting, as well as extra-heavy crosshairs on their 2x for woods hunting. Leupold's original 2x and 4x have been joined by the second-highest power variable on the market, the 2.5-8x. Everybody makes a 2x and a variable from 2.5-7x, with the Thompson/Center having an option for controlled lighting of their crosshairs. Bushnell's 2-6x is the favorite of a number of handgun hunters for all-around use. Most dealers stock a good variety of these, and you'll have to do some thinking in selecting your choice.

Grips

I didn't personally see anything new in grips at the SHOT Show, but I can't think of anything that hasn't been addressed by the manufacturers. If you have an unfulfilled dream or a custom gun, you might talk to one of the custom gripmakers. I've had some beautiful and functional grips made at Blue Magnum, in Colorado, that add a special touch to a treasured gun, but production manufacturers have gone well past that extra mile to satisfy consumer needs. Check Hogue, Pachmayr, and Uncle Mike's for rubber grips that soften and soothe the interface of gun and hand. They all have slightly different design features that might resolve your particular concerns. Hogue also makes some very attractive wood grips in different designs for production guns. Pachmayr makes the combination wood/rubber sets that provide both softness and the "woody" look. Your dealer probably stocks some of the synthetic grips designed to provide a custom touch to your hardware. If not, ask to see catalogs from various manufacturers to get an idea of how different materials would look on your gun.

One last item: If you're shooting the big boomers, and available grips are not meeting all your needs, check on some of the shooting gloves available. Chemere makes lightly padded gloves with full fingers that help you hold onto a slippery single action in recoil. PAST makes more heavily padded gloves with no fingers that absorb recoil punishment before it gets to your hand. Michaels has introduced their new padded gloves with cut-off fingers, but with an extended pad to protect the middle finger of the shooting hand that gets whacked by the trigger guard, particularly by the Dragoon-style guard on the older Ruger 44s. Don't trade any part of your body for a moment of macho; it isn't worth it, and it's not necessary. ●

COMPETITION SCENE

by GARY ANDERSON

PISTOLS AND PISTOL shooters who win Olympic medals have a special fascination for many gun enthusiasts. Much of their romance comes from someone just trying to be the best in the world at any sports event in the world's greatest sports competition, whether it's running, fencing, wrestling or shooting. Olympic shooting has a special appeal because it demands such a high degree of human precision. Moreover, the pistols and the people who shoot them in Olympic-style competition are highly interesting themselves.

Shooting is one of the biggest and most popular Olympic sports. Significantly, five of its fifteen events feature handguns. Olympic pistol rules are established by shooting's world governing body, the International Shooting Union, usually called the UIT from its French name. UIT rules offer both tradition and modern media-age innovation. The current target and course of fire for the Free Pistol event were adopted over 100 years ago. Today's new competition format with finals concluding each event successfully presents shooting's true excitement to spectators, media and television.

UIT rules strongly emphasize the shooter as an athlete. Olympic medals are supposed to be won by the best-trained athletes, not the ones who are lucky or have better equipment. To truly test shooters' abilities, the targets, courses of fire and shooting conditions are very difficult. Free Pistol shooters shoot at a ten ring about the size of a silver dollar over half a football field away. No telescopic or optical sights, only metallic sights, are permitted. Two-handed shooting or the use of supports is unheard of; all UIT-style handgunning is done standing with one arm extended.

The finals put tremendous additional pressure on the top shooters. Everyone shoots the "qualification round" over a standard course of fire. Then the top eight shooters advance, with their qualification round scores, to the "final round." In the final, the eight leaders shoot ten additional shots with all shots scored in tenths. When the difference between a good ten and a bad nine is nearly two points, finals become extremely exciting because the shooters' places routinely change after each shot. Winners are recognized immediately after the last shot.

Past efforts to develop guns to win Olympic medals produced fabled pistols like the Walther Olympia of the 1930s, the classic Hämmerli free pistol of the 1950s and 1960s and the "upside down" Russian rapid-fire pistol of the 1950s. Then or today, these pistols had to be exceptionally accurate, extremely reliable and have painstakingly designed grips, frame designs and recoil-control characteristics.

The Hämmerli M162 Free Pistol is one of the top guns for the difficult 50-meter event. It is an electric-trigger version of the M160. Extremely light trigger pulls of 1/2- to 1-ounce are standard in Free Pistol shooting.

What are today's best handguns for Olympic events? A great way to answer that question is to find out what the best shooters use. During the 1996 UIT World Cup at the Wolf Creek Olympic Shooting Complex in Atlanta, a comprehensive equipment survey was taken. This was both the biggest World Cup in UIT history and an official pre-Olympic competition, so virtually all of the world's best shooters were there. Information from that survey will help answer this question.

Free Pistol shooting is the ultimate in human precision with a handgun. The target is 50 meters (54.7 yds.) away and has a 50mm (1.97-inch) ten ring. It is a classic slow-fire event with two full hours to shoot unlimited sighting shots and sixty record shots in the qualification round.

The Hämmerli Company of Lenzburg, Switzerland, the legendary Swiss target rifle maker, became the leading free pistol manufacturer after World War II and still is. Its only strong challenger has been the Russian Vostok TOZ-35. In the Atlanta World Cup survey, there were thirty-three Hämmerlis, mostly M160s and a few M162s with electric triggers, twenty-six Russian and fourteen Morini 84E (Switzerland) free pistols. The Pardini K50 (Italy) and Steyr FP (Austria) were also used by several shooters.

All true free pistols are single shots, and most have falling block actions. Set triggers with extremely light 15- to 30-gram (1/2- to 1-ounce) trigger pulls let shooters touch off their

The Walther OSP Rapid-Fire Pistol pictured here is used by 1992 and 1996 U.S. Olympic team member Roger Mar. It was modified by Mar's coach, Gary Spychalski, who added Bo-Mar sights and a ported Douglas barrel. The wrap-around grip is common in rapid-fire guns where consistent control of the pistol through a series of shots is required.

The Walther LP200 incorporates two new trends in air pistol technology, the use of pre-compressed air instead of CO_2 gas, and a ported muzzle. Even with low-recoil air pistols, ported barrels reduce recoil jump and can improve scores.

The FAS M607 Sport Pistol, manufactured in Italy, is shown with the 25m precision and rapid fire targets used in this event. Most top shooters replace or modify the factory grips with specially fitted custom grips. Federal's Gold Medal Match ammo suits it perfectly.

In the Olympic Games, Sport Pistol is a women's event. The shooter is firing at the smaller precision targets where the 25-meter target has a 2-inch ten ring. The pistol is the FAS M607 that, like all pistols designed for the Olympic shooting events, locates the barrel as low as possible in the hand.

shots at the optimum moment. A dominating feature of modern free pistol design is placement of the axis of the bore as low as possible in the hand to minimize recoil jump.

Hämmerli and Vostok free pistols both feature low action placement and acutely angled grips to align the bore with the web of the hand and give better recoil control. The new Steyr FP advances this technology a step further by placing a small cylindrical falling block and the barrel directly in front of the trigger, so recoil goes straight into the arm.

Rapid-Fire Pistol originated with 19th-century practice sessions for dueling. Its original man-shaped targets evolved into rectangular targets with oval scoring rings and finally into square targets with round scoring rings. When semi-automatic rimfire handguns became reliable, the event shifted from dueling's single shots to shooting five shots at five different targets. To reduce recoil that makes precise track-

ing from target to target more difficult, shooters use pistols chambered for low-recoil 22 Short cartridges.

Rapid-Fire Pistol targets are 25 meters away, with ten-rings measuring a scant 100mm (3.94 inches). The shooter begins with a loaded pistol in the "ready" position, pointed down at a 45-degree angle, then shoots twelve successive five-shot series in 8, then 6 and finally 4 seconds. Starting from a ready position and hitting five different palm-sized ten-rings in just 4 seconds is a difficult enough feat that perfect 50s are always cheered. The final is two additional 4-second series.

At the Atlanta World Cup, twenty shooters used Walther OSPs and fourteen used Pardini GP rapid-fire pistols. Various Russian models and the FAS M601 (Italy) were also well represented. The Walther OSP has a great reputation for out-of-the-box reliability, a critical factor in a competition where

COMPETITION

alibis are costly. The Walther OSP and Pardini GP have magazines and loading ports in front of the trigger guard, while the Russian and FAS pistols have magazines in the grip. The new Pardini Model GP Schumann, named after the world's best Rapid-Fire shooter, Ralf Schumann of Germany, offers an extended rear sight to increase the sight radius that is compromised by the forward magazine location.

Sport Pistol is a women's Olympic event that was first contested in 1984. A thirty-shot precision stage is shot on the free pistol target at 25 meters. In the 30-shot Rapid-Fire stage, shooters load five shots, and after coming to the ready position, have 3 seconds to raise the pistol, aim and fire. Shooters return to the ready position after each shot to begin a new 3-second shot opportunity. The final is ten shots at the precision target.

The best Sport Pistol shooters all use 22 LR semi-automatic pistols. At the Atlanta World Cup, there were twenty-eight Hämmerlis and sixteen Pardini SP models. Russian, Walther GSP and FAS M607 pistols also were used by many shooters. The Hämmerlis included both the M208s classic standard with its magazine in the grip and the newer M280 with its magazine in front of the trigger guard and frame of carbon-fiber-reinforced synthetics.

Air Pistol, the newest Olympic pistol event, is quickly gaining popularity because it can be shot in almost every country in the world. Air pistols are shot at targets with an 11.5mm (0.45-inch) ten ring that are 10 meters (33 feet) away. Women shoot forty shots, and men sixty. Both finals consists of ten additional shots. Target air pistols look like free pistols at a distance. Shooters consider trigger reliability and consistency, balance, accuracy and recoil characteristics in choosing their guns. Most new air pistols now feature recoil compensators.

Air pistols with CO_2 and compressed air systems are the most popular. Pistols using pre-compressed air are relatively new, but enjoy growing popularity. Pneumatic or hand-cocking air pistols have all but disappeared because the effort required to cock disturbs the consistent grip necessary for top performances.

The Steyr LP-1 was the air pistol of choice in Atlanta. It is well designed and supported with an aggressive marketing program to get it into the hands of the world's top shooters. There were thirty-five in the men's and thirty-seven in the women's events. Feinwerkbau air pistols followed in both events with twenty-three and thirteen. Many Walther, Pardini, Morini and Hämmerli air pistols also were used. Indeed, there are a wealth of excellent choices among target air pistols.

American shooters, most of whom are trained at the USA Shooting Resident Athlete Program at Colorado Springs, or by the U.S. Army Marksmanship Unit at Fort Benning, are strong international pistol contenders. American arms companies, on the other hand, have not developed pistols that are competitive in international competition. A High Standard Olympic rapid-fire pistol was used to win an Olympic gold medal in 1960. High Standard tried to develop a free pistol during that same period. Smith & Wesson put considerable developmental work into a rapid-fire pistol in the 1980s. Unfortunately, those laudable efforts did not continue. Today, a shooter who is excited by the challenge of an Olympic pistol event must choose a pistol made in Europe, but there are many outstanding pistols that can produce gold-medal results.

[*Editor's note: High Standard just introduced a new rapid-fire pistol in 22 Short, with wrap-around grip.*] ●

1996 Olympic Handgun Events, Atlanta

Event	Medal	Medalist	Country	Handgun
Free Pistol	Gold	Boris Kokorev	Russia	Toz 3S
	Silver	Igor Basinski	Belarus	Toz 3S
	Bronze	Roberto Di Donna	Italy	Toz 3S
Rapid-Fire Pistol	Gold	Ralf Schumann	Germany	Pardini GP Schumann
	Silver	Emil Milev	Bulgaria	Walther OSP
	Bronze	Vladimir Vokhmyanin	Kazakhstan	XPG88 Prototype, Russian
Air Pistol (women)	Gold	Olga Klochneva	Russia	Walther CPM 1
	Silver	Marina Logvinenko	Russia	Steyr Compensator
	Bronze	Mariya Grozdeva	Bulgaria	Steyr Compensator
Air Pistol (men)	Gold	Roberto Di Donna	Italy	Pardini K58
	Silver	Yifa Wang	People's Rep. of China	Morini CM162E
	Bronze	Tanu Kiriakov	Bulgaria	Hämmerli 480
Sport Pistol (women)	Gold	Duihong Li	People's Rep. of China	Donfeng (Chinese)
	Silver	Diana Yorgova	Bulgaria	Hämmerli 208s
	Bronze	Marina Logvinenko	Russia	Hämmerli 280

HANDGUNS 97

Handgun Hunting

Half-inchers make big holes, page 178.

Kinetic energy isn't the last word, page 184.

Chasing the elusive pig, page 188.

The author with the 50 AE, an eland, and a 50-caliber smile.

THE
BIG
FIFTIES
by DICK WILLIAMS

IN AUTOMOBILE ENGINES, there is no substitute for displacement. In handguns, there is no substitute for bore size. These are axioms. They relate to two different worlds in which being bigger is better. In both worlds, you can give the illusion of being bigger by using things like turbos and expanding bullets. But if you're big enough, you need not resort to trickery. Guns like the 50 Action Express and the 500 Linebaugh launch bullets with a frontal area about 35 percent larger than the 44 Magnum and 25 percent larger than the 45-calibers. These projectiles begin their journeys with a diameter that other calibers seek to achieve after striking their targets.

Why do such guns exist? One reason is that shooters seem fascinated with bigger, more powerful guns and ammo. John Linebaugh calls guns sold to these kind of buyers "coffee-table guns." Their primary purpose is to be displayed, admired, and envied. If the owner engages in a little boasting during that

Heavy-horsepower handguns in a pair of big fifties. The 500 Linebaugh (top) with five rounds of its 450-grain ammo, and the Freedom Arms 50 AE with five 380-grainers.

There are differences between the two that you can see and feel. The Ruger Bisley grip of the Linebaugh does not have the hammer bolsters at the top, which can cut your hand.

process, so much the better. But a more practical use for one of these big fifties is hunting anything that can hunt back. Even for the non-hunter operating in the environment of large, cranky critters, e.g. salmon fishermen in brown bear country, a 500 Linebaugh or 50 AE on the hip is a better prescription for potential maladies than anything smaller.

The first 500 Linebaugh on the Ruger Bisley frame was built for gun writer Ross Seyfried, who, I believe, wanted to use it on African lion. I don't know if he ever did so, but it ought to have worked well, given the right bullet. As I learned earlier this year, the 50 AE, even with the lighter 325-grain JHP from Speer, is capable of shooting clear through African game like wildebeest, zebra and kudu. Make no mistake, heavy 50-caliber bullets at 1200 to 1300 fps will penetrate and kill large animals, despite the fact that kinetic energy and momentum formulas make no reference to bullet diameter.

There are several "manufacturers" of 50-calibers. Quotes are used because the exact dividing line between production and custom-built handguns is not clearly defined. Magnum Research's and

Freedom Arms' manufacturing numbers are in the thousands per year, but these numbers include guns of lesser calibers than the 50 AE. L.A.R. Manufacturing produces fewer of their Grizzly handguns per year, and again, not all are fifties. AMT made a one-time production run of 3000 50-caliber handguns and closed that production line forever.

There are also two custom shops where highly regarded and nationally recognized gunsmiths, specifically John Linebaugh and Hamilton Bowen, make 50-caliber handguns (and other sizes as well) by fitting custom barrels and cylinders to some other manufacturer's frame. Their annual handgun output is probably fewer than 100. The 500 Linebaugh is actually not the most powerful handgun John Linebaugh makes. He makes an even larger fifty called the 500 Maximum, or Linebaugh Long, which uses a case 0.2-inch longer than the 500 Linebaugh. Hamilton Bowen also makes a 50 Special, which is on a slightly shorter case. The 500 Maximum surpasses the 500 Linebaugh in power (and cost), while the 50 Special is less powerful than the 50 AE.

There is another major distinction

between production guns and custom models. The production 50s are all in caliber 50 Action Express, a cartridge designed for semi-automatic handguns. It features a rebated rim and utilizes .500-inch bullets to match its groove diameter. Brass is available from numerous sources.

The custom handguns in 50 Special, 500 Linebaugh or 500 Maximum are all revolvers with .510-inch groove diameters, and they shoot cast bullets sized to around .511-inch from rimmed cartridge cases. The cases (at least so far) are made from 348 Winchester brass.

The bore diameter difference stems from a U.S. State Department ruling that restricts imported handguns to those no larger than 50-caliber. The first gun for the 50 AE, called the Desert Eagle, was imported from Israel, so its groove diameter was held to .500-inch to insure there would be no last-minute "interpretation" problems that could prevent importation. The bore diameter (across the lands) runs about .490-inch.

Linebaugh and Bowen measure their half-inch across the lands, and their guns have a .510-inch groove diameter.

Bullets for the Linebaugh and Bowen guns must be cast in custom moulds. Other than doing your own casting, there are several sources for hard-cast, sized and lubed bullets in a variety of weights. I understand some custom bullet manufacturers make jacketed bullets of .510-inch diameter, but I couldn't find any before this article was due.

One of the guns for this article was to be mine, and I chose the 50 AE Freedom Arms revolver over any of the semi-autos. There were several reasons for this. First, ammunition for semi-automatic handguns must be tailored to cycle the firearm's action; you don't have the flexibility of loading up or down like you can with a revolver. The Desert Eagle's gas operation also precludes the use of lead bullets, because they might block the gas channel with lead particles. I wanted the option of using lead slugs. The design of semi-autos and their magazines also restrict overall cartridge length and bullet design. Also, I thought it to be necessary to use revolvers for both calibers in order to get any kind of meaningful comparison between the two big fifties.

Editor Ray Ordorica had wanted a 500 Linebaugh for a long time, and when the chance for a meaningful comparison with the 50 AE rolled around, he ordered a 500 from John Linebaugh, and arranged delivery to me for comparison testing.

Cases for the 500 Linebaugh are made from 348 Winchester brass, and you can either make them yourself using RCBS case-forming dies, or buy them ready-made from Golden Bear Bullets. If you buy the cases already formed, all you'll need is some 500 Linebaugh loading dies, also available from RCBS. Unless you have the correct power tools for reaming the inside of the shortened 348 case, I suggest you buy the 500 Linebaugh brass ready-made by Golden Bear. Reaming the inside of a straight-wall case by hand is an ugly job. All 500 Linebaugh cases used in this article came from Golden Bear.

A nice additional custom touch is getting the cases properly headstamped. Just send the formed cases to John Linebaugh; he removes enough of the head surface to delete the "348 Winchester" and replaces it with "500 Linebaugh." No, it doesn't mess up the headspace. I obtained cast bullets sized

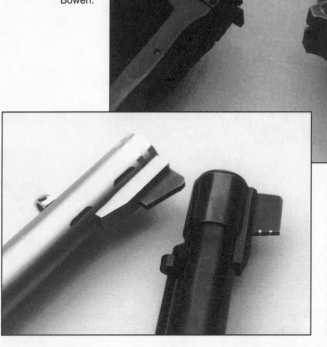

Adjustable rear sights on the two guns are different, but both present excellent sight pictures. The Linebaugh sight (left) is by Hamilton Bowen.

The stainless Freedom has Mag-Na-Port slots and interchangeable front sight blades of different heights. The blued Linebaugh has a barrel-band front sight with gold inlays for long-range shooting, an extra-cost item, as is the Bowen rear sight.

.511-inch diameter in four different weights: 350 and 450 grains from Penny's, 415 grains from Black Diamond, and 425 grains from Roger Barnes.

The 50 AE was a little easier to deal with since Speer makes a variety of loaded ammo, plus brass and bullets for reloaders. Packaged under the Magnum Research logo are two loaded rounds, one with 300-grain JHP bullets and the other with 350-grain softpoints. Under its own label, Speer offers loaded ammo with the 325-grain JHP, or the same bullet and new brass for the reloader. Roger Barnes sent two different hard-cast bullets sized .500-inch. The lighter was a 345-grainer with a large meplat, the heavyweight was 380 grains with a slightly smaller meplat.

It would have been interesting, and easier for "apples to apples" comparisons, to have a Freedom Arms revolver chambered for the rimmed 500 Linebaugh caliber. Because revolvers lend themselves to rimmed cases, and Freedom would not have had to deal with import restrictions on bore size, I explored this possibility with Randy Smith at the Wyoming factory. While they could have used a bigger barrel with no problem, the larger rim of the 348 case would have forced them to make some major retooling and manufacturing changes. The larger rim would have interfered with the hand and cylinder rotation mechanism in the existing Freedom frames. In addition, they would have lost all the advantages of capitalizing on an existing factory round. As it turns out, we came close to an "apples to apples" scenario with a couple of the components. But before we discuss performance of cartridges, let's look at the guns themselves.

Both are five-shooters. The Linebaugh begins life as a Ruger Bisley in either 44 Magnum or 45 Colt. John removes the factory cylinder and barrel from the gun, then he carefully fits and installs his own custom-made 500 Linebaugh cylinders and barrels (in this case a 5.5-inch length). A steel ejector-rod housing also replaces the Ruger original. The barrel has an integral

(Left) Because the 500 Linebaugh cylinder is not recessed for the cartridge rims, a case must be in front of the loading gate to prevent the gate from bending under massive recoil.

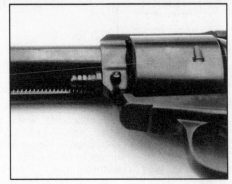

A set screw has been added to the cylinder rod on the Linebaugh to prevent the rod from sliding forward under recoil. Big guns are big kickers.

The Freedom 50 AE with a zebra shot by author Dick Williams. He discoverd the Speer factory loads would shoot completely through such game.

band at the muzzle that helps retain the front sight base under extreme recoil. The barrel band also helps keep the ejector rod housing on the gun. The front sight blade is held by an Allen screw.

Editor Ordorica asked John Linebaugh to install Linebaugh's version of the Keith gold-bar front sight, useful for long-range shooting. The blade has two inlaid horizontal gold lines, or bars. The gold lines are placed so that when the top of the front sight is flush with the top of the rear sight, the gold bars are not visible. They're below the bottom of the rear notch so they don't interfere with the sight picture. When the top gold bar is elevated to the top of the rear sight for long-range shooting, the bottom gold bar is still not visible. The range for which the gold bars are calibrated depends on the loads you're using. The Editor will have to work that out for his favorite load.

To use this system, you elevate one of the gold bars to the top of the rear notch, then put your target on top of that. You can see everything and the sight picture is repeatable. If you've figured range correctly, you can make uncanny hits at extreme long range. Elmer Keith worked out and mastered this technique long ago.

John retains the Bisley-style hammer and Ruger trigger, but polishes and tunes the trigger to a very smooth and consistent 3-pound pull. John replaced the Ruger's rear sight with a new, adjustable one manufactured by Hamilton Bowen. The back of the blade is flat and black, making for a very clean, uncluttered sight picture with no distractions or reflections. The Ruger cylinder release mechanism is still controlled by rotating the loading gate to the open position, but John has disconnected the ratchet mechanism leaving the cylinder free to rotate in both directions as long as the loading gate is open. This is a big improvement over the standard Ruger mechanism which "locks" the cylinder midway in rotation so that the extractor rod cannot enter the chamber until the cylinder is moved halfway to the next position and held carefully in place.

The new 500 cylinder is not recessed for the cartridge rims, so there is a large space between the cylinder and the face of the loading gate. John specifies that a cartridge case must be under the loading gate when the gun is fired to avoid the gate bending forward into the cylinder under the forces of recoil. If you only load four rounds and forget to add a fifth before firing, cocking the gun for the first shot rotates the empty chamber in line with the loading gate, leaving the gate free to flex. The 500 retains the Ruger's transfer-bar safety system so you can safely carry the cylinder with a full five rounds. The gun retains the original Ruger Bisley grips, and they fit almost as well as custom grips. The Linebaugh gun has a very attractive blue finish which nicely complements this extremely well-built handgun.

While it is technically a production gun, a Freedom Arms revolver is hand built. The cylinders on all guns are carefully fitted before being line bored to their respective calibers. All components are made at the Wyoming plant, including their standard adjustable sights and grips. The rear sight is nicely integrated into a slot machined in the top of the frame. The result is a hell-for-stout adjustable sight in a slot that can also be used for mounting an equally stout scope base from either Leupold or SSK Industries. The rear sight can be changed from the standard square notch to a V-notch express sight which is also adjustable. The front sight blade fits into a notch in the sight base and is retained/changed by an Allen screw in the front of the base. Options include ramped blades of various heights for the square-notch rear sight, or gold beads for the V-notch express sight. Trigger pull on all Freedom Arms revolvers is carefully set at 3 pounds.

Since the Linebaugh was to be a custom piece with a few fancy extras specified by our esteemed Editor, I thought it would be fair to have this particular Freedom revolver receive the ministrations of Ken Kelly at Mag-Na-Port. I truly appreciate muzzle-braking devices on any heavy-recoiling handgun that I'm going to shoot a lot, as in doing load development for an article. Ken cut the Freedom barrel to 5.75 inches and

THE BIG FIFTIES

installed a tapered crown that protects the rifling from bumps and dings around the muzzle. (Hey, I'm clumsy!)

The Mag-Na-Porting is his standard four-slot arrangement, but he can vary this if you have any personal desires or a specific application in mind. The bead-blasted finish is enhanced by several polished bands on the cylinder, barrel and extractor housing, a jeweled hammer and action, and the polishing of a few other miscellaneous spots including the loading gate. Jeweling the action resulted in the trigger pull dropping to a crisp 2.75 pounds. The Blue Magnum grips are custom laminated wood with an oil finish. The end result is a beautifully built firearm enhanced by some personal artistic touches.

When he builds you one of his 500s, John Linebaugh will send you some loading data and suggestions. Read them; they're excellent. There was close correlation between his loads and my test results. Even when using different bullet designs and weights, I was able to extrapolate from his data to find suggested starting points. The one exception was my "lightweight" 350-grain bullet for which he had no data. Using slow-burning powder and regular pistol primers, four rounds ranged from 900 to 1100 fps with the fifth round squibbing and lodging in the barrel. I traced the problem to the regular primer not igniting the powder. In a test program, you're only supposed to change one parameter at a time to isolate the cause of a failure. I changed several parameters for the rest of the program and had no further problems:

1. I switched to CCI Magnum pistol primers for all loads. (Don't use rifle primers. They are slightly taller and may not seat flush in the altered primer pocket of the custom 500 Linebaugh cases.)

2. I used the .496-inch expander plug of the 50 AE dies rather than the .509-inch expander plug of the 500 Linebaugh dies for loading all 500 Linebaugh cases to ensure maximum bullet tension. If the 500 Linebaugh dies were mine, I would polish that expander plug to be about .507-inch.

3. For the lighter bullet, I switched to a faster powder. Twelve grains of W-W 231 gave velocities around 1000 fps, and 27 grains AA#9 gave velocities around 1200 fps.

Shooting sessions with the 500

The boxes contain factory loads for the 50 AE. Cast bullet handloads from left: a pair of 50 AEs with 345- and 380-grain bullets; four 500 Linebaughs with bullets of 350, 415, 425 and 450 grains.

Cast bullet loads, left to right, 357 Mag./158-grain, 44 Mag./240-grain, 50 AE/380-grain, and 500 Linebaugh/450-grain. The fifties dwarf the other "magnums." The 500 Linebaugh case is noticeably longer than the 50 AE case (1.400 vs. 1.285 inches). The 500 Linebaugh Long case (not shown) is a full 1.6 inches long.

The 325-grain Speer Gold Dot bullet (at left), fired from 50 AE, was recovered from a big kudu and still weighs 325 grains. Next is another bullet recovered from an eland, and it weighs 292 grains, having clipped the shoulder blade. Then there's an unfired Speer 325-grain JHP Gold Dot and a Speer factory 325-grain round. With limited testing, author found JHPs to work better on this size game than cast bullets.

Table 1

500 Linebaugh Data

Powder (Grs. Wt./Type)	—Bullet—Wgt. Grs.	Type	MV* (fps)	Comments
29/H110	450	cast	1201	
30/H110	450	cast	1247	2"; heavy recoil
30/H110	425	cast	1219	
31/H110	425	cast	1235	1.5"
31/H110	415	cast	1239	
32/H110	415	cast	1278	3" (3 in 1")
12/WW231	350	cast	1000	light load
27/AA#9	350	cast	1200	

Use large pistol magnum primers for all loads.
*Five-shot average

Linebaugh were kept short due to a limited supply of brass and my limited tolerance for heavy recoil. Bullets weighing over 400 grains and traveling at velocities between 1200 and 1300 fps begin to exceed my idea of fun. Yet spending a lot of time with reduced loads didn't seem like a worthwhile exploration of the 500 Linebaugh's capabilities. Utilizing the three heaviest bullets available, I worked my way up to the loads listed in Table 1 with the results as shown. I suspect the gun will handle higher loads, but I don't know that, and some of these loads are already a grain or so over John's suggestions. As always, back off a bit and find your own horizons. I suspect you'll reach your personal limits before you

exceed the gun's. All accuracy testing was done shooting offhand at the On Target indoor range in Southern California.

The 50 AE has some reloads listed in the reloading manuals, but not for the heavy cast bullets used in this article. Please note that the overall lengths of cast bullet loads listed here are too long for semi-automatic handguns; data shown here for cast bullets are to be used *only in 50 AE Freedom Arms revolvers!* The Freedom revolver was easier to test than the Linebaugh simply because the recoil was less ferocious. No magic: bullets under 400 grains in a Mag-Na-Ported gun are gentler than heavier bullets in a non-Mag-Na-Ported gun. But while shooting sessions could last longer, they were still not all-day affairs. The heavier 50 AE bullets still produced enough recoil that they were difficult to test from sandbags. I needed all of me to absorb energy without overstressing hands and wrists.

A couple of comments regarding the 50 AE:

The Speer factory ammo shown in Table 2 is their new loading. The original Speer 325-grain ammo produced significantly lower velocities than this.

Loads of 29 and 30 grains of WW 296 with the 380-grain cast bullet were tested in a different gun, but velocities progressed uniformly at about 50 fps per grain increase of powder, and groups stayed at or under the 2-inch mark.

For testing the 50 AE, I used Chemere full-fingered shooting gloves with the light padding. They stopped the grip from slipping in my hand during recoil, and were so comfortable I later wore them for a ten-day hunt with the 50 AE. In order to save my knuckle from the recoil of the heavier loads in the 500 Linebaugh, I had to use Uncle Mike's new shooting gloves with the padding extended over the middle finger. The heavier padding makes it more difficult for short-fingered people to reach the trigger, but the softening effect throughout your hand and fingers is well worth the extended reach. Without these gloves, shooting sessions with the 500 would not have exceeded five to ten rounds.

As a quick test, several shooters compared felt recoil of the 27/AA#9/350-grain loads at 1200 fps from the Linebaugh with the 30/296/345-grain loads at 1200fps from the Freedom. Those with normal to large hands claimed the

Freedom felt softer. But despite the Freedom's advantage of Mag-Na-Porting, guys with very large hands and long fingers preferred the extra length of the Ruger Bisley grip frame and said it was easier to hang onto the Linebaugh. Absolutely nobody liked the heaviest loads in the Linebaugh. In fact, some trauma in the form of shaking hands was noticed in most shooters after firing the 450-grain bullets.

As it turned out, only the Freedom/Mag-Na-Port 50 AE had a real-life performance evaluation. A short-notice opportunity for a ten-day safari presented itself and the Freedom and I were off to South Africa with some Speer 325-grain JHP factory rounds and some cast-bullet handloads. The hoped-for buffalo hunt didn't materialize, so I tried the cast bullets on a large blue wildebeest at about 70 yards. The bullet's dust cloud behind the animal was so large I thought I had missed, but the blood and bits of lung on the trail indicated otherwise. Although the lung shot ultimately proved fatal, it did little internal damage and the animal evaded us for a few days before succumbing to his wounds.

A consultation with Andre Booysen, the professional hunter, resulted in my switching to the Speer factory 325-grain JHP load. Except for one blown shot attributed to pilot error, performance of the factory round was superb. I took an impala, a wildebeest and a zebra, and all bullets totally penetrated the animals. A kudu bull had one shot completely penetrate the chest area and exit the far side without striking bone, while the finishing shot was recovered just under the hide on the off side. It

retained its entire 325-grain weight and was nearly a picture-perfect mushroom shape. A bullet recovered from the chest of an eland weighed 292 grains and was slightly deformed from glancing off the edge of the shoulder bone. Kudu are about the size of our elk, while eland are comparable to our moose.

Since some sort of comparison between the two guns/calibers is inevitable, let's do it. Clearly we have the two biggest-bore handgun calibers available here, with the 500 Linebaugh having about 4 percent more frontal area than the 50 AE. In terms of size and weight, available bullets also favor the Linebaugh with Joel Penny's 450-grain cast slug edging out Roger Barnes' 380-grain cast bullet for the 50 AE. I understand moulds for the 50 AE are being built that will cast heavier bullets and close the bullet weight gap a little, but the 500 Linebaugh will still have an edge over the 50 AE in loading volume. *[Moulds are available for the Linebaugh that cast 470-grain bullets. Ed.]*

The availability of ammo and components favors the 50 AE since it is a production round. To a non-reloader, this is a huge factor. In the previously mentioned African hunt, the Speer 325-grain JHP load performed so well on animals ranging from impala to eland there was no need for heavy handloads with cast bullets. Even for a reloader, the availability of standard dies, factory brass and a greater selection of bullets might sway a decision to the 50 AE.

However, unless you can find a 50 Freedom Arms on your dealer's shelf (and occasionally you can), the factory's current backlog of three to four months may negate the inherent advantage of a production gun versus a custom gun. Price doesn't seem to be the deciding factor; starting price for a basic gun from either Freedom Arms or John Linebaugh is around $1300. Freedom has a catalog with factory prices on the most popular upgrades. You would have to call or write John to explore the costs and schedules associated with your custom preferences.

To me, the major factor in choosing between the two guns boils down to personal preferences and ergonomics. Either one can be loaded to the maximum performance that remains within your individual tolerance of recoil. To put it succinctly, let pain be your guide. Depending on your individual paw print, one gun's grip may be noticeably more comfortable than the other. Pride of ownership won't suffer with either gun; both are superb pieces of hardware that will well serve the dedicated handgunner who wants all the power of one of the big fifties. ●

Slow-burning powder, big bullets and RCBS dies; you're ready to load the big fifties.

Table 2

50 AE Data				
Powder	—Bullet—		MV	Comments
(Grs. Wt./Type)	Wgt. Grs.	Type	(fps)	
Factory	300	MR JHP	1437	<1.8″
Factory	350	MR SP	1232	>2″
Factory	325	Speer JHP	1369	<1.5″
29/WW 296	345	cast	1150	<2″
30/WW 296	345	cast	1201	<2″
31/WW 296	345	cast	1249	1.5″
32/WW 296	345	cast	1342	1.5″
28/WW 296	380	cast	1182	<3″
31/WW 296	380	cast	1321	1.5″
MR = Magnum Research				

THE NUMBER OF states with "shall issue" concealed carry laws has increased to the point where many of us can at least begin thinking about what gun we might need or want to carry as a personal self-protection weapon. The amount of folklore, legend and pure myth that surrounds the selection of a gun for this purpose is simply mind boggling. To reduce all this confusion to something we can actually use may be impossible. Still, if we don't try to look at the selection process in some sort of rational manner we'll never even get close to making a decision, except purely on the basis of emotion, and that's absolutely the last basis we should be using.

Stated simply, the problem boils down to selecting a gun that is comfortable and convenient to carry, and at the same time is "big enough" to get our job done. To make the selection process a little more manageable, I think it helps to reduce the gun sizes to three simple categories of small, medium and large. These aren't completely arbitrary size distinctions as we'll see in a little while. Let's begin by defining these terms.

Starting with the automatic pistols,

The Smith & Wesson 10mm Model 1076, while physically a little smaller than the Model 1911A1 is, by any measure, a large gun. The FBI test concluded that it was big enough for their purposes.

MOMENTUM

A BETTER MEASURE OF KILLING POWER

by BOB FORKER

my definition of small includes the 22s (both Long Rifle and WMR), the 25 Auto and the 32 Auto. This group is generally accepted to be not enough gun for serious defensive purposes, but we'll get into that later.

Continuing with the definitions of gun size classes, the medium pistols include the 380 Auto and the 9mm Parabellum (Luger) calibers. It also includes 38 Special revolvers.

Finally, we come to the large guns. In this class the autos would include the 357 SIG, 40 S&W, 10mm Auto and 45 ACP. In revolvers, we're talking about any caliber 357 Magnum or larger. We can even include the 50 Action Express auto and the 44 Magnum revolvers in this category, but although they're top choices for hunting, they certainly aren't serious choices for concealed carry guns; very few people can shoot these big cannons really well.

The fundamental problem then comes down to making the tradeoffs necessary to select the most suitable size group. The exact choice of caliber within any group or the choice of gun make and model can be left to personal preference. If you look at small, medium and large guns you can easily see that small means light and easy to conceal, but they're not very high on the list of effective "stoppers." Conversely, large implies heavy, bulky guns with impressive recoil and equally impressive effects on the target.

The Browning Model 1905 (Vest Pocket) in 25 Auto is a good example of the "small" size category: tiny, light—and ineffective!

Walther's PPK in 380 Auto is, in both size and effectiveness, a "medium" category gun.

A "big" but very effective gun is the Colt 1911A1 in 45 ACP.

That boils the selection process down to a factor that's simple to state but not simple to accurately measure. The best choice will be the smallest gun that's big enough. "Big enough" will be defined by the caliber, not (in general) by the make and model of the gun. It does bring our selection process down to manageable proportions, but it's still far from trivial and certainly very subjective. Still, this selection process could literally someday become a matter of life and death...for you!

Let's make something very clear here. The factors that are important in selecting a concealed-carry gun are very different from the factors you would use to select a gun for personal defense in the home. For the home-defense application, concealability (size) and carrying comfort (weight) are pretty unimportant. That means that you shouldn't be willing to trade away any effectiveness to obtain these features. For this application, "big enough" tends to limit the selection process to the large guns, so long as the shooter can manage the caliber.

We can look to some numerical values for the different calibers for some help but we still have to make some of the basic decisions for ourselves. Before we do that we should consider our bullet selection. The gun launches the bullet, but then the gun's job is over. It's the performance of the bullet on the target that will make the difference between the "gun" being enough or not enough.

Every major manufacturer of ammunition sells a line of premium-performance bullets for their pistol ammunition. Most manufacturers also make lower-cost ammunition, and much of that lower cost comes from a lower cost (read inferior, from a terminal performance standpoint) bullet. You can save about 25 cents a round by some careful shopping for low-cost ammo. Think about that for a minute. If you seriously think your life isn't worth two bits, why are you bothering to spend the money to buy a gun? A while back I stood in our local gun shop while a customer took delivery on his brand-new Beretta 9mm auto. He then proceeded to buy the cheapest surplus junk ammo available, not for target work but for his personal defense ammunition. Unbelievable!

For my money, there's only one kind of ammo to buy for self protection, and

MOMENTUM

that's the very best you can get. For this application, the very best means one of the jacketed, controlled expansion, core-bonded, hollowpoint bullets that have been developed in the last six years or so. If you don't use effective bullets, nothing else in the selection process will matter.

To be effective, a bullet must penetrate deeply, expand without fragmenting, and leave an open wound channel. There is an ongoing argument about whether these characteristics derive from high bullet energy (usually related to light bullets at high velocities) or some momentum-related factor that in pistols seems to be best produced by heavy bullets at about 1000 fps velocity. This momentum factor is the basis for the RSP (Relative Stopping Power) index that was first defined by Gen. Julian Hatcher. RSP is defined by bullet mass times velocity times bullet cross sectional area times a factor based on bullet shape and type. For the hollowpoint bullets used here, that factor is about 1250. By comparison, bullet energy equals one-half of bullet mass times velocity times velocity again (velocity squared). The velocity squared term is why energy factors favor faster (resulting from being lighter) bullets.

There is another momentum-based measure of weapon effectiveness. It's the Taylor KO (Knock Out) index, developed after years of practical experience by John "Pondoro" Taylor. The KO index was originally developed for African rifles and since, like the RSP index, the KO index uses bullet momentum as a major factor, it also favors heavy bullets. Not surprisingly, it agrees with the basic British belief that African guns should drive very large bullets at modest velocities. The KO value is computed by multiplying bullet weight (grains) times velocity (fps) times bullet diameter (inches) divided by 7000. A careful look at the two momentum-based indices shows that the major difference is that RSP uses bullet area and Taylor uses bullet diameter. The RSP numbers and the KO numbers can't be compared directly with each other. They can only be compared with similar values for different calibers.

It's important to remember that the velocity we are talking about here is striking velocity, not muzzle velocity. Pistol bullets, and especially those with large hollow points, have very poor ballistic shapes. As a result, velocities fall off rather rapidly with distance. The good news here is that it is hard to

imagine a realistic personal self-defense encounter taking place at a range in excess of 10 yards or so. The comparisons in our performance table are based on velocities at a 10-yard range, rather than muzzle velocities.

What happens if you do want to use your gun at some range longer than the 10 yards in our example? To show what happens, we have plotted a curve of bullet energy versus range (out to 100 yards) for the 25 Auto, for the 10mm Auto and for the 44 Magnum cartridge fired out of a rifle-length barrel. This curve underscores just one reason why pistols are not the weapon of choice at long ranges. Even the 10mm is getting into the medium energy class by the time it reaches 100 yards.

We also plotted a curve of bullet path for the same three guns. We chose a 50-yard zero. Even the worst trajectory curve out to that distance (the 25 Auto) shows only 1.2 inches high at 25 yards. That's closer than most people can shoot a 2-inch barreled gun. But look what happens past 50 yards. Both pistols just fall off a cliff.

The law enforcement high-performance requirements include delivering stopping power after having to penetrate car doors, windshields, or other obstructions to reach their intended target. For basic law enforcement applications, effectiveness nearly always comes before concealability or carrying comfort. Because of this, the best gun for law enforcement may be too big for an individual. While the small guns might very well satisfy law enforcement people for a backup gun for their own personal defense needs, they are inadequate for routine law enforcement purposes.

Table 1 compares striking energy, RSP index and KO index for bullets fired from a selection of small-, medium- and large-class calibers and guns.

As you review these figures it's easy to see that, no matter which effectiveness factor you wish to use, the small, medium and large categories are quite clear. The break points for energy are at about 165 and 350 foot pounds of striking energy. To put those numbers into another perspective, it just doesn't matter very much whether the bullet energy is 384 or 386 foot pounds. The energy measure isn't nearly precise enough for this difference to have any significance. Worrying about those small differences gets into the category of pulling the wings off flies. But a bullet with an energy in the neighborhood of 500 foot pounds is indisputably going to be a lot more effective than one that's down around 100 foot pounds.

If you belong to the large group of shooters who believe that heavy and slow bullets are more effective, you will probably prefer to use the RSP or KO indices instead of energy. It really doesn't make a whole lot of difference in our selection process here. For the RSP index, the break-point numbers are about 40 and 85. The KO index break points are about 4.0 and 8.0. No matter which factor you use, the same clear size classes result.

I don't believe that any one of these measures is really accurate enough to predict the difference between two similar guns, for instance, between the 10mm Auto and the 45 ACP. Comparing these two cartridges illustrates that selecting either the energy or

Table 1

	Comparison of Cartridge Effectiveness						
Cartridge	Bullet Wgt. Grs./Type	Vel.* (fps)	Bullet Dia. (ins.)	Barrel (ins.)	Impact (fpe)	RSP Index	KO Index
22 LR	36/Remington HP	825	.223	2	54	6.4	0.9
22 WMR	50/Federal JHP	950	.223	2	100	10.3	1.5
25 Auto	35/Hornady XTP	885	.251	2	61	8.5	1.1
32 Auto	71/Magtech JHP	895	.312	4	153	29.7	3.1
380 Auto	95/Winchester SXT	940	.356	3³/₄	186	49.4	4.5
38 Special	140/Hornady XTP	890	.358	4	246	69.6	6.4
9mm Luger	147/Winchester SXT	980	.356	5	313	80.5	7.4
357 Magnum	158/Federal HydraShok	1210	.358	4	514	106.0	9.8
357 SIG	125/CCI Gold Dot	1315	.357	4	480	91.4	8.4
40 S&W	180/CCI Gold Dot	980	.400	4	384	123.0	10.1
10mm Auto	200/Hornady XTP	1040	.400	5	480	145.0	11.9
45 Auto	230/Rem. Golden Saber	870	.451	5	386	177.0	12.9
44 Magnum	240/PMC Starfire	1315	.430	7¹/₂	922	254.0	19.4

*Velocities measured 10 yards from muzzle.

momentum criteria shows only slight differences in their numerical ratings. The 10mm comes out a little ahead when evaluated on the basis of striking energy. The 45 is a little better when you use RSP or KO indices. Both cartridges clearly fall into the "large" category, and the detail features of the individual guns themselves are more important than the numerical effec-

This shows the typical expansion of a Winchester 9mm SXT bullet, with unfired bullet for comparison. Bullet effectiveness requires good expansion, weight retention and deep penetration.

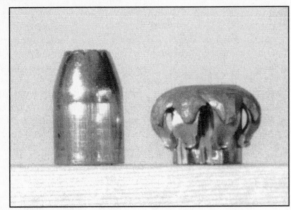

Here's what happens to the Winchester SXT bullet when it's fired from a 10mm Auto.

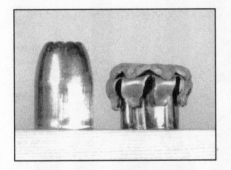

Big guns can make their big bullets even bigger with today's technology. The Winchester SXT bullet fired from a 45 ACP.

tiveness values of the cartridges they use.

Even though none of these comparison factors are precise enough to clearly select between a 45 and a 10mm, they do show that both guns have a clear superiority over something like the 9mm Luger caliber. The comparison between the 357 SIG and the 40 S&W provides another good example of light and fast versus slow and heavy. An energy basis will favor the SIG, but the momentum indices favor the 40 S&W. I don't think there is enough data on the SIG's effectiveness to come down firmly on one side or the other. It would be a close call since both are in the large-gun category by any measure.

Even with the numbers to help us, we're still left with a pretty serious decision. In the final analysis, our choice boils down to deciding exactly what we

expect the gun to do for us. We know that something well in excess of ninety percent of documented gun encounters involving non-law-enforcement people end without a shot being fired. That suggests that for the overwhelming portion of our protection needs, a small gun will get the job done almost as well as some big cannon. We're not talking here about either a gun for home defense, nor are we talking about the primary weapon for a police officer. If you think you are going to need to effectively fire your protection weapon, then the small guns simply aren't up to the job. You are going to have to pay the price in convenience and comfort for some better ballistic performance.

For my money, and this conclusion came directly from reading the results of the FBI tests in 1988 and '89, even the medium guns aren't really enough

gun if you are serious about wanting to stop a bad guy. I know this is going to start a lot of folks frothing at the mouth, but I consider the both the 9mm Luger and the 38 Special to be marginal, although I admit they're near the upper end of their category. This puts the medium class of guns literally right on the fence in the middle of everything. They're clearly not as convenient as the guns in the small group and if you really need to shoot, they may or may not be quite big enough.

But even the large guns won't be "enough" if you can't hit where you want. Recoil and controllability get to be factors in our ability to shoot accurately. This pretty much eliminates the 44 Magnum from nearly everybody's list even though it's clearly tops in all three indices. But no matter what gun and cartridge size you select, plenty of practice with your gun—actually firing, not simply waving the gun around—is going to pay big dividends in your ability to effectively use it in an emergency.

There are two separate factors to this effectiveness equation. The first is that no bullet, not even the ones with the greatest RSP indices or those with the greatest striking energies, are going to do much of anything if you can't shoot well enough to put the bullet where you're looking, and that means both on the target and into an effective spot. That ability is something that only comes with practice. The second factor is that the gun isn't going to be a bit useful unless you know how to use it. That may sound like double talk, but you do have to be able to get the gun out of its carrying place, get it cocked, and get the safety off without fumbling, and do it all without having to look down at the gun.

Practice bullets don't have to be premium quality, because, after all, you're only shooting paper. But it is important that the gun feels and shoots very much like it will with the premium loads. You don't want to do too much practicing with wimpy target loads and then load big blasters into the gun for your defense application.

Let's sum up the elements that lead to an effective self-defense weapon. They are: enough gun, effective bullets, and plenty of practice. Taken together, these factors lead to confidence that you can mount an effective defense should it ever become necessary. In the final accounting, it may be that very confidence, expressed in your demeanor as you face potential danger, that may ultimately be far more important than the caliber of your gun in deciding the outcome of a threatening incident. ●

MY FRIEND WAS packing a 357 Magnum against my advice, but he was a good shot and an excellent woodsman. We were in the Virgin River area near the Arizona/Nevada border, and we had spotted a big boar at the edge of a plowed field near the river bottom. After a careful stalk he was able to place himself undetected at a location from which to shoot. His 6-inch Python barked, sending a linotype-cast Keith 158-grain SWC on its way, punched out with a maximum load of 15.5 grains of Hercules 2400. The large boar, feeding only twenty-five meters away, was hit squarely in the chest. He merely started, looked up, spotted my friend and charged, showing no signs of discomfort, much less serious injury.

My friend immediately shot him in the chest five more times with no visible effect, then decided that discretion might indeed be the better part of valor and quit the field, with the boar in hot pursuit....

First introduced to North America in 1893 by Austin Corbin as an exotic game animal for his private preserve, *Sus scrofa*, the European Wild Boar, has not only survived but flourished. Originally found only in small quantities in the areas where he was first released, this tough, intelligent creature has now proliferated widely throughout much of the United States. Indeed, in some areas such as northern California, his numbers have reached epidemic proportions, causing considerable alarm to wildlife conservation officers and property owners alike.

Unlike his domestic barnyard relative or European cousin, the North American wild pig doesn't become fat or complacent. Because he lives in a more competitive environment, he must rely on brains and speed to survive, and therefore must remain "lean and mean." Thus, not surprisingly, he only occasionally grows to body weights above 400 pounds, far short of his European cousins in the food-rich forests of Bavaria, who have been known to reach 600 pounds.

Wild hogs are dangerous, formidable creatures because of their tusks, which can reach nine inches in length. Moreover, they are famous for demonstrating an attitude problem, in that they tend to viciously attack anything they encounter at close quarters.

Aside from his razor-sharp tusks, which are really canine fangs, ol' *Scrofa* has forty-two teeth in a huge mouth, and a tremendous bite pressure with which to use them, the result of constant rooting for food. These are attached to a neck an NFL linebacker would envy, shoulders that dwarf Arnold Schwartzenegger's and a breastplate of 2-inch thick armor extending from behind each shoulder across his chest.

Although his eyes are small, his vision is good and his hearing excellent, due to 5-inch long ears that are kept erect at all times. His sense of smell is nothing short of superb and is perhaps his most efficient detection mechanism.

In contrast to what their portly appearance might suggest, wild hogs are capable of astonishing speed and agility and can run nearly as fast as a deer—and can do it in thickets a human would need a chain saw to negotiate. As if this isn't enough, he is also a good swimmer and a decent climber, making his way across streams even with strong currents and up rock-strewn hillsides with relative ease. He is big boned and heavily muscled, with a nervous system that resists shock.

Wild boars tend to remain in a ten-square-mile home area as long as the food supply remains plentiful, but have been known to travel as much as fifty miles to new feeding grounds when necessary. Like the shark, they are nearly perfect eating machines, even demonstrating omnivorous tendencies when required. They prefer roots, nuts, pecans, tubers, grass, fruits and berries when possible and literally rip up large

WILD BOAR SECRETS

by CHUCK TAYLOR

Author Chuck Taylor with a 375-pound boar, taken with a single shot from a camouflaged blind, as it emerged from brush at the edge of a milo field. Attention to camouflage and careful recon of the area to pinpoint the boar's feeding/travel habits allowed the author to place the blind to give the best chance for a quick, precise shot.

WILD BOAR SECRETS

areas of ground seeking them. However, they also eat mice, the eggs of ground-nesting birds, rabbits, salamanders, frogs, deer fawns, rattlesnakes—whose poison to which they are immune—and, when the fancy strikes them, *each other*!

While wild hogs enjoy a good wallow to escape heat and insects, they are anything but filthy. If they are unable to find a suitable wallow, they often root into the ground to lie on the moist soil beneath. In cold weather, they often pile grass into a mattress for warmth. This being insufficient, they will also sleep together in a heap to maximize the effects of their collective body warmth.

They communicate via a series of grunts when at leisure, but when aroused or alarmed they emit loud, shrill squeals that can be heard at great distances. While hunting in river canyon country, I have heard the sounds of two boars locked in combat from over a mile distant.

Novices often confuse wild hogs with southwestern javelina. However, javelina are quite small, normally weighing about 50 pounds, while wild hogs often reach more than 400 pounds.

About the Author

An internationally renowned weapons and tactics consultant and author, Chuck Taylor is also a big-game hunter with worldwide experience that includes Africa and Alaska.

He has put a dozen animals into three separate record books. His trophies include elk, wild boar, whitetail, Sitka and fallow deer, blackbuck antelope, Catalina goat and Corsican ram. Many of these were taken with a handgun.

When he hunts with a handgun, Chuck uses only iron-sighted, service types chambered for traditional pistol cartridges. He prefers the 6-inch Smith & Wesson M29 44 Magnum, but occasionally uses the 1911 Colt 45 ACP, 7½-inch Colt New Frontier in 44 Special, Glock M22 40 S&W, Colt Python 357 and Colt Diamondback 38 Special.

Their mating season typically occurs in December, with the sow coming into heat for two or three days at a time. If she is not fertilized within this period, she will again come into heat about twenty-one days later, the cycle repeating itself until the breeding process is complete. Piglets are thus born at different times of the year in groups of from three to twelve animals after a 112-115 day gestation period.

And, yes, the piglets *are* cute, with nine or ten white stripes running the length of their bodies. The sight of a sow sauntering through the bush with her entourage of piglets trailing along behind is enough to cause even the

most serious hunter to break into a grin.

Wild pigs have a highly developed social order and for protection often travel in groups of from a dozen to as many as fifty animals. When threatened, the group will respond with what bears a remarkable resemblance to a military perimeter defense. Most predators give them a wide berth, lacking the power, speed and courage to take on a mature pig. However, the black bear has been known to tangle with them, and wild dogs, wolves, bobcats and foxes pose a constant threat to youngsters.

Successful hunting of these creatures, especially with a handgun, requires some forethought. They are highly dangerous, being perfectly capable of tearing a human limb from limb,

The payoff! After several days of examining the residing animals' habits, the author took this photo of two good hogs emerging from their river-bottom bedding area just before dark.

and are thought by many to be the most dangerous game animal in North America, eclipsing even the grizzly bear in ferocity. Add to this the distressing fact that they will, without hesitation, confront anything that gets in their way, and the picture is complete.

In many parts of the country, wild hogs are hunted with dogs, but being a handgun-hunting purist, I prefer to match them on a more equal—and difficult—basis. This means that I must work harder, use my head more and take more risks, thus enhancing the quality of the hunt.

Extensive scouting is required to locate the areas they inhabit, travel routes, bedding locations and feeding preferences. This accomplished, two tactics are available—ambush or bait-

ing. I have used both with about equal success, sometimes in conjunction with one another. Although wild pigs love the same pungent slop that domestic pigs enjoy, baiting is effective only when proper scouting has been performed. Otherwise, it becomes a completely coincidental effort. Ambush, too, is dependent upon a knowledge of the animal's travel routes and times and resultant selection of a suitable ambush location.

If baiting is chosen, try to obtain restaurant garbage, placing it in plastic bags small enough to carry in a rucksack, although animal carcasses and even grain will do. The bait is placed for several days at a suitable spot in the pig's habitat to attract them, allowing you to make an examination of tracks,

dung and, often, even a visual analysis of the animals themselves.

As previously mentioned, pigs are highly intelligent, meaning that they are also highly competitive. Once the bait is discovered, they will make the site a regular stop on their feeding circuit and come from considerable distances to reach it before another animal gets there.

Ambush is best executed at a suitable spot along one of their routes to or from feeding areas and, depending upon the terrain and vegetation, can work very well in conjunction with baiting. However, proper care must be taken with camouflage, including movement, sound, scent and ultra-violet light reflection.

Pigs are by nature suspicious, but are also very curious, so even if they spot you, they may not immediately flee or attack. Instead, they may actually approach, seeking friend or foe identification. Once they realize what you are—something normally confirmed via their superb sense of smell—*be ready*, remembering that whatever happens, it will happen *fast!*

Equally "purist" are my feelings about what kind of handgun to utilize. I forgo using optically sighted weapons or rifle-powered "carbines without a buttstock," preferring instead to rely upon standard handguns and my own skill with them. Sure, it makes things tougher, but that is the whole point. I *want* a tougher challenge; one that requires my entire concentration to conquer. And if increased personal hazard is part of it, then so be it.

As previously stated, wild pigs are heavily muscled, with large bones and a two-inch thick "chest plate" of dense, leathery hide. This means that care must be taken not only in handgun and caliber selection but in what kind of bullet is used as well. Except perhaps in the larger calibers, JHP/JSP bullets just don't give adequate penetration. They increase the potential for a mishap and/or personal injury. For this reason, I recommend the heaviest hard-cast SWC bullet available in any given caliber.

We left my friend running from a boar at the beginning of this article. The ineffectiveness of the 357, even with a stout load, indicates the toughness of these animals, and the need to use enough gun. My friend was running away from the boar, and unfortunately his chosen path of withdrawal

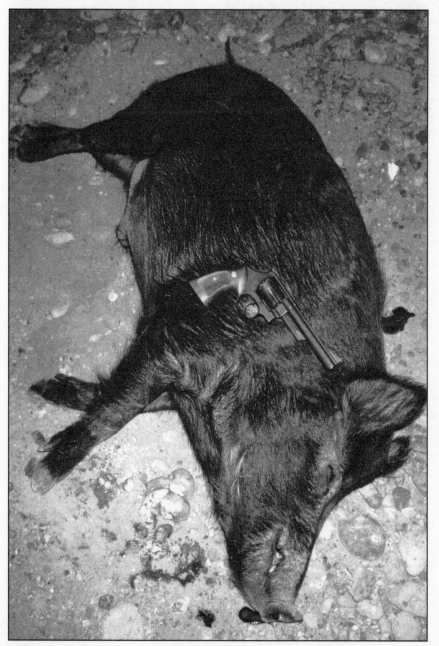

This excellent young boar weighed 324 pounds and was taken with a single shot behind the shoulder with the author's preferred S&W M29 44 Mag.

inadvertently placed him between the boar and me, preventing my entry into the fray. However, running laterally across a plowed field probably saved his life because he was able to run across the tops of the furrows, while in order to pursue, the boar was forced to diagonally negotiate the bottoms as well.

Nonetheless, the boar gained steadily, tusks snapping furiously at my friend's heels. My friend reached the

Considered by many to be the most dangerous North American big game animal, the wild boar requires "enough gun." Wild boars came from the Old World in the 1890s and proliferated.

(Below) A "purist" handgun hunter who uses only standard handgun calibers and weapons, Taylor believes the 44 Magnum to be the best for wild hogs because of its penetration capability and large-diameter bullet. He also prefers 6-inch or longer barrels for best sight radius and cartridge performance on this intelligent and highly dangerous game animal.

The 44 Magnum offers a variety of good bullets in factory loads or reloads. The round-nose, fourth from left, is about the worst. The best, says Taylor, is the semi-wadcutter, as used in the two loads at right.

truck and unceremoniously launched himself headlong into the bed. The boar, still coming full tilt, slammed into the left rear wheel, bounced off, and then did his absolute level best to join my friend up in the truck, smashing the fender and flattening the left rear tire in the process.

He then circled the truck twice, continuing his rampage. The next time around, as he emerged into my view from the front of the truck, the boar took a lino-cast 250-grain Keith SWC from my 6-inch S&W M29 44 Magnum on the joint of his left shoulder. Having reacted to my associate's precarious situation, I had taken advantage of the boar's preoccupation with him to also move across the field and approach unnoticed to within twenty meters.

The bullet smashed both shoulders and exited, ricocheting off the frozen ground and howling away across the field. He collapsed, squealed loudly, then flipped over and regained his feet, then collapsed again. A second 250-grain Keith bullet finished it.

Subsequent examination disclosed that all six 357s had failed to penetrate his frontal armor, thus inflicting little more than superficial wounds. You can bet my friend believes me now!

This is why I recommend the bigger, heavier bullets and a minimum of 40-caliber/900 fps for general-purpose use on these beasties. Penetration and bone-breaking ability are critical here, just like they are with any other kind of dangerous game. You *must* be able to anchor the animal with the first shot or the situation can quickly get out of hand, with potentially disastrous consequences.

Several additional points are also illustrated by this story: 1) Understand field shooting positions and be able to quickly assume them. 2) Understand your firearm, its capabilities and limitations, as well as your own as a marksman. 3) Develop your shooting ability until you can hit virtually any kind of target quickly, regardless of its size, color or shape. To settle for less is asking for trouble.

In conclusion, "purist" handgunning of these impressive animals clearly isn't for everyone. They're tough, smart, mean and big, and won't hesitate to prove it to you if you give them half a chance. But if you're looking for a hunting challenge that demands the ultimate from both the hunter and his equipment—and if you're good enough—then it just *might* be your cup of tea. After a lifetime of hunting all over the world, I've found with great satisfaction that it's mine.

The barbecued ribs aren't bad, either! ●

HANDGUNS 97

CATALOG

CENTERFIRE HANDGUN CARTRIDGES—BALLISTICS AND PRICES

Caliber	Bullet Wgt. Grs.	Velocity (fps) MV	Velocity 50 yds.	Velocity 100 yds.	Energy (ft. lbs.) ME	Energy 50 yds.	Energy 100 yds.	Mid-Range Traj. (in.) 50 yds.	Mid-Range Traj. 100 yds.	Bbl. Lgth. (in.)	Est. Price /box
221 Rem. Fireball	50	2650	2380	2130	780	630	505	0.2	0.8	10.5"	$15
25 Automatic	35	900	813	742	63	51	43	NA	NA	2"	$18
25 Automatic	45	815	730	655	65	55	40	1.8	7.7	2"	$21
25 Automatic	50	760	705	660	65	55	50	2.0	8.7	2"	$17
7.5mm Swiss	107	1010	NA	NA	240	NA	NA	NA	NA	NA	NEW
7.62mm Tokarev	87	1390	NA	NA	365	NA	NA	0.6	NA	4.5"	NA
7.62mm Nagant	97	1080	NA	NA	350	NA	NA	NA	NA	NA	NEW
7.63mm Mauser	88	1440	NA	NA	405	NA	NA	NA	NA	NA	NEW
30 Luger	93†	1220	1110	1040	305	255	225	0.9	3.5	4.5"	$34
30 Carbine	110	1790	1600	1430	785	625	500	0.4	1.7	10"	$28
32 S&W	88	680	645	610	90	80	75	2.5	10.5	3"	$17
32 S&W Long	98	705	670	635	115	100	90	2.3	10.5	4"	$17
32 Short Colt	80	745	665	590	100	80	60	2.2	9.9	4"	$19
32 H&R Magnum	85	1100	1020	930	230	195	165	1.0	4.3	4.5"	$21
32 H&R Magnum	95	1030	940	900	225	190	170	1.1	4.7	4.5"	$19
32 Automatic	60	970	895	835	125	105	95	1.3	5.4	4"	$22
32 Automatic	71	905	855	810	130	115	95	1.4	5.8	4"	$19
8mm Lebel Pistol	111	850	NA	NA	180	NA	NA	NA	NA	NA	NEW
8mm Steyr	113	1080	NA	NA	290	NA	NA	NA	NA	NA	NEW
8mm Gasser	126	850	NA	NA	200	NA	NA	NA	NA	NA	NEW
380 Automatic	60	1130	960	NA	170	120	NA	1.0	NA	NA	NA
380 Automatic	85/88	990	920	870	190	165	145	1.2	5.1	4"	$20
380 Automatic	90	1000	890	800	200	160	130	1.2	5.5	3.75"	$10
380 Automatic	95/100	955	865	785	190	160	130	1.4	5.9	4"	$20
38 Super Auto +P	115	1300	1145	1040	430	335	275	0.7	3.3	5"	$26
38 Super Auto +P	125/130	1215	1100	1015	425	350	300	0.8	3.6	5"	$26
38 Super Auto +P	147	1100	1050	1000	395	355	325	0.9	4.0	5"	NA
9x18mm Makarov	95	1000	NA	NA	NA	NA	NA	NA	NA	NA	NEW
9x18mm Ultra	100	1050	NA	NA	240	NA	NA	NA	NA	NA	NEW
9x23mm Largo	124	1190	1055	966	390	306	257	0.7	3.7	4"	NA
9mm Steyr	115	1180	NA	NA	350	NA	NA	NA	NA	NA	NEW
9mm Luger	88	1500	1190	1010	440	275	200	0.6	3.1	4"	$24
9mm Luger	90	1360	1112	978	370	247	191	NA	NA	4"	$26
9mm Luger	95	1300	1140	1010	350	275	215	0.8	3.4	4"	NA
9mm Luger	100	1180	1080	NA	305	255	NA	0.9	NA	4"	NA
9mm Luger	115	1155	1045	970	340	280	240	0.9	3.9	4"	$21
9mm Luger	123/125	1110	1030	970	340	290	260	1.0	4.0	4"	$23
9mm Luger	140	935	890	850	270	245	225	1.3	5.5	4"	$23
9mm Luger	147	990	940	900	320	290	265	1.1	4.9	4"	$26
9mm Luger +P	90	1475	NA	NA	437	NA	NA	NA	NA	NA	NA
9mm Luger +P	115	1250	1113	1019	399	316	265	0.8	3.5	4"	$27
9mm Federal	115	1280	1130	1040	420	330	280	0.7	3.3	4"V	$24
9mm Luger Vector	115	1155	1047	971	341	280	241	NA	NA	4"	NA
9mm Luger +P	124	1180	1089	1021	384	327	287	0.8	3.8	4"	NA
38 S&W	146	685	650	620	150	135	125	2.4	10.0	4"	$19
38 Short Colt	125	730	685	645	150	130	115	2.2	9.4	6"	$19
38 Special	100	950	900	NA	200	180	NA	1.3	NA	4"V	NA
38 Special	110	945	895	850	220	195	175	1.3	5.4	4"V	$23
38 Special	130	775	745	710	175	160	120	1.9	7.9	4"V	$22
38 (Multi-Ball)	140	830	730	505	215	130	80	2.0	10.6	4"V	$10**
38 Special	148	710	635	565	165	130	105	2.4	10.6	4"V	$17
38 Special	158	755	725	690	200	185	170	2.0	8.3	4"V	$18
38 Special +P	95	1175	1045	960	290	230	195	0.9	3.9	4"V	$23
38 Special +P	110	995	925	870	240	210	185	1.2	5.1	4"V	$23
38 Special +P	125	975	929	885	264	238	218	1	5.2	4"	NA
38 Special +P	125	945	900	860	250	225	205	1.3	5.4	4"V	$23
38 Special +P	129	945	910	870	255	235	215	1.3	5.3	4"V	$11
38 Special +P	130	925	887	852	247	227	210	1.3	5.50	4"V	NA
38 Special +P	147/150(c)	884	NA	NA	264	NA	NA	NA	NA	4"V	$27
38 Special +P	158	890	855	825	280	255	240	1.4	6.0	4"V	$20
357 SIG	115	1520	NA	NA	593	NA	NA	NA	NA	NA	NA
357 SIG	124	1450	NA	NA	578	NA	NA	NA	NA	NA	NA
357 SIG	125	1350	1190	1080	510	395	325	0.7	3.1	4"	NA
357 SIG	150	1130	1030	970	420	355	310	0.9	4.0	NA	NA
356 TSW	115	1520	NA	NA	593	NA	NA	NA	NA	NA	NA
356 TSW	124	1450	NA	NA	578	NA	NA	NA	NA	NA	NA
356 TSW	135	1280	1120	1010	490	375	310	0.8	3.50	NA	NA
356 TSW	147	1220	1120	1040	485	410	355	0.8	3.5	5"	NA
357 Magnum	110	1295	1095	975	410	290	230	0.8	3.5	4"V	$25
357 (Med. Vel.)	125	1220	1075	985	415	315	270	0.8	3.7	4"V	$25
357 Magnum	125	1450	1240	1090	585	425	330	0.6	2.8	4"V	$25
357 (Multi-Ball)	140	1155	830	665	420	215	135	1.2	6.4	4"V	$11**
357 Magnum	140	1360	1195	1075	575	445	360	0.7	3.0	4"V	$25
357 Magnum	145	1290	1155	1060	535	430	360	0.8	3.5	4"V	$26
357 Magnum	150/158	1235	1105	1015	535	430	360	0.8	3.5	4"V	$25
357 Magnum	165	1290	1189	1108	610	518	450	0.7	3.1	8 3/8"	NA
357 Magnum	180	1145	1055	985	525	445	390	0.9	3.9	4"V	$25
357 Rem. Maximum	158	1825	1590	1380	1170	885	670	0.4	1.7	10.5"	$14**
40 S&W	135	1140	1070	NA	390	345	NA	0.9	NA	4"	NA
40 S&W	155	1140	1026	958	447	362	309	0.9	4.1	4"	$14***
40 S&W	165	1150	NA	NA	485	NA	NA	NA	NA	4"	$18***
40 S&W	180	985	936	893	388	350	319	1.4	5.0	4"	$14***
40 S&W	180	1015	960	914	412	368	334	1.3	4.5	4"	NA
10mm Automatic	155	1125	1046	986	436	377	335	0.9	3.9	5"	$26
10mm Automatic	170	1340	1165	1145	680	510	415	0.7	3.2	5"	$31
10mm Automatic	175	1290	1140	1035	650	505	420	0.7	3.3	5.5"	$11**
10mm Auto.(FBI)	180	950	905	865	361	327	299	1.5	5.4	4"	$16**
10mm Automatic	180	1030	970	920	425	375	340	1.1	4.7	5"	$16**
10mm Auto H.V.	180†	1240	1124	1037	618	504	430	0.8	3.4	5"	$27
10mm Automatic	200	1160	1070	1010	495	510	430	0.9	3.8	5"	$14**
10.4mm Italian	177	950	NA	NA	360	NA	NA	NA	NA	NA	NEW
41 Action Exp.	180	1000	947	903	400	359	326	0.5	4.2	5"	$13**
41 Rem. Magnum	170	1420	1165	1015	760	515	390	0.7	3.2	4"V	$33
41 Rem. Magnum	175	1250	1120	1030	605	490	410	0.8	3.4	4"V	$14**
41 (Med. Vel.)	210	965	900	840	435	375	330	1.3	5.4	4"V	$30
41 Rem. Magnum	210	1300	1160	1060	790	630	535	0.7	3.2	4"V	$33
44 S&W Russian	247	780	NA	NA	335	NA	NA	NA	NA	NA	NA
44 S&W Special	180	980	NA	NA	383	NA	NA	NA	NA	6.5"	NA
44 S&W Special	180	1000	935	882	400	350	311	NA	NA	7.5"V	NA
44 S&W Special	200†	875	825	780	340	302	270	1.2	6.0	6"	$13**
44 S&W Special	200	1035	940	865	475	390	335	1.1	4.9	6.5"	$13**
44 S&W Special	240/246	755	725	695	310	285	265	2.0	8.3	6.5"	$26
44 Rem. Magnum	180	1610	1365	1175	1035	745	550	0.5	2.3	4"V	$18***
44 Rem. Magnum	200	1400	1192	1053	870	630	492	0.6	NA	6.5"	$20
44 Rem. Magnum	210	1495	1310	1165	1040	805	635	0.6	2.5	6.5"	$18***
44 (Med. Vel.)	240	1000	945	900	535	475	435	1.1	4.8	6.5"	$17
44 R.M.(Jacketed)	240	1180	1080	1010	740	625	545	0.9	3.7	4"V	$18***
44 R.M. (Lead)	240	1350	1185	1070	970	750	610	0.7	3.1	4"V	$29
44 Rem. Magnum	250	1180	1100	1040	775	670	600	0.8	3.6	6.5"V	$21
44 Rem. Magnum	275	1235	1142	1070	931	797	699	0.8	3.3	6.5"	NA
44 Rem. Magnum	300	1200	1100	1026	959	806	702	NA	NA	7.5"	$17
450 Short Colt	226	830	NA	NA	350	NA	NA	NA	NA	NA	NEW
45 Automatic	165	1030	930	NA	385	315	NA	1.2	NA	5"	NA
45 Automatic	185	1000	940	890	410	360	325	1.1	4.9	5"	$28
45 Auto. (Match)	185	770	705	650	245	204	175	2.0	8.7	5"	$28
45 Auto. (Match)	200	940	890	840	392	352	312	2.0	8.6	5"	$20
45 Automatic	200	975	917	860	421	372	328	1.4	5.0	5"	$18
45 Automatic	230	830	800	675	355	325	300	1.6	6.8	5"	$27
45 Automatic	230	880	846	816	396	366	340	1.5	6.1	5"	NA
45 Automatic +P	165	1250	NA	NA	573	NA	NA	NA	NA	NA	NA
45 Automatic +P	185	1140	1040	970	535	445	385	0.9	4.0	5"	$31
45 Automatic +P	200	1055	982	925	494	428	380	NA	NA	5"	NA
45 Win. Magnum	230	1400	1230	1105	1000	775	635	0.6	2.8	5"	$14**
45 Win. Magnum	260	1250	1137	1053	902	746	640	0.8	3.3	5"	$16**
455 Webley MKII	262	850	NA	NA	420	NA	NA	NA	NA	NA	NA
45 Colt	200	1000	938	889	444	391	351	1.3	4.8	5.5"	$21
45 Colt	225	960	890	830	460	395	345	1.3	5.5	5.5"	$22
45 Colt	250/255	860	820	780	410	375	340	1.6	6.6	5.5"	$27
50 Action Exp.	325	1400	1209	1075	1414	1055	835	0.2	2.3	6"	$24**

Notes: Blanks are available in 32 S&W, 38 S&W, and 38 Special. V after barrel length indicates test barrel was vented to produce ballistics similar to a revolver with a normal barrel-to-cylinder gap. Ammo prices are per 50 rounds except when marked with an ** which signifies a 20 round box; *** signifies a 25-round box. Not all loads are available from all ammo manufacturers. Listed loads are those made by Remington, Winchester, Federal, and others. DISC. is a discontinued load. Prices are rounded to nearest whole dollar and will vary with brand and retail outlet. †= new bullet weight this year; "c" indicates a change in data.

RIMFIRE AMMUNITION—BALLISTICS AND PRICES

Cartridge type	Bullet Wt. Grs.	Velocity (fps) 22½" Barrel Muzzle	50 Yds.	100 Yds.	Energy (ft. lbs.) 22½" Barrel Muzzle	50 Yds.	100 Yds.	Velocity (fps) 6" Barrel Muzzle	50 Yds.	Energy (ft. lbs) 6" Barrel Muzzle	50 Yds.	Approx. Price Per Box 50 Rds.	100 Rds.
22 Short Blank		Not applicable										$4	NA
22 CB Short	30	725	667	610	34	29	24	706	—	32	—	$2	NA
22 Short Match	29	830	752	695	44	36	31	786	—	39	—	—	NA
22 Short Std. Vel.	29	1045	—	810	70	—	42	865	—	48	—	Discontinued	
22 Short High Vel.	29	1095	—	903	77	—	53	—	—	—	—	$2	NA
22 Short H.V. H.P.	27	1120	—	904	75	—	49	—	—	—	—	—	NA
22 CB Long	30	725	667	610	34	29	24	706	—	32	—	$2	NA
22 Long Std. Vel.	29	1180	1038	946	90	69	58	1031	—	68	—	—	—
22 Long High Vel.	29	1240	—	962	99	—	60	—	—	—	—	$2	NA
22 L.R. Sub Sonic	38/40	1070	970	890	100	80	70	940	—	—	—	$2	NA
22 L.R. Std. Vel.	40	1138	1047	975	116	97	84	1027	925	93	76	$2	NA
22 L.R. High Vel.	40	1255	1110	1017	140	109	92	1060	—	100	—	$2	NA
22 L.R. H.V. Sil.	42	1220	—	1003	139	—	94	1025	—	98	—	$2	NA
22 L.R. H.V. H.P.	36/38	1280	1126	1010	131	101	82	1089	—	95	—	$2	NA
22 L.R. Shot	#11 or #12	1047	—	—	—	—	—	950	—	—	—	$5	NA
22 L.R. Hyper Vel	36	1410	1187	1056	159	113	89	—	—	—	—	$2	NA
22 L.R. Hyper H.P	32/33/34	1500	1240	1075	165	110	85	—	—	—	—	$2	NA
22 WRF	45	1320	—	1055	175	—	111	—	—	—	—	NA	$5
22 Win. Mag.	30	2200	1750	1373	322	203	127	1610	—	—	—	—	NA
22 Win. Mag.	40	1910	1490	1326	324	197	156	1428	—	181	—	$6	NA
22 Win. Mag.	50	1650	—	1280	300	180	—	—	—	—	—	NA	NA
22 Win. Mag. Shot	#11	1126	—	—	—	—	—	—	—	—	—	NA	NA

Note: The actual ballistics obtained with your firearm can vary considerably from the advertised ballistics. Also ballistics can vary from lot to lot with the same brand and type load. Prices can vary with manufacturer and retail outlet. NA in the price column indicates this size packaging currently unavailable.

Includes models suitable for several forms of competition and other sporting purposes.

AA ARMS AP9 PISTOL Caliber: 9mm Para., 10-shot magazine. **Barrel:** 5″. **Weight:** 3.5 lbs. **Length:** 12″ overall. **Stocks:** Checkered black synthetic. **Sights:** Post front adjustable for elevation, rear adjustable for windage **Features:** Ventilated barrel shroud; blue or electroless nickel finish. Made in U.S. by AA Arms.
Price: Blue $299.00
Price: Nickel $312.00
Price: AP9 Target 11″ barrel $399.00

AA Arms AP9 Mini, AP9 Mini/5 Pistol Similar to AP9 except scaled-down dimensions with 3″ or 5″ barrel.
Price: 3″ barrel, blue $239.00
Price: 3″ barrel, electroless nickel $259.00
Price: Mini/5, 5″ barrel, blue $259.00
Price: Mini/5, 5″ barrel, electroless nickel $279.00

Accu-Tek AT-9SS

ACCU-TEK MODEL AT-9SS AUTO PISTOL Caliber: 9mm Para., 8-shot magazine. **Barrel:** 3.2″. **Weight:** 28 oz. **Length:** 6.25″ overall. **Stocks:** Black checkered nylon. **Sights:** Blade front, rear adjustable for windage; three-dot system. **Features:** Stainless steel construction. Double action only. Firing pin block with no external safeties. Lifetime warranty. Introduced 1992. Made in U.S. by Accu-Tek.
Price: Satin stainless $317.00

Accu-Tek AT-40SS Auto Pistol Same as the Model AT-9 except chambered for 40 S&W, 7-shot magazine. Introduced 1992.
Price: Stainless $317.00

Accu-Tek AT-45SS Auto Pistol Same as the Model AT-9SS except chambered for 45 ACP, 6-shot magazine. Introduced 1995. Made in U.S. by Accu-Tek.
Price: Stainless steel $327.00

Accu-Tek AT-45SS

ACCU-TEK MODEL AT-380SS AUTO PISTOL Caliber: 380 ACP, 5-shot magazine. **Barrel:** 2.75″. **Weight:** 20 oz. **Length:** 5.6″ overall. **Stocks:** Grooved black composition. **Sights:** Blade front, rear adjustable for windage. **Features:** Stainless steel frame and slide. External hammer; manual thumb safety; firing pin block, trigger disconnect. Lifetime warranty. Introduced 1991. Made in U.S. by Accu-Tek.
Price: Satin stainless $191.00
Price: Black finish over steel (AT-380B) $196.00

ACCU-TEK MODEL HC-380SS AUTO PISTOL Caliber: 380 ACP, 10-shot magazine. **Barrel:** 2.75″. **Weight:** 28 oz. **Length:** 6″ overall. **Stocks:** Checkered black composition. **Sights:** Blade front, rear adjustable for windage. **Features:** External hammer; manual thumb safety with firing pin and trigger disconnect; bottom magazine release. Stainless finish. Introduced 1993. Made in U.S. by Accu-Tek.
Price: Satin stainless $243.00
Price: Black finish over stainless $248.00

Accu-Tek HC-380SS

Acc-Tek AT-380SS

Consult our Directory pages for the location of firms mentioned.

Accu-Tek Model AT-32SS Auto Pistol Same as the AT-380SS except chambered for 32 ACP. Introduced 1991.
Price: Satin stainless $185.00
Price: Black finish over steel (AT-32B) $190.00

American Arms Escort

AMERICAN ARMS ESCORT AUTO PISTOL Caliber: 380 ACP, 7-shot magazine. **Barrel:** 3³/₈″. **Weight:** 19 oz. **Length:** 6¹/₈″ overall. **Stocks:** Soft polymer. **Sights:** Blade front, rear adjustable for windage. **Features:** Double-action-only trigger; stainless steel construction; chamber loaded indicator. Introduced 1995. From American Arms, Inc.
Price: $349.00

American Arms PK22

AMERICAN ARMS MODEL PK22 DA AUTO PISTOL Caliber: 22 LR, 8-shot magazine. **Barrel:** 3.3″. **Weight:** 22 oz. **Length:** 6.3″ overall. **Stocks:** Checkered plastic. **Sights:** Fixed. **Features:** Double action. Polished blue finish. Slide-mounted safety. Made in the U.S. by American Arms, Inc.
Price: $199.00

AMERICAN ARMS MODEL P-98 AUTO PISTOL Caliber: 22 LR, 8-shot magazine. **Barrel:** 5″. **Weight:** 25 oz. **Length:** 8¹/₈″ overall. **Stocks:** Grooved black polymer. **Sights:** Blade front, rear adjustable for windage. **Features:** Double action with hammer-block safety, magazine disconnect safety. Alloy frame. Has external appearance of the Walther P-38 pistol. Introduced 1989. Made in U.S. by American Arms, Inc.
Price: $209.00

American Arms P-98

AMERICAN ARMS AUSSIE PISTOL Caliber: 9mm Para., 40 S&W, 10-shot magazine. **Barrel:** 4³/₄″. **Weight:** 23 oz. **Length:** 7⁷/₈″ overall. **Stocks:** Integral; checkered polymer. **Sights:** Blade front, rear adjustable for windage. **Features:** Double action only. Polymer frame. Has five safeties—firing pin block; positive trigger safety; magazine safety; slide lock safety; loaded chamber indicator. Introduced 1996. From American Arms, Inc.
Price: $425.00

ARMSCOR M-1911-A1P AUTOLOADING PISTOL Caliber: 45 ACP, 7- or 10-shot magazine. **Barrel:** 5″. **Weight:** 38 oz. **Length:** 8³/₄″ overall. **Stocks:** Checkered. **Sights:** Blade front, rear drift adjustable for windage; three-dot system. **Features:** Skeletonized combat hammer and trigger; beavertail grip safety; extended slide release; oversize thumb safety; Parkerized finish. Introduced 1996. Imported from the Philippines by K.B.I., Inc.
Price: $399.99

Armscor M-1911-A1P

AMT 45 ACP HARDBALLER Caliber: 45 ACP. **Barrel:** 5″. **Weight:** 39 oz. **Length:** 8¹/₂″ overall. **Stocks:** Wrap-around rubber. **Sights:** Adjustable. **Features:** Extended combat safety, serrated matte slide rib, loaded chamber indicator, long grip safety, beveled magazine well, adjustable target trigger. All stainless steel. From AMT.
Price: $549.95
Price: Government model (as above except no rib, fixed sights) $489.99

AMT 45 ACP HARDBALLER LONG SLIDE Caliber: 45 ACP. **Barrel:** 7″. **Length:** 10¹/₂″ overall. **Stocks:** Wrap-around rubber. **Sights:** Fully adjustable rear sight. **Features:** Slide and barrel are 2″ longer than the standard 45, giving less recoil, added velocity, longer sight radius. Has extended combat safety, serrated matte rib, loaded chamber indicator, wide adjustable trigger. From AMT.
Price: $595.99

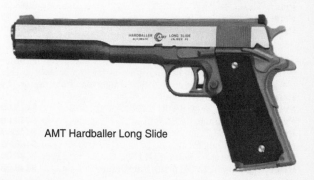

AMT Hardballer Long Slide

AMT AUTOMAG II AUTO PISTOL Caliber: 22 WMR, 9-shot magazine (7-shot with 3⅜" barrel). **Barrel:** 3⅜", 4½", 6". **Weight:** About 23 oz. **Length:** 9⅜" overall. **Stocks:** Grooved carbon fiber. **Sights:** Blade front, adjustable rear. **Features:** Made of stainless steel. Gas-assisted action. Exposed hammer. Slide flats have brushed finish, rest is sandblast. Squared trigger guard. Introduced 1986. From AMT.
Price: $405.95

AMT AUTOMAG III PISTOL Caliber: 30 Carbine, 8-shot magazine. **Barrel:** 6⅜". **Weight:** 43 oz. **Length:** 10½" overall. **Stocks:** Carbon fiber. **Sights:** Blade front, adjustable rear. **Features:** Stainless steel construction. Hammer-drop safety. Slide flats have brushed finish, rest is sandblasted. Introduced 1989. From AMT.
Price: $469.79

AMT AUTOMAG IV PISTOL Caliber: 45 Winchester Magnum, 6-shot magazine. **Barrel:** 6.5". **Weight:** 46 oz. **Length:** 10.5" overall. **Stocks:** Carbon fiber. **Sights:** Blade front, adjustable rear. **Features:** Made of stainless steel with brushed finish. Introduced 1990. Made in U.S. by AMT.
Price: $699.99

AMT BACK UP II AUTO PISTOL Caliber: 380 ACP, 5-shot magazine. **Barrel:** 2½". **Weight:** 18 oz. **Length:** 5" overall. **Stocks:** Carbon fiber. **Sights:** Fixed, open, recessed. **Features:** Concealed hammer, blowback operation; manual and grip safeties. All stainless steel construction. Smallest domestically-produced pistol in 380. From AMT.
Price: $309.99

AMT Back Up Double Action Only Pistol Similar to the standard Back Up except has double-action-only mechanism, enlarged trigger guard, slide is rounded ar rear. Has 5-shot magazine. Introduced 1992. From AMT.
Price: $329.99
Price: 9mm Para., 38 Super, 40 S&W, 45 ACP $449.99

ARGENTINE HI-POWER 9MM AUTO PISTOL Caliber: 9mm Para., 10-shot magazine. **Barrel:** 4²¹/₃₂". **Weight:** 32 oz. **Length:** 7¾" overall. **Stocks:** Checkered walnut. **Sights:** Blade front, adjustable rear. **Features:** Produced in Argentina under F.N. Browning license. Introduced 1990. Imported by Century International Arms, Inc.
Price: About $299.95

ASTRA A-70 AUTO PISTOL Caliber: 9mm Para., 8-shot; 40 S&W, 7-shot magazine. **Barrel:** 3.5". **Weight:** 29.3 oz. **Length:** 6.5" overall. **Stocks:** Checkered black plastic. **Sights:** Blade front, rear adjustable for windage. **Features:** All steel frame and slide. Checkered grip straps and trigger guard. Nickel or blue finish. Introduced 1992. Imported from Spain by European American Armory.
Price: Blue, 9mm Para. $360.00
Price: Blue, 40 S&W $360.00
Price: Nickel, 9mm Para. $385.00
Price: Nickel, 40 S&W $385.00
Price: Stainless steel, 9mm $450.00
Price: Stainless steel, 40 S&W $450.00

Astra A-75 Decocker Auto Pistol Same as the A-70 except has decocker system, double or single action, different trigger, contoured pebble-grain grips. Introduced 1993. Imported from Spain by European American Armory.
Price: Blue, 9mm or 40 S&W $415.00
Price: Nickel, 9mm or 40 S&W $440.00
Price: Blue, 45 ACP $445.00
Price: Nickel, 45 ACP $460.00
Price: Stainless steel, 9mm, 40 S&W $495.00
Price: Featherweight (23.5 oz.), 9mm, blue $440.00

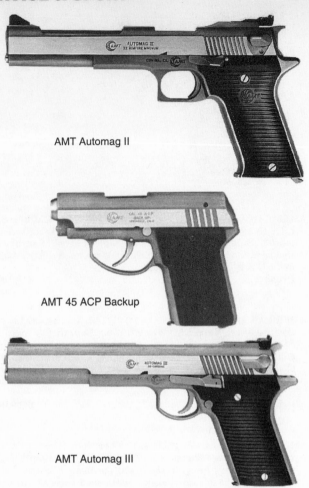

AMT Automag II

AMT 45 ACP Backup

AMT Automag III

Argentine Hi-Power Detective Model Similar to the standard model except has 3.8" barrel, 6.9" overall length and weighs 33 oz. Grips are finger-groove, checkered soft rubber. Matte black finish. Introduced 1994. Imported by Century International Arms, Inc.
Price: About $310.00

Astra A-75

ASTRA A-100 AUTO PISTOL Caliber: 9mm Para., 10-shot; 40 S&W, 10-shot; 45 ACP, 9-shot magazine. **Barrel:** 3.9". **Weight:** 29 oz. **Length:** 7.1" overall. **Stocks:** Checkered black plastic. **Sights:** Blade front, interchangeable rear blades for elevation, screw adjustable for windage. **Features:** Double action. Decocking lever permits lowering hammer onto locked firing pin. Automatic firing pin block. Side button magazine release. Introduced 1993. Imported from Spain by European American Armory.
Price: Blue, 9mm, 40 S&W, 45 ACP $450.00
Price: As above, nickel $475.00

AUTO-ORDNANCE 1911A1 AUTOMATIC PISTOL Caliber: 9mm Para., 38 Super, 9-shot; 10mm, 45 ACP, 7-shot magazine. **Barrel:** 5". **Weight:** 39 oz. **Length:** 8½" overall. **Stocks:** Checkered plastic with medallion. **Sights:** Blade front, rear adjustable for windage. **Features:** Same specs as 1911A1 military guns—parts interchangeable. Frame and slide blued; each radius has non-glare finish. Made in U.S. by Auto-Ordnance Corp.
Price: 45 ACP, blue $397.50
Price: 45 ACP, Parkerized $389.95
Price: 45 ACP, satin nickel $425.95
Price: 9mm, 38 Super $435.00
Price: 10mm (has three-dot combat sights, rubber wrap-around grips) $435.00
Price: 45 ACP General Model (Commander style) $465.00
Price: Duo Tone (nickel frame, blue slide, three-dot sight system, textured black wrap-around grips) $435.00

Auto-Ordnance ZG-51 Pit Bull Auto Same as the 1911A1 except has 3½" barrel, weighs 36 oz. and has an over-all length of 7¼". Available in 45 ACP only; 7-shot magazine. Introduced 1989.
Price: $455.00

Auto-Ordnance 1911A1 Competition Model Similar to the standard Model 1911A1 except has barrel compensator. Commander hammer, flat mainspring housing, three-dot sight system, low-profile magazine funnel, Hi-Ride beavertail grip safety, full-length recoil spring guide system, black-textured rubber, wrap-around grips, and extended slide stop, safety and magazine catch. In 45 or 38 Super. Introduced 1994. Made in U.S. by Auto-Ordnance Corp.
Price: $635.00

BABY EAGLE AUTO PISTOL Caliber: 9mm Para., 40 S&W, 41 A.E. **Barrel:** 4.37". **Weight:** 35 oz. **Length:** 8.14" overall. **Stocks:** High-impact black polymer. **Sights:** Combat. **Features:** Double-action mechanism; polygonal rifling; ambidextrous safety. Model 9mm F has frame-mounted safety on left side of pistol; Model 9mm FS has frame-mounted safety and 3.62" barrel. Introduced 1992. Imported by Magnum Research.
Price: 40 S&W, 41 A.E., 9mm (9mm F, 9mm FS), black finish $569.00
Price: Conversion kit, 9mm Para. to 41 A.E. $239.00
Price: 9mm FS, chrome finish $659.00
Price: 9mm FSS, matte black finish, frame-mounted safety, short grip, short barrel $569.00
Price: As above, chrome finish $659.00

BAER 1911 CONCEPT I AUTO PISTOL Caliber: 45 ACP, 7-shot magazine. **Barrel:** 5". **Weight:** 37 oz. **Length:** 8.5" overall. **Stocks:** Checkered rosewood. **Sights:** Baer dovetail front, Bo-Mar deluxe low-mount rear with hidden leaf. **Features:** Baer forged steel frame, slide and barrel with Baer stainless bushing; slide fitted to frame; double serrated slide; Baer beavertail grip safety, checkered slide stop, tuned extractor, extended ejector, deluxe hammer and sear, match disconnector; lowered and flared ejection port; fitted recoil link; polished feed ramp, throated barrel; Baer fitted speed trigger, flat serrated mainspring housing. Blue finish. Made in U.S. by Les Baer Custom, Inc.
Price: $1,428.00
Price: Concept II (with Baer adjustable rear sight) ...$1,428.00

Astra A-100

Auto-Ordnance 1911A1

Baby Eagle FS

Les Baer Concept IV

Baer 1911 Concept III Auto Pistol Same as the Concept I except has forged stainless frame with blued steel slide, Bo-Mar rear sight, 30 lpi checkering on front strap. Made in U.S. by Les Baer Custom, Inc.
Price: $1,500.00
Price: Concept IV (with Baer adjustable rear sight) ...$1,499.00
Price: Concept V (all stainless, Bo-Mar sight, checkered front strap) $1,598.00
Price: Concept VI (stainless, Baer adjustable sight, checkered front strap).............................$1,598.00

Baer Custom Carry

Baer Premier II

Consult our Directory pages for the location of firms mentioned.

Baer 1911 Prowler III Auto Pistol Same as the Premier II except also has tapered cone stub weight and reverse recoil plug. Made in U.S. by Les Baer Custom, Inc.
Price: Standard size, blued $1,795.00

Biakal IJ-70

BAIKAL IJ-70 DA AUTO PISTOL Caliber: 9x18mm Makarov, 8-shot magazine. **Barrel:** 4″. **Weight:** 25 oz. **Length:** 6.25″ overall. **Stocks:** Checkered composition. **Sights:** Blade front, rear adjustable for windage and elevation. **Features:** Double action; all-steel construction; frame-mounted safety with decocker. Comes with two magazines, cleaning rod, universal tool. Introduced 1994. Imported from Russia by Century International Arms, K.B.I., Inc.
Price: 9x18mm, blue $199.00
Price: IJ-70HC, 9x18, 10-shot magazine, from K.B.I. . . .$239.00
Price: As above, 380 ACP (K.B.I.) $249.00

Baer 1911 Concept VII Auto Pistol Same as the Concept I except reduced Commanche size with 4.25″ barrel, weighs 27.5 oz., 7.75″ overall. Blue finish, checkered front strap. Made in U.S. by Les Baer Custom, Inc.
Price: $1,480.00
Price: Concept VIII (stainless frame and slide, Baer adjustable rear sight) $1,598.00

Baer 1911 Concept IX Auto Pistol Same as the Commanche Concept VII except has Baer lightweight forged aluminum frame, blued steel slide, Baer adjustable rear sight. Chambered for 45 ACP, 7-shot magazine. Made in U.S. by Les Baer Custom, Inc.
Price: $1,598.00
Price: Concept X (as above with stainless slide) $1,598.00

BAER 1911 CUSTOM CARRY AUTO PISTOL Caliber: 45 ACP, 7- or 10-shot magazine. **Barrel:** 5″. **Weight:** 37 oz. **Length:** 8.5″ overall. **Stocks:** Checkered walnut. **Sights:** Baer improved ramp-style dovetailed front, Novak low-mount rear. **Features:** Baer forged NM frame, slide and barrel with stainless bushing; fitted slide to frame; double serrated slide (full-size only); Baer speed trigger with 4-lb. pull; Baer deluxe hammer and sear, tactical-style extended ambidextrous safety, beveled magazine well; polished feed ramp and throated barrel; tuned extractor; Baer extended ejector, checkered slide stop; lowered and flared ejection port, full-length recoil guide rod; recoil buff. Made in U.S. by Les Baer Custom, Inc.
Price: Standard size, blued $1,490.00
Price: Standard size, stainless $1,580.00
Price: Commanche size, blued $1,490.00
Price: Commanche size, stainless $1,580.00
Price: Commanche size, aluminum frame, blued slide .$1,530.00
Price: Commanche size, aluminum frame, stainless slide $1,590.00

BAER 1911 S.R.P. PISTOL Caliber: 45 ACP. **Barrel:** 5″. **Weight:** 37 oz. **Length:** 8.5″ overall. **Stocks:** Checkered walnut. **Sights:** Trijicon night sights. **Features:** Similar to the F.B.I. contract gun except uses Baer forged steel frame. Has Baer match barrel with supported chamber, Wolff springs, complete tactical action job. All parts Mag-na-fluxed; deburred for tactical carry. Has Baer Ultra Coat finish. Tuned for reliability. Contact Baer for complete details. Introduced 1996. Made in U.S. by Les Baer Custom, Inc.
Price: Government or Commanche length $2,495.00

BAER 1911 PREMIER II AUTO PISTOL Caliber: 45 ACP, 7- or 10-shot magazine. **Barrel:** 5″. **Weight:** 37 oz. **Length:** 8.5″ overall. **Stocks:** Checkered rosewood, double diamond pattern. **Sights:** Baer dovetailed front, low-mount Bo-Mar rear with hidden leaf. **Features:** Baer NM forged steel frame and barrel with stainless bushing; slide fitted to frame; double serrated slide; lowered, flared ejection port; tuned, polished extractor; Baer extended ejector, checkered slide stop, aluminum speed trigger with 4-lb. pull, deluxe Commander hammer and sear, beavertail grip safety with pad, beveled magazine well, extended ambidextrous safety; flat mainspring housing; polished feed ramp and throated barrel; 30 lpi checkered front strap. Made in U.S. by Les Baer Custom, Inc.
Price: Blued $1,428.00
Price: Stainless $1,559.00
Price: 6″ model, blued $1,690.00

BAER LIGHTWEIGHT 22 Caliber: 22 LR. **Barrel:** 5″. **Weight:** 25 oz. **Length:** 8.5″ overall. **Stocks:** Checkered walnut. **Sights:** Blade front. **Features:** Aluminum frame and slide. Baer beavertail grip safety with pad, checkered slide stop, deluxe hammer and sear, match disconnector, flat serrated mainspring housing, Baer fitted speed trigger, tuned extractor. Has total reliability tuning package, action job. Baer Ultra Coat finish. Introduced 1996. Made in U.S. by Les Baer Custom, Inc.
Price: Government model size, fixed sights $1,428.00
Price: Government model, Bo-Mar sights $1,498.00
Price: Commanche size, fixed sights $1,428.00

BERETTA MODEL 80 CHEETAH SERIES DA PISTOLS **Caliber:** 380 ACP, 10-shot magazine (M84); 8-shot (M85); 22 LR, 7-shot (M87), 22 LR, 8-shot (M89). **Barrel:** 3.82″. **Weight:** About 23 oz. (M84/85). 20.8 oz. (M87). **Length:** 6.8″ overall. **Stocks:** Glossy black plastic (wood optional at extra cost). **Sights:** Fixed front, drift-adjustable rear. **Features:** Double action, quick takedown, convenient magazine release. Introduced 1977. Imported from Italy by Beretta U.S.A.
Price: Model 84 Cheetah, plastic grips $529.00
Price: Model 84 Cheetah, wood grips $557.00
Price: Model 84 Cheetah, wood grips, nickel finish $600.00
Price: Model 85 Cheetah, plastic grips, 8-shot $499.00
Price: Model 85 Cheetah, wood grips, 8-shot $530.00
Price: Model 85 Cheetah, wood grips, nickel, 8-shot $599.00
Price: Model 87 Cheetah wood, 22 LR, 7-shot $493.00

Beretta 84 Cheetah

Beretta Model 86 Cheetah Similar to the 380-caliber Model 85 except has tip-up barrel for first-round loading. Barrel length is 4.33″, overall length of 7.33″. Has 8-shot magazine, walnut grips. Introduced 1989.
Price: $514.00

Beretta 86 Cheetah

BERETTA MODEL 92FS PISTOL **Caliber:** 9mm Para., 10-shot magazine. **Barrel:** 4.9″. **Weight:** 34 oz. **Length:** 8.5″ overall. **Stocks:** Checkered black plastic; wood optional at extra cost. **Sights:** Blade front, rear adjustable for windage. Tritium night sights available. **Features:** Double action. Extractor acts as chamber loaded indicator, squared trigger guard, grooved front- and backstraps, inertia firing pin. Matte finish. Introduced 1977. Made in U.S. and imported from Italy by Beretta U.S.A.
Price: With plastic grips $626.00
Price: With wood grips $647.00
Price: Tritium night sights, add $90.00

Beretta 87 Cheetah

Beretta Model 92D Pistol Same as the Model 92FS except double-action-only and has bobbed hammer, no external safety. Introduced 1992.
Price: With plastic grips, three-dot sights $586.00
Price: As above with tritium sights $676.00

Beretta Model 92F Stainless Pistol Same as the Model 92FS except has stainless steel barrel and slide, and frame of aluminum-zirconium alloy. Has three-dot sight system. Introduced 1992.
Price: $757.00
Price: For tritium sights, add $90.00

Beretta 92FS

Beretta Model 96 Auto Pistol Same as the Model 92F except chambered for 40 S&W. Ambidextrous safety mechanism with passive firing pin catch, slide safety/decocking lever, trigger bar disconnect. Has 10-shot magazine. Available with tritium or three-dot sights. Introduced 1992.
Price: Model 96, plastic grips $643.00
Price: Model 96D, double-action-only, three-dot sights .. $607.00
Price: For tritium sights, add $90.00

Beretta Models 92FS/96 Centurion Pistols Identical to the Model 92FS and 96F except uses shorter slide and barrel (4.3″). Tritium or three-dot sight systems. Plastic or wood grips. Available in 9mm or 40 S&W. Also available in D Models (double-action-only). Introduced 1992.
Price: Model 92FS Centurion, three-dot sights, plastic grips .. $626.00
Price: Model 92FS Centurion, wood grips $647.00
Price: Model 96 Centurion, three-dot sights, plastic grips $643.00
Price: Model 92D Centurion $586.00
Price: Model 96D Centurion $607.00
Price: For tritium sights, add $90.00

Beretta 96D

BERETTA MODEL 950 JETFIRE AUTO PISTOL Caliber: 25 ACP, 8-shot. **Barrel:** 2.4". **Weight:** 9.9 oz. **Length:** 4.7" overall. **Stocks:** Checkered black plastic or walnut. **Sights:** Fixed. **Features:** Single action, thumb safety; tip-up barrel for direct loading/unloading, cleaning. From Beretta U.S.A.
Price: Jetfire plastic, blue $187.00
Price: Jetfire plastic, nickel $221.00
Price: Jetfire wood, engraved $267.00
Price: Jetfire plastic, matte blue $159.00

Beretta 950 Jetfire

Beretta Model 21 Bobcat Pistol Similar to the Model 950 BS. Chambered for 22 LR or 25 ACP. Both double action. Has 2.4" barrel, 4.9" overall length; 7-round magazine on 22 cal.; 8 rounds in 25 ACP, 9.9 oz., available in nickel, matte, engraved or blue finish. Plastic or walnut grips. Introduced in 1985.
Price: Bobcat, 22-cal. $244.00
Price: Bobcat, nickel, 22-cal. $254.00
Price: Bobcat, 25-cal. $244.00
Price: Bobcat, nickel, 25-cal. $254.00
Price: Bobcat wood, engraved, 22 or 25 . . . .$294.00
Price: Bobcat plastic matte, 22 or 25 . . . .$194.00

Beretta 3032 Tomcat

BERETTA MODEL 3032 TOMCAT PISTOL Caliber: 32 ACP, 7-shot magazine. **Barrel:** 2.45". **Weight:** 15 oz. **Length:** 5" overall. **Stocks:** Checkered black plastic. **Sights:** Blade front, drift-adjustable rear. **Features:** Double action with exposed hammer; tip-up barrel for direct loading/unloading; thumb safety; polished or matte blue finish. Imported from Italy by Beretta U.S.A. Introduced 1996.
Price: Polished blue $299.00
Price: Matte blue $240.00

BERETTA MODEL 8000/8040 COUGAR PISTOL Caliber: 9mm Para., 10-shot, 40 S&W, 10-shot magazine. **Barrel:** 3.6". **Weight:** 33.5 oz. **Length:** 7" overall. **Stocks:** Checkered plastic. **Sights:** Blade front, rear drift adjustable for windage. **Features:** Slide-mounted safety; rotating barrel; exposed hammer. Matte black Bruniton finish. Announced 1994. Imported from Italy by Beretta U.S.A.
Price: $699.00
Price: D models $663.00

Beretta M8000/8040 Cougar

BERNARDELLI PO18 DA AUTO PISTOL Caliber: 9mm Para., 10-shot magazine. **Barrel:** 4.8". **Weight:** 34.2 oz. **Length:** 8.23" overall. **Stocks:** Checkered plastic; walnut optional. **Sights:** Blade front, rear adjustable for windage and elevation; low profile, three-dot system. **Features:** Manual thumb half-cock, magazine and auto-locking firing pin safeties. Thumb safety decocks hammer. Reversible magazine release. Imported from Italy by Mitchell Arms.
Price: Blue $505.00
Price: Chrome $568.00

Bernadelli PO18

Bernardelli PO18 Compact DA Auto Pistol Similar to the PO18 except has 4" barrel, 7.44" overall length, 10-shot magazine. Weighs 31.7 oz. Imported from Italy by Mitchell Arms.
Price: Blue $552.00
Price: Chrome $600.00

BERNARDELLI MODEL USA AUTO PISTOL Caliber: 22 LR, 10-shot, 380 ACP, 7-shot magazine. **Barrel:** 3.5". **Weight:** 26.5 oz. **Length:** 6.5" overall. **Stocks:** Checkered plastic with thumbrest. **Sights:** Ramp front, white outline rear adjustable for windage and elevation. **Features:** Hammer-block slide safety; loaded chamber indicator; dual recoil buffer springs; serrated trigger; inertia-type firing pin. Imported from Italy by Mitchell Arms.
Price: Blue, either caliber $387.00
Price: Chrome, either caliber $412.00
Price: Model AMR (6" barrel, target sights) $440.00

Bernadelli USA

BERNARDELLI P. ONE DA AUTO PISTOL Caliber: 9mm Para., 16-shot, 40 S&W, 10-shot magazine. **Barrel:** 4.8″. **Weight:** 34 oz. **Length:** 8.35″ overall. **Stocks:** Checkered black plastic. **Sights:** Blade front, rear adjustable for windage and elevation; three dot system. **Features:** Forged steel frame and slide; full-length slide rails; reversible magazine release; thumb safety/decocker; squared trigger guard. Introduced 1994. Imported from Italy by Mitchell Arms.
Price: 9mm Para., blue/black $530.00
Price: 9mm Para., chrome $580.00
Price: 40 S&W, blue/black $530.00
Price: 40 S&W, chrome $580.00

Bernardelli P. One Practical VB Pistol Similar to the P. One except chambered for 9x21mm, two- or four-port compensator, straight trigger, micro-adjustable rear sight. Introduced 1994. Imported from Italy by Mitchell Arms.
Price: Blue/black, two-port compensator $1,425.00
Price: As above, four-port compensator $1,475.00
Price: Chrome, two-port compensator $1,498.00
Price: As above, four-port compensator $1,540.00
Price: Customized VB, four-plus-two-port
        compensator $2,150.00
Price: As above, chrome $2,200.00

BERSA THUNDER 22 AUTO PISTOL Caliber: 22 LR, 10-shot magazine. **Barrel:** 3.5″. **Weight:** 24.2 oz. **Length:** 6.6″ overall. **Stocks:** Black polymer. **Sights:** Blade front, notch rear adjustable for windage; three-dot system. **Features:** Double action; firing pin and magazine safeties. Available in blue or nickel. Introduced 1995. Distributed by Eagle Imports, Inc.
Price: Blue $249.95
Price: Nickel $266.95

BERSA THUNDER 380 AUTO PISTOLS Caliber: 380 ACP, 7-shot (Thunder 380), 10-shot magazine (Thunder 380 Plus). **Barrel:** 3.5″. **Weight:** 25.75 oz. **Length:** 6.6″ overall. **Stocks:** Black rubber. **Sights:** Blade front, notch rear adjustable for windage; three-dot system. **Features:** Double action; firing pin and magazine safeties. Available in blue or nickel. Introduced 1995. Distributed by Eagle Imports, Inc.
Price: Thunder 380, 7-shot, deep blue finish $249.95
Price: As above, satin nickel $266.95
Price: Thunder 380 Plus, 10-shot, matte blue $316.95
Price: As above, satin nickel $349.95

BERSA SERIES 95 AUTO PISTOL Caliber: 380 ACP, 7-shot magazine. **Barrel:** 3.5″. **Weight:** 22 oz. **Length:** 6.6″ overall. **Stocks:** Wrap-around textured rubber. **Sights:** Blade front, rear adjustable for windage; three-dot system. **Features:** Double action; firing pin and magazine safeties; combat-style trigger guard. Matte blue or satin nickel. Introduced 1992. Distributed by Eagle Imports, Inc.
Price: Matte blue $224.95
Price: Satin nickel $241.95

BERSA THUNDER 9 AUTO PISTOL Caliber: 9mm Para., 10-shot magazine. **Barrel:** 4″. **Weight:** 30 oz. **Length:** $7^3/_8$″ overall. **Stocks:** Checkered black polymer. **Sights:** Blade front, rear adjustable for windage and elevation; three-dot system. **Features:** Double action. Ambidextrous safety, decocking levers and slide release; internal automatic firing pin safety; reversible extended magazine release; adjustable trigger stop; alloy frame. Link-free locked breech design. Matte blue finish. Introduced 1993. Imported from Argentina by Eagle Imports, Inc.
Price: Matte finish $474.95
Price: Satin nickel $524.95
Price Duo-Tone finish $491.95

Bersa Thunder 22

Bersa Thunder 380

Bersa Series 95

Bersa Thunder 9

BROLIN LEGEND L45 STANDARD PISTOL Caliber: 45 ACP, 7-shot magazine. **Barrel:** 5″. **Weight:** 36 oz. **Length:** 8.5″ overall. **Stocks:** Checkered walnut. **Sights:** Orange ramp front, white outline rear. **Features:** Throated match barrel; polished feed ramp; lowered and flared ejection port; beveled magazine well; flat top slide; flat mainspring housing; lightened aluminum match trigger; slotted Commander hammer; modified high-relief grip safety; matte blue finish. Introduced 1996. Made in U.S. by Brolin Arms.
Price: $449.00

Brolin Legend L45

Brolin Legend L45C Compact Pistol Similar to the L45 Standard pistol except has 4″ barrel with conical lock up; overall length 7.5″; weighs 32 oz. Matte blue finish. Introduced 1996. Made in U.S. by Brolin Arms.
Price: $459.00

BROLIN PATRIOT P45 STANDARD CARRY COMP Caliber: 45 ACP, 7-shot magazine. **Barrel:** 4″. **Weight:** 37 oz. **Length:** 8.5″ overall. **Stocks:** Checkered wood. **Sights:** Orange ramp front, white outline rear. **Features:** Dual-port compensator is integral with the throated match barrel; conical lock-up system; polished feed ramp; lowered and flared ejection port; beveled magazine well; flat-top slide; four-legged sear spring; serrated flat mainspring housing; high relief cut front strap; adjustable aluminum match trigger; beavertail grip safety; slotted Commander hammer. Introduced 1996. Made in U.S. by Brolin Arms.
Price: Blue or two-tone $649.00

Brolin L45C Compact

Brolin P45C Compact Carry Comp Similar to the P45 Standard Carry Comp except has 3.25″ barrel with integral milled compensator; overall length 7.5″; weighs 33 oz. Introduced 1996. Made in U.S. by Brolin Arms.
Price: Blue or two-tone $679.00

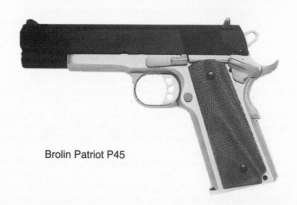
Brolin Patriot P45

Browning Hi-Power Adjustable Sight

BROWNING HI-POWER 9mm AUTOMATIC PISTOL Caliber: 9mm Para., 40 S&W, 10-shot magazine. **Barrel:** $4^{21}/_{32}$″. **Weight:** 32 oz. **Length:** $7^3/_4$″ overall. **Stocks:** Walnut, hand checkered, or black Polyamide. **Sights:** $^1/_8$″ blade front; rear screw-adjustable for windage and elevation. Also available with fixed rear (drift-adjustable for windage). **Features:** External hammer with half-cock and thumb safeties. A blow on the hammer cannot discharge a cartridge; cannot be fired with magazine removed. Fixed rear sight model available. Ambidextrous safety available only with matte finish, moulded grips. Imported from Belgium by Browning.
Price: Fixed sight model, walnut grips $584.75
Price: 9mm with rear sight adj. for w. and e., walnut grips $635.95
Price: Mark III, standard matte black finish, fixed sight, moulded grips, ambidextrous safety $550.75
Price: Silver chrome, adjustable sight, Pachmayr grips .$650.95

Browning Hi-Power Silver Chrome

Browning 40 S&W Hi-Power Mark III Pistol Similar to the standard Hi-Power except chambered for 40 S&W, 10-shot magazine, weighs 35 oz., and has $4^3/_4$″ barrel. Comes with matte blue finish, low profile front sight blade, drift-adjustable rear sight, ambidextrous safety, moulded polyamide grips with thumb rest. Introduced 1993. Imported from Belgium by Browning.
Price: Mark III $550.95

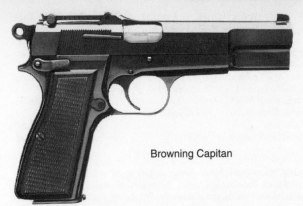

Browning Capitan

Browning Capitan Hi-Power Pistol Similar to the standard Hi-Power except has adjustable tangent rear sight authentic to the early-production model. Also has Commander-style hammer. Checkered walnut grips, polished blue finish. Reintroduced 1993. Imported from Belgium by Browning.
Price: 9mm only $692.95

Browning Hi-Power HP-Practical Pistol Similar to the standard Hi-Power except has silver-chromed frame with blued slide, wrap-around Pachmayr rubber grips, round-style serrated hammer and removable front sight, fixed rear (drift-adjustable for windage). Available in 9mm Para. or 40 S&W. Introduced 1991.
Price: $629.75
Price: With fully adjustable rear sight $681.95

Browning Hi-Power HP Practical

BROWNING BDM DA AUTO PISTOL Caliber: 9mm Para., 10-shot magazine. **Barrel:** 4.73″. **Weight:** 31 oz. **Length:** 7.85″ overall. **Stocks:** Moulded black composition; checkered, with thumbrest on both sides. **Sights:** Low profile removable blade front, rear screw adjustable for windage. **Features:** Mode selector allows switching from DA pistol to "revolver" mode via a switch on the slide. Decocking lever/safety on the frame. Two redundant, passive, internal safety systems. All steel frame; matte black finish. Introduced 1991. Made in the U.S. From Browning.
Price: $612.95

Browning BDM

BROWNING FN BDA/BDAO PISTOLS Caliber: 9mm Para., 10-shot magazine. **Barrel:** 4⅝″. **Weight:** 31 oz. **Length:** 7⅞″ overall. **Stocks:** Checkered, contoured composition. **Sights:** Low profile three-dot system; blade front, rear adjustable for windage. **Features:** All-steel slide and frame; tilt-barrel design; reversible magazine release; grooved front strap; matted blue finish; ambidextrous decocking lever on BDA. Available as DA or DAO. Introduced 1996. Imported from Belgium by Browning.
Price: Double action or double-action-only $612.95

BROWNING BDA-380 DA AUTO PISTOL Caliber: 380 ACP, 10-shot magazine. **Barrel:** 3¹³/₁₆″. **Weight:** 23 oz. **Length:** 6¾″ overall. **Stocks:** Smooth walnut with inset Browning medallion. **Sights:** Blade front, rear drift-adjustable for windage. **Features:** Combination safety and decocking lever will automatically lower a cocked hammer to half-cock and can be operated by right- or left-hand shooters. Inertia firing pin. Introduced 1978. Imported from Italy by Browning.
Price: Blue $563.95
Price: Nickel $606.95

Browning BDA 380

Browning FN BDA

Browning Buck Mark Plus

Browning Micro Buck Mark Blue

Browning Micro Buck Mark Nickel

Browning Buck Mark Varmint

Bryco Model 38

Bryco Model 48

BROWNING BUCK MARK 22 PISTOL Caliber: 22 LR, 10-shot magazine. **Barrel:** 5½". **Weight:** 32 oz. **Length:** 9½" overall. **Stocks:** Black moulded composite with skip-line checkering. **Sights:** Ramp front, Browning Pro Target rear adjustable for windage and elevation. **Features:** All steel, matte blue finish or nickel, gold-colored trigger. Buck Mark Plus has laminated wood grips. Made in U.S. Introduced 1985. From Browning.
Price: Buck Mark, blue $256.95
Price: Buck Mark, nickel finish with contoured rubber
   stocks $301.95
Price: Buck Mark Plus $313.95

Browning Micro Buck Mark Same as the standard Buck Mark and Buck Mark Plus except has 4" barrel. Available in blue or nickel. Has 16-click Pro Target rear sight. Introduced 1992.
Price: Blue $256.95
Price: Nickel $301.95
Price: Micro Buck Mark Plus $313.95

Browning Buck Mark Varmint Same as the Buck Mark except has 9⅞" heavy barrel with .900" diameter and full-length scope base (no open sights); walnut grips with optional forend, or finger-groove walnut. Overall length is 14", weighs 48 oz. Introduced 1987.
Price: $390.95

BRYCO MODEL 38 AUTO PISTOLS Caliber: 22 LR, 32 ACP, 380 ACP, 6-shot magazine. **Barrel:** 2.8". **Weight:** 15 oz. **Length:** 5.3" overall. **Stocks:** Polished resin-impregnated wood. **Sights:** Fixed. **Features:** Safety locks sear and slide. Choice of satin nickel, bright chrome or black Teflon finishes. Introduced 1988. From Jennings Firearms.
Price: 22 LR, 32 ACP, about $109.95
Price: 380 ACP, about $129.95

BRYCO MODEL 48 AUTO PISTOLS Caliber: 22 LR, 32 ACP, 380 ACP, 6-shot magazine. **Barrel:** 4". **Weight:** 19 oz. **Length:** 6.7" overall. **Stocks:** Polished resin-impregnated wood. **Sights:** Fixed. **Features:** Safety locks sear and slide. Choice of satin nickel, bright chrome or black Teflon finishes. Announced 1988. From Jennings Firearms.
Price: 22 LR, 32 ACP, about $139.00
Price: 380 ACP, about $139.00

BRYCO MODEL 59 AUTO PISTOL Caliber: 9mm Para., 10-shot magazine. **Barrel:** 4". **Weight:** 33 oz. **Length:** 6.5" overall. **Stocks:** Black composition. **Sights:** Blade front, fixed rear. **Features:** Striker-fired action; manual thumb safety; polished blue finish. Comes with two magazines. Introduced 1994. From Jennings Firearms.
Price: About $169.00
Price: Model 58 (5.5" overall length, 30 oz.) $169.00

CALICO M-110 AUTO PISTOL Caliber: 22 LR. 100-shot magazine. **Barrel:** 6". **Weight:** 3.7 lbs. (loaded). **Length:** 17.9" overall. **Stocks:** Moulded composition. **Sights:** Adjustable post front, notch rear. **Features:** Aluminum alloy frame; flash suppressor; pistol grip compartment; ambidextrous safety. Uses same helical-feed magazine as M-100 Carbine. Introduced 1986. Made in U.S. From Calico.
Price: $359.00

Calico M-110

CENTURY FEG P9R PISTOL Caliber: 9mm Para., 10-shot magazine. **Barrel:** 4.6". **Weight:** 35 oz. **Length:** 8" overall. **Stocks:** Checkered walnut. **Sights:** Blade front, rear drift adjustable for windage. **Features:** Double action with hammer-drop safety. Polished blue finish. Comes with spare magazine. Imported from Hungary by Century International Arms.
Price: About $263.00
Price: Chrome finish, about $375.00

Century FEG P9RK Auto Pistol Similar to the P9R except has 4.12" barrel, 7.5" overall length and weighs 33.6 oz. Checkered walnut grips, fixed sights, 10-shot magazine. Introduced 1994. Imported from Hungary by Century International Arms, Inc.
Price: About $290.00

Century FEG P9RK

COLT 22 AUTOMATIC PISTOL Caliber: 22 LR, 10-shot magazine. **Barrel:** 4.5". **Weight:** 33 oz. **Length:** 8.62" overall. **Stocks:** Textured black polymer. **Sights:** Blade front, rear drift adjustable for windage. **Features:** Stainless steel construction; ventilated barrel rib; single action mechanism; cocked striker indicator; push-button safety. Introduced 1994. Made in U.S. by Colt's Mfg. Co.
Price: $248.00

Colt 22 Target Pistol Similar to the Colt 22 pistol except has 6" bull barrel, full-length sighting rib with lightening cuts and mounting rail for optical sights; fully adjustable rear sight; removable sights; two-point factory adjusted trigger travel. Stainless steel frame. Introduced 1995. Made in U.S. by Colt's Mfg. Co.
Price: $377.00

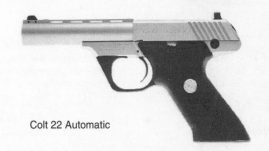

Colt 22 Automatic

COLT DOUBLE EAGLE MKII/SERIES 90 DA PISTOL Caliber: 45 ACP, 8-shot magazine. **Barrel:** 4½", 5". **Weight:** 39 oz. **Length:** 8½" overall. **Stocks:** Black checkered Xenoy thermoplastic. **Sights:** Blade front, rear adjustable for windage. High profile three-dot system. Colt Accro adjustable sight optional. **Features:** Made of stainless steel with matte finish. Checkered and curved extended trigger guard, wide steel trigger; decocking lever on left side; traditional magazine release; grooved frontstrap; beveled magazine well; extended grip guard; rounded, serrated combat-style hammer. Announced 1989.
Price: $727.00
Price: Combat Comm., 45, 4½" bbl. $727.00

Colt 22 Target

Colt Double Eagle Officer's ACP Similar to the regular Double Eagle except 45 ACP only, 3½" barrel, weighs 35 oz., 7¼" overall length. Has 5¼" sight radius. Introduced 1991.
Price: $727.00

COLT COMBAT COMMANDER AUTO PISTOL Caliber: 38 Super, 9-shot; 45 ACP, 8-shot. **Barrel:** 4¼". **Weight:** 36 oz. **Length:** 7¾" overall. **Stocks:** Checkered rubber composite. **Sights:** Fixed, glare-proofed blade front, square notch rear; three-dot system. **Features:** Long trigger; arched housing; grip and thumb safeties.
Price: 45, blue $735.00
Price: 45, stainless $789.00
Price: 38 Super, stainless $789.00

Colt Double Eagle Combat

Colt Lightweight Commander MK IV/Series 80 Same as Commander except high strength aluminum alloy frame, checkered rubber composite stocks, weighs 27½ oz. 45 ACP only.
Price: Blue $735.00

COLT GOVERNMENT MODEL MK IV/SERIES 80 **Caliber:** 38 Super, 9-shot; 45 ACP, 8-shot magazine. **Barrel:** 5″. **Weight:** 38 oz. **Length:** 8½″ overall. **Stocks:** Black composite. **Sights:** Ramp front, fixed square notch rear; three-dot system. **Features:** Grip and thumb safeties and internal firing pin safety, long trigger.

Price: 45 ACP, blue	$735.00
Price: 45 ACP, stainless	$789.00
Price: 45 ACP, bright stainless	$863.00
Price: 38 Super, blue	$735.00
Price: 38 Super, stainless	$789.00
Price: 38 Super, bright stainless	$863.00

Colt 10mm Delta Elite Similar to the Government Model except chambered for 10mm auto cartridge. Has three-dot high profile front and rear combat sights, checkered rubber composite stocks, internal firing pin safety, and new recoil spring/buffer system. Introduced 1987.

Price: Blue	$807.00
Price: Stainless	$860.00

Colt Combat Elite MK IV/Series 80 Similar to the Government Model except has stainless frame with ordnance steel slide and internal parts. High profile front, rear sights with three-dot system, extended grip safety, beveled magazine well, checkered rubber composite stocks. Introduced 1986.

Price: 45 ACP, STS/B	$895.00
Price: 38 Super, STS/B	$895.00

COLT MODEL 1991 A1 AUTO PISTOL **Caliber:** 45 ACP, 7-shot magazine. **Barrel:** 5″. **Weight:** 38 oz. **Length:** 8.5″ overall. **Stocks:** Checkered black composition. **Sights:** Ramped blade front, fixed square notch rear, high profile. **Features:** Parkerized finish. Continuation of serial number range used on original G.I. 1911 A1 guns. Comes with one magazine and moulded carrying case. Introduced 1991.

Price:	$538.00
Price: Stainless	$590.00

Colt Model 1991 A1 Compact Auto Pistol Similar to the Model 1991 A1 except has 3½″ barrel. Overall length is 7″, and gun is ⅜″ shorter in height. Comes with one 6-shot magazine, moulded case. Introduced 1993.

Price:	$538.00

Colt Model 1991 A1 Commander Auto Pistol Similar to the Model 1991 A1 except has 4¼″ barrel. Parkerized finish. 7-shot magazine. Comes in moulded case. Introduced 1993.

Price:	$538.00

COLT COMBAT TARGET MODEL **Caliber:** 45 ACP, 7-shot magazine. **Barrel:** 5″. **Weight:** 39 oz. **Length:** 8½″ overall. **Stocks:** Black composition. **Sights:** Patridge-style front, Colt Accro adjustable rear. **Features:** Steel target trigger with cut-out; flat-top slide; flared and lowered ejection port; beveled magazine well. Introduced 1996. Made in U.S. by Colt's Mfg. Co.

Price: Matte blue	$768.00
Price: Matte stainless	$820.00

COLT GOVERNMENT MODEL 380 **Caliber:** 380 ACP, 7-shot magazine. **Barrel:** 3¼″. **Weight:** 21¾ oz. **Length:** 6″ overall. **Stocks:** Checkered composition. **Sights:** Ramp front, square notch rear, fixed. **Features:** Scaled-down version of the 1911 A1 Colt G.M. Has thumb and internal firing pin safeties. Introduced 1983.

Price: Blue	$462.00
Price: Stainless	$493.00
Price: Pocketlite 380, blue	$462.00

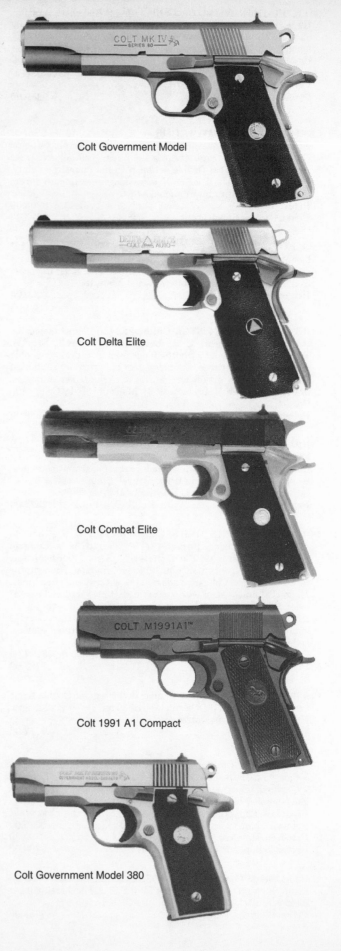

Colt Government Model

Colt Delta Elite

Colt Combat Elite

Colt 1991 A1 Compact

Colt Government Model 380

Colt Mustang 380, Mustang Pocketlite Similar to the standard 380 Government Model. Mustang has steel frame (18.5 oz.), Pocketlite has aluminum alloy (12.5 oz.). Both are 1/2″ shorter than 380 G.M., have 2³/₄″ barrel. Introduced 1987.
Price: Mustang 380, blue $462.00
Price: As above, stainless $493.00
Price: Mustang Pocketlite, blue $462.00
Price: Mustang Pocketlite STS/N $493.00

Colt Mustang Plus II Similar to the 380 Government Model except has the shorter barrel and slide of the Mustang. Introduced 1988.
Price: Blue $462.00
Price: Stainless $493.00

COLT OFFICER'S ACP MK IV/SERIES 80 Caliber: 45 ACP, 6-shot magazine. **Barrel:** 3¹/₂″. **Weight:** 34 oz. (steel frame); 24 oz. (alloy frame). **Length:** 7¹/₄″ overall. **Stocks:** Checkered rubber composite. **Sights:** Ramp blade front with white dot, square notch rear with two white dots. **Features:** Trigger safety lock (thumb safety), grip safety, firing pin safety; long trigger; flat mainspring housing. Also available with lightweight alloy frame and in stainless steel. Introduced 1985.
Price: Blue $735.00
Price: L.W., blue finish $789.00
Price: Stainless $735.00
Price: Bright stainless $863.00

COONAN 357 MAGNUM PISTOL Caliber: 357 Mag., 7-shot magazine. **Barrel:** 5″. **Weight:** 42 oz. **Length:** 8.3″ overall. **Stocks:** Smooth walnut. **Sights:** Interchangeable ramp front, rear adjustable for windage. **Features:** Stainless steel construction. Unique barrel hood improves accuracy and reliability. Linkless barrel. Many parts interchange with Colt autos. Has grip, hammer, half-cock safeties, extended slide latch. Made in U.S. by Coonan Arms, Inc.
Price: 5″ barrel $720.00
Price: 6″ barrel $755.00
Price: With 6″ compensated barrel $999.00
Price: Classic model (Teflon black two-tone finish, 8-shot magazine, fully adjustable rear sight, integral compensated barrel) $1,400.00

Coonan Compact Cadet 357 Magnum Pistol Similar to the 357 Magnum full-size gun except has 3.9″ barrel, shorter frame, 6-shot magazine. Weight is 39 oz., overall length 7.8″. Linkless bull barrel, full-length recoil spring guide rod, extended slide latch. Introduced 1993. Made in U.S. by Coonan Arms, Inc.
Price: $841.00

CZ 75 9mm

CZ 75 AUTO PISTOL Caliber: 9mm Para., 40 S&W, 10-shot magazine. **Barrel:** 4.7″. **Weight:** 34.3 oz. **Length:** 8.1″ overall. **Stocks:** High impact checkered plastic. **Sights:** Square post front, rear adjustable for windage; three-dot system. **Features:** Single action/double action design; choice of black polymer, matte or high-polish blue finishes. All-steel frame. Imported from the Czech Republic by Magnum Research.
Price: Black polymer finish $539.00
Price: Nickel $569.00

Colt Mustang 380

Colt Mustang Pocketlite

Colt Officer's ACP

Coonan 357 Magnum

Coonan Compact Cadet 357

CZ 75 Compact Auto Pistol Similar to the CZ 75 except has 10-shot magazine, 3.9″ barrel and weighs 32 oz. Has removable front sight, non-glare ribbed slide top. Trigger guard is squared and serrated; combat hammer. Introduced 1993. Imported from the Czech Republic by Magnum Research.
Price: Black polymer finish $539.00

CZ 75 Semi-Compact Auto Pistol Uses the shorter slide and barrel of the CZ 75 Compact with the full-size frame of the standard CZ 75. Has 10-shot magazine; 9mm Para. only. Introduced 1994. Imported from the Czech Republic by Magnum Research.
Price: Black polymer finish $519.00
Price: Matte blue finish $539.00
Price: High-polish blue finish $559.00

CZ 75 Compact

CZ 85

CZ 83 380

Daewoo DP51 Fastfire

Daewoo DP51C Compact

CZ 85 Auto Pistol Same gun as the CZ 75 except has ambidextrous slide release and safety-levers; non-glare, ribbed slide top; squared, serrated trigger guard; trigger stop to prevent overtravel. Introduced 1986. Imported from the Czech Republic by Magnum Research.
Price: Black polymer finish $549.00

CZ 85 Combat Auto Pistol Same as the CZ 85 except has walnut grips, round combat hammer, fully adjustable rear sight, extended magazine release. Trigger parts coated with friction-free beryllium copper. Introduced 1992. Imported from the Czech Republic by Magnum Research.
Price: Black polymer finish $649.00

CZ 83 DOUBLE-ACTION PISTOL Caliber: 32, 380 ACP, 10-shot magazine. **Barrel:** 3.8″. **Weight:** 26.2 oz. **Length:** 6.8″ overall. **Stocks:** High impact checkered plastic. **Sights:** Removable square post front, rear adjustable for windage; three-dot system. **Features:** Single action/double action; ambidextrous magazine release and safety. Blue finish; non-glare ribbed slide top. Imported from the Czech Republic by Magnum Research.
Price: $409.00

CZ 100 AUTO PISTOL Caliber: 9mm Para., 40 S&W, 10-shot magazine. **Barrel:** 3.7″. **Weight:** 24 oz. **Length:** 6.9″ overall. **Stocks:** Grooved polymer. **Sights:** Blade front with dot, white outline rear drift adjustable for windage. **Features:** Double action only with firing pin block; polymer frame, steel slide; has laser sight mount. Introduced 1996. Imported from the Czech Republic by Magnum Research.
Price: $489.00

DAEWOO DP51 FASTFIRE AUTO PISTOL Caliber: 9mm Para., 40 S&W, 10-shot magazine. **Barrel:** 4.1″. **Weight:** 28.2 oz. **Length:** 7.5″ overall. **Stocks:** Checkered composition. **Sights:** 1/8″ blade front, square notch rear drift adjustable for windage. Three dot system. **Features:** Patented Fastfire mechanism. Ambidextrous manual safety and magazine catch, automatic firing pin block. Alloy frame, squared trigger guard. Matte black finish. Introduced 1991. Imported from South Korea by Kimber of America, distributed by Kimber and Nationwide Sports Dist.
Price: DP51 ....$400.00
Price: DH40 (40 S&W) $450.00

Daewoo DP51C, DP51S Auto Pistols Same as the DP51 except DP51C has 3.6″ barrel, 1/4″ shorter grip frame, flat mainspring housing, and is 2 oz. lighter. Model DP51S has 3.6″ barrel, same grip as standard DP51, weighs 27 oz. Introduced 1995. Imported from South Korea by Kimber of America, Inc., distributed by Kimber and Nationwide Sports Dist.
Price: DP51C $445.00
Price: DP51S $420.00

Daewoo DP52

Davis P-32

Consult our Directory pages for the location of firms mentioned.

Desert Eagle Magnum

Desert Industries War Eagle

DAEWOO DP52, DH380 AUTO PISTOLS **Caliber:** 22 LR, 10-shot magazine. **Barrel:** 3.8". **Weight:** 23 oz. **Length:** 6.7" overall. **Stocks:** Checkered black composition with thumbrest. **Sights:** 1/8" blade front, rear drift adjustable for windage; three-dot system. **Features:** All-steel construction with polished blue finish. Dual safety system with hammer block. Introduced 1994. Imported from South Korea by Kimber of America, distributed by Kimber and Nationwide Sports Distributors.
Price: $380.00
Price: DH380 (as above except 380 ACP, 7-shot
    magazine) $410.00

DAVIS P-32 AUTO PISTOL **Caliber:** 32 ACP, 6-shot magazine. **Barrel:** 2.8". **Weight:** 22 oz. **Length:** 5.4" overall. **Stocks:** Laminated wood. **Sights:** Fixed. **Features:** Choice of black Teflon or chrome finish. Announced 1986. Made in U.S. by Davis Industries.
Price: $87.50

DAVIS P-380 AUTO PISTOL **Caliber:** 32 ACP, 6-shot, 380 ACP, 5-shot magazine. **Barrel:** 2.8". **Weight:** 22 oz. **Length:** 5.4" overall. **Stocks:** Black composition. **Sights:** Fixed. **Features:** Choice of chrome or black Teflon finish. Introduced 1991. Made in U.S. by Davis Industries.
Price: $98.00

DESERT EAGLE MAGNUM PISTOL **Caliber:** 357 Mag., 9-shot; 44 Mag., 8-shot; 50 Magnum, 7-shot. **Barrel:** 6", 10", interchangeable. **Weight:** 357 Mag.—62 oz.; 41 Mag., 44 Mag.—69 oz.; 50 Mag.—72 oz. **Length:** 10 1/4" overall (6" bbl.). **Stocks:** Hogue rubber. **Sights:** Blade on ramp front, combat-style rear. Adjustable available. **Features:** Rotating three-lug bolt; ambidextrous safety; combat-style trigger guard; adjustable trigger optional. Military epoxy finish. Satin, bright nickel, hard chrome, polished and blued finishes available. Made in U.S. From Magnum Research, Inc.
Price: 357, 6" bbl., standard pistol $979.00
Price: 44 Mag., 6", standard pistol $999.00
Price: 50 Magnum, 6" bbl., standard pistol $1,049.00

DESERT INDUSTRIES WAR EAGLE PISTOL **Caliber:** 380 ACP, 8- or 10-shot; 9mm Para., 14-shot; 10mm, 10-shot; 40 S&W, 10-shot; 45 ACP, 10-shot. **Barrel:** 4". **Weight:** 35.5 oz. **Length:** 7.5" overall. **Stocks:** Rosewood. **Sights:** Fixed. **Features:** Double action; matte finish stainless steel; slide mounted ambidextrous safety. Announced 1986. From Desert Industries, Inc.
Price: $795.00
Price: 380 ACP $725.00

Desert Industries Double Deuce

DESERT INDUSTRIES DOUBLE DEUCE, TWO BIT SPECIAL PISTOLS **Caliber:** 22 LR, 6-shot; 25 ACP, 5-shot. **Barrel:** 2 1/2". **Weight:** 15 oz. **Length:** 5 1/2" overall. **Stocks:** Rosewood. **Sights:** Special order. **Features:** Double action; stainless steel construction with matte finish; ambidextrous slide-mounted safety. From Desert Industries, Inc.
Price: 22 ....$399.95
Price: 25 (Two-Bit Special) $399.95

E.A.A. WITNESS DA AUTO PISTOL Caliber: 9mm Para., 10-shot magazine; 38 Super, 40 S&W, 10-shot magazine; 45 ACP, 10-shot magazine. **Barrel:** 4.50″. **Weight:** 35.33 oz. **Length:** 8.10″ overall. **Stocks:** Checkered rubber. **Sights:** Undercut blade front, open rear adjustable for windage. **Features:** Double-action trigger system; round trigger guard; frame-mounted safety. Introduced 1991. Imported from Italy by European American Armory.

Price: 9mm, blue $399.00
Price: 9mm, satin chrome $425.00
Price: 9mm Compact, blue, 10-shot $399.00
Price: As above, chrome $425.00
Price: 40 S&W, blue $425.00
Price: As above, chrome $450.00
Price: 40 S&W Compact, 8-shot, blue $425.00
Price: As above, chrome $450.00
Price: 45 ACP, blue $525.00
Price: As above, chrome $550.00
Price: 45 ACP Compact, 8-shot, blue $525.00
Price: As above, chrome $550.00
Price: 9mm/40 S&W Combo, blue, compact or full size ..$595.00
Price: 9mm or 40 S&W Carry Comp, blue $550.00

E.A.A. EUROPEAN MODEL AUTO PISTOLS Caliber: 32 ACP or 380 ACP, 7-shot magazine. **Barrel:** 3.88″. **Weight:** 26 oz. **Length:** 7³⁄₈″ overall. **Stocks:** European hardwood. **Sights:** Fixed blade front, rear drift-adjustable for windage. **Features:** Chrome or blue finish; magazine, thumb and firing pin safeties; external hammer; safety-lever takedown. Imported from Italy by European American Armory.

Price: Blue $160.00
Price: Chrome $175.00
Price: Ladies Model $225.00

ERMA KGP68 AUTO PISTOL Caliber: 32 ACP, 6-shot, 380 ACP, 5-shot. **Barrel:** 4″. **Weight:** 22¹⁄₂ oz. **Length:** 7³⁄₈″ overall. **Stocks:** Checkered plastic. **Sights:** Fixed. **Features:** Toggle action similar to original "Luger" pistol. Action stays open after last shot. Has magazine and sear disconnect safety systems. Imported from Germany by Mandall Shooting Supplies.

Price: $499.95

FEG B9R AUTO PISTOL Caliber: 380 ACP, 10-shot magazine. **Barrel:** 4″. **Weight:** 25 oz. **Length:** 7″ overall. **Stocks:** Hand-checkered walnut. **Sights:** Blade front, drift-adjustable rear. **Features:** Hammer-drop safety; grooved backstrap; squared trigger guard. Comes with spare magazine. Introduced 1993. Imported from Hungary by Century International Arms.

Price: About $312.00

FEG FP9 AUTO PISTOL Caliber: 9mm Para., 10-shot magazine. **Barrel:** 5″. **Weight:** 35 oz. **Length:** 7.8″ overall. **Stocks:** Checkered walnut. **Sights:** Blade front, windage-adjustable rear. **Features:** Full-length ventilated rib. Polished blue finish. Comes with extra magazine. Introduced 1993. Imported from Hungary by Century International Arms.

Price: About $269.00

FEG GKK-45C DA AUTO PISTOL Caliber: 45 ACP, 8-shot magazine. **Barrel:** 4¹⁄₈″. **Weight:** 36 oz. **Length:** 7³⁄₄″ overall. **Stocks:** Hand-checkered walnut. **Sights:** Blade front, rear adjustable for windage; three-dot system. **Features:** Combat-type trigger guard. Polished blue finish. Comes with two magazines, cleaning rod. Introduced 1995. Imported from Hungary by K.B.I., Inc.

Price: Blue $399.00
Price: GKK-40C (40 S&W, 9-shot magazine) $399.00

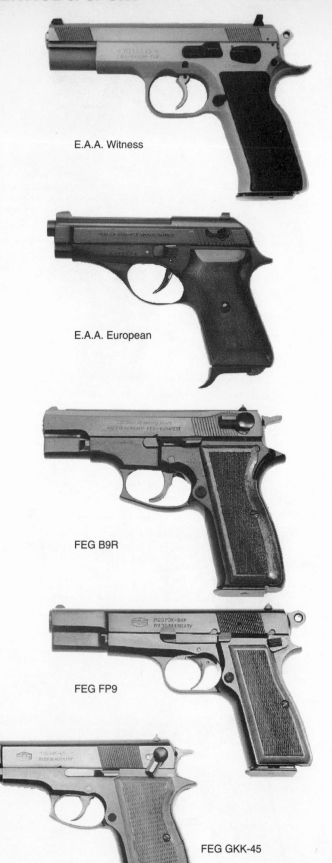

E.A.A. Witness

E.A.A. European

FEG B9R

FEG FP9

FEG GKK-45

FEG PJK-9HP AUTO PISTOL Caliber: 9mm Para., 10-shot magazine. **Barrel:** 4.75″. **Weight:** 32 oz. **Length:** 8″ overall. **Stocks:** Hand-checkered walnut. **Sights:** Blade front, rear adjustable for windage; three dot system. **Features:** Single action; polished blue or hard chrome finish; rounded combat-style serrated hammer. Comes with two magazines and cleaning rod. Imported from Hungary by K.B.I., Inc.
Price: Blue **$349.00**
Price: Hard chrome **$429.00**

FEG P9R AUTO PISTOL Caliber: 9mm Para., 10-shot magazine. **Barrel:** 4.6″. **Weight:** 35 oz. **Length:** 7.9″ overall. **Stocks:** Checkered walnut. **Sights:** Blade front, rear adjustable for windage. **Features:** Double-action mechanism; slide-mounted safety. All-Steel construction with polished blue finish. Comes with extra magazine. Introduced 1993. Imported from Hungary by Century International Arms.
Price: About **$262.00**

FEG SMC-22 DA AUTO PISTOL Caliber: 22 LR, 8-shot magazine. **Barrel:** 3.5″. **Weight:** 18.5 oz. **Length:** 6.12″ overall. **Stocks:** Checkered composition with thumbrest. **Sights:** Blade front, rear adjustable for windage. **Features:** Patterned after the PPK pistol. Alloy frame, steel slide; blue finish. Comes with two magazines, cleaning rod. Introduced 1994. Imported from Hungary by K.B.I., Inc.
Price: **$279.00**

FEG SMC-380 AUTO PISTOL Caliber: 380 ACP, 6-shot magazine. **Barrel:** 3.5″. **Weight:** 18.5 oz. **Length:** 6.1″ overall. **Stocks:** Checkered composition with thumbrest. **Sights:** Blade front, rear adjustable for windage. **Features:** Patterned after the PPK pistol. Alloy frame, steel slide; double action. Blue finish. Comes with two magazines, cleaning rod. Imported from Hungary by K.B.I., Inc.
Price: **$279.00**

FEG SMC-918 Auto Pistol Same as the SMC-380 except chambered for 9x18 Makarov. Alloy frame, steel slide, blue finish. Comes with two magazines, cleaning rod. Introduced 1995. Imported from Hungary by K.B.I., Inc.
Price: **$279.00**

GAL COMPACT AUTO PISTOL Caliber: 45 ACP, 8-shot magazine. **Barrel:** 4.25″. **Weight:** 36 oz. **Length:** 7.75″ overall. **Stocks:** Rubberized wrap-around. **Sights:** Low profile, fixed, three-dot system. **Features:** Forged steel frame and slide; competition trigger, hammer, slide stop magazine release, beavertail grip safety; front and rear slide grooves; two-tone finish. Introduced 1996. Imported from Israel by J.O. Arms, Inc.
Price: **$525.00**

GLOCK 17 AUTO PISTOL Caliber: 9mm Para., 10-shot magazine. **Barrel:** 4.49″. **Weight:** 21.9 oz. (without magazine). **Length:** 7.28″ overall. **Stocks:** Black polymer. **Sights:** Dot on front blade, white outline rear adjustable for windage. **Features:** Polymer frame, steel slide; double-action trigger with "Safe Action" system; mechanical firing pin safety, drop safety; simple takedown without tools; locked breech, recoil operated action. Adopted by Austrian armed forces 1983. NATO approved 1984. Imported from Austria by Glock, Inc.
Price: With extra magazine, magazine loader, cleaning
kit **$606.00**
Price: Model 17L (6″ barrel) **$790.00**

Glock 19 Auto Pistol Similar to the Glock 17 except has a 4″ barrel, giving an overall length of 6.85″ and weight of 20.99 oz. Magazine capacity is 10 rounds. Fixed or adjustable rear sight. Introduced 1988.
Price: **$606.00**

FEG PJK-9HP

FEG SMC-22

GAL Compact

Glock 17

Glock 19

Glock 20 10mm Auto Pistol Similar to the Glock Model 17 except chambered for 10mm Automatic cartridge. Barrel length is 4.60″, overall length is 7.59″, and weight is 26.3 oz. (without magazine). Magazine capacity is 10 rounds. Fixed or adjustable rear sight. Comes with an extra magazine, magazine loader, cleaning rod and brush. Introduced 1990. Imported from Austria by Glock, Inc.
Price: $658.00

Glock 21 Auto Pistol Similar to the Glock 17 except chambered for 45 ACP, 10-shot magazine. Overall length is 7.59″, weight is 25.2 oz. (without magazine). Fixed or adjustable rear sight. Introduced 1991.
Price: $658.00

Glock 21

Glock 22 Auto Pistol Similar to the Glock 17 except chambered for 40 S&W, 10-shot magazine. Overall length is 7.28″, weight is 22.3 oz. (without magazine). Fixed or adjustable rear sight. Introduced 1990.
Price: $606.00

Glock 23 Auto Pistol Similar to the Glock 19 except chambered for 40 S&W, 10-shot magazine. Overall length is 6.85″, weight is 20.6 oz. (without magazine). Fixed or adjustable rear sight. Introduced 1990.
Price: $606.00

Glock 27 40 S&W

GLOCK 26, 27 AUTO PISTOLS Caliber: 9mm Para. (M26), 10-shot magazine; 40 S&W (M27), 9-shot magazine. **Barrel:** 3.47″. **Weight:** 21.75 oz. **Length:** 6.3″ overall. **Stocks:** Integral. Stippled polymer. **Sights:** Dot on front blade, fixed or fully adjustable white outline rear. **Features:** Subcompact size. Polymer frame, steel slide; double-action trigger with "Safe Action" system, three safeties. Matte black Tenifer finish. Hammer-forged barrel. Imported from Austria by Glock, Inc. Introduced 1996.
Price: Fixed sight $606.00
Price: Adjustable sight $634.00

GOLAN AUTO PISTOL Caliber: 9mm Para., 40 S&W, 10-shot magazine. **Barrel:** 3.9″. **Weight:** 34 oz. **Length:** 7″ overall. **Stocks:** Textured composition. **Sights:** Fixed. **Features:** Fully ambidextrous double/single action; forged steel slide, alloy frame; matte blue finish. Introduced 1994. Imported from Israel by J.O. Arms, Inc.
Price: $684.50

Golan Auto

HECKLER & KOCH USP AUTO PISTOL Caliber: 9mm Para., 10-shot magazine, 40 S&W, 10-shot magazine. **Barrel:** 4.25″. **Weight:** 28 oz. (USP40). **Length:** 6.9″ overall. **Stocks:** Non-slip stippled black polymer. **Sights:** Blade front, rear adjustable for windage. **Features:** New HK design with polymer frame, modified Browning action with recoil reduction system, single control lever. Special "hostile environment" finish on all metal parts. Available in SA/DA, DAO, left- and right-hand versions. Introduced 1993. Imported from Germany by Heckler & Koch, Inc.
Price: Right-hand $636.00
Price: Left-hand $656.00
Price: Stainless steel, right-hand $681.00
Price: Stainless steel, left-hand $701.00

Heckler & Koch USP

HECKLER & KOCH MARK 23 SPECIAL OPERATIONS PISTOL Caliber: 45 ACP, 10-shot magazine. **Barrel:** 5.87″. **Weight:** 43 oz. **Length:** 9.65″ overall. **Stocks:** Integral with frame; black polymer. **Sights:** Blade front, rear drift adjustable for windage; three-dot. **Features:** Polymer frame; double action; exposed hammer; short recoil, modified Browning action. Civilian version of the SOCOM pistol. Introduced 1996. Imported from Germany by Heckler & Koch, Inc.
Price: $1,995.00

Heckler & Koch Mark 23

AUTOLOADERS, SERVICE & SPORT

Heckler & Koch USP 45 Auto Pistol Similar to the 9mm and 40 S&W USP except chambered for 45 ACP, 10-shot magazine. Has 4.13" barrel, overall length of 7.87" and weighs 30.4 oz. Has adjustable three-dot sight system. Available in SA/DA, DAO, left- and right-hand versions. Introduced 1995. Imported from Germany by Heckler & Koch, Inc.
Price: Right-hand **$696.00**
Price: Left-hand **$716.00**
Price: Stainless steel right-hand **$696.00**
Price: Stainless steel left-hand **$716.00**

Heckler & Koch USP 45

HECKLER & KOCH P7M8 AUTO PISTOL Caliber: 9mm Para., 8-shot magazine. **Barrel:** 4.13". **Weight:** 29 oz. **Length:** 6.73" overall. **Stocks:** Stippled black plastic. **Sights:** Blade front, adjustable rear; three dot system. **Features:** Unique "squeeze cocker" in frontstrap cocks the action. Gas-retarded action. Squared combat-type trigger guard. Blue finish. Compact size. Imported from Germany by Heckler & Koch, Inc.
Price: P7M8, blued **$1,187.00**

HERITAGE STEALTH AUTO PISTOL Caliber: 9mm Para., 40 S&W, 10-shot magazine. **Barrel:** 3.9". **Weight:** 20.2 oz. **Length:** 6.3" overall. **Stocks:** Black polymer; integral. **Sights:** Blade front, rear drift adjustable for windage. **Features:** Gas retarded blowback action; polymer frame, 17-4 stainless slide; frame mounted ambidextrous trigger safety, magazine safety. Introduced 1996. Made in U.S. by Heritage Mfg., Inc.
Price: **$299.95**

Heckler & Koch P7M8

HI-POINT FIREARMS 40 S&W AUTO Caliber: 40 S&W, 8-shot magazine. **Barrel:** 4.5". **Weight:** 39 oz. **Length:** 7.72" overall. **Stocks:** Checkered acetal resin. **Sights:** Fixed; low profile. **Features:** Internal drop-safe mechansim; all aluminum frame. Introduced 1991. From MKS Supply, Inc.
Price: Matte black **$148.95**

HI-POINT FIREARMS 45 CALIBER PISTOL Caliber: 45 ACP, 7-shot magazine. **Barrel:** 4.5". **Weight:** 39 oz. **Length:** 7.95" over-all. **Stocks:** Checkered acetal resin. **Sights:** Fixed; low profile. **Features:** Internal drop-safe mechanism; all aluminum frame. Introduced 1991. From MKS Supply, Inc.
Price: Matte black **$148.95**

Hi-Point 40 S&W

HI-POINT FIREARMS 9MM AUTO PISTOL Caliber: 9mm Para., 9-shot magazine. **Barrel:** 4.5". **Weight:** 39 oz. **Length:** 7.72" over-all. **Stocks:** Textured acetal plastic. **Sights:** Fixed, low profile. **Features:** Single-action design. Scratch-resistant, non-glare blue finish. Introduced 1990. From MKS Supply, Inc.
Price: Matte black **$139.95**

Heritage Stealth

Hi-Point 9mm Compact

HI-POINT FIREARMS 9MM COMPACT PISTOL Caliber: 380 ACP, 9mm Para., 8-shot magazine. **Barrel:** 3.5". **Weight:** 29 oz. **Length:** 6.7" overall. **Stocks:** Textured acetal plastic. **Sights:** Combat-style fixed three-dot system; low profile. **Features:** Single-action design; frame-mounted magazine release. Scratch-resistant matte finish. Introduced 1993. From MKS Supply, Inc.
Price: **$124.95**
Price: With polymer frame (29 oz.), non-slip grips **$132.95**
Price: 380 ACP **$89.95**

Intratec Cat 9

Jennings J-25

Kahr K9

Kareen MK II

Kareen Mk II Compact

HUNGARIAN T-58 AUTO PISTOL Caliber: 7.62mm and 9mm Para., 8-shot magazine. **Barrel:** 4.5″. **Weight:** 31 oz. **Length:** 7.68″ overall. **Stocks:** Grooved composition. **Sights:** Blade front, rear adjustable for windage. **Features:** Comes with both barrels and magazines. Thumb safety locks hammer. Blue finish. Imported by Century International Arms.
Price: About $187.00

INTRATEC PROTEC-22, 25 AUTO PISTOLS Caliber: 22 LR, 10-shot; 25 ACP, 8-shot magazine. **Barrel:** 2½″. **Weight:** 14 oz. **Length:** 5″ overall. **Stocks:** Wraparound composition in gray, black or driftwood color. **Sights:** Fixed. **Features:** Double-action only trigger mechanism. Choice of black, satin or TEC-KOTE finish. Announced 1991. Made in U.S. by Intratec.
Price: 22 or 25, black finish $112.00
Price: 22 or 25, satin or TEC-KOTE finish $117.00

INTRATEC SPORT 22 AUTO PISTOL Caliber: 22 LR, 10-shot magazine. **Barrel:** 4″. **Weight:** 28 oz. **Length:** 11³⁄₁₆″ overall. **Stocks:** Moulded composition. **Sights:** Protected post front, adjustable for windage, rear adjustable elevation. **Features:** Ambidextrous cocking knobs and safety. Matte black finish. Accepts any 10/22-type magazine. Introduced 1988. Made in U.S. by Intratec.
Price: $130.00

INTRATEC CAT 9 AUTO PISTOL Caliber: 380 ACP, 9mm Para., 7-shot magazine. **Barrel:** 3″. **Weight:** 21 oz. **Length:** 5.5″ overall. **Stocks:** Textured black polymer. **Sights:** Fixed channel. **Features:** Black polymer frame. Introduced 1993. Made in U.S. by Intratec.
Price: About $235.00

INTRATEC CAT 45 Caliber: 40 S&W, 45 ACP; 6-shot magazine. **Barrel:** 3.25″. **Weight:** 19 oz. **Length:** 6.35″ overall. **Stocks:** Moulded composition. **Sights:** Fixed, channel. **Features:** Black polymer frame. Introduced 1996. Made in U.S. by Intratec.
Price: $255.00

JENNINGS J-22, J-25 AUTO PISTOLS Caliber: 22 LR, 25 ACP, 6-shot magazine. **Barrel:** 2½″. **Weight:** 13 oz. (J-22). **Length:** 4¹⁵⁄₁₆″ overall (J-22). **Stocks:** Walnut on chrome or nickel models; grooved black Cycolac or resin-impregnated wood on Teflon model. **Sights:** Fixed. **Features:** Choice of bright chrome, satin nickel or black Teflon finish. Introduced 1981. From Jennings Firearms.
Price: J-22, about $79.95
Price: J-25, about $79.95

KAHR K9 DA AUTO PISTOL Caliber: 9mm Para., 7-shot magazine. **Barrel:** 3.5″. **Weight:** 25 oz. **Length:** 6″ overall. **Stocks:** Wraparound textured soft polymer. **Sights:** Blade front, rear drift adjustable for windage; bar-dot combat style. **Features:** Trigger-cocking double-action mechanism with passive firing pin block. Made of 4140 ordnance steel with matte black finish. Introduced 1994. Made in U.S. by Kahr Arms.
Price: $595.00
Price: Matte black, night sights $692.00
Price: Matte nickel finish $678.00
Price: Nickel, night sights $775.00

KAREEN MK II AUTO PISTOL Caliber: 9mm Para., 10-shot magazine. **Barrel:** 4.75″. **Weight:** 34 oz. **Length:** 7.85″ overall. **Stocks:** Textured composition. **Sights:** Blade front, rear adjustable for windage. **Features:** Single-action mechanism; ambidextrous external hammer safety; magazine safety; combat trigger guard. Two-tone finish. Introduced 1985. Imported from Israel by J.O. Arms & Ammunition.
Price: $425.00
Price: Kareen Mk II Compact 9mm (3.75″ barrel, 30 oz., 6.75″ overall length) $495.00

KEL-TEC P-11 AUTO PISTOL **Caliber:** 9mm Para., 10-shot magazine. **Barrel:** 3.1″. **Weight:** 14 oz. **Length:** 5.6″ overall. **Stocks:** Checkered black polymer. **Sights:** Blade front, rear adjustable for windage. **Features:** Ordnance steel slide, aluminum frame. Double-action-only trigger mechanism. Introduced 1995. Made in U.S. by Kel-Tec CNC Industries, Inc.
Price: Blue $309.00
Price: Stainless $407.00
Price: Parkerized $350.00

Kel-Tec P-11

KIMBER CLASSIC 45 CUSTOM AUTO PISTOL **Caliber:** 45 ACP, 8-shot magazine. **Barrel:** 5″. **Weight:** 38 oz. **Length:** 8.5″ overall. **Stocks:** Black synthetic. **Sights:** McCormick dovetailed front, low combat rear. **Features:** Uses Chip McCormick Corp. forged frame and slide, match-grade barrel, extended combat thumb safety, high beavertail grip safety, skeletonized lightweight composite trigger, skeletonized Commander-type hammer, elongated Commander ejector, and 8-shot magazine. Bead-blasted black oxide finish; flat mainspring housing; lowered and flared ejection port; serrated front and rear of slide; relief cut under trigger guard; Wolff spring set; beveled magazine well. Introduced 1995. Made in U.S. by Kimber of America, Inc.
Price: Custom $575.00
Price: Custom Stainless $650.00

Kimber Classic 45 Custom

Kimber Classic 45 Custom Royal Auto Pistol Same as the Custom model except has checkered diamond-pattern walnut grips, long guide rod, polished blue finish, and comes with two 8-shot magazines. Introduced 1995. Made in U.S. by Kimber of America, Inc.
Price: $715.00

Kimber Classic 45 Gold Match Auto Pistol Same as the Custom Royal except also has Bo-Mar BMCS low-mount adjustable rear sight, fancy walnut grips, tighter tolerances. Comes with one 10-shot and one 8-shot magazine and factory proof target. Introduced 1995. Made in U.S. by Kimber of America, Inc.
Price: $925.00

Kimber Classic 45 Gold Match

L.A.R. GRIZZLY WIN MAG MK I PISTOL **Caliber:** 357 Mag., 357/45, 10mm, 44 Mag., 45 Win. Mag., 45 ACP, 7-shot magazine. **Barrel:** 5.4″, 6.5″. **Weight:** 51 oz. **Length:** 10¹⁄₂″ overall. **Stocks:** Checkered rubber, non-slip combat-type. **Sights:** Ramped blade front, fully adjustable rear. **Features:** Uses basic Browning/Colt 1911A1 design; interchangeable calibers; beveled magazine well; combat-type flat, checkered rubber mainspring housing; lowered and back-chamfered ejection port; polished feed ramp; throated barrel; solid barrel bushings. Available in satin hard chrome, matte blue, Parkerized finishes. Introduced 1983. From L.A.R. Mfg., Inc.
Price: 45 Win. Mag. $1,000.00
Price: 357 Mag. $1,014.00
Price: Conversion units (357 Mag.) $248.00
Price: As above, 45 ACP, 10mm, 45 Win. Mag., 357/45 Win. Mag. $233.00

L.A.R. Girzzly MK I

L.A.R. Grizzly 50 Mark V Pistol Similar to the Grizzly Win Mag Mark I except chambered for 50 Action Express with 6-shot magazine. Weight, empty, is 56 oz., overall length 10⁵⁄₈″. Choice of 5.4″ or 6.5″ barrel. Has same features as Mark I, IV pistols. Introduced 1993. From L.A.R. Mfg., Inc.
Price: $1,152.00

L.A.R. Grizzly 44 Mag MK IV Similar to the Win Mag Mk I except chambered for 44 Magnum, has beavertail grip safety. Matte blue finish only. Has 5.4″ or 6.5″ barrel. Introduced 1991. From L.A.R. Mfg., Inc.
Price: $1,014.00

L.A.R. Grizzly 50

Laseraim Arms Series I

Laseraim Series III

Llama Max-I

Llama Large Frame

Llama Compact Frame

LASERAIM ARMS SERIES I AUTO PISTOL Caliber: 10mm Auto, 8-shot, 45 ACP, 7-shot magazine. **Barrel:** 6″, with compensator. **Weight:** 46 oz. **Length:** 9.75″ overall. **Stocks:** Pebble-grained black composite. **Sights:** Blade front, fully adjustable rear. **Features:** Single action; barrel compensator; stainless steel construction; ambidextrous safety-levers; extended slide release; matte black Teflon finish; integral mount for laser sight. Introduced 1993. Made in U.S. by Laseraim Technologies, Inc.

Price: Standard, fixed sight	**$552.95**
Price: Standard, Compact (4³/₈″ barrel), fixed sight	**$552.95**
Price: Adjustable sight	**$579.95**
Price: Standard, fixed sight, Auto Illusion red dot sight system	**$649.95**
Price: Standard, fixed sight, Laseraim Laser with Hotdot	**$694.95**

Laseraim Arms Series II Auto Pistol Similar to the Series I except without compensator, has matte stainless finish. Standard Series II has 5″ barrel, weighs 43 oz., Compact has 3³/₈″ barrel, weighs 37 oz. Blade front sight, rear adjustable for windage or fixed. Introduced 1993. Made in U.S. by Laseraim Technologies, Inc.

Price: Standard or Compact (3³/₈″ barrel), fixed sight	**$399.95**
Price: Adjustable sight, 5″ only	**$429.95**
Price: Standard, fixed sight, Auto Illustion red dot sight	**$499.95**
Price: Standard, fixed sight, Laseraim Laser	**$499.95**

Laseraim Arms Series III Auto Pistol Similar to the Series II except has 5″ barrel only, with dual-port compensator; weighs 43 oz.; overall length is 7⁵/₈″. Choice of fixed or adjustable rear sight. Introduced 1994. Made in U.S. by Laseraim Technologies, Inc.

Price: Fixed sight	**$533.95**
Price: Adjustable sight	**$559.95**
Price: Fixed sight Dream Team Laseraim laser sight	**$629.95**

Consult our Directory pages for the location of firms mentioned.

LLAMA MAX-I AUTO PISTOLS Caliber: 9mm Para., 9-shot, 45 ACP, 7-shot. **Barrel:** 4¹/₄″ (Compact); 5¹/₈″ (Government). **Weight:** 34 oz. (Compact); 36 oz. (Government). **Length:** 7³/₈″ overall (Compact). **Stocks:** Black rubber. **Sights:** Blade front, rear adjustable for windage; three-dot system. **Features:** Single-action trigger; skeletonized combat-style hammer; steel frame; extended manual and grip safeties. Introduced 1995. Imported from Spain by Import Sports, Inc.

Price: 9mm, 9-shot, Government model	**$349.95**
Price: As above, Compact model	**$349.95**
Price: 45 ACP, 7-shot, Government model	**$349.95**
Price: As above, Duo-Tone finish	**$366.95**
Price: As above, Compact model	**$382.95**

LLAMA IX-D COMPACT FRAME AUTO PISTOL Caliber: 45 ACP, 10-shot. **Barrel:** 4¹/₄″. **Weight:** 39 oz. **Stocks:** Black rubber. **Sights:** Blade front, rear adjustable for windage; three-dot system. **Features:** Scaled-down version of the Large Frame gun. Locked breech mechanism; manual and grip safeties. Introduced 1995. Imported from Spain by Import Sports, Inc.

Price: Matte finish	**$399.95**

LLAMA IX-C LARGE FRAME AUTO PISTOL Caliber: 45 ACP, 10-shot. **Barrel:** 5¹/₈″. **Weight:** 41 oz. **Length:** 8¹/₂″ overall. **Stocks:** Black rubber. **Sights:** Blade front, rear adjustable for windage; three-dot system. **Features:** Grip and manual safeties, ventilated rib. Imported from Spain by Import Sports, Inc.

Price: Matte finish	**$399.95**

LLAMA III-A SMALL FRAME AUTO PISTOL Caliber: 380 ACP. **Barrel:** 3¹¹/₁₆″. **Weight:** 23 oz. **Length:** 6½″ overall. **Stocks:** Checkered polymer, thumbrest. **Sights:** Fixed front, adjustable notch rear. **Features:** Ventilated rib, manual and grip safeties. Imported from Spain by Import Sports, Inc.
Price: Blue $248.95
Price: Satin Chrome $291.95

Llama Small Frame

LLAMA MINIMAX SERIES Caliber: 9mm Para., 40 S&W, 45 ACP, 6-shot magazine. **Barrel:** 3½″. **Weight:** 35 oz. **Length:** 7¹/₃″ overall. **Stocks:** Checkered rubber. **Sights:** Three-dot combat. **Features:** Single action, skeletonized combat-style hammer, extended slide release, cone-style barrel, flared ejection port. Introduced 1996. Imported from Spain by Import Sports, Inc.
Price: Blue $366.95
Price: Duo-Tone finish (45 only) $382.95
Price: Satin chrome $408.95
Price: Stainless steel finish $432.95

Llama Minimax

LLAMA MAX-I COMPENSATOR Caliber: 45 ACP, 7-, 10-shot magazine. **Barrel:** 4⁷/₈″ (without compensator, 6¹/₃″ with). **Weight:** 42 oz. (7-shot). **Length:** 9⁷/₈″ overall. **Stocks:** Checkered rubber. **Sights:** Dovetail blade front, fully adjustable rear. **Features:** Extended beavertail grip safety, skeletonized combat hammer, extended slide release. Introduced 1996. Imported from Spain by Import Sports, Inc.
Price: 7-shot $491.95
Price: 10-shot $516.95

Llama Max-1 Compensator

LORCIN L-22 AUTO PISTOL Caliber: 22 LR, 9-shot magazine. **Barrel:** 2.5″. **Weight:** 16 oz. **Length:** 5.25″ overall. **Stocks:** Black combat, or pink or pearl. **Sights:** Fixed three-dot system. **Features:** Available in chrome or black Teflon finish. Introduced 1989. From Lorcin Engineering.
Price: About $89.00

LORCIN L9MM AUTO PISTOL Caliber: 9mm Para., 10-shot magazine. **Barrel:** 4.5″. **Weight:** 31 oz. **Length:** 7.5″ overall. **Stocks:** Grooved black composition. **Sights:** Fixed; three-dot system. **Features:** Matte black finish; hooked trigger guard; grip safety. Introduced 1994. Made in U.S. by Lorcin Engineering.
Price: $159.00

Lorcin L9MM

LORCIN L-25, LT-25 AUTO PISTOLS Caliber: 25 ACP, 7-shot magazine. **Barrel:** 2.4″. **Weight:** 14.5 oz. **Length:** 4.8″ overall. **Stocks:** Smooth composition. **Sights:** Fixed. **Features:** Available in choice of finishes: chrome, black Teflon or camouflage. Introduced 1989. From Lorcin Engineering.
Price: L-25 . . . .$69.00
Price: LT-25 . . . .$79.00

LORCIN L-32, L-380 AUTO PISTOLS Caliber: 32 ACP, 380 ACP, 7-shot magazine. **Barrel:** 3.5″. **Weight:** 27 oz. **Length:** 6.6″ overall. **Stocks:** Grooved composition. **Sights:** Fixed. **Features:** Black Teflon or chrome finish with black grips. Introduced 1992. From Lorcin Engineering.
Price: L-32 32 ACP $89.00
Price: L-380 380 ACP $100.00

Lorcin L-25

MITCHELL 45 GOLD STANDARD MODEL Caliber: 45 ACP, 8-shot magazine. **Barrel:** 5″. **Weight:** 32 oz. **Length:** 8.75″ overall. **Stocks:** Wrap-around rubber. **Sights:** Blade front, fixed rear. **Features:** Stainless steel with bright/satin finish; front and rear slide serrations; flat grooved mainspring housing; full-length mainspring guide rod; Commander hammer; beavertail grip safety. Announced 1994. Made in U.S. by Mitchell Arms.
Price: $675.00

Mitchell 45 Gold Tactical Model Similar to the Standard model except fixed or adjustable sight; adjustable trigger; ambidextrous safety; extended slide stop; checkered walnut grips; skeleton hammer. Announced 1996. Made in U.S. by Mitchell Arms.
Price: With fixed sight $750.00
Price: With adjustable sight $775.00

Mitchell 45 Gold Wide Body Standard Similar to the 45 Gold Standard except comes with 10-shot magazine; rear slide serrations only; satin-finished slide; walnut composite grips. Announced 1994. Made in U.S. by Mitchell Arms.
Price: $775.00

Mitchell 45 Gold Wide Body Tactical Similar to the 45 Gold Standard except 10-shot magazine; adjustable sight; ambidextrous safety; checkered mainspring housing; adjustable trigger; extended slide release; match barrel; skeleton Commander hammer; polished slide; black composite grips. Announced 1994. Made in U.S. by Mitchell Arms.
Price: $895.00

MITCHELL ARMS ALPHA AUTO PISTOL Caliber: 45 ACP, 8- and 10-shot magazine. **Barrel:** 5″. **Weight:** 41 oz. **Length:** 8.5″ overall. **Stocks:** Smooth polymer. **Sights:** Interchangeable blade front, fully adjustable rear or drift adjustable rear. **Features:** Interchangeable trigger modules permit double-action-only, single-action-only or SA/DA fire. Accepts any single-column, 8-shot 1911-style magazine. Frame-mounted decocker/safety; extended ambidextrous safety; extended slide latch; serrated combat hammer; beveled magazine well; heavy bull barrel (no bushing design); extended slide underlug; full-length recoil spring guide system. Introduced 1995. Made in U.S. From Mitchell Arms, Inc.
Price: Blue, fixed sight $695.00
Price: Blue, adjustable sight $725.00
Price: Stainless, fixed sight $725.00
Price: Stainless, adjustable sight $749.00

MITCHELL GOLD SERIES AMBIDEXTROUS AUTO Caliber: 9mm Para., 40 S&W. **Barrel:** 4.4″. **Weight:** 33 oz. **Length:** NA. **Stocks:** Checkered wood. **Sights:** Dovetail blade front, drift-adjustable rear; three-dot system. **Features:** Ambidextrous controls, including magazine release; chrome lined barrel; forged steel slide, aluminum frame. Announced 1996. Made in U.S. by Mitchell Arms.
Price: Black pearl $650.00
Price: Diamond $725.00
Price: Gold $795.00

MITCHELL JEFF COOPER SIGNATURE AUTO Caliber: 45 ACP, 8-shot magazine. **Barrel:** 5″ heavy match, no bushing. **Weight:** 32 oz. **Length:** NA. **Stocks:** Thin checkered composite. **Sights:** Ramped front, fixed rear. **Features:** Cooper's signature roll-marked on slide; slenderized frame; completely dehorned; short adjustable trigger; grooved arched mainspring housing; extended safety; military slide serrations; military guide rod; burn hammer. Announced 1996. Made in U.S. by Mitchell Arms.
Price: Satin black finish $795.00

Mitchell Jeff Cooper Commemorative Model Similar to the Signature model except has polished frame; engraved signature; polished and gold-plated trigger; checkered walnut grips with medallion; gold-filled lettering. Limited edition gun comes with red and Marine gold lanyard with gold trim, certificate of authenticity, special case. Announced 1996. Made in U.S. by Mitchell Arms.
Price: $1,895.00

MITCHELL 44 MAGNUM AUTO PISTOL Caliber: 44 Mag., 6-shot magazine. **Barrel:** 5.5″. **Weight:** 46 oz. **Length:** NA. **Stocks:** Checkered walnut. **Sights:** Dovetail blade front, fully adjustable rear. **Features:** Front and rear slide serrations; skeleton hammer. Announced 1996. Made in U.S. by Mitchell Arms.
Price: $1,190.00

Mitchell Arms Alpha

Mitchell Gold Series

Mitchell 45 Gold Tactical

Mitchell Sportster

MITCHELL ARMS SPORTSTER AUTO PISTOL Caliber: 22 LR, 10-shot magazine. **Barrel:** 4.5″, 6.75″. **Weight:** 39 oz. (4.5″ barrel). **Length:** 9″ overall (4.5″ barrel). **Stocks:** Checkered black plastic. **Sights:** Blade front, rear adjustable for windage. **Features:** Military grip; standard trigger; push-button barrel takedown. Stainless steel or blue. Introduced 1992. From Mitchell Arms, Inc.
Price: $325.00

Mountain Eagle Target

Para-Ordnance P12.45

Para-Ordnance P16.40

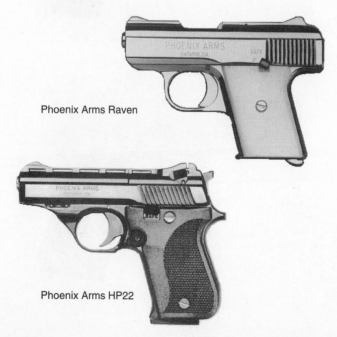

Phoenix Arms Raven

Phoenix Arms HP22

MOUNTAIN EAGLE AUTO PISTOL Caliber: 22 LR, 10-shot magazine. **Barrel:** 4.5″, 6.5″, 8″. **Weight:** 21 oz., 23 oz. **Length:** 10.6″ overall (with 6.5″ barrel). **Stocks:** One-piece impact-resistant polymer in "conventional contour"; checkered panels. **Sights:** Serrated ramp front with interchangeable blades, rear adjustable for windage and elevation; interchangeable blades. **Features:** Injection moulded grip frame, alloy receiver; hybrid composite barrel replicates shape of the Desert Eagle pistol. Flat, smooth trigger. Introduced 1992. From Magnum Research.
Price: Mountain Eagle Compact $199.00
Price: Mountain Eagle Standard $239.00
Price: Mountain Eagle Target Edition (8″ barrel) $279.00

NORTH AMERICAN MUNITIONS MODEL 1996 Caliber: 9mm Para., 9-shot magazine. **Barrel:** 4.5″. **Weight:** 40 oz. **Length:** 8.38″ overall. **Stocks:** Black polycarbonate. **Sights:** Blade front, adjustable rear; three-dot system. **Features:** Gas-delayed blowback system; no external safeties; fixed 10-groove barrel. Introduced 1996. Made in U.S. From Intercontinental Munitions Distributors, Ltd.
Price: $275.00

PARA-ORDNANCE P-SERIES AUTO PISTOLS Caliber: 40 S&W, 45 ACP, 10-shot magazine. **Barrel:** 5″. **Weight:** 28 oz. (alloy frame). **Length:** 8.5″ overall. **Stocks:** Textured composition. **Sights:** Blade front, rear adjustable for windage. High visibility three-dot system. **Features:** Available with alloy, steel or stainless steel frame with black finish (silver or stainless gun). Steel and stainless steel frame guns weighs 38 oz. (P14.45), 35 oz. (P13.45), 33 oz. (P12.45). Grooved match trigger, rounded combat-style hammer. Beveled magazine well. Manual thumb, grip and firing pin lock safeties. Solid barrel bushing. Contact maker for full details. Introduced 1990. Made in Canada by Para-Ordnance.
Price: P14.45ER (steel frame) $750.00
Price: P14.45RR (alloy frame) $705.00
Price: P12.45RR (3¹/₂″ bbl., 24 oz., alloy) $705.00
Price: P13.45RR (4¹/₄″ barrel, 28 oz., alloy) $705.00
Price: P12.45ER (steel frame) $750.00
Price: P16.40ER (steel frame) $750.00

PHOENIX ARMS MODEL RAVEN AUTO PISTOL Caliber: 25 ACP, 6-shot magazine. **Barrel:** 2⁷/₁₆″. **Weight:** 15 oz. **Length:** 4³/₄″ overall. **Stocks:** Ivory-colored or black slotted plastic. **Sights:** Ramped front, fixed rear. **Features:** Available in blue, nickel or chrome finish. Made in U.S. Available from Phoenix Arms.
Price: $79.00

PHOENIX ARMS HP22, HP25 AUTO PISTOLS Caliber: 22 LR, 10-shot (HP22), 25 ACP, 10-shot (HP25). **Barrel:** 3″. **Weight:** 20 oz. **Length:** 5¹/₂″ overall. **Stocks:** Checkered composition. **Sights:** Blade front, adjustable rear. **Features:** Single action, exposed hammer; manual hold-open; button magazine release. Available in satin nickel, polished blue finish. Introduced 1993. Made in U.S. by Phoenix Arms.
Price: $99.00

Piranha Pistol

PIRANHA AUTOLOADING PISTOL Caliber: 9mm Para., 9mm Largo, 30 Luger, 10-shot magazine. **Barrel:** 4″, 6″, 8″, 10″, 16″. **Weight:** About 2.7 lbs. **Length:** 9″ overall with 4″ barrel. **Stocks:** Smooth walnut. **Sights:** Blade front, rear adjustable for windage. **Features:** Nearly recoilless action; stainless steel construction; fires from closed bolt; change caliber by changing barrel. Introduced 1996. Made in U.S. by Recoillers Technologies, Inc.
Price: $600.00

PSA-25 AUTO PISTOL Caliber: 25 ACP, 6-shot magazine. **Barrel:** 2¹⁄₈″. **Weight:** 9.5 oz. **Length:** 4¹⁄₈″ overall. **Stocks:** Checkered black plastic. **Sights:** Fixed. **Features:** All steel construction with polished finish. Introduced 1984. Made in the U.S. by PSP.
Price: Black oxide $249.00
Price: Brushed satin chrome $301.00
Price: Featherweight $375.00

PSA-25 Pistol

ROCKY MOUNTAIN ARMS PATRIOT PISTOL Caliber: 223, 10-shot magazine. **Barrel:** 7″, with muzzle brake. **Weight:** 5 lbs. **Length:** 20.5″ overall. **Stocks:** Black composition. **Sights:** None furnished. **Features:** Milled upper receiver with enhanced Weaver base; milled lower receiver from billet plate; machined aluminum National Match handguard. Finished in DuPont Teflon-S matte black or NATO green. Comes with black nylon case, one magazine. Introduced 1993. From Rocky Mountain Arms, Inc.
Price: With A-2 handle top ....$2,500.00 to $2,800.00
Price: Flat top model ....$3,000.00 to $3,500.00

Ruger P89

RUGER P89 AUTOMATIC PISTOL Caliber: 9mm Para., 10-shot magazine. **Barrel:** 4.50″. **Weight:** 32 oz. **Length:** 7.84″ overall. **Stocks:** Grooved black Xenoy composition. **Sights:** Square post front, square notch rear adjustable for windage, both with white dot inserts. **Features:** Double action with ambidextrous slide-mounted safety-levers. Slide is 4140 chrome-moly steel or 400-series stainless steel, frame is a lightweight aluminum alloy. Ambidextrous magazine release. Blue or stainless steel. Introduced 1986; stainless introduced 1990.
Price: P89, blue, with extra magazine and magazine loading tool, plastic case $410.00
Price: KP89, stainless, with extra magazine and magazine loading tool, plastic case $452.00

Ruger P89D Decocker Automatic Pistol Similar to the standard P89 except has ambidextrous decocking levers in place of the regular slide-mounted safety. The decocking levers move the firing pin inside the slide where the hammer can not reach it, while simultaneously blocking the firing pin from forward movement—allows shooter to decock a cocked pistol without manipulating the trigger. Conventional thumb decocking procedures are therefore unnecessary. Blue or stainless steel. Introduced 1990.
Price: P89D, blue with extra magazine and loader, plastic case $410.00
Price: KP89D, stainless, with extra magazine, plastic case $452.00

Ruger KP89D

Ruger P89 Double-Action-Only Automatic Pistol Same as the KP89 except operates only in the double-action mode. Has a spurless hammer, gripping grooves on each side of the rear of the slide; no external safety or decocking lever. An internal safety prevents forward movement of the firing pin unless the trigger is pulled. Available in 9mm Para., stainless steel only. Introduced 1991.
Price: With lockable case, extra magazine, magazine loading tool $452.00

Ruger P89DAO

Ruger KP89DAC

RUGER P90 SAFETY MODEL AUTOMATIC PISTOL **Caliber:** 45 ACP, 7-shot magazine. **Barrel:** 4.50″. **Weight:** 33.5 oz. **Length:** 7.87″ overall. **Stocks:** Grooved black Xenoy composition. **Sights:** Square post front, square notch rear adjustable for windage, both with white dot inserts. **Features:** Double action with ambidextrous slide-mounted safety-levers which move the firing pin inside the slide where the hammer can not reach it, while simultaneously blocking the firing pin from forward movement. Stainless steel only. Introduced 1991.
Price: KP90 with plastic case, extra magazine, loader . .**$488.65**

Ruger KP90

> Consult our Directory pages for
> the location of firms mentioned.

Ruger P90 Decocker Automatic Pistol Similar to the P90 except has a manual decocking system. The ambidextrous decocking levers move the firing pin inside the slide where the hammer can not reach it, while simultaneously blocking the firing pin from forward movement—allows shooter to decock a cocked pistol without manipulating the trigger. Available only in stainless steel. Overall length 7.87″, weighs 34 oz. Introduced 1991.
Price: P90D with lockable case, extra magazine, and magazine loading tool **$488.65**

Ruger P93 DAO

RUGER P93 COMPACT AUTOMATIC PISTOL Caliber: 9mm Para., 10-shot magazine. **Barrel:** 3.9″. **Weight:** 31 oz. **Length:** 7.3″ overall. **Stocks:** Grooved black Xenoy composition. **Sights:** Square post front, square notch rear adjustable for windage. **Features:** Front of slide is crowned with a convex curve; slide has seven finger grooves; trigger guard bow is higher for a better grip; 400-series stainless slide, lightweight alloy frame. Decocker-only or DAO-only. Introduced 1993. Made in U.S. by Sturm, Ruger & Co.
Price: **$520.00**

Ruger KP94 Automatic Pistol Sized midway between the full-size P-Series and the compact P93. Has 4.25″ barrel, 7.5″ overall length and weighs about 33 oz. KP94 is manual safety model; KP94DAO is double-action-only (both 9mm Para., 10-shot magazine); KP94D is decocker-only in 40 S&W with 10-shot magazine. Slide gripping grooves roll over top of slide. KP94 has ambidextrous safety-levers; KP94DAO has no external safety, full-cock hammer position or decocking lever; KP94D has ambidextrous decocking levers. Matte finish stainless slide, barrel, alloy frame. Introduced 1994. Made in U.S. by Sturm, Ruger & Co.
Price: KP94 (9mm), KP944 (40) **$520.00**
Price: KP94DAO (9mm), KP944DAO (40) **$520.00**
Price: KP94D (9mm), KP9440 (40 S&W) **$520.00**

Ruger KP94

Ruger P94L Automatic Pistol Same as the KP94 except mounts a laser sight in a housing cast integrally with the frame. Allen-head screws control windage and elevation adjustments. Announced 1994. Made in U.S. by Sturm, Ruger & Co.
Price: For law enforcement only .... **NA**

RUGER P95 AUTOMATIC PISTOL Caliber: 9mm Para., 10-shot magazine. **Barrel:** 3.9″. **Weight:** 27 oz. **Length:** 7.3″ overall. **Stocks:** Grooved; integral with frame. **Sights:** Blade front, rear drift adjustable for windage; three-dot system. **Features:** Moulded grip frame, stainless steel or chrome-moly slide. Suitable for +P+ ammunition. Decocker or DAO. Introduced 1996. Made in U.S. by Sturm, Ruger & Co. Comes with lockable plastic case, spare magazine, loading tool.
Price: P95 DAO double-action-only **$343.00**
Price: P95D decocker only **$351.00**

Ruger KP95D

Ruger Mark II

Ruger P512 22/45

Ruger MK-4B Compact

Safari Arms Enforcer

Schuetzen Big Deuce

RUGER MARK II STANDARD AUTO PISTOL Caliber: 22 LR, 10-shot magazine. **Barrel:** 4³/₄" or 6". **Weight:** 25 oz. (4³/₄" bbl.). **Length:** 8⁵/₁₆" (4³/₄" bbl.). **Stocks:** Checkered plastic. **Sights:** Fixed, wide blade front, square notch rear adjustable for windage. **Features:** Updated design of the original Standard Auto. Has new bolt hold-open latch. 10-shot magazine, magazine catch, safety, trigger and new receiver contours. Introduced 1982.
Price: Blued (MK 4, MK 6) $252.00
Price: In stainless steel (KMK 4, KMK 6) $330.25

Ruger 22/45 Mark II Pistol Similar to the other 22 Mark II autos except has grip frame of Zytel that matchs the angle and magazine latch of the Model 1911 45 ACP pistol. Available in 4³/₄" standard and 5¹/₂" bull barrel. Introduced 1992.
Price: KP4 (4³/₄" barrel) $280.00
Price: KP512 (5¹/₂" bull barrel) $330.00
Price: P512 (5¹/₂" bull barrel, all blue) $237.50

Ruger MK-4B Compact Pistol Similar to the Mark II Standard pistol except has 4" bull barrel, Patridge-type front sight, fully adjustable rear, and smooth laminated hardwood thumbrest stocks. Weighs 38 oz., overall length of 8³/₁₆". Comes with extra magazine, plastic case, lock. Introduced 1996. Made in U.S. by Sturm, Ruger & Co.
Price: $336.50

SAFARI ARMS GI SAFARI PISTOL Caliber: 45 ACP, 7-shot magazine. **Barrel:** 5", 416 stainless. **Weight:** 39.9 oz. **Length:** 8.5" overall. **Stocks:** Checkered walnut. **Sights:** G.I.-style blade front, drift-adjustable rear. **Features:** Beavertail grip safety; extended thumb safety and slide release; Commander-style hammer. Parkerized finish. Reintroduced 1996.
Price: ....$585.00.

SAFARI ARMS ENFORCER PISTOL Caliber: 45 ACP, 6-shot magazine. **Barrel:** 3.8", stainless. **Weight:** 36 oz. **Length:** 7.3" overall. **Stocks:** Smooth walnut with etched black widow spider logo. **Sights:** Ramped blade front, LPA adjustable rear. **Features:** Extended safety, extended slide release; Commander-style hammer; beavertail grip safety; throated, polished, tuned. Parkerized matte black or satin stainless steel finishes. Made in U.S. by Safari Arms.
Price: $740.00

SAFARI ARMS COHORT PISTOL Caliber: 45 ACP, 7-shot magazine. **Barrel:** 3.8", 416 stainless. **Weight:** 37 oz. **Length:** 8.5" overall. **Stocks:** Smooth walnut with laser-etched black widow logo. **Sights:** Ramped blade front, LPA adjustable rear. **Features:** Combines the Enforcer model, slide and MatchMaster frame. Beavertail grip safety; extended thumb safety and slide release; Commander-style hammer. Throated, polished and tuned. Satin stainless finish. Introduced 1996. Made in U.S. by Safari Arms, Inc.
Price: $780.00

SCHUETZEN PISTOL WORKS BIG DEUCE PISTOL Caliber: 45 ACP, 7-shot magazine. **Barrel:** 6", 416 stainless steel. **Weight:** 40.3 oz. **Length:** 9.5" overall. **Stocks:** Smooth walnut. **Sights:** Ramped blade front, LPA adjustable rear. **Features:** Beavertail grip safety; extended thumb safety and slide release; Commander-style hammer. Throated, polished and tuned. Parkerized matte black slide with satin stainless steel frame. Introduced 1995. Made in U.S. by Safari Arms, Inc.
Price: $849.00

SCHUETZEN PISTOL WORKS RENEGADE Caliber: 45 ACP, 7-shot magazine. **Barrel:** 5", 416 stainless steel. **Weight:** 39 oz. **Length:** 8.5" overall. **Stocks:** Checkered walnut. **Sights:** Ramped blade, LPA adjustable rear. **Features:** True left-hand pistol. Beavertail grip safety; long aluminum trigger; full-length recoil spring guide; Commander-style hammer; satin stainless finish. Throated, polished and tuned. Introduced 1996. Made in U.S. by Safari Arms, Inc.
Price: $1,075.00

SCHUETZEN PISTOL WORKS GRIFFON PISTOL **Caliber:** 45 ACP, 10-shot magazine. **Barrel:** 5", 416 stainless steel. **Weight:** 40.5 oz. **Length:** 8.5" overall. **Stocks:** Smooth walnut. **Sights:** Ramped blade front, LPA adjustable rear. **Features:** 10+1 1911 enhanced 45. Beavertail grip safety; long aluminum trigger; full-length recoil spring guide; Commander-style hammer. Throated, polished and tuned. Grip size comparable to standard 1911. Satin stainless steel finish. Introduced 1996. Made in U.S. by Olympic Arms, Inc.
Price: $910.00

Schuetzen Pistol Works Enforcer Carrycomp II Pistol Similar to the Enforcer except has Wil Schueman-designed hybrid compensator system. Introduced 1993. Made in U.S. by Safari Arms, Inc.
Price: 3.8" barrel $1,150.00
Price: 5" barrel $1,300.00

SCHUETZEN PISTOL WORKS RELIABLE PISTOL **Caliber:** 45 ACP, 7-shot magazine. **Barrel:** 5", 416 stainless steel. **Weight:** 39 oz. **Length:** 8.5" overall. **Stocks:** Checkered walnut. **Sights:** Ramped blade front, LPA adjustable rear. **Features:** Beavertail grip safety; long aluminum trigger; full-length recoil spring guide; Commander-style hammer. Throated, polished and tuned. Satin stainless steel finish. Introduced 1996. Made in U.S. by Safari Arms, Inc.
Price: $815.00

Schuetzen Pistol Works Reliable 4-Star Pistol Similar to the Reliable except has 4.5" barrel, 7.5" overall length, and weighs 35.7 oz. Introduced 1996. Made in U.S. by Safari Arms, Inc.
Price: $875.00

SEECAMP LWS 32 STAINLESS DA AUTO **Caliber:** 32 ACP Win. Silvertip, 6-shot magazine. **Barrel:** 2", integral with frame. **Weight:** 10.5 oz. **Length:** 4 1/8" overall. **Stocks:** Glass-filled nylon. **Sights:** Smooth, no-snag, contoured slide and barrel top. **Features:** Aircraft quality 17-4 PH stainless steel. Inertia-operated firing pin. Hammer fired double-action-only. Hammer automatically follows slide down to safety rest position after each shot—no manual safety needed. Magazine safety disconnector. Polished stainless. Introduced 1985. From L.W. Seecamp.
Price: $375.00

SIG SAUER P220 "AMERICAN" AUTO PISTOL **Caliber:** 38 Super, 45 ACP, (9-shot in 38 Super, 7 in 45). **Barrel:** 4 3/8". **Weight:** 28 1/4 oz. (9mm). **Length:** 7 3/4" overall. **Stocks:** Checkered black plastic. **Sights:** Blade front, drift adjustable rear for windage. **Features:** Double action. Decocking lever permits lowering hammer onto locked firing pin. Squared combat-type trigger guard. Slide stays open after last shot. Imported from Germany by SIGARMS, Inc.
Price: "American," blue (side-button magazine release, 45 ACP only) $805.00
Price: 45 ACP, blue, Siglite night sights $905.00
Price: K-Kote finish $850.00
Price: K-Kote, Siglite night sights $950.00

SIG SAUER P225 DA AUTO PISTOL **Caliber:** 9mm Para., 8-shot magazine. **Barrel:** 3.8". **Weight:** 26 oz. **Length:** 7 3/32" overall. **Stocks:** Checkered black plastic. **Sights:** Blade front, rear adjustable for windage. Optional Siglite night sights. **Features:** Double action. Decocking lever permits lowering hammer onto locked firing pin. Square combat-type trigger guard. Shortened, lightened version of P220. Imported from Germany by SIGARMS, Inc.
Price: Blue, SA/DA or DAO $780.00
Price: With Siglite night sights, blue, SA/DA or DAO ...$880.00
Price: K-Kote finish $850.00
Price: K-Kote with Siglite night sights $950.00

Seecamp LWS 32

SIG Sauer P220 American

SIG Sauer P225

SIG Sauer P226 DA Auto Pistol Similar to the P220 pistol except has 4.4" barrel, and weighs 26 1/2 oz. 357 SIG or 9mm. Imported from Germany by SIGARMS, Inc.
Price: Blue $825.00
Price: With Siglite night sights $925.00
Price: Blue, double-action-only $825.00
Price: Blue, double-action-only, Siglite night sights $925.00
Price: K-Kote finish $875.00
Price: K-Kote, Siglite night sights $975.00
Price: K-Kote, double-action-only $875.00
Price: K-Kote, double-action-only, Siglite night sights ..$975.00

SIG Sauer P228 DA Auto Pistol Similar to the P226 except has 3.86" barrel, with 7.08" overall length and 3.35" height. Chambered for 9mm Para. only, 10-shot magazine. Weight is 29.1 oz. with empty magazine. Introduced 1989. Imported from Germany by SIGARMS, Inc.

Price: Blue $825.00
Price: Blue, with Siglite night sights $925.00
Price: Blue, double-action-only $825.00
Price: Blue, double-action-only, Siglite night sights $975.00
Price: K-Kote finish $875.00
Price: K-Kote, Siglite night sights $975.00
Price: K-Kote, double-action-only $875.00
Price: K-Kote, double-action-only, Siglite night sights ..$975.00

SIG Sauer P228

SIG Sauer P229 DA Auto Pistol Similar to the P228 except chambered for 9mm Para., 40 S&W, 357 SIG. Has 3.86" barrel, 7.08" overall length and 3.35" height. Weight is 30.5 oz. Introduced 1991. Frame made in Germany, stainless steel slide assembly made in U.S.; pistol assembled in U.S. From SIGARMS, Inc.

Price: Blue $875.00
Price: With nickel slide $900.00
Price: Blue, double-action-only $875.00
Price: With Siglite night sights $975.00

SIG SAUER P230 DA AUTO PISTOL **Caliber:** 32 ACP, 8-shot; 380 ACP, 7-shot. **Barrel:** 3³/₄". **Weight:** 16 oz. **Length:** 6¹/₂" overall. **Stocks:** Checkered black plastic. **Sights:** Blade front, rear adjustable for windage. **Features:** Double action/single action or DAO. Same basic action design as P220. Blowback operation, stationary barrel. Introduced 1977. Imported from Germany by SIGARMS, Inc.

Price: Blue $510.00
Price: In stainless steel (P230 SL) $595.00
Price: With stainless steel slide, blue frame $545.00

SIG Sauer P230

SIG P-210-2 AUTO PISTOL **Caliber:** 7.65mm or 9mm Para., 8-shot magazine. **Barrel:** 4³/₄". **Weight:** 31³/₄ oz. (9mm). **Length:** 8¹/₂" overall. **Stocks:** Checkered black composition. **Sights:** Blade front, rear adjustable for windage. **Features:** Lanyard loop; matte finish. Conversion unit for 22 LR available. Imported from Switzerland by Mandall Shooting Supplies.

Price: P-210-2 Service Pistol $3,500.00

SIG P210-6 AUTO PISTOL **Caliber:** 9mm Para., 8-shot magazine. **Barrel:** 4³/₄". **Weight:** 32 oz. **Length:** 8¹/₂" overall. **Stocks:** Checkered walnut. **Sights:** Blade front, notch rear drift adjustable for windage. **Features:** Mechanically locked, short-recoil operation; single action only; target trigger with adjustable stop; magazine safety; all-steel construction with matte blue finish. Optional 22 LR conversion kit consists of barrel, slide, recoil spring and magazine. Imported from Switzerland by SIGARMS, Inc.

Price: $2,300.00
Price: With 22LR conversion kit $2,900.00

Smith & Wesson Model 422

SMITH & WESSON MODEL 410 DA AUTO PISTOL **Caliber:** 40 S&W, 10-shot magazine. **Barrel:** 4". **Weight:** 28.5 oz. **Length:** 7.5 oz. **Stocks:** One-piece Xenoy, wrap-around with straight backstrap. **Sights:** Post front, fixed rear; three-dot system. **Features:** Aluminum alloy frame; blued carbon steel slide; traditional double action with left-side slide-mountd decocking lever. Introduced 1996. Made in U.S. by Smith & Wesson.

Price: $490.00

SMITH & WESSON MODEL 422, 622 AUTO **Caliber:** 22 LR, 10-shot magazine. **Barrel:** 4¹/₂", 6". **Weight:** 22 oz. (4¹/₂" bbl.). **Length:** 7¹/₂" overall (4¹/₂" bbl.). **Stocks:** Checkered simulated woodgrain polymer. **Sights:** Field—serrated ramp front, fixed rear; Target—serrated ramp front, adjustable rear. **Features:** Aluminum frame, steel slide, brushed stainless steel or blue finish; internal hammer. Introduced 1987. Model 2206 introduced 1990.

Price: Blue, 4¹/₂", 6", fixed sight $235.00
Price: As above, adjustable sight $290.00
Price: Stainless (Model 622), 4¹/₂", 6", fixed sight $284.00
Price: As above, adjustable sight $337.00

Smith & Wesson Model 410

Smith & Wesson Model 2213, 2214 Sportsman Auto Similar to the Model 422 except has 3″ barrel, 8-shot magazine; dovetail Patridge front sight with white dot, fixed rear with two white dots; matte blue finish, black composition grips with checkered panels. Overall length 6 1/8″, weight 18 oz. Introduced 1990.
Price: $269.00
Price: Model 2213 (stainless steel) $314.00

Smith & Wesson Model 2214

Smith & Wesson Model 622 VR Auto Similar to the Model 622 except 6″ barrel only with ventilated rib, glass-beaded serrated sight line with revised ramped front sight; matte black trigger, barrel and extractor; revised trigger guard. Introduced 1996. Made in U.S. by Smith & Wesson.
Price: $310.00

Smith & Wesson Model 2206 Auto Similar to the Model 422/622 except made entirely of stainless steel with non-reflective finish. Weight is 39 oz. Introduced 1990.
Price: With adjustable sight $385.00

Smith & Wesson Model 622 VR

Smith & Wesson Model 2206 Target Auto Same as the Model 2206 except 6″ barrel only; Millett Series 100 fully adjustable sight system; Patridge front sight; smooth contoured Herrett walnut target grips with thumbrest; serrated trigger with adjustable stop. Frame is bead-blasted along sighting plane, drilled and tapped for optics mount. Introduced 1994. Made in U.S. by Smith & Wesson.
Price: $433.00

SMITH & WESSON MODEL 457 DA AUTO PISTOL Caliber: 45 ACP, 7-shot magazine. **Barrel:** 3 3/4″. **Weight:** 29 oz. **Length:** 7 1/4″ overall. **Stocks:** One-piece Xenoy, wrap-around with straight backstrap. **Sights:** Post front, fixed rear, three-dot system. **Features:** Aluminum alloy frame, matte blue carbon steel slide; bobbed hammer; smooth trigger. Introduced 1996. Made in U.S. by Smith & Wesson.
Price: $490.00

Smith & Wesson Model 457

SMITH & WESSON MODEL 908 AUTO PISTOL Caliber: 9mm Para., 8-shot magazine. **Barrel:** 3 1/2″. **Weight:** 26 oz. **Length:** 6 13/16″. **Stocks:** One-piece Xenoy, wrap-around with straight backstrap. **Sights:** Post front, fixed rear, three-dot system. **Features:** Aluminum alloy frame, matte blue carbon steel slide; bobbed hammer; smooth trigger. Introduced 1996. Made in U.S. by Smith & Wesson.
Price: $443.00

SMITH & WESSON MODEL 909, 910 DA AUTO PISTOLS Caliber: 9mm Para., 10-shot magazine. **Barrel:** 4″. **Weight:** 28 oz. **Length:** 7 3/8″ overall. **Stocks:** One-piece Xenoy, wrap-around with straight backstrap. **Sights:** Post front with white dot, fixed two-dot rear. **Features:** Alloy frame, blue carbon steel slide. Slide-mounted decocking lever. Introduced 1995.
Price: Model 910 ....$443.00
Price: Model 909 (9-shot magazine, curved backstrap, 27 oz.) $443.00

Smith & Wesson Model 910

SMITH & WESSON MODEL 3913 DOUBLE ACTION Caliber: 9mm Para., 8-shot magazine. **Barrel:** 3 1/2″. **Weight:** 26 oz. **Length:** 6 13/16″ overall. **Stocks:** One-piece Delrin wrap-around, textured surface. **Sights:** Post front with white dot, Novak LoMount Carry with two dots, adjustable for windage. **Features:** Aluminum alloy frame, stainless slide (M3913) or blue steel slide (M3914). Bobbed hammer with no half-cock notch; smooth .304″ trigger with rounded edges. Straight backstrap. Extra magazine included. Introduced 1989.
Price: $622.00

Smith & Wesson Model 3913 LadySmith Auto Similar to the standard Model 3913 except has frame that is upswept at the front, rounded trigger guard. Comes in frosted stainless steel with matching gray grips. Grips are ergonomically correct for a woman's hand. Novak LoMount Carry rear sight adjustable for windage, smooth edges for snag resistance. Extra magazine included. Introduced 1990.
Price: $640.00

Smith & Wesson Model 3953DA Pistol Same as the Model 3913 except double-action-only. Model 3953 has stainless slide with alloy frame. Overall length 7″; weighs 25.5 oz. Extra magazine included. Introduced 1990.
Price: $622.00

SMITH & WESSON MODEL 4006 DA AUTO Caliber: 40 S&W, 10-shot magazine. **Barrel:** 4″. **Weight:** 38.5 oz. **Length:** 7⅞″ overall. **Stocks:** Xenoy wrap-around with checkered panels. **Sights:** Replaceable post front with white dot, Novak LoMount Carry fixed rear with two white dots, or micro. click adjustable rear with two white dots. **Features:** Stainless steel construction with non-reflective finish. Straight back-strap. Extra magazine included. Introduced 1990.
Price: With adjustable sights $775.00
Price: With fixed sight $745.00
Price: With fixed night sights $855.00

Smith & Wesson Model 4046 DA Pistol Similar to the Model 4006 except is double-action-only. Has a semi-bobbed hammer, smooth trigger, 4″ barrel; Novak LoMount Carry rear sight, post front with white dot. Overall length is 7½″, weighs 28 oz. Extra magazine included. Introduced 1991.
Price: $745.00
Price: With fixed night sights $855.00

SMITH & WESSON MODEL 4013, 4053 AUTOS Caliber: 40 S&W, 8-shot magazine. **Barrel:** 3½″. **Weight:** 26 oz. **Length:** 7″ overall. **Stocks:** One-piece Xenoy wrap-around with straight backstrap. **Sights:** Post front with white dot, fixed Novak LoMount Carry rear with two white dots. **Features:** Model 4013 is traditional double action; Model 4053 is double-action-only; stainless slide on alloy frame. Introduced 1991.
Price: Model 4013 ....$722.00
Price: Model 4053 ....$722.00

SMITH & WESSON MODEL 4500 SERIES AUTOS Caliber: 45 ACP, 7-shot (M4516), 8-shot magazine for M4506, 4566/4586. **Barrel:** 3¾″ (M4516), 5″ (M4506). **Weight:** 41 oz. (4506). **Length:** 7⅛″ overall (4516). **Stocks:** Xenoy one-piece wrap-around, arched or straight backstrap on M4506, straight only on M4516. **Sights:** Post front with white dot, adjustable or fixed Novak LoMount Carry on M4506. **Features:** M4506 has serrated hammer spur. Extra magazine included. Contact Smith & Wesson for complete data. Introduced 1989.
Price: Model 4506, fixed sight $774.00
Price: Model 4506, adjustable sight $806.00
Price: Model 4516, fixed sight $774.00
Price: Model 4566 (stainless, 4¼″, traditional DA, ambidextrous
safety, fixed sight) $774.00
Price: Model 4586 (stainless, 4¼″, DA only) $774.00

Smith & Wesson Model 6904/6906 Double-Action Autos Similar to the Models 5904/5906 except with 3½″ barrel, 10-shot magazine, fixed rear sight, .260″ bobbed hammer. Extra magazine included. Introduced 1989.
Price: Model 6904, blue $614.00
Price: Model 6906, stainless $677.00
Price: Model 6906 with fixed night sights $788.00
Price: Model 6946 (stainless, DA only, fixed sights) $677.00

Smith & Wesson 3913 LadySmith

Smith & Wesson Model 4053

Smith & Wesson Model 4506

SMITH & WESSON MODEL 5900 SERIES AUTO PISTOLS Caliber: 9mm Para., 10-shot magazine. **Barrel:** 4″. **Weight:** 28½ to 37½ oz. (fixed sight); 38 oz. (adjustable sight). **Length:** 7½″ overall. **Stocks:** Xenoy wrap-around with curved backstrap. **Sights:** Post front with white dot, fixed or fully adjustable with two white dots. **Features:** All stainless, stainless and alloy or carbon steel and alloy construction. Smooth .304″ trigger, .260″ serrated hammer. Extra magazine included. Introduced 1989.
Price: Model 5903 (stainless, alloy frame, traditional DA, fixed sight,
ambidextrous safety) $690.00
Price: Model 5904 (blue, alloy frame, traditional DA, adjustable sight, ambidextrous safety) $642.00
Price: Model 5906 (stainless, traditional DA, adjustable sight, ambidextrous safety) $742.00
Price: As above, fixed sight $707.00
Price: With fixed night sights $817.00
Price: Model 5946 (as above, stainless frame and slide) .$707.00

SMITH & WESSON SIGMA SW380 AUTO Caliber: 380 ACP, 6-shot magazine. **Barrel:** 3″. **Weight:** 14 oz. **Length:** 5.8″ overall. **Stocks:** Integral. **Sights:** Fixed groove in the slide. **Features:** Polymer frame; double-action-only trigger mechanism; grooved/serrated front and rear straps; two passive safeties. Introduced 1995. Made in U.S. by Smith & Wesson.
Price: **$308.00**

SMITH & WESSON SIGMA SERIES PISTOLS Caliber: 9mm Para., 40 S&W, 10-shot magazine. **Barrel:** 4.5″. **Weight:** 26 oz. **Length:** 7.4″ overall. **Stocks:** Integral. **Sights:** White dot front, fixed rear; three-dot system. Tritium night sights available. **Features:** Ergonomic polymer frame; low barrel centerline; internal striker firing system; corrosion-resistant slide; Teflon-filled, electroless-nickel coated magazine. Introduced 1994. Made in U.S. by Smith & Wesson.
Price: Model SW9F (9mm Para.) **$593.00**
Price: Model SW40F (40 S&W) **$593.00**
Price: Model Compact, SW9C, SW 40C (4″ bbl., 24.4 oz.) **$593.00**
Price: With fixed tritium night sights **$697.00**

SPHINX AT-380 AUTO PISTOL Caliber: 380 ACP, 10-shot magazine. **Barrel:** 3.27″. **Weight:** 25 oz. **Length:** 6.03″ overall. **Stocks:** Checkered plastic. **Sights:** Fixed. **Features:** Double-action-only mechanism, Chamber loaded indicator; ambidextrous magazine release and slide latch. Introduced 1993. Imported from Switzerland by Sphinx USA, Inc.
Price: Two-tone **$493.95**
Price: Black finish **$513.95**
Price: Nickel/Palladium finish **$564.95**

SPHINX AT-2000S DOUBLE-ACTION PISTOL Caliber: 9mm Para., 9x21mm, 40 S&W, 10-shot magazine. **Barrel:** 4.53″. **Weight:** 36.3 oz. **Length:** 8.03″ overall. **Stocks:** Checkered neoprene. **Sights:** Fixed, three-dot system. **Features:** Double-action mechanism changeable to double-action-only. Stainless frame, blued slide. Ambidextrous safety, magazine release, slide latch. Introduced 1993. Imported from Switzerland by Sphinx USA, Inc.
Price: 9mm, two-tone **$1,090.00**
Price: 40 S&W, two-tone **$1,120.00**

Sphinx AT-2000P, AT-2000PS Auto Pistols Same as the AT-2000S except AT-2000P has shortened frame, 3.74″ barrel, 7.25″ overall length, and weighs 34 oz. Model AT-2000PS has full-size frame. Both have stainless frame with blued slide. Introduced 1993. Imported from Switzerland by Sphinx USA, Inc.
Price: 9mm, two-tone **$940.00**
Price: 40 S&W, two-tone **$980.00**

Smith & Wesson Sigma SW380

Smith & Wesson Sigma

Smith & Wesson Sigma Compact

Sphinx AT-380M

Sphinx AT-2000P

Sphinx AT-2000S

Sphinx AT-2000H Auto Pistol Similar to the AT-2000P except has shorter slide with 3.54″ barrel, shorter frame, 10-shot magazine, with 7″ overall length. Weight is 32.2 oz. Stainless frame with blued slide. Introduced 1993. Imported from Switzerland by Sphinx USA, Inc.
Price: 9mm, two-tone **$940.00**
Price: 40 S&W, two-tone **$980.00**

Springfield Standard

Springfield 1911A1 Factory Comp

Springfield Champion

Springfield Champion Comp

Springfield V10 Ultra Compact

SPRINGFIELD, INC. 1911A1 AUTO PISTOL **Caliber:** 9mm Para., 9-shot; 38 Super, 9-shot; 45 ACP, 8-shot. **Barrel:** 5″. **Weight:** 35.6 oz. **Length:** 8⅝″ overall. **Stocks:** Checkered plastic or walnut. **Sights:** Fixed three-dot system. **Features:** Beveled magazine well; lowered and flared ejection port. All forged parts, including frame, barrel, slide. All new production. Introduced 1990. From Springfield, Inc.
Price: Basic, 45 ACP, Parkerized $476.00
Price: Standard, 45 ACP, blued $527.00
Price: Basic, 45 ACP, stainless $572.00
Price: Lightweight (28.6 oz., matte finish) $527.00
Price: Standard, 9mm, 38 Super, blued $557.00
Price: Standard, 9mm, stainless steel $587.00

Springfield, Inc. 1911A1 Custom Carry Gun Similar to the standard 1911A1 except has fixed three-dot low profile sights, Videki speed trigger, match barrel and bushing; extended thumb safety, beavertail grip safety; beveled, polished magazine well, polished feed ramp and throated barrel; match Commander hammer and sear, tuned extractor; lowered and flared ejection port; recoil buffer system, full-length spring guide rod; walnut grips. Comes with two magazines with slam pads, plastic carrying case. Available in all popular calibers. Introduced 1992. From Springfield, Inc.
Price: $1,388.00

Consult our Directory pages for
the location of firms mentioned.

Springfield, Inc. N.R.A. PPC Pistol Specifically designed to comply with NRA rules for PPC competition. Has custom slide-to-frame fit; polished feed ramp; throated barrel; total internal honing; tuned extractor; recoil buffer system; fully checkered walnut grips; two fitted magazines; factory test target; custom carrying case. Introduced 1995. From Springfield, Inc.
Price: $1,632.00

Springfield, Inc. 1911A1 Factory Comp Similar to the standard 1911A1 except comes with bushing-type dual-port compensator, adjustable rear sight, extended thumb safety, Videki speed trigger, and beveled magazine well. Checkered walnut grips standard. Available in 38 Super or 45 ACP, blue only. Introduced 1992.
Price: 38 Super $947.00
Price: 45 ACP $984.00

Springfield, Inc. 1911A1 Champion Pistol Similar to the standard 1911A1 except slide is 4.025″. Has low-profile three-dot sight system. Comes with skeletonized hammer and walnut stocks. Available in 45 ACP only; blue or stainless. Introduced 1989.
Price: Blue $543.00
Price: Stainless $582.00
Price: Mil-Spec $476.00
Price: Champion Comp (single-port compensator) $871.00

Springfield, Inc. 1911A1 Defender Pistol Similar to the 1911A1 Champion except has tapered cone dual-port compensator system, rubberized grips. Has reverse recoil plug, full-length recoil spring guide, serrated frontstrap, extended thumb safety, skeletonized hammer with modified grip safety to match and a Videki speed trigger. Bi-Tone finish. Introduced 1991.
Price: 45 ACP $993.00

Springfield, Inc. V10 Ultra Compact Pistol Similar to the 1911A1 Compact except has shorter slide, 3.5″ barrel, recoil reducing compensator built into the barrel and slide. Beavertail grip safety, beveled magazine well, "hi-viz" combat sights, Videki speed trigger, flared ejection port, stainless steel frame, blued slide, match grade barrel, walnut grips. Introduced 1996. From Springfield, Inc.
Price: V10 45 ACP $659.00
Price: Ultra Compact (no compensator), 45 ACP $569.00

Springfield High Capacity Factory Comp

Star Firestar

Star Firestar Plus

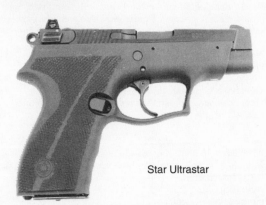

Star Ultrastar

Springfield, Inc. 1911A1 Compact Pistol Similar to the Champion model except has a shortened frame height, 7.75″ overall length. Magazine capacity is 7 shots. Has shortened hammer, checkered walnut grips. Available in 45 ACP only. Introduced 1989.

Price: Blued $543.00
Price: Stainless $582.00
Price: Compact Lightweight $543.00
Price: Mil-Spec $476.00

Springfield, Inc. 1911A1 High Capacity Pistol Similar to the Standard 1911A1 except available in 45 ACP and 9mm with 10-shot magazine (45 ACP). Has Commander-style hammer, walnut grips, ambidextrous thumb safety, beveled magazine well, plastic carrying case. Introduced 1993. From Springfield, Inc.

Price: 45 ACP $622.00
Price: 9mm $638.00
Price: 45 ACP Factory Comp $964.00
Price: 45 ACP Comp Lightweight, matte finish $840.00
Price: 45 ACP Compact, blued $609.00
Price: As above, stainless steel $648.00

STAR FIRESTAR AUTO PISTOL Caliber: 9mm Para., 7-shot; 40 S&W, 6-shot. **Barrel:** 3.39″. **Weight:** 30.35 oz. **Length:** 6.5″ overall. **Stocks:** Checkered rubber. **Sights:** Blade front, fully adjustable rear; three-dot system. **Features:** Low-profile, combat-style sights; ambidextrous safety. Available in blue or weather-resistant Starvel finish. Introduced 1990. Imported from Spain by Interarms.

Price: Blue, 9mm $450.00
Price: Starvel finish 9mm $450.00
Price: Blue, 40 S&W $465.00
Price: Starvel finish, 40 S&W $465.00

Star Firestar M45 Auto Pistol Similar to the standard Firestar except chambered for 45 ACP with 6-shot magazine. Has 3.6″ barrel, weighs 35 oz., 6.85″ overall length. Reverse-taper Acculine barrel. Introduced 1992. Imported from Spain by Interarms.

Price: Blue $490.00
Price: Starvel finish $490.00

Star Firestar Plus Auto Pistol Same as the standard Firestar except has 10-shot magazine. Introduced 1994. Imported from Spain by Interarms.

Price: Blue, 9mm $460.00
Price: Starvel, 9mm $485.00

STAR ULTRASTAR DOUBLE-ACTION PISTOL Caliber: 9mm Para., 9-shot magazine; 40 S&W, 8-shot. **Barrel:** 3.57″. **Weight:** 26 oz. **Length:** 7″ overall. **Stocks:** Checkered black polymer. **Sights:** Blade front, rear adjustable for windage; three-dot system. **Features:** Polymer frame with inside steel slide rails; ambidextrous two-position safety (Safe and Decock). Introduced 1994. Imported from Spain by Interarms.

Price: $490.00

Stoeger American Eagle Luger

STOEGER AMERICAN EAGLE LUGER Caliber: 9mm Para., 7-shot magazine. **Barrel:** 4″, 6″. **Weight:** 32 oz. **Length:** 9.6″ overall. **Stocks:** Checkered walnut. **Sights:** Blade front, fixed rear. **Features:** Recreation of the American Eagle Luger pistol in stainless steel. Chamber loaded indicator. Introduced 1994. From Stoeger Industries.

Price: $695.00
Price: Navy Model, 6″ barrel $695.00

Sundance BOA

Sundance Laser 25

Taurus PT 25

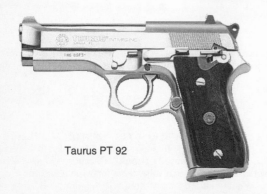

Taurus PT 92

Taurus PT99AF

SUNDANCE MODEL A-25 AUTO PISTOL Caliber: 25 ACP, 7-shot magazine. **Barrel:** 2.5". **Weight:** 16 oz. **Length:** 4⅞" overall. **Stocks:** Grooved black ABS or simulated smooth pearl; optional pink. **Sights:** Fixed. **Features:** Manual rotary safety; button magazine release. Bright chrome or black Teflon finish. Introduced 1989. Made in U.S. by Sundance Industries, Inc.
Price: $79.95

SUNDANCE BOA AUTO PISTOL Caliber: 25 ACP, 7-shot magazine. **Barrel:** 2½". **Weight:** 16 oz. **Length:** 4⅞". **Stocks:** Grooved ABS or smooth simulated pearl; optional pink. **Sights:** Fixed. **Features:** Patented grip safety, manual rotary safety; button magazine release; lifetime warranty. Bright chrome or black Teflon finish. Introduced 1991. Made in the U.S. by Sundance Industries, Inc.
Price: $95.00

SUNDANCE LASER 25 PISTOL Caliber: 25 ACP, 7-shot magazine. **Barrel:** 2½". **Weight:** 18 oz. **Length:** 4⅞" overall. **Stocks:** Grooved black ABS. **Sights:** Class IIIa laser, 670 NM, 5mW, and fixed open. **Features:** Factory installed and sighted laser sight activated by squeezing the grip safety; manual rotary safety; button magazine release. Bright chrome or black finish. Introduced 1995. Made in U.S. by Sundance Industries, Inc.
Price: With laser $219.00
Price: Lady Laser (as above except different name, bright chrome only) $219.00

TAURUS MODEL PT 22/PT 25 AUTO PISTOLS Caliber: 22 LR, 9-shot (PT 22); 25 ACP, 8-shot (PT 25). **Barrel:** 2.75". **Weight:** 12.3 oz. **Length:** 5.25" overall. **Stocks:** Smooth Brazilian hardwood. **Sights:** Blade front, fixed rear. **Features:** Double action. Tip-up barrel for loading, cleaning. Blue or stainless. Introduced 1992. Made in U.S. by Taurus International.
Price: 22 LR or 25 ACP $187.00
Price: Nickel $195.00

TAURUS MODEL PT58 AUTO PISTOL Caliber: 380 ACP, 10-shot magazine. **Barrel:** 4.01". **Weight:** 30 oz. **Length:** 7.2" overall. **Stocks:** Brazilian hardwood. **Sights:** Integral blade on slide front, notch rear adjustable for windage. Three-dot system. **Features:** Double action with exposed hammer; inertia firing pin. Introduced 1988. Imported by Taurus International.
Price: Blue $429.00
Price: Stainless steel $470.00

TAURUS MODEL PT 92AF AUTO PISTOL Caliber: 9mm Para., 10-shot magazine. **Barrel:** 4.92". **Weight:** 34 oz. **Length:** 8.54" overall. **Stocks:** Brazilian hardwood. **Sights:** Fixed notch rear. Three-dot sight system. **Features:** Double action, exposed hammer, chamber loaded indicator, ambidextrous safety, inertia firing pin. Imported by Taurus International.
Price: Blue $479.00
Price: Blue, Deluxe Shooter's Pak (extra magazine, case) $477.00
Price: Stainless steel $493.00
Price: Stainless, Deluxe Shooter's Pak (extra magazine, case) $522.00

Taurus PT 92AFC Compact Pistol Similar to the PT-92 except has 4.25" barrel, 10-shot magazine, weighs 31 oz. and is 7.5" overall. Available in stainless steel or blue. Introduced 1991. Imported by Taurus International.
Price: Blue $449.00
Price: Stainless steel $493.00

Taurus PT 99AF Auto Pistol Similar to the PT-92 except has fully adjustable rear sight, smooth Brazilian walnut stocks and is available in stainless steel or polished blue. Introduced 1983.
Price: Blue $471.00
Price: Blue, Deluxe Shooter's Pak (extra magazine, case)$500.00
Price: Stainless steel $518.00
Price: Stainless, Deluxe Shooter's Pak (extra magazine, case) $546.00

TAURUS MODEL PT 100 AUTO PISTOL Caliber: 40 S&W, 10-shot magazine. **Barrel:** 5". **Weight:** 34 oz. **Stocks:** Smooth Brazilian hardwood. **Sights:** Fixed front, drift-adjustable rear. Three-dot combat. **Features:** Double action, exposed hammer. Ambidextrous hammer-drop safety; inertia firing pin; chamber loaded indicator. Introduced 1991. Imported by Taurus International.
Price: Blue **$469.00**
Price: Blue, Deluxe Shooter's Pak (extra magazine,
 case) **$497.00**
Price: Stainless **$514.00**
Price: Stainless, Deluxe Shooter's Pak (extra magazine,
 case) **$542.00**

Taurus PT 101 Auto Pistol Same as the PT 100 except has micro-click rear sight adjustable for windage and elevation, three-dot combat-style. Introduced 1991.
Price: Blue **$491.00**
Price: Blue, Deluxe Shooter's Pak (extra magazine, case)**$519.00**
Price: Stainless **$537.00**
Price: Stainless, Deluxe Shooter's Pak (extra magazine,
 case) **$565.00**

TAURUS MODEL PT-908 AUTO PISTOL Caliber: 9mm Para., 8-shot magazine. **Barrel:** 3.8". **Weight:** 30 oz. **Length:** 7.05" overall. **Stocks:** Santoprene II. **Sights:** Drift-adjustable front and rear; three-dot combat. **Features:** Double action, exposed hammer; manual ambidextrous hammer-drop; inertia firing pin; chamber loaded indicator. Introduced 1993. Imported by Taurus International.
Price: Blue **$435.00**
Price: Stainless steel **$473.00**
Price: Blue, Deluxe Shooter's Pak **$459.00**
Price: Stainless, Deluxe Shooter's Pak **$496.00**

Taurus PT-940 Auto Pistol Same as the PT-908 except chambered for 40 siW, 9-shot magazine. Introduced 1996. Imported by Taurus International.
Price: Blue **$453.00**
Price: Stainless **$497.00**
Price: Blue, Deluxe Shooter's Pak **$476.00**
Price: Stainless, Deluxe Shooter's Pack **$520.00**

TAURUS MODEL PT-945 AUTO PISTOL Caliber: 45 ACP, 8-shot magazine. **Barrel:** 4.25". **Weight:** 29.5 oz. **Length:** 7.48" overall. **Stocks:** Santoprene II. **Sights:** Drift-adjustable front and rear; three-dot system. **Features:** Double-action mechanism. Has manual ambidextrous hammer drop safety, intercept notch, firing pin block, chamber loaded indicator, last-shot hold-open. Introduced 1995. Imported by Taurus International.
Price: Blue **$453.00**
Price: Stainless **$497.00**
Price: Blue, Deluxe Shooter's Pak **$476.00**
Price: Stainless, Deluxe Shooter's Pak **$520.00**

WALTHER P-5 AUTO PISTOL Caliber: 9mm. **Barrel:** 3.6" **Weight:** 28 oz. **Length:** 7" overall. **Stocks:** Checkered polymer. **Sights:** Blade front, adjustable rear. **Features:** Uses the basic Walther P-38 double-action mechanism. Polished blue finish. Imported from Germany by Interarms.
Price: **$900.00**

Walther P-5 Compact Similar to the P-5 except has 3.2" barrel, weighs 26 oz., and has magazine release on left side of grip. Imported from Germany by Interarms.
Price: **$900.00**

WALTHER PP AUTO PISTOL Caliber: 32 ACP, 380 ACP, 7-shot magazine. **Barrel:** 3.86". **Weight:** 23½ oz. **Length:** 6.7" overall. **Stocks:** Checkered plastic. **Sights:** Fixed, white markings. **Features:** Double action; manual safety blocks firing pin and drops hammer; chamber loaded indicator on 32 and 380; extra finger rest magazine provided. Imported from Germany by Interarms.
Price: 32 . . . .**$999.00**
Price: 380 . . . .**$999.00**
Price: Engraved models . . . . **On Request**

Taurus PT 101

Taurus PT-908

Taurus PT 945

Walther P-5 Compact

Walther PP

Walther PPK American Auto Pistol Similar to Walther PPK/S except weighs 21 oz., has 6-shot capacity. Made in the U.S. Introduced 1986.
Price: Stainless, 380 ACP only $540.00
Price: Blue, 380 ACP only $540.00

Walther PPK/S American Auto Pistol Similar to Walther PP except made entirely in the United States. Has 3.27″ barrel with 6.1″ length overall. Introduced 1980.
Price: 380 ACP only, blue $540.00
Price: As above, stainless $540.00

Walther PPK/S

WALTHER MODEL TPH AUTO PISTOL Caliber: 22 LR, 25 ACP, 6-shot magazine. **Barrel:** 2¼″. **Weight:** 14 oz. **Length:** 5⅜″ overall. **Stocks:** Checkered black composition. **Sights:** Blade front, rear drift-adjustable for windage. **Features:** Made of stainless steel. Scaled-down version of the Walther PP/PPK series. Made in U.S. Introduced 1987. From Interarms.
Price: Blue or stainless steel, 22 or 25 ....$440.00

WALTHER P88 COMPACT PISTOL Caliber: 9mm Para., 10-shot magazine. **Barrel:** 3.93″. **Weight:** 28 oz. **Length:** NA. **Stocks:** Checkered black polymer. **Sights:** Blade front, drift adjustable rear. **Features:** Double action with ambidextrous decocking lever and magazine release; alloy frame; loaded chamber indicator; matte blue finish. Imported from Germany by Interarms.
Price: $900.00

Walther TPH

WILKINSON "SHERRY" AUTO PISTOL Caliber: 22 LR, 8-shot magazine. **Barrel:** 2⅛″. **Weight:** 9¼ oz. **Length:** 4⅜″ overall. **Stocks:** Checkered black plastic. **Sights:** Fixed, groove. **Features:** Cross-bolt safety locks the sear into the hammer. Available in all blue finish or blue slide and trigger with gold frame. Introduced 1985.
Price: $195.00

WILKINSON "LINDA" AUTO PISTOL Caliber: 9mm Para. **Barrel:** 8⁵⁄₁₆″. **Weight:** 4 lbs., 13 oz. **Length:** 12¼″ overall. **Stocks:** Checkered black plastic pistol grip, walnut forend. **Sights:** Protected blade front, aperture rear. **Features:** Fires from closed bolt. Semi-auto only. Straight blowback action. Cross-bolt safety. Removable barrel. From Wilkinson Arms.
Price: $533.33

Walther P88 Compact

WILDEY AUTOMATIC PISTOL Caliber: 10mm Wildey Mag., 11mm Wildey Mag., 30 Wildey Mag., 357 Peterbuilt, 45 Win. Mag., 475 Wildey Mag., 7-shot magazine. **Barrel:** 5″, 6″, 7″, 8″, 10″, 12″, 14″ (45 Win. Mag.); 8″, 10″, 12″, 14″ (all other cals.). Interchangeable. **Weight:** 64 oz. (5″ barrel). **Length:** 11″ overall (7″ barrel). **Stocks:** Hardwood. **Sights:** Ramp front (interchangeable blades optional), fully adjustable rear. Scope base available. **Features:** Gas-operated action. Made of stainless steel. Has three-lug rotary bolt. Double or single action. Polished and matte finish. Made in U.S. by Wildey, Inc.
Price: ....$1,175.00 to $1,495.00

Wilkinson Sherry

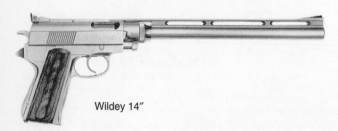

Wildey 14″

Wildey 8″

Includes models suitable for several forms of competition and other sporting purposes.

AUTO-ORDNANCE 1911A1 COMPETITION MODEL **Caliber:** 45 ACP. **Barrel:** 5″. **Weight:** 42 oz. **Length:** 10″ overall. **Stocks:** Black textured rubber wrap-around. **Sights:** Blade front, rear adjustable for windage; three-dot system. **Features:** Machined compensator, combat Commander hammer; flat mainspring housing; low profile magazine funnel; metal form magazine bumper; high-ride beavertail grip safety; full-length recoil spring guide system; extended slide stop, safety and magazine catch; Videcki adjustable speed trigger; extended combat ejector. Introduced 1994. Made in U.S. by Auto-Ordnance Corp.
Price: $635.50

BAER 1911 ULTIMATE MASTER COMBAT PISTOL Caliber: 45 ACP (others available), 10-shot magazine. **Barrel:** 5″; Baer NM. **Weight:** 37 oz. **Length:** 8.5″ overall. **Stocks:** Checkered rosewood. **Sights:** Baer dovetail front, low-mount Bo-Mar rear with hidden leaf. **Features:** Full-house competition gun. Baer forged NM blued steel frame and double serrated slide; Baer triple port, tapered cone compensator; fitted slide to frame; lowered, flared ejection port; Baer reverse recoil plug; full-length guide rod; recoil buff; beveled magazine well; Baer Commander hammer, sear; Baer extended ambidextrous safety, extended ejector, checkered slide stop, beavertail grip safety with pad, extended magazine release button; Baer speed trigger. Made in U.S. by Les Baer Custom, Inc.
Price: Compensated, open sights $1,996.00
Price: Uncompensated "Limited" Model $1,843.00
Price: Compensated, with Baer optics mount $2,360.00

Baer 1911 Ultimate Master "Steel Special" Pistol Similar to the Ultimate Master except chambered for 38 Super with supported chamber (other calibers available), lighter slide, bushing-type compensator; two-piece guide rod. Designed for maximum 150 power factor. Comes without sights—scope and mount only. Hard chrome finish. Made in U.S. by Les Baer Custom, Inc.
Price: $2,670.00

BAER 1911 NATIONAL MATCH HARDBALL PISTOL **Caliber:** 45 ACP, 7-shot magazine. **Barrel:** 5″. **Weight:** 37 oz. **Length:** 8.5″ overall. **Stocks:** Checkered walnut. **Sights:** Baer dovetail front with undercut post, low-mount Bo-Mar rear with hidden leaf. **Features:** Baer NM forged steel frame, double serrated slide and barrel with stainless bushing; slide fitted to frame; Baer match trigger with 4-lb. pull; polished feed ramp, throated barrel; checkered front strap, arched mainspring housing; Baer beveled magazine well; lowered, flared ejection port; tuned extractor; Baer extended ejector, checkered slide stop; recoil buff. Made in U.S. by Les Baer Custom, Inc.
Price: $1,180.00

Baer 1911 Target Master Pistol Similar to the National Match Hardball except available in 45 ACP and other calibers, has Baer post-style dovetail front sight, flat serrated mainspring housing, standard trigger. Made in U.S. by Les Baer Custom, Inc.
Price: $1,263.00
Price: With 6″ barrel $1,540.00

Baer 1911 Bullseye Wadcutter Pistol Similar to the National Match Hardball except designed for wadcutter loads only. Has polished feed ramp and barrel throat; Bo-Mar rib on slide; full-length recoil rod; Baer speed trigger with 3½-lb. pull; Baer deluxe hammer and sear; Baer beavertail grip safety with pad; flat mainspring housing checkered 20 lpi. Blue finish; checkered walnut grips. Made in U.S. by Les Baer Custom, Inc.
Price: $1,347.00
Price: With 6″ barrel $1,597.00

Auto-Ordnance Competition Model

Baer 1911 Ultimate Master

Baer 1911 Bullseye Wadcutter

Benelli MP95E

BENELLI MP95E MATCH PISTOL **Caliber:** 22 LR, 9-shot magazine, or 32 S&W WC, 5-shot magazine. **Barrel:** 4.33″. **Weight:** 38.8 oz. **Length:** 11.81″ overall. **Stocks:** Checkered walnut match type; anatomically shaped. **Sights:** Match type. Blade front, click-adjustable rear for windage and elevation. **Features:** Removable, trigger assembly. Special internal weight box on subframe below barrel. Cut for scope rails. Introduced 1993. Imported from Italy by European American Armory.
Price: Blue $550.00
Price: Chrome $599.00
Price: MP90S (competition version of MP95E), 22 LR .$1,295.00
Price: As above, 32 S&W $1,495.00

BERNARDELLI MODEL 69 TARGET PISTOL **Caliber:** 22 LR, 10-shot magazine. **Barrel:** 5.9″. **Weight:** 38 oz. **Length:** 9″ overall. **Stocks:** Wrap-around, hand-checkered walnut with thumbrest. **Sights:** Fully adjustable and interchangeable target type. **Features:** Conforms to U.I.T. regulations. Has 7.1″ sight radius, .27″ wide grooved trigger. Manual thumb safety and magazine safety. Introduced 1987. Imported from Italy by Mitchell Arms.
Price: $612.00

BERETTA MODEL 89 GOLD STANDARD PISTOL **Caliber:** 22 LR, 8-shot magazine. **Barrel:** 6″ **Weight:** 41 oz. **Length:** 9.5″ overall. **Stocks:** Target-type walnut with thumbrest. **Sights:** Interchangeable blade front, fully adjustable rear. **Features:** Single action target pistol. Matte black, Bruniton finish. Imported from Italy by Beretta U.S.A.
Price: $736.00

BF SINGLE SHOT PISTOL **Caliber:** 22 LR, 357 Mag., 44 Mag., 7-30 Waters, 30-30 Win., 375 Win., 45-70; custom chamberings from 17 Rem. through 45-cal. **Barrel:** 10″, 10.75″, 12″, 15+″. **Weight:** 52 oz. **Length:** NA. **Stocks:** Custom Herrett finger-groove grip and forend. **Sights:** Undercut Patridge front, 1/2-MOA match-quality fully adjustable RPM Iron Sight rear; barrel or receiver mounting. Drilled and tapped for scope mounting. **Features:** Rigid barrel/receiver; falling block action with short lock time; automatic ejection; air-gauged match barrels by Wilson or Douglas; matte black oxide finish standard, electroless nickel optional. Barrel has 11-degree recessed target crown. Introduced 1988. Made in U.S. by E.A. Brown Mfg.
Price: 10″, no sights $499.95
Price: 10″, RPM sights $564.95
Price: 10.75″, no sights $529.95
Price: 10.75″, RPM sights $594.95
Price: 12″, no sights $562.95
Price: 12″, RPM sights $643.75
Price: 15″, no sights $592.95
Price: 15″, RPM sights $675.00
Price: 10.75″ Ultimate Silhouette (heavy barrel, special forend, RPM rear sight with hooded front, gold-plated trigger) $687.95

BROLIN PRO-STOCK COMPETITION PISTOL **Caliber:** 45 ACP, 8-shot magazine. **Barrel:** 5″. **Weight:** 37 oz. **Length:** 8.5″ overall. **Stocks:** Checkered with Brolin logo. **Sights:** Ramp front, fully adjustable rear. **Features:** Throated heavy match barrel; full-length recoil spring guide; polished feed ramp; lowered and flared ejection port; beveled magazine well; flat-top slide; serrated flat mainspring housing; high relief front strap cut; four-legged sear spring; adjustable match trigger; slotted Commander hammer; beavertail grip safety; ambidextrous thumb safety; front slide serrations. Introduced 1996. Made in U.S. by Brolin Arms.
Price: Blue $779.00
Price: Blue/stainless two-tone $799.00

Brolin Pro-Comp Competition Pistol Similar to the Pro-Stock model except has integral milled DPC Comp on the heavy match barrel; barrel length 4″, overall length 8.5″; weighs 37 oz.; 8-shot magazine. Introduced 1996. Made in U.S. by Brolin Arms.
Price: Blue $909.00
Price: Blue/stainless two-tone $929.00

BROWNING BUCK MARK SILHOUETTE **Caliber:** 22 LR, 10-shot magazine. **Barrel:** 9 7/8″. **Weight:** 53 oz. **Length:** 14″ overall. **Stocks:** Smooth walnut stocks and forend, or finger-groove walnut. **Sights:** Post-type hooded front adjustable for blade width and height; Pro Target rear fully adjustable for windage and elevation. **Features:** Heavy barrel with .900″ diameter; 12 1/2″ sight radius. Special sighting plane forms scope base. Introduced 1987. Made in U.S. From Browning.
Price: $434.95

Browning Buck Mark Unlimited Match Same as the Buck Mark Silhouette except has 14″ heavy barrel. Conforms to IHMSA 15″ maximum sight radius rule. Introduced 1991.
Price: $535.95

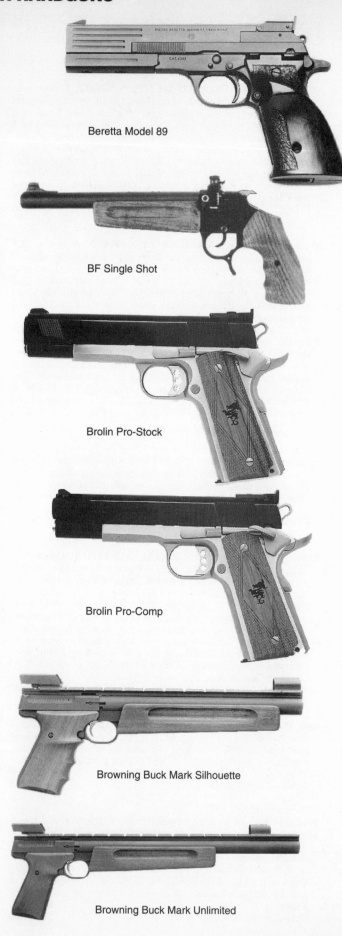

Beretta Model 89

BF Single Shot

Brolin Pro-Stock

Brolin Pro-Comp

Browning Buck Mark Silhouette

Browning Buck Mark Unlimited

Browning Buck Mark Bullseye

Browning Buck Mark Target 5.5

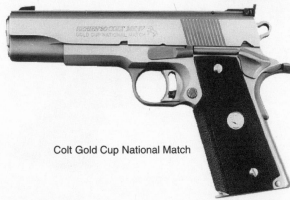

Colt Gold Cup National Match

Competitor Single Shot

E.A.A. Witness Gold Team

Browning Buck Mark Bullseye Similar to the Buck Mark Silhouette except has 7¼″ heavy barrel with three flutes per side; trigger is adjustable from 2½ to 5 lbs.; specially designed rosewood target or three-finger-groove stocks with competition-style heel rest, or with contoured rubber grip. Overall length is 11⁵⁄₁₆″, weighs 36 oz. Introduced 1996. Made in U.S. From Browning.
Price: With rubber stocks $376.95
Price: With rosewood stocks $484.95

Browning Buck Mark Target 5.5 Same as the Buck Mark Silhouette except has a 5½″ barrel with .900″ diameter. Has hooded sights mounted on a scope base that accepts an optical or reflex sight. Rear sight is a Browning fully adjustable Pro Target, front sight is an adjustable post that customizes to different widths, and can be adjusted for height. Contoured walnut grips with thumbrest, or finger-groove walnut. Matte blue finish. Overall length is 9⁵⁄₈″, weighs 35½ oz. Has 10-shot magazine. Introduced 1990. From Browning.
Price: $411.95
Price: Target 5.5 Gold (as above with gold anodized frame and
    top rib) $462.95
Price: Target 5.5 Nickel (as above with nickel frame and
    top rib) $462.95

Browning Buck Mark Field 5.5 Same as the Target 5.5 except has hoodless ramp-style front sight and low profile rear sight. Matte blue finish, contoured or finger-groove walnut stocks. Introduced 1991.
Price: $411.95

COLT GOLD CUP NATIONAL MATCH MK IV/SERIES 80 Caliber: 45 ACP, 8-shot magazine. **Barrel:** 5″, with new design bushing. **Weight:** 39 oz. **Length:** 8½″. **Stocks:** Checkered rubber composite with silver-plated medallion. **Sights:** Patridge-style front, Colt-Elliason rear adjustable for windage and elevation, sight radius 6¾″. **Features:** Arched or flat housing; wide, grooved trigger with adjustable stop; ribbed-top slide, hand fitted, with improved ejection port.
Price: Blue $937.00
Price: Stainless $1,003.00
Price: Bright stainless $1,073.00
Price: Delta Gold Cup (10mm, stainless) $1,027.00

COMPETITOR SINGLE SHOT PISTOL Caliber: 22 LR through 50 Action Express, including belted magnums. **Barrel:** 14″ standard; 10.5″ silhouette; 16″ optional. **Weight:** About 59 oz. (14″ bbl.). **Length:** 15.12″ overall. **Stocks:** Ambidextrous; synthetic (standard) or laminated or natural wood. **Sights:** Ramp front, adjustable rear. **Features:** Rotary canon-type action cocks on opening; cammed ejector; interchangeable barrels, ejectors. Adjustable single stage trigger, sliding thumb safety and trigger safety. Matte blue finish. Introduced 1988. From Competitor Corp., Inc.
Price: 14″, standard calibers, synthetic grip $399.95
Price: Extra barrels, from $149.95

E.A.A. WITNESS GOLD TEAM AUTO Caliber: 9mm Para., 9x21, 38 Super, 40 S&W, 45 ACP. **Barrel:** 5.1″. **Weight:** 41.6 oz. **Length:** 9.6″ overall. **Stocks:** Checkered walnut, competition style. **Sights:** Square post front, fully adjustable rear. **Features:** Triple-chamber cone compensator; competition SA trigger; extended safety and magazine release; competition hammer; beveled magazine well; beavertail grip. Hand-fitted major components. Hard chrome finish. Match-grade barrel. From E.A.A. Custom Shop. Introduced 1992. From European American Armory.
Price: $2,195.00

E.A.A. Witness Silver Team Auto Similar to the Witness Gold Team except has double-chamber compensator, oval magazine release, black rubber grips, double-dip blue finish. Comes with Super Sight and drilled and tapped for scope mount. Built for the intermediate competition shooter. Introduced 1992. From European American Armory Custom Shop.
Price: 9mm Para., 9x21, 38 Super, 40 S&W, 45 ACP ...$975.00

ERMA ER MATCH REVOLVER Caliber: 32 S&W Long, 6-shot. **Barrel:** 6″. **Weight:** 47.3 oz. **Length:** 11.2″ overall. **Stocks:** Stippled walnut, adjustable match-type. **Sights:** Blade front, micrometer rear adjustable for windage and elevation. **Features:** Polished blue finish. Introduced 1989. Imported from Germany by Precision Sales International.
Price: 32 S&W Long **$1,248.00**

ERMA ESP 85A MATCH PISTOL Caliber: 22 LR, 6-shot; 32 S&W, 6-shot magazine. **Barrel:** 6″. **Weight:** 39 oz. **Length:** 10″ overall. **Stocks:** Match-type of stippled walnut; adjustable. **Sights:** Interchangeable blade front, micrometer adjustable rear with interchangeable leaf. **Features:** Five-way adjustable trigger; exposed hammer and separate firing pin block allow unlimited dry firing practice. Blue or matte chrome; right- or left-hand. Introduced 1989. Imported from Germany by Precision Sales International.
Price: 22 LR **$1,695.00**
Price: 22 LR, left-hand **$1,735.00**
Price: 22 LR, matte chrome **$1,890.00**
Price: 32 S&W **$1,790.00**
Price: 32 S&W, left-hand **$1,830.00**
Price: 32 S&W, matte chrome **$2,095.00**
Price: 32 S&W, matte chrome, left-hand **$2,135.00**

Erma ESP Junior Match Pistol Similar to the ESP 85A Match except chambered only for 22 LR, blue finish only. Stippled non-adjustable walnut match grips (adjustable grips optional). Introduced 1995. Imported from Germany by Precision Sales International.
Price: **$1,295.00**

FAS 607 MATCH PISTOL Caliber: 22 LR, 5-shot. **Barrel:** 5.6″. **Weight:** 37 oz. **Length:** 11″ overall. **Stocks:** Walnut wrap-around; sizes small, medium, large or adjustable. **Sights:** Match. Blade front, open notch rear fully adjustable for windage and elevation. Sight radius is 8.66″. **Features:** Line of sight is only $^{11}/_{32}$″ above centerline of bore; magazine is inserted from top; adjustable and removable trigger mechanism; single lever takedown. Full 5-year warranty. Imported from Italy by Nygord Precision Products.
Price: **$1,175.00**
Price: Model 603 (32 S&W) **$1,175.00**

FAS 601 Match Pistol Similar to Model 607 except has different match stocks with adjustable palm shelf, 22 Short only for rapid fire shooting; weighs 40 oz., 5.6″ bbl.; has gas ports through top of barrel and slide to reduce recoil; slightly different trigger and sear mechanisms. Imported from Italy by Nygord Precision Products.
Price: **$1,250.00**

FORTH WORTH MATCH MASTER STANDARD PISTOL Caliber: 22 LR, 10-shot magazine. **Barrel:** 3$^7/_8$″, 4$^1/_2$″, 5$^1/_2$″. **Weight:** 44 oz. **Length:** 9$^1/_2$″ overall. **Stocks:** Checkered walnut. **Sights:** Undercut ramp front, integral adjustable rear mounted on the slide. **Features:** Made of stainless steel. Double extractors; quick-release magazine latch; beveled magazine well; flared slide for easier cocking; low-profile frame. Introduced 1996. Made in U.S. by Fort Worth Firearms.
Price: **$388.00**

FORTH WORTH MATCH MASTER DELUXE PISTOL Caliber: 22 LR, 10-shot magazine. **Barrel:** 3$^7/_8$″, 4$^1/_2$″, 5$^1/_2$″, 7$^1/_2$″, 10″. **Weight:** 46 oz. **Length:** 9$^1/_2$″ overall. **Stocks:** Checkered walnut. **Sights:** Undercut ramp front, micro-click rear adjustable for windage and elevation. Comes with Weaver-style rib. **Features:** Made of stainless steel. Dual extractors; quick-release magazine latch; beveled magazine well. Flared slide for easier cocking. Introduced 1996. Made in U.S. by Fort Worth Firearms.
Price: **$537.00**
Price: Match Master Dovetail (as above except dovetail-style scope mount, 3$^7/_8$″, 4$^1/_2$″, 5$^1/_2$″ only) **$472.00**

Erma ER Match Revolver

Erma ESP 85A

FAS 607 Match

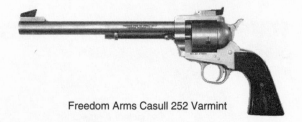

Freedom Arms Casull 252 Varmint

FREEDOM ARMS CASULL MODEL 252 SILHOUETTE Caliber: 22 LR, 5-shot cylinder. **Barrel:** 9.95″. **Weight:** 63 oz. **Length:** NA **Stocks:** Black micarta, western style. **Sights:** $^1/_8$″ Patridge front, Iron Sight Gun Works silhouette rear, click adjustable for windage and elevation. **Features:** Stainless steel. Built on the 454 Casull frame. Two-point firing pin, lightened hammer for fast lock time. Trigger pull is 3 to 5 lbs. with pre-set overtravel screw. Introduced 1991. From Freedom Arms.
Price: Silhouette Class **$1,509.00**
Price: Extra fitted 22 WMR cylinder **$253.00**

Freedom Arms Casull Model 252 Varmint Similar to the Silhouette Class revolver except has 7.5″ barrel, weighs 59 oz., has black and green laminated hardwood grips, and comes with brass bead front sight, express shallow V rear sight with windage and elevation adjustments. Introduced 1991. From Freedom Arms.
Price: Varmint Class **$1,454.00**
Price: Extra fitted 22 WMR cylinder **$253.00**

Glock 24 Competition

Hammerli Model 160

Hammerli Model 208s

Hammerli Model 280

GAUCHER GP SILHOUETTE PISTOL Caliber: 22 LR, single shot. **Barrel:** 10″. **Weight:** 42.3 oz. **Length:** 15.5″ overall. **Stocks:** Stained hardwood. **Sights:** Hooded post on ramp front, open rear adjustable for windage and elevation. **Features:** Matte chrome barrel, blued bolt and sights. Other barrel lengths available on special order. Introduced 1991. Imported by Mandall Shooting Supplies.
Price: **$425.00**

GLOCK 17L COMPETITION AUTO Caliber: 9mm Para., 10-shot magazine. **Barrel:** 6.02″. **Weight:** 23.3 oz. **Length:** 8.85″ overall. **Stocks:** Black polymer. **Sights:** Blade front with white dot, fixed or adjustable rear. **Features:** Polymer frame, steel slide; double-action trigger with "Safe Action" system; mechanical firing pin safety, drop safety; simple takedown without tools; locked breech, recoil operated action. Introduced 1989. Imported from Austria by Glock, Inc.
Price: **$790.00**

GLOCK 24 COMPETITION MODEL PISTOL Caliber: 40 S&W, 10-shot magazine. **Barrel:** 6.02″. **Weight:** 29.5 oz. **Length:** 8.85″ overall. **Stocks:** Black polymer. **Sights:** Blade front with dot, white outline rear adjustable for windage. **Features:** Long-slide competition model available as compensated or non-compensated gun. Factory-installed competition trigger; drop-free magazine. Introduced 1994. Imported from Austria by Glock, Inc.
Price: **$790.00**

HAMMERLI MODEL 160/162 FREE PISTOLS Caliber: 22 LR, single shot. **Barrel:** 11.30″. **Weight:** 46.94 oz. **Length:** 17.52″ overall. **Stocks:** Walnut; full match style with adjustable palm shelf. Stippled surfaces. **Sights:** Changeable blade front, open, fully adjustable match rear. **Features:** Model 160 has mechanical set trigger; Model 162 has electronic trigger; both fully adjustable with provisions for dry firing. Introduced 1993. Imported from Switzerland by Sigarms, Inc.
Price: Model 160, about **$2,085.00**
Price: Model 162, about **$2,295.00**

HAMMERLI MODEL 208s PISTOL Caliber: 22 LR, 8-shot magazine. **Barrel:** 5.9″. **Weight:** 37.5 oz. **Length:** 10″ overall. **Stocks:** Walnut, target-type with thumbrest. **Sights:** Blade front, open fully adjustable rear. **Features:** Adjustable trigger, including length; interchangeable rear sight elements. Imported from Switzerland by Sigarms, Inc.
Price: About **$1,925.00**

HAMMERLI MODEL 280 TARGET PISTOL Caliber: 22 LR, 6-shot; 32 S&W Long WC, 5-shot. **Barrel:** 4.5″. **Weight:** 39.1 oz. (32). **Length:** 11.8″ overall. **Stocks:** Walnut match-type with stippling, adjustable palm shelf. **Sights:** Match sights, micrometer adjustable; interchangeable elements. **Features:** Has carbon-reinforced synthetic frame and bolt/barrel housing. Trigger is adjustable for pull weight, take-up weight, let-off, and length, and is interchangeable. Interchangeable metal or carbon fiber counterweights. Sight radius of 8.8″. Comes with barrel weights, spare magazine, loading tool, cleaning rods. Introduced 1990. Imported from Sigarms, Inc.
Price: 22-cal., about **$1,565.00**
Price: 32-cal., about **$1,765.00**

HARRIS GUNWORKS SIGNATURE JR. LONG RANGE PISTOL Caliber: Any suitable caliber. **Barrel:** To customer specs. **Weight:** 5 lbs. **Stock:** Gunworks fiberglass. **Sights:** None furnished; comes with scope rings. **Features:** Right- or left-hand benchrest action of titanium or stainless steel; single shot or repeater. Comes with bipod. Introduced 1992. Made in U.S. by Harris Gunworks, Inc.
Price: **$2,400.00**

HIGH STANDARD 10X MODEL TARGET PISTOL Caliber: 22 LR, 10-shot magazine. **Barrel:** 5.5″; push-button takedown. **Weight:** 44 oz. **Length:** 9.5″ overall. **Stocks:** Checkered black epoxied walnut; ambidextrous. **Sights:** Undercut ramp front, micro-click rear adjustable for windage and elevation. **Features:** Hand built with select parts. Adjustable trigger and sear; Parkerized finish; stippled front grip and backstrap. Barrel weights optional. Comes with test target, extended warranty. Reintroduced 1994. From High Standard Mfg. Co., Inc.
Price: ....**$869.00 to $1,095.00**

HIGH STANDARD OLYMPIC MILITARY Caliber: 22 Short, 5-shot magazine. **Barrel:** 5.5″ bull. **Weight:** 44 oz. **Length:** 9.50″ overall. **Stocks:** Checkered hardwood with thumbrest. **Sights:** Undercut ramp front, micro-click rear adjustable for windage and elevation. **Features:** Removable barrel stabilizer; high strength aluminum slide, carbon steel frame; adjustable trigger and sear. Overall blue finish. Reintroduced 1994. Made in U.S. by High Standard Mfg. Co., Inc.
Price: **$536.00**

HIGH STANDARD OLYMPIC RAPID FIRE Caliber: 22 Short, 5-shot magazine. **Barrel:** 4″. **Weight:** 46 oz. **Length:** 11.5″ overall. **Stocks:** International-style stippled hardwood. **Sights:** Undercut ramp front, fully adjustable rear. **Features:** Integral muzzle brake and forward mounted compensator; trigger adjustable for weight of pull, travel; gold-plated trigger, slide stop, safety, magazine release; stippled front and backstraps; push-button barrel takedown. Introduced 1996. Made in U.S. by High Standard Mfg. Co.
Price: **$1,995.00**

High Standard Olympic Rapid Fire

HIGH STANDARD SUPERMATIC TOURNAMENT PISTOL Caliber: 22 LR, 10-shot magazine. **Barrel:** 5.5″; push-button takedown. **Weight:** 43 oz. **Length:** 8.5″ overall. **Stocks:** Black rubber; ambidextrous. **Sights:** Undercut ramp front, micro-click rear adjustable for windage and elevation. **Features:** Slide-mounted rear sight. Blue finish. Reintroduced 1994. From High Standard Mfg. Co., Inc.
Price: **$399.00**

High Standard Tournament

HIGH STANDARD SUPERMATIC TROPHY PISTOL Caliber: 22 LR, 10-shot magazine. **Barrel:** 5.5″ or 7.25″; push-button takedown; drilled and tapped for scope mount. **Weight:** 44 oz. **Length:** 9.5″ overall. **Stocks:** Checkered hardwood with thumbrest. **Sights:** Undercut ramp front, micro-click rear adjustable for windage and elevation. **Features:** Gold-plated trigger, slide lock, safety-lever and magazine release; stippled front grip and backstrap; adjustable trigger and sear. Barrel weights optional. A 22 Short version is available. Reintroduced 1994. From High Standard Mfg. Co., Inc.
Price: **$516.00**

High Standard Supermatic Trophy

High Standard Supermatic Citation Pistol Same as the Supermatic Trophy except has nickel-plated trigger, slide lock, safety lever, magazine release, and has slightly heavier trigger pull. Has stippled front-grip and backstrap, checkered hardwood thumbrest grips, adjustable trigger and sear. Matte blue finish. 5.5″ barrel only. Conversion unit for 22 Short available. Reintroduced 1994. From High Standard Mfg. Co., Inc.
Price: **$446.00**
Price: With scope mount, rings, no sights **$416.00**

High Standard Supermatic Citation MS Same as the Supermatic Citation except has 10″ barrel and RPM sights. Introduced 1996. Made in U.S. by High Standard Mfg. Co., Inc.
Price: **$695.00**

High Standard Citation MS

HIGH STANDARD VICTOR TARGET PISTOL Caliber: 22 LR, 10-shot magazine. **Barrel:** 4.5″ or 5.5″; push-button takedown. **Weight:** 46 oz. **Length:** 9.5″ overall. **Stocks:** Checkered hardwood with thumbrest. **Sights:** Undercut ramp front, micro-click rear adjustable for windage and elevation. Also available with scope mount, rings, no sights. **Features:** Full-length aluminum vent rib (steel optional). Gold-plated trigger, slide lock, safety-lever and magazine release; stippled front grip and backstrap; adjustable trigger and sear. Comes with barrel weight. Blue or Parkerized finish. Reintroduced 1994. From High Standard Mfg. Co., Inc.
Price: **$532.00**
Price: Victor 10X **$1,195.00**
Price: With scope mount, rings, no sights **$479.00**

High Standard Victor

MITCHELL ARMS BARON PISTOL Caliber: 22 LR, 10-shot magazine. **Barrel:** 5.5″ bull. **Weight:** 45 oz. **Length:** 10.25″ overall. **Stocks:** Checkered walnut. **Sights:** Ramp front, slide-mounted square notch rear adjustable for windage and elevation. **Features:** Military grip. Slide lock; smooth grip straps; push-button takedown; drilled and tapped for barrel weights. Introduced 1992. From Mitchell Arms, Inc.
Price: Stainless steel, blue or combo **$395.00**

Mitchell Arms Baron

MITCHELL ARMS MEDALIST AUTO PISTOL Caliber: 22 Short, 22 LR, 10-shot magazine. **Barrel:** 6.75″ round tapered, with stabilizer. **Weight:** 40 oz. **Length:** 11.25″ overall. **Stocks:** Checkered walnut with thumbrest. **Sights:** Undercut ramp front, frame-mounted click adjustable square notch rear. **Features:** Integral stabilizer with two removable weights. Trigger adjustable for pull and over-travel; blue finish or stainless or combo; stippled front and backstraps; push-button barrel takedown. Announced 1992. From Mitchell Arms.
Price: $599.00

MITCHELL ARMS MONARCH PISTOL Caliber: 22 LR, 10-shot magazine. **Barrel:** 5.5″ bull, 7.25″ fluted. **Weight:** 44.5 oz. **Length:** 9.75″ overall (5.5″ barrel). **Stocks:** Checkered walnut with thumbrest. **Sights:** Undercut ramp front, click-adjsutable frame-mounted rear. **Features:** Grip duplicates feel of military 45; positive action magazine latch; front and rear straps stippled. Trigger adjustable for pull, over-travel; gold-filled roll marks, gold-plated trigger, safety, magazine release; push-button barrel takedown. Introduced 1992. From Mitchell Arms, Inc.
Price: Stainless steel or blue $489.00

Mitchell Arms Monarch II Pistol Same as the Monarch except has nickel-plated trigger, safety and magazine release, and has silver-filled roll marks. Available in satin finish stainless steel or blue. Introduced 1992. From Mitchell Arms, Inc.
Price: $498.00

MITCHELL ARMS SOVEREIGN AUTO PISTOL Caliber: 22 LR, 10-shot magazine. **Barrel:** 4.5″ vent rib, 5.5″ vent, dovetail or Weaver ribs. **Weight:** 44 oz. **Length:** 9.75″ overall. **Stocks:** Military-type checkered walnut with thumbrest. **Sights:** Blade front, fully adjustable rear mounted on rib. **Features:** Push-button takedown for barrel interchangeability. Bright stainless steel combo or royal blue finish. Introduced 1994. Made in U.S. From Mitchell Arms.
Price: Vent rib, 4.5″ barrel $595.00
Price: Dovetail rib, 5.5″ barrel $595.00
Price: Weaver rib, 5.5″ barrel $675.00

MITCHELL ARMS 45 BULLSEYE MODEL Caliber: 45 ACP, 8-shot magazine. **Barrel:** 5″, match. **Weight:** 32 oz. **Length:** 8.75″ overall. **Stocks:** Checkered walnut. **Sights:** Blade front, adjustable rear. **Features:** Stainless steel construction; adjustable trigger; flat checkered mainspring housing; extended slide stop; front and rear slide serrations; checkered front strap; full-length guide rod; wadcutter recoil spring. Announced 1996. Made in U.S. by Mitchell Arms.
Price: $950.00

Mitchell Arms 45 Gold IPSC Limited Model Similar to the Bullseye model except has hard-chromed frame; ghost-ring or adjustable sight; match trigger tuning; ambidextrous safety; fitted barrel and slide; extended magazine release; hex-head grip screws. Announced 1996. Made in U.S. by Mitchell Arms.
Price: $1,195.00

MORINI MODEL 84E FREE PISTOL Caliber: 22 LR, single shot. **Barrel:** 11.4″. **Weight:** 43.7 oz. **Length:** 19.4″ overall. **Stocks:** Adjustable match type with stippled surfaces. **Sights:** Interchangeable blade front, match-type fully adjustable rear. **Features:** Fully adjustable electronic trigger. Introduced 1995. Imported from Switzerland by Nygord Precision Products.
Price: $1,495.00

PARDINI GP RAPID FIRE MATCH PISTOL Caliber: 22 Short, 5-shot magazine. **Barrel:** 4.6″. **Weight:** 43.3 oz. **Length:** 11.6″ overall. **Stocks:** Wrap-around stippled walnut. **Sights:** Interchangeable post front, fully adjustable match rear. **Features:** Model GP Schuman has extended rear sight for longer sight radius. Introduced 1995. Imported from Italy by Nygord Precision Products.
Price: Model GP $995.00
Price: Model GP Schuman $1,395.00

Mitchell Arms Medalist

Mitchell Arms Sovereign

> Consult our Directory pages for the location of firms mentioned.

Mitchell Arms 45 Bullseye

PARDINI K50 FREE PISTOL Caliber: 22 LR, single shot. **Barrel:** 9.8″. **Weight:** 34.6 oz. **Length:** 18.7″ overall. **Stocks:** Wrap-around walnut; adjustable match type. **Sights:** Interchangeable post front, fully adjustable match open rear. **Features:** Removable, adjustable match trigger. Barrel weights mount above the barrel. Introduced 1995. Imported from Italy by Nygord Precision Products.
Price: $995.00

PARDINI MODEL SP, HP TARGET PISTOLS Caliber: 22 LR, 32 S&W, 5-shot magazine. **Barrel:** 4.7″. **Weight:** 38.9 oz. **Length:** 11.6″ overall. **Stocks:** Adjustable; stippled walnut; match type. **Sights:** Interchangeable blade front, interchangeable, fully adjustable rear. **Features:** Fully adjustable match trigger. Introduced 1995. Imported from Italy by Nygord Precision Products.
Price: Model SP (22 LR) $950.00
Price: Model HP (32 S&W) $1,095.00

RUGER MARK II TARGET MODEL AUTO PISTOL Caliber: 22 LR, 10-shot magazine. **Barrel:** 6⁷/₈". **Weight:** 42 oz. **Length:** 11¹/₈" overall. **Stocks:** Checkered hard plastic. **Sights:** .125" blade front, micro-click rear, adjustable for windage and elevation. Sight radius 9³/₈". **Features:** Introduced 1982.
Price: Blued (MK-678) $310.50
Price: Stainless (KMK-678) $389.00

Ruger Mark II Target

Ruger Mark II Bull Barrel Same gun as the Target Model except has 5¹/₂" or 10" heavy barrel (10" meets all IHMSA regulations). Weight with 5¹/₂" barrel is 42 oz., with 10" barrel, 51 oz.
Price: Blued (MK-512) $310.50
Price: Blued (MK-10) $294.50
Price: Stainless (KMK-10) $373.00
Price: Stainless (KMK-512) $389.00

Ruger Mark II Bull Stainless

Ruger Mark II Government Target Model Same gun as the Mark II Target Model except has 6⁷/₈" barrel, higher sights and is roll marked "Government Target Model" on the right side of the receiver below the rear sight. Identical in all aspects to the military model used for training U.S. armed forces except for markings. Comes with factory test target. Introduced 1987.
Price: Blued (MK-678G) $356.50
Price: Stainless (KMK-678G) $427.25

Ruger Government Target

Ruger Stainless Government Competition Model 22 Pistol Similar to the Mark II Government Target Model stainless pistol except has 6⁷/₈" slab-sided barrel; the receiver top is drilled and tapped for a Ruger scope base adaptor of blued, chrome moly steel; comes with Ruger 1" stainless scope rings with integral bases for mounting a variety of optical sights; has checkered laminated grip panels with right-hand thumbrest. Has blued open sights with 9¹/₄" radius. Overall length is 11¹/₈", weight 45 oz. Introduced 1991.
Price: KMK-678GC $441.00

Ruger Mark II Government Competition

SMITH & WESSON MODEL 41 TARGET Caliber: 22 LR, 10-shot clip. **Barrel:** 5¹/₂", 7". **Weight:** 44 oz. (5¹/₂" barrel). **Length:** 9" overall (5¹/₂" barrel). **Stocks:** Checkered walnut with modified thumbrest, usable with either hand. **Sights:** ¹/₈" Patridge on ramp base; micro-click rear adjustable for windage and elevation. **Features:** ³/₈" wide, grooved trigger; adjustable trigger stop.
Price: S&W Bright Blue, either barrel $753.00

SPHINX AT-2000C, CS COMPETITOR PISTOL Caliber: 9mm Para., 9x21mm, 40 S&W, 10-shot. **Barrel:** 5.31". **Weight:** 40.56 oz. **Length:** 9.84" overall. **Stocks:** Checkered neoprene. **Sights:** Fully adjustable Bo-Mar or Tasco Pro-Point dot sight in Sphinx mount. **Features:** Extended magazine release. Competition slide with dual-port compensated barrel. Two-tone finish only. Introduced 1993. Imported from Switzerland by Sphinx U.S.A., Inc.
Price: With Bo-Mar sights $1,902.00
Price: With Tasco Pro-Point and mount (AT-2000CS) .$2,189.00

Sphinx AT-2000C Competitor

Smith & Wesson Model 41

Sphinx AT-2000GM Grand Master Pistol Similar to the AT-2000C except has single-action-only trigger mechanism, squared trigger guard, extended beavertail grip, safety and magazine release; notched competition slide for easier cocking. Two-tone finish only. Has dual-port compensated barrel. Available with fully adjustable Bo-Mar sights or Tasco Pro-Point and Sphinx mount. Introduced 1993. Imported from Switzerland by Sphinx U.S.A., Inc.
Price: With Bo-Mar sights (AT-2000GMS) $2,894.00
Price: With Tasco Pro-Point and mount (AT-2000GM) $2,972.00

SAFARI ARMS MATCHMASTER PISTOL Caliber: 45 ACP, 7-shot magazine. **Barrel:** 5″, 6″; stainless steel. **Weight:** 38 oz. **Length:** 8.5″ overall. **Stocks:** Smooth walnut with etched scorpion logo. **Sights:** Ramped blade front, LPA adjustable rear. **Features:** Beavertail grip safety, extended safety, extended slide release, Commander-style hammer; throated, polished, tuned. Finishes: Parkerized matte black, or satin stainless steel. Made in U.S. by Safari, Inc.
Price: 5″ barrel $715.00
Price: 6″ barrel $844.00

Safari Arms Matchmaster Carrycomp I Similar to the Matchmaster except has Wil Schueman-designed hybrid compensator system. Introduced 1993. Made in U.S. by Safari Arms, Inc.
Price: 3.8″ barrel $1,150.00
Price: 5″ barrel $1,300.00

SPRINGFIELD, INC. 1911A1 BULLSEYE WADCUTTER PISTOL Caliber: 45 ACP. **Barrel:** 5″. **Weight:** 45 oz. **Length:** 8.59″ overall (5″ barrel). **Stocks:** Checkered walnut. **Sights:** Bo-Mar rib with undercut blade front, fully adjustable rear. **Features:** Built for wadcutter loads only. Has full-length recoil spring guide rod, fitted Videki speed trigger with 3.5-lb. pull; match Commander hammer and sear; beavertail grip safety; lowered and flared ejection port; tuned extractor; fitted slide to frame; recoil buffer system; beveled and polished magazine well; checkered front strap and steel mainspring housing (flat housing standard); polished and throated National Match barrel and bushing. Comes with two magazines with slam pads, plastic carrying case, test target. Introduced 1992. From Springfield, Inc.
Price: $1,665.00

Springfield, Inc. Basic Competition Pistol Has low-mounted Bo-Mar adjustable rear sight, undercut blade front; match throated barrel and bushing; polished feed ramp; lowered and flared ejection port; fitted Videki speed trigger with tuned 3.5-lb. pull; fitted slide to frame; recoil buffer system; checkered walnut grips; serrated, arched mainspring housing. Comes with two magazines with slam pads, plastic carrying case. Introduced 1992. From Springfield, Inc.
Price: 45 ACP, blue, 5″ only $1,439.00

Springfield, Inc. Competition Pistol Similar to the 1911A1 Basic Competition Wadcutter Pistol except has brazed, serrated improved ramp front sight; Videki speed trigger with 3½-lb. pull; extended ambidextrous thumb safety; match Commander hammer and sear; serrated rear slide; Pachmayr flat mainspring housing; extended magazine release; beavertail grip safety; full-length recoil spring guide; Pachmayr wrap-around grips. Comes with two magazines with slam pads, plastic carrying case. Introduced 1992. From Springfield, Inc.
Price: 45 ACP, blue $1,598.00

Springfield, Inc. Expert Pistol Similar to the Competition Pistol except has triple-chamber tapered cone compensator on match barrel with dovetailed front sight; lowered and flared ejection port; fully tuned for reliability; fitted slide to frame; extended ambidextrous thumb safety, extended magazine release button; beavertail grip safety; Pachmayr wrap-around grips. Comes with two magazines, plastic carrying case. Introduced 1992. From Springfield, Inc.
Price: 45 ACP, Duotone finish $1,915.00
Price: Expert Ltd. $1,804.00

Sphinx AT-2000GM Grand Master

Safari Arms Matchmaster

Springfield 1911A1 Trophy Match

Springfield, Inc. Distinguished Pistol Has all the features of the 1911A1 Expert except is full-house pistol with deluxe Bo-Mar low-mounted adjustable rear sight; full-length recoil spring guide rod and recoil spring retainer; checkered frontstrap; S&A magazine well; walnut grips. Hard chrome finish. Comes with two magazines with slam pads, plastic carrying case. From Springfield, Inc.
Price: 45 ACP $2,717.00
Price: Distinguished Limited $2,606.00

Springfield, Inc. 1911A1 N.M. Hardball Pistol Has Bo-Mar adjustable rear sight with undercut front blade; fitted match Videki trigger with 4-lb. pull; fitted slide to frame; throated National Match barrel and bushing, polished feed ramp; recoil buffer system; tuned extractor; Herrett walnut grips. Comes with two magazines, plastic carrying case, test target. Introduced 1992. From Springfield, Inc.
Price: 45 ACP, blue $1,485.00

Springfield, Inc. 1911A1 Trophy Match Pistol Similar to the 1911A1 except factory accurized, Videki speed trigger, skeletonized hammer; has 4- to 5½-lb. trigger pull, click adjustable rear sight, match-grade barrel and bushing. Comes with checkered walnut grips. Introduced 1994. From Springfield, Inc.
Price: Blue $954.00
Price: Stainless steel $985.00

STOEGER PRO SERIES 95 VENT RIB Caliber: 22 LR, 10-shot magazine. **Barrel:** 5¹/₂″. **Weight:** 48 oz. **Length:** 9⁵/₈″ overall. **Stocks:** Pachmayr wrap-around checkered rubber. **Sights:** Blade front, fully adjustable micro-click rear mounted on rib. **Features:** Stainless steel construction; full-length ventilated rib; gold-plated trigger, slide lock, safety-lever and magazine release; adjustable trigger; interchangeable barrels. Introduced 1996. From Stoeger Ind.
Price: $565.00

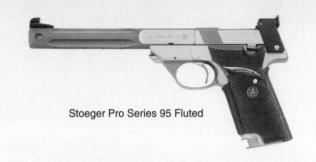

Stoeger Pro Series 95 Fluted

Stoeger Pro Series 95 Bull Barrel Similar to the Vent Rib model except has 5¹/₂″ bull barrel, rear sight mounted on slide bridge. Introduced 1996. From Stoeger Ind.
Price: $460.00

Stoeger Pro Series 95 Fluted Barrel Similar to the Vent Rib model except has 7¹/₂″ heavy fluted barrel, rear sight mounted on slide bridge. Overall length 11¹/₄″, weighs 50 oz. Introduced 1996. From Stoeger Ind.
Price: $490.00

Thompson/Center Super 14 Contender

THOMPSON/CENTER SUPER 14 CONTENDER Caliber: 22 LR, 222 Rem., 223 Rem., 7mm TCU, 7-30 Waters, 30-30 Win., 35 Rem., 357 Rem. Maximum, 44 Mag., 10mm Auto, 445 Super Mag., single shot. **Barrel:** 14″. **Weight:** 45 oz. **Length:** 17¹/₄″ overall. **Stocks:** T/C "Competitor Grip" (walnut and rubber). **Sights:** Fully adjustable target-type. **Features:** Break-open action with auto safety. Interchangeable barrels for both rimfire and centerfire calibers. Introduced 1978.
Price: Blued $473.80
Price: Stainless steel $504.70
Price: Extra barrels, blued $244.00
Price: Extra barrels, stainless steel $239.50

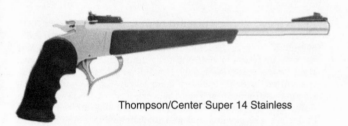

Thompson/Center Super 14 Stainless

Consult our Directory pages for the location of firms mentioned.

Thompson/Center Super 16 Contender Same as the T/C Super 14 Contender except has 16¹/₄″ barrel. Rear sight can be mounted at mid-barrel position (10³/₄″ radius) or moved to the rear (using scope mount position) for 14³/₄″ radius. Overall length is 20¹/₄″. Comes with T/C Competitor Grip of walnut and rubber. Available in 22 LR, 22 WMR, 223 Rem., 7-30 Waters, 30-30 Win., 35 Rem., 44 Mag., 45-70 Gov't. Also available with 16″ vent rib barrel with internal choke, caliber 45 Colt/410 shotshell.
Price: Blue $478.90
Price: Stainless steel $509.90
Price: 45-70 Gov't., blue $484.10
Price: As above, stainless steel $530.50
Price: Super 16 Vent Rib, blued $509.90
Price: As above, stainless steel $540.80
Price: Extra 16″ barrel, blued $229.20
Price: As above, stainless steel $244.50
Price: Extra 45-70 barrel, blued $234.30
Price: As above, stainless steel $265.50
Price: Extra Super 16 vent rib barrel, blue $260.10
Price: As above, stainless steel $265.50

Thompson/Center Super 16 Contender

Unique D.E.S. 69U

UNIQUE D.E.S. 69U TARGET PISTOL Caliber: 22 LR, 5-shot magazine. **Barrel:** 5.91″. **Weight:** 35.3 oz. **Length:** 10.5″ overall. **Stocks:** French walnut target-style with thumbrest and adjustable shelf; hand-checkered panels. **Sights:** Ramp front, micro. adjustable rear mounted on frame; 8.66″ sight radius. **Features:** Meets U.I.T. standards. Comes with 260-gram barrel weight; 100, 150, 350-gram weights available. Fully adjustable match trigger; dry-firing safety device. Imported from France by Nygord Precision Products.
Price: Right-hand, about $1,250.00
Price: Left-hand, about $1,290.00

UNIQUE D.E.S. 32U TARGET PISTOL Caliber: 32 S&W Long wadcutter. **Barrel:** 5.9″. **Weight:** 40.2 oz. **Stocks:** Anatomically shaped, adjustable stippled French walnut. **Sights:** Blade front, micrometer click rear. **Features:** Trigger adjustable for weight and position; dry firing mechanism; slide stop catch. Optional sleeve weights. Introduced 1990. Imported from France by Nygord Precision Products.
Price: Right-hand, about $1,350.00
Price: Left-hand, about $1,380.00

WALTHER GSP MATCH PISTOL Caliber: 22 LR, 32 S&W Long (GSP-C), 5-shot magazine. **Barrel:** 4.22″. **Weight:** 44.8 oz. (22 LR), 49.4 oz. (32). **Length:** 11.8″ overall. **Stocks:** Walnut. **Sights:** Post front, match rear adjustable for windage and elevation. **Features:** Available with either 2.2-lb. (1000 gm) or 3-lb. (1360 gm) trigger. Spare magazine, barrel weight, tools supplied. Imported from Germany by Nygord Precision Products.
Price: GSP, with case $1,495.00
Price: GSP-C, with case $1,595.00

WICHITA SILHOUETTE PISTOL Caliber: 308 Win. F.L., 7mm IHMSA, 7mm-308. **Barrel:** 14¹⁵⁄₁₆″. **Weight:** 4¹⁄₂ lbs. **Length:** 21³⁄₈″ overall. **Stock:** American walnut with oil finish. Glass bedded. **Sights:** Wichita Multi-Range sight system. **Features:** Comes with left-hand action with right-hand grip. Round receiver and barrel. Fluted bolt, flat bolt handle. Wichita adjustable trigger. Introduced 1979. From Wichita Arms.
Price: Center grip stock $1,417.50
Price: As above except with Rear Position Stock and target-type Lightpull trigger $1,417.50

Wichita Silhouette

WICHITA CLASSIC SILHOUETTE PISTOL Caliber: All standard calibers with maximum overall length of 2.800″. **Barrel:** 11¹⁄₄″. **Weight:** 3 lbs., 15 oz. **Stocks:** AAA American walnut with oil finish, checkered grip. **Sights:** Hooded post front, open adjustable rear. **Features:** Three locking lug bolt, three gas ports; completely adjustable Wichita trigger. Introduced 1981. From Wichita Arms.
Price: $3,450.00

DOUBLE-ACTION REVOLVERS, SERVICE & SPORT

Includes models suitable for hunting and competitive courses for fire, both police and international.

ARMSCOR M-200DC REVOLVER Caliber: 38 Spec., 6-shot cylinder. **Barrel:** 2¹⁄₂″, 4″. **Weight:** 22 oz. (2¹⁄₂″ barrel). **Length:** 7³⁄₈″ overall (2¹⁄₂″ barrel). **Stocks:** Checkered rubber. **Sights:** Blade front, fixed notch rear. **Features:** All-steel construction; floating firing pin, transfer bar ignition; shrouded ejector rod; blue finish. Reintroduced 1996. Imported from the Philippines by K.B.I., Inc.
Price: $199.99

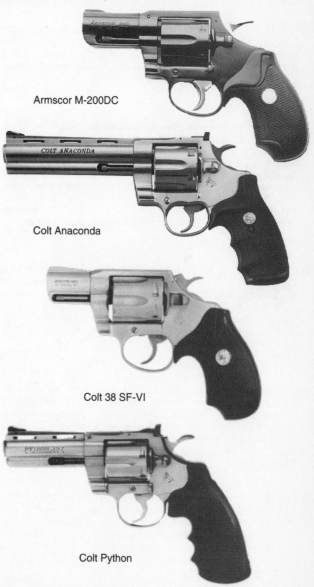

Armscor M-200DC

COLT ANACONDA REVOLVER Caliber: 44 Rem. Magnum, 45 Colt, 6-shot. **Barrel:** 4″, 6″, 8″. **Weight:** 53 oz. (6″ barrel). **Length:** 11⁵⁄₈″ overall. **Stocks:** TP combat style with finger grooves. **Sights:** Red insert front, adjustable white outline rear. **Features:** Stainless steel; full-length ejector rod housing; ventilated barrel rib; offset bolt notches in cylinder; wide spur hammer. Introduced 1990.
Price: $612.00
Price: 45 Colt, 6″, 8″ barrel only $612.00
Price: With complete Realtree camouflage coverage $740.00
Price: As above with scope and mount $999.00

Colt Anaconda

COLT 38 SF-VI REVOLVER Caliber: 38 Special, 6-shot. **Barrel:** 2″. **Weight:** 21 oz. **Length:** 7″ overall. **Stocks:** Checkered black composition. **Sights:** Ramp front, fixed rear. **Features:** Has new lockwork. Made of stainless steel. Introduced 1995. From Colt's Mfg. Co.
Price: $408.00

Colt 38 SF-VI

COLT KING COBRA REVOLVER Caliber: 357 Magnum, 6-shot. **Barrel:** 4″, 6″. **Weight:** 42 oz. (4″ bbl.). **Length:** 9″ overall (4″ bbl.). **Stocks:** TP combat style. **Sights:** Red insert ramp front, adjustable white outline rear. **Features:** Full-length contoured ejector rod housing, barrel rib. Introduced 1986.
Price: Stainless $455.00

COLT PYTHON REVOLVER Caliber: 357 Magnum (handles all 38 Spec.), 6-shot. **Barrel:** 4″, 6″ or 8″, with ventilated rib. **Weight:** 38 oz. (4″ bbl.). **Length:** 9¹⁄₄″ (4″ bbl.). **Stocks:** Hogue Monogrip (4″), TP combat style (6″, 8″). **Sights:** ¹⁄₈″ ramp front, adjustable notch rear. **Features:** Ventilated rib; grooved, crisp trigger; swing-out cylinder; target hammer.
Price: Royal blue, 4″, 6″, 8″ $815.00
Price: Stainless, 4″, 6″, 8″ $904.00
Price: Bright stainless, 4″, 6″, 8″ $935.00

Colt Python

E.A.A. STANDARD GRADE REVOLVERS **Caliber:** 22 LR, 22 LR/22 WMR, 8-shot; 38 Spec., 6-shot; 357 magnum, 6-shot. **Barrel:** 4″, 6″ (22 rimfire); 2″, 4″ (38 Spec.). **Weight:** 38 oz. (22 rimfire, 4″). **Length:** 8.8″ overall (4″ bbl.). **Stocks:** Rubber with finger grooves. **Sights:** Blade front, fixed or adjustable on rimfires; fixed only on 32, 38. **Features:** Swing-out cylinder; hammer block safety; blue finish. Introduced 1991. Imported from Germany by European American Armory.
Price: 38 Special 2″ $180.00
Price: 38 Special, 4″ $199.00
Price: 357 Magnum $199.00
Price: 22 LR, 6″ $199.00
Price: 22 LR/22 WMR combo, 4″ $200.00
Price: As above, 6″ $200.00

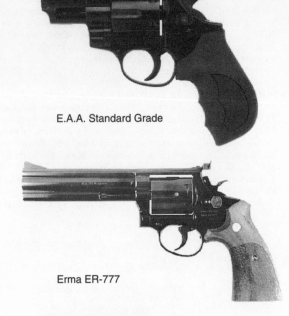

E.A.A. Standard Grade

> Consult our Directory pages for
> the location of firms mentioned.

ERMA ER-777 SPORTING REVOLVER **Caliber:** 357 Mag., 6-shot. **Barrel:** 5½″. **Weight:** 43.3 oz. **Length:** 9½″ overall (4″ barrel). **Stocks:** Stippled walnut service-type. **Sights:** Interchangeable blade front, micro-adjustable rear for windage and elevation. **Features:** Polished blue finish. Adjustable trigger. Imported from Germany by Precision Sales Int'l. Introduced 1988.
Price: $1,019.00

Erma ER-777

HARRINGTON & RICHARDSON AMERICAN REVOLVERS **Caliber:** 38 Spec., 5-shot. **Barrel:** 2″, 3″. **Weight:** 24 oz. **Length:** 7⅛″ overall. **Stocks:** Pachmayr rubber. **Sights:** Ramp front, fixed notch rear. **Features:** Available in blue or nickel. Introduced 1996. Made in U.S. by Amtec 2000.
Price: ....**NA**

Harrington & Richardson American

HARRINGTON & RICHARDSON 929 SIDEKICK **Caliber:** 22 LR, 9-shot cylinder. **Barrel:** 4″ heavy. **Weight:** 30 oz. **Length:** NA. **Stocks:** Cinnamon-color laminated wood. **Sights:** Blade front, notch rear. **Features:** Double action; swing-out cylinder, traditional loading gate; blued frame and barrel. Comes with lockable storage case, Uncle Mike's Sidekick holster. Introduced 1996. Made in U.S. by H&R 1871, Inc.
Price: $159.95
Price: NTA Trapper Edition, special rollmark, gray laminate grips $174.95

HARRINGTON & RICHARDSON 939 PREMIER REVOLVER **Caliber:** 22 LR, 9-shot cylinder. **Barrel:** 6″ heavy. **Weight:** 36 oz. **Length:** NA. **Stocks:** Walnut-finished hardwood. **Sights:** Blade front, fully adjustable rear. **Features:** Swing-out cylinder with plunger-type ejection; solid barrel rib; high-polish blue finish; double-action mechanism; Western-style grip. Introduced 1995. Made in U.S. by H&R 1871, Inc.
Price: $189.95

Harrington & Richardson 939

HARRINGTON & RICHARDSON 949 WESTERN REVOLVER **Caliber:** 22 LR, 9-shot cylinder. **Barrel:** 5½″, 7½″. **Weight:** 36 oz. **Length:** NA. **Stocks:** Walnut-stained hardwood. **Sights:** Blade front, adjustable rear. **Features:** Color case-hardened frame and backstrap, traditional loading gate and ejector rod. Introduced 1994. Made in U.S. by H&R 1871, Inc.
Price: About $189.95

Harrington & Richardson 949

HARRINGTON & RICHARDSON 999 SPORTSMAN REVOLVER **Caliber:** 22 Short, Long, Long Rifle, 9-shot. **Barrel:** 4″, 6″. **Weight:** 30 oz. (4″ barrel). **Length:** 8.5″ overall. **Stocks:** Walnut-finished hardwood. **Sights:** Blade front adjustable for elevation, rear adjustable for windage. **Features:** Top-break loading; polished blue finish; automatic shell ejection. Reintroduced 1992. From H&R 1871, Inc.
Price: $279.95

Harrington & Richardson 999 Sportsman

Heritage Sentry

Manurhin MR73 Sport Revolver

Manurhin MR 96

New England Lady Ultra

New England Ultra

HERITAGE SENTRY DOUBLE-ACTION REVOLVERS Caliber: 38 Spec., 6-shot. **Barrel:** 2". **Weight:** 23 oz. **Length:** 6¼" overall (2" barrel). **Stocks:** Checkered plastic. **Sights:** Ramp front, fixed rear. **Features:** Pull-pin-type ejection; serrated hammer and trigger. Polished blue or nickel finish. Introduced 1993. Made in U.S. by Heritage Mfg., Inc.
Price: . . . .**$129.95 to $139.95**

MANURHIN MR 73 SPORT REVOLVER Caliber: 357 Magnum, 6-shot cylinder. **Barrel:** 6". **Weight:** 37 oz. **Length:** 11.1" overall. **Stocks:** Checkered walnut. **Sights:** Blade front, fully adjustable rear. **Features:** Double action with adjustable trigger. High-polish blue finish, straw-colored hammer and trigger. Comes with extra sight. Introduced 1984. Imported from France by Century International Arms.
Price: About **$1,500.00**

MANURHIN MR 73 REVOLVER Caliber: 32 S&W, 38 Spec., 357 Mag. **Barrel:** 3", 4", 5¼", 5¾", 6". **Weight:** 38 oz. (6" barrel). **Length:** 11" overall (6" barrel). **Stocks:** Checkered hardwood. **Sights:** Blade front, fully adjustable rear. **Features:** Polished bright blue finish; hammer-forged barrel. Imported from France by Sphinx U.S.A., Inc.
Price: Police model, 3" or 4" barrel **$1,885.00**
Price: Sport model, 5¼" or 6" barrel, undercut blade front sight **$1,885.00**
Price: 38 Spec. Match, 5¾" barrel, single action only . .**$1,975.00**
Price: 32 S&W Match, 6" barrel, single action only . . .**$1,975.00**

MANURHIN MR 88 REVOLVER Caliber: 357 Magnum, 6-shot. **Barrel:** 4", 5¼", 6". **Weight:** 33.5 oz. **Length:** 8.1" overall. **Stocks:** Checkered wood. **Sights:** Blade front, fully adjustable rear. **Features:** Stainless steel construction; hammer-forged barrel. Imported from France by Sphinx U.S.A., Inc.
Price: **$877.95**

MANURHIN MR 96 REVOLVER Caliber: 357 Magnum, 6-shot. **Barrel:** 3", 4", 5¼", 6". **Weight:** 38.4 oz. **Length:** 8.8" overall. **Stocks:** Checkered rubber. **Sights:** Blade front, fully adjustable rear. **Features:** Polished blue finish; removable sideplate holds action parts; separate barrel and shroud. Introduced 1996. Imported from France by Sphinx U.S.A., Inc.
Price: **$857.95**

MEDUSA MODEL 47 REVOLVER Caliber: Any 38/357/380/9mm, interchangeable, 6-shot. **Barrel:** 2½", 3", 4", 5", 6". **Weight:** 34 oz. **Length:** 9½" overall. **Stocks:** Checkered rubber. **Sights:** Red ramp front, fully adjustable rear. **Features:** Designed to use almost any cartridge using .357" or 38-caliber bullets interchangeably. Matte finish. Interchangeable front sight blades. Introduced 1996. Made in U.S. by Phillips & Rogers, Inc.
Price: **$899.00**

NEW ENGLAND FIREARMS LADY ULTRA REVOLVER Caliber: 32 H&R Mag., 5-shot. **Barrel:** 3". **Weight:** 31 oz. **Length:** 7.25" overall. **Stocks:** Walnut-finished hardwood with NEF medallion. **Sights:** Blade front, fully adjustable rear. **Features:** Swing-out cylinder; polished blue finish. Comes with lockable storage case. Introduced 1992. From New England Firearms.
Price: **$174.95**

NEW ENGLAND FIREARMS ULTRA REVOLVER Caliber: 22 LR, 9-shot; 22 WMR, 6-shot. **Barrel:** 4", 6". **Weight:** 36 oz. **Length:** 10⅝" overall (6" barrel). **Stocks:** Walnut-finished hardwood with NEF medallion. **Sights:** Blade front, fully adjustable rear. **Features:** Blue finish. Bull-style barrel with recessed muzzle, high "Lustre" blue/black finish. Introduced 1989. From New England Firearms.
Price: **$174.95**
Price: Ultra Mag 22 WMR **$174.95**

NEW ENGLAND FIREARMS STANDARD REVOLVERS Caliber: 22 LR, 9-shot; 32 H&R Mag., 5-shot. **Barrel:** 2½", 4". **Weight:** 26 oz. (22 LR, 2½"). **Length:** 8½" overall (4" bbl.). **Stocks:** Walnut-finished American hardwood with NEF medallion. **Sights:** Fixed. **Features:** Choice of blue or nickel finish. Introduced 1988. From New England Firearms.
Price: 22 LR, 32 H&R Mag., blue **$134.95**
Price: 22 LR, 2½", 4", nickel, 32 H&R Mag. 2½" nickel .**$144.95**

ROSSI LADY ROSSI REVOLVER **Caliber:** 38 Spec., 5-shot. **Barrel:** 2″, 3″. **Weight:** 21 oz. **Length:** 6.5″ overall (2″ barrel). **Stocks:** Smooth rosewood. **Sights:** Fixed. **Features:** High-polish stainless steel with "Lady Rossi" engraved on frame. Comes with velvet carry bag. Introduced 1995. Imported from Brazil by Interarms.
Price: $285.00

ROSSI MODEL 68 REVOLVER **Caliber:** 38 Spec. **Barrel:** 2″, 3″. **Weight:** 22 oz. **Stocks:** Checkered wood and rubber. **Sights:** Ramp front, low profile adjustable rear. **Features:** All-steel frame, thumb latch operated swing-out cylinder. Introduced 1978. Imported from Brazil by Interarms.
Price: 38, blue, 3″, wood or rubber grips $225.00
Price: M68/2 (2″ barrel), wood or rubber grips $225.00
Price: 3″, nickel $225.00

ROSSI MODEL 88 STAINLESS REVOLVER **Caliber:** 38 Spec., 5-shot. **Barrel:** 2″, 3″. **Weight:** 22 oz. **Length:** 7.5″ overall. **Stocks:** Checkered wood, service-style, and rubber. **Sights:** Ramp front, square notch rear drift adjustable for windage. **Features:** All metal parts except springs are of 440 stainless steel; matte finish; small frame for concealability. Introduced 1983. Imported from Brazil by Interarms.
Price: 3″ barrel, wood or rubber grips $255.00
Price: 2″ barrel, wood or rubber grips $255.00

ROSSI MODEL 515, 518 REVOLVERS **Caliber:** 22 LR (Model 518), 22 WMR (Model 515), 6-shot. **Barrel:** 4″. **Weight:** 30 oz. **Length:** 9″ overall. **Stocks:** Checkered wood and finger-groove wrap-around rubber. **Sights:** Blade front with red insert, rear adjustable for windage and elevation. **Features:** Small frame; stainless steel construction; solid integral barrel rib. Introduced 1994. Imported from Brazil by Interarms.
Price: Model 518, 22 LR $255.00
Price: Model 515, 22 WMR $270.00

ROSSI MODEL 720 REVOLVER **Caliber:** 44 Spec., 5-shot. **Barrel:** 3″. **Weight:** 27.5 oz. **Length:** 8″ overall. **Stocks:** Checkered rubber, combat style. **Sights:** Red insert front on ramp, fully adjustable rear. **Features:** All stainless steel construction; solid barrel rib; full ejector rod shroud. Introduced 1992. Imported from Brazil by Interarms.
Price: $290.00
Price: Model 720C, spurless hammer, DA only $290.00

ROSSI MODEL 851 REVOLVER **Caliber:** 38 Spec., 6-shot. **Barrel:** 3″ or 4″. **Weight:** 27.5 oz. (3″ bbl.). **Length:** 8″ overall (3″ bbl.). **Stocks:** Checkered Brazilian hardwood. **Sights:** Blade front with red insert, rear adjustable for windage. **Features:** Medium-size frame; stainless steel construction; ventilated barrel rib. Introduced 1991. Imported from Brazil by Interarms.
Price: $255.00

ROSSI MODEL 877 REVOLVER **Caliber:** 357 Mag., 6-shot cylinder. **Barrel:** 2″. **Weight:** 26 oz. **Length:** NA. **Stocks:** Stippled synthetic. **Sights:** Blade front, fixed groove rear. **Features:** Stainless steel construction; fully enclosed ejector rod. Introduced 1996. Imported from Brazil by Interarms.
Price: $290.00

ROSSI MODEL 971 REVOLVER **Caliber:** 357 Mag., 6-shot. **Barrel:** 2½″, 4″, 6″, heavy. **Weight:** 36 oz. **Length:** 9″ overall. **Stocks:** Checkered Brazilian hardwood. Stainless models have checkered, contoured rubber. **Sights:** Blade front, fully adjustable rear. **Features:** Full-length ejector rod shroud; matted sight rib; target-type trigger, wide checkered hammer spur. Introduced 1988. Imported from Brazil by Interarms.
Price: 4″, stainless $290.00
Price: 6″, stainless $290.00
Price: 4″, blue $255.00
Price: 2½″, stainless $290.00

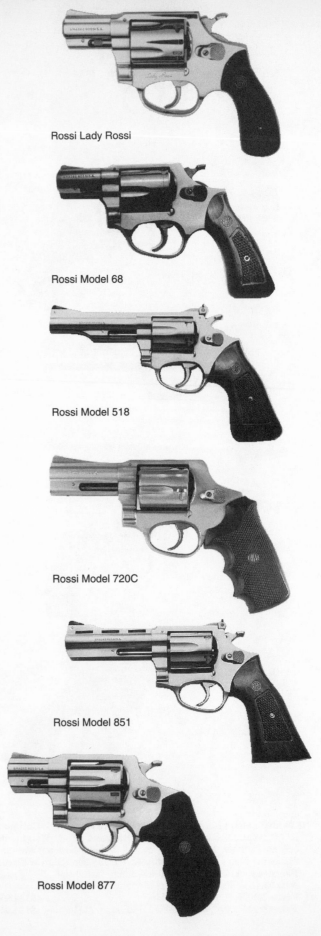

Rossi Lady Rossi

Rossi Model 68

Rossi Model 518

Rossi Model 720C

Rossi Model 851

Rossi Model 877

Rossi Model 971 VRC Revolver Similar to the Model 971 except has Rossi's 8-port Vented Rib Compensator; checkered finger-groove rubber grips; stainless steel construction. Available with 2.5", 4", 6" barrel; weighs 30 oz. with 2⅝" barrel. Introduced 1996. Imported from Brazil by Interarms.
Price: **$340.00**

Rossi Model 971 VRC

Rossi Model 971 Comp Gun Same as the Model 971 stainless except has 3¼" barrel with integral compensator. Overall length is 9", weighs 32 oz. Has red insert front sight, fully adjustable rear. Checkered, contoured rubber grips. Introduced 1993. Imported from Brazil by Interarms.
Price: **$290.00**

Rossi Model 971 Comp

RUGER GP-100 REVOLVERS Caliber: 38 Spec., 357 Mag., 6-shot. **Barrel:** 3", 3" heavy, 4", 4" heavy, 6", 6" heavy. **Weight:** 3" barrel—35 oz., 3" heavy barrel—36 oz., 4" barrel—37 oz., 4" heavy barrel—38 oz. **Sights:** Fixed; adjustable on 4" heavy, 6", 6" heavy barrels. **Stocks:** Ruger Santoprene Cushioned Grip with Goncalo Alves inserts. **Features:** Uses action and frame incorporating improvements and features of both the Security-Six and Redhawk revolvers. Full length and short ejector shroud. Satin blue and stainless steel. Available in high-gloss stainless steel finish. Introduced 1988.
Price: GP-141 (357, 4" heavy, adj. sights, blue) **$440.00**
Price: GP-160 (357, 6", adj. sights, blue) **$440.00**
Price: GP-161 (357, 6" heavy, adj. sights, blue) **$440.00**
Price: GPF-331 (357, 3" heavy), GPF-831 (38 Spec.) . . .**$423.00**
Price: GPF-340 (357, 4"), GPF-840 (38 Spec.) **$423.00**
Price: GPF-341 (357, 4" heavy), GPF-841 (38 Spec.) **$423.00**
Price: KGP-141 (357, 4" heavy, adj. sights, stainless) . .**$474.00**
Price: KGP-160 (357, 6", adj. sights, stainless) **$474.00**
Price: KGP-161 (357, 6" heavy, adj. sights, stainless) . .**$474.00**
Price: KGPF-330 (357, 3", stainless), KGPF-830 (38
Spec.) **$457.00**
Price: KGPF-331 (357, 3" heavy, stainless), KGPF-831 (38
Spec.) **$457.00**
Price: KGPF-340 (357, 4", stainless), KGPF-840 (38
Spec.) **$457.00**
Price: KGPF-341 (357, 4" heavy, stainless), KGPF-841 (38
Spec.) **$457.00**

Ruger GP-100

RUGER SP101 REVOLVERS Caliber: 22 LR, 32 H&R Mag., 6-shot, 9mm Para., 38 Spec. +P, 357 Mag., 5-shot. **Barrel:** 2¼", 3¹/₁₆", 4". **Weight:** 2¼"—25 oz.; 3¹/₁₆"—27 oz. **Sights:** Adjustable on 22, 32, fixed on others. **Stocks:** Ruger Santoprene Cushioned Grip with Xenoy inserts. **Features:** Incorporates improvements and features found in the GP-100 revolvers into a compact, small frame, double-action revolver. Full-length ejector shroud. Stainless steel only. Available with high-polish finish. Introduced 1988.
Price: KSP-821 (2½", 38 Spec.) **$443.00**
Price: KSP-831 (3¹/₁₆", 38 Spec.) **$443.00**
Price: KSP-221 (2¼", 22 LR) **$443.00**
Price: KSP-240 (4", 22 LR) **$443.00**
Price: KSP-241 (4" heavy bbl., 22 LR) **$443.00**
Price: KSP-3231 (3¹/₁₆", 32 H&R) **$443.00**
Price: KSP-921 (2¼", 9mm Para.) **$443.00**
Price: KSP-931 (3¹/₁₆", 9mm Para.) **$443.00**
Price: KSP-321 (2¼", 357 Mag.) **$443.00**
Price: KSP-331 (3¹/₁₆", 357 Mag.) **$443.00**

Ruger SP101/KSP-240

Ruger SP101 Double-Action-Only Revolver Similar to the standard SP101 except is double-action-only with no single-action sear notch. Has spurless hammer for snag-free handling, floating firing pin and Ruger's patented transfer bar safety system. Available with 2¼" barrel in 38 Special +P and 357 Magnum only. Weighs 25½ oz., overall length 7.06". Natural brushed satin or high-polish stainless steel. Introduced 1993.
Price: KSP821L (38 Spec.), KSP321XL (357 Mag.) **$443.00**

Ruger SP101 DAO

Ruger Redhawk

RUGER REDHAWK Caliber: 44 Rem. Mag., 6-shot. **Barrel:** 5½", 7½". **Weight:** About 54 oz. (7½" bbl.). **Length:** 13" overall (7½" barrel). **Stocks:** Square butt Goncalo Alves. **Sights:** Interchangeable Patridge-type front, rear adjustable for windage and elevation. **Features:** Stainless steel, brushed satin finish, or blued ordnance steel. Has a 9½" sight radius. Introduced 1979.
Price: Blued, 44 Mag., 5½", 7½" **$490.00**
Price: Blued, 44 Mag., 7½", with scope mount, rings . . .**$527.00**
Price: Stainless, 44 Mag., 5½", 7½" **$547.00**
Price: Stainless, 44 Mag., 7½", with scope mount, rings .**$589.00**

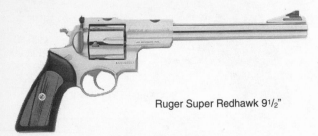

Ruger Super Redhawk 9½"

Ruger Super Redhawk Revolver Similar to the standard Redhawk except has a heavy extended frame with the Ruger Integral Scope Mounting System on the wide topstrap. The wide hammer spur has been lowered for better scope clearance. Incorporates the mechanical design features and improvements of the GP-100. Choice of 7½" or 9½" barrel, both with ramp front sight base with Redhawk-style Interchangeable Insert sight blades, adjustable rear sight. Comes with Ruger "Cushioned Grip" panels of Santoprene with Goncalo Alves wood panels. Satin or high-polished stainless steel. Introduced 1987.
Price: KSRH-7 (7½"), KSRH-9 (9½") **$589.00**

> Consult our Directory pages for the location of firms mentioned.

Smith & Wesson Model 10

SMITH & WESSON MODEL 10 M&P REVOLVER Caliber: 38 Spec., 6-shot. **Barrel:** 2", 4". **Weight:** 30 oz. **Length:** 9⁵⁄₁₆" overall. **Stocks:** Uncle Mike's Combat soft rubber; square butt. Wood optional. **Sights:** Fixed, ramp front, square notch rear.
Price: Blue **$383.00**

Smith & Wesson Model 10 38 M&P Heavy Barrel Same as regular M&P except has heavy 4" ribbed barrel with square butt grips. Weighs 33½ oz.
Price: Blue **$390.00**

SMITH & WESSON MODEL 13 H.B. M&P Caliber: 357 Mag. and 38 Spec., 6-shot. **Barrel:** 3" or 4". **Weight:** 34 oz. **Length:** 9⁵⁄₁₆" overall (4" bbl.). **Stocks:** Uncle Mike's Combat soft rubber; wood optional. **Sights:** ⅛" serrated ramp front, fixed square notch rear. **Features:** Heavy barrel, K-frame, square butt (4"), round butt (3").
Price: Blue **$394.00**

Smith & Wesson Model 65LS

Smith & Wesson Model 65 Revolver Similar to the Model 13 except made of stainless steel. Has Uncle Mike's Combat grips, smooth combat trigger, fixed notch rear sight. Made in U.S. by Smith & Wesson.
Price: 3" or 4" **$427.00**

SMITH & WESSON MODEL 14 FULL LUG REVOLVER Caliber: 38 Spec., 6-shot. **Barrel:** 6", full lug. **Weight:** 47 oz. **Length:** 11⅛" overall. **Stocks:** Hogue soft rubber; wood optional. **Sights:** Pinned Patridge front, adjustable micrometer click rear. **Features:** Has .500" target hammer, .312" smooth combat trigger. Polished blue finish. Reintroduced 1991. Limited production.
Price: **$465.00**

Smith & Wesson Model 14

SMITH & WESSON MODEL 15 COMBAT MASTERPIECE Caliber: 38 Spec., 6-shot. **Barrel:** 4". **Weight:** 32 oz. **Length:** 9⁵⁄₁₆" (4" bbl.). **Stocks:** Uncle Mike's Combat soft rubber; wood optional. **Sights:** Front, Baughman Quick Draw on ramp, micro-click rear adjustable for windage and elevation.
Price: Blued **$419.00**

DOUBLE-ACTION REVOLVERS, SERVICE & SPORT

Smith & Wesson Model 17

Smith & Wesson Model 19

Smith & Wesson Model 629

Smith & Wesson Model 629 PowerPort

Smith & Wesson Model 37

SMITH & WESSON MODEL 17 K-22 MASTERPIECE Caliber: 22
LR, 10-shot cylinder. **Barrel:** 6". **Weight:** 42 oz. **Length:** 11⅛"
overall. **Stocks:** Hogue rubber. **Sights:** Pinned Patridge front,
fully adjustable rear. **Features:** Polished blue finish; smooth combat trigger; semi-target hammer. The 10-slot version of this model
introduced 1996.
Price: $490.00

SMITH & WESSON MODEL 19 COMBAT MAGNUM Caliber: 357
Mag. and 38 Spec., 6-shot. **Barrel:** 2½", 4", 6". **Weight:** 36 oz.
Length: 9⁹⁄₁₆" (4" bbl.). **Stocks:** Uncle Mike's Combat soft rubber; wood optional. **Sights:** Serrated ramp front 2½" or 4" bbl.,
red ramp on 4", 6" bbl., micro-click rear adjustable for windage
and elevation.
Price: S&W Bright Blue, adj. sights ....$416.00 to $430.00

SMITH & WESSON MODEL 29, 629 REVOLVERS Caliber: 44
Magnum, 6-shot. **Barrel:** 6", 8⅜" (Model 29); 4", 6", 8⅜" (Model
629). **Weight:** 47 oz. (6" bbl.). **Length:** 11⅜" overall (6" bbl.).
Stocks: Soft rubber; wood optional. **Sights:** ⅛" red ramp front,
micro-click rear, adjustable for windage and elevation.
Price: S&W Bright Blue, 6" $554.00
Price: S&W Bright Blue, 8⅜" $566.00
Price: Model 629 (stainless steel), 4" $587.00
Price: Model 629, 6" $592.00
Price: Model 629, 8⅜" barrel $606.00

Smith & Wesson Model 629 Classic Revolver Similar to the standard
Model 629 except has full-lug 5", 6½" or 8⅜" barrel; chamfered
front of cylinder; interchangable red ramp front sight with
adjustable white outline rear; Hogue grips with S&W monogram;
the frame is drilled and tapped for scope mounting. Factory accurizing and endurance packages. Overall length with 5" barrel is
10½"; weighs 51 oz. Introduced 1990.
Price: Model 629 Classic (stainless), 5", 6½" $629.00
Price: As above, 8 ⅜" $650.00

Smith & Wesson Model 629 Classic PowerPort Revolver Similar to the
Model 629 Classic with 6½" full-lug barrel except has PowerPort
compensator. Introduced 1996. Made in U.S. by Smith & Wesson.
Price: 6½" barrel only $629.00

Smith & Wesson Model 629 Classic DX Revolver Similar to the Model
629 Classic except offered only with 6½" or 8⅜" full-lug barrel;
comes with five front sights: 50-yard red ramp; 50-yard black
Patridge; 100-yard black Patridge with gold bead; 50-yard black
ramp; and 50-yard black Patridge with white dot. Comes with
Hogue combat-style round butt grip. Introduced 1991.
Price: Model 629 Classic DX, 6½" $811.00
Price: As above, 8⅜" $838.00

**SMITH & WESSON MODEL 36, 37 CHIEFS SPECIAL & AIR-
WEIGHT Caliber:** 38 Spec., 5-shot. **Barrel:** 2". **Weight:** 19½ oz.
(2" bbl.); 13½ oz. (Airweight). **Length:** 6½" (2" bbl. and round
butt). **Stocks:** Round butt soft rubber; wood optional. **Sights:**
Fixed, serrated ramp front, square notch rear.
Price: Blue, standard Model 36 ....$377.00
Price: Blue, Airweight Model 37, 2" only $412.00

Smith & Wesson Model 637 Airweight Revolver Similar to the Model 37
Airweight except has stainless steel barrel, cylinder and yoke;
Uncle Mike's Boot Grip. Introduced 1996. Made in U.S. by Smith
& Wesson.
Price: $428.00

Smith & Wesson Model 60 Chiefs Special Stainless Same as Model 36
except 357 Magnum or 38 Special (only). All stainless construction, 2" bbl. and round butt only.
Price: Stainless steel $431.00

Smith & Wesson Model 36LS, 60LS LadySmith Similar to the standard Model 36. Available with 2″ barrel. Comes with smooth, contoured rosewood grips with the S&W monogram. Has a speedloader cutout. Comes in a fitted carry/storage case. Introduced 1989.
Price: Model 36LS $408.00
Price: Model 60LS (as above except in stainless) $461.00

Smith & Wesson Model 60LS

Smith & Wesson Model 60 3″ Full-Lug Revolver Similar to the Model 60 Chief's Special except has 3″ full-lug barrel, adjustable micrometer click black blade rear sight; rubber Uncle Mike's Custom Grade Boot Grip. Overall length 7½″; weighs 24½ oz. Introduced 1991.
Price: $458.00

SMITH & WESSON MODEL 38 BODYGUARD Caliber: 38 Spec., 5-shot. **Barrel:** 2″. **Weight:** 14½ oz. **Length:** 6⁵/₁₆″ overall. **Stocks:** Soft rubber; wood optional. **Sights:** Fixed serrated ramp front, square notch rear. **Features:** Alloy frame; internal hammer.
Price: Blue $444.00
Price: Nickel $460.00

Smith & Wesson Model 60 3"

Smith & Wesson Model 49, 649 Bodyguard Revolvers Same as Model 38 except steel construction, weighs 20½ oz.
Price: Blued, Model 49 ....$409.00
Price: Stainless, Model 649 ....$469.00

SMITH & WESSON MODEL 63 KIT GUN Caliber: 22 LR, 6-shot. **Barrel:** 2″, 4″. **Weight:** 24 oz. (4″ bbl.). **Length:** 8³/₈″ (4″ bbl. and round butt). **Stocks:** Round butt soft rubber; wood optional. **Sights:** Red ramp front, micro-click rear adjustable for windage and elevation. **Features:** Stainless steel construction.
Price: 2″ $458.00
Price: 4″ $462.00

Smith & Wesson Model 649

SMITH & WESSON MODEL 65LS LADYSMITH Caliber: 357 Magnum, 6-shot. **Barrel:** 3″. **Weight:** 31 oz. **Length:** 7.94″ overall. **Stocks:** Rosewood, round butt. **Sights:** Serrated ramp front, fixed notch rear. **Features:** Stainless steel with frosted finish. Smooth combat trigger, service hammer, shrouded ejector rod. Comes with soft case. Introduced 1992.
Price: $461.00

SMITH & WESSON MODEL 64 STAINLESS M&P Caliber: 38 Spec., 6-shot. **Barrel:** 2″, 3″, 4″. **Weight:** 34 oz. **Length:** 9⁵/₁₆″ overall. **Stocks:** Soft rubber; wood optional. **Sights:** Fixed, ⅛″ serrated ramp front, square notch rear. **Features:** Satin finished stainless steel, square butt.
Price: 2″ $415.00
Price: 3″, 4″ $423.00

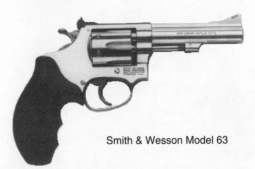

Smith & Wesson Model 63

SMITH & WESSON MODEL 66 STAINLESS COMBAT MAGNUM Caliber: 357 Mag. and 38 Spec., 6-shot. **Barrel:** 2½″, 4″, 6″. **Weight:** 36 oz. (4″ barrel). **Length:** 9⁹/₁₆″ overall. **Stocks:** Soft rubber; wood optional. **Sights:** Red ramp front, micro-click rear adjustable for windage and elevation. **Features:** Satin finish stainless steel.
Price: 2½″ $466.00
Price: 4″, 6″ $471.00

SMITH & WESSON MODEL 67 COMBAT MASTERPIECE Caliber: 38 Special, 6-shot. **Barrel:** 4″. **Weight:** 32 oz. **Length:** 9⁵/₁₆″ overall. **Stocks:** Soft rubber; wood optional. **Sights:** Red ramp front, micro-click rear adjustable for windage and elevation. **Features:** Stainless steel with satin finish. Smooth combat trigger, semi-target hammer. Introduced 1994.
Price: $467.00

Smith & Wesson Model 65LS

Smith & Wesson Model 686

Smith & Wesson Model 625

Smith & Wesson Model 640

Smith & Wesson Model 442

Smith & Wesson Model 642

SMITH & WESSON MODEL 586, 686 DISTINGUISHED COMBAT MAGNUMS Caliber: 357 Magnum. **Barrel:** 4″, 6″, full shroud. **Weight:** 46 oz. (6″), 41 oz. (4″). **Stocks:** Soft rubber; wood optional. **Sights:** Baughman red ramp front, four-position click-adjustable front, S&W micrometer click rear. Drilled and tapped for scope mount. **Features:** Uses L-frame, but takes all K-frame grips. Full-length ejector rod shroud. Smooth combat-type trigger, semi-target type hammer. Trigger stop on 6″ models. Also available in stainless as Model 686. Introduced 1981.
Price: Model 586, blue, 4″, from $461.00
Price: Model 586, blue, 6″ $466.00
Price: Model 686, 6″, ported barrel $528.00
Price: Model 686, 8³/₈″ $515.00
Price: Model 686, 2¹/₂″ $481.00

Smith & Wesson Model 686 Magnum Plus Revolver Similar to the Model 686 except has 7-shot cylinder, 2¹/₂″, 4″ or 6″ barrel. Weighs 34¹/₂ oz., overall length 7¹/₂″ (2¹/₂″ barrel). Hogue rubber grips. Introduced 1996. Made in U.S. by Smith & Wesson.
Price: 2¹/₂″ barrel $498.00
Price: 4″ barrel $506.00
Price: 6″ barrel $514.00

SMITH & WESSON MODEL 617 FULL LUG REVOLVER Caliber: 22 LR, 6-shot. **Barrel:** 4″, 6″, 8³/₈″. **Weight:** 42 oz. (4″ barrel). **Length:** NA. **Stocks:** Soft rubber; wood optional. **Sights:** Patridge front, adjustable rear. Drilled and tapped for scope mount. **Features:** Stainless steel with satin finish; 4″ has .312″ smooth trigger, .375″ semi-target hammer; 6″ has either .312″ combat or .400″ serrated trigger, .375″ semi-target or .500″ target hammer; 8³/₈″ with .400″ serrated trigger, .500″ target hammer. Introduced 1990.
Price: 4″ $460.00
Price: 6″, target hammer, combat trigger $490.00
Price: 8³/₈″ $501.00

SMITH & WESSON MODEL 625 REVOLVER Caliber: 45 ACP, 6-shot. **Barrel:** 5″. **Weight:** 46 oz. **Length:** 11.375″ overall. **Stocks:** Soft rubber; wood optional. **Sights:** Patridge front on ramp, S&W micrometer click rear adjustable for windage and elevation. **Features:** Stainless steel construction with .400″ semi-target hammer, .312″ smooth combat trigger; full lug barrel. Introduced 1989.
Price: $597.00

SMITH & WESSON MODEL 640 CENTENNIAL Caliber: 357 Mag., 38 Spec., 5-shot. **Barrel:** 2¹/₈″. **Weight:** 25 oz. **Length:** 6³/₄″ overall. **Stocks:** Uncle Mike's Boot Grip. **Sights:** Serrated ramp front, fixed notch rear. **Features:** Stainless steel version of the original Model 40 but without the grip safety. Fully concealed hammer, snag-proof smooth edges. Introduced 1995 in 357 Magnum.
Price: $469.00
Price: Model 940 (9mm Para.) $474.00

Smith & Wesson Model 442 Centennial Airweight Similar to the Model 640 Centennial except has alloy frame giving weight of 15.8 oz. Chambered for 38 Special, 2″ carbon steel barrel; carbon steel cylinder; concealed hammer; Uncle Mike's Custom Grade Santoprene grips. Fixed square notch rear sight, serrated ramp front. Introduced 1993.
Price: Blue $427.00

Smith & Wesson Model 642 Airweight Revolver Similar to the Model 442 Centennial Airweight except has stainless steel barrel, cylinder and yoke with matte finish; Uncle Mike's Boot Grip; weights 15.8 oz. Introduced 1996. Made in U.S. by Smith & Wesson.
Price: $442.00

Smith & Wesson Model 642LS LadySmith Revolver Same as the Model 642 except has smooth combat wood grips, and comes with case; frosted matte finish. Introduced 1996. Made in U.S. by Smith & Wesson.
Price: $471.00

SMITH & WESSON MODEL 651 REVOLVER Caliber: 22 WMR, 6-shot cylinder. **Barrel:** 4″. **Weight:** 24½ oz. **Length:** 8¹¹/₁₆″ overall. **Stocks:** Soft rubber; wood optional. **Sights:** Red ramp front, adjustable micrometer click rear. **Features:** Stainless steel construction with semi-target hammer, smooth combat trigger. Reintroduced 1991. Limited production.
Price: $460.00

SMITH & WESSON MODEL 657 REVOLVER Caliber: 41 Mag., 6-shot. **Barrel:** 6″. **Weight:** 48 oz. **Length:** 11³/₈″ overall. **Stocks:** Soft rubber; wood optional. **Sights:** Pinned ¹/₈″ red ramp front, micro-click rear adjustable for windage and elevation. **Features:** Stainless steel construction.
Price: $528.00

TAURUS MODEL 44 REVOLVER Caliber: 44 Mag., 6-shot. **Barrel:** 4″, 6½″, 8³/₈″. **Weight:** 44³/₄ oz. (4″ barrel). **Length:** NA. **Stocks:** Soft black rubber. **Sights:** Serrated ramp front, micro-click rear adjustable for windage and elevation. **Features:** Heavy solid rib on 4″, vent rib on 6½″, 8³/₈″. Compensated barrel. Blued model has color case-hardened hammer and trigger. Introduced 1994. Imported by Taurus International.
Price: Blue, 4″ $425.00
Price: Blue, 6½″, 8³/₈″ $443.00
Price: Stainless, 4″ $484.00
Price: Stainless, 6½″, 8³/₈″ $504.00

TAURUS MODEL 66 REVOLVER Caliber: 357 Mag., 6-shot. **Barrel:** 2.5″, 4″, 6″. **Weight:** 35 oz.(4″ barrel). **Stocks:** Soft black rubber. **Sights:** Serrated ramp front, micro-click rear adjustable for windage and elevation. Red ramp front with white outline rear on stainlees models only. **Features:** Wide target-type hammer spur, floating firing pin, heavy barrel with shrouded ejector rod. Introduced 1978. Imported by Taurus International.
Price: Blue, 2.5″, 4″, 6″ $318.00
Price: Stainless, 2.5″, 4″, 6″ $392.00

Taurus Model 65 Revolver Same as the Model 66 except has fixed rear sight and ramp front. Available with 2.5″ or 4″ barrel only, round butt grip. Imported by Taurus International.
Price: Blue, 2.5″, 4″ $290.00
Price: Stainless, 2.5″, 4″ $357.00

TAURUS MODEL 80 STANDARD REVOLVER Caliber: 38 Spec., 6-shot. **Barrel:** 3″ or 4″. **Weight:** 30 oz. (4″ bbl.). **Length:** 9¹/₄″ overall (4″ bbl.). **Stocks:** Soft black rubber. **Sights:** Serrated ramp front, square notch rear. **Features:** Imported by Taurus International.
Price: Blue $252.00
Price: Stainless $299.00

TAURUS MODEL 82 HEAVY BARREL REVOLVER Caliber: 38 Spec., 6-shot. **Barrel:** 3″ or 4″, heavy. **Weight:** 34 oz. (4″ bbl.). **Length:** 9¹/₄″ overall (4″ bbl.). **Stocks:** Soft black rubber. **Sights:** Serrated ramp front, square notch rear. **Features:** Imported by Taurus International.
Price: Blue $252.00
Price: Stainless $295.00

Smith & Wesson Model 651

Smith & Wesson Model 657

Taurus Model 44

Taurus Model 66

Taurus Model 80

Taurus Model 82

TAURUS MODEL 83 REVOLVER **Caliber:** 38 Spec., 6-shot. **Barrel:** 4" only, heavy. **Weight:** 34 oz. **Stocks:** Soft black rubber. **Sights:** Ramp front, micro-click rear adjustable for windage and elevation. **Features:** Blue or nickel finish. Introduced 1977. Imported by Taurus International.
Price: Blue $265.00
Price: Stainless $309.00

TAURUS MODEL 85 REVOLVER **Caliber:** 38 Spec., 5-shot. **Barrel:** 2", 3". **Weight:** 21 oz. **Stocks:** Black rubber, boot grip. **Sights:** Ramp front, square notch rear. **Features:** Blue finish or stainless steel. Introduced 1980. Imported by Taurus International.
Price: Blue, 2", 3" $239.00
Price: Stainless steel $287.00

Taurus Model 85CH Revolver Same as the Model 85 except has 2" barrel only and concealed hammer. Soft rubber boot grip. Introduced 1991. Imported by Taurus International.
Price: Blue $239.00
Price: Stainless $287.00

TAURUS MODEL 94 REVOLVER **Caliber:** 22 LR, 9-shot cylinder. **Barrel:** 3", 4", 5". **Weight:** 25 oz. **Stocks:** Soft black rubber. **Sights:** Serrated ramp front, click-adjustable rear for windage and elevation. **Features:** Floating firing pin, color case-hardened hammer and trigger. Introduced 1989. Imported by Taurus International.
Price: Blue $293.00
Price: Stainless $339.00

TAURUS MODEL 96 REVOLVER **Caliber:** 22 LR, 6-shot. **Barrel:** 6". **Weight:** 34 oz. **Length:** NA. **Stocks:** Soft black rubber. **Sights:** Patridge-type front, micrometer click rear adjustable for windage and elevation. **Features:** Heavy solid barrel rib; target hammer; adjustable target trigger. Blue only. Imported by Taurus International.
Price: $358.00

TAURUS MODEL 441/431 REVOLVERS **Caliber:** 44 Spec., 5-shot. **Barrel:** 3", 4", 6". **Weight:** 40.4 oz. (6" barrel). **Length:** NA. **Stocks:** Soft black rubber. **Sights:** Serrated ramp front, micrometer click rear adjustable for windage and elevation. **Features:** Heavy barrel with solid rib and full-length ejector shroud. Introduced 1992. Imported by Taurus International.
Price: Model 441, Blue, 3", 4", 6" $298.00
Price: Model 441, Stainless, 3", 4", 6" $374.00
Price: Model 431 (fixed sights), blue, 2", 3", 4" $256.00
Price: Model 431 (fixed sights), stainless, 2", 3", 4" $350.00

TAURUS MODEL 605 REVOLVER **Caliber:** 357 Mag., 5-shot. **Barrel:** 2¼", 3". **Weight:** 24.5 oz. **Length:** NA. **Stocks:** Finger-groove Santoprene I. **Sights:** Serrated ramp front, fixed notch rear. **Features:** Heavy, solid rib barrel; floating firing pin. Blue or stainless. Introduced 1995. Imported by Taurus International.
Price: Blue $262.00
Price: Stainless $312.00
Price: Model 605CH (concealed hammer) 2¼", blue $262.00
Price: Model 605CH, stainless, 2¼" $312.00

TAURUS MODEL 607 REVOLVER **Caliber:** 357 Mag., 7-shot. **Barrel:** 4", 6½". **Weight:** 44 oz. **Length:** NA. **Stocks:** Santoprene I with finger grooves. **Sights:** Serrated ramp front, fully adjustable rear. **Features:** Ventilated rib with built-in compensator on 6½" barrel. Available in blue or stainless. Introduced 1995. Imported by Taurus international.
Price: Blue, 4" $425.00
Price: Blue, 6½" $443.00
Price: Stainless, 4" $484.00
Price: Stainless, 6½" $504.00

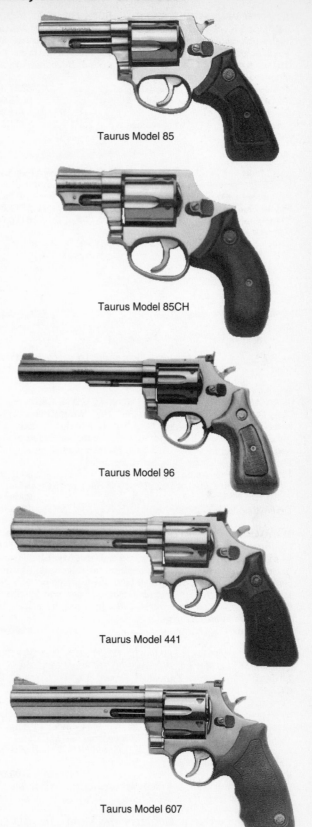

Taurus Model 85

Taurus Model 85CH

Taurus Model 96

Taurus Model 441

Taurus Model 607

Taurus Model 608 Revolver Same as the Model 607 except has 8-shot cylinder. Introduced 1996. Imported by Taurus International.
Price: Blue, 4" $425.00
Price: Blue, 6½" $443.00
Price: Stainless, 4" $484.00
Price: Stainless, 6½" $504.00

TAURUS MODEL 669 REVOLVER **Caliber:** 357 Mag., 6-shot. **Barrel:** 4″, 6″. **Weight:** 37 oz., (4″ bbl.). **Stocks:** Black rubber. **Sights:** Serrated ramp front, micro-click rear adjustable for windage and elevation. **Features:** Wide target-type hammer, floating firing pin, full-length barrel shroud. Introduced 1988. Imported by Taurus International.
Price: Blue, 4″, 6″ $327.00
Price: Blue, 4″, 6″ compensated $346.00
Price: Stainless, 4″, 6″ $401.00
Price: Stainless, 4″, 6″ compensated $421.00

Taurus Model 669

Taurus Model 689 Revolver Same as the Model 669 except has full-length ventilated barrel rib. Available in blue or stainless steel. Introduced 1990. From Taurus International.
Price: Blue, 4″ or 6″ $341.00
Price: Stainless, 4″ or 6″ $415.00

TAURUS MODEL 941 REVOLVER **Caliber:** 22 WMR, 8-shot. **Barrel:** 3″, 4″. **Weight:** 27.5 oz. (4″ barrel). **Length:** NA. **Stocks:** Soft black rubber. **Sights:** Serrated ramp front, rear adjustable for windage and elevation. **Features:** Solid rib heavy barrel with full-length ejector rod shroud. Blue or stainless steel. Introduced 1992. Imported by Taurus International.
Price: Blue $315.00
Price: Stainless $366.00

SINGLE-ACTION REVOLVERS

Both classic six-shooters and modern adaptations for hunting and sport.

AMERICAN ARMS REGULATOR SINGLE-ACTIONS **Caliber:** 357 Mag. 44-40, 45 Colt. **Barrel:** 4³/₄″, 5¹/₂″, 7¹/₂″. **Weight:** 32 oz. (4³/₄″ barrel). **Length:** 8¹/₆″ overall (4³/₄″ barrel). **Stocks:** Smooth walnut. **Sights:** Blade front, groove rear. **Features:** Blued barrel and cylinder, brass trigger guard and backstrap. Introduced 1992. Imported from Italy by American Arms, Inc.
Price: Regulator, single cylinder $349.00
Price: Regulator, dual cylinder (44-40/44 Spec. or 45 Colt/45 ACP) $399.00
Price: Regulator DLX (all steel) $395.00

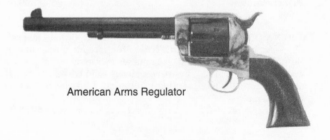

American Arms Regulator

AMERICAN FRONTIER POCKET RICHARDS & MASON NAVY **Caliber:** 32, 5-shot cylinder. **Barrel:** 4³/₄″, 5¹/₂″. **Weight:** NA. **Length:** NA. **Stocks:** Varnished walnut. **Sights:** Blade front, fixed rear. **Features:** Shoots metallic-cartridge ammunition. Non-rebated cylinder; high-polish blue, silver-plated brass backstrap and trigger guard; ejector assembly; color case-hardened hammer and trigger. Introduced 1996. Imported from Italy by American Frontier Firearms Co.
Price: From $495.00

American Frontier 1871-1872 Open-Top

AMERICAN FRONTIER 1871-1872 OPEN-TOP REVOLVERS **Caliber:** 38, 44. **Barrel:** 4³/₄″, 5¹/₂″, 7¹/₂″, 8″ round. **Weight:** NA. **Length:** NA. **Stocks:** Varnished walnut. **Sights:** Blade front, fixed rear. **Features:** Reproduction of the early cartridge conversions from percussion. Made for metallic cartridges. High polish blued steel, silver-plated brass backstrap and trigger guard, color case-hardened hammer; straight non-rebated cylinder with naval engagement engraving; stamped with original patent dates. Does not have conversion breechplate. Introduced 1996. Imported from Italy by American Frontier Firearms Co.
Price: $795.00
Price: Tiffany model with Tiffany grips, silver and gold finish with engraving $995.00

American Frontier Remington

AMERICAN FRONTIER REMINGTON NEW MODEL REVOLVER **Caliber:** 38, 44. **Barrel:** 5¹/₂″, 7¹/₂″. **Weight:** NA. **Length:** NA. **Stocks:** Varnished walnut. **Sights:** Blade front, fixed rear. **Features:** Replica of the factory conversions by Remington between 1863 and 1875. High polish blue or silver finish with color case-hardened hammer; with or without ejector rod and loading gate. Introduced 1996. Imported from Italy by American Frontier Firearms Co.
Price: $695.00

AMERICAN FRONTIER 1871-1872 POCKET MODEL REVOLVER **Caliber:** 32, 5-shot cylinder. **Barrel:** 4³/₄″, 5¹/₂″ round. **Weight:** NA. **Length:** NA. **Stocks:** Varnished walnut or Tiffany. **Sights:** Blade front, fixed rear. **Features:** Based on the 1862 Police percussion revolver converted to metallic cartridge. High polish blue finish with silver-plated brass backstrap and trigger guard, color case-hardened hammer. Introduced 1996. Imported from Italy by American Frontier Firearms Co.
Price: From $495.00

SINGLE-ACTION REVOLVERS

AMERICAN FRONTIER RICHARDS 1860 ARMY **Caliber:** 38, 44. **Barrel:** 4³/₄″, 5¹/₂″, 7¹/₂″, round. **Weight:** NA. **Length:** NA. **Stocks:** Varnished walnut, Army size. **Sights:** Blade front, fixed rear. **Features:** Shoots metallic cartridge ammunition. Rebated cylinder; available with or without ejector assembly; high-polish blue including backstrap; silver-plated trigger guard; color case-hardened hammer and trigger. Introduced 1996. Imported from Italy by American Frontier Firearms Co.
Price: **$695.00**

AMERICAN FRONTIER 1851 NAVY CONVERSION **Caliber:** 38, 44. **Barrel:** 4³/₄″, 5¹/₂″, 7¹/₂″, octagon. **Weight:** NA. **Length:** NA. **Stocks:** Varnished walnut, Navy size. **Sights:** Blade front, fixed rear. **Features:** Shoots metallic cartridge ammunition. Non-rebated cylinder; blued steel backstrap and trigger guard; color case-hardened hammer, trigger, ramrod, plunger; no ejector rod assembly. Introduced 1996. Imported from Italy by American Frontier Firearms Co.
Price: **$695.00**

American Frontier 1851 Navy Richards & Mason Conversion Similar to the 1851 Navy Conversion except has Mason ejector assembly. Introduced 1996. Imported from Italy by American Frontier Firearms Co.
Price: **$695.00**

CENTURY GUN DIST. MODEL 100 SINGLE-ACTION **Caliber:** 30-30, 375 Win., 444 Marlin, 45-70, 50-70. **Barrel:** 6¹/₂″ (standard), 8″, 10″, 12″. **Weight:** 6 lbs. (loaded). **Length:** 15″ overall (8″ bbl.). **Stocks:** Smooth walnut. **Sights:** Ramp front, Millett adjustable square notch rear. **Features:** Highly polished high tensile strength manganese bronze frame, blue cylinder and barrel; coil spring trigger mechanism. Calibers other than 45-70 start at $2,000.00. Contact maker for full price information. Introduced 1975. Made in U.S. From Century Gun Dist., Inc.
Price: 6¹/₂″ barrel, 45-70 . . . .**$1,250.00**

CIMARRON U.S. CAVALRY MODEL SINGLE-ACTION **Caliber:** 45 Colt **Barrel:** 7¹/₂″. **Weight:** 42 oz. **Length:** 13¹/₂″ overall. **Stocks:** Walnut. **Sights:** Fixed. **Features:** Has "A.P. Casey" markings; "U.S." plus patent dates on frame, serial number on backstrap, trigger guard, frame and cylinder, "APC" cartouche on left grip; color case-hardened frame and hammer, rest charcoal blue. Exact copy of the original. Imported by Cimarron Arms.
Price: **$469.00**

Cimarron Rough Rider Artillery Model Single-Action Similar to the U.S. Cavalry model except has 5¹/₂″ barrel, weighs 39 oz., and is 11¹/₂″ overall. U.S. markings and cartouche, case-hardened frame and hammer; 45 Colt only.
Price: **$469.00**

CIMARRON 1873 FRONTIER SIX SHOOTER **Caliber:** 38 WCF, 357 Mag., 44 WCF, 44 Spec., 45 Colt. **Barrel:** 4³/₄″, 5¹/₂″, 7¹/₂″. **Weight:** 39 oz. **Length:** 10″ overall (4″ barrel). **Stocks:** Walnut. **Sights:** Blade front, fixed or adjustable rear. **Features:** Uses "old model" blackpowder frame with "Bullseye" ejector or New Model frame. Imported by Cimarron Arms.
Price: 4³/₄″ barrel **$439.95**
Price: 5¹/₂″ barrel **$439.95**
Price: 7¹/₂″ barrel **$439.95**

COLT SINGLE ACTION ARMY REVOLVER **Caliber:** 44-40, 45 Colt, 6-shot. **Barrel:** 4³/₄″, 5¹/₂″, 7¹/₂″. **Weight:** 40 oz. (4³/₄″ barrel). **Length:** 10¹/₄″ overall (4³/₄″ barrel). **Stocks:** Black Eagle composite. **Sights:** Blade front, notch rear. **Features:** Available in full nickel finish with nickel grip medallions, or Royal Blue with color case-hardened frame, gold grip medallions. Reintroduced 1992.
Price: **$1,213.00**

American Frontier 1851 Mason

Century Model 100

Cimarron Frontier Six Shooter

Colt Single Action Army

Cimarron New Thunderer

CIMARRON NEW THUNDERER REVOLVER **Caliber:** 357 Mag., 44 WCF, 44 Spec., 45 Colt, 6-shot. **Barrel:** 3¹/₂″, 4³/₄″, with ejector. **Weight:** 38 oz. (3¹/₂″ barrel). **Length:** NA. **Stocks:** Hand-checkered walnut. **Sights:** Blade front, notch rear. **Features:** Thunderer grip; color case-hardened frame with balance blued, or nickel finish. Introduced 1993. Imported by Cimarron Arms.
Price: Color case-hardened **$439.95**
Price: Nickeled **$559.95**

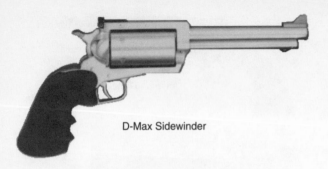

D-Max Sidewinder

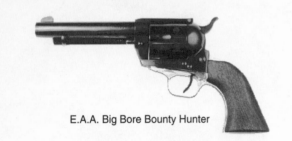

E.A.A. Big Bore Bounty Hunter

EMF Hartford

Freedom Arms Premier

FREEDOM ARMS PREMIER SINGLE-ACTION REVOLVER
Caliber: 44 Mag., 454 Casull with 45 Colt, 45 ACP, 45 Win. Mag. optional cylinders, 5-shot. Barrel: 4³/₄", 6", 7¹/₂", 10". Weight: 50 oz. Length: 14" overall (7¹/₂" bbl.). Stocks: Impregnated hardwood. Sights: Blade front, notch or adjustable rear. Features: All stainless steel construction; sliding bar safety system. Lifetime warranty. Made in U.S. by Freedom Arms, Inc.
Price: Field Grade (matte finish, Pachmayr grips), adjustable
  sights, 4³/₄", 6", 7¹/₂", 10" $1,301.00
Price: Field Grade, fixed sights, 4³/₄", 6", 7¹/₂", 10" $1,207.00
Price: Field Grade, 44 Rem. Mag., adjustable sights, all
  lengths $1,253.00
Price: Premier Grade 454 (brush finish, impregnated hardwood
  grips) adjustable sights, 4³/₄", 6", 7¹/₂", 10" $1,677.00
Price: Premier Grade, fixed sights, all barrel lengths . .$1,568.00
Price: Premier Grade, 44 Rem. Mag., adjustable sights, all
  lengths $1,627.00
Price: Fitted 45 ACP, 45 Colt or 45 Win. Mag cylinder,
  add $253.00

D-MAX SIDEWINDER REVOLVER Caliber: 45 Colt/410 shotshell, 6-shot. Barrel: 6.5", 7.5". Weight: 57 oz. (6.5"). Length: 14.1" (6.5" barrel). Stocks: Hogue black rubber with finger grooves. Sights: Blade on ramp front, fully adjustable rear. Features: Stainless steel construction. Has removable choke for firing shotshells. Grooved, wide-spur hammer; transfer bar ignition; satin stainless finish. Introduced 1992. Made in U.S. by D-Max, Inc.
Price: $750.00

E.A.A. BIG BORE BOUNTY HUNTER SA REVOLVERS Caliber: 357 Mag., 44 Mag., 45 Colt, 6-shot. Barrel: 4¹/₂", 7¹/₂". Weight: 2.5 lbs. Length: 11" overall (4⁵/₈" barrel). Stocks: Smooth walnut. Sights: Blade front, grooved topstrap rear. Features: Transfer bar safety; three position hammer; hammer forged barrel. Introduced 1992. Imported by European American Armory.
Price: Blue $299.00
Price: Color case-hardened frame $310.00

> Consult our Directory pages for
> the location of firms mentioned.

EMF DAKOTA 1875 OUTLAW REVOLVER Caliber: 357 Mag., 44-40, 45 Colt. Barrel: 7¹/₂". Weight: 46 oz. Length: 13¹/₂" overall. Stocks: Smooth walnut. Sights: Blade front, fixed groove rear. Features: Authentic copy of 1875 Remington with firing pin in hammer; color case-hardened frame, blue cylinder, barrel, steel backstrap and brass trigger guard. Also available in nickel, factory engraved. Imported by E.M.F.
Price: All calibers $465.00
Price: Nickel $550.00
Price: Engraved $600.00
Price: Engraved Nickel $710.00

EMF Dakota 1890 Police Revolver Similar to the 1875 Outlaw except has 5¹/₂" barrel, weighs 40 oz., with 12¹/₂" overall length. Has lanyard ring in butt. No web under barrel. Calibers 357, 44-40, 45 Colt. Imported by E.M.F.
Price: All calibers $470.00
Price: Nickel $560.00
Price: Engraved $620.00
Price: Engraved nickel $725.00

EMF Dakota New Model Single-Action Revolvers Similar to the standard Dakota except has color case-hardened forged steel frame, black nickel backstrap and trigger guard. Calibers 357 Mag., 44-40, 45 Colt only.
Price: $460.00
Price: Nickel $585.00

EMF HARTFORD SINGLE-ACTION REVOLVERS Caliber: 22 LR, 357 Mag., 32-20, 38-40, 44-40, 44 Spec., 45 Colt. Barrel: 4³/₄", 5¹/₂", 7¹/₂". Weight: 45 oz. Length: 13" overall (7¹/₂" barrel). Stocks: Smooth walnut. Sights: Blade front, fixed rear. Features: Identical to the original Colts with inspector cartouche on left grip, original patent dates and U.S. markings. All major parts serial numbered using original Colt-style lettering, numbering. Bullseye ejector head and color case-hardening on frame and hammer. Introduced 1990. From E.M.F.
Price: $600.00
Price: Cavalry or Artillery $655.00
Price: Nickel plated $725.00
Price: Engraved, nickel plated $840.00
Price: Pinkerton (bird's-head grip), 45 Colt, 4" barrel . . .$680.00

EMF 1894 Target Bisley Revolver Similar to the Hartford single-action revolver except has special grip frame and trigger guard, wide spur hammer; available in 45 Colt only, 5¹/₂" or 7¹/₂" barrel. Introduced 1995. Imported by E.M.F.
Price: Blue $680.00
Price: Nickel $805.00

SINGLE-ACTION REVOLVERS

Freedom Arms Model 353 Revolver Similar to the Premier 454 Casull except chambered for 357 Magnum with 5-shot cylinder; 4³/₄", 6", 7¹/₂" or 9" barrel. Weighs 59 oz. with 7¹/₂" barrel. Field grade model has adjustable sights, matte finish, Pachmayr grips, 7¹/₂" or 10" barrel; Silhouette has 9" barrel, Patridge front sight, Iron Sight Gun Works Silhouette adjustable rear, Pachmayr grips, trigger over-travel adjustment screw. All stainless steel. Introduced 1992.
Price: Field Grade $1,253.00
Price: Premier Grade (brushed finish, impregnated hardwood
  grips, Premier Grade sights) $1,627.00
Price: Silhouette (9", 357 Mag., 10", 44 Mag.) $1,347.00

Heritage Rough Rider

Freedom Arms Model 555 Revolver Same as the 454 Casull except chambered for the 50 A.E. (Action Express) cartridge. Offered in Premier and Field Grades with adjustable sights, 4³/₄", 6", 7¹/₂" or 10" barrel. Introduced 1994. Made in U.S. by Freedom Arms, Inc.
Price: Premier Grade $1,677.00
Price: Field Grade $1,301.00

HERITAGE ROUGH RIDER REVOLVER Caliber: 22 LR, 22 LR/22 WMR combo, 6-shot. **Barrel:** 2³/₄", 3¹/₂", 4³/₄", 6¹/₂", 9". **Weight:** 31 to 38 oz. **Length:** NA **Stocks:** Exotic hardwood. **Sights:** Blade front, fixed rear. **Features:** Hammer block safety. High polish blue or nickel finish. Introduced 1993. Made in U.S. by Heritage Mfg., Inc.
Price: . . . .$109.95 to $169.95
Price: 2³/₄", 3¹/₂", 4³/₄" birdshead grip . . . .$129.95 to $149.95

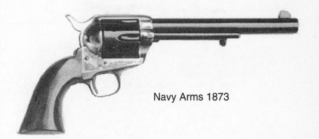

Navy Arms 1873

NAVY ARMS 1873 SINGLE-ACTION REVOLVER Caliber: 44-40, 45 Colt, 6-shot cylinder. **Barrel:** 3", 4³/₄", 5¹/₂", 7¹/₂". **Weight:** 36 oz. **Length:** 10³/₄" overall (5¹/₂" barrel). **Stocks:** Smooth walnut. **Sights:** Blade front, groove in topstrap rear. **Features:** Blue with color case-hardened frame, or nickel. Introduced 1991. Imported by Navy Arms.
Price: Blue $390.00
Price: Nickel $455.00
Price: 1873 U.S. Cavalry Model (7¹/₂", 45 Colt, arsenal
  markings) $480.00
Price: 1895 U.S. Artillery Model (as above, 5¹/₂" barrel) .$480.00

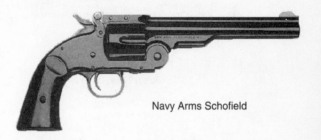

Navy Arms Schofield

NAVY ARMS 1875 SCHOFIELD REVOLVER Caliber: 44-40, 44 S&W Spec., 45 Colt, 6-shot cylinder. **Barrel:** 5", 7". **Weight:** 39 oz. **Length:** 10³/₄" overall (5" barrel). **Stocks:** Smooth walnut. **Sights:** Blade front, notch rear. **Features:** Replica of Smith & Wesson Model 3 Schofield. Single-action, top-break with automatic ejection. Polished blue finish. Introduced 1994. Imported by Navy Arms.
Price: Wells Fargo (5" barrel, Wells Fargo markings) . . .$795.00
Price: U.S. Cavalry model (7" barrel, military markings) $795.00

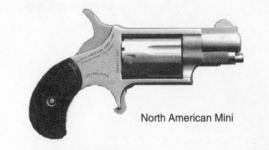

North American Mini

NORTH AMERICAN MINI-REVOLVERS Caliber: 22 Short, 22 LR, 22 WMR, 5-shot. **Barrel:** 1¹/₈", 1⁵/₈". **Weight:** 4 to 6.6 oz. **Length:** 3⁵/₈" to 6¹/₈" overall. **Stocks:** Laminated wood. **Sights:** Blade front, notch fixed rear. **Features:** All stainless steel construction. Polished satin and matte finish. Engraved models available. From North American Arms.
Price: 22 Short, 22 LR, 1¹/₈" bbl. $157.00
Price: 22 LR, 1⁵/₈" bbl. $157.00
Price: 22 WMR, 1⁵/₈" bbl. $178.00
Price: 22 WMR, 1¹/₈" or 1⁵/₈" bbl. with extra 22 LR
  cylinder $210.00

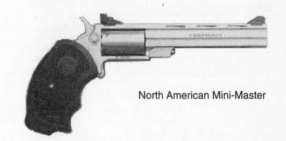

North American Mini-Master

North American Black Widow Revolver Similar to the Mini-Master except has 2" heavy vent barrel. Built on the 22 WMR frame. Non-fluted cylinder, black rubber grips. Available with either Millett Low Profile fixed sights or Millett sight adjustable for elevation only. Overall length 5⁷/₈", weighs 8.8 oz. From North American Arms.
Price: Adjustable sight, 22 LR or 22 WMR $249.00
Price: As above with extra WMR/LR cylinder $285.00
Price: Fixed sight, 22 LR or 22 WMR $235.00
Price: As above with extra WMR/LR cylinder $270.00

NORTH AMERICAN MINI-MASTER Caliber: 22 LR, 22 WMR, 5-shot cylinder. **Barrel:** 4". **Weight:** 10.7 oz. **Length:** 7.75" overall. **Stocks:** Checkered hard black rubber. **Sights:** Blade front, white outline rear adjustable for elevation, or fixed. **Features:** Heavy vent barrel; full-size grips. Non-fluted cylinder. Introduced 1989.
Price: Adjustable sight, 22 WMR or 22 LR $279.00
Price: As above with extra WMR/LR cylinder $317.00
Price: Fixed sight, 22 WMR or 22 LR $264.00
Price: As above with extra WMR/LR cylinder $302.00

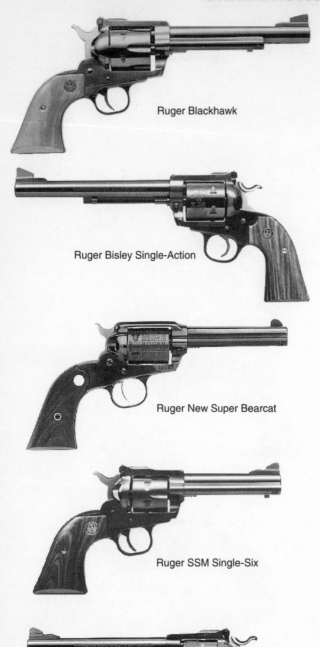

Ruger Blackhawk

Ruger Bisley Single-Action

Ruger New Super Bearcat

Ruger SSM Single-Six

Ruger Bisley Small Frame

RUGER BLACKHAWK REVOLVER Caliber: 30 Carbine, 357 Mag./38 Spec., 41 Mag., 45 Colt, 6-shot. **Barrel:** 4⁵/₈″ or 6¹/₂″, either caliber; 7¹/₂″ (30 Carbine, 45 Colt only). **Weight:** 42 oz. (6¹/₂″ bbl.). **Length:** 12¹/₄″ overall (6¹/₂″ bbl.). **Stocks:** American walnut. **Sights:** ¹/₈″ ramp front, micro-click rear adjustable for windage and elevation. **Features:** Ruger transfer bar safety system, independent firing pin, hardened chrome-moly steel frame, music wire springs throughout.
Price: Blue, 30 Carbine (7¹/₂″ bbl.), BN31 . . . .$360.00
Price: Blue, 357 Mag. (4⁵/₈″, 6¹/₂″), BN34, BN36 . . . .$360.00
Price: Blue, 357/9mm Convertible (4⁵/₈″, 6¹/₂″), BN34X, BN36X $360.00
Price: Blue, 41 Mag., 45 Colt (4⁵/₈″, 6¹/₂″), BN41, BN42, BN45 . . . .$360.00
Price: Stainless, 357 Mag. (4⁵/₈″, 6¹/₂″), KBN34, KBN36 .$443.00
Price: High-gloss stainless, 357 Mag. (4⁵/₈″, 6¹/₂″), GKBN34, GKBN36 . . . .$443.00
Price: High-gloss stainless, 45 Colt (4⁵/₈″, 7¹/₂″), GKBN44, GKBN45 . . . .$443.00

Ruger Bisley Single-Action Revolver Similar to standard Blackhawk except the hammer is lower with a smoothly curved, deeply checkered wide spur. The trigger is strongly curved with a wide smooth surface. Longer grip frame has a hand-filling shape. Adjustable rear sight, ramp-style front. Has an unfluted cylinder and roll engraving, adjustable sights. Chambered for 357, 41, 44 Mags. and 45 Colt; 7¹/₂″ barrel; overall length of 13″. Introduced 1985.
Price: $430.00

RUGER SUPER BLACKHAWK Caliber: 44 Mag., 6-shot. Also fires 44 Spec. **Barrel:** 4⁵/₈″, 5¹/₂″, 7¹/₂″, 10¹/₂″. **Weight:** 48 oz. (7¹/₂″ bbl.), 51 oz. (10¹/₂″ bbl.). **Length:** 13³/₈″ overall (7¹/₂″ bbl.). **Stocks:** American walnut. **Sights:** ¹/₈″ ramp front, micro-click rear adjustable for windage and elevation. **Features:** Ruger transfer bar safety system, non-fluted cylinder, steel grip and cylinder frame, square back trigger guard, wide serrated trigger and wide spur hammer.
Price: Blue (S45N, S47N, S411N) $413.00
Price: Stainless (KS45N, KS47N, KS411N) $450.00
Price: High-gloss stainless (4⁵/₈″, 5¹/₂″, 7¹/₂″), GKS458N, GKS45N, GKS47N $450.00

RUGER NEW SUPER BEARCAT SINGLE-ACTION Caliber: 22 LR, 6-shot. **Barrel:** 4″. **Weight:** 23 oz. **Length:** 8⁷/₈″ overall. **Stocks:** Smooth rosewood with Ruger medallion. **Sights:** Blade front, fixed notch rear. **Features:** Reintroduction of the Ruger Super Bearcat with slightly lengthened frame, Ruger patented transfer bar safety system. Available in blue only. Introduced 1993. From Sturm, Ruger & Co.
Price: SBC4, blue $298.00

RUGER SUPER SINGLE-SIX CONVERTIBLE Caliber: 22 LR, 6-shot; 22 WMR in extra cylinder. **Barrel:** 4⁵/₈″, 5¹/₂″, 6¹/₂″, or 9¹/₂″ (6-groove). **Weight:** 34¹/₂ oz. (6¹/₂″ bbl.). **Length:** 11¹³/₁₆″ overall (6¹/₂″ bbl.). **Stocks:** Smooth American walnut. **Sights:** Improved Patridge front on ramp, fully adjustable rear protected by integral frame ribs; or fixed sight. **Features:** Ruger transfer bar safety system, gate-controlled loading, hardened chrome-moly steel frame, wide trigger, music wire springs throughout, independent firing pin.
Price: 4⁵/₈″, 5¹/₂″, 6¹/₂″, 9¹/₂″ barrel, blue, fixed or adjustable sight (5¹/₂″, 6¹/₂″) $313.00
Price: 5¹/₂″, 6¹/₂″ bbl. only, high-gloss stainless steel, fixed or adjustable sight $353.00

Ruger Bisley Small Frame Revolver Similar to the Single-Six except frame is styled after the classic Bisley "flat-top." Most mechanical parts are unchanged. Hammer is lower and smoothly curved with a deeply checkered spur. Trigger is strongly curved with a wide smooth surface. Longer grip frame designed with a hand-filling shape, and the trigger guard is a large oval. Adjustable dovetail rear sight; front sight base accepts interchangeable square blades of various heights and styles. Has an unfluted cylinder and roll engraving. Weighs about 41 oz. Chambered for 22 LR and 32 H&R Mag., 6¹/₂″ barrel only. Introduced 1985.
Price: $360.00

Ruger SSM Single-Six Revolver Similar to the Super Single-Six revolver except chambered for 32 H&R Magnum (also handles 32 S&W and 32 S&W Long). Weighs about 34 oz. with 6¹/₂″ barrel. Barrel lengths: 4⁵/₈″, 5¹/₂″, 6¹/₂″, 9¹/₂″. Introduced 1985.
Price: $313.00

Ruger Vaquero

Texas Longhorn Grover's No. Five

Texas Longhorn Border Special

Texas Longhorn South Texas Army

Texas Longhorn Flat Top

RUGER VAQUERO SINGLE-ACTION REVOLVER Caliber: 44-40, 44 Mag., 45 Colt, 6-shot. **Barrel:** 4⅝", 5½", 7½". **Weight:** 41 oz. **Length:** 13⅜" overall (7½" barrel). **Stocks:** Smooth rosewood with Ruger medallion. **Sights:** Blade front, fixed notch rear. **Features:** Uses Ruger's patented transfer bar safety system and loading gate interlock with classic styling. Blued model has color case-hardened finish on the frame, the rest polished and blued. Stainless model has high-gloss polish. Introduced 1993. From Sturm, Ruger & Co.
Price: BNV44 (4⅝"), BNV445 (5½"), BNV45 (7½"), blue $434.00
Price: KBNV44 (4⅝"), KBNV455 (5½"), KBNV45 (7½"), stainless $434.00

> Consult our Directory pages for the location of firms mentioned.

TEXAS LONGHORN ARMS GROVER'S IMPROVED NO. FIVE Caliber: 44 Mag., 6-shot. **Barrel:** 5½". **Weight:** 44 oz. **Length:** 11½" overall. **Stocks:** Smooth walnut. **Sights:** Square blade front on ramp, fully adjustable rear. **Features:** Music wire coil spring action with double locking bolt; polished blue finish. Handmade in limited 1,200-gun production. Grip contour, straps, over-sized base pin, lever latch and lockwork identical copies of Elmer Keith design. Lifetime warranty to original owner. Introduced 1988.
Price: $1,195.00

TEXAS LONGHORN ARMS RIGHT-HAND SINGLE-ACTION Caliber: All centerfire pistol calibers. **Barrel:** 4¾". **Weight:** 40 oz. **Length:** 10¼" overall. **Stocks:** One-piece fancy walnut. **Sights:** Blade front, grooved topstrap rear. **Features:** Loading gate and ejector housing on left side of gun. Cylinder rotates to the left. All steel construction; color case-hardened frame; high polish blue; music wire coil springs. Lifetime guarantee to original owner. Introduced 1984. From Texas Longhorn Arms.
Price: South Texas Army Limited Edition—handmade, only 1,000 to be produced; "One of One Thousand" engraved on barrel $1,595.00

Texas Longhorn Arms Sesquicentennial Model Revolver Similar to the South Texas Army Model except has ¾-coverage Nimschke-style engraving, antique golden nickel plate finish, one-piece elephant ivory grips. Comes with handmade solid walnut presentation case, factory letter to owner. Limited edition of 150 units. Introduced 1986.
Price: $2,500.00

Texas Longhorn Arms Texas Border Special Similar to the South Texas Army Limited Edition except has 4" barrel, bird's-head style grip. Same special features. Introduced 1984.
Price: $1,595.00

Texas Longhorn Arms West Texas Flat Top Target Similar to the South Texas Army Limited Edition except choice of barrel length from 7½" through 15"; flat-top style frame; ⅛" contoured ramp front sight, old model steel micro-click rear adjustable for windage and elevation. Same special features. Introduced 1984.
Price: $1,595.00

Texas Longhorn Arms Cased Set Set contains one each of the Texas Longhorn Right-Hand Single-Actions, all in the same caliber, same serial numbers (100, 200, 300, 400, 500, 600, 700, 800, 900). Ten sets to be made (#1000 donated to NRA museum). Comes in hand-tooled leather case. All other specs same as Limited Edition guns. Introduced 1984.
Price: $5,750.00
Price: With ¾-coverage "C-style" engraving $7,650.00

SINGLE-ACTION REVOLVERS

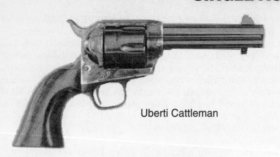

Uberti Cattleman

Uberti 1875 Army

U.S. PATENT FIRE ARMS SINGLE ACTIONS Caliber: 22 LR/22 WMR, 38 Spec., 357 Mag., 38-40, 44-40, 44 Spec., 45 ACP, 45 Colt. **Barrel:** 3″, 4″ (44-40 and 45 Colt only), 4³/₄″, 5¹/₂″, 7¹/₂″. **Weight:** 37 oz. (7¹/₂″ barrel). **Length:** 13″ overall (7¹/₂″ barrel). **Stocks:** Smooth walnut. **Sights:** Blade front, grooved topstrap rear. **Features:** Available in blue with color case-hardening, nickel, or all blue. Recreation of original Colt-style revolvers, finishes and engraving; many options offered. (No ejector on 3″, 4″ barrels. Introduced 1996. From United States Patent Fire Arms Mfg. Co.
Price: From . . . .$737.00 to $750.00
Price: Nickel plated . . . .$789.00 to $811.00

UBERTI 1873 CATTLEMAN SINGLE ACTIONS Caliber: 22 LR/22 WMR, 38 Spec., 357 Mag., 44 Spec., 44-40, 45 Colt/45 ACP, 6-shot. **Barrel:** 4³/₄″, 5¹/₂″, 7¹/₂″; 44-40, 45 Colt also with 3″, 3¹/₂″, 4″. **Weight:** 38 oz. (5¹/₂″ bbl.). **Length:** 10³/₄″ overall (5¹/₂″ bbl.). **Stocks:** One-piece smooth walnut. **Sights:** Blade front, groove rear; fully adjustable rear available. **Features:** Steel or brass backstrap, trigger guard; color case-hardened frame, blued barrel, cylinder. Imported from Italy by Uberti U.S.A.
Price: Steel backstrap, trigger guard, fixed sights $435.00
Price: Brass backstrap, trigger guard, fixed sights $365.00
Price: Bisley model $435.00

Uberti 1873 Buckhorn Single Action A slightly larger version of the Cattleman revolver. Available in 44 Magnum or 44 Magnum/44-40 convertible, otherwise has same specs.
Price: Steel backstrap, trigger guard, fixed sights $410.00
Price: Convertible (two cylinders) $475.00

UBERTI 1875 SA ARMY OUTLAW REVOLVER Caliber: 357 Mag., 44-40, 45 Colt, 45 Colt/45 ACP convertible, 6-shot. **Barrel:** 5¹/₂″, 7¹/₂″. **Weight:** 44 oz. **Length:** 13³/₄″ overall. **Stocks:** Smooth walnut. **Sights:** Blade front, notch rear. **Features:** Replica of the 1875 Remington S.A. Army revolver. Brass trigger guard, color case-hardened frame, rest blued. Imported by Uberti U.S.A.
Price: $435.00
Price: 45 Colt/45 ACP convertible $475.00

UBERTI 1890 ARMY OUTLAW REVOLVER Caliber: 357 Mag., 44-40, 45 Colt, 45 Colt/45 ACP convertible, 6-shot. **Barrel:** 5¹/₂″, 7¹/₂″. **Weight:** 37 oz. **Length:** 12¹/₂″ overall. **Stocks:** American walnut. **Sights:** Blade front, groove rear. **Features:** Replica of the 1890 Remington single-action. Brass trigger guard, rest is blued. Imported by Uberti U.S.A.
Price: $435.00
Price: 45 Colt/45 ACP convertible $475.00

MISCELLANEOUS HANDGUNS

Specially adapted single-shot and multi-barrel arms.

American Derringer Model 1

American Derringer Model 4 Similar to the Model 1 except has 4.1″ barrel, overall length of 6″, and weighs 16¹/₂ oz.; chambered for 357 Mag., 357 Maximum, 45-70, 3″ 410-bore shotshells or 45 Colt or 44 Mag. Made of stainless steel. Manual hammer block safety. Introduced 1985.
Price: 3″ 410/45 Colt $352.00
Price: 3″ 410/45 Colt or 45-70 (Alaskan Survival model) .$388.00
Price: 44 Mag. with oversize grips $422.00
Price: Alaskan Survival model (45-70 upper, 410 or 45 Colt lower) $388.00

AMERICAN DERRINGER MODEL 1 Caliber: 22 LR, 22 WMR, 30 Carbine, 30 Luger, 30-30 Win., 32 H&R Mag., 32-20, 380 ACP, 38 Super, 38 Spec., 38 Spec. shotshell, 38 Spec. +P, 9mm Para., 357 Mag., 357 Mag./45/410, 357 Maximum, 10mm, 40 S&W, 41 Mag., 38-40, 44-40 Win., 44 Spec., 44 Mag., 45 Colt, 45 Win. Mag., 45 ACP, 45 Colt/410, 45-70 single shot. **Barrel:** 3″. **Weight:** 15¹/₂ oz. (38 Spec.). **Length:** 4.82″ overall. **Stocks:** Rosewood, Zebra wood. **Sights:** Blade front. **Features:** Made of stainless steel with high-polish or satin finish. Two-shot capacity. Manual hammer block safety. Introduced 1980. Available in almost any pistol caliber. Contact the factory for complete list of available calibers and prices. From American Derringer Corp.
Price: 22 LR $245.00
Price: 38 Spec. $245.00
Price: 357 Maximum $265.00
Price: 357 Mag. $257.00
Price: 9mm, 380, ...$245.00
Price: 40 S&W $257.00
Price: 44 Spec., ...$320.00
Price: 44-40 Win., 45 Colt $320.00
Price: 30-30, 41, 44 Mags., 45 Win. Mag. . . . .$375.00 to $385.00
Price: 45-70, single shot $312.00
Price: 45 Colt, 410, 2¹/₂″ $320.00
Price: 45 ACP, 10mm Auto $257.00

American Derringer Model 10 Lightweight Similar to the Model 1 except frame is of aluminum, giving weight of 10 oz. Stainless barrels. Available in 38 Spec., 45 Colt or 45 ACP only. Matte gray finish. Introduced 1989.
Price: 45 Colt $320.00
Price: 45 ACP $257.00
Price: 38 Spec. $240.00

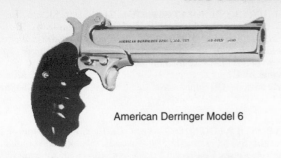

American Derringer Model 6

Anschutz Exemplar

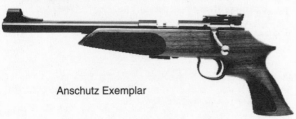

Anschutz Exemplar Hornet

Davis 22 Derringer

Davis D-38 Derringer

DAVIS DERRINGERS Caliber: 22 LR, 22 WMR, 25 ACP, 32 ACP. **Barrel:** 2.4″. **Weight:** 9.5 oz. **Length:** 4″ overall. **Stocks:** Laminated wood. **Sights:** Blade front, fixed notch rear. **Features:** Choice of black Teflon or chrome finish; spur trigger. Introduced 1986. Made in U.S. by Davis Industries.
Price: $75.00

DAVIS D-SERIES DERRINGERS Caliber: 22 WMR, 32 H&R, 38 Spec.. **Barrel:** 2.75″. **Weight:** 11.5 oz. **Length:** 4.65″ overall. **Stocks:** Textured black synthetic. **Sights:** Blade front, fixed notch rear. **Features:** Alloy frame, steel-lined barrels, steel breech block. Plunger-type safety with integral hammer block. Chrome or black Teflon finish. Introduced 1992. Made in U.S. by Davis Industries.
Price: $98.00

American Derringer Model 6 Similar to the Model 1 except has 6″ barrel chambered for 3″ 410 shotshells or 22 WMR, 357 Mag., 45 ACP, 45 Colt; rosewood stocks; 8.2″ o.a.l. and weighs 21 oz. Shoots either round for each barrel. Manual hammer block safety. Introduced 1986.
Price: 22 WMR $300.00
Price: 357 Mag. $300.00
Price: 45 Colt/410 ....$363.00
Price: 45 ACP $345.00

American Derringer Model 7 Ultra Lightweight Similar to Model 1 except made of high strength aircraft aluminum. Weighs 7½ oz., 4.82″ o.a.l., rosewood stocks. Available in 22 LR, 22 WMR, 32 H&R Mag., 380 ACP, 38 Spec., 44 Spec. Introduced 1986.
Price: 22 LR, WMR $240.00
Price: 38 Spec. $240.00
Price: 380 ACP $240.00
Price: 32 H&R Mag. $240.00
Price: 44 Spec. $500.00

American Derringer Lady Derringer Same as the Model 1 except has tuned action, is fitted with scrimshawed synthetic ivory grips; chambered for 32 H&R Mag. and 38 Spec.; 357 Mag., 45 Colt. Deluxe Grade is highly polished; Deluxe Engraved is engraved in a pattern similar to that used on 1880s derringers. All come in a French fitted jewelry box. Introduced 1991.
Price: 32 H&R Mag. $280.00
Price: 357 Mag. $300.00
Price: 38 Spec. $200.00
Price: 45 Colt $345.00

American Derringer Texas Commemorative A Model 1 Derringer with solid brass frame, stainless steel barrel and rosewood grips. Available in 38 Spec., 44-40 Win., or 45 Colt. Introduced 1987.
Price: 38 Spec. $280.00
Price: 44-40 or 45 Colt $345.00

AMERICAN DERRINGER DA 38 MODEL Caliber: 22 LR, 9mm Para., 38 Spec., 357 Mag., 40 S&W. **Barrel:** 3″. **Weight:** 14.5 oz. **Length:** 4.8″ overall. **Stocks:** Rosewood, walnut or other hardwoods. **Sights:** Fixed. **Features:** Double-action only; two-shots. Manual safety. Made of satin-finished stainless steel and aluminum. Introduced 1989. From American Derringer Corp.
Price: 22 LR, 38 Spec. $300.00
Price: 9mm Para. $325.00
Price: 357 Mag., 40 S&W $350.00

ANSCHUTZ EXEMPLAR BOLT-ACTION PISTOL Caliber: 22 LR, 5-shot; 22 Hornet, 5-shot. **Barrel:** 10″. **Weight:** 3½ lbs. **Length:** 17″ overall. **Stock:** European walnut with stippled grip and forend. **Sights:** Hooded front on ramp, open notch rear adjustable for windage and elevation. **Features:** Uses Match 64 action with left-hand bolt; Anschutz #5091 two-stage trigger set at 9.85 oz. Receiver grooved for scope mounting; open sights easily removed. The 22 Hornet version uses Match 54 action with left-hand bolt, Anschutz #5099 two-stage trigger set at 19.6 oz. Introduced 1987. Imported from Germany by AcuSport Corp.
Price: 22 LR $580.75
Price: 22 LR, left-hand $473.14
Price: 22 Hornet (no sights, 10″ bbl.) $1,009.89

DAVIS LONG-BORE DERRINGERS Caliber: 22 WMR, 32 H&R Mag., 38 Spec., 9mm Para. **Barrel:** 3.5″. **Weight:** 16 oz. **Length:** 5.4″ overall. **Stocks:** Textured black synthetic. **Sights:** Fixed. **Features:** Chrome or black teflon finish. Larger than Davis D-Series models. Introduced 1995. Made in U.S. by Davis Industries.
Price: $104.00
Price: Big-Bore models (same calibers, ¾″ shorter barrels) $98.00

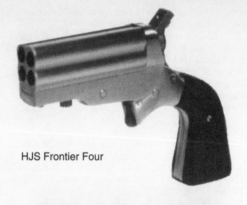

HJS Frontier Four

Magnum Research Lone Eagle

Mitchell Guardian Angel

Maximum Single Shot

GAUCHER GN1 SILHOUETTE PISTOL Caliber: 22 LR, single shot. **Barrel:** 10″. **Weight:** 2.4 lbs. **Length:** 15.5″ overall. **Stocks:** European hardwood. **Sights:** Blade front, open adjustable rear. **Features:** Bolt action, adjustable trigger. Introduced 1990. Imported from France by Mandall Shooting Supplies.
Price: About **$525.00**
Price: Model GP Silhouette **$425.00**

HJS FRONTIER FOUR DERRINGER Caliber: 22 LR. **Barrel:** 2″. **Weight:** 5½ oz. **Length:** 3¹⁵/₁₆″ overall. **Stocks:** Brown plastic. **Sights:** None. **Features:** Four barrels fire with rotating firing pin. Stainless steel construction. Introduced 1993. Made in U.S. by HJS Arms, Inc.
Price: **$165.00**

HJS Antigua Derringer Same as the Frontier Four except blued barrel, brass frame, brass pivot pins. Brown plastic grips. Introduced 1994. Made in U.S. by HJS Arms, Inc.
Price: **$180.00**

HJS LONE STAR DERRINGER Caliber: 380 ACP. **Barrel:** 2″. **Weight:** 6 oz. **Length:** 3¹⁵/₁₆″ overall. **Stocks:** Brown plastic. **Sights:** Groove. **Features:** Stainless steel construction. Beryllium copper firing pin. Button-rifled barrel. Introduced 1993. Made in U.S. by HJS Arms, Inc.
Price: **$185.00**

LORCIN OVER/UNDER DERRINGER Caliber: 38 Spec./357 Mag., 45 ACP. **Barrel:** 3.5″. **Weight:** NA. **Length:** 6.5″ overall. **Stocks:** Black composition. **Sights:** Blade front, fixed rear. **Features:** Stainless steel construction. Rebounding hammer. Introduced 1996. Made in U.S. by Lorcin Engineering.
Price: **$129.00**

MAGNUM RESEARCH LONE EAGLE SINGLE SHOT PISTOL Caliber: 22 Hornet, 223, 22-250, 243, 7mm BR, 7mm-08, 30-30, 7.62x39, 308, 30-06, 357 Max., 35 Rem., 358 Win., 44 Mag., 444 Marlin. **Barrel:** 14″, interchangable. **Weight:** 4lbs., 3 oz. to 4 lbs., 7 oz. **Length:** 15″ overall. **Stocks:** Ambidextrous. **Sights:** None furnished; drilled and tapped for scope mounting and open sights. Open sights optional. **Features:** Cannon-type rotating breech with spring-activated ejector. Ordnance steel with matte blue finish. Cross-bolt safety. External cocking lever on left side of gun. Introduced 1991. Available from Magnum Research, Inc.
Price: Complete pistol **$408.00**
Price: Barreled action only **$289.00**
Price: Scope base **$14.00**
Price: Adjustable open sights **$35.00**

MANDALL/CABANAS PISTOL Caliber: 177, pellet or round ball; single shot. **Barrel:** 9″. **Weight:** 51 oz. **Length:** 19″ overall. **Stock:** Smooth wood with thumbrest. **Sights:** Blade front on ramp, open adjustable rear. **Features:** Fires round ball or pellets with 22 blank cartridge. Automatic safety; muzzlebrake. Imported from Mexico by Mandall Shooting Supplies.
Price: **$139.95**

MITCHELL ARMS GUARDIAN ANGEL PISTOL Caliber: 22 LR, 22 WMR, 2-shot. **Barrel:** 1¾″. **Weight:** 7½ oz. **Length:** 4¾″ overall. **Stocks:** Checkered black synthetic. **Sights:** Fixed channel. **Features:** Uses a pre-loaded, drop-in 2-shot removable breechblock; double-action-only. Available in nickel, black nickel, satin steel, gold finishes. Deluxe comes in jewel box with angel charm. Introduced 1996. Made in U.S. by Mitchell Arms.
Price: ....**$142.95** to **$199.95**

MAXIMUM SINGLE SHOT PISTOL Caliber: 22 LR, 22 Hornet, 22 BR, 22 PPC, 223 Rem., 22-250, 6mm BR, 6mm PPC, 243, 250 Savage, 6.5mm-35M, 270 MAX, 270 Win., 7mm TCU, 7mm BR, 7mm-35, 7mm INT-R, 7mm-08, 7mm Rocket, 7mm Super Mag., 30 Herrett, 30 Carbine, 30-30, 308 Win., 30x39, 32-20, 350 Rem. Mag., 357 Mag., 357 Maximum, 358 Win., 44 Mag., 454 Casull. **Barrel:** 8¾″, 10½″, 14″. **Weight:** 61 oz. (10½″ bbl.); 78 oz. (14″ bbl.). **Length:** 15″, 18½″ overall (with 10½″ and 14″ bbl., respectively). **Stocks:** Smooth walnut stocks and forend. Also available with 17° finger groove grip. **Sights:** Ramp front, fully adjustable open rear. **Features:** Falling block action; drilled and tapped for M.O.A. scope mounts; integral grip frame/receiver; adjustable trigger; Douglas barrel (interchangeable). Introduced 1983. Made in U.S. by M.O.A. Corp.
Price: Stainless receiver, blue barrel **$653.00**
Price: Stainless receiver, stainless barrel **$711.00**
Price: Extra blued barrel **$164.00**
Price: Extra stainless barrel **$222.00**
Price: Scope mount **$52.00**

NEW ADVANTAGE ARMS DERRINGER Caliber: 22 LR, 22 WMR, 4-shot. **Barrel:** 2½". **Weight:** 15 oz. **Length:** 4½" overall. **Stocks:** Smooth walnut. **Sights:** Fixed. **Features:** Double-action mechanism, four barrels, revolving hammer with four firing pins. Rebounding hammer. Blue or stainless. Reintroduced 1989. From New Advantage Arms Corp.
Price: 22 LR, 22 WMR, blue, about $249.99
Price: As above, stainless, about $249.99

New Advantage Derringer

RPM XL SINGLE SHOT PISTOL Caliber: 22 LR through 45-70. **Barrel:** 8", 10¾", 12", 14". **Weight:** About 60 oz. **Length:** NA. **Stocks:** Smooth Goncalo Alves with thumb and heel rests. **Sights:** Hooded front with interchangeable post, or Patridge; ISGW rear adjustable for windage and elevation. **Features:** Barrel drilled and tapped for scope mount. Visible cocking indicator. Spring-loaded barrel lock, positive hammer-block safety. Trigger adjustable for weight of pull and over-travel. Contact maker for complete price list. Made in U.S. by RPM.
Price: Hunter model (stainless frame, 5/16" underlug, latch lever and positive extractor) $1,195.00
Price: Silhouette model (chrome-moly frame, blue or hard chrome finish) $857.50
Price: Extra barrel, 8" through 10¾" $287.50
Price: Muzzle brake $100.00

RPM XL Pistol

SUNDANCE POINT BLANK O/U DERRINGER Caliber: 22 LR, 2-shot. **Barrel:** 3". **Weight:** 8 oz. **Length:** 4.6" overall. **Stocks:** Grooved composition. **Sights:** Blade front, fixed notch rear. **Features:** Double-action trigger, push-bar safety, automatic chamber selection. Fully enclosed hammer. Matte black finish. Introduced 1994. Made in U.S. by Sundance Industries.
Price: $99.00

Sundance Point Blank

TEXAS ARMORY DEFENDER DERRINGER Caliber: 9mm Para., 357 Mag., 44 Mag., 45 ACP, 45 Colt/410. **Barrel:** 3". **Weight:** 21 oz. **Length:** 5" overall. **Stocks:** Smooth wood. **Sights:** Blade front, fixed rear. **Features:** Interchangeable barrels; retracting firing pins; rebounding hammer; cross-bolt safety; removable trigger guard; automatic extractor. Blasted finish stainless steel. Introduced 1993. Made in U.S. by Texas Armory.
Price: $310.00
Price: Extra barrel $100.00

Texas Armory Defender

TEXAS LONGHORN "THE JEZEBEL" PISTOL Caliber: 22 Short, Long, Long Rifle, single shot. **Barrel:** 6". **Weight:** 15 oz. **Length:** 8" overall. **Stocks:** One-piece fancy walnut grip (right- or left-hand), walnut forend. **Sights:** Bead front, fixed rear. **Features:** Handmade gun. Top-break action; all stainless steel; automatic hammer block safety; music wire coil springs. Barrel is half-round, half-octagon. Announced 1986. From Texas Longhorn Arms.
Price: About $250.00

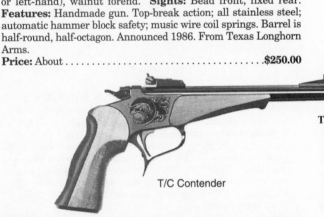
T/C Contender

THE JUDGE SINGLE SHOT PISTOL Caliber: 22 Hornet, 22 K-Hornet, 218 Bee, 7-30 Waters, 30-30. **Barrel:** 10" or 16.2". **Weight:** NA. **Length:** NA. **Stocks:** Walnut. **Sights:** Bead on ramp front, open adjustable rear. **Features:** Break-open design; made of 17-4 stainless steel. Also available as a kit. Introduced 1995. Made in U.S. by Cumberland Mountain Arms.
Price: ....NA

THOMPSON/CENTER CONTENDER Caliber: 7mm TCU, 30-30 Win., 22 LR, 22 WMR, 22 Hornet, 223 Rem., 270 Ren, 7-30 Waters, 32-20 Win., 357 Mag., 357 Rem. Max., 44 Mag., 10mm Auto, 445 Super Mag., 45/410, single shot. **Barrel:** 10", tapered octagon, bull barrel and vent. rib. **Weight:** 43 oz. (10" bbl.). **Length:** 13¼" (10" bbl.). **Stocks:** T/C "Competitor Grip." Right or left hand. **Sights:** Under-cut blade ramp front, rear adjustable for windage and elevation. **Features:** Break-open action with automatic safety. Single-action only. Interchangeable bbls., both caliber (rim & centerfire), and length. Drilled and tapped for scope. Engraved frame. See T/C catalog for exact barrel/caliber availability.
Price: Blued (rimfire cals.) $463.50
Price: Blued (centerfire cals.) $463.50
Price: Extra bbls. (standard octagon) $213.70
Price: 45/410, internal choke bbl. $218.90

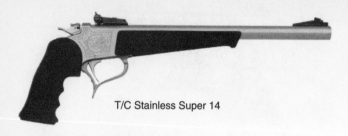

T/C Stainless Super 14

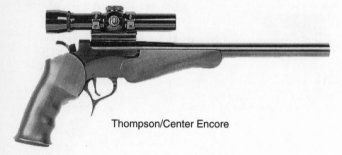

Thompson/Center Encore

Uberti Rolling Block

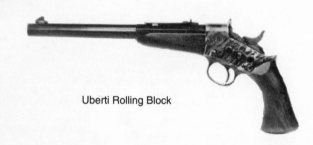

Ultra Light Model 20

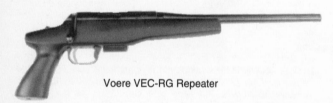

Voere VEC-RG Repeater

Thompson/Center Stainless Super 14, Super 16 Contender Same as the standard Super 14 and Super 16 except they are made of stainless steel with blued sights. Both models have black Rynite forend and finger-groove, ambidextrous grip with a built-in rubber recoil cushion that has a sealed-in air pocket. Receiver has a different cougar etching. Available in 22 LR, 22 LR Match, 22 Hornet, 223 Rem., 30-30 Win., 35 Rem. (Super 14), 45-70 (Super 16 only), 45 Colt/410. Introduced 1993.
Price: 14" bull barrel $504.70
Price: 16¼" bull barrel $509.90
Price: 45 Colt/410, 14" $535.60
Price: 45 Colt/410, 16" $530.50

Thompson/Center Contender Hunter Package Package contains the Contender pistol in 223, 7-30 Waters, 30-30, 375 Win., 357 Rem. Maximum, 35 Rem., 44 Mag. or 45-70 with 14" barrel with T/C's Muzzle Tamer, a 2.5x Recoil Proof Long Eye Relief scope with lighted reticle, q.d. sling swivels with a nylon carrying sling. Comes with a suede leather case with foam padding and fleece lining. Introduced 1990. From Thompson/Center Arms.
Price: Blued $798.00
Price: Stainless $829.00

Thompson/Center Stainless Contender Same as the standard Contender except made of stainless steel with blued sights, black Rynite forend and ambidextrous finger-groove grip with a built-in rubber recoil cushion that has a sealed-in air pocket. Receiver has a different cougar etching. Available with 10" bull barrel in 22 LR, 22 LR Match, 22 Hornet, 223 Rem., 30-30 Win., 357 Mag., 44 Mag., 45 Colt/410. Introduced 1993.
Price: $494.40
Price: 45 Colt/410 . . . .$499.60
Price: With 22 LR match chamber $504.70

THOMPSON/CENTER ENCORE PISTOL Caliber: 22-250, 223, 7mm-08, 308, 30-06, single shot. **Barrel:** 10", 15", tapered round. **Weight:** NA **Length:** 19" overall with 10" barrel. **Stocks:** American walnut with finger grooves, walnut forend. **Sights:** Blade on ramp front, adjustable rear, or none. **Features:** Interchangeable barrels; action opens by squeezing the trigger guard; drilled and tapped for scope mounting; blue finish. Announced 1996. Made in U.S. by Thompson/Center Arms.
Price: About $500.00

UBERTI ROLLING BLOCK TARGET PISTOL Caliber: 22 LR, 22 WMR, 22 Hornet, 357 Mag., 45 Colt, single shot. **Barrel:** 9⅞", half-round, half-octagon. **Weight:** 44 oz. **Length:** 14" overall. **Stocks:** Walnut grip and forend. **Sights:** Blade front, fully adjustable rear. **Features:** Replica of the 1871 rolling block target pistol. Brass trigger guard, color case-hardened frame, blue barrel. Imported by Uberti U.S.A.
Price: $410.00

ULTRA LIGHT ARMS MODEL 20 REB HUNTER'S PISTOL Caliber: 22-250 thru 308 Win. standard. Most silhouette calibers and others on request. 5-shot magazine. **Barrel:** 14", Douglas No. 3. **Weight:** 4 lbs. **Stock:** Composite Kevlar, graphite reinforced. Du Pont Imron paint in green, brown, black and camo. **Sights:** None furnished. Scope mount included. **Features:** Timney adjustable trigger; two-position, three-function safety; benchrest quality action; matte or bright stock and metal finish; right- or left-hand action. Shipped in hard case. Introduced 1987. From Ultra Light Arms.
Price: $1,600.00

VOERE VEC-95CG SINGLE SHOT PISTOL Caliber: 5.56mm, 6mm UCC caseless, single shot. **Barrel:** 12", 14". **Weight:** 3 lbs. **Length:** NA. **Stock:** Black synthetic; center grip. **Sights:** None furnished. **Features:** Fires caseless ammunition via electronic ignition; two batteries in the grip last about 500 shots. Bolt action has two forward locking lugs. Tang safety. Drilled and tapped for scope mounting. Introduced 1995. Imported from Austria by JagerSport, Ltd.
Price: $1,495.00

Voere VEC-RG Repeater pistol Similar to the VEC-95CG except has rear grip stock and detachable 5-shot magazine. Available with 12" or 14" barrel. Introduced 1995. Imported from Austria by JagerSport, Ltd.
Price: $1,495.00

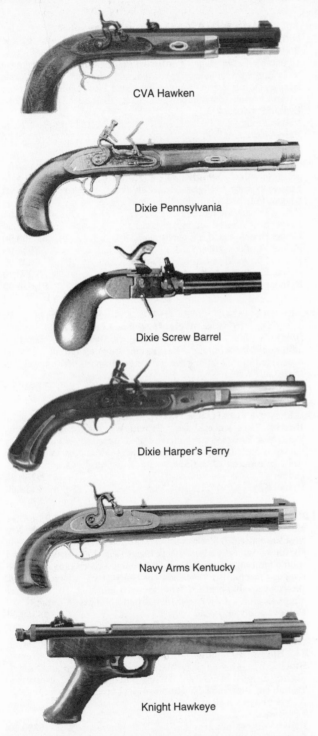

CVA Hawken

Dixie Pennsylvania

Dixie Screw Barrel

Dixie Harper's Ferry

Navy Arms Kentucky

Knight Hawkeye

CVA HAWKEN PISTOL Caliber: 50. **Barrel:** 9³/₄"; ¹⁵/₁₆" flats. **Weight:** 50 oz. **Length:** 16¹/₂" overall. **Stock:** Select hardwood. **Sights:** Beaded blade front, fully adjustable open rear. **Features:** Color case-hardened lock, polished brass wedge plate, nose cap, ramrod thimble, trigger guard, grip cap. Imported by CVA.
Price: $149.95
Price: Kit $119.95
Price: With laminated stock $159.95

DIXIE PENNSYLVANIA PISTOL Caliber: 44 (.430" round ball). **Barrel:** 10" (⁷/₈" octagon). **Weight:** 2¹/₂ lbs. **Stock:** Walnut-stained hardwood. **Sights:** Blade front, open rear drift-adjustable for windage; brass. **Features:** Available in flint only. Brass trigger guard, thimbles, nosecap, wedgeplates; high-luster blue barrel. Imported from Italy by Dixie Gun Works.
Price: Finished $159.95
Price: Kit $119.95

DIXIE SCREW BARREL PISTOL Caliber: .445". **Barrel:** 2¹/₂". **Weight:** 8 oz. **Length:** 6¹/₂" overall. **Stock:** Walnut. **Features:** Trigger folds down when hammer is cocked. Close copy of the originals once made in Belgium. Uses No. 11 percussion caps. From Dixie Gun Works.
Price: $99.95
Price: Kit $79.95

> Consult our Directory pages for
> the location of firms mentioned.

FRENCH-STYLE DUELING PISTOL Caliber: 44. **Barrel:** 10". **Weight:** 35 oz. **Length:** 15³/₄" overall. **Stock:** Carved walnut. **Sights:** Fixed. **Features:** Comes with velvet-lined case and accessories. Imported by Mandall Shooting Supplies.
Price: $295.00

HARPER'S FERRY 1806 PISTOL Caliber: 58 (.570" round ball). **Barrel:** 10". **Weight:** 40 oz. **Length:** 16" overall. **Stock:** Walnut. **Sights:** Fixed. **Features:** Case-hardened lock, brass-mounted browned barrel. Replica of the first U.S. Gov't.-made flintlock pistol. Imported by Navy Arms, Dixie Gun Works.
Price: ....$275.00 to $405.00
Price: Kit (Dixie) $199.95
Price: Cased set (Navy Arms) $335.00

KENTUCKY FLINTLOCK PISTOL Caliber: 44, 45. **Barrel:** 10¹/₈". **Weight:** 32 oz. **Length:** 15¹/₂" overall. **Stock:** Walnut. **Sights:** Fixed. **Features:** Specifications, including caliber, weight and length may vary with importer. Case-hardened lock, blued barrel; available also as brass barrel flint Model 1821. Imported by Navy Arms (44 only), The Armoury.
Price: ....$145.00 to $225.00
Price: In kit form, from ....$90.00 to $112.00
Price: Single cased set (Navy Arms) $350.00
Price: Double cased set (Navy Arms) $580.00

Kentucky Percussion Pistol Similar to flint version but percussion lock. Imported by The Armoury, Navy Arms, CVA (50-cal.).
Price: ....$129.95 to $250.00
Price: Steel barrel (Armoury) $179.00
Price: Single cased set (Navy Arms) $335.00
Price: Double cased set (Navy Arms) $550.00

KNIGHT HAWKEYE PISTOL Caliber: 50. **Barrel:** 12", 1:20" twist. **Weight:** 3¹/₄ lbs. **Length:** 20" overall. **Stock:** Black composite, autumn brown or shadow black laminate. **Sights:** Bead front on ramp, open fully adjustable rear. **Features:** In-line ignitiion design; patented double safety system; removable breech plug; fully adjustable trigger; receiver drilled and tapped for scope mounting. Made in U.S. by Modern Muzzle Loading, Inc.
Price: Blued $359.95
Price: Stainless $429.95

Lyman Plains Pistol

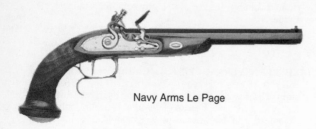

Navy Arms Le Page

Pedersoli Mang

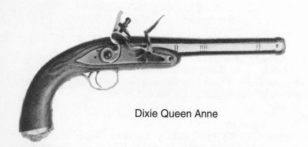

Dixie Queen Anne

Thompson/Center Scout

Traditions Buckhunter

LE PAGE PERCUSSION DUELING PISTOL Caliber: 44. **Barrel:** 10″, rifled. **Weight:** 40 oz. **Length:** 16″ overall. **Stock:** Walnut, fluted butt. **Sights:** Blade front, notch rear. **Features:** Double-set triggers. Blued barrel; trigger guard and buttcap are polished silver. Imported by Dixie Gun Works.
Price: $425.00

LYMAN PLAINS PISTOL Caliber: 50 or 54. **Barrel:** 8″, 1:30″ twist, both calibers. **Weight:** 50 oz. **Length:** 15″ overall. **Stock:** Walnut half-stock. **Sights:** Blade front, square notch rear adjustable for windage. **Features:** Polished brass trigger guard and ramrod tip, color case-hardened coil spring lock, spring-loaded trigger, stainless steel nipple, blackened iron furniture. Hooked patent breech, detachable belt hook. Introduced 1981. From Lyman Products.
Price: Finished $224.95
Price: Kit $179.95

NAVY ARMS LE PAGE DUELING PISTOL Caliber: 44. **Barrel:** 9″, octagon, rifled. **Weight:** 34 oz. **Length:** 15″ overall. **Stock:** European walnut. **Sights:** Adjustable rear. **Features:** Single-set trigger. Polished metal finish. From Navy Arms.
Price: Percussion $500.00
Price: Single cased set, percussion $775.00
Price: Double cased set, percussion $1,300.00
Price: Flintlock, rifled $625.00
Price: Flintlock, smoothbore (45-cal.) $625.00
Price: Flintlock, single cased set $900.00
Price: Flintlock, double cased set $1,575.00

PEDERSOLI MANG TARGET PISTOL Caliber: 38. **Barrel:** 10.5″, octagonal; 1:15″ twist, **Weight:** 2.5 lbs. **Length:** 17.25″ overall. **Stock:** Walnut with fluted grip. **Sights:** Blade front, open rear adjustable for windage. **Features:** Browned barrel, polished breech plug, rest color case-hardened. Imported from Italy by Dixie Gun Works.
Price: $749.00

QUEEN ANNE FLINTLOCK PISTOL Caliber: 50 (.490″ round ball). **Barrel:** 7½″, smoothbore. **Stock:** Walnut. **Sights:** None. **Features:** Browned steel barrel, fluted brass trigger guard, brass mask on butt. Lockplate left in the white. Made by Pedersoli in Italy. Introduced 1983. Imported by Dixie Gun Works.
Price: $189.95
Price: Kit $138.50

THOMPSON/CENTER SCOUT PISTOL Caliber: 45, 50 and 54. **Barrel:** 12″, interchangeable. **Weight:** 4 lbs., 6 oz. **Length:** NA. **Stocks:** American black walnut stocks and forend. **Sights:** Blade on ramp front, fully adjustable Patridge rear. **Features:** Patented in-line ignition system with special vented breech plug. Patented trigger mechanism consists of only two moving parts. Interchangeable barrels. Wide grooved hammer. Brass trigger guard assembly. Introduced 1990. From Thompson/Center.
Price: 45-, 50- or 54-cal. $350.00

TRADITIONS BUCKHUNTER PRO IN-LINE PISTOL Caliber: 50, 54. **Barrel:** 10″ round. **Weight:** 48 oz. **Length:** 14″ overall. **Stocks:** Smooth walnut or black epoxy coated grip and forend. **Sights:** Beaded blade front, folding adjustable rear. **Features:** Thumb safety; removable stainless steel breech plug; adjustable trigger, barrel drilled and tapped for scope mounting. From Traditions.
Price: With walnut grip $230.00
Price: Nickel with black grip $247.00

TRADITIONS BUCKSKINNER PISTOL Caliber: 50. **Barrel:** 10″ octagonal, ⅞″ flats, 1:20″ twist. **Weight:** 40 oz. **Length:** 15″ overall. **Stocks:** Stained beech or laminated wood. **Sights:** Blade front, fixed rear. **Features:** Percussion ignition. Blackened furniture. Imported by Traditions.
Price: Beech stocks $165.00
Price: Laminated stocks $180.00

BLACKPOWDER SINGLE SHOT PISTOLS—FLINT & PERCUSSION

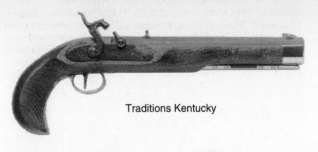

Traditions Kentucky

Traditions Pioneer

Traditions Trapper

TRADITIONS KENTUCKY PISTOL Caliber: 50. **Barrel:** 10"; octagon with 7/8" flats; 1:20" twist. **Weight:** 40 oz. **Length:** 15" overall. **Stock:** Stained beech. **Sights:** Blade front, fixed rear. **Features:** Birds-head grip; brass thimbles; color case-hardened lock. Percussion only. Introduced 1995. From Traditions.
Price: Finished $142.00
Price: Kit $115.00

TRADITIONS PIONEER PISTOL Caliber: 45. **Barrel:** 9 5/8", 13/16" flats, 1:16" twist. **Weight:** 31 oz. **Length:** 15" overall. **Stock:** Beech. **Sights:** Blade front, fixed rear. **Features:** V-type mainspring. Single trigger. German silver furniture, blackened hardware. From Traditions.
Price: $157.00
Price: Kit $126.00

TRADITIONS TRAPPER PISTOL Caliber: 50. **Barrel:** 9 3/4", 7/8" flats, 1:20" twist. **Weight:** 2 3/4 lbs. **Length:** 16" overall. **Stock:** Beech. **Sights:** Blade front, adjustable rear. **Features:** Double-set triggers; brass buttcap, trigger guard, wedge plate, forend tip, thimble. From Traditions.
Price: Percission $190.00
Price: Flintlock $207.00
Price: Kit $148.00

TRADITIONS WILLIAM PARKER PISTOL Caliber: 50. **Barrel:** 10 3/8", 15/16" flats; polished steel. **Weight:** 37 oz. **Length:** 17 1/2" overall. **Stock:** Walnut with checkered grip. **Sights:** Brass blade front, fixed rear. **Features:** Replica dueling pistol with 1:20" twist, hooked breech. Brass wedge plate, trigger guard, cap guard; separate ramrod. Double-set triggers. Polished steel barrel, lock. Imported by Traditions.
Price: $282.00

BLACKPOWDER REVOLVERS

Uberti 1860 Army

American Arms 1860 Army

Army 1851

ARMY 1851 PERCUSSION REVOLVER Caliber: 44, 6-shot. **Barrel:** 7 1/2". **Weight:** 45 oz. **Length:** 13" overall. **Stocks:** Walnut finish. **Sights:** Fixed. **Features:** 44-caliber version of the 1851 Navy. Imported by The Armoury, Armsport.
Price: $129.00

ARMY 1860 PERCUSSION REVOLVER Caliber: 44, 6-shot. **Barrel:** 8". **Weight:** 40 oz. **Length:** 13 5/8" overall. **Stocks:** Walnut. **Sights:** Fixed. **Features:** Engraved Navy scene on cylinder; brass trigger guard; case-hardened frame, loading lever and hammer. Some importers supply pistol cut for detachable shoulder stock, have accessory stock available. Imported by American Arms, Cabela's (1860 Lawman), E.M.F., Navy Arms, The Armoury, Cimarron, Dixie Gun Works (half-fluted cylinder, not roll engraved), Euroarms of America (brass or steel model), Armsport, Traditions (brass or steel), Uberti U.S.A. Inc.
Price: About ....$92.95 to $300.00
Price: Hartford model, steel frame, German silver trim, cartouches (E.M.F.) $215.00
Price: Single cased set (Navy Arms) $300.00
Price: Double cased set (Navy Arms) $490.00
Price: 1861 Navy: Same as Army except 36-cal., 7 1/2" bbl., weighs 41 oz., cut for shoulder stock; round cylinder (fluted available), from CVA (brass frame, 44-cal.)
................................$99.95 to $249.00
Price: Steel frame kit (E.M.F., Euroarms) ...$125.00 to $216.25
Price: Colt Army Police, fluted cyl., 5 1/2", 36-cal. (Cabela's) $124.95

BLACKPOWDER REVOLVERS

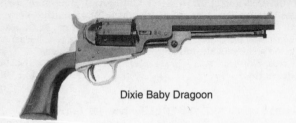

Dixie Baby Dragoon

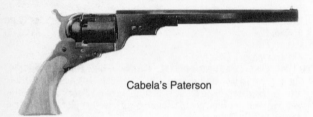

Cabela's Paterson

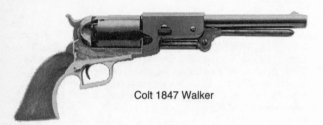

Colt 1847 Walker

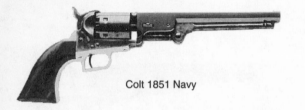

Colt 1851 Navy

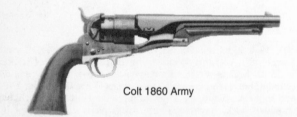

Colt 1860 Army

Colt 1860 "Cavalry Model" Percussion Revolver Similar to the 1860 Army except has fluted cylinder. Color case-hardened frame, hammer, loading lever and plunger; blued barrel, backstrap and cylinder, brass trigger guard. Has four-screw frame cut for optional shoulder stock. From Colt Blackpowder Arms Co.
Price: $465.00

COLT 1861 NAVY PERCUSSION REVOLVER Caliber: 36. **Barrel:** 7½". **Weight:** 42 oz. **Length:** 13⅛" overall. **Stocks:** One-piece walnut. **Sights:** Blade front, hammer notch rear. **Features:** Color case-hardened frame, loading lever, plunger; blued barrel, backstrap, trigger guard; roll-engraved cylinder and barrel. From Colt Blackpowder Arms Co.
Price: $465.00

BABY DRAGOON 1848, 1849 POCKET, WELLS FARGO Caliber: 31. **Barrel:** 3", 4", 5", 6"; seven-groove, RH twist. **Weight:** About 21 oz. **Stocks:** Varnished walnut. **Sights:** Brass pin front, hammer notch rear. **Features:** No loading lever on Baby Dragoon or Wells Fargo models. Unfluted cylinder with stagecoach holdup scene; cupped cylinder pin; no grease grooves; one safety pin on cylinder and slot in hammer face; straight (flat) mainspring. From Armsport, Dixie Gun Works, Uberti USA Inc., Cabela's.
Price: 6" barrel, with loading lever (Dixie Gun Works) ..$254.95
Price: 4" (Cabela's, Uberti USA Inc.) $169.95

CABELA'S PATERSON REVOLVER Caliber: 36, 5-shot cylinder. **Barrel:** 7½". **Weight:** 24 oz. **Length:** 11½" overall. **Stocks:** One-piece walnut. **Sights:** Fixed. **Features:** Recreation of the 1836 gun. Color case-hardened frame, steel backstrap; roll-engraved cylinder scene. Imported by Cabela's.
Price: $229.95

COLT 1847 WALKER PERCUSSION REVOLVER Caliber: 44. **Barrel:** 9", 7 groove, right-hand twist. **Weight:** 73 oz. **Stocks:** One-piece walnut. **Sights:** German silver front sight, hammer notch rear. **Features:** Made in U.S. Faithful reproduction of the original gun, including markings. Color case-hardened frame, hammer, loading lever and plunger. Blue steel backstrap, brass square-back trigger guard. Blue barrel, cylinder, trigger and wedge. From Colt Blackpowder Arms Co.
Price: $442.50

COLT 1849 POCKET DRAGOON REVOLVER Caliber: 31. **Barrel:** 4". **Weight:** 24 oz. **Length:** 9½" overall. **Stocks:** One-piece walnut. **Sights:** Fixed. Brass pin front, hammer notch rear. **Features:** Color case-hardened frame. No loading lever. Unfluted cylinder with engraved scene. Exact reproduction of original. From Colt Blackpowder Arms Co.
Price: $390.00

COLT 1851 NAVY PERCUSSION REVOLVER Caliber: 36. **Barrel:** 7½", octagonal, 7 groove left-hand twist. **Weight:** 40½ oz. **Stocks:** One-piece oiled American walnut. **Sights:** Brass pin front, hammer notch rear. **Features:** Faithful reproduction of the original gun. Color case-hardened frame, loading lever, plunger, hammer and latch. Blue cylinder, trigger, barrel, screws, wedge. Silver-plated brass backstrap and square-back trigger guard. From Colt Blackpowder Arms Co.
Price: $427.50

Uberti 1861 Navy Percussion Revolver Similar to 1851 Navy except has round 7½" barrel, rounded trigger guard, German silver blade front sight, "creeping" loading lever. Available with fluted or round cylinder. Imported by Uberti USA Inc.
Price: Steel backstrap, trigger guard, cut for stock $300.00

Stone Mountain Arms Sheriff's Model Similar to the Uberti 1861 Navy except has 5½" barrel, brass or steel frame, semi-fluted cylinder. In 44-caliber only.
Price: Steel frame, finished $179.95
Price: Brass frame (Armsport) $155.00
Price: Steel frame (Armsport) $193.00

COLT 1860 ARMY PERCUSSION REVOLVER Caliber: 44. **Barrel:** 8", 7 groove, left-hand twist. **Weight:** 42 oz. **Stocks:** One-piece walnut. **Sights:** German silver front sight, hammer notch rear. **Features:** Steel backstrap cut for shoulder stock; brass trigger guard. Cylinder has Navy scene. Color case-hardened frame, hammer, loading lever. Reproduction of original gun with all original markings. From Colt Blackpowder Arms Co.
Price: $427.50

BLACKPOWDER REVOLVERS

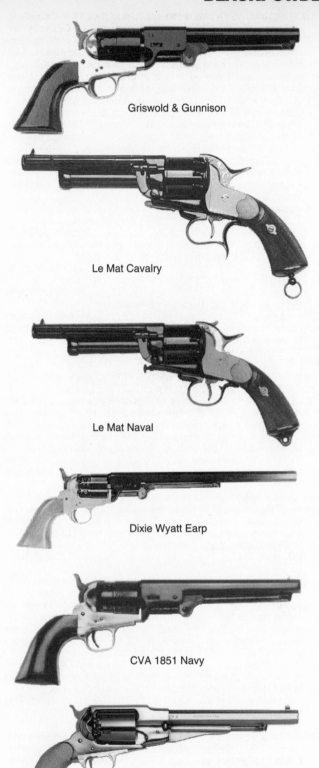

Griswold & Gunnison

Le Mat Cavalry

Le Mat Naval

Dixie Wyatt Earp

CVA 1851 Navy

Navy Arms 1858 Remington

NAVY ARMS DELUXE 1858 REMINGTON-STYLE REVOLVER
Caliber: 44. **Barrel:** 8″. **Weight:** 2 lbs., 13 oz. **Stocks:** Smooth walnut. **Sights:** Dovetailed blade front. **Features:** First exact reproduction—correct in size and weight to the original, with progressive rifling; highly polished with blue finish, silver-plated trigger guard. From Navy Arms.
Price: Deluxe model $415.00

COLT 1862 POCKET POLICE "TRAPPER MODEL" REVOLVER
Caliber: 36. **Barrel:** 3½″. **Weight:** 20 oz. **Length:** 8½″ overall. **Stocks:** One-piece walnut. **Sights:** Blade front, hammer notch rear. **Features:** Has separate 4⅝″ brass ramrod. Color case-hardened frame and hammer; silver-plated backstrap and trigger guard; blued semi-fluted cylinder, blued barrel. From Colt Blackpowder Arms Co.
Price: $442.50

COLT THIRD MODEL DRAGOON **Caliber:** 44. **Barrel:** 7½″. **Weight:** 66 oz. **Length:** 13¾″ overall. **Stocks:** One-piece walnut. **Sights:** Blade front, hammer notch rear. **Features:** Color case-hardened frame, hammer, lever and plunger; round trigger guard; flat mainspring; hammer roller; rectangular bolt cuts. From Colt Blackpowder Arms Co.
Price: Three-screw frame with brass grip straps $487.50
Price: Four-screw frame with blued steel grip straps, shoulder stock cuts, dovetailed folding leaf rear sight $502.50

DIXIE WYATT EARP REVOLVER **Caliber:** 44. **Barrel:** 12″ octagon. **Weight:** 46 oz. **Length:** 18″ overall. **Stocks:** Two-piece walnut. **Sights:** Fixed. **Features:** Highly polished brass frame, backstrap and trigger guard; blued barrel and cylinder; case-hardened hammer, trigger and loading lever. Navy-size shoulder stock ($45) will fit with minor fitting. From Dixie Gun Works.
Price: $130.00

GRISWOLD & GUNNISON PERCUSSION REVOLVER **Caliber:** 36 or 44, 6-shot. **Barrel:** 7½″. **Weight:** 44 oz. (36-cal.). **Length:** 13″ overall. **Stocks:** Walnut. **Sights:** Fixed. **Features:** Replica of famous Confederate pistol. Brass frame, backstrap and trigger guard; case-hardened loading lever; rebated cylinder (44-cal. only). Rounded Dragoon-type barrel. Imported by Navy Arms as Reb Model 1860.
Price: $115.00
Price: Kit $90.00
Price: Single cased set $235.00
Price: Double cased set $365.00

LE MAT REVOLVER **Caliber:** 44/65. **Barrel:** 6¾″ (revolver); 4⅞″ (single shot). **Weight:** 3 lbs., 7 oz. **Stocks:** Hand-checkered walnut. **Sights:** Post front, hammer notch rear. **Features:** Exact reproduction with all-steel construction; 44-cal. 9-shot cylinder, 65-cal. single barrel; color case-hardened hammer with selector; spur trigger guard; ring at butt; lever-type barrel release. From Navy Arms.
Price: Cavalry model (lanyard ring, spur trigger guard) .$595.00
Price: Army model (round trigger guard, pin-type barrel release) $595.00
Price: Naval-style (thumb selector on hammer) $595.00
Price: Engraved 18th Georgia cased set $795.00
Price: Engraved Beauregard cased set $1,000.00

NAVY MODEL 1851 PERCUSSION REVOLVER **Caliber:** 36, 44, 6-shot. **Barrel:** 7½″. **Weight:** 44 oz. **Length:** 13″ overall. **Stocks:** Walnut finish. **Sights:** Post front, hammer notch rear. **Features:** Brass backstrap and trigger guard; some have 1st Model square-back trigger guard, engraved cylinder with navy battle scene; case-hardened frame, hammer, loading lever. Imported by American Arms, The Armoury, Cabela's, Navy Arms, E.M.F., Dixie Gun Works, Euroarms of America, Armsport, CVA (36-cal. only), Traditions (44 only), Uberti USA Inc., Stone Mountain Arms.
Price: Brass frame . . . .$99.95 to $280.00
Price: Steel frame . . . .$130.00 to $285.00
Price: Kit form . . . .$110.00 to $123.95
Price: Engraved model (Dixie Gun Works) $139.95
Price: Single cased set, steel frame (Navy Arms) $280.00
Price: Double cased set, steel frame (Navy Arms) $455.00
Price: Confederate Navy (Cabela's) $69.95
Price: Hartford model, steel frame, German silver trim, cartouche (E.M.F.) $190.00

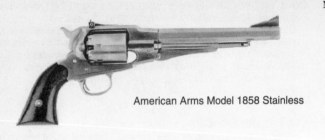

American Arms Model 1858 Stainless

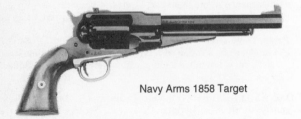

Navy Arms 1858 Target

North American Companion

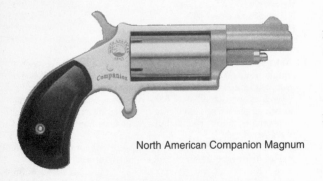

North American Companion Magnum

Uberti 1862 Police

Euroarms Rogers & Spencer

NEW MODEL 1858 ARMY PERCUSSION REVOLVER Caliber: 36 or 44, 6-shot. **Barrel:** 6½″ or 8″. **Weight:** 38 oz. **Length:** 13½″ overall. **Stocks:** Walnut. **Sights:** Blade front, groove-in-frame rear. **Features:** Replica of Remington Model 1858. Also available from some importers as Army Model Belt Revolver in 36-cal., a shortened and lightened version of the 44. Target Model (Uberti USA Inc., Navy Arms) has fully adjustable target rear sight, target front, 36 or 44. Imported by American Arms, Cabela's, Cimarron, CVA (as 1858 Army, steel or brass frame, 44 only), Dixie Gun Works, Navy Arms, The Armoury, E.M.F., Euroarms of America (engraved, stainless and plain), Armsport, Traditions (44 only), Uberti USA Inc. Stone Mountain Arms.
Price: Steel frame, about ....$99.95 to $280.00
Price: Steel frame kit (Euroarms, Navy Arms)$115.95 to $242.00
Price: Single cased set (Navy Arms) $290.00
Price: Double cased set (Navy Arms) $480.00
Price: Stainless steel Model 1858 (American Arms, Euroarms, Uberti USA Inc., Cabela's, Navy Arms, Armsport, Traditions) ....$169.95 to $380.00
Price: Target Model, adjustable rear sight (Cabela's, Euroarms, Uberti USA Inc., Navy Arms, Stone Mountain Arms) ....$95.95 to $399.00
Price: Brass frame (CVA, Cabela's, Traditions, Navy Arms) ....$79.95 to $212.95
Price: As above, kit (Dixie Gun Works, Navy Arms) ....$145.00 to $188.95
Price: Buffalo model, 44-cal. (Cabela's) $129.95
Price: Hartford model, steel frame, German silver trim, cartouche (E.M.F.) $215.00

NORTH AMERICAN COMPANION PERCUSSION REVOLVER Caliber: 22. **Barrel:** 1⅛″. **Weight:** 5.1 oz. **Length:** 4⁵/₁₀″ overall. **Stocks:** Laminated wood. **Sights:** Blade front, notch fixed rear. **Features:** All stainless steel construction. Uses standard #11 percussion caps. Comes with bullets, powder measure, bullet seater, leather clip holster, gun rag. Long Rifle or Magnum frame size. Introduced 1996. Made in U.S. by North American Arms.
Price: Long Rifle frame $160.00
Price: Magnum frame (1⅝″ barrel) $180.00

North American Magnum Companion Percussion Revolver Similar to the Companion except has larger frame. Weighs 7.2 oz., has 1⅝″ barrel, measures 5⁷/₁₆″ overall. Comes with bullets, powder measure, bullet seater, leather clip holster, gun rug. Introduced 1996. Made in U.S. by North American Arms.
Price: $180.00

POCKET POLICE 1862 PERCUSSION REVOLVER Caliber: 36, 5-shot. **Barrel:** 4½″, 5½″, 6½″, 7½″. **Weight:** 26 oz. **Length:** 12″ overall (6½″ bbl.). **Stocks:** Walnut. **Sights:** Fixed. **Features:** Round tapered barrel; half-fluted and rebated cylinder; case-hardened frame, loading lever and hammer; silver or brass trigger guard and backstrap. Imported by CVA (7½″ only), Navy Arms (5½″ only), Uberti USA Inc. (5½″, 6½″ only).
Price: About ....$139.95 to $310.00
Price: Single cased set with accessories (Navy Arms) ...$365.00
Price: Hartford model, steel frame, German silver trim, cartouche (E.M.F.) $215.00

ROGERS & SPENCER PERCUSSION REVOLVER Caliber: 44. **Barrel:** 7½″. **Weight:** 47 oz. **Length:** 13¾″ overall. **Stocks:** Walnut. **Sights:** Cone front, integral groove in frame for rear. **Features:** Accurate reproduction of a Civil War design. Solid frame; extra large nipple cut-out on rear of cylinder; loading lever and cylinder easily removed for cleaning. From Euroarms of America (standard blue, engraved, burnished, target models), Navy Arms, Stone Mountain Arms.
Price: ....$160.00 to $289.00
Price: Nickel-plated $215.00
Price: Engraved (Euroarms) $287.00
Price: Kit version ....$245.00 to $252.00
Price: Target version (Euroarms, Navy Arms)
.................................$239.00 to $270.00
Price: Burnished London Gray (Euroarms, Navy Arms) ....$245.00 to $270.00

Ruger Old Army

Ruger Old Army Stainless

Sheriff Model 1851

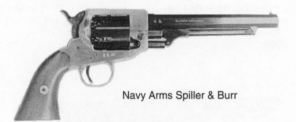

Navy Arms Spiller & Burr

Texas Paterson

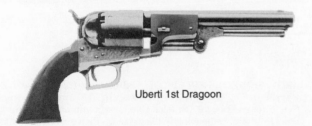

Uberti 1st Dragoon

RUGER OLD ARMY PERCUSSION REVOLVER Caliber: 45, 6-shot. Uses .457″ dia. lead bullets. **Barrel:** 7¹/₂″ (6-groove, 16″ twist). **Weight:** 46 oz. **Length:** 13³/₄″ overall. **Stocks:** Smooth walnut. **Sights:** Ramp front, rear adjustable for windage and elevation; or fixed (groove). **Features:** Stainless steel; standard size nipples, chrome-moly steel cylinder and frame, same lockwork as in original Super Blackhawk. Also available in stainless steel. Made in USA. From Sturm, Ruger & Co.
Price: Stainless steel (Model KBP-7) $465.00
Price: Blued steel (Model BP-7) $413.00
Price: Stainless steel, fixed sight (KBP-7F) $465.00
Price: Blued steel, fixed sight (BP-7F) $413.00

SHERIFF MODEL 1851 PERCUSSION REVOLVER Caliber: 36, 44, 6-shot. **Barrel:** 5″. **Weight:** 40 oz. **Length:** 10¹/₂″ overall. **Stocks:** Walnut. **Sights:** Fixed. **Features:** Brass backstrap and trigger guard; engraved navy scene; case-hardened frame, hammer, loading lever. Imported by E.M.F., Stone Mountain Arms (5¹/₂″ barrel).
Price: Steel frame (E.M.F.) $172.00
Price: Brass frame (E.M.F.) $140.00
Price: Steel frame (Stone Mountain Arms) $159.95

SPILLER & BURR REVOLVER Caliber: 36 (.375″ round ball). **Barrel:** 7″, octagon. **Weight:** 2¹/₂ lbs. **Length:** 12¹/₂″ overall. **Stocks:** Two-piece walnut. **Sights:** Fixed. **Features:** Reproduction of the C.S.A. revolver. Brass frame and trigger guard. Also available as a kit. From Cabela's, Dixie Gun Works, Navy Arms.
Price: . . . .$89.95 to $199.00
Price: Kit form $129.95
Price: Single cased set (Navy Arms) $270.00
Price: Double cased set (Navy Arms) $430.00

TEXAS PATERSON 1836 REVOLVER Caliber: 36 (.375″ round ball). **Barrel:** 7¹/₂″. **Weight:** 42 oz. **Stocks:** One-piece walnut. **Sights:** Fixed. **Features:** Copy of Sam Colt's first commercially-made revolving pistol. Has no loading lever but comes with loading tool. From Dixie Gun Works, Navy Arms, Uberti USA Inc.
Price: About . . . .$325.00 to $395.00
Price: With loading lever (Uberti USA Inc.) $450.00
Price: Engraved (Navy Arms) $465.00

UBERTI 1862 POCKET NAVY PERCUSSION REVOLVER Caliber: 36, 5-shot. **Barrel:** 5¹/₂″, 6¹/₂″, octagonal, 7-groove, LH twist. **Weight:** 27 oz. (5¹/₂″ barrel). **Length:** 10¹/₂″ overall (5¹/₂″ bbl.). **Stocks:** One-piece varnished walnut. **Sights:** Brass pin front, hammer notch rear. **Features:** Rebated cylinder, hinged loading lever, brass or silver-plated backstrap and trigger guard, color-cased frame, hammer, loading lever, plunger and latch, rest blued. Has original-type markings. From Uberti USA Inc.
Price: With brass backstrap, trigger guard $310.00

UBERTI 1st MODEL DRAGOON Caliber: 44. **Barrel:** 7¹/₂″, part round, part octagon. **Weight:** 64 oz. **Stocks:** One-piece walnut. **Sights:** German silver blade front, hammer notch rear. **Features:** First model has oval bolt cuts in cylinder, square-back flared trigger guard, V-type mainspring, short trigger. Ranger and Indian scene roll-engraved on cylinder. Color case-hardened frame, loading lever, plunger and hammer; blue barrel, cylinder, trigger and wedge. Available with old-time charcoal blue or standard blue-black finish. Polished brass backstrap and trigger guard. From Uberti USA Inc.
Price: $325.00

Uberti 1862 Pocket

BLACKPOWDER REVOLVERS

Uberti 3rd Dragoon

U.S. PATENT FIRE ARMS WHITNEYVILLE WALKER 1847 Caliber: 44, 6-shot. **Barrel:** 9″, half-round. **Weight:** 4 lbs., 9 oz. **Stocks:** Smooth walnut. **Sights:** Fixed. **Features:** Color case-hardened frame, lever and hammer, blued barrel and cylinder. Has Ranger and Indian fight cylinder scene. Introduced 1996. From United States Patent Fire Arms Mfg. Co.
Price: $420.00

U.S. PATENT FIRE ARMS 1848/1849 POCKET REVOLVER Caliber: 31, 5-shot. **Barrel:** 4″, octagonal. **Weight:** 1 lb., 7 oz. **Stocks:** One-piece walnut. **Sights:** Fixed. **Features:** Color case-hardened frame and hammer, blued barrel. Silver-plated brass grip straps. Has stagecoach holdup cylinder scene. Introduced 1996. From United States Patent Fire Arms Mfg. Co.
Price: Model 1848 ....$296.00
Price: Model 1849, with loading lever $300.00

U.S. Patent Fire Arms 1862 Police Similar to the 1862 Navy model except with round barrel, different loading lever and ball loading port. Takes 36-caliber bullet or ball. Introduced 1996. From United States Patent Fire Arms Mfg. Co.
Price: $322.00

U.S. PATENT FIRE ARMS 1860 ARMY Caliber: 44, 6-shot. **Barrel:** 7¹/₂″, round. **Weight:** 2 lbs., 10 oz. **Stocks:** One-piece walnut. **Sights:** Fixed. **Features:** Color case-hardened frame, lever and hammer, blued barrel and cylinder. Silver-plated grip straps. Fluted or standard rebated cylinder. Introduced 1996. From United States Patent Fire Arms Mfg. Co.
Price: $370.00

WALKER 1847 PERCUSSION REVOLVER Caliber: 44, 6-shot. **Barrel:** 9″. **Weight:** 84 oz. **Length:** 15¹/₂″ overall. **Stocks:** Walnut. **Sights:** Fixed. **Features:** Case-hardened frame, loading lever and hammer; iron backstrap; brass trigger guard; engraved cylinder. Imported by Cabela's, CVA, Navy Arms, Dixie Gun Works, Uberti USA Inc., E.M.F., Cimarron, Traditions.
Price: About ....$225.00 to $360.00
Price: Single cased set (Navy Arms) $405.00
Price: Deluxe Walker with French fitted case (Navy
   Arms) $505.00
Price: Hartford model, steel frame, German silver trim,
   cartouche (E.M.F.) $295.00

Uberti 2nd Model Dragoon Revolver Similar to the 1st Model except distinguished by rectangular bolt cuts in the cylinder.
Price: $325.00

Uberti 3rd Model Dragoon Revolver Similar to the 2nd Model except for oval trigger guard, long trigger, modifications to the loading lever and latch. Imported by Uberti USA Inc.
Price: Military model (frame cut for shoulder stock, steel back-
   strap) $330.00
Price: Civilian (brass backstrap, trigger guard) $325.00

U.S. PATENT FIRE ARMS DRAGOON MODELS 1848-1851 Caliber: 44, 6-shot. **Barrel:** 7¹/₂″, half-round. **Weight:** 4 lbs., 2 oz. **Stocks:** One-piece walnut. **Sights:** Blade front, hammer-notch rear. **Features:** Color case-hardened frame, lever and hammer, blued barrel and cylinder; silver-plated grip straps. Introduced 1996. From United States Patent Fire Arms Mfg. Co.
Price: 1st Model $400.00
Price: 2nd Model $396.00
Price: 3rd Model $396.00

U.S. Patent Fire Arms 1862 Navy Similar to the 1848/1849 Pocket models except with rebated cylinder for 36-caliber balls; 4¹/₂″, 5¹/₂″ or 6¹/₂″ barrel with loading lever. Introduced 1996. From United States Patent Fire Arms Mfg. Co.
Price: $310.00

U.S. PATENT FIRE ARMS 1851 NAVY Caliber: 36, 6-shot. **Barrel:** 7¹/₂″, octagonal. **Weight:** 2 lbs., 10 oz. **Stocks:** One-piece walnut. **Sights:** Fixed. **Features:** Color case-hardened frame, lever and hammer, blued barrel and cylinder, engraved naval cylinder scene. Introduced 1996. From United States Patent Fire Arms Mfg. Co.
Price: $359.00

U.S. Patent Fire Arms 1861 Navy Similar to the 1851 Navy except has round barrel, different loading lever and loading port. Introduced 1996. From United States Patent Fire Arms Mfg. Co.
Price: $349.00

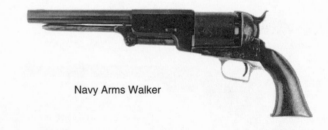

Navy Arms Walker

AIRGUNS

Airrow Model A6

AIRROW MODEL A6 AIR PISTOL Caliber: #2512 10.75″ arrow. **Barrel:** 10.75″. **Weight:** 1.75 lbs. **Length:** 16.5″ overall. **Power:** CO_2 or compressed air. **Stocks:** Checkered composition. **Sights:** Bead front, fully adjustable Williams rear. **Features:** Velocity to 375 fps. Pneumatic air trigger. Floating barrel. All aircraft aluminum and stainless steel construction; Mil-spec materials and finishes. Announced 1993. From Swivel Machine Works, Inc.
Price: About $597.00

ANICS A-101 AIR PISTOL Caliber: 177, 4.5mm, BB; 15-shot magazine. **Barrel:** 4.5" steel smoothbore. **Weight:** 35 oz. **Length:** 7" overall. **Power:** CO₂ **Stocks:** Checkered plastic. **Sights:** Blade front, fixed rear. **Features:** Velocity to 460 fps. Semi-automatic action; double action only; cross-bolt safety; black and silver finish. Comes with two 15-shot magazines. Introduced 1996. Imported by Anics, Inc.
Price: With case, about **$65.00**

Anics A-101 Magnum Air Pistol Similar to the A-101 except has 6" barrel with compensator, gives about 490 fps. Introduced 1996. Imported by Anics, Inc.
Price: With case, about **$72.00**

ANICS A-201 AIR REVOLVER Caliber: 177, 4.5mm, BB; 36-shot cylinder. **Barrel:** 4", 6" steel smoothbore. **Weight:** 36 oz. **Length:** 9.75" overall. **Power:** CO₂ **Stocks:** Checkered plastic. **Sights:** Blade front, fully adjustable rear. **Features:** Velocity about 425 fps. Fixed barrel; single/double action; rotating cylinder; manual cross-bolt safety; blue and silver finish. Introduced 1996. Imported by Anics, Inc.
Price: **$75.00**

> Consult our Directory pages for
> the location of firms mentioned.

BEEMAN P1 MAGNUM AIR PISTOL Caliber: 177, 5mm, single shot. **Barrel:** 8.4". **Weight:** 2.5 lbs. **Length:** 11" overall. **Power:** Top lever cocking; spring-piston. **Stocks:** Checkered walnut. **Sights:** Blade front, square notch rear with click micrometer adjustments for windage and elevation. Grooved for scope mounting. **Features:** Dual power for 177 and 20-cal.: low setting gives 350-400 fps; high setting 500-600 fps. Rearward expanding mainspring simulates firearm recoil. All Colt 45 auto grips fit gun. Dry-firing feature for practice. Optional wooden shoulder stock. Introduced 1985. Imported by Beeman.
Price: 177, 5mm **$405.00**

Beeman P2 Match Air Pistol Similar to the Beeman P1 Magnum except shoots only 177 pellets; completely recoilless single-stroke pnuematic action. Weighs 2.2 lbs. Choice of thumbrest match grips or standard style. Introduced 1990.
Price: 177, 5mm, standard grip **$435.00**
Price: 177, match grip **$465.00**

BEEMAN/FEINWERKBAU 102 PISTOL Caliber: 177, single shot. **Barrel:** 10.1", 12-groove rifling. **Weight:** 2.5 lbs. **Length:** 16.5" overall. **Power:** Single-stroke pneumatic, underlever cocking. **Stocks:** Stippled walnut with adjustable palm shelf. **Sights:** Blade front, open rear adjustable for windage and elevation. Notch size adjustable for width. Interchangeable front blades. **Features:** Velocity 460 fps. Fully adjustable trigger. Cocking effort 12 lbs. Introduced 1988. Imported by Beeman.
Price: Right-hand **$1,530.00**
Price: Left-hand **$1,580.00**

BEEMAN/FEINWERKBAU 65 MKII AIR PISTOL Caliber: 177, single shot. **Barrel:** 6.1", removable bbl. wgt. available. **Weight:** 42 oz. **Length:** 13.3" overall. **Power:** Spring, sidelever cocking. **Stocks:** Walnut, stippled thumbrest; adjustable or fixed. **Sights:** Front, interchangeable post element system, open rear, click adjustable for windage and elevation and for sighting notch width. Scope mount available. **Features:** New shorter barrel for better balance and control. Cocking effort 9 lbs. Two-stage trigger, four adjustments. Quiet firing, 525 fps. Programs instantly for recoil or recoilless operation. Permanently lubricated. Steel piston ring. Imported by Beeman.
Price: Right-hand **$1,170.00**
Price: Left-hand **$1,220.00**

Anics A-101 Magnum

Beeman P1

Beeman P2 Match

Beeman/Feinwekbau 102

Beeman/FWB P30

BEEMAN/FWB P30 MATCH AIR PISTOL Caliber: 177, single shot. **Barrel:** 10⁵/₁₆", with muzzlebrake. **Weight:** 2.4 lbs. **Length:** 16.5" overall. **Power:** Pre-charged pneumatic. **Stocks:** Stippled walnut; adjustable match type. **Sights:** Undercut blade front, fully adjustable match rear. **Features:** Velocity to 525 fps; up to 200 shots per CO₂ cartridge. Fully adjustable trigger; built-in muzzlebrake. Introduced 1995. Imported from Germany by Beeman.
Price: Right-hand **$1,530.00**
Price: Left-hand **$1,580.00**

Beeman/FWB C55

Beeman HW70A

Beeman/Webley Nemesis

Beeman/Webley Tempest

Benjamin Sheridan CO$_2$

BRNO Tau-7 Match

BEEMAN/FWB C55 CO$_2$ RAPID FIRE PISTOL Caliber: 177, single shot or 5-shot magazine. **Barrel:** 7.3". **Weight:** 2.5 lbs. **Length:** 15" overall. **Power:** Special CO$_2$ cylinder. **Stocks:** Anatomical, adjustable. **Sights:** Interchangeable front, fully adjustable open micro-click rear with adjustable notch size. **Features:** Velocity 510 fps. Has 11.75" sight radius. Built-in muzzlebrake. Introduced 1993. Imported by Beeman Precision Airguns.
Price: Right-hand $1,705.00
Price: Left-hand $1,755.00

BEEMAN HW70A AIR PISTOL Caliber: 177, single shot. **Barrel:** 6^1/$_4$", rifled. **Weight:** 38 oz. **Length:** 12^3/$_4$" overall. **Power:** Spring, barrel cocking. **Stocks:** Plastic, with thumbrest. **Sights:** Hooded post front, square notch rear adjustable for windage and elevation. Comes with scope base. **Features:** Adjustable trigger, 24-lb. cocking effort, 410 fps MV; automatic barrel safety. Imported by Beeman.
Price: $215.00
Price: HW70S, black grip, silver finish $240.00

BEEMAN/WEBLEY NEMESIS AIR PISTOL Caliber: 177, single shot. **Barrel:** 7". **Weight:** 2.2 lbs. **Length:** 9.8" overall. **Power:** Single-stroke pneumatic. **Stocks:** Checkered black composition. **Sights:** Blade on ramp front, fully adjustable rear. Integral scope rail. **Features:** Velocity to 400 fps. Adjustable two-stage trigger, manual safety. Recoilless action. Introduced 1995. Imported from England by Beeman.
Price: $190.00

BEEMAN/WEBLEY TEMPEST AIR PISTOL Caliber: 177, 22, single shot. **Barrel:** 6^7/$_8$". **Weight:** 32 oz. **Length:** 8.9" overall. **Power:** Spring-piston, break barrel. **Stocks:** Checkered black plastic with thumbrest. **Sights:** Blade front, adjustable rear. **Features:** Velocity to 500 fps (177), 400 fps (22). Aluminum frame; black epoxy finish; manual safety. Imported from England by Beeman.
Price: $200.00

Beeman/Webley Hurricane Air Pistol Similar to the Tempest except has extended frame in the rear for a click-adjustable rear sight; hooded front sight; comes with scope mount. Imported from England by Beeman.
Price: $225.00

BENJAMIN SHERIDAN PNEUMATIC PELLET PISTOLS Caliber: 177, 20, 22, single shot. **Barrel:** 9^3/$_8$", rifled brass. **Weight:** 38 oz. **Length:**13^1/$_8$" overall. **Power:** Underlever pnuematic, hand pumped. **Stocks:** Walnut stocks and pump handle. **Sights:** High ramp front, fully adjustable notch rear. **Features:** Velocity to 525 fps (variable). Bolt action with cross-bolt safety. Choice of black or nickel finish. Made in U.S. by Benjamin Sheridan Co.
Price: Black finish, HB17 (177), HB20 (20), HB22 (22),
    about $106.00
Price: Nickel finish, H17 (177), H20 (20), H22 (22),
    about $112.75

BENJAMIN SHERIDAN CO$_2$ PELLET PISTOLS Caliber: 177, 20, 22, single shot. **Barrel:** 6^3/$_8$", rifled brass. **Weight:** 29 oz. **Length:** 9.8" overall. **Power:** 12-gram CO$_2$ cylinder. **Stocks:** Walnut. **Sights:** High ramp front, fully adjustable notch rear. **Features:** Velocity to 500 fps. Turn-bolt action with cross-bolt safety. Gives about 40 shots per CO$_2$ cylinder. Black or nickel finish. Made in U.S. by Benjamin Sheridan Co.
Price: Black finish, EB17 (177), EB20 (20), EB22 (22),
    about $97.25
Price: Nickel finish, E17 (177), E20 (20), E22 (22),
    about $110.50

BRNO TAU-7 CO$_2$ MATCH PISTOL Caliber: 177. **Barrel:** 10.24". **Weight:** 37 oz. **Length:** 15.75" overall. **Power:** 12.5-gram CO$_2$ cartridge. **Stocks:** Stippled hardwood with adjustable palm rest. **Sights:** Blade front, open fully adjustable rear. **Features:** Comes with extra seals and counterweight. Blue finish. Imported by Century International Arms, Great Lakes Airguns.
Price: About $326.50

AIRGUNS

BSA 240 Magnum

Crosman Auto Air II

Crossman 357 8"

Crosman Model 1008

Crosman Model 1322

BSA 240 MAGNUM AIR PISTOL Caliber: 177, 22 **Barrel:** 5½", rifled. **Weight:** 28 oz. **Length:** 8½" overall. **Power:** Spring-air. **Stocks:** Oil-finish hardwood. **Sights:** Post front, fully adjustable rear. **Features:** Velocity about 390 fps (177). Automatic safety; adjustable trigger; matte finish. Introduced 1996. Imported frmo England by Great Lakes Airguns.
Price: $224.75

COPPERHEAD BLACK VENOM PISTOL Caliber: 177 pellets, BB, 17-shot magazine. **Barrel:** 4.75" smoothbore. **Weight:** 16 oz. **Length:** 10.8" overall. **Power:** Spring. **Stocks:** Checkered. **Sights:** Blade front, adjustable rear. **Features:** Velocity to 260 fps (BBs), 250 fps (pellets). Spring-fed magazine; cross-bolt safety. Introduced 1996. Made in U.S. by Crosman Corp.
Price: About $16.00

COPPERHEAD BLACK FANG PISTOL Caliber: 177 BB, 17-shot magazine. **Barrel:** 4.75" smoothbore. **Weight:** 10 oz. **Length:** 10.8" overall. **Power:** Spring. **Stocks:** Checkered. **Sights:** Blade front, fixed notch rear. **Features:** Velocity to 240 fps. Spring-fed magazine; cross-bolt safety. Introduced 1996. Made in U.S. by Crosman Corp.
Price: About $14.00

CROSMAN AUTO AIR II PISTOL Caliber: BB, 17-shot magazine, 177 pellet, single shot. **Barrel:** 8⅝" steel, smoothbore. **Weight:** 13 oz. **Length:** 10¾" overall. **Power:** CO₂ Powerlet. **Stocks:** Grooved plastic. **Sights:** Blade front, adjustable rear; highlighted system. **Features:** Velocity to 480 fps (BBs), 430 fps (pellets). Semi-automatic action with BBs, single shot with pellets. Silvered finish. Introduced 1991. From Crosman.
Price: About $29.00

CROSMAN MODEL 357 AIR PISTOL Caliber: 177, 6- and 10-shot pellet clips. **Barrel:** 4" (Model 357-4), 6" (Model 357-6), rifled steel; 8" (Model 357-8), rifled brass. **Weight:** 32 oz. (6"). **Length:** 11⅜" overall (357-6). **Power:** CO₂ Powerlet. **Stocks:** Checkered wood-grain plastic. **Sights:** Ramp front, fully adjustable rear. **Features:** Average 430 fps (Model 357-6). Break-open barrel for easy loading. Single or double action. Vent. rib barrel. Wide, smooth trigger. Two cylinders come with each gun. Model 357-8 has matte gray finish, black grips. From Crosman.
Price: 4" or 6", about $46.50
Price: 8", about $53.25
Price: Model 1357 (same gun as above, except shoots BBs, has 6-shot clip), about $46.50

CROSMAN MODEL 1008 REPEAT AIR Caliber: 177, 8-shot pellet clip **Barrel:** 4.25", rifled steel. **Weight:** 17 oz. **Length:** 8.625" overall. **Power:** CO₂ Powerlet. **Stocks:** Checkered plastic. **Sights:** Post front, adjustable rear. **Features:** Velocity about 430 fps. Break-open barrel for easy loading; single or double semi-automatic action; two 8-shot clips included. Optional carrying case available. Introduced 1992. From Crosman.
Price: About $45.00
Price: With case, about $55.00
Price: Model 1008SB (silver and black finish), about $47.00

CROSMAN MODEL 1322, 1377 AIR PISTOLS Caliber: 177 (M1377), 22 (M1322), single shot. **Barrel:** 8", rifled steel. **Weight:** 39 oz. **Length:** 13⅝". **Power:** Hand pumped. **Sights:** Blade front, rear adjustable for windage and elevation. **Features:** Moulded plastic grip, hand size pump forearm. Cross-bolt safety. Model 1377 also shoots BBs. From Crosman.
Price: About $53.00

DAISY MODEL 288 AIR PISTOL Caliber: 177 pellets, 24-shot. **Barrel:** Smoothbore steel. **Weight:** .8 lb. **Length:** 12.1" overall. **Power:** Single stroke spring-air. **Stocks:** Moulded resin with checkering and thumbrest. **Sights:** Blade and ramp front, open fixed rear. **Features:** Velocity to 215 fps. Cross-bolt trigger block safety. Black finish. From Daisy Mfg. Co.
Price: About $26.00

DAISY MODEL 91 MATCH PISTOL **Caliber:** 177, single shot. **Barrel:**10.25″, rifled steel. **Weight:** 2.5 lbs. **Length:** 16.5″ overall. **Power:** CO_2, 12-gram cylinder. **Stocks:** Stippled hardwood; anatomically shaped and adjustable. **Sights:** Blade and ramp front, changeable-width rear notch with full micrometer adjustments. **Features:** Velocity to 476 fps. Gives 55 shots per cylinder. Fully adjustable trigger. Imported by Daisy Mfg. Co.
Price: About **$670.00**

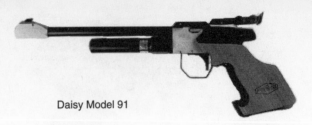

Daisy Model 91

Daisy Model 500

Daisy/Power Line 45

Daisy/Power Line 93

DAISY/POWER LINE MATCH 777 PELLET PISTOL **Caliber:** 177, single shot. **Barrel:** 9.61″ rifled steel by Lothar Walther. **Weight:** 32 oz. **Length:** 13½″ overall. **Power:** Sidelever, single-pump pneumatic. **Stocks:** Smooth hardwood, fully contoured with palm and thumbrest. **Sights:** Blade and ramp front, match-grade open rear with adjustable width notch, micro. click adjustments. **Features:** Adjustable trigger; manual cross-bolt safety. MV of 385 fps. Comes with cleaning kit, adjustment tool and pellets. From Daisy Mfg. Co.
Price: About **$335.00**

DAISY MODEL 500 RAVEN AIR PISTOL **Caliber:** 177 pellets, single shot. **Barrel:** Rifled steel. **Weight:** 36 oz. **Length:** 8.5″ overall. **Power:** CO_2. **Stocks:** Moulded plastic with checkering. **Sights:** Blade front, fixed rear. **Features:** Velocity up to 500 fps. Hammer-block safety. Resembles semi-auto centerfire pistol. Barrel tips up for loading. Introduced 1993. From Daisy Mfg. Co.
Price: About **$65.00**

DAISY/POWER LINE 44 REVOLVER **Caliber:** 177 pellets, 6-shot. **Barrel:** 6″, rifled steel; interchangeable 4″ and 8″. **Weight:** 2.7 lbs. **Power:** CO_2. **Stocks:** Moulded plastic with checkering. **Sights:** Blade on ramp front, fully adjustable notch rear. **Features:** Velocity up to 400 fps. Replica of 44 Magnum revolver. Has swingout cylinder and interchangeable barrels. Introduced 1987. From Daisy Mfg. Co.
Price: **$70.00**

DAISY/POWER LINE 45 AIR PISTOL **Caliber:** 177, 13-shot clip. **Barrel:** 5″, rifled steel. **Weight:** 1.25 lbs. **Length:** 8.5″ overall. **Power:** CO_2. **Stocks:** Checkered plastic. **Sights:** Fixed. **Features:** Velocity 400 fps. Semi-automatic repeater with double-action trigger. Manually operated lever-type trigger block safety; magazine safety. Introduced 1990. From Daisy Mfg. Co.
Price: About **$80.00**
Price: Model 645 (nickel-chrome plated), about **$85.00**

DAISY/POWER LINE 93 PISTOL **Caliber:** 177, BB, 15-shot clip. **Barrel:** 5″, steel. **Weight:** 17 oz. **Length:** NA. **Power:** CO_2. **Stocks:** Checkered plastic. **Sights:** Fixed. **Features:** Velocity to 400 fps. Semi-automatic repeater. Manual lever-type trigger-block safety. Introduced 1991. From Daisy Mfg. Co.
Price: About **$80.00**
Price: Model 693 (nickel-chrome plated), about **$85.00**

DAISY/POWER LINE 400 BB PISTOL **Caliber:** BB, 20-shot magazine. **Barrel:** Smoothbore steel. **Weight:** 1.4 lbs. **Length:** 10.7″ overall. **Power:** 12-gram CO_2. **Stocks:** Moulded black checkered plastic. **Sights:** Blade front, fixed open rear. **Features:** Velocity to 420 fps. Blowback slide cycles automatically on firing. Rotary trigger block safety. Introduced 1994. From Daisy Mfg. Co.
Price: About **$83.00**

DAISY/POWER LINE 717 PELLET PISTOL **Caliber:** 177, single shot. **Barrel:** 9.61″. **Weight:** 2.8 lbs. **Length:** 13½″ overall. **Stocks:** Moulded wood-grain plastic, with thumbrest. **Sights:** Blade and ramp front, micro-adjustable notch rear. **Features:** Single pump pneumatic pistol. Rifled steel barrel. Cross-bolt trigger block. Muzzle velocity 385 fps. From Daisy Mfg. Co. Introduced 1979.
Price: About **$80.00**

Daisy/Power Line 747 Pistol Similar to the 717 pistol except has a 12-groove rifled steel barrel by Lothar Walther, and adjustable trigger pull weight. Velocity of 360 fps. Manual cross-bolt safety.
Price: About **$160.00**

DAISY/POWER LINE 1140 PELLET PISTOL **Caliber:** 177, single shot. **Barrel:** Rifled steel. **Weight:** 1.3 lbs. **Length:** 11.7″ overall. **Power:** Single-stroke barrel cocking. **Stocks:** Checkered resin. **Sights:** Hooded post front, open adjustable rear. **Features:** Velocity to 325 fps. Made of black lightweight engineering resin. Introduced 1995. From Daisy.
Price: About **$45.50**

Daisy/Power Line 1140

Daisy/Power Line 1200

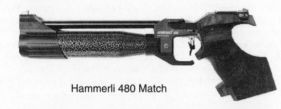

Hammerli 480 Match

Marksman 1015

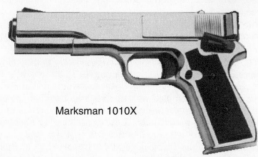

Marksman 1010X

PARDINI K58 MATCH AIR PISTOL Caliber: 177, single shot. **Barrel:** 9.0″. **Weight:** 37.7 oz. **Length:** 15.5″ overall. **Power:** Pre-charged compressed air; single-stroke cocking. **Stocks:** Adjustable match type; stippled walnut. **Sights:** Interchangeable post front, fully adjustable match rear. **Features:** Fully adjustable trigger. Introduced 1995. Imported from Italy by Nygord Precision Products.
Price: **$650.00**
Price: K60 model (CO_2) **$650.00**

DAISY/POWER LINE CO_2 1200 PISTOL Caliber: BB, 177. **Barrel:** $10^{1}/_{2}$″, smooth. **Weight:** 1.6 lbs. **Length:** 11.1″ overall. **Power:** Daisy CO_2 cylinder. **Stocks:** Contoured, checkered moulded wood-grain plastic. **Sights:** Blade ramp front, fully adjustable square notch rear. **Features:** 60-shot BB reservoir, gravity feed. Cross-bolt safety. Velocity of 420-450 fps for more than 100 shots. From Daisy Mfg. Co.
Price: About **$37.50**

DAISY/POWER LINE 1700 AIR PISTOL Caliber: 177 BB, 60-shot magazine. **Barrel:** Smoothbore steel. **Weight:** 1.4 lbs. **Length:** 11.2″ overall. **Power:** CO_2. **Stocks:** Moulded checkered plastic. **Sights:** Blade front, adjustable rear. **Features:** Velocity to 420 fps. Cross-bolt trigger block safety; matte finish. Has $^3/_8$″ dovetail mount for scope or point sight. Introduced 1994. From Daisy Mfg. Co.
Price: About **$40.00**

"GAT" AIR PISTOL Caliber: 177, single shot. **Barrel:** $7^{1}/_{2}$″ cocked, $9^{1}/_{2}$″ extended. **Weight:** 22 oz. **Power:** Spring-piston. **Stocks:** Cast checkered metal. **Sights:** Fixed. **Features:** Shoots pellets, corks or darts. Matte black finish. Imported from England by Stone Enterprises, Inc.
Price: **$21.95**

HAMMERLI 480 MATCH AIR PISTOL Caliber: 177, single shot. **Barrel:** 9.8″. **Weight:** 37 oz. **Length:** 16.5″ overall. **Power:** Air or CO_2. **Stocks:** Walnut with 7-degree rake adjustment. Stippled grip area. **Sights:** Undercut blade front, fully adjustable open match rear. **Features:** Under-barrel cannister charges with air or CO_2 for power supply; gives 320 shots per filling. Trigger adjustable for position. Introduced 1994. Imported from Switzerland by Hammerli Pistols U.S.A.
Price: **$1,325.00**

> Consult our Directory pages for the location of firms mentioned.

Hammerli 480k Match Air Pistol Similar to the 480 except has a short, detachable aluminum air cylinder for use only with compressed air; can be filled while on the gun or off; special adjustable barrel weights. Muzzle velocity of 470 fps, gives about 180 shots. Has stippled black composition grip with adjustable palm shelf and rake angle. Comes with air pressure gauge. Introduced 1996. Imported from Switzerland by SIGARMS, Inc.
Price: **$1,155.00**

MARKSMAN 1010 REPEATER PISTOL Caliber: 177, 18-shot repeater. **Barrel:** $2^{1}/_{2}$″, smoothbore. **Weight:** 24 oz. **Length:** $8^{1}/_{4}$″ overall. **Power:** Spring. **Features:** Velocity to 200 fps. Thumb safety. Black finish. Uses BBs, darts or pellets. Repeats with BBs only. From Marksman Products.
Price: Matte black finish **$25.50**
Price: Model 1010X (as above except nickel-plated) **$33.50**

MARKSMAN 1015 SPECIAL EDITION AIR PISTOL Caliber: 177, 24-shot repeater. **Barrel:** 3.8″, rifled. **Weight:** 22 oz. **Length:** 10.3″ overall. **Power:** Spring-air. **Stocks:** Checkered brown composition. **Sights:** Fixed. **Features:** Velocity about 230 fps. Skeletonized trigger, extended barrel with "ported compensator." Shoots BBs, pellets, darts or bolts. From Marksman Products.
Price: **$31.75**

MORINI 162E MATCH AIR PISTOL Caliber: 177, single shot. **Barrel:** 9.4″. **Weight:** 32 oz. **Length:** 16.1″ overall. **Power:** Pre-charged CO_2. **Stocks:** Adjustable match type. **Sights:** Interchangeable blade front, fully adjustable match-type rear. **Features:** Power mechanism shuts down when pressure drops to a pre-set level. Adjustable electronic trigger. Introduced 1995. Imported from Switzerland by Nygord Precision Products.
Price: **$950.00**

Record Champion Repeater

Record Jumbo

RWS/Diana Model 5G

RWS/Diana Model 6M

Steyr Match LP1

RECORD CHAMPION REPEATER PISTOL Caliber: 177, 12-shot magazine. **Barrel:** 7.6″, rifled. **Weight:** 2.8″, rifled. **Length:** 10.2″ overall. **Power:** Spring-air. **Stocks:** Oil-finished walnut. **Sights:** Post front, fully adjustable rear. **Features:** Velocity about 420 fps. Magazine loads through bottom of the grip. Full-length dovetail for scope mounting. Manual safety. Introduced 1996. Imported from Germany by Great Lakes Airguns.
Price: **$161.50**

RECORD JUMBO DELUXE AIR PISTOL Caliber: 177, single shot. **Barrel:** 6″, rifled. **Weight:** 1.9 lbs. **Length:** 7.25″ overall. **Power:** Spring-air, lateral cocking lever. **Stocks:** Smooth walnut. **Sights:** Blade front, fully adjustable open rear. **Features:** Velocity to 322 fps. Thumb safety. Grip magazine compartment for extra pellet storage. Introduced 1983. Imported from Germany by Great Lakes Airguns.
Price: **$121.34**

RWS/DIANA MODEL 5G AIR PISTOL Caliber: 177, single shot. **Barrel:** 7″. **Weight:** 2¾ lbs. **Length:** 15″ overall. **Power:** Spring-air, barrel cocking. **Stocks:** Plastic, thumbrest design. **Sights:** Tunnel front, micro-click open rear. **Features:** Velocity of 450 fps. Adjustable two-stage trigger with automatic safety. Imported from Germany by Dynamit Nobel-RWS, Inc.
Price: **$260.00**

RWS/DIANA MODEL 6M MATCH AIR PISTOL Caliber: 177, single shot. **Barrel:** 7″. **Weight:** 3 lbs. **Length:** 15″ overall. **Power:** Spring-air, barrel cocking. **Stocks:** Walnut-finished hardwood with thumbrest. **Sights:** Adjustable front, micro. click open rear. **Features:** Velocity of 410 fps. Recoilless double piston system, movable barrel shroud to protect from sight during cocking. Imported from Germany by Dynamit Nobel-RWS, Inc.
Price: Right-hand **$585.00**
Price: Left-hand **$640.00**

RWS/Diana Model 6G Air Pistols Similar to the Model 6M except does not have the movable barrel shroud. Has click micrometer rear sight, two-stage adjustable trigger, interchangeable tunnel front sight. Available in right- or left-hand models.
Price: Right-hand **$450.00**
Price: Left-hand **$490.00**

STEYR CO_2 MATCH LP1 PISTOL Caliber: 177, single shot. **Barrel:** 9″. **Weight:** 38.7 oz. **Length:** 15.3″ overall. **Power:** Pre-compressed CO_2 cylinders. **Stocks:** Fully adjustable Morini match with palm shelf; stippled walnut. **Sights:** Interchangeable blade in 4mm, 4.5mm or 5mm widths, fully adjustable open rear with interchangeable 3.5mm or 4mm leaves. **Features:** Velocity about 500 fps. Adjustable trigger, adjustable sight radius from 12.4″ to 13.2″. Imported from Austria by Nygord Precision Products.
Price: About **$1,095.00**
Price: LP1C (compensated) **$1,150.00**

STEYR LP5 MATCH PISTOL Caliber: 177, 5-shot magazine. **Barrel:** NA. **Weight:** 40.2 oz. **Length:** 13.39″ overall. **Power:** Pre-compressed CO_2 cylinders. **Stocks:** Adjustable Morini match with palm shelf; stippled walnut. **Sights:** Movable 2.5mm blade front; 2-3mm interchangeable in .2mm increments; fully adjustable open match rear. **Features:** Velocity about 500 fps. Fully adjustable trigger; has dry-fire feature. Barrel and grip weights available. Introduced 1993. Imported from Austria by Nygord Precision Products.
Price: About **$1,250.00**

STEYR LP 5C MATCH AIR PISTOL Caliber: 177, 5-shot magazine. **Barrel:** NA. **Weight:** 40.7 oz. **Length:** 15.2″ overall. **Power:** Pre-charged air cylinder. **Stocks:** Adjustable match type. **Sights:** Interchangeable blade front, fully adjustable match rear. **Features:** Adjustable sight radius; fully adjustable trigger. Has barrel compensator. Introduced 1995. Imported from Austria by Nygord Precision Products.
Price: **$1,325.00**

WALTHER CPM-1 CO_2 MATCH PISTOL Caliber: 177, single shot. **Barrel:** 8.66″. **Weight:** NA. **Length:** 15.1″ overall. **Power:** CO_2. **Stocks:** Orthopaedic target type. **Sights:** Undercut blade front, open match rear fully adjustable for windage and elevation. **Features:** Adjustable velocity; matte finish. Introduced 1995. Imported from Germany by Nygord Precision Products.
Price: **$950.00**

A

A&M Sales, 23 W. North Ave., Northlake, IL 60264/708-562-8190

Accu-Tek, 4525 Carter Ct., Chino, CA 91710/909-627-2404; FAX: 909-627-7817

Accuracy Gun Shop, 1240 Hunt Ave., Columbus, GA 31907/706-561-6386

Accuracy Gun Shop, Inc., 5903 Boulder Highway, Las Vegas, NV 89122/702-458-3330

Ace Custom 45's, 1880½ Upper Turtle Creek Rd., Kerrville, TX 78028/210-257-4290; FAX: 210-257-5724

Adventure A.G.R., 2991 St. Jude, Waterford, MI 48329/810-673-3090

Ahlman's Custom Gun Shop, Inc., 9525 West 230th St., Morristown, MN 55052/507-685-4244

Aimpoint, Inc., 580 Herndon Parkway, Suite 500, Herndon, VA 22070/703-471-6828; FAX: 703-689-0575

Aimtech Mount Systems, P.O. Box 223, 101 Inwood Acres, Thomasville, GA 31799/912-226-4313; FAX: 912-227-0222

Air Arms, Hailsham Industrial Park, Diplocks Way, Hailsham, E. Sussex, BN27 3JF ENGLAND/011-0323-845853 (U.S. importers—Air Werks International; World Class Airguns)

Air Gun Shop, The, 2312 Elizabeth St., Billings, MT 59102/406-656-2983

Air Guns Unlimited, 15866 Main St., La Puente, CA 91744/818-333-4991

Air Venture, 9752 E. Flower St., Bellflower, CA 90706/310-867-6355

Air Werks International, 403 W. 24th St., Norfolk, VA 23517-1204/800-247-9375

Airgun Repair Centre, 3227 Garden Meadows, Lawrenceburg, IN 47025/812-637-1463; FAX: 812-637-1463

Airguns International, 3451 G Airway Dr, Santa Rosa, CA 95403/707-578-7900; FAX: 707-578-0951

Airrow (See Swivel Machine Works, Inc.)

Alessandri and Son, Lou, 24 French St., Rehoboth, MA 02769/508-252-3436, 800-248-5652; FAX: 508-252-3436

Alexander, Gunsmith, W.R., 1406 Capitol Circle N.E. #D, Tallahassee, FL 32308/904-656-6176

All Game Sport Center, 6076 Guinea Pike, Milford, OH 45150/513-575-0134

Allison & Carey Gun Works, 17311 S.E. Stark, Portland, OR 97233/503-256-5166

American Arms & Ordnance, Inc., P.O. Box 2691, 1303 S. College Ave., Bryan, TX 77805/409-822-4983

American Arms, Inc., 715 Armour Rd., N. Kansas City, MO 64116/816-474-3161; FAX: 816-474-1225

American Derringer Corp., 127 N. Lacy Dr., Waco, TX 76705/800-642-7817, 817-799-9111; FAX: 817-799-7935

Ammo Load, Inc., 1560 E. Edinger, Suite G, Santa Ana, CA 92705/714-558-8858; FAX: 714-569-0319

AMT, 6226 Santos Diaz St., Irwindale, CA 91702/818-334-6629; FAX: 818-969-5247

Anderson Manufacturing Co., Inc., P.O. Box 2640, 2741 N. Crosby Rd., Oak Harbor, WA 98277/360-675-7300; FAX: 360-675-3939

Anderson, Inc., Andy, 2125 NW Expressway, Oklahoma City, OK 73112/405-842-3305

Anschutz GmbH, Postfach 1128, D-89001 Ulm, Donau, GERMANY (U.S. importer—PSI, Inc.)

Answer Products Co., 1519 Westbury Drive, Davison, MI 48423/810-653-2911

Argonaut Gun Shop, 607 McHenry Ave., Modesto, CA 95350/209-522-5876

Armadillo Air Gun Repair, 5892 Hampshire Rd., Corpus Christi, TX 78408/512-289-5458

Armas Azor, J.A. (See U.S. importer—Armes de Chasse)

Armes de Chasse, P.O. Box 827, Chadds Ford, PA 19317/610-388-1146; FAX: 610-388-1147

Armi Sport (See U.S. importers—Cape Outfitters; Taylor's & Co., Inc.)

Armoury, Inc., The, Rt. 202, Box 2340, New Preston, CT 06777/203-868-0001

Armscorp USA, Inc., 4424 John Ave., Baltimore, MD 21227/410-247-6200; FAX: 410-247-6205

Armurier De L'Outaouais, 28 Rue Bourque, Hull, Quebec, CANADA J8Y 1X1/819-777-9824

Astra Sport, S.A., Apartado 3, 48300 Guernica, Espagne, SPAIN/34-4-6250100; FAX: 34-4-6255186 (U.S. importer—E.A.A. Corp.)

ATIS Armi S.A.S., via Gussalli 24, Zona Industriale-Loc. Fornaci, 25020 Brescia, ITALY

Atlantic Guns, Inc., 944 Bonifant St., Silver Spring, MD 20910/301-585-4448/301-279-7983

Atlas Gun Repair, 4908 E. Judge Perez Dr., Violet, LA 70092/504-277-4229

Auto Electric & Parts, Inc., 24 W. Baltimore Ave., Media, PA 19063/215-565-2432

Auto-Ordnance Corp., Williams Lane, West Hurley, NY 12491/914-679-4190; FAX: 914-679-2698

Autumn Sales, Inc. (Blaser), 1320 Lake St., Fort Worth, TX 76103/817-335-1634; FAX: 817-338-0119

AWC Systems Technology, P.O. Box 41938, Phoenix, AZ 85080-1938/602-780-1050

B

B&B Supply Co., 4501 Minnehaha Ave., Minneapolis, MN 55406/612-724-5230

B&T, Inc., 1777 Central Ave., Albany, NY 12205/518-869-7934

B&W Gunsmithing, 505 Main Ave. N.W., Cullman, AL 35055/205-737-9595

B-Square Company, Inc., P.O. Box 11281, 2708 St. Louis Ave., Ft. Worth, TX 76110/817-923-0964, 800-433-2909; FAX: 817-926-7012

Bachelder Custom Arms, 1229 Michigan N.E., Grand Rapids, MI 49503/616-459-3636

Badger Gun & Ammo, Inc., 2339 S. 43rd St., West, Milwaukee, WI 53219/414-383-0855

Badger's Shooters Supply, Inc., 202 N. Harding, Owen, WI 54460/715-229-2101; FAX: 715-229-2332

Baer Custom, Inc., Les, 29601 34th Ave., Hillsdale, IL 61257/309-658-2716; FAX: 309-658-2610

Bain & Davis, Inc., 307 E. Valley Blvd., San Gabriel, CA 91776-3522/818-573-4241, 213-283-7449

Baity's Custom Gunworks, 2623 Boone Trail, N. Wilkesboro, NC 28659/919-667-8785

Baltimore Gunsmiths, 218 South Broadway, Baltimore, MD 21231/410-276-6908

Barrett Firearms Manufacturer, Inc., P.O. Box 1077, Murfreesboro, TN 37133/615-896-2938; FAX: 615-896-7313

Bausch & Lomb Sports Optics Div., 9200 Cody, Overland Park, KS 66214/913-752-3400, 800-423-3537; FAX: 913-752-3550

Bausch & Lomb, Inc., 42 East Ave., Rochester, NY 14603/913-752-3433, 800-828-5423; FAX: 913-752-3489

Beard's Sport Shop, 811 Broadway, Cape Girardeau, MO 63701/314-334-2266

Beauchamp & Son, Inc., 160 Rossiter Rd., Richmond, MA 01254/413-698-3822; FAX: 413-698-3866

Bedlan's Sporting Goods, Inc., 1318 E. Street, P.O. Box 244, Fairbury, NE 68352/402-729-6112

Beeman Precision Airguns, 5454 Argosy Dr., Huntington Beach, CA 92649/714-890-4800; FAX: 714-890-4808

Bell's Legendary Country Wear, 22 Circle Dr., Bellmore, NY 11710/516-679-1158

Belleplain Supply, Inc., Box 346, Handsmill Rd., Belleplain, NJ 08270/609-861-2345

Bellrose & Son, L.E., 21 Forge Pond Rd., Granby, MA 01033-0184/413-467-3637

Ben's Gun Shop, 1151 S. Cedar Ridge, Duncanville, TX 75137/214-780-1807

Benjamin (See page 291)

Benson Gun Shop, 35 Middle Country Rd., Coram L.I., NY 11727/516-736-0065

Benton & Brown Firearms, Inc., 311 W. First, P.O. Box 326, Delhi, LA 71232-0326/318-878-2499; FAX: 817-284-9300

Beretta Firearms, Pietro, 25063 Gardone V.T., ITALY (U.S. importer—Beretta U.S.A. Corp.)

Beretta U.S.A. Corp., 17601 Beretta Drive, Accokeek, MD 20607/301-283-2191; FAX: 301-283-0435

Beretta, Dr. Franco, via Rossa, 4, Concesio (BC), Italy I-25062/030-2751955; FAX: 030-218-0414 (U.S. importer—Nevada Cartridge Co.)

Bernardelli Vincenzo S.p.A., 125 Via Matteotti, P.O. Box 74, Gardone V.T., Brescia ITALY, 25063/39-30-8912851-2-3; FAX: 39-30-8910249 (U.S. importer—Armsport, Inc.)

Bertuzzi (See U.S. importers—Cape Outfitters; Moore & Co., Wm. Larkin; New England Arms Co.)

Bickford's Gun Repair, 426 N. Main St., Joplin, MO 64801/417-781-6440

Billings Gunsmiths, Inc., 1940 Grand Ave., Billings, MT 59102/406-652-3104

Blaser Jagdwaffen GmbH, D-88316 Isny Im Allgau, GERMANY (U.S. importer—Autumn Sales, Inc.)

Blount, Inc., Sporting Equipment Div., 2299 Snake River Ave., P.O. Box 856, Lewiston, ID 83501/800-627-3640, 208-746-2351; FAX: 208-746-2915

Blue Ridge Outdoor Sports, Inc., 2314 Spartansburg Hwy., E. Flat Rock, NC 28726/704-697-3006

Bob's Crosman Repair, 2510 E. Henry Ave., Cudahy, WI 53110/414-769-8256

Bob's Gun & Tackle Shop, (Blaustein & Reich, Inc.), 746 Granby St., Norfolk, VA 23510/804-627-8311/804-622-9786

Boggus Gun Shop, 1402 W. Hopkins St., San Marcos, TX 78666/512-392-3513

Bohemia Arms Co., 17101 Los Modelos, Fountain Valley, CA 92708/619-442-7005; FAX: 619-442-7005

Bolsa Gunsmithing, 7404 Bolsa Ave., Westminster, CA 92683/714-894-9100

Boracci, E. John, Village Sport Center, 38-10 Merrick Rd., Seaford L.I., NY 11783/516-785-7110

Borden's Accuracy, RD 1, Box 250BC, Springville, PA 18844/717-965-2505; FAX: 717-965-2328

Borgheresi, Enrique, 106 E. Tallalah, P.O. Box 8063, Greenville, SC 29604/803-271-2664

Bosis (See U.S. importer—New England Arms Co.)

Boudreaux, Gunsmith, Preston, 412 W. School St., Lake Charles, LA 70605/318-478-0640

Bradys Sportsmans Surplus, P.O. Box 4166, Missoula, MT 59806/406-721-5500; FAX: 406-721-5581

Braverman Corp., R.J., 88 Parade Rd., Meridith, NH 03293/800-736-4867

Brenner Sport Shop, Charlie, 344 St. George Ave., Rahway, NJ 07065/908-382-4066

Bretton, 19, rue Victor Grignard, F-42026 St.-Etienne (Cedex 1) FRANCE/77-93-54-69; FAX: 77-93-57-98 (U.S. importer—Mandall Shooting Supplies, Inc.)

Bridge Sportsmen's Center, 1319 Spring St., Paso Robles, CA 93446/805-238-4407

BRNO (See U.S. importers—Bohemia Arms Co.)

Broadway Arms, 4116 E. Broadway, N. Little Rock, AR 72117/501-945-9348

Brock's Gunsmithing, Inc., North 2104 Division St., Spokane, WA 99207/509-328-9788

Brolin Arms, 2755 Thompson Creek Rd., Pomona, CA 91767/909-392-2345; FAX: 909-392-2354

Brown Co., E. Arthur, 3404 Pawnee Dr., Alexandria, MN 56308/612-762-8847

Brown, Don, Gunsmith, 1085 Tunnel Rd., Ashville, NC 28805/704-298-4867

Browning (See page 291)

Browning Arms Co. (Parts & Service), 3005 Arnold Tenbrook Rd., Arnold, MO 63010-9406/314-287-6800; FAX: 314-287-9751

Bryan & Associates, 201 S. Gosset, Anderson, SC 29623/803-261-6810

Bryco Arms (See U.S. distributor—Jennings Firearms, Inc.)

BSA Guns Ltd., Armoury Rd. Small Heath, Birmingham, ENGLAND B11 2PX/011-021-772-8543; FAX: 011-021-773-0845 (U.S. importer—John Groenewold)

Buffalo Arms, 123 S. Third, Suite 6, Sandpoint, ID 83864/208-263-6953; FAX: 208-265-2096

Buffalo Gun Center, Inc., 3385 Harlem Rd., Buffalo, NY 14225/716-835-1546

Bullseye Gun Works, 7949 E. Frontage Rd., Overland Park, KS 66204/913-648-4867

Burby, Inc. Guns & Gunsmithing, Rt. 7 South RR #3, Box 345, Middlebury, VT 05753/802-388-7365

Burgins Gun Shop, RD #1 Box 66, Mericksville Rd., Sidney Center, NY 13839/607-829-8668

Burris Co., Inc., P.O. Box 1747, 331 E. 8th St., Greeley, CO 80631/303-356-1670; FAX: 303-356-8702

Burton Hardware, 200 N. Huntington, Sulphur, LA 70663/318-527-8651

Bushmaster Firearms (See Quality Parts Co./Bushmaster Firearms)

Bushnell (See Bausch & Lomb)

C

C-H Tool & Die Corp. (See 4-D Custom Die Co.)

Cabanas (See U.S. importer—Mandall Shooting Supplies, Inc.)

Cabela's, 812 13th Ave., Sidney, NE 69160/308-254-6644; FAX: 308-254-6669

Cal's Customs, 110 E. Hawthorne, Fallbrook, CA 92028/619-728-5230

Calico Light Weapon Systems, 405 E. 19th St., Bakersfield, CA 93305/805-323-1327; FAX: 805-323-7844

Camdex, Inc., 2330 Alger, Troy, MI 48083/810-528-2300; FAX: 810-528-0989

Cape Outfitters, 599 County Rd. 206, Cape Girardeau, MO 63701/314-335-4103; FAX: 314-335-1555

Capitol Sports & Western Wear, 1092 Helena Ave., Helena, MT 59601/406-443-2978

Carl's Gun Shop, 100 N. Main, El Dorado Springs, MO 64744/417-876-4168

Carpenter's Gun Works, RD 1 Box 43D, Newton Rd., Proctorsville, VT 05153/802-226-7690

Carroll's Gun Shop, Inc., 1610 N. Alabama Rd., Wharton, TX 77488/409-532-3175

Carter's Country, 8925 Katy Freeway, Houston, TX 77024/713-461-1844

Casey's Gun Shop, 59 Des E Rables, P.O. Box 100, Rogersville, New Brunswick E0A 2T0 CANADA/506-775-6822

Catfish Guns, 900 Jeffco-Executive Park, Imperial, MO 63052/314-464-1217

CBC, Avenida Humberto de Campos, 3220, 09400-000 Ribeirao Pires-SP-BRAZIL/55-11-742-7500; FAX: 55-11-459-7385 (U.S. importer—MAGTECH Recreational Products, Inc.)

Central Ohio Police Supply, c/o Wammes Guns, 225 South Main St., Bellefontaine, OH 43311

Century Gun Dist., Inc., 1467 Jason Rd., Greenfield, IN 46140/317-462-4524

Century International Arms, Inc., P.O. Box 714, St. Albans, VT 05478-0714/802-527-1252; FAX: 802-527-0470

Cervera, Albert J., Rt. 1 Box 808, Hanover, VA 23069/804-994-5783

CHAA, Ltd., P.O. Box 565, Howell, MI 48844/800-677-8737; FAX: 313-894-6930

Charlie's Sporting Goods, Inc., 7401-H Menaul Blvd. N.E., Albuquerque, NM 87110/505-884-4545
Charlton Co., Ltd., M.D., Box 153, Brentwood Bay, B.C., CANADA V0S 1A0/604-652-5266
Charter Arms (See CHARCO)
Cherry Corners, Inc., 11136 Congress Rd., P.O. Box 38, Lodi, OH 44254/216-948-1238
Chet Paulson Outfitters, 1901 South 72nd St., Suite A-14, Tacoma, WA 98408/206-475-8831
Christopher Firearms Co., E., Inc., Route 128 & Ferry St., Miamitown, OH 45041/513-353-1321
Chuck's Gun Shop, P.O. Box 597, Waldo, FL 32694/904-468-2264
Chung, Gunsmith, Mel, 8 Ing Rd., P.O. Box 1008, Kaunakakai, HI 96748/808-553-5888
Cimarron Arms, P.O. Box 906, Fredericksburg, TX 78624-0906/210-997-9090; FAX: 210-997-0802
Clark's Custom Guns, Inc., P.O. Box 530, 11462 Keatchie Rd., Keithville, LA 71047/318-925-0836; FAX: 318-925-9425
Colabaugh Gunsmith, Inc., Craig, R.D. 4, Box 4168 Gumm St., Stroudsburg, PA 18360/717-992-4499
Coleman, Inc., Ron, 1600 North I-35 #106, Carrollton, TX 75006/214-245-3030
Coliseum Gun Traders, Ltd., 1180 Hempstead Turnpike, Uniondale, NY 11553/516-481-3593
Colonial Repair, P.O. Box 372, Hyde Park, MA 02136-9998/617-469-4951
Colt Blackpowder Arms Co., 5 Centre Market Place, New York, NY 10013/212-925-2159; FAX: 212-966-4986
Colt's Mfg. Co., Inc., P.O. Box 1868, Hartford, CT 06144-1868/800-962-COLT, 203-236-6311; FAX: 203-244-1449
Competitor Corp., Inc., P.O. Box 244, 293 Townsend Rd., West Groton, MA 01472/508-448-3521; FAX: 508-448-6691
Connecticut Valley Arms Co. (See CVA)
Connecticut Valley Classics, P.O. Box 2068, 12 Taylor Lane, Westport, CT 06880/203-435-4600; FAX: 203-256-1180
Coonan Arms, 1465 Selby Ave., St. Paul, MN 55104/612-641-1263; FAX: 612-641-1173
Cooper Arms, P.O. Box 114, Stevensville, MT 59870/406-777-5534; FAX: 406-777-5228
Corbin, Inc., 600 Industrial Circle, P.O. Box 2659, White City, OR 97503/503-826-5211; FAX: 503-826-8669
Cosmi Americo & Figlio s.n.c., Via Flaminia 307, Ancona, ITALY I-60020/071-888208; FAX: 071-887008 (U.S. importer—New England Arms Co.)
Creekside Gun Shop, Inc., East Main St., Holcomb, NY 14469/716-657-6131; FAX: 716-657-7900
Crosman (See page 291)
Crosman Airguns, Rts. 5 and 20, E. Bloomfield, NY 14443/716-657-6161; FAX: 716-657-5405
Cumberland Arms, Rt. I, Box 1150 Shafer Rd., Blantons Chapel, Manchester, TN 37355/800-797-8414
Cumberland Knife & Gun Works, 5661 Bragg Blvd., Fayetteville, NC 28303/919-867-0009
Custom Firearms Shop, The, 1133 Indiana Ave., Sheboygan, WI 53081/414-457-3320
Custom Gun Service, 1104 Upas Ave., McAllen, TX 78501/210-686-4670
Custom Gun Shop, 12505 97th St., Edmonton, Alberta, CANADA T5G 1Z8/403-477-3737
Custom Gun Works, 4952 Johnston St., Lafayette, LA 70503/318-984-0721
CVA, 5988 Peachtree Corners East, Norcross, GA 30071/800-251-9412; FAX: 404-242-8546
Cylinder & Slide, Inc., William R. Laughridge, 245 E. 4th St., Fremont, NE 68025/402-721-4277; FAX: 402-721-0263
CZ (See U.S. importer—Magnum Research, Inc.)

D

D&D Sporting Goods, 108 E. Main, Tishomingo, OK 73460/405-371-3571
D&J Bullet Co., 426 Ferry St., Russel, KY 41169/606-836-2663
D&J Coleman Service, 4811 Guadalupe Ave., Hobbs, NM 88240/505-392-5318
D&L Gunsmithing/Guns & Ammo, 3615 Summer Ave., Memphis, TN 38122/901-327-4384
D&L Shooting Supplies, 2663 W. Shore Rd., Warwick, RI 02886/401-738-1889
D-Max, Inc., RR1, Box 473, Bagley, MN 56621/218-785-2278
Daenzer, Charles E., 142 Jefferson Ave., Otisville, MI 48463/810-631-2415
Daisy Mfg. Co., P.O. Box 220, Rogers, AR 72757/501-636-1200; FAX: 501-636-1601
Dakota (See U.S. importer—EMF Co., Inc.)
Dale's Guns & Archery Center, 3915 Eighteenth Ave., S.W. Rte. 8, Rochester, MN 55902/507-289-8308
Damiano's Field & Stream, 172 N. Highland Ave., Ossining, NY 10562/914-941-6005
Danny's Gun Repair, Inc., 811 East Market St., Louisville, KY 40206/502-583-7100
Darnall's Gun Works, RR #3, Box 274, Bloomington, IL 61704/309-379-4331
Daryl's Gun Shop, Inc., R.R. #2 Highway 30 West, Box 145, State Center, IA 50247/515-483-2656
Dave's Airgun Service, 1525 E. LaVieve Ln., Tempe, AZ 85284/602-491-8304
Davidson's of Canada, 584 Neal Dr., Box 479, Peterborough, Ontario, CANADA K9J 6Z6/705-742-5405; 800-461-7663
Davis Industries, 15150 Sierra Bonita Ln., Chino, CA 91710/909-597-4726; FAX: 909-393-9771
Dayton Traister, 4778 N. Monkey Hill Rd., P.O. Box 593, Oak Harbor, WA 98277/206-679-4657; FAX:206-675-1114
Delhi Small Arms, 22B Argyle Ave., Delhi, Ontario, CANADA N4B 1J3/519-582-0522
Delisle Thompson Sporting Goods, Ltd., 1814A Loren Ave., Saskatoon, Saskatchewan, CANADA S7H 1Y4/306-653-2171
Denver Instrument Co., 6542 Fig St., Arvada, CO 80004/800-321-1135, 303-431-7255; FAX: 303-423-4831
Desert Industries, Inc., P.O. Box 93443, Las Vegas, NV 89193-3443/702-597-1066; FAX: 702-871-9452
Dillon Precision Products, Inc., 8009 East Dillon's Way, Scottsdale, AZ 85260/602-948-8009, 800-762-3845; FAX: 602-998-2786
Dixie Gun Works, Inc., Hwy. 51 South, Union City, TN 38261/901-885-0561, order 800-238-6785; FAX: 901-885-0440
Dollar Drugs, Inc., 15A West 3rd, Lee's Summit, MO 64063/816-524-7600
Don & Tim's Gun Shop, 3724 Northwest Loop 410 and Fredricksburg, San Antonio, TX 78229/512-736-0263
Don's Sport Shop, Inc., 7803 E. McDowell Rd., Scottsdale, AZ 85257/602-945-4051
Dorn's Outdoor Center, 4388 Mercer University Drive, Macon, GA 31206/912-471-0304
Douglas Sporting Goods, 138 Brick Street, Princeton, WV 24740/304-425-8144
Down Under Gunsmiths, 318 Driveway, Fairbanks, AK 99701/907-456-8500
Dubbs, Gunsmith, Dale R., 32616 U.S. Hwy. 90, Seminole, AL 36574/205-946-3245
Duncan Gun Shop, Inc., 414 Second St., North Wilksboro, NC 28659/919-838-4851
Duncan's Gunworks, Inc., 1619 Grand Ave., San Marcos, CA 92069/619-727-0515
Dynamit Nobel-RWS, Inc., 81 Ruckman Rd., Closter, NJ 07624/201-767-7971; FAX: 201-767-1589

E

E&L Mfg., Inc., 4177 Riddle by Pass Rd., Riddle, OR 97469/503-874-2137; FAX: 503-874-3107
E.A.A. Corp., P.O. Box 1299, Sharpes, FL 32959/407-639-4842, 800-536-4442; FAX: 407-639-7006
Eagle Arms, Inc., 128 E. 23rd Ave., Coal Valley, IL 61240/309-799-5619, 800-336-0184; FAX: 309-799-5150
Ed's Gun & Tackle Shop, Inc., Suite 90, 2727 Canton Rd. (Hwy. 5), Marietta, GA 30066/404-425-8461
Elbe Arms Co., Inc., 610 East 27th St., Cheyenne, WY 82001/307-634-5731
Ellett Bros., P.O. Box 128, 267 Columbia Ave., Columbia, SC 29036/803-345-3751, 800-845-3711; FAX: 803-345-1820
Emerging Technologies, Inc., 721 Main St., Little Rock, AR 72201/501-375-2227; FAX: 501-372-1445
EMF Co., Inc., 1900 E. Warner Ave. Suite 1-D, Santa Ana, CA 92705/714-261-6611; FAX: 714-756-0133
Enstad & Douglas, 211 Hedges, Oregon City, OR 97045/503-655-3751
Epps, Ellwood, RR 3, Hwy. 11 North, Orillia, Ontario CANADA L3V 6H3/705-689-5333
Erma Werke GmbH, Johan Ziegler St., 13/15/FeldiglSt., D-8060 Dachau, GERMANY (U.S. importers—Mandall Shooting Supplies, Inc.; PSI, Inc.)
Ernie's Gun Shop, Ltd., 1031 Marion St., Winnipeg, Manitoba, CANADA R2J 0L1/204-233-1928
Essex Arms, P.O. Box 345, Island Pond, VT 05846/802-723-4313
Euroarms of America, Inc., 208 E. Piccadilly St., Winchester, VA 22601/703-662-1863; FAX: 703-662-4464
Europtik Ltd., P.O. Box 319, Dunmore, PA 18512/717-347-6049; FAX: 717-969-4330
Eversull, Ken, #1 Tracemont, Boyce, LA 71409/318-793-8728
Ewell Cross Gun Shop, Inc., 8240 Interstate 30W, Ft. Worth, TX 76108/817-246-4622
Eyster Heritage Gunsmiths, Inc., Ken, 6441 Bishop Rd., Centerburg, OH 43011/614-625-6131

F

F&D Guns, 5140 Westwood Drive, St. Charles, MO 63304/314-441-5897
FAS, Via E. Fermi, 8, 20019 Settimo Milanese, Milano, ITALY/02-3285846; FAX: 02-33500196 (U.S. importer—Nygord Precision Products)
Fausti Cav. Stefano & Figlie snc, Via Martiri Dell Indipendenza, 70, Marcheno, ITALY 25060 (U.S. importer—American Arms, Inc.)
Feather Industries, Inc., 37600 Liberty Dr., Trinidad, CO 81082/719-846-2699; FAX: 719-846-2644
Federal Engineering Corp., 1090 Bryn Mawr, Bensenville, IL 60106/708-860-1938; FAX: 708-860-2085
Federal Firearms Co., Inc., 5035 Thom's Run Rd., Oakdale, PA 15071/412-221-0300
FEG, Budapest, Soroksariut 158, H-1095 HUNGARY (U.S. importers—Century International Arms, Inc.; K.B.I., Inc.)
Feinwerkbau Westinger & Altenburger GmbH (See FWB)
Felton, James, Custom Gunsmith, 1033 Elizabeth St., Eugene, OR 97402/503-689-1687
Fiocchi Munizioni s.p.a. (See U.S. importer—Fiocchi of America)
Fiocchi of America, Inc., 5030 Fremont Rd., Ozark, MO 65721/417-725-4118, 800-721-2666; FAX: 417-725-1039
Firearms Co. Ltd./Alpine (See U.S. importer—Mandall Shooting Supplies, Inc.)
Firearms Repair & Refinish Shoppe, 639 Hoods Mill Rd., Woodbine, MD 21797/410-795-5859
Firearms Service Center, 2140 Old Shepherdsville Rd., Louisville, KY 40218/502-458-1148
Fix Gunshop, Inc., Michael D., 334 Mt. Penn Rd., Reading, PA 19607/215-775-2067
FN Herstal, Voie de Liege 33, Herstal 4040, BELGIUM/(32)41.40.82.83; FAX: (32)41.40.86.79
Foothills Shooting Center, 7860 W. Jewell Ave., Lakewood, CO 80226/303-985-4417
Forgett Jr., Valmore J., 689 Bergen Blvd., Ridgefield, NJ 07657/201-945-2500; FAX: 201-945-6859
Forster Products, 82 E. Lanark Ave., Lanark, IL 61046/815-493-6360; FAX: 815-493-2371
Four Seasons, 76 R Winn St., Woburn, MA 01801/617-932-3133/3255
4-D Custom Die Co., 711 N. Sandusky St., P.O. Box 889, Mt. Vernon, OH 43050-0889/614-397-7214; FAX: 614-397-6600
Fox & Company, 2211 Dutch Valley Rd., Knoxville, TN 37918/615-687-7411
Franklin Sports, Inc., 3941 Atlanta Hwy., Bogart, GA 30622/706-543-7803
Freedom Arms, Inc., P.O. Box 1776, Freedom, WY 83120/307-883-2468, 800-833-4432 (orders only); FAX: 307-883-2005
Freer's Gun Shop, Building B-1, 8928 Spring Branch Dr., Houston, TX 77080/713-467-3016
Fremont Tool Works, 1214 Prairie, Ford, KS 67842/316-369-2327
Friedman's Army Surplus, 2617 Nolenville Rd., Nashville, TN 37211/615-244-1653
Frontiersman's Sports, 6925 Wayzata Blvd., Minneapolis, MN 55426/612-544-3775
FWB, Neckarstrasse 43, 78727 Oberndorf a. N., GERMANY/07423-814-0; FAX: 07423-814-89 (U.S. importer—Beeman Precision Airguns, Inc.)

G

G.H. Outdoor Sports, 520 W. "B" St., McCook, NE 69001/308-345-1250
G.I. Loan Shop, 1004 W. Second St., Grand Island, NE 68801/308-382-9573
G.U. Inc., 4325 S. 120th St., Omaha, NE 68137/402-330-4492; FAX: 402-330-8029
Galaxy Imports Ltd., Inc., P.O. Box 3361, Victoria, TX 77903/512-573-4867; FAX: 512-576-9622
Galazan, Div. of Connecticut Shotgun Mfg. Co., P.O. Box 622, 35 Woodland St., New Britain, CT 06051-0622/203-225-6581; FAX: 203-832-8707
Gander Mountain, Inc., P.O. Box 128, Hwy. W, Wilmot, WI 53192/414-862-2331
Gander Mt. Inc., 1307 Miller Trunk Highway, Duluth, MN 55811/218-726-1100
Garfield Gunsmithing, 237 Wessington Ave., Garfield, NJ 07026/201-478-0171
Garrett Gunsmiths, Inc., Peter, 838 Monmouth St., Newport, KY 41071-1821/606-261-1855
Gart Brothers Sporting Goods, 1000 Broadway, Denver, CO 80203/303-861-1122
Gary's Gun Shop, 905 W. 41st St., Sioux Falls, SD 57104/605-332-6119
Gene's Gunsmithing, Box 34 GRP 326 R.R. 3, Selkirk, Manitoba, CANADA R1A 2A8/204-757-4413
Genecco Gun Works, K., 10512 Lower Sacramento Rd., Stockton, CA 95210/209-951-0706
Gentry Custom Gunmaker, David, 314 N. Hoffman, Belgrade, MT 59714/406-388-4867
GFR Corp., P.O. Box 430, Andover, NH 03216/603-735-5300
Giacomo Sporting, Inc., Delta Plaza, Rt. 26N, Rome, NY 13440
Gibbs Rifle Co., Inc., Cannon Hill Industrial Park, Rt. 2, Box 214 Hoffman, Rd./Martinsburg, WV 25401/304-274-0458; FAX: 304-274-0078
Gilbert Equipment Co., Inc., 960 Downtowner Rd., Mobile, AL 36609/205-344-3322
Girard, Florent, Gunsmith, 598 Verreault, Chicoutimi, Quebec, CANADA G7H 2B8/418-696-3329
Glades Gunworks, 4360 Corporate Square, Naples, FL 33942/813-643-2922
Glenn's Reel & Rod Repair, 2210 E. 9th St., Des Moines, IA 50316/515-262-2990
Glock GmbH, P.O. Box 50, A-2232 Deutsch Wagram, AUSTRIA (U.S. importer—Glock, Inc.)
Glock, Inc., 6000 Highlands Parkway, Smyrna, GA 30082/404-432-1202; FAX: 404-433-8719
Gonic Arms, Inc., 134 Flagg Rd., Gonic, NH 03839/603-332-8456, 603-332-8457
Gonzalez Guns, Ramon B., P.O. Box 370, Monticello, NY 12701/914-794-4515
Gordon's Wigwam, 501 S. St. Francis, Wichita, KS 67202/316-264-5891
Gorenflo Gunsmithing, 1821 State St., Erie, PA 16501/814-452-4855
Great Lakes Airguns, 6175 S. Park Ave., Hamburg, NY 14075/716-648-6666; FAX: 716-648-5279
Green Acres Sporting Goods, Inc., 8774 Normandy Blvd., Jacksonville, FL 32221/904-786-5166
Greene's Gun Shop, 4778 Monkey Hill Rd., Oak Harbor, WA 98277/206-675-3421
Greenwood Precision, P.O. Box 468, Nixa, MO 65714-0468/417-725-2330
Grenada Gun Works, 942 Lakeview Drive, Grenada, MS 38901/601-226-9272
Grice Gun Shop, Inc., 216 Reed St., P.O. 1028, Clearfield, PA 16830/814-765-9273
Griffiths & Sons, E.J., 1014 N. McCullough St., Lima OH 45801/419-228-2141
Groenwold, John, P.O. Box 830, Mundelein, IL 60060-0830/708-566-2365
Grundman's, Inc., 75 Wildwood Ave., Rio Dell, CA 95562/707-764-5744

GSI, Inc., 108 Morrow Ave., P.O. Box 129, Trussville, AL 35173/205-655-8299; FAX: 205-655-7078

Gun & Tackle Store, The, 6041 Forrest Ln., Dallas, TX 75230/214-239-8181

Gun Ace Gunsmithing, 3975 West I-40 North, Hurricane, UT 84737/801-635-5212

Gun Center, The, 5831 Buckeystown Pike, Frederick, MD 21701/301-694-6887

Gun City USA, Inc., 573 Murfreesboro Rd., Nashville, TN 37210/615-256-6127

Gun City, 212 W. Main Ave., Bismarck, ND 58501/701-223-2304

Gun Corral, Inc., 2827 East College Ave., Decatur, GA 30030/404-299-0288

Gun Doc, Inc., 5405 N.W. 82nd Ave., Miami, FL 33166/305-477-2777

Gun Exchange, Inc., 5317 W. 65th St., Little Rock, AR 72209/501-562-4668

Gun Hospital, The, 45 Vineyard Ave., E. Providence, RI 02914/401-438-3495

Gun Rack, Inc., The, 213 Richland Ave., Aiken, SC 29801/803-648-7100

Gun Room, The, 201 Clark St., Chapin, SC 29036/803-345-2199

Gun Shop, The, 5550 S. 900 East, Salt Lake City, UT 84117/801-263-3633

Gun World, 392 Fifth Street, Elko, NV 89801/702-738-2666

Gunshop, Inc., The, 44633 N. Sierra Hwy., Lancaster CA 93534/805-942-8377

Gunsite Training Center, P.O. Box 700, Paulden, AZ 86334/602-636-4565; FAX: 602-636-1236

Gunsmith Co., The, 3435 S. State St., Salt Lake City, UT 84115/801-467-8244; FAX: 801-467-8256

Gunsmith, Inc., The, 1410 Sunset Blvd., West Columbia, SC 29169/803-791-0250

Gunsmithing Ltd., 57 Unquowa Rd., Fairfield, CT 06430/203-254-0436

Gunsmithing Specialties Co., 110 North Washington St., Papillion, NE 68046/402-339-1222

H

H&B Service, Inc., 7150 S. Platte Canyon Road, Littleton, CO 80123/970-979-5447

H&R 1871, Inc., 60 Industrial Rowe, Gardner, MA 01440/508-632-9393; FAX: 508-632-2300

H-S Precision, Inc., 1301 Turbine Dr., Rapid City, SD 57701/605-341-3006; FAX: 605-342-8964

Hagstrom, E.G., 2008 Janis Dr., Memphis, TN 38116/901-398-5333

Hal's Gun Supply, 320 Second Avenue SE, Cullman, AL 35055/205-734-7546

Hämmerli Ltd., Seonerstrasse 37, CH-5600 Lenzburg, SWITZERLAND/064-50 11 44; FAX: 064-51 38 27 (U.S. importer—Hammerli USA)

Hammerli USA, 19296 Oak Grove Circle, Groveland, CA 95321/209-962-5311; FAX: 209-962-5931

Hampel's, Inc., 710 Randolph, Traverse City, MI 49684/616-946-5485

Harris-McMillan Gunworks, 302 W. Melinda Lane, Phoenix, AZ 85027/602-582-9627; FAX: 602-582-5178

Harry's Army & Navy Store, 691 NJSH Rt. 130, Yardville, NJ 08691/609-585-5450

Hart & Son, Inc., Robert W., 401 Montgomery St., Nescopeck, PA 18635/717-752-3655, 800-368-3656; FAX: 717-752-1088

Hart's Gun Supply, Ed, U.S. Route 415, Bath, NY 14810/607-776-4228

Hatfield Gun Co., Inc., 224 N. 4th St., St. Joseph, MO 64501/816-279-8688; FAX: 816-279-2716

Hawken Shop, The (See Dayton Traister)

Heckler & Koch GmbH, Postfach 1329, D-7238 Oberndorf, Neckar, GERMANY (U.S. importer—Heckler & Koch, Inc.)

Heckler & Koch, Inc., 21480 Pacific Blvd., Sterling, VA 20166-8903/703-450-1900; FAX: 703-450-8160

Heckman Arms Company, 1736 Skyline Dr., Richmond Heights, OH 44143/216-289-9182

Helwan (See U.S. importer—Interarms)

Hemlock Gun Shop, Box 149, Rt. 590 & Crane Rd., Lakeville, PA 18438/717-226-9410

Henry's Airguns, 1204 W. Locust, Belvidere, IL 61008/815-547-5091

Herold's Gun Shoppe, 1498 E. Main Street, Box 350, Waynesboro, PA 17268/717-762-4010

Hi-Grade Imports, 8655 Monterey Rd., Gilroy, CA 95021/408-842-9301; FAX: 408-842-2374

Hi-Point Firearms, 5990 Philadelphia Dr., Dayton, OH 45415/513-275-4991; FAX: 513-275-4991

High Standard Mfg. Co., Inc., 264 Whitney St., Hartford, CT 06105-2270/203-586-8220; FAX: 203-231-0411

Hill Top Gunsmithing, Rt. 3, Box 85, Canton, NY 13617/315-386-4875

Hill's Hardware & Sporting Goods, 1234 S. Second St., Union City, TN 38261/901-885-1510

Hill's, Inc., 1720 Capital Blvd., Raleigh, NC 27604/919-833-4884

HJS Arms, Inc., P.O. Box 3711, Brownsville, TX 78523-3711/800-453-2767, 210-542-2767

Hobbs Bicycle & Gun Sales, 406 E. Broadway, Hobbs, NM 88240/505-393-9815

Hodson & Son Pell Gun Repair, 4500 S. 100 E., Anderson, IN 46013/317-643-2055

Hoffman's Gun Center, Inc., 2208 Berlin Turnpike, Newington, CT 06111/203-666-8827

Hollywood Engineering, 10642 Arminta St., Sun Valley, CA 91352/818-842-8376

Holston Ent., Inc., P.O. Box 493, Piney Flats, TN 37686

Horchler's Gun Shop, 100 Ratlum Rd. RFD, Collinsville, CT 06022/203-379-1977

Hornady Mfg. Co., P.O. Box 1848, Grand Island, NE 68802/800-338-3220, 308-382-1390; FAX: 308-382-5761

Houma Gun Works, 1520 Grand Caillou Rd., Houma, LA 70363/504-872-2782

Howa Machinery, Ltd., Sukaguchi, Shinkawa-cho, Nishikasugai-gun, Aichi 452, JAPAN (U.S. importer—Interarms)

Huntington Die Specialties, 601 Oro Dam Blvd., Oroville, CA 95965/916-534-1210; FAX: 916-534-1212

Hutch's, 50 E. Main St., Lehi, UT 84043/801-768-3461

Hutchinson's Gun Repair, 507 Clifton St., Pineville, LA 71360/318-640-4315

I

IAI, 6226 Santos Diaz St., Irwindale, CA 91702/818-334-1200

Imbert & Smithers, Inc., 1144 El Camino Real, San Carlos, CA 94070/415-593-4207

IMI, P.O. Box 1044, Ramat Hasharon 47100, ISRAEL/972-3-5485222 (U.S. importer—Magnum Research, Inc.)

Interarms, 10 Prince St., Alexandria, VA 22314/703-548-1400; FAX: 703-549-7826

Intermountain Arms & Tackle, Inc., 105 E. Idaho St., Meridian, ID 83642/208-888-4911; FAX: 208-888-4381

Intermountain Arms & Tackle, Inc., 1375 E. Fairfield Ave., Meridian, ID 83642/208-888-4911; FAX: 208-888-4381

Intratec, 12405 SW 130th St., Miami, FL 33186/305-232-1821; FAX: 305-253-7207

Island Pond Gunshop, P.O. Box 428 Cross St., Island Pond, VT 05846/802-723-4546

J

J&G Gunsmithing, 625 Vernon St., Roseville, CA 95678/916-782-7075

J&T Services, 12¹⁄₂ Woodlawn Ave., Bradford, PA 16701/814-368-3034

J.O. Arms Inc., 5709 Hartsdale, Houston, TX 77036/713-789-0745; FAX: 713-789-7513

Jack First, 1201 Turbine Drive, Rapid City, SD 57701/605-343-9544

Jack's Lock & Gun Shop, 32 4th St., Fond Du Lac, WI 54935/414-922-4420

Jackalope Gun Shop, 1048 S. 5th St., Douglas, WY 82633/307-358-3441

Jackson, Inc., Bill, 9501 U.S. 19 N., Pinellas Park, FL 34666/813-576-4169

Jacobsen's Gun Center, 612 Broadway St., Story City, IA 50248/515-733-2995

Jaeger, Inc., Paul/Dunn's, P.O. Box 449, 1 Madison Ave., Grand Junction, TN 38039/901-764-6909; FAX: 901-764-6503

JagerSport, Ltd., One Wholesale Way, Cranston, RI 02920/800-962-4867, 401-944-9682; FAX: 401-946-2587

Jansma, Jack J., 4320 Kalamazoo Ave., Grand Rapids, MI 49508/616-455-7810; FAX: 616-455-5212

Jay's Sports, Inc., North 88 West 15263 Main St., Menomonee Falls, WI 53051/414-251-0550

Jennings Firearms, Inc., 17692 Cowan, Irvine, CA 92714/714-252-7621; FAX: 714-252-7626

Jensen's Custom Ammunition, 5146 E. Pima, Tucson, AZ 85712/602-325-3346; FAX: 602-322-5704

Jerry's Gun Shop, P.O. Box 88, 100 Main St., Glenarm, IL 62536/217-483-4606

Jim's Gun & Service Center, 514 Tenth Ave. S.E., Aberdeen, SD 57401/605-225-9111

Jim's Trading Post, #10 Southwest Plaza, Pine Bluff, AR 71603/501-534-8591

Joe's Gun Shop, 4430 14th St., Dorr, MI 49323/616-877-4615

Joe's Gun Shop, 5215 W. Edgemont Ave., Phoenix, AZ 85035/602-233-0694

John Q's Quality Gunsmithing, 5165 Auburn Blvd., Sacramento, CA 95841/916-344-7669

Johnson Service, Inc., W., 3654 N. Adrian Rd., Adrian, MI 49221/517-265-2545

Jones, J.D. (See SSK Industries)

Jordan Gun Shop, 28 Magnolia Dr., Tifton, GA 31794/912-382-4251

JSL (Hereford) Ltd., 35 Church St., Hereford HR1 2LR ENGLAND/0432-355416; FAX: 0432-355242 (U.S. importer—Specialty Shooters Supply, Inc.)

K

K&M Industries, Inc., Box 66, 510 S. Main, Troy, ID 83871/208-835-2281; FAX: 208-835-5211

K.B.I., Inc., P.O. Box 5440, Harrisburg, PA 17110-0440/717-540-8518; FAX: 717-540-8567

Kahles U.S.A., P.O. Box 81071, Warwick, RI 02888/800-752-4537; FAX: 401-946-2587

Kahnke Gunworks, 206 West 11th St., Redwood Falls, MN 56283/507-637-2901

Kahr Arms, P.O. Box 220, 630 Route 303, Blauvelt, NY 10913/914-353-5996; FAX: 914-353-7833

Karrer's Gunatorium, 5323 N. Argonne Rd., Spokane, WA 99212/509-924-3030

Keidel's Gunsmithing Service, 927 Jefferson Ave., Washington, PA 15301/412-222-6379

Kel-Tec CNC Industries, Inc., P.O. Box 3427, Cocoa, FL 32924/407-631-0068; FAX: 407-631-1169

Kelbly, Inc., 7222 Dalton Fox Lake Rd., North Lawrence, OH 44666/216-683-4674; FAX: 216-683-7349

Keller's Co., Inc., 511 Spielman Hwy., Rt. 4, Burlington, CT 06013/203-583-2220

Keng's Firearms Specialty, Inc., 875 Wharton Dr. SW, Atlanta, GA 30336/404-691-7611; FAX: 404-505-8445

Kesselring Gun Shop, 400 Hwy. 99 North, Burlington, WA 98233/206-724-3113; FAX: 206-724-7003

Kesselring Gun Shop, 400 Pacific Hwy. 99 North, Burlington, WA 98233/206-724-3113; FAX: 206-724-7003

Kick's Sport Center, 300 Goodge St., Claxton, GA 30417/912-739-1734

Kielon, Gunsmith, Dave, 57 Kittleberger Park, Webster, NY 14580/716-872-2256

Kimber of America, Inc., 9039 SE Jannsen Rd., Clackamas, OR 97015/503-656-1704, 800-880-2418; FAX: 503-656-5357

Kimel Industries, 3800 Old Monroe Rd., P.O. Box 335, Matthews, NC 28105/800-438-9288; FAX: 704-821-6339

King's Gun Shop, Inc., 32301 Walter's Hwy., Franklin, VA 23851/804-562-4725

Kingyon, Paul L., 607 N. 5th St., Burlington, IA 52601/319-752-4465

Kirkpatrick, Gunsmith, Larry, 707 79th St., Lubbock, TX 79404/806-745-5308

Knight's Mfg. Co., 7750 9th St. SW, Vero Beach, FL 32968/407-562-5697; FAX: 407-569-2955

Kopp, Prof. Gunsmith, Terry K., 1301 Franklin, Lexington, MO 64067/816-259-2636

Korth, Robert-Bosch-Str. 4, P.O. Box 1320, 23909 Ratzeburg, GERMANY/0451-4991497; FAX: 0451-4993230 (U.S. importers—Interarms; Mandall Shooting Supplies, Inc.)

Kotila Gun Shop, 726 County Rd. 3SW, Cokato, MN 55321/612-286-5636

Kowa Optimed, Inc., 20001 S. Vermont Ave., Torrance, CA 90502/310-327-1913; FAX: 310-327-4177

Krebs Gunsmithing, 7417 N. Milwaukee Ave., Niles, IL 60714/708-647-6994

Krico/Kriegeskorte GmbH, A., Nurnbergerstrasse 6, D-90602 Pyrbaum GERMANY/0911-796092; FAX: 0911-796074 (U.S. importer—Mandall Shooting Supplies, Inc.)

KSN Industries, Ltd. (See U.S. importer—J.O. Arms Inc.)

L

L&S Technologies, Inc. (See Aimtech Mount Systems)

L'Armurier Alain Bouchard, Inc., 420 Route 143, Ulverton, Quebec CANADA J0B 2J0/819-826-6611

L.A.R. Mfg., Inc., 4133 W. Farm Rd., West Jordan, UT 84088/801-280-3505; FAX: 801-280-1972

Labs Air Gun Shop, 2307 N. 62nd St., Omaha, NE 68104/402-553-0990

LaFrance Specialties, P.O. Box 178211, San Diego, CA 92177-8211/619-293-3373

Laib's Gunsmithing, North Hwy. 23, R.R. 1, Spicer, MN 56288/612-796-2686

Lakefield Arms Ltd., 248 Water St., P.O. Box 129, Lakefield, Ont. K0L 2H0, CANADA/705-652-6735, 705-652-8000; FAX: 705-652-8431

Lapua Ltd., P.O. Box 5, Lapua, FINLAND SF-62101/64-310111; FAX: 64-4388951 (U.S. importers—Champion's Choice; Keng's Firearms Specialty, Inc.)

Laser Devices, Inc., 2 Harris Ct. A-4, Monterey, CA 93940/408-373-0701; FAX: 408-373-0903

Laseraim, Inc. (See Emerging Technologies, Inc.)

Lawson's Custom Firearms, Inc., Art, 313 S. Magnolia Ave., Ocala, FL 32671/904-629-7793

Lee Precision, Inc., 4275 Hwy. U, Hartford, WI 53027/414-673-3075

Leica USA, Inc., 156 Ludlow Ave., Northvale, NJ 07647/201-767-7500; FAX: 201-767-8666

Leo's Custom Stocks, 1767 Washington Ave., Library, PA 15129/412-835-4126

Les Gun & Pawn Shop, 1423 New Boston Rd., Texarkana, TX 75501/903-793-2201

Leupold & Stevens, Inc., P.O. Box 688, Beaverton, OR 97075/503-646-9171; FAX: 503-526-1455

Levan's Sporting Goods, 433 N. Ninth St., Lebanon, PA 17042/717-273-3148

Lew's Mountaineer Gunsmithing, Route 2, Box 330A, Charleston, WV 25314/304-344-3745

Lewis Arms, 1575 Hooksett Rd., Hooksett, NH 03106/603-485-7334

Llama Gabilondo Y Cia, Apartado 290, E-01080, Victoria, SPAIN (U.S. importer—SGS Importers International, Inc.)

Lock Stock & Barrel, 115 SW H St., Grants Pass, OR 97526/503-474-0775

Loftin & Taylor, 2619 N. Main St., Jacksonville, FL 32206/904-353-9634

Log Cabin Sport Shop, 8010 Lafayette Rd., Lodi, OH 44254/216-948-1082

Lolo Sporting Goods, 1026 Main St., Lewiston, ID 83501/208-743-1031

Lone Star Guns, Inc., 2452 Avenue K, Plano, TX 75074/214-424-4501; 800-874-7923

Long Beach Uniform Co., Inc., 2789 Long Beach Blvd., Long Beach, CA 90806/310-424-0220

Longacres, Inc., 358 Chestnut St., Abilene, TN 79602/915-672-9521

Longs Gunsmithing Ltd., W.R., P.O. Box 876, 2 Coverdale St., Cobourg, Ontario CANADA K9A 4H1/416-372-5955

Lorcin Engineering Co., Inc., 10427 San Sevaine Way, Ste. A, Mira Loma, CA 91752/909-360-1406; FAX: 909-360-0623

Lounsbury Sporting Goods, Bob, 104 North St., Middletown, NY 10940/914-343-1808

Lusignant, Armurier, A. Richard, 15820 St. Michel, St. Hyacinthe, Quebec, CANADA, J2T 3R7/514-773-7997

Lutter, Robert E., 3547 Auer Dr., Ft. Wayne, IN 46835/219-485-8319

Lyman Products Corp., Rt. 147, Middlefield, CT 06455/203-349-3421, 800-22-LYMAN; FAX: 203-349-3586

M

M.O.A. Corp., 2451 Old Camden Pike, Eaton, OH 45320/513-456-3669
Mac-1 Distributors, 13974 Van Ness Ave., Gardena, CA 90249/310-327-3582
Magasin Latulippe, Inc., 637 West St. Vallier, P.O. Box 395, Quebec City, Quebec, CANADA G1K 6W8/418-529-0024; FAX: 418-529-6381
Magma Engineering Co., P.O. Box 161, 20955 E. Ocotillo Rd., Queen Creek, AZ 85242/602-987-9008; FAX: 602-987-0148
Magnum Gun Service, 357 Welsh Track Rd., Newark, DE 19702/302-454-0141
Magnum Research, Inc., 7110 University Ave. NE, Minneapolis, MN 55432/612-574-1868; FAX: 612-574-0109
MAGTECH Recreational Products, Inc., 4737 College Park, Ste. 101, San Antonio, TX 78249/210-493-4427; FAX: 210-493-9534
Mandall Shooting Supplies, Inc., 3616 N. Scottsdale Rd., Scottsdale, AZ 85252/602-945-2553; FAX: 602-949-0734
Marksman Products, 5482 Argosy Dr., Huntington Beach, CA 92649/714-898-7535, 800-822-8005; FAX: 714-372-3041
Marlin Firearms Co., 100 Kenna Dr., New Haven, CT 06473/203-239-5621; FAX: 203-234-7991
Martin Gun Shop, Henry, 206 Kay Lane, Shreveport, LA 71115/318-797-1119
Martin's Gun Shop, 3600 Laurel Ave., Natchez, MS 39120/601-442-0784
Mashburn Arms Co., Inc., 1218 North Pennsylvania Ave., Oklahoma City, OK 73107/405-236-5151
Mason, Guns & Ammo Co., Tom, 68 Lake Avenue, Danbury, CT 06810/203-778-6421
Master Gunsmiths, Inc., 12621 Tyconderoga, Houston, TX 77044/713-459-1631
Matt's 10X Gunsmithing, Inc., 5906 Castle Rd., Duluth, MN 55803/218-721-4210
Mauser Werke Oberndorf Waffensysteme GmbH, Postfach 1349, 78722 Oberndorf/N. GERMANY (U.S. importer—Gibbs Rifle Co., Inc.)
Maverick Arms, Inc., 7 Grasso Ave., P.O. Box 497, North Haven, CT 06473/203-230-5300; FAX: 203-230-5420
May & Company, Inc., P.O. Box 1111, 838 W. Capitol St., Jackson, MS 39203/601-354-5781
McBride's Guns, Inc., 2915 San Gabriel, Austin, TX 78705/512-472-3532
McBros Rifle Co., P.O. Box 86549, Phoenix, AZ 85080/602-780-2115; FAX: 602-581-3825
McCann's Machine & Gun Shop, P.O. Box 641, Spanaway, WA 98387/206-537-6919; FAX: 206-537-6993
McClelland Gun Shop, 1533 Centerville Rd., Dallas, TX 75228-2597/214-321-0231
McDaniel Co., Inc., B., 8880 Pontiac Tr., P.O. Box 119, South Lyon, MI 48178/313-437-8989
McGuns, W.H., N. 22nd Ave. at Osborn St., Humboldt, TN 38343/901-784-5742
MCS, Inc., 34 Delmar Dr., Brookfield, CT 06804/203-775-1013; FAX: 203-775-9462
MEC, Inc., 715 South St., Mayville, WI 53050/414-387-4500; FAX: 414-387-5802
MEC-Gar S.R.L., Via Madonnina 64, Gardone V.T., Brescia, ITALY 25063/39-30-8912687; FAX: 39-30-8910065 (U.S. importer—MEC-Gar U.S.A., Inc.)
MEC-Gar U.S.A., Inc., Box 112, 500B Monroe Turnpike, Monroe, CT 06468/203-635-8662; FAX: 203-635-8662
Metro Rod & Reel, 236 S.E. Grand Ave., Portland, OR 97214/503-232-3193
Meydag, Peter, 12114 East 16th, Tulsa, OK 74128/918-437-1928
Miclean, Bill, 499 Theta Ct., San Jose, CA 95123/408-224-1445
Midwestern Shooters Supply, Inc., 150 Main St., Lomira, WI 53048/414-269-4995
Mike's Crosman Service, 5995 Renwood Dr., Winston-Salem, NC 27106/910-922-1031
Mill Creek Sport Center, 8180 Main St., Dexter, MI 48104/313-426-3445
Miller Arms, Inc., P.O. Box 260 Purl St., St. Onge, SD 57779/605-642-5160; FAX: 605-642-5160
Miller's Sport Shop, 2 Summit View Dr., Mountaintop, PA 18707/717-474-6931
Millers Gun Shop, 915 23rd St., Gulfport, MS 39501/601-684-1765
Milliken's Gun Shop, Rt. 2, Box 167, Elm Grove, WV 26003/304-242-0827
Mines Gun Shack, Rt. 4 Box 4623, Tullahoma, TN 37388/615-455-1414
Mirador Optical Corp., P.O. Box 11614, Marina Del Rey, CA 90295-7614/310-821-5587; FAX: 310-305-0386
Mitchell Arms, Inc., 3400-I W. MacArthur Blvd., Santa Ana, CA 92704/714-957-5711; FAX: 714-957-5732
MKS Supply, Inc., 174 S. Mulberry St., Mansfield, OH 44902/419-522-8330; FAX: 513-522-8330
Mo's Competitor Supplies (See MCS, Inc.)
Moates Sport Shop, Bob, 10418 Hull St. Rd., Midlothian, VA 23112/804-276-2293
Modern Guncraft, 148 N. Branford Rd., Wallingford, CT 06492/203-265-1015
Modern MuzzleLoading, Inc., 234 Airport Rd., P.O. Box 130, Centerville, IA 52544/515-856-2626; FAX: 515-856-2628
Moneymaker Guncraft Corp., 1420 Military Ave., Omaha, NE 68131/402-556-0226
Montana Armory, Inc., 100 Centennial Dr., Big Timber, MT 59011/406-932-4353
Montana Gun Works, 3017 10th Ave. S., Great Falls, MT 59405/406-761-4346
Moore & Co., Wm. Larkin, 31360 Via Colinas, Suite 109, Westlake Village, CA 91361/818-889-1986
Moreau, Gunsmith, Pete, 1807 S. Erie, Bay City, MI 48706/517-893-7106
Morrison Gun Shop, Middle Rd., Bradford, ME 04410/207-327-1116
Mossberg (See page 291)
Mowrey Gun Works, P.O. Box 246, Waldron, IN 46182/317-525-6181; FAX: 317-525-6181
Mueschke Manufacturing Co., 1003 Columbia St., Houston, TX 77008/713-869-7073
Mulvey's Marine & Sport Shop, 994 E. Broadway, Monticello, NY 12701/914-794-2000

N

N.A. Guns, Inc., 10220 Florida Blvd., Baton Rouge, LA 70815/504-272-3620
Nagel Gun Shop, Inc., 6201 San Pedro Ave., San Antonio, TX 78216/210-342-5420; 210-342-9893
Nationwide Sports Distributors, Inc., 70 James Way, Southampton, PA 18966/215-322-2050, 800-355-3006; FAX: 702-358-2093
Navy Arms Co., 689 Bergen Blvd., Ridgefield, NJ 07657/201-945-2500; FAX: 201-945-6859
NCP Products, Inc., 721 Maryland Ave. SW, Canton, OH 44710
Nelson's Engine Shop, 620 State St., Cedar Falls, IA 50613/319-266-4497
Nesika Bay Precision, 22239 Big Valley Rd., Poulsbo, WA 98370/206-697-3830
Nevada Air Guns, 3297 "J" Las Vegas Blvd. N., Las Vegas, NV 89115/702-643-8532
Nevada Cartridge Co., 44 Montgomery St., Suite 500, San Francisco, CA 94104/415-925-9394; FAX: 415-925-9396
New Advantage Arms Corp., 2843 N. Alvernon Way, Tucson, AZ 85712/602-881-7444; FAX: 602-323-0949
New England Arms Co., Box 278, Lawrence Lane, Kittery Point, ME 03905/207-439-0593; FAX: 207-439-6726
New England Firearms, 60 Industrial Rowe, Gardner, MA 01440/508-632-9393; FAX: 508-632-2300
Newby, Stewart, Gunsmith, Main & Cross Streets, Newburgh, Ontario CANADA K0K 2S0/613-378-6613
Nicholson's Gunsmithing, 35 Hull St., Shelton, CT 06484/203-924-5635
Nikon, Inc., 1300 Walt Whitman Rd., Melville, NY 11747/516-547-8623; FAX: 516-547-0309
Noreen, Peter H., 5075 Buena Vista Dr., Belgrade, MT 59714/406-586-7383
Norinco, 7A, Yun Tan N Beijing, CHINA (U.S. importers—Century International Arms, Inc.; Interarms)
Norma Precision AB (See U.S. importers—Dynamit Nobel-RWS Inc.; Paul Co. Inc., The)
Norman Custom Gunstocks, Jim, 14281 Cane Rd., Valley Center, CA 92082/619-749-6252
Norrell Arms, John, 2608 Grist Mill Rd., Little Rock, AR 72207/501-225-7864
North American Arms, Inc., 2150 South 950 East, Provo, UT 84606-6285/800-821-5783, 801-374-9990; FAX: 801-374-9998
Northern Precision Airguns, 1161 Grove St., Tawas City, MI 48763/517-362-6949
Northern Virginia Gun Works, Inc., 7518-K Fullerton Road, Springfield, VA 22153/703-644-6504
Northland Sport Center, 1 Mile W. on U.S. Rt. 2, Bagley, MN 56621/218-694-2464
Northwest Arms Service, 720 S. Second St., Atwood, KS 67730/913-626-3700
Nu-Line Guns, Inc., 1053 Caulks Hill Rd., Harvester, MO 63304/314-441-4500; FAX: 314-447-5018
Nusbaum Enterprises, Inc., 1364 Ridgewood Dr., Mobile, AL 36608/205-344-1079
Nygord Precision Products, P.O. Box 8394, La Crescenta, CA 91224/818-352-3027; FAX: 818-352-3378

O

Old Dominion Engravers, 100 Progress Drive, Lynchburg, VA 24502/804-237-4450
Old Western Scrounger, Inc., 12924 Hwy. A-12, Montague, CA 96064/916-459-5445; FAX: 916-459-3944
Olympic Arms, 620-626 Old Pacific Hwy. SE, Olympic, WA 98503/360-456-3471; FAX: 360-491-3447
On Target Gunshop, Inc., 6984 West Main St., Kalamazoo, MI 49009/616-375-4570
Oregon Arms, Inc., 790 Stevens St., Medford, OR 97504-6746/503-560-4040
Orvis Co., The, Rt. 7, Manchester, VT 05254/802-362-3622 ext. 283; FAX: 802-362-3525
Oshman's Sporting Goods, Inc., 975 Gessner, Houston, TX 77024/713-467-1155
Ott's Gun Service, Rt. 2, Box 169A, Atmore, AL 36502/205-862-2588
Outdoor America Store, 1925 N. MacArthur Blvd., Oklahoma City, OK 73127/405-789-0051
Outdoorsman Sporting Goods Co., The, 1707 Radner Ct., Geneva, IL 60134/708-232-9518
Outdoorsman, The, Village West Shopping Center, Fargo, ND 58103/701-282-0131
Outpost, The, 2451 E. Maple Rapids Rd., Eureka, MI 48833/517-224-9562
Ozark Shooters, Inc., P.O. Box 6518, Branson, MO 65616/417-587-3093

P

Pace Marketing, Inc., P.O. Box 2039, Stuart, FL 34995/407-223-2189; FAX: 407-286-9547
Pachmayr, Ltd., 1875 S. Mountain Ave., Monrovia, CA 91016/818-357-7771, 800-423-9704; FAX: 818-358-7251
Pacific International Service Co., Mountain Way, P.O. Box 3, Janesville, CA 96114/916-253-2218
Paducah Shooters Supply, Inc., 3919 Cairo St., Paducah, KY 42001/502-443-3758
Para-Ordnance Mfg., Inc., 3411 McNicoll Ave., Unit 14, Scarborough, Ont. M1V 2V6, CANADA/416-297-7855; FAX: 416-297-1289 (U.S. importer—Para-Ordnance, Inc.)
Para-Ordnance, Inc., 1919 NE 45th St., Ft. Lauderdale, FL 33308
Pardini Armi Srl, Via Italica 154, 55043 Lido Di Camaiore Lu, ITALY/584-90121; FAX: 584-90122 (U.S. importers—MCS, Inc.; Nygord Precision Products)
Pasadena Gun Center, 206 E. Shaw, Pasadena, TX 77506/713-472-0417; FAX: 713-472-1322
Paul Co., The, 27385 Pressonville Rd., Wellsville, KS 66092/913-883-4444; FAX: 913-883-2525
Pedersoli Davide & C., Via Artigiani 57, Gardone V.T., Brescia, ITALY 25063/030-8912402; FAX: 030-8911019 (U.S. importers—Beauchamp & Son, Inc.; Cabela's; Cape Outfitters; Dixie Gun Works; EMF Co., Inc.; Navy Arms Co.; Taylor's & Co., Inc.)
Pederson Co., C.R., 2717 S. Pere Marquette, Ludington, MI 49431/616-843-2061
Pekin Gun & Sporting Goods, 1304 Derby St., Pekin, IL 61554/309-347-6060
Pentax Corp., 35 Inverness Dr. E., Englewood, CO 80112/303-799-8000; FAX: 303-790-1131
Peregrine Sporting Arms, Inc., 14155 Brighton Rd., Brighton, CO 80601/303-654-0850
Perry's Gunshop, P.O. Box 10, 21 E. Third St., Wendell, NC 27591/919-365-4200
Pete's Gun Shop, 31 Columbia St., Adams, MA 01220/413-743-0780
Peters Stahl GmbH, Stettiner Strasse 42, D-33106 Paderborn, GERMANY/05251-750025; FAX: 05251-75611 (U.S. importers—Harris-McMillan Gunworks; Olympic Arms)
Phillips, D.J., Gunsmith, Rt. 1, N31-W22087 Shady Ln., Pewaukee, WI 53072/414-691-2165
Phoenix Armoury, Inc., 248 Miami Ave., Norristown, PA 19403/215-539-0733
Phoenix Arms, 1420 S. Archibald Ave., Ontario, CA 91761/909-947-4843; FAX: 909-947-6798
PHOXX Shooters Supply, 5807 Watt Ave., N. Highlands, CA 95660/800-280-8668
Pietta (See U.S. importers—Navy Arms Co.; Taylor's & Co., Inc.)
Pintos Gun Shop, 827 N. Central #102, Kent, WA 98032/206-859-6333
Pioneer Arms Co., 355 Lawrence Rd., Broomall, PA 19008/215-356-5203
Plaza Gunworks, Inc., 983 Gasden Highway, Birmingham, AL 35235/205-836-6206
Ponsness/Warren, P.O. Box 8, Rathdrum, ID 83858/208-687-2231; FAX: 208-687-2233
Poor Borch's, Inc., 1204 E. College Dr., Marshall, MN 56258/507-532-4880
Potter Gunsmithing, 13960 Boxhorn Dr., Muskego, WI 53150/414-425-4830
Powell & Son (Gunmakers) Ltd., William, 35-37 Carrs Lane, Birmingham B4 7SX ENGLAND/21-643-0689; FAX: 21-631-3504 (U.S. importer—The William Powell Agency)
Powell Agency, William, The, 22 Circle Dr., Bellmore, NY 11710/516-679-1158
Prairie River Arms, 1220 N. Sixth St., Princeton, IL 61356/815-875-1616; FAX: 815-875-1402
Precision Airgun Sales, Inc., 5139 Warrensville Center Rd., Maple Hts., OH 44137-1906/216-587-5005
Precision Arms & Gunsmithing Ltd., Hwy. 27 & King Road Box 809, Nobleton, Ontario, CANADA L0G 1N0/416-859-0965
Precision Gun Works, 4717 State Rd. 44, Oshkosh, WI 54904/414-233-2274
Precision Gunsmithing, 2723 W. 6th St., Amarillo, TX 79106/806-376-7223
Precision Pellet, 1016 Erwin Dr., Joppa, MD 21085/410-679-8179
Precision Reloading, Inc., P.O. Box 122, Stafford Springs, CT 06076/203-684-7979; FAX: 203-684-6788
Precision Sales International, Inc., P.O. Box 1776, Westfield, MA 01086/413-562-5055; FAX: 413-562-5056
Precision Small Arms, 155 Carlton Rd., Charlottesville, VA 22902/804-293-6124; FAX: 804-295-0780
Precision Sport Optics, 15571 Producer Lane, Unit G, Huntington Beach, CA 92649/714-891-1309; FAX: 714-892-6920
Preuss Gun Shop, 4545 E. Shepherd, Clovis, CA 93612/209-299-6248
Professional Armaments, Inc., 3695 South Redwood Rd., West Valley City, UT 84119/801-975-7422

Q

Quad City Gun Repair, 220 N. Second St., Eldridge, IA 52748/319-285-4153
Quality Arms, Inc., Box 19477, Dept. GD, Houston, TX 77224/713-870-8377; FAX: 713-870-8524
Quality Firearms of Idaho, Inc., 114 13th Ave. S., Nampa, ID 83651/208-466-1631
Quality Parts Co./Bushmaster Firearms, 999 Roosevelt Trail, Bldg. 3, Windham, ME 04062/800-998-7928, 207-892-2005; FAX: 207-892-8068

R

R&R Shooters Supply, W6553 North Rd., Mauston, WI 53948/608-847-4562
R.D.P. Tool Co., Inc., 49162 McCoy Ave., East Liverpool, OH 43920/216-385-5129
R.L. "Skeet" Hill Gun Shop, 209½ Raymond Street, P.O. Box 457, Verona, MS 38879/601-566-8353

Rajo Corporation, 2106 W. Franklin St., Evansville, IN 47712/812-422-6945

Ralph's Gun Shop, 200 Fourth St., South, Niverville, Manitoba, CANADA R0A 1E0/204-338-4581

Ram-Line, Inc., 545 Thirty-One Rd., Grand Junction, CO 81504/303-434-4500; FAX: 303-434-4004

Randy's Gun Repair, P.O. Box 106, 231 Hierlihy High, Tabustinac, N.B. CANADA E0C 2A0/506-779-4768

Ranging, Inc., Routes 5 & 20, East Bloomfield, NY 14443/716-657-6161; FAX: 716-657-5405

Rapids Gun Shop, 7811 Buffalo Ave., Niagara Falls, NY 14304/716-283-7873

Ravell Ltd., 289 Diputacion St., 08009, Barcelona SPAIN

Ray's Gunsmith Shop, 3199 Elm Ave., Grand Junction, CO 81504/970-434-6162

Ray's Liquor and Sporting Goods, 1956 Solano St., Box 677, Corning, CA 96021/916-824-5625

Ray's Rod & Reel Service, 414 Pattie St., Wichita, KS 67211/316-267-9462

Ray's Sport Shop, Inc., 559 Route 22, North Plainfield, NJ 07060/908-561-4400

Ray's Sporting Goods, 730 Singleton Blvd., Dallas, TX 75212/214-747-7916

RCBS, Div. of Blount, Inc., 605 Oro Dam Blvd., Oroville, CA 95965/800-533-5000, 916-533-5191; FAX: 916-533-1647

Red's Gunsmithing, P.O. Box 1251, Chickaloon, AK 99674/907-745-4500

Redding Reloading Equipment, 1089 Starr Rd., Cortland, NY 13045/607-753-3331; FAX: 607-756-8445

Redfield, Inc., 5800 E. Jewell Ave., Denver, CO 80227/303-757-6411; FAX: 303-756-2338

Reliable Gun & Tackle, Ltd., 3227 Fraser St., Vancouver, British Columbia CANADA V5V 4B8/604-874-4710

Reloading Center, 515 W. Main St., Burley, ID 83318/208-678-5053

Remington (See page 291)

Reynold's Gun Shop, Inc., 3502A S. Broadway, Tyler, TX 75702/903-592-1531

Reynolds Gun Shop, 314 N. Western Ave., Peoria, IL 61606/309-674-5790

Richland Gun Shop, 207 Park St., Box 645, Richland, PA 17087/717-866-4246

Richmond Gun Shop, 517 E. Main St., Richmond, VA 23219/804-644-7207

Rigby & Co., John, 66 Great Suffolk St., London SE1 OBU, ENGLAND

River Bend Sport Shop, 230 Grand Seasons Dr., Waupaca, WI 54981/715-258-3583

Robinson's Sporting Goods, Ltd., 1307 Broad St., Victoria, British Columbia CANADA V8W 2A8/604-385-3429

Rocking S Gun Shop, 316 VC Ranches, Hwy. 287, P.O. Box 1469, Ennis, MT 59729/406-682-5229

Rocky Mountain Arms, Inc., 600 S. Sunset, Unit C, Longmont, CO 80501/303-768-8522; FAX: 303-678-8766

Ron's Gun Repair, 1212 Benson Road, Sioux Falls, SD 57104/605-338-7398

Rossi S.A., Amadeo, Rua: Amadeo Rossi, 143, Sao Leopoldo, RS, BRAZIL 93030-220/051-592-5566 (U.S. importer—Interarms)

Ruko Products, Inc., 2245 Kenmore Ave., No. 102, Buffalo, NY 14207/716-874-2707; FAX: 905-826-1353

Rusk Gun Shop, Inc., 6904 Watts Rd., Madison, WI 53719/608-274-8740

Russell's Sporting Goods, 8228 Macleod Trail SE, Calgary, Alberta, CANADA T2M 2B8/403-276-9222

Rutko Corp. d/b/a Stonewall Range, 100 Ken-Mar Dr., Broadview Heights, OH 44147/216-526-0029

RWS (See U.S. importer—Dynamit Nobel-RWS, Inc.)

S

S.E.M. Gun Works, 3204 White Horse Rd., Greenville, SC 29611/803-295-2948

S.K. Guns, Inc., 302 25th St. South, Suite A, Fargo, ND 58103/701-293-4867; FAX: 701-232-0001

Safari Arms/SWG (See Olympic Arms)

Sams Gunsmithing, David, 225 Front St., Lititz, PA 17543/717-626-0021

San Marco (See U.S. importers—Cape Outfitters; EMF Co., Inc.)

Sanders Custom Gun Service, 2358 Tyler Ln., Louisville, KY 40205/502-454-3338

Sanders Custom Gun Shop, P.O. Box 5967, 2031 Bloomingdale Ave., Augusta, GA 30906/706-798-5220

Sanders Gun Shop, 3001 Fifth St., P.O. Box 4181, Meridian, MS 39301/601-485-5301

Saskatoon Gunsmith Shoppe, Ltd., 2310 Avenue C North, Saskatoon, Saskachewan, CANADA S7L 5X5/306-244-2023

Sauer (See U.S. importer—Paul Co., The)

Saville Iron Co. (See Greenwood Precision)

Scalzo's Sporting Goods, 1520 Farm to Market Road, Endwell, NY 13760/607-746-7586

Scattergun Technologies, Inc., 518 3rd Ave. S., Nashville, TN 37202/615-254-1441; FAX: 615-254-1449

Scharch Mfg., Inc., 10325 Co. Rd. 120, Unit C, Salida, CO 81201/719-539-7242; FAX: 719-539-3021

Schmidt & Bender, Inc., Brook Rd., P.O. Box 134, Meriden, NH 03770/603-469-3565, 800-468-3450; FAX: 603-469-3471

Schultheis Sporting Goods, 8 Main St., Arkport, NY 14807/607-295-7485

Sea Gull Marina, 1400 Lake, Two Rivers, WI 54241/414-794-7533

Seecamp Co., Inc., L.W., P.O. Box 255, New Haven, CT 06502/203-877-3429

Selin Gunsmith, Ltd., Del, 2803 23rd Street, Vernon, British Columbia, CANADA V1T 4Z5/604-545-6413

SGS Importers International, Inc., 1750 Brielle Ave., Unit B1, Wanamassa, NJ 07712/908-493-0302; FAX: 908-493-0301

Shaler Eagle, 102 Arrow Wood, Jonesbrough, TN 37659/615-753-7620

Shamburg's Wholesale Spt. Gds., 403 Frisco Ave., Clinton, OK 73601/405-323-0209

Shapel's Gun Shop, 1708 N. Liberty, Boise, ID 83704/208-375-6159

Sharp (See U.S. importer—Great Lakes Airguns)

Sharps Arms Co., Inc., C. (See Montana Armory, Inc.)

Shepherd Scope Ltd., Box 189, Waterloo, NE 68069/402-779-2424; FAX: 402-779-4010

Sheridan USA, Inc., Austin, P.O. Box 577, 36 Haddam Quarter Rd., Durham, CT 06422/203-349-1772; FAX: 203-349-1771

Shockley, Harold, 2204 E. Farmington Road, Hanna City, IL 61536/309-565-4524

Shooters Supply, 1120 Tieton Dr., Yakima, WA 98902/509-482-1181; FAX: 509-575-0315

Shooting Gallery, The, 249 Seneca, Weirton, WV 26062/304-723-3298

Siegle's Gunshop, Inc., 508 W. MacArthur Blvd., Oakland, CA 94609/415-655-8789

Sievert's Guns 4107 W. Northern, Pueblo, CO 81005/719-564-0035

SIG, CH-8212 Neuhausen, SWITZERLAND (U.S. importer—Mandall Shooting Supplies, Inc.)

SIG-Sauer (See U.S. importer—Sigarms, Inc.)

Sigarms, Inc., Corporate Park, Exeter, NH 03833/603-772-2302; FAX: 603-772-9082

Sile Distributors, Inc., 7 Centre Market Pl., New York, NY 10013/212-925-4111; FAX: 212-925-3149

Sillman, Hal, Associated Services, 1514 NE 205 Terrace, Miami, FL 33179/305-651-4450

Simmons Enterprises, Ernie, 709 East Elizabethtown Rd., Manheim, PA 17545/717-664-4040

Simmons Gun Repair, 700 S. Rodgers Rd., Olathe, KS 66062/913-782-3131

Simmons Outdoor Corp., 2120 Killearney Way, Tallahassee, FL 32308-3402/904-878-5100; FAX: 904-878-0300

Sipes Gun Shop, 7415 Asher Ave., Little Rock, AR 72204/501-565-8480

Skip's Gunshop, 3 Pleasant St., Bristol, NH 03222/603-744-3100

Smith & Smith Gun Shop, Inc., 2589 Oscar Johnson Drive, North Charleston, SC 29405/803-744-2024

Smith & Wesson (See page 291)

Smith's Lawn & Marine Svc., 9100 Main St., Clarence, NY 14031/716-633-7868

Societa Armi Bresciane Srl. (See U.S. importer—Gamba, USA)

Sodak Sport & Bait, 850 South Hwy 281, Aberdeen, SD 57401/605-225-2737

Solvay Home & Outdoor Center, 102 First St., Solvay, NY 13209/315-468-6285

Southland Gun Works, Inc., 1134 Hartsville Rd., Darlington, SC 29532/803-393-6291

Southwest Airguns, 3311 Ryan St., Lake Charles, LA 70601/318-474-6038

Southwest Shooters Supply, Inc., 1940 Linwood Blvd., Oklahoma City, OK 73106/405-235-4476; FAX: 405-235-7022

Specialty Shooters Supply, Inc., 3325 Griffin Rd., Suite 9mm, Fort Lauderdale, FL 33317

Speer Products, Div. of Blount, Inc., P.O. Box 856, Lewiston, ID 83501/208-746-2351; FAX: 208-746-2915

Sporting Arms Mfg., Inc., 801 Hall Ave., Littlefield, TX 79339/806-385-5665; FAX: 806-385-3394

Sports Mart, The, 828 Ford St., Ogdensburg, NY 13669/315-393-2865

Sports Shop, The, 8055 Airline Highway, Baton Rouge, LA 70815/504-927-2600

Sports World, Inc., 5800 S. Lewis Ave., Suite 154, Tulsa, OK 74105/918-742-4027

Sports World, Route 52, Liberty, NY 12754/914-292-3077

Sportsman's Center, U.S. Hwy. 130, Box 731, Bordentown, NJ 08505/609-298-5300

Sportsman's Depot, 644 Miami St., Urban, OH 43078/513-653-4429

Sportsman's Haven, 14695 E. Pike Rd., Cambridge, OH 43725/614-432-7243

Sportsman's Paradise Gunsmith, 640 Main St., Pineville, LA 71360/318-443-6041

Sportsman's Shop, 101 W. Main St., New Holland, PA 17557/717-354-4311

Sportsmen's Exchange & Western Gun Traders, Inc., 560 South C St., Oxnard, CA 93030/805-483-1917

Sportsmen's Repair Ctr., Inc., 106 S. High St., Box 134, Columbus Groves, OH 45830/419-659-5818

Spradlin's, 113 Arthur St., Pueblo, CO 81004/719-543-9462

Springfield, Inc., 420 W. Main St., Geneseo, IL 61254/309-944-5631; FAX: 309-944-3676

SSK Industries, 721 Woodvue Lane, Wintersville, OH 43952/614-264-0176; FAX: 614-264-2257

Stalwart Corporation, P.O. Box 357, Pocatello, ID 83204/208-232-7899; FAX: 208-232-0815

Stan's Gun Repair, RR #2 Box 48, Westbrook, MN 56183-9521/507-274-5649

Star Bonifacio Echeverria S.A., Torrekva 3, Eibar, SPAIN 20600/43-107340; FAX: 43-101524 (U.S. importer—Interarms)

Star Machine Works, 418 10th Ave., San Diego, CA 92101/619-232-3216

Starnes, Ken, 32900 SW Laurelview Rd., Hillsboro, OR 97123/503-628-0705

Steyr Mannlicher AG, Mannlicherstrasse 1, P.O.B. 1000, A-4400 Steyr, AUSTRIA/0043-7252-896-0; FAX: 0043-7252-68621 (U.S. importer—GSI, Inc.)

Stocker's Shop, 5199 Mahoning Ave., Warren, OH 44483/216-847-9579

Stoeger (See page 291)

Stoeger Industries, 5 Mansard Ct., Wayne, NJ 07470/201-872-9500, 800-631-0722; FAX: 201-872-0722

Sundance Industries, Inc., 25163 W. Avenue Stanford, Valencia, CA 91355/805-257-4807

Surplus Center, 515 S.E. Spruce Street, Roseburg, OR 97470/503-672-4312

Survival Arms, Inc., 4500 Pine Cone Place, Cocoa, FL 32922/407-633-4880; FAX: 407-633-4975

Swarovski Optik North America Ltd., One Wholesale Way, Cranston, RI 02920/401-942-3380, 800-426-3089; FAX: 401-946-2587

Swift Instruments, Inc., 952 Dorchester Ave., Boston, MA 02125/617-436-2960; FAX: 617-436-3232

Swivel Machine Works, Inc., 167 Cherry St., Suite 286, Milford, CT 06460/203-926-1840; FAX: 203-874-9212

T

T.J.'s Firing Line Gunsmith, 692-A Peoria Street, Aurora, CO 80011/303-363-1911

Tanfoglio S.r.l., Fratelli, via Valtrompia 39, 41, 25068 Gardone V.T., Brescia, ITALY/30-8910361; FAX: 30-8910183 (U.S. importer—E.A.A. Corp.)

Tank's Rifle Shop, P.O. Box 474, Fremont, NE 68025/402-727-1317; FAX: 402-721-2573

Tanner (See U.S. importer—Mandall Shooting Supplies, Inc.)

Tapco, Inc., 3615 Kennesaw N. Ind. Pkwy, Kennesaw, GA 30144/800554-1445; FAX: 404-425-1510

Tasco Sales, Inc., 7600 NW 26th St., Miami, FL 33156/305-591-3670; FAX: 305-592-5895

Taurus Firearms, Inc., 16175 NW 49th Ave., Miami, FL 33014/305-624-1115; FAX: 305-623-7506

Taurus International Firearms (See U.S. importer—Taurus Firearms, Inc.)

Taylor & Vadney, Inc., 303 Central Ave., Albany, NY 12206/518-472-9183

Taylor's & Co., Inc., 304 Lenoir Dr., Winchester, VA 22603/703-722-2017; FAX: 703-722-2018

Taylor's Sporting Goods, Gene, 445 W. Gunnison Ave., Grand Junction, CO 81505/303-242-8165

Ted's Gun & Reel Repair, 311 Natchitoches St. Box 1635, W. Monroe, LA 71291/318-323-0661

Ten Ring Service, 2227 West Lou Dr., Jacksonville, FL 32216/904-724-7419

Texas Armory, P.O. Box 154906, Waco, TX 76715/817-867-6972

Texas Longhorn Arms, Inc., 5959 W. Loop South, Suite 424, Bellaire, TX 77401/713-341-0775; FAX: 713-660-0493

Theoben Engineering, Stephenson Road, St. Ives, Huntingdon, Cambs., PE17 4WJ ENGLAND/011-0480-461718

Thompson's Gunshop, Inc., 10254 84th St., Alto, MI 49302/616-891-0440

Thompson/Center (See page 291)

300 Gunsmith Service Inc., at Cherry Creek Park Shooting Center, 12500 E. Bellview Ave., Englewood, CO 80111/303-690-3300

Thunder Mountain Arms, P.O. Box 593, Oak Harbor, WA 98277/206-679-4657; FAX: 206-675-1114

Time Precision, Inc., 640 Federal Rd., Brookfield, CT 06804/203-775-8343

TOZ (See Nygord Precision Products)

Traders, The, 885 E. 14th St., San Leandro, CA 94577/510-569-0555

Trading Post, The, 412 Erie St. S., Massillon, OH 44646/216-833-7761

Traditions, Inc., P.O. Box 235, Deep River, CT 06417/203-526-9555; FAX: 203-526-4564

Trester, Inc., Verne, 3604 West 16th St., Indianapolis, IN 46222/317-638-6921

Trijicon, Inc., 49385 Shafer Ave., P.O. Box 6029, Wixom, MI 48393-6029/810-960-7700; FAX: 810-960-7725

U

U.S. General Technologies, Inc., 145 Mitchell Ave., South San Francisco, CA 94080/415-634-8440; FAX: 415-634-8452

Uberti USA, Inc., 362 Limerock Rd., P.O. Box 509, Lakeville, CT 06039/203-435-8068; FAX: 203-435-8146

Uberti, Aldo, Casella Postale 43, I-25063 Gardone V.T., ITALY (U.S. importers—American Arms, Inc.; Cape Outfitters; Cimarron Arms; Dixie Gun Works; EMF Co., Inc.; Forgett Jr., Valmore J.; Navy Arms Co; Taylor's & Co., Inc.; Uberti USA, Inc.)

Ultimate Accuracy, 121 John Shelton Rd., Jacksonville, AR 72076/501-985-2530

Ultralux (See U.S. importer—Keng's Firearms Specialty, Inc.)

Unertl Optical Co., Inc., John, 308 Clay Ave., P.O. Box 818, Mars, PA 16046-0818/412-625-3810

Unique Sporting Goods, 1538 Columbia St., Lorreto, PA 15940/814-674-8889

Unique/M.A.P.F., 10, Les Allees, 64700 Hendaye, FRANCE 64700/33-59 20 71 93 (U.S. importer—Nygord Precision Products)

Upper Missouri Trading Co., 304 Harold St., Crofton, NE 68730/402-388-4844

Upton's Gun Shop, 810 Croghan St., Fremont, OH 43420/419-332-1326

V

Valley Gun Shop, 7719 Harford Rd., Baltimore, MD 21234/410-668-2171

Valley Gunsmithing, John A. Foster, 619 Second St., Webster City, IA 50595/515-832-5102

Valor Corp., 5555 NW 36th Ave., Miami, FL 33142/305-633-0127; FAX: 305-634-4536

Van's Gunsmith Service, Rt. 69A, Parish, NY 13131/315-625-7251

VanBurnes Gun Shop, 2706 Sylvania Ave., Toledo, OH 43613/419-475-9526

Voere-KGH m.b.H., P.O. Box 416, A-6333 Kufstein, Tirol, AUSTRIA/0043-5372-62547; FAX: 0043-5372-65752 (U.S. importers—JagerSport, Ltd.)

Volquartsen Custom Ltd., RR 1, Box 33A, P.O. Box 271, Carroll, IA 51401/712-792-4238; FAX: 712-792-2542

W

Walker Arms Co., Inc., 499 County Rd. 820, Selma, AL 36701/334-872-6231

Wallace & Cockrell Gunsmiths, Inc., 8240 I-30 West, Fort Worth, TX 76108/817-246-4622

Wallace Gatlin Gun Repair, 140 Gatlin Rd., Oxford, AL 36203/205-831-6993

Walther GmbH, Carl, B.P. 4325, D-89033 Ulm, GERMANY (U.S. importer—Interarms)

Warren's Sports Hdqts., 240 W. Main St., Washington, NC 27889/919-946-0960

Way It Was Sporting, The, 620 Chestnut Street, Moorestown, NJ 08057/609-231-0111

Weapon Works, The, 7017 N. 19th Ave., Phoenix, AZ 85021/602-995-3010

Weatherby (See page 291)

Weaver Scope Repair Service, 1121 Larry Mahan Dr., Suite B, El Paso, TX 79925/915-593-1005

Weihrauch KG, Hermann, Industriestrasse 11, 8744 Mellrichstadt, GERMANY/09776-497-498 (U.S. importers—Beeman Precision Airguns; E.A.A. Corp.)

Welsh, Bud, 80 New Road, E. Amherst, NY 14051/716-688-6344

Wessel Gun Service, 4000 E. 9-Mile Rd., Warren, MI 48091/313-756-2660

Wessinger Custom Guns & Engraving, 268 Limestone Rd., Chapin, SC 29036/803-345-5677

West Gate Gunsports, Inc., 10116 175th Street, Edmonton, Alberta, CANADA T5S 1A1/403-489-9633

West Luther Gun Repair, R.R. #1, Conn, Ontario, CANADA N0G 1N0/519-848-6260

Wheeler Gun Shop, C., 1908 George Washington Way Bldg. F, Richland, WA 99352/509-946-4634

White Dog Gunsmithing, 62 Central Ave., Ilion, NY 13357/315-894-6211

White Shooting Systems, Inc., 25 E. Hwy. 40, Box 330-12, Roosevelt, UT 84066/801-722-3085; FAX: 801-722-3054

Wholesale Sports, 12505 97 St., Edmonton, Alberta, CANADA T5G 1Z8/403-426-4417; 403-477-3737

Wichita Arms, Inc., 923 E. Gilbert, P.O. Box 11371, Wichita, KS 67211/316-265-0661; FAX: 316-265-0760

Wichita Guncraft, Inc., 4607 Barnett Rd., Wichita Falls, TX 76310/817-692-5622

Wild West Guns, Inc., 7521 Old Seward Highway #A, Anchorage, Alaska 99518/907-344-4500; FAX: 907-344-4005

Wildey, Inc., P.O. Box 475, Brookfield, CT 06804/203-355-9000; FAX: 203-354-7759

Wilkinson Arms, 26884 Pearl Rd., Parma, ID 83660/208-722-6771; FAX: 208-722-5197

Will's Gun Shop, 5603 N. Hubbard Lake Rd., Spruce, MI 48762/517-727-2500

Willborn Outdoors & Feed, 505 Main Avenue N.W., Cullman, AL 35055/205-737-9595

William's Gun Shop, Ben, 1151 S. Cedar Ridge, Duncanville, TX 75137/214-780-1807

Williams Gun Sight & Outfitters, 7389 Lapeer Rd., Rt. #1, Davison, MI 48423/313-653-2131, 800-530-9028; FAX: 313-658-2140

Williams Gunsmithing, 4985 Cole Rd., Saginaw, MI 48601/517-777-1240

Williamson Precision Gunsmithing, 117 W. Pipeline, Hurst, TX 76053/817-285-0064; FAX: 817-285-0064

Winchester (See page 291)

Windsor Gun Shop, 8410 Southeastern Ave., Indianapolis, IN 46239/317-862-2512

Wiseman and Co., Bill, P.O. Box 3427, Bryan, TX 77805/409-690-3456; FAX: 409-690-0156

Wisner's Gun Shop, Inc., 287 NW Chehalis Ave., Chehalis, WA 98532/206-748-8942; FAX: 206-748-7011

Wolf Custom Gunsmithing, Gregory, c/o Albright's Gun Shop, 36 E. Dover St., Easton, MD 21601/410-820-8811

Wolfer Brothers, Inc., 1701 Durham, Houston, TX 77007/713-869-7640

Woodman's Sporting Goods, 223 Main Street, Norway, ME 04268/207-743-6602

World Class Airguns, 2736 Morningstar Dr., Indianapolis, IN 46229/317-897-5548

Wortner Gun Works, Ltd., 433 Queen St., Chatham, Ont., CANADA N7M 5K5/519-352-0924

Wright's Hardwood Gunstock Blanks, 8540 SE Kane Rd., Gresham, OR 97080/503-666-1705

Wyoming Armory, Inc., Box 28, Farson, WY 82932/307-273-5556

Y

Ye Olde Blk Powder Shop, 994 W. Midland Rd., Auburn, MI 48611/517-662-2271; FAX: 512-662-2666

Z

Zanes Gun Rack, 4167 N. High St., Columbus, OH 43214/614-263-0369

Zeiss Optical, Carl, 1015 Commerce St., Petersburg, VA 23803/804-861-0033; FAX: 804-733-4024

Warranty Service Centers

BE=Benjamin BR=Browning CR=Crosman MO=Mossberg RE=Remington ST=Stoeger SW=Smith & Wesson TC=Thompson/Center WN=Winchester WE=Weatherby

SERVICE CENTER	CITY	BE	BR	CR	MO	RE	ST	SW	TC	WN	WE
ALABAMA											
B&W Gunsmithing	Cullman					●					
Dubbs, Gunsmith, Dale R.	Seminole					●					
Hat's Gun Supply	Cullman		●								
Nusbaum Enterprises, Inc.	Mobile				●						
Ott's Gun Service	Atmore		●			●					
Plaza Gunworks, Inc.	Birmingham				●	●	●		●	●	
Walker Arms Co., Inc.	Selma		●		●	●	●		●	●	●
Wallace Gatlin Gun	Oxford									●	
Wilborn Outdoors & Feed	Cullman								●	●	
ALASKA											
Down Under Gunsmiths	Fairbanks										●
Red's Gunsmithing	Chickaloon		●		●	●		●			
Wild West Guns, Inc.	Anchorage				●				●		
ARIZONA											
Dave's Airgun Service	Tempe	●									
Don's Sport Shop, Inc.	Scottsdale		●	●	●	●			●	●	
Jensen's Custom Ammunition	Tucson		●		●	●		●	●	●	
Joe's Gun Shop	Phoenix			●		●					
Weapon Works, The	Phoenix								●		
ARKANSAS											
Broadway Arms	North Little Rock					●				●	
Gun Exchange, Inc.	Little Rock				●	●		●			
Jim's Trading Post	Pine Bluff		●		●						
Sipes Gun Shop	Little Rock		●		●	●			●		
CALIFORNIA											
Air Guns Unlimited	La Puente				●	●					
Air Venture Air Guns	Bellflower	●		●							
Airguns International	Santa Rosa	●		●							
Argonaut Gun Shop	Modesto					●					
Bain & Davis	San Gabriel				●	●					●
Beeman Precision Arms, Inc.	Santa Rosa	●									
Bolsa Gunsmithing	Westminster		●		●	●	●			●	●
Bridge Sportsman's Ctr.	Paso Robles					●	●				
Cal's Customs	Fallbrook		●		●						

SERVICE CENTER	CITY	BE	BR	CR	MO	RE	ST	SW	TC	WN	WE
Duncan's Gunworks	San Marcos										●
Grundman's	Rio Dell										
Gunshop, Inc., The	Lancaster		●		●	●				●	
Huntington Sportsman's Store	Oroville		●			●				●	●
Imbert & Smithers, Inc.	San Carlos		●			●				●	
J&G Gunsmithing	Roseville					●					
John Q's Quality Gunsmithing	Sacramento										
Long Beach Uniform Co., Inc.	Long Beach			●							
Mac-1	Gardena	●		●		●		●			
Miclean, Bill	San Jose	●		●		●		●			
Pacific International Service Co.	Janesville								●		
PHOXX Shooters Supply	N. Highlands	●	●		●	●				●	
Preuss Gun Shop	Clovis	●		●							
Ray's Liquor and Sporting Goods	Corning			●	●	●					
Siegle's Gunshop, Inc.	Oakland			●		●					
Sportsman's Exchange, Inc.	Oxnard				●						
Traders, The	San Leandro			●		●					
COLORADO											
Foothills Shooting Ctr.	Lakewood	●			●	●				●	
Gart Brothers Sporting Goods	Denver				●	●					
H&B Service, Inc.	Littleton	●	●			●			●		
Ray's Gunsmith Shop	Grand Junction	●	●								
Sievert's Guns	Pueblo										
Spradlin's	Pueblo					●					
Taylor's Sporting Goods, Gene	Grand Junction					●			●	●	●
300 Gunsmith Service (Wichita Guncraft)	Englewood					●				●	
T.J.'s Firing Line Gunsmith	Aurora				●	●		●			
CONNECTICUT											
Gunsmithing Limited	Fairfield		●			●				●	
Hoffman's Gun Center, Inc.	Newington				●	●					
Horchler's Gun Shop	Collinsville			●							
Keller's Co. Inc.	Burlington					●					
Mason, Gun & Ammo Co., Tom	Danbury										
Modern Guncraft	Wallingford	●		●	●						
Nicholson's Gunsmithing	Shelton				●	●			●	●	
DELAWARE											
Magnum Gun Service	Newark					●					

See page 285 for Service Center addresses.

Warranty Service Centers (cont.)

BE=Benjamin ■ BR=Browning ■ CR=Crosman ■ MO=Mossberg ■ RE=Remington ■ ST=Stoeger ■ SW=Smith & Wesson ■ TC=Thompson/Center ■ WN=Winchester ■ WE=Weatherby

SERVICE CENTER	CITY	BE	BR	CR	MO	RE	ST	SW	TC	WN	WE
FLORIDA											
Air Gun Rifle Repair	Sebring			•							
Alexander, Gunsmith, W.R.	Tallahassee					•					
Glades Gunworks	Naples				•	•		•			
Green Acres Sporting Goods, Inc.	Jacksonville		•	•	•	•		•		•	
Gun Doc, Inc.	Miami		•	•		•					
Jackson, Inc., Bill	Pinellas Park									•	
Lawsons Custom Firearms, Inc., Art	Ocala				•	•					
Loftin & Taylor	Jacksonville			•		•					
Sillman, Hal, Associated Services	Miami	•									
Ten Ring Service	Jacksonville								•		
GEORGIA											
Accuracy Gun Shop	Columbus		•		•	•				•	
Dorn's Outdoor Center	Macon		•	•	•	•				•	
Ed's Gun & Tackle Shop, Inc.	Marietta	•	•	•							
Franklin Sports, Inc.	Bogart		•			•		•		•	
Gun Corral, Inc.	Decatur					•					
Jordan Gun & Pawn Shop	Tifton		•								
Kick's Sport Center	Claxton										
Sanders Custom Gun Shop	Augusta			•		•				•	
HAWAII											
Chung, Gunsmith, Mel	Kaunakakai		•	•	•	•		•		•	•
IDAHO											
Intermountain Arms & Tackle, Inc.	Meridian		•	•	•	•		•		•	•
Lolo Sporting Goods	Lewiston		•		•	•				•	•
Quality Firearms	Nampa			•	•	•					
Reloading Center	Burley			•		•					
Shapel's Gun Shop	Boise					•					
ILLINOIS											
A&M Sales	North Lake	•		•	•						
Darnall's Gun Works	Bloomington			•	•	•					
Groenwald, John	Mundelein		•	•							
Henry's Airguns	Belvidere			•							
Jerry's Gunshop	Glenarm					•					
Krebs Gunsmithing	Niles										
Outdoorsman Sporting Goods Co.	Geneva	•			•	•					
Pekin Gun & Sporting Goods	Pekin			•	•						
Reynolds Gun Shop	Peoria		•								
Shockley, Harold	Hanna City		•								
INDIANA											
Airgun Centre, Ltd.	Lawrenceburg			•	•						
Hodson & Son Pell Gun Repair	Anderson			•	•						

SERVICE CENTER	CITY	BE	BR	CR	MO	RE	ST	SW	TC	WN	WE
Lutter, Robert E.	Ft. Wayne		•	•							
Rajo Corporation	Evansville		•	•							
Trester, Inc.	Indianapolis				•	•					
Windsor Gun Shop	Indianapolis			•	•	•					
IOWA											
Daryl's Gun Shop, Inc.	State Center		•			•					
Glenn's Reel & Rod Repair	Des Moines		•			•					
Jacobson's Gun Center	Story City			•		•					•
Nelson's Engine Shop	Cedar Falls					•					
Quad City Gun Repair	Eldridge				•	•				•	
Valley Gunsmithing, John A. Foster	Webster City				•	•				•	
KANSAS											
Bullseye Gun Works	Overland Park			•		•					
Gordon's Wigwam	Wichita		•	•		•					
Northwest Arms Service	Atwood			•		•				•	
Ray's Rod & Reel Service	Wichita					•					
Simmons Gun Repair	Olathe					•		•			
KENTUCKY											
D&J Bullet Co.	Russel										
Danny's Gun Repair, Inc.	Louisville			•		•		•			
Firearms Service Center	Louisville			•	•	•					
Garrett Gunsmiths, Inc.	Newport					•					
Paducah Shooters Supply, Inc.	Paducah				•					•	
LOUISIANA											
Atlas Gun Repair	Violet		•			•		•			
Boudreaux, Gunsmith	Lake Charles					•				•	
Burton Hardware	Sulphur							•			
Clark's Custom Guns, Inc.	Keithville							•			
Custom Gun Works	Lafayette		•			•					
Eversull, Ken	Boyce	•	•								
Houma Gun Works	Houma		•								
Hutchinson's Gun Repair	Pineville									•	
Martin Gun Shop	Shreveport					•					
N.A. Guns, Inc.	Baton Rouge					•					
Southwest Airguns	Lake Charles	•								•	
Sports Shop, The	Baton Rouge		•			•					
Sportsman's Paradise Gunsmith	Pineville										
Ted's Gun & Reel Repair	W. Monroe										
MAINE											
Brunswick Gun Shop	Brunswick				•	•		•		•	•
Morrison Gun Shop	Bradford									•	•
Woodman's Sporting Goods	Norway					•					

See page 285 for Service Center addresses.

■BE=Benjamin ■BR=Browning ■CR=Crosman ■MO=Mossberg ■RE=Remington ■ST=Stoeger ■SW=Smith & Wesson ■TC=Thompson/Center ■WN=Winchester ■WE=Weatherby

SERVICE CENTER	CITY	BE	BR	CR	MO	RE	ST	SW	TC	WN	WE
MARYLAND											
Atlantic Guns, Inc.	Silver Spring		•		•	•		•		•	
Baltimore Gunsmiths	Baltimore				•						
Firearms Repair & Refinish Shoppe	Woodbine										•
Gun Center, The	Frederick			•							
Precision Pellet	Joppa	•									
Valley Gun Shop	Baltimore		•	•	•	•				•	
Wolf Custom Gunsmithing, Gregory, c/o Albright's Gun Shop	Easton		•	•	•	•					
MASSACHUSETTS											
Bellrose & Son, L.E.	Granby			•							
Four Seasons	Woburn				•	•					
Pete's Gun Shop	Adams										
MICHIGAN											
Adventure A.G.R.	Waterford			•	•	•	•	•		•	•
Bachelder Custom Arms	Grand Rapids				•	•	•	•		•	•
Daenzer, Charles E.	Otisville	•		•							
Hampel's, Inc.	Traverse City										
Joe's Gun Shop	Dorr			•							
Johnson Service, Inc., W.	Adrian					•					
McDaniel Co., Inc., B.	South Lyon				•	•					
Mill Creek Sport Center	Dexter										
Moreau, Gunsmith, Pete	Bay City	•		•							
Northern Precision Airguns	Tawas City										
On Target Gunshop, Inc.	Kalamazoo				•	•					
Outpost, The	Eureka			•		•			•		
Pederson Co., C.R.	Ludington										
MINNESOTA											
Ahlman's Custom Gun Shop, Inc.	Morristown	•	•		•	•	•	•		•	•
B&B Supply Co.	Minneapolis										
Dale's Gunshop	Rochester										
Gander Mt., Inc.	Duluth				•						
Frontiersman's Sports	Minneapolis		•								
Kotila Gun Shop	Cokato				•	•					
Laib's Gunsmithing	Spicer										
Matt's 10X Gunsmithing, Inc.	Duluth				•	•	•			•	
Northland Sport Center	Bagley				•	•	•	•		•	•

SERVICE CENTER	CITY	BE	BR	CR	MO	RE	ST	SW	TC	WN	WE
Poor Borch's, Inc.	Marshall					•					
Stan's Gun Repair	Westbrook					•				•	
MISSISSIPPI											
Grenada Gun Works	Grenada				•	•					
Martins Gun Shop	Natchez			•	•	•					
May & Company, Inc.	Jackson			•					•		
Millers Gun Shop	Gulfport										
Saffle Repair Service	Jackson		•								
R.L. "Skeet" Hill Gun Shop	Verona		•								
MISSOURI											
Beard's Sport Shop	Cape Girardeau			•		•					
Bickford's Gun Repair	Joplin				•	•				•	•
Carl's Gun Shop	El Dorado Springs				•	•					
Catfish Guns	Imperial							•			
Dollar Drugs, Inc.	Lee's Summit	•		•							•
F&D Guns	St. Charles				•	•		•		•	
Kopp, Prof. Gunsmith, Terry K.	Lexington		•		•	•		•		•	
Nu-Line Guns, Inc.	Harvester		•		•	•		•		•	•
Ozark Shooters, Inc.	Branson			•	•	•					
MONTANA											
Air Gun Shop, The	Billings		•		•						
Billings Gunsmiths	Billings				•	•				•	
Brady's Sportsmans Surplus	Missoula			•	•						
Capitol Sports & Western Wear	Helena				•	•				•	•
Montana Gun Works	Great Falls			•		•		•			
Rocking S Gunshop	Ennis		•						•		
NEBRASKA											
Bedlan's Sporting Goods, Inc.	Fairbury		•		•						
Cylinder & Slide, Inc.	Fremont				•	•		•			
G.H. Outdoor Sports	McCook										
G.I. Loan Shop	Grand Island				•					•	•
Gunsmithing Specialties. Co.	Papillion		•			•					
Labs Air Gun Shop	Omaha			•							
Moneymaker Gun Craft, Inc.	Omaha	•				•			•	•	
Upper Missouri Trading Co., Inc.	Crofton	•		•	•	•					
NEVADA											
Accuracy Gun Shop, Inc.	Las Vegas				•	•				•	
Gun World	Elko				•	•					
Nevada Air Guns	Las Vegas	•									
NEW HAMPSHIRE											
Lewis Arms	Hooksett		•		•	•			•	•	
Skip's Gunshop	Bristol		•		•	•				•	

See page 285 for Service Center addresses.

Warranty Service Centers (cont.)

■BE=Benjamin ■BR=Browning ■CR=Crosman ■MO=Mossberg ■RE=Remington ■ST=Stoeger ■SW=Smith & Wesson ■TC=Thompson/Center ■WN=Winchester ■WE=Weatherby

SERVICE CENTER	CITY	BE	BR	CR	MO	RE	ST	SW	TC	WN	WE
NEW JERSEY											
Belleplain Supply, Inc.	Belleplain		●								
Brenner Sport Shop, Charlie	Rahway	●		●							
Garfield Gunsmithing	Garfield				●	●					
Harry's Army & Navy Store	Robbinsville			●	●	●					
Ray's Sport Shop, Inc.	North Plainfield			●	●	●		●			
Sportsman's Center	Bordentown				●	●					
The Way It Was Sporting	Moorestown				●					●	
NEW MEXICO											
Charlie's Sporting Goods, Inc.	Albuquerque					●		●		●	●
D&J Coleman Service	Hobbs			●		●					
Hobbs Bicycle & Gun Sales	Hobbs	●									
NEW YORK											
Alpine Arms Corp.	Brooklyn										
B&T, Inc.	Albany				●						
Benson Gun Shop	Coram L.I.	●		●							
Boracci, E. John, Village Sport Ctr.	Seaford L.I.	●		●							
Buffalo Gun Center, Inc.	Buffalo										
Burgins Gun Shop	Sidney Center				●	●					
Coliseum Gun Traders, Ltd.	Uniondale				●	●					
Creekside Gun Shop	Holcomb	●						●			
Damiano's Field & Stream	Ossining			●		●		●		●	
Hart's Gun Supply, Ed	Bath					●					
Hill Top Gunsmithing	Canton					●					
Kielon, Gunsmith, Dave	Webster			●	●						
LeFever & Sons, Inc., Frank	Lee Center	●							●		
Lounsbury Sporting Goods, Bob	Middletown			●	●	●					
Mulvey's Marine & Sport Shop	Monticello			●	●	●					
Rapids Gun Shop	Niagara Falls			●	●						
Scalzo's Sporting Goods	Endwell			●	●						
Schultheis Sporting Goods	Arkport					●					
Smith's Lawn & Marine Svc.	Clarence			●		●					
Solvay Home & Outdoor Center	Solvay							●			●
Sports Mart, The	Ogdensburg					●					
Sports World	Liberty	●									
Taylor & Vadney, Inc.	Albany			●	●	●					
Van's Gunsmith Service	Parish					●					
White Dog Gunsmithing	Ilion					●		●			
NORTH CAROLINA											
Baity's Custom Gunworks	North Wilksboro				●	●			●	●	
Blue Ridge Outdoor Sports, Inc.	E. Flat Rock		●		●	●					
Brown, Don, Gunsmith	Ashville			●							
Cumberland Knife & Gun Works	Fayetteville									●	

SERVICE CENTER	CITY	BE	BR	CR	MO	RE	ST	SW	TC	WN	WE
Duncan Gun Shop, Inc.	North Wilksboro										●
Hill's, Inc.	Raleigh		●			●			●		
Mike's Crosman Service	Winston-Salem	●	●			●			●		
Perry's Gunshop	Wendell		●		●	●					
Warren's Sports Hdqts.	Washington				●	●				●	
NORTH DAKOTA											
Gun City, Inc.	Bismarck		●		●	●					
Outdoorsman, The	Fargo		●		●	●					●
S.K. Guns, Inc.	Fargo									●	
OHIO											
All Game Sport Center	Milford			●		●					●
Central Ohio Police Supply, c/o Wammes Guns	Bellefontaine			●		●					
Cherry Corners, Inc.	Lodi		●			●		●		●	
Eyster Heritage Gunsmiths, Ken	Centerburg				●						
Griffiths & Sons, E.J.	Lima										
Heckman Arms Company	Richmond Heights										
Log Cabin Sport Shop	Lodi					●					
Precision Airgun Sales	Maple Heights	●		●							
Rutko Corp. (Stonewall Range)	Broadview Heights			●	●	●					
Sportsman's Depot	Urban			●		●		●		●	
Sportsman's Haven	Cambridge		●	●		●		●	●	●	●
Sportsmen's Repair Ctr., Inc.	Columbus Groves			●		●					
Stocker's Shop	Warren			●							
Trading Post, The	Massillon	●		●							
Upton's Gun Shop	Fremont			●							
VanBurne's Gun Rack	Toledo										
Zanes Gun Rack	Columbus			●							
OKLAHOMA											
Anderson, Andy	Oklahoma City		●								
D&D Sporting Goods	Tishomingo			●		●					
Mashburn Arms Co., Inc.	Oklahoma City		●	●		●		●		●	
Meydag, Peter	Tulsa				●						
Outdoor America Store	Oklahoma City				●	●			●		
Shamburg's Wholesale Spt. Gds.	Clinton	●									
Skeet's Gun Shop	Tahlequah			●							
Southwest Shooters Supply, Inc.	Oklahoma City		●	●	●	●		●		●	●
Sports World, Inc.	Tulsa		●	●	●	●		●		●	
OREGON											
Allison & Carey Gun Works	Portland		●			●				●	
Enstad & Douglas	Oregon City								●		
Felton, James	Eugene									●	

See page 285 for Service Center addresses.

■BE=Benjamin ■BR=Browning ■CR=Crosman ■MO=Mossberg ■RE=Remington ■ST=Stoeger ■SW=Smith & Wesson ■TC=Thompson/Center ■WN=Winchester ■WE=Weatherby

SERVICE CENTER	CITY	BE	BR	CR	MO	RE	ST	SW	TC	WN	WE
Lock Stock & Barrel	Grants Pass									•	
Metro Rod & Reel	Portland	•									
Starnes, Gunmaker, Ken	Hillsboro					•					
Surplus Center	Roseburg				•	•					
PENNSYLVANIA											
Auto Electric & Parts, Inc.	Media			•							
Colabaugh Gunsmith, Inc., Craig	Stroudsburg			•	•	•					
Federal Firearms Co., Inc.	Oakdale			•	•	•					
Fix Gunshop, Inc., Michael D.	Reading			•		•					
Gorenflo Gunsmithing	Erie					•					
Grice Gun Shop, Inc.	Clearfield									•	
Hart & Son, Robert W.	Nescopeck			•		•					
Hemlock Gun Shop	Lakeville			•		•					
Herold's Gun Shoppe	Waynesboro		•								
J&T Services	Bradford			•		•					
Keidel's Gunsmithing Service	Washington				•	•					
Leo's Custom Stocks	Library		•			•				•	
Levan's Sporting Goods	Lebanon	•		•		•					
Miller's Sport Shop	Mountaintop				•						
Phoenix Armoury, Inc.	Norristown			•							
Richland Gun Shop	Richland					•					
Sams Gunsmithing, David	Lititz					•					
Sportsman's Shop	New Holland		•	•		•					
Unique Sporting Goods	Loretto					•					
RHODE ISLAND											
D&L Shooting Supplies	Warwick					•				•	
Gun Hospital, The	E. Providence			•							
SOUTH CAROLINA											
Borgheresi, Enrique	Greenville			•							
Bryan & Associates	Anderson					•					
Gun Rack, Inc., The	Aiken				•	•					
Gun Room, The	Chapin				•			•			
Gunsmith, Inc., The	West Columbia				•	•					
S.E.M. Gun Works	Greenville		•								
Smith & Smith Gun Shop, Inc.	North Charleston			•							
Southland Gun Works, Inc.	Darlington					•					
SOUTH DAKOTA											
Gary's Gun Shop	Sioux Falls				•	•					
Jack First	Rapid City				•						
Jim's Gun & Service Center	Aberdeen			•	•	•				•	
Ron's Gun Repair	Sioux Falls		•	•	•	•				•	
Sodak Sport & Bait	Aberdeen		•	•		•				—	

SERVICE CENTER	CITY	BE	BR	CR	MO	RE	ST	SW	TC	WN	WE
TENNESSEE											
D&L Gunsmithing/Guns & Ammo	Memphis	•				•					
Fox & Company	Knoxville					•					
Friedman's Army Surplus	Nashville			•							
Gun City USA, Inc.	Nashville	•	•		•	•		•	•	•	
Hagstrom, E.G.	Memphis			•							
Hill's Hardware & Sporting Goods	Union City				•	•					
McGuns, W.H.	Humboldt		•			•				•	
Mines Gun Shack	Tullahoma			•		•		•	•		
Shaler Eagle	Jonesbrough			•							
TEXAS											
Armadillo Air Gun Repair	Corpus Christi	•		•		•					
Ben's Gun Shop	Duncanville	•		•		•					
Boggus Gun Shop	San Marcos					•					
Carroll's Gun Shop, Inc.	Wharton		•		•	•					
Carter's Country	Houston					•					
Coleman, Inc., Ron	Carrollton			•	•	•					
Custom Gun Service	McAllen			•							
Don & Tim's Gun Shop	San Antonio				•						
Ewell Cross Gun Shop, Inc.	Ft. Worth		•	•		•					
Freer's Gun Shop	Houston		•			•					
Gun & Tackle Store, The	Dallas					•					
Kirkpatrick, Gunsmith, Larry	Lubbock			•		•					
Les Gun & Pawn Shop	Texarkana									•	
Lone Star Guns, Inc.	Plano				•	•		•			•
Longacre's, Inc.	Abilene			•		•					
Master Gunsmiths, Inc.	Houston		•	•	•	•	•	•		•	
McBride's Guns, Inc.	Austin		•			•				•	
McClelland Gun Shop	Dallas		•		•	•	•	•		•	
Mueschke Manufacturing Co.	Houston					•					
Nagel Gun Shop, Inc.	San Antonio					•		•		•	
Oshman's Sporting Goods, Inc.	Houston	•			•	•				—	
Pasadena Gun Center	Pasadena					•	•		•		
Precision Gunsmithing	Amarillo					•					
Ray's Sporting Goods	Dallas					•				•	
Reynol's Gun Shop, Inc.	Tyler			•		•				•	
Wallace & Cockrell, Gunsmiths, Inc.	Fort Worth					•					
Wichita Guncraft, Inc.	Wichita Falls					•			•		
Williamson Precision	Hurst			•			•			•	
Wolfer Brothers, Inc.	Houston				•	•				•	
UTAH											
Gun Ace Gunsmithing	Hurricane		•		•	•				•	
Gun Shop, The	Salt Lake City			•							

See page 285 for Service Center addresses.

Legend: ■BE=Benjamin ■BR=Browning ■CR=Crosman ■MO=Mossberg ■RE=Remington ■ST=Stoeger ■SW=Smith & Wesson ■TC=Thompson/Center ■WN=Winchester ■WE=Weatherby

SERVICE CENTER	CITY	BE	BR	CR	MO	RE	ST	SW	TC	WN	WE
Gunsmith Co., The	Salt Lake City				•	•			•		
Hutch's	Lehi			•	•	•					
Professional Armaments, Inc.	West Valley City			•	•	•		•		•	
VERMONT											
Burby, Inc. Guns & Gunsmithing	Middlebury					•			•		
Carpenter's Gun Works	Proctorsville										
Island Pond Gunshop	Island Pond					•				•	
VIRGINIA											
Bob's Gun & Tackle Shop, (Blaustein & Reich, Inc.)	Norfolk		•		•	•		•		•	
Cervera, Albert J.	Hanover			•							
King's Gun Shop, Inc.	Franklin		•			•					
Moates Sport Shop, Bob	Midlothian		•								
Northern Virginia Gun Works, Inc.	Springfield		•		•	•		•		•	
Old Dominion Engraver, Inc.	Lynchburg					•				•	
Richmond Gun Shop	Richmond		•			•					
WASHINGTON											
Brock's Gunsmithing, Inc.	Spokane		•			•				•	
Chet Paulson Outfitters	Tacoma					•					
Greene's Gun Shop	Oak Harbor					•		•			
Karrer's Gunatorium	Spokane		•		•	•					
Kesselring Gun Shop	Burlington					•					
Pintos Gun Shop	Kent	•									
Shooters Supply	Yakima								•		
Wisner's Gun Shop, Inc.	Chehalis		•		•	•			•	•	
Wheeler Gun Shop, C.	Richland			•		•				•	
WEST VIRGINIA											
Douglas Sporting Goods	Princeton					•					
Lew's Mountaineer Gunsmithing	Charleston				•	•				•	
Milliken's Gun Shop	Elm Grove			•		•					
Shooting Gallery, The	Weirton	•									•
WISCONSIN											
Badger Gun & Ammo, Inc.	Milwaukee					•					
Badger's Shooters Supply, Inc.	Owen					•	•				
Bob's Crosman Repair	Cudahy			•							
Custom Firearms Shop, The	Sheboygan		•		•	•		•		•	
Gander Mountain, Inc.	Wilmot		•		•	•					
Jack's Lock & Gun Shop	Fond Du Lac			•		•					
Jay's Sports, Inc.	Menomonee Falls	•	•								
Midwestern Shooters Supply, Inc.	Lomira	•	•								
Phillips, D.J. Gunsmith	Pewaukee										

SERVICE CENTER	CITY	BE	BR	CR	MO	RE	ST	SW	TC	WN	WE
Potter Gunsmithing	Muskego					•					
Precision Gun Works	Oshkosh				•	•					
River Bend Sport Shop	Waupaca				•	•					
R&R Shooters Supply	Mauston	•									
Rusk Gun Shop, Inc.	Madison		•			•				•	•
Sea Gull Marina	Two Rivers			•						•	
WYOMING											
Elbe Arms Co., Inc.	Cheyenne					•		•		•	
Jackalope Gun Shop	Douglas					•					
CANADA											
Armurier De L'Outaouais	Hull, PQ				•	•		•		•	
Casey's Gun Shop	Rogersville, NB		•		•	•		•		•	
Charlton Co., Ltd., M.D.	Brentwood Bay, BC							•			
Custom Gun Shop	Edmonton, AB		•		•	•				•	
Davidson's of Canada	Peterborough, ON					•				•	
Delhi Small Arms	Delhi, ON					•				•	
Delisle Thompson Sport Goods	Saskatoon, SK					•			•		
Epps, Ellwood	Orillia, ON				•	•			•		
Ernie's Gun Shop, Ltd.	Winnipeg, MB					•					
Gene's Gunsmithing	Selkirk, MB										
Girard, Florent, Gunsmith	Chicoutimi, PQ					•					
L'Armurier Alain Bouchard, Inc.	Ulverton, PQ		•			•			•	•	
Longs Gunsmithing Ltd. W.R.	Coburg, ON				•	•				•	
Lusignant Armurier, A. Richard	St. Hyacinthe, PQ		•			•			•	•	
Magasin Latulippe, Inc.	Quebec City, PQ					•					
Newby, Stewart, Gunsmith	New Burgh, ON					•		•			
Precision Arms & Gunsmithing Ltd.	Nobleton, ON		•		•	•				•	
Ralph's Gun Shop	Niverville, MB					•				•	
Randy's Gun Repair	Tabusintac, NB				•	•		•		•	
Reliable Gun & Tackle, Ltd.	Vancouver, BC					•				•	•
Robinson's Sporting Goods, Ltd.	Victoria, BC									•	
Russell's Sporting Goods	Calgary, AB					•				•	
Saskatoon Gunsmith Shoppe, Ltd.	Saskatoon, SK				•	•				•	
Selin Gunsmith, Ltd., Del	Vernon, BC				•	•					
West Gate Gunsports, Inc.	Edmonton, AB					•					•
West Luther Gun Repair	Conn., ON					•					
Wholesale Sports	Edmonton, AB					•				•	
Wortner Gun Works, Ltd.	Chatham, ON		•			•				•	

See page 285 for Service Center addresses.

METALLIC SIGHTS

Handgun Sights

BO-MAR DELUXE BMCS Gives $3/8''$ windage and elevation adjustment at 50 yards on Colt Gov't 45; sight radius under 7". For GM and Commander models only. Uses existing dovetail slot. Has shield-type rear blade.
Price:	$65.95
Price: BMCS-2 (for GM and 9mm)	$65.95
Price: Flat bottom	$65.95
Price: BMGC (for Colt Gold Cup), angled serrated blade, rear	$65.95
Price: BMGC front sight	$12.00
Price: BMCZ-75 (for CZ-75, TZ-75, P-9 and most clones. Works with factory front	$65.95

BO-MAR FRONT SIGHTS Dovetail style for S&W 4506, 4516, 1076; undercut style (.250", .280", $5/16''$ high); Fast Draw style (.210", .250", .230" high).
Price:	$12.00

BO-MAR BMU XP-100/T/C CONTENDER No gunsmithing required; has .080" notch.
Price:	$77.00

BO-MAR BMML For muzzleloaders; has .062" notch, flat bottom.
Price:	$65.95
Price: With $3/8''$ dovetail	$65.95

BO-MAR RUGER "P" ADJUSTABLE SIGHT Replaces factory front and rear sight.
Price: Rear sight	$65.95
Price: Front sight	$12.00

BO-MAR BMR Fully adjustable rear sight for Ruger MKI, MKII Bull barrel autos.
Price: Rear	$65.95
Price: Undercut front sight	$12.00

Bo-Mar BMSW
(photo: Brownells, Inc.)

BO-MAR BMSW SMITH & WESSON SIGHTS Replace the S&W Novak-style fixed sights. A .385" high front sight and minor machining required. For models 4506, 4516, 1076; all 9mms with $5^3/4''$ and $6^3/16''$ radius.
Price:	$65.95
Price: .385" front sight	$12.00
Price: BM-645 rear sight (for S&W 645, 745), uses factory front	$65.95
Price: BMSW-52 rear sight (for Model 52), fits factory dovetail, uses factory front	$65.95

BO-MAR LOW PROFILE RIB & ACCURACY TUNER Streamlined rib with front and rear sights; $7^1/8''$ sight radius. Brings sight line closer to the bore than standard or extended sight and ramp. Weight 5 oz. Made for Colt Gov't 45, Super 38, and Gold Cup 45 and 38.
Price:	$123.00

BO-MAR COMBAT RIB For S&W Model 19 revolver with 4" barrel. Sight radius $5^3/4''$, weight $5^1/2$ oz.
Price:	$110.00

BO-MAR HUNTER REAR SIGHT Replacement rear sight in two models—S&W K and L frames use $2^3/4''$ Bo-Mar base with $7/16''$ overhang, has two screw holes; S&W N frame has 3" base, three screw holes. A .200" taller front blade is required.
Price:	$79.00

BO-MAR WINGED RIB For S&W 4" and 6" length barrels—K-38, M10, HB 14 and 19. Weight for the 6" model is about $7^1/4$ oz.
Price:	$123.00

BO-MAR COVER-UP RIB Adjustable rear sight, winged front guards. Fits right over revolver's original front sight. For S&W 4" M-10HB, M-13, M-58, M-64 & 65, Ruger 4" models SDA-34, SDA-84, SS-34, SS-84, GF-34, GF-84.
Price:	$117.00

C-MORE SIGHTS Replacement front sight blades offered in two types and five styles. Made of Du Pont Acetal, they come in a set of five high-contrast colors: blue, green, pink, red and yellow. Easy to install. Patridge style for Colt Python (all barrels), Ruger Super Blackhawk ($7^1/2''$), Ruger Blackhawk ($4^5/8''$); ramp style for Python (all barrels), Blackhawk ($4^5/8''$), Super Blackhawk ($7^1/2''$ and $10^1/2''$). From C-More Systems.
Price: Per set	$19.95

JP GHOST RING Replacement bead front, ghost ring rear for Glock and M1911 pistols. From JP Enterprises.
Price:	$79.95
Price: Bo-Mar replacement leaf with JP dovetail front bead	$99.95

MMC COMBAT FIXED REAR SIGHT (Colt 1911-Type Pistols) This veteran MMC sight is well known to those who prefer a true combat sight for "carry" guns. Steel construction for long service. Choose from a wide variety of front sights.
Price: Combat Fixed Rear, plain	$19.35
Price: As above, white outline	$24.80
Price: Combat Front Sight for above, six styles, from	$6.15

MMC STANDARD ADJUSTABLE REAR SIGHT Available for Colt 1911 type, Ruger Standard Auto, and now for S&W 469, and 659 pistols. No front sight change is necessary, as this sight will work with the original factory front sight.
Price: Standard Adjustable Rear Sight, plain leaf	$48.40
Price: Standard Adjustable Rear Sight, white outline	$53.85

MMC MINI-SIGHT Miniature size for carrying, fully adjustable, for maximum accuracy with your pocket auto. MMC's Mini-Sight will work with the factory front sight. No machining is necessary; easy installation. Available for Walther PP, PPK, and PPK/S pistols. Will also fit fixed sight Browning Hi-Power (P-35).
Price: Mini-Sight, plain	$60.00
Price: Mini-Sight, white bar	$60.00

MEPROLIGHT TRITIUM NIGHT SIGHTS Replacement sight assemblies for use in low-light conditions. Available for rifles, shotguns, handguns and bows. **TRU-DOT** models carry a 12-year warranty on the useable illumination, while non-TRU-DOT have a 5-year warranty. Contact Hesco, Inc. for complete details.
Price: Shotgun bead sight	$22.95
Price: AR-15/M-16 front sight only	$34.95
Price: AR-15/M-16 sight sets, Rem. rifle sights	$89.95
Price: TRU-DOT fixed sight sets	$94.95
Price: TRU-DOT adjustable sight sets, pistols	$139.95
Price: TRU-DOT adjustable sights for Python, King Cobra, Taurus 669, Ruger GP-100	$124.95
Price: H&K MP5, SR9 front sight only	$49.95
Price: H&K MP5, SR9 sight sets	$94.95

MILLETT DOVETAIL FRONT All-steel replacement front sights with highly visible white or orange bar, serrated ramp, or 3-dot. For Browning, SIG Sauer and S&W autos.
Price:	$16.00

Bo-Mar BMCG Gold Cup

Bo-Mar "P" Series
(photo: Brownells, Inc.)

MMC Mini-Sight
(photo: Brownells, Inc.)

MILLETT SERIES 100 REAR SIGHTS All-steel highly visible, click adjustable. Blades in white outline, target black, silhouette, 3-dot, and tritium bars. Fit most popular revolvers and autos.
Price:	$49.30 to $55.60

MILLETT ULTRA SIGHT Fully adjustable rear works with factory front. Steel and carbon fiber. Easy to install. For most automatics. White outline, target black or 3-dot.
Price:	$49.95

MILLETT BAR-DOT-BAR TRITIUM NIGHT SIGHTS Replacement front and rear combos fit most automatics. Horizontal tritium bars on rear, dot front sight.
Price:	$145.00

MILLETT 3-DOT SYSTEM SIGHTS The 3-Dot System sights use a single white dot on the front blade and two dots flanking the rear notch. Fronts available in Dual-Crimp and Wide Stake-On styles, as well as special applications. Adjustable rear sight available for most popular auto pistols and revolvers.
Price: Front, from	$16.00
Price: Adjustable rear	$55.60 to $56.80

MILLETT REVOLVER FRONT SIGHTS All-steel replacement front sights with either white or orange bar. Easy to install. For Ruger GP-100, Redhawk, Security-Six, Police-Six, Speed-Six, Colt Trooper, Diamondback, King Cobra, Peacemaker, Python, Dan Wesson 22 and 15-2.
Price: ....$13.60 to $16.00

MILLETT DUAL-CRIMP FRONT SIGHT Replacement front sight for automatic pistols. Dual-Crimp uses an all-steel two-point hollow rivet system. Available in eight heights and four styles. Has a skirted base that covers the front sight pad. Easily installed with the Millett Installation Tool Set. Available in Blaze Orange Bar, White Bar, Serrated Ramp, Plain Post.
Price: $16.00

MILLETT STAKE-ON FRONT SIGHT Replacement front sight for automatic pistols. Stake-On sights have skirted base that covers the front sight pad. Easily installed with the Millet Installation Tool Set. Available in seven heights and four styles—Blaze Orange Bar, White Bar, Serrated Ramp, Plain Post.
Price: $16.00

OMEGA OUTLINE SIGHT BLADES Replacement rear sight blades for Colt and Ruger single action guns and the Interarms Virginian Dragoon. Standard Outline available in gold or white notch outline on blue metal. From Omega Sales, Inc.
Price: $8.95

OMEGA MAVERICK SIGHT BLADES Replacement "peep-sight" blades for Colt, Ruger SAs, Virginian Dragoon. Three models available—No. 1, Plain; No. 2, Single Bar; No. 3, Double Bar Rangefinder. From Omega Sales, Inc.
Price: Each $6.95

P-T TRITIUM NIGHT SIGHTS Self-luminous tritium sights for most popular handguns, Colt AR-15, H&K rifles and shotguns. Replacement handgun sight sets available in 3-Dot style (green/green, green/yellow, green/orange) with bold outlines around inserts; Bar-Dot available in green/green with or without white outline rear sight. Functional life exceeds 15 years. From Innovative Weaponry, Inc.
Price: Handgun sight sets $99.95
Price: Rifle sight sets $99.95
Price: Rifle, front only $49.95
Price: Shotgun, front only $49.95

Millett Dual Crimp (top), Stake-On front sights

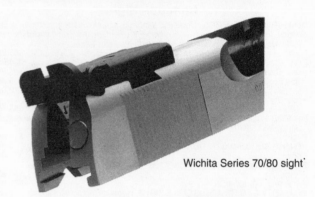

Wichita Series 70/80 sight

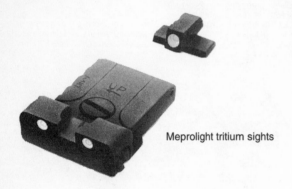

Meprolight tritium sights

Trijicon three-dot fixed

Trijicon three-dot adjustable

Merit Optical Attachment

TRIJICON NIGHT SIGHTS Three-dot night sight system uses tritium inserts in the front and rear sights. Tritium "lamps" are mounted in silicone rubber inside a metal cylinder. A polished crystal sapphire provides protection and clarity. Inlaid white outlines provide 3-dot aiming in daylight also. Available for most popular handguns with fixed or adjustable sights. From Trijicon, Inc.
Price: ....$19.95 to $175.00

THOMPSON/CENTER SILHOUETTE SIGHTS Replacement front and rear sights for the T/C Contender. Front sight has three interchangeable blades. Rear sight has three notch widths. Rear sight can be used with existing soldered front sights.
Price: Front sight $35.80
Price: Rear sight $92.40

WICHITA SERIES 70/80 SIGHT Provides click windage and elevation adjustments with precise repeatability of settings. Sight blade is grooved and angled back at the top to reduce glare. Available in Low Mount Combat or Low Mount Target styles for Colt 45s and their copies, S&W 645, Hi-Power, CZ 75 and others.
Price: Rear sight, target or combat $75.02
Price: Front sight, Patridge or ramp $12.60

WICHITA GRAND MASTER DELUXE RIBS Ventilated rib has wings machined into it for better sight acquisition and is relieved for Mag-Na-Porting. Milled to accept Weaver see-thru-style rings. Made of stainless or blued steel; front and rear sights blued. Has Wichita Multi-Range rear sight system, adjustable front sight. Made for revolvers with 6" barrel.
Price: Model 301S, 301B (adj. sight K frames with custom bbl. of 1" to 1.032" dia. L and N frame with 1.062" to 1.100" dia. bbl.) $180.60
Price: Model 303S, 303B (adj. sight K, L, N frames with factory barrel) . .$180.60

Sight Attachments

MERIT IRIS SHUTTER DISC Eleven clicks give 12 different apertures. No. 3 Disc and Master, primarily target types, 0.22" to .125"; No. 4, 1/2" dia. hunting type, .025" to .155". Available for all popular sights. The Master Deluxe, with flexible rubber light shield, is particularly adapted to extension, scope height, and tang sights. All Merit Deluxe models have internal click springs; are hand fitted to minimum tolerance.
Price: Master Deluxe $66.00
Price: No. 3 Disc $55.00
Price: No. 4 Hunting Disc $45.00

MERIT LENS DISC Similar to Merit Iris Shutter (Model 3 or Master) but incorporates provision for mounting prescription lens integrally. Lens may be obtained locally from your optician. Sight disc is 7/16" wide (Model 3), or 3/4" wide (Master). Model 3 Target.
Price: $68.00
Price: Master Deluxe $78.00

MERIT OPTICAL ATTACHMENT For revolver and pistol shooters, instantly attached by rubber suction cup to regular or shooting glasses. Any aperture .020" to .156".
Price: Deluxe (swings aside) $63.00

HANDGUN SCOPES

Maker and Model	Magn.	Field at 100 Yds. (feet)	Eye Relief (in.)	Length (in.)	Tube Dia. (in.)	W&E Adjustments	Weight (ozs.)	Price	Other Data
AAL OPTICS									[1]Brightness-adjustable fiber optic red dot reticle. Waterproof, nitrogen-filled one-piece tube tube. Tinted see-through lens covers and battery included. [2]Parallax adjustable. [3]Ultra-Dot sights include rings, battery, polarized filter, and 5-year warranty. All models available in black or satin finish. [4]Illuminated red dot has eleven brightness settings. Shock-proof aluminum tube. [5]Fiber optic red dot has five brightness settings. Shock-proof polymer tube. From AAL Optics.
Micro-Dot Scopes[1]									
1.5-4.5x20 Rifle	1.5-4.5	80-26	3	9.8	1	Int.	10.5	$287.00	
2-7x32	2-7	54-18	3	11.0	1	Int.	12.1	299.00	
3-9x40	3-9	40-14	3	12.2	1	Int.	13.3	319.00	
4x-12x56[2]	4-12	30-10	3	14.3	1	Int.	18.3	409.00	
Ultra-Dot Sights[3]									
Ultra-Dot 25[4]	1	—	—	5.1	1	Int.	3.9	139.00	
Ultra-Dot 30[4]	1	—	—	5.1	30mm	Int.	4.0	149.00	
Ultra Dot Patriot[5]	1	—	—	5.1	1	Int.	2.9	119.00	
ADCO									[1]Multi-Color Dot system changes from red to green. [2]For airguns, paintball, rimfires. Uses common lithium wafer battery. [3]Comes with standard dovetail mount. [4]3/8" dovetail mount; poly body; adj. intensity diode. [5] Adj. dot size—5, 10, 15 MOA.
MiRAGE Ranger 1"	0	—	—	5.2	1	Int.	3.9	159.00	
MiRAGE Ranger 30mm	0	—	—	5.5	30mm	Int.	5.0	179.00	
MiRAGE Sportsman[1]	0	—	—	5.2	1	Int.	4.5	249.00	
MiRAGE Competitor[1]	0	—	—	5.5	30mm	Int.	5.5	269.00	
MiRAGE Trident[5]	0	—	—	6.0	30mm	Int.	6.5	499.00	
IMP Sight[2]	0	—	—	4.5	—	Int.	1.3	19.95	
Square Shooter[3]	0	—	—	5.0	—	Int.	5	129.00	
MiRAGE Eclipse[1]	0	—	—	5.5	30mm	Int.	5.5	249.00	
MiRAGE Champ Red Dot	0	—	—	4.5	—	Int.	2	39.95	
AIMPOINT									Illuminates red dot in field of view. Noparallax (dot does not need to be centered). Unlimited field of view and eye relief. On/off, adj. intensity. Dot covers 3" @ 100 yds. Mounts avail. for all sights and scopes. [1]Comes with 30mm rings, battery, lens cloth. [2]Requires 1" rings. Black or stainless finish. 3x scope attachment (for rifles only), $129.95. [3]Projects red dot of visible laser light onto target. Black finish (LSR-2B) or stainless (LSR-2S); or comes with rings and accessories. Optional toggle switch, $34.95. [4]Lithium battery life up to 15 hours. Black finish (AP 5000-B) or stainless (AP 5000-S); avail. with regular 3-min. or 10-min. Mag Dot as B2 or S2. [5]For Beretta, Browning, Colt Gov't., Desert Eagle, Glock, Ruger, SIG-Sauer, S&W. [6]For Colt, S&W. From Aimpoint U.S.A.
Comp	0	—	—	4.6	30mm	Int.	4.3	308.00	
Series 5000[4]	0	—	—	5.75	30mm	Int.	5.8	277.00	
Series 3000 Universal[2]	0	—	—	5.5	1	Int.	5.5	232.00	
Series 5000/2x[1]	2	—	—	7	30mm	Int.	9	367.00	
Laserdot[3]	—	—	—	3.5	1	Int.	4.0	319.95	
Autolaser[5]	—	—	—	3.75	1	Int.	4.3	351.00	
Revolver Laser[6]	—	—	—	3.5	1	Int.	3.6	339.00	
ARMSON O.E.G.									Shows red dot aiming point. No batteries needed. Standard model fits 1" ring mounts (not incl.). Other models available for many popular shotguns, para-military rifles and carbines. [1]Daylight Only Sight with 3/8" dovetail mount for 22s. Does not contain tritium. From Trijicon, Inc.
Standard	0	—	—	5 1/8	1	Int.	4.3	175.00	
22 Day/Night	0	—	—	3 3/4	—	Int.	3.0	146.00	
Colt Pistol	0	—	—	3 3/4	—	Int.	3.0	209.00	
BAUSCH & LOMB									[1]Also in silver finish, $321.95. [2]Also in silver finish, $432.95 Partial listing shown. Contact Bausch & Lomb Sports Optics Div. for details.
Elite 3000 Handguns									
30-2028G[1]	2	23	9-26	8.4	1	Int.	6.9	301.95	
30-2632G[2]	2-6	10-4	20	9.0	1	Int.	10.0	413.95	
BEEMAN									All scopes have 5-point reticle, all glass, fully coated lenses. Includes mount. [1]Also as 66RL with lighted color reticle, $355.00. [3]Also as SS-2L 3x with color 4pt. reticle. Imported by Beeman
Blue Ribbon SS-3[1]	1.5-4	42-25	3	5.8	7/8	Int.	8.5	300.00	
Blue Ribbon 66R[2]	2-7	62-16	3	11.4	1	Int.	14.9	315.00	
Blue Ribbon SS-2[1,3]	4	25	3.5	7.0	1.4	Int.	13.7	305.00	
Blue Ribbon 25 Pistol	2	19	10-24	9.1	1	Int.	7.4	155.00	
B-SQUARE									[1]Blue finish; stainless, $209.95. T-slot mount; cord or integral switch. [2]Blue finish; stainless, $259.95. T-slot mount; cord or integral switch. Uses common A76 batteries. [3]High intensity 635 beam, $349.95 (blue), $359.95 (stainless). Dimensions 1.1"x1.1"x.6". From B-Square.
BSL-1[1]	—	—	—	2.75	.75	Int.	2.25	199.95	
Mini-Laser[2,3]	—	—	—	1.1		Int.	2.9	239.95	
BURRIS									All scopes avail. in Plex reticle. Steel-on-steel click adjustments. [1]Dot reticle on some models. [2]Matte satin finish. [3]Available with parallax adjustment (standard on 10x, 12x, 4-12x, 6-12x, 6-18x, 6x HBR and 3-12x Signature). [4]Silver matte finish extra. [5]Target knobs avail. standard on silhouette models, LER and XER with P.A., 6x HBR. [6]Available with Posi-Lock.
Handgun									
1 1/2-4x LER[1,5,10]	1.6-3.	16-11	11-25	10 1/4	1	Int.	11	365.00	
2-7x LER[3,4,5,10]	2-6.5	21-7	7-27	9.5	1	Int.	12.6	358.00	
3-9x LER[4,5,10]	3.4-8.4	12-5	22-14	11	1	Int.	14	402.00	
1x LER[1]	1.1	27	10-24	8 3/4	1	Int.	6.8	228.00	
2x LER[4,5,6]	1.7	21	10-24	8 3/4	1	Int.	6.8	235.00	
3x LER[4,6]	2.7	17	10-20	8 7/8	1	Int.	6.8	252.00	
4x LER[1,4,5,6,10]	3.7	11	10-22	9 5/8	1	Int.	9.0	262.00	
7x IER[1,4,5,6]	6.5	6.5	10-16	11 1/4	1	Int.	10	329.00	
10x IER[1,4,6]	9.5	4	8-12	13 1/2	1	Int.	14	388.00	
BUSHNELL									[1]Also silver finish, $205.95. [2]Also silver finish, $267.95. [3]Variable intensity; interchangeable extra reticles (Dual Rings, Open Cross Hairs, Rising Dot) $128.95; fits Weaver-style base.
HOLO SIGHT[3]	1	—	—	6	—	Int.	8.7	599.95	
Trophy Handgun									
73-0232[1]	2	20	9-26	8.7	1	Int.	7.7	190.95	
73-2632[2]	2-6	21-7	9-26	9.1	1	Int.	9.6	252.95	

CAUTION: PRICES SHOWN ARE SUPPLIED BY THE MANUFACTURER OR IMPORTER. CHECK YOUR LOCAL GUNSHOP.

HANDGUN SCOPES

Maker and Model	Magn.	Field at 100 Yds. (feet)	Eye Relief (in.)	Length (in.)	Tube Dia. (in.)	W&E Adjustments	Weight (ozs.)	Price	Other Data
INTERAIMS									Intended for handguns. Comes with rings. Dot size less than 1½" @ 100 yds. Waterproof. Battery life 50-10,000 hours. Black or nickel finish. 2x booster, 1" or 30mm, **$139.00** Imported by Stoeger.
One V	0	—	—	4.5	1	Int.	4	159.95	
One V 30	0	—	—	4.5	30mm	Int.	4	176.95	
KILHAM									Unlimited eye relief; internal click adjustments; crosshair reticle. Fits Thompson/Center rail mounts, for S&W K, N, Ruger Blackhawk, Super, Super Single-Six, Contender.
Hutson Handgunner II	1.7	8	—	5½	⅞	Int.	5.1	119.95	
Hutson Handgunner	3	8	10-12	6	⅞	Int.	5.3	119.95	
LASERAIM									[1]Red dot/laser combo; 300-yd. range: LA3XHD Hotdot has 500-yd. range **$249.00**; 4 MOA dot size, laser gives 2" dot size at 100 yds. [3]30mm obj. lens; 4 MOA dot at 100 yds.; fits Weaver base. [4]300-yd. range; 2" dot at 100 yds.; rechargeable Nicad battery. [5]1.5-mile range; 1" dot at 100 yds.; 20+ hrs. batt. life. [6]1.5-mile range; 1" dot at 100 yds.; rechargeable Nicad battery (comes with in-field charger); [8]Black or satin finish. With mount, **$169.00**. [7]Laser projects 2" dot at 100 yds.; with rotary switch; with Hotdot **$237.00**; with Hotdot, touch switch **$357.00**. [9]For Glock 17-27; G1 Hotdot **$299.00**; price installed. [10]Fits std. Weaver base, no rings required; 6-MOA dot; seven brightness settings. All have w&e adj.; black or satin silver finish. From Laseraim Technologies, Inc.
LA3X Dualdot[1]	—	—	—	6	—	Int.	12	199.00	
LA5[3]	—	—	—	2	.75	Int.	1.2	236.00	
LA10 Hotdot[4]	—	—	—	3.87	.75	Int.	NA	396.00	
LA11 Hotdot[5]	—	—	—	2.75	.75	Int.	NA	292.00	
LA14	—	—	—	NA	NA	Int.	NA	314.00	
LA16 Hotdot Mighty Sight[6]	—	—	—	1.5	NA	Int.	1.5	169.00	
Red Dot Sights									
LA93 Illusion III[2]	—	—	—	6.0	—	Int.	5.0	139.00	
LA9750 Grand Illusion[10]	—	—	—	5.5	50mm	Int.	7.0	199.00	
Lasers									
MA3 Mini Aimer[7]	—	—	—	1.5	⅝	Int.	1.0	155.00	
G1 Laser[8]	—	—	—	1.5	—	Int.	2.0	289.00	
LASER DEVICES									Projects high intensity beam of laser light onto target as an aiming point. Adj. for w. & e. Diode laser system. From Laser Devices, Inc.
He Ne FA-6	—	—	—	6.2	—	Int.	11	229.50	
He Ne FA-9	—	—	—	12	—	Int.	16	299.00	
He Ne FA-9P	—	—	—	9	—	Int.	14	299.00	
FA-4[1]	—	—	—	4.5	—	Int.	3.5	299.00	
LEUPOLD									Constantly centered reticles, choice of Duplex, tapered CPC, Leupold Dot, Crosshair and Dot. CPC and Dot reticles extra. [1]2x and 4x scopes have from 12"-24" of eye relief and are suitable for handguns, top ejection arms and muzzleloaders. [2]Battery life 60 min.; dot size .625" @ 25 yds. Black matte finish Partial listing shown. **Contact Leupold for complete details.**
Vari-X III 3.5x10 STD Tactical	3.5-10	29.5-10.7	3.6-4.6	12.5	1	Int.	13.5	716.10	
M8-2X EER[1]	1.7	21.2	12-24	7.9	1	Int.	6.0	271.40	
M8-2X EER Silver[1]	1.7	21.2	12-24	7.9	1	Int.	6.0	292.90	
M8-4X EER[1]	3.7	9	12-24	8.4	1	Int.	7.0	367.90	
M8-4X EER Silver[1]	3.7	9	12-24	8.4	1	Int.	7.0	367.90	
Vari-X 2.5-8 EER	2.5-8.0	13-4.3	11.7-12	9.7	1	Int.	10.9	530.40	
Laser									
LaserLight[2]	—	—	—	1.18	NA	Int.	.5	292.90	
MILLETT									Full coated lenses; parallax-free; three lenses; 30mm has 10-min. dot, 1-Inch has 3-min. dot. Black or silver finish. From Millett Sights.
Red Dot 1 Inch	1	36.65	—	NA	1	Int.	NA	189.95	
Red Dot 30mm	1	58	—	NA	30mm	Int.	NA	289.95	
NIKON									Super multi-coated lenses and blackening of all internal metal parts for maximum light gathering capability; positive ¼-MOA; fogproof; waterproof; shockproof; luster and matte finish. From Nikon, Inc.
1.5-4.5x24 EER	1.5-4.4	13.7-5.8	24-18	8.9	1	Int.	9.3	352.00	
2x20 EER	2	22	26.4	8.1	1	Int.	6.3	213.00	
PENTAX									[1]Glossy finish; satin chrome, **$260.00**. [2]Glossy finish; satin chrome, **$380.00**. [3]Glossy finish; satin chrome, **$390.00**. Imported by Pentax Corp.
Pistol									
2x[1]	2	21	10-24	8.8	1	Int.	6.8	230.00	
1.5-4x[2]	1.5-4	16-11	11-25, 11-18	10.0	1	Int.	11.0	350.00	
2.5-7x[3]	2.5-7	12-7.5	11-28, 9-14	12.0	1	Int.	12.5	370.00	
REDFIELD									*Accutrac feature avail. on these scopes at extra cost. Traditionals have round lenses. 4-Plex reticle is standard. **Contact Redfield for full data.**
Handgun Scopes									
Golden Five Star 2x	2	24	9.5-20	7.88	1	Int.	6	223.95	
Golden Five Star 4x	4	75	13-19	8.63	1	Int.	6.1	223.95	
Golden Five Star 2½-7x	2½-7	11-3.75	11-26	9.4	1	Int.	9.3	303.95	
SIGHTRON									[1]Black finish; also stainless. [2]3 MOA dot; also with 5 or 10 MOA dot. [3]Variable 3, 5, 10 MOA dot; black finish; also stainless. Electronic Red Dot scopes come with ring mounts, front and rear extension tubes, polarizing filter, battery, haze filter caps, wrench. Pistol scopes have aluminum tubes, Exac Trak adjustments. Lifetime warranty. From Sightron, Inc.
Electronic Red Dot									
S33-3[1,2]	1	58	—	5.15	33mm	Int.	5.43	279.99	
S33-30[3]	1	58	—	5.74	33mm	Int.	6.27	369.99	
Pistol									
SII 1x28P[1]	1	30	9.0-24.0	9.44	1	Int.	8.46	197.99	
SII 2x28P[1]	2	16-10	9.0-24.0	9.56	1	Int.	8.28	196.99	
SIMMONS									[1]Black polish. [2]Black or silver matte. **Only selected models shown.** Contact Simmons Outdoor Corp. for complete details.
Master Red Dot									
51004[2]	1	40	—	5.25	30mm	Int.	4.8	269.95	
Gold Medal Handgun									
22002[1]	2.5-7	9.7-4.0	8.9-19.4	9.25	1	Int.	9.0	329.95	
22004[1]	2	3.9	8.6-19.5	7.3	1	Int.	7.4	229.95	
22006[1]	4	8.9	9.8-18.7	9	1	Int.	8.8	269.95	
SWIFT									All Swift scopes, with the exception of the 4x15, have Quadraplex reticles and are fogproof and waterproof. The 4x15 has crosshair reticle and is non-waterproof. [1]Available in black or silver finish—same price. From Swift Instruments.
Pistol Scopes									
661 4x32	4	90	10-22	9.2	1	Int.	9.5	115.00	
662 2.5x32	2.5	14.3	9-22	8.9	1	Int.	9.3	110.00	
663 2x20[1]	2	18.3	9-21	7.2	1	Int.	8.4	115.00	

CAUTION: PRICES SHOWN ARE SUPPLIED BY THE MANUFACTURER OR IMPORTER. CHECK YOUR LOCAL GUNSHOP.

HANDGUN SCOPES

Maker and Model	Magn.	Field at 100 Yds. (feet)	Eye Relief (in.)	Length (in.)	Tube Dia. (in.)	W&E Adjustments	Weight (ozs.)	Price	Other Data
TASCO									[1]Electronic dot reticle with rheostat; coated optics; adj. for windage and elevation; waterproof, shockproof, fogproof; Lithium battery; 3x power booster avail.; matte black or matte aluminum finish; dot or T-3 reticle. [2]Also matte aluminum finish. [3]Also with crosshair reticle. [4]Dot size 1.5" at 100 yds.; waterproof. [5]Black matte or stainless finish. [6]Available with 5-min. or 10-min. dot. [7]Available with 10, 15, 20-min. dot. **Contact Tasco for details on complete line.**
World Class Pistol									
PWC2x22[2]	2	25	11-20	8.75	1	Int.	7.3	288.00	
PWC4x28[2]	4	8	12-19	9.45	1	Int.	7.9	340.00	
P1.254x28[2]	1.25-4	23-9	15-23	9.25	1	Int.	8.2	339.00	
Propoint									
PDP2[1,2,6]	1	40	—	5	30mm	Int.	5	254.00	
PDP3[1,2,6]	1	52	—	5	30mm	Int.	5	367.00	
PDP4[5,7]	1	82	—	—	45mm	Int.	6.1	458.00	
PB1[3]	3	35	3	5.5	30mm	Int.	6.0	183.00	
PB3	2	30	—	1.25	30mm	Int.	2.6	214.00	
PDP3CMP	1	68	—	4.75	33mm	Int.	—	390.00	
PDP5	1	82	—	5.5	45mm	Int.	9.1	340.00	
LaserPoint LP2[4]	—	—	—	2	5/8	Int.	.75	374.00	
THOMPSON/CENTER RECOIL PROOF SCOPES									[1]Black finish; silver, **$269.00**. [2]Rail mount. [3]Black finish; silver, **$357.00**. [4]Black; silver, **$305.00**. [5]Lighted reticle, black, rail mount; std. mount, **$314.00**; silver, std., **$329**. [6]Lighted reticle, black. [7]Red dot scope. From Thompson/Center.
Pistol Scopes									
8356[1]	2	22.1	10.5-26.4	7 4/5	1	Int.	6.4	264.00	
8312[2]	2.5	15	9-21	7 2/5	1	Int.	6.6	227.00	
8315[3]	2.5-7	15-5	8-21, 8-11	9 1/4	1	Int.	9.2	324.00	
8352[4]	4	22.1	10.5-26.4	7 4/5	1	Int.	6.4	300.00	
8320[5]	2.5	15	9-21	7 2/5	1	Int.	8.2	342.00	
8326[6]	2.5-7	15-5	8-21, 8-11	9 1/4	1	Int.	10.5	389.00	
8650[7]	1	40	—	5 1/4	30mm	Int.	4.8	265.00	
WEAVER									All have Dual-X reticle. One-piece aluminum tube, satin finish, nitrogen filled, multi-coated lenses, waterproof. [1]4 MOA red dot; also with 12 MOA dot; comes with Weaver q.d. rings. [2]Variable 4, 8, 12 MOA red dot; comes with Weaver q.d. rings; matte finish **$382.34**. [3]4 MOA, 12 MOA, variable 4, 8, 12 MOA **$364.86**; matte finish **$383.11**. [4]Stainless finish, **$226.42**. [5]Stainless finish, **$232.04**. [6]Stainless finish, **$287.58**. [7]Gloss; matte **$285.04**; stainless **$292.36**. From Weaver.
Quick Point									
QP30[3]	1	12.6	—	5.39	30mm	Int.	5.3	235.81	
QP33[4]	1	14.4	—	5.74	33mm	Int.	6.3	383.11	
QP45[5]	1	21.8	—	4.8	45mm	Int.	8.46	296.19	
Handgun									
2x28[6]	2	21	4-29	8.5	1	Int.	6.7	214.52	
VH8 2.5-8x28[9]	2.5-8	8.5-3.7	12-16	9.3	1	Int.	8.3	280.58	
4x28[7]	4	18	11.5-18	8.5	1	Int.	6.7	226.42	
1.5-4x20[8]	1.5-4	13.5-5.8	12-24, 10.5-17	8.6	1	Int.	8.1	275.68	

Hunting scopes in general are furnished with a choice of reticle—crosshairs, post with crosshairs, tapered or blunt post, or dot crosshairs, etc. The great majority of target and varmint scopes have medium or fine crosshairs but post or dot reticles may be ordered. W—Windage E—Elevation MOA—Minute of angle or 1" (approx.) at 100 yards, etc.

Bushnell HOLOsight

Thompson/Center 8356

Laseraim G1/G1 HOT

ADCO Mirage Ranger 1" Red Dot

CAUTION: PRICES SHOWN ARE SUPPLIED BY THE MANUFACTURER OR IMPORTER. CHECK YOUR LOCAL GUNSHOP.

9th ANNUAL EDITION **301**

Maker, Model, Type	Adjust.	Scopes	Price
AIMPOINT	No	1"	$49.95-89.95
Laser Mounts[1]	No	1", 30mm	51.95

Mounts/rings for all Aimpoint sights and 1" scopes. For many popular revolvers, auto pistols, shotguns, military-style rifles/carbines, sporting rifles. Most require no gunsmithing. [1]Mounts Aimpoint Laser-dot below barrel; many popular handguns, military-style rifles. Contact Aimpoint.

AIMTECH			
Handguns			
AMT Auto Mag II, III	No	1"	56.99-64.95
Auto Mag IV	No	1"	64.95
Astra revolvers	No	1"	63.25
Beretta/Taurus auto	No	1"	63.25
Browning Buck Mark/Challenger II	No	1"	56.99
Browning Hi-Power	No	1"	63.25
Glock 17, 17L, 19, 22, 23	No	1"	63.25
Govt. 45 Auto	No	1"	63.25
Rossi revolvers	No	1"	63.25
Ruger Mk I, Mk II	No	1"	49.95
S&W K,L,N frame	No	1"	63.25
S&W Model 41 Target	No	1"	63.25
S&W Model 52 Target	No	1"	63.25
S&W 45, 9mm autos	No	1"	56.99
S&W 422/622/2206	No	1"	56.99
Taurus revolvers	No	1"	63.25
TZ/CZ/P9 9mm	No	1"	63.25

Mount scopes, lasers, electronic sights using Weaver-style base. All mounts allow use of iron sights; no gunsmithing. Available in satin black or satin stainless finish. **Partial listing shown.** Contact maker for full details. From L&S Technologies, Inc.

B-SQUARE			
Pistols			
Beretta/Taurus 92/99[6]	—	1"	69.95
Browning Buck Mark[6]	No	1"	49.95
Colt 45 Auto	E only	1"	69.95
Colt Python/MkIV, 4",6",8"[1,5]	E	1"	59.95
Dan Wesson Clamp-On[2,5]	E	1"	59.95
Ruger 22 Auto Mono-Mount[3]	No	1"	59.95
Ruger Single-Six[4]	No	1"	59.95
Ruger Blackhawk, Super B'hwk[6]	W&E	1"	59.95
Ruger GP-100[7]	No	1"	59.95
Ruger Redhawk[6]	W&E	1"	59.95
S&W 422/2206[7]	No	1"	59.95
Taurus 66[7]	No	1"	59.95
S&W K, L, N frame[2,5]	No	1"	59.95
T/C Contender (Dovetail Base)	W&E	1"	39.95
BSL Laser Mounts			
Scope Tube Clamp[8,9,10]	No	—	39.95
45 Auto[8,9,10]	No	—	39.95
SIG P226[8,9,10]	No	—	39.95
Beretta 92F/Taurus PT99[8,9,10]	No	—	39.95
Colt King Cobra, Python, MkV[8,9,10]	No	—	39.95
S&W L Frame[9,10]	No	—	39.95
Browning HP[8,9,10]	No	—	39.95
Glock	No	—	39.95
Star Firestar[6,9,10]	No	—	39.95
Rossi small frame revolver[6,9,10]	No	—	39.95
Taurus 85 revolver[6,9,10]	No	—	39.95

[1]Clamp-on, blue finish; stainless finish **$59.95**. [2]Blue finish; stainless finish **$59.95**. [3]Clamp-on, blue; stainless finish **$59.95**. [4]Dovetail; stainless finish **$59.95**. [5]Weaver-style rings. Rings not included with Weaver-type bases; stainless finish add $10. [6]Blue; stainless finish **$69.96**. [7]Blue; stainless finish **$69.50**. [8]Stainless finish add $10. [9]Under-barrel mount, no gunsmithing. [10]Used with B-Square BSL-1 Laser Sight only. Mounts for many shotguns, airguns, military and law enforcement guns also available. **Partial listing of mounts shown here. Contact B-Square for more data.**

BURRIS			
L.E.R. (LU) Mount Bases[1]	W only	1" split rings	25.00-66.00
L.E.R. No Drill-No Tap Bases[1,2,3]	W only	1" split rings	46.00-52.00

[1]Universal dovetail; accept Burris, Universal, Redfield, Leupold rings. For Dan Wesson, S&W, Virginian, Ruger Blackhawk, Win. 94. [2]Selected rings and bases available with matte Safari or silver finish. [3]For S&W K,L,N frames, Colt Python, Dan Wesson with 6" or longer barrels.

CONETROL			
Pistol Bases, 2 or 3-ring[1]	W only	1" scopes	—

[1]For XP-100, T/C Contender, Colt SAA, Ruger Blackhawk, S&W. Three-ring mount available for T/C Contender and other pistols in Conetrol's three grades. Any Conetrol mount available in stainless or Teflon for double regular cost of grade.

IRONSIGHTER			
Ironsighter Handguns[1]	No	1" split rings	38.95

[1]For 1" dia. extended eye relief scopes.

Aimtech Glock

B-Square Beretta 92

Burris Zee Rings

Laseraim LA93 Illusion III

CAUTION: PRICES SHOW ARE SUPPLIED BY THE MANUFACTURER OR IMPORTER. CHECK YOUR LOCAL GUNSHOP.

SCOPE MOUNTS

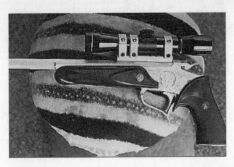

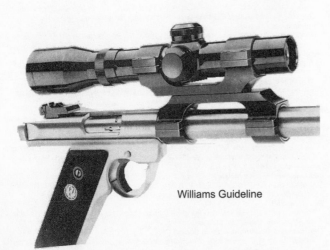

SSK T'SOB

Thompson/Center Weaver-Style

Leupold LTD Casull

Williams Guideline

Maker, Model, Type	Adjust.	Scopes	Price
KRIS MOUNTS			
One Piece (T)[1]	No	1", 26mm split rings	12.98
[1]Blackhawk revolver. Mounts have oval hole to permit use of iron sights.			
LASER AIM	No	Laser Aim	19.00-69.00
Mounts Laser Aim above or below barrel. Avail. for most popular handguns, rifles, shotguns, including militaries. From Laseraim Technologies, Inc.			
LEUPOLD			
STD Handgun mounts[1]	No	—	57.00
[1]Base and two rings; Casull, Ruger, S&W, T/C; add $5.00 for silver finish.			
MILLETT			
Handgun Bases, Rings[1]	—	1"	34.60-69.15
[1]Two and three-ring sets for Colt Python, Trooper, Diamondback, Peacekeeper, Dan Wesson, Ruger Redhawk, Super Redhawk. From Millett Sights.			
REDFIELD			
Three-Ring Pistol System SMP[1]	No	1" split rings (three)	56.95-62.95
[1]Used with MP scopes for: S&W K, L or N frame, XP-100, T/C Contender, Ruger receivers.			
SSK INDUSTRIES			
T'SOB	No	1"	65.00-145.00
Quick Detachable	No	1"	From 160.00
Custom installation using from two to four rings (included). For T/C Contender, most 22 auto pistols, Ruger and other S.A. revolvers, Ruger, Dan Wesson, S&W, Colt DA revolvers. Black or white finish. Uses Kimber rings in two- or three-ring sets. In blue or SSK Khrome. For T/C Contender or most popular revolvers. Standard, non-detachable model also available, from **$65.00**.			
TASCO			
Handgun Revolver	No	1"	33.50-58.00
Handgun Competition	No	1"	103.00
Handgun bases have w&e adj. From Tasco.			
THOMPSON/CENTER			
Contender 9741[1]	No	2½, 4 RP	20.00
Duo-Ring Mount[2]	No	1"	65.00
Weaver-Style Bases[3]	No	—	13.00
Weaver-Style Rings[4]	No	1"	29.00-41.00
Quick Release System[5]	No	1"	Rings 56.00
			Base 30.00
[1]T/C rail mount scopes; all Contenders except vent. rib. [2]Attaches directly to T/C Contender bbl., no drilling/tapping; also for T/C M/L rifles, needs base adapter; blue or stainless; for M/L guns, **$59.80**. [3]For T/C ThunderHawk, FireHawk rifles; blue; silver; **$37.00**. [4]Medium and high; blue or silver finish. [5]For Contender pistol, Carbine, Scout. From Thompson/Center.			
WEAVER			
Mount Base System[1]			
Blue Finish	No	1"	75.00
Stainless Finish	No	1"	105.00
[1]No drilling, tapping. For Colt Python, Trooper, 357, Officer's Model, Ruger Blackhawk & Super, Mini-14, Security-Six, 22 auto pistols, Single-Six 22, Redhawk, Blackhawk SRM 357, S&W current K, L with adj. sights. From Weaver.			
WEIGAND			
1911 PDP4[1]	No	40mm, PDP4	69.95
1911 General Purpose[2]	No	—	59.95
Ruger Mark II[3]	No	—	49.95
3rd Generation[4]	No	—	99.95
Pro Ringless[5]	No	30mm	99.95
Stabilizer I Ringless[6,7]	No	30mm	99.95
Revolver Mount[8]	No	—	35.50
[1]For Tasco PDP4 and similar 40mm sights. [2]Weaver rail; takes any standard rings. [3]No drilling, tapping. [4]For M1911; grooved top for Weaver-style rings; requires drilling, tapping. [5]Two-piece design; for M1911, P9/EA-9, CZ-75 copies; integral rings; silver alum. finish. [6]Three-piece design; fits M1911, P9/EA-9, TZ, CZ-75 copies; silver alum. finish. [7]Stabilizer II —more forward position; for M1911, McCormick frames. [8]Frame mount. From Weigand Combat Handguns, Inc.			
WILLIAMS			
Guideline Handgun[1]	No	1" split rings.	61.75
[1]No drilling, tapping required; heat treated alloy. For Ruger MkII Bull Barrel (**$61.75**); Streamline Top Mount for T/C Contender (**$41.15**), Scout Rifle, (**$24.00**), High Top Mount with sub-base (**$51.45**). From Williams Gunsight Co.			
NOTES			
(S)—Side Mount (T)—Top Mount; 22mm=.866"; 25.4mm=1.024"; 26.5mm=1.045"; 30mm=1.81"			

AAFTA News (M)
5911 Cherokee Ave., Tampa, FL 33604. Official newsletter of the American Airgun Field Target Assn.

Action Pursuit Games Magazine (M)
CFW Enterprises, Inc., 4201 W. Vanowen Pl., Burbank, CA 91505 818-845-2656. $3.95 single copy U.S., $4.50 Canada. Editor: Jessica Sparks, 818-845-2656. World's leading magazine of paintball sports.

Air Gunner Magazine
4 The Courtyard, Denmark St., Wokingham, Berkshire RG11 2AZ, England/011-44-734-771677. $U.S. $44 for 1 yr. Leading monthly airgun magazine in U.K.

Airgun Ads
Box 33, Hamilton, MT 59840/406-363-3805. $35 1 yr. (for first mailing; $20 for second mailing; $35 for Canada and foreign orders.) Monthly tabloid with extensive For Sale and Wanted airgun listings.

The Airgun Letter
Gapp, Inc., 4614 Woodland Rd., Ellicott City, MD 21042-6329/410-730-5496; airgnltr@clark.net; http://www.airgun-letter.com. $18 U.S., $21 Canada, $24 Mexico and $30 other foreign orders, 1 yr. Monthly newsletter for airgun users and collectors.

Airgun World
4 The Courtyard, Denmark St., Wokingham, Berkshire RG40 2AZ, England/011-44-734-771677. Call for subscription rates. Oldest monthly airgun magazine in the U.K., now a sister publication to *Air Gunner*.

Alaska Magazine
4220 B St., Suite 210, Achorage, AK 99503. $24.00 yr. Hunting, Fishing and Life on the Last Frontier articles of Alaska and western Canada. Outdoors Editor, Ken Marsh.

American Firearms Industry
Nat'l. Assn. of Federally Licensed Firearms Dealers, 2455 E. Sunrise Blvd., Suite 916, Ft. Lauderdale, FL 33304. $35.00 yr. For firearms retailers, distributors and manufacturers.

American Gunsmith
Belvoir Publications, Inc., 75 Holly Hill Lane, Greenwich, CT 06836-2626/203-661-6111. $49.00 (12 issues). Technical journal of firearms repair and maintenance.

American Handgunner
591 Camino de la Reina, Suite 200, San Diego, CA 92108. $16.75 yr. Articles for handgun enthusiasts, competitors, police and hunters.

American Hunter (M)
National Rifle Assn., 11250 Waples Mill Rd., Fairfax, VA 22030 (Same address for both.) Publications Div. $35.00 yr. Wide scope of hunting articles.

American Survival Guide
McMullen Angus Publishing, Inc., 774 S. Placentia Ave., Placentia, CA 92670-6846. 12 issues $19.95/714-572-2255; FAX: 714-572-1864.

American West
American West Management Corp., 7000 E. Tanque Verde Rd., Suite #30, Tucson, AZ 85715. $15.00 yr.

Arms Collecting (Q)
Museum Restoration Service, P.O. Box 70, Alexandria Bay, NY 13607-0070. $22.00 yr.; $62.00 3 yrs.; $112.00 5 yrs.

Australian Shooters Journal
Sporting Shooters' Assn. of Australia, Inc., P.O. Box 2066, Kent Town SA 5071, Australia. $45.00 yr. locally; $55.00 yr. overseas surface mail only. Hunting and shooting articles.

The Backwoodsman Magazine
P.O. Box 627, Westcliffe, CO 81252. $16.00 for 6 issues per yr.; $30.00 for 2 yrs.; sample copy $2.75. Subjects include muzzle-loading, woodslore, primitive survival, trapping, homesteading, blackpowder cartridge guns, 19th century how-to.

Black Powder Cartridge News (Q)
SPG, Inc., P.O. Box 761, Livingston, MT 59047. $17 yr. (4 issues). For the blackpowder cartridge enthusiast.

Black Powder Times
P.O. Box 234, Lake Stevens, WA 98258. $20.00 yr.; add $5 per year for Canada, $10 per year other foreign. Tabloid newspaper for blackpowder activities; test reports.

Blade Magazine*
700 East State St., Iola, WI 54990-0001. $19.95 for 12 issues. Foreign price (including Canada-Mexico) $50.00. A magazine for all enthusiasts of handmade, factory and antique knives.

Caliber
GFI-Verlag, Theodor-Heuss Ring 62, 50668 K"ln, Germany. For hunters, target shooters and reloaders.

The Caller (Q) (M)
National Wild Turkey Federation, P.O. Box 530, Edgefield, SC 29824. Tabloid newspaper for members; 4 issues per yr. (membership fee $25.00)

Cartridge Journal (M)
Robert Mellichamp, 907 Shirkmere, Houston, TX 77008/713-869-0558. Dues $12 for U.S. and Canadian members (includes the newsletter); 6 issues.

The Cast Bullet*(M)
Official journal of The Cast Bullet Assn. Director of Membership, 4103 Foxcraft Dr., Traverse City, MI 49684. Annual membership dues $14, includes 6 issues.

COLTELLI, che Passione (Q)
Casella postale N.519, (-20101 Milano, Italy/Fax:02-48402857. $15 1 yr., $27 2 yrs. Covers all types of knives—collecting, combat, historical. Italian text.

Combat Handguns*
Harris Publications, Inc., 1115 Broadway, New York, NY 10010. Single copy $3.25 U.S.A.; $3.75 Canada.

The Derringer Peanut (M)
The National Association of Derringer Collectors, P.O. Box 20572, San Jose, CA 95160. A newsletter dedicated to developing the best derringer information. Write for details.

Deutsches Waffen Journal
Journal-Verlag Schwend GmbH, Postfach 100340, D-74503 Schwäbisch Hall, Germany/0791-404-500; FAX:0791-404-505 and 404-424. DM102 p. yr. (interior); DM125.30 (abroad), postage included. Antique and modern arms and equipment. German text.

The Engraver (M) (Q)
P.O. Box 4365, Estes Park, CO 80517. Mike Dubber, editor. The journal of firearms engraving.

The Field
King's Reach Tower, Stamford St., London SE1 9LS England. £36.40 U.K. 1 yr.; 49.90 (overseas, surface mail) yr.; £82.00 (overseas, air mail) yr. Hunting and shooting articles, and all country sports.

Field & Stream
Times Mirror Magazines, Two Park Ave., New York, NY 10016. $11.94 yr. Monthly shooting column. Articles on hunting and fishing.

FIRE
Euro-Editions, Boulevard Lambermont 140, B1030 Brussels, Belgium. Belg. Franc 2100 for 6 issues. Arms, shooting, ammunition. French text.

Fur-Fish-Game
A.R. Harding Pub. Co., 2878 E. Main St., Columbus, OH 43209. $15.95 yr. "Gun Rack" column by Don Zutz.

The Gottlieb-Tartaro Report
Second Amendment Foundation, James Madison Bldg., 12500 NE 10th Pl., Bellevue, WA 98005/206-454-7012;Fax:206-451-3959. $30 for 12 issues. An insiders guide for gun owners.

Gray's Sporting Journal
Gray's Sporting Journal, P.O. Box 1207, Augusta, GA 30903. $36.95 per yr. for 6 consecutive issues. Hunting and fishing journals. Expeditions and Guides Book (Annual Travel Guide).

Gun List†
700 E. State St., Iola, WI 54990. $29.95 yr. (26 issues); $54.95 2 yrs. (52 issues). Indexed market publication for firearms collectors and active shooters; guns, supplies and services.

Gun New Digest (Q)
Second Amendment Fdn., P.O. Box 488, Station C, Buffalo, NY 14209/716-885-6408;Fax:716-884-4471. $10 U.S.; $20 foreign.

The Gun Report
World Wide Gun Report, Inc., Box 38, Aledo, IL 61231-0038. $33.00 yr. For the antique and collectable gun dealer and collector.

Gunmaker (M) (Q)
ACGG, P.O. Box 812, Burlington, IA 52601-0812. The journal of custom gunmaking.

The Gunrunner
Div. of Kexco Publ. Co. Ltd., Box 565G, Lethbridge, Alb., Canada T1J 3Z4. $23.00 yr., sample $2.00. Monthly newspaper, listing everything from antiques to artillery.

Gun Show Calendar (Q)
700 E. State St., Iola, WI 54990. $14.95 yr. (4 issues). Gun shows listed; chronologically and by state.

Gun Tests
11 Commerce Blvd., Palm Coast, FL 32142. The consumer resource for the serious shooter. Write for information.

Gun Trade News
Bruce Publishing Ltd., Manor Farm The Green, Uffington, Oxon SN7 7RB, England/44-1367-820-882;Fax:44-1367-820-113. Britain's only "trade only" magazine exclusive to the gun trade.

Gun Week†
Second Amendment Foundation, P.O. Box 488, Station C, Buffalo, NY 14209. $35.00 yr. U.S. and possessions; $40.00 yr. other countries. Tabloid paper on guns, hunting, shooting and collecting (36 issues).

Gun World
Gallant/Charger Publications, Inc., 34249 Camino Capistrano, Capistrano Beach, CA 92624. $22.50 yr. For the hunting, reloading and shooting enthusiast.

Guns & Ammo
Petersen Publishing Co., 6420 Wilshire Blvd., Los Angeles, CA 90048. $21.94 yr. Guns, shooting, and technical articles.

Guns
Guns Magazine, P.O. Box 85201, San Diego, CA 92138. $19.95 yr.; $34.95 2 yrs.; $46.95 3 yrs. In-depth articles on a wide range of guns, shooting equipment and related accessories for gun collectors, hunters and shooters.

Guns and Gear
Creative Arts, Inc., 4901 Northwest 17th Way, Fort Lauderdale, FL 33309/305-772-2788; FAX:305-351-0484. Single copy $4.95. Covering all aspects of the shooting sports.

Guns Review
Ravenhill Publishing Co. Ltd., Box 35, Standard House, Bonhill St., London EC 2A 4DA, England. œ20.00 sterling (approx. U.S. & Canada) yr. For collectors and shooters.

H.A.C.S. Newsletter (M)
Harry Moon, Pres., P.O. Box 50117, South Slope RPO, Burnaby BC, V5J 5G3, Canada/604-438-0950;Fax:604-277-3646. $25 p. yr. U.S. and Canada. Official newsletter of The Historical Arms Collectors of B.C. (Canada).

Handgunner*
Richard A.J. Munday, Seychelles house, Brightlingsen, Essex CO7 ONN, England/012063-305201. £ 18.00 (sterling).

Handgunning*
PJS Publications, News Plaza, P.O. Box 1790, Peoria, IL 61656. Cover price $3.95; subscriptions $19.98 for 6 issues. Premier journal for multi-sport handgunners: hunting, reloading, law enforcement, practical pistol and target shooting, and home defense.

Handgun Times
Creative Arts, Inc., 4901 NW 17th Way, Fort Lauderdale, FL 33309/305-772-2788; FAX: 305-351-0484. Single copy $4.95. Technical evaluations, detailed information and testing by handgun experts.

Handloader*
Wolfe Publishing Co., 6471 Airpark Dr., Prescott, AZ 86301/520-445-7810;Fax:520-778-5124. $22.00 yr. The journal of ammunition reloading.

Hunting Horizons
Wolfe Publishing Co., 6471 Airpark Dr., Prescott, AZ 86301. $6.95 Annual. Dedicated to the finest pursuit of the hunt.

INSIGHTS*
NRA, 11250 Waples Mill Rd., Fairfax, VA 22030. Editor, John E. Robbins. $15.00 yr., which includes NRA junior membership; $10.00 for adult subscriptions (12 issues). Plenty of details for the young hunter and target shooter; emphasizes gun safety, marksmanship training, hunting skills.

International Arms & Militaria Collector (Q)
Arms & Militaria Press, P.O. Box 80, Labrador, Qld. 4215, Australia. A$39.50 yr. (U.S. & Canada), 2 yrs. A$77.50; A$37.50 (others), 1 yr., 2 yrs. $73.50. Editor: Ian D. Skennerton.

International Shooting Sport*/UIT Journal
International Shooting Union (UIT), Bavariaring 21, D-80336 Munich, Germany. Europe: (Deutsche Mark) DM44.00 yr., 2 yrs. DM83.00; outside Europe: DM50.00 yr., 2 yrs. DM95.00 (air mail postage included.) For international sport shooting.

Internationales Waffen-Magazin
Habegger-Verlag Zürich, Postfach 9230, CH-8036 Zürich, Switzerland. SF 107.00 (approx. U.S. $87.00) surface mail for 10 issues. Modern and antique arms, self-defense. German text; English summary of contents.

IPPA News (M)
International Paintball Players Assn., P.O. Box 26669, San Diego, CA 92196-0669/619-695-8882. Call or write for subscription rates. Newsletter for members of the IPPA.

The Journal of the Arms & Armour Society (M)
A. Dove, P.O. Box 10232, London, SW19 2ZD England. œ15.00 surface mail; œ20.00 airmail sterling only yr. Articles for the historian and collector.

PERIODICAL PUBLICATIONS

Knife World
Knife World Publications, P.O. Box 3395, Knoxville, TN 37927. $15.00 yr.; $25.00 2 yrs. Published monthly for knife enthusiasts and collectors. Articles on custom and factory knives; other knife-related interests, monthly column on knife identification, military knives.

Machine Gun News
Lane Publishing, P.O. Box 459, Dept. GD, Lake Hamilton, AR 71951/501-525-7514;Fax:501-525-7519. $34.95 yr. (12 issues); $5.00 sample copy. Informative articles on machine guns, tactical firearms, and suppressors; contains interviews, question & answer columns, legislative updates, ATF ruling, classified and display ads.

Man At Arms*
P.O. Box 460, Lincoln, RI 02865. $27.00 yr.; $52.00 2 yrs. plus $8.00 for foreign subscribers. The N.R.A. magazine of arms collecting-investing, with excellent articles for the collector of antique arms and militaria.

MAN/MAGNUM
S.A. Man (Pty) Ltd., P.O. Box 35204, Northway, Durban 4065, Republic of South Africa. SA Rand 125.00 for 12 issues. Africa's only publication on hunting, shooting, firearms, bushcraft, knives, etc.

Muzzle Blasts (M)
National Muzzle Loading Rifle Assn., P.O. Box 67, Friendship, IN 47021. $30.00 yr. annual membership. For the blackpowder shooter.

Muzzleloader Magazine*
Scurlock Publishing Co., Inc., Dept. Gun, Route 5, Box 347-M, Texarkana, TX 75501. $18.00 U.S.; $22.50 U.S. for foreign subscribers a yr. The publication for blackpowder shooters.

National Defense (M)*
American Defense Preparedness Assn., Two Colonial Place, Suite 400, 2101 Wilson Blvd., Arlington, VA 22201-3061/703-522-1820; FAX: 703-522-1885. $35.00 yr. Articles on both military and civil defense field, including weapons, materials technology, management.

National Knife Magazine (M)
Natl. Knife Coll. Assn., 7201 Shallowford Rd., P.O. Box 21070, Chattanooga, TN 37424-0070. Membership $35 yr.; $65.00 International yr.

National Rifle Assn. Journal (British) (Q)
Natl. Rifle Assn. (BR.), Bisley Camp, Brookwood, Woking, Surrey, England. GU24, OPB. œ22.00 Sterling including postage.

National Wildlife*
Natl. Wildlife Fed., 1400 16th St. NW, Washington, DC 20036, $16.00 yr. (6 issues); *International Wildlife*, 6 issues, $16.00 yr. Both, $22.00 yr., includes all membership benefits. Write attn.: Membership Services Dept., for more information.

New Zealand GUNS*
Waitekauri Publishing, P.O. 45, Waikino 3060, New Zealand. $NZ90.00 (6 issues) yr. Covers the hunting and firearms scene in New Zealand.

New Zealand Wildlife (Q)
New Zealand Deerstalkers Assoc., Inc., P.O. Box 6514, Wellington, N.Z. $30.00 (N.Z.). Hunting, shooting and firearms/game research articles.

North American Hunter* (M)
P.O. Box 3401, Minnetonka, MN 55343. $18.00 yr. (7 issues). Articles on all types of North American hunting.

Outdoor Life
Times Mirror Magazines, Two Park Ave., New York, NY 10016. Special 1-yr. subscription, $11.97. Extensive coverage of hunting and shooting. Shooting column by Jim Carmichel.

La Passion des Courteaux (Q)
Phenix Editions, 25 rue Mademoiselle, 75015 Paris, France. French text.

Paintball Consumer Reports
14573-C Jefferson Davis Highway, Woodridge, VA 22191/703-491-6199. $19.95 1 yr. U.S., $27.95 foreign. Product testing for the paintball industry.

Paintball Games International Magazine
Aceville Publications, Castle House, 97 High St., Colchester, Essex, England CO1 1TH/011-44-206-564840. Write for subscription rates. Leading magazine in the U.K. covering competitive paintball activities.

Paintball Hotline†
American Paintball Media and Marketing, 15507 S. Normandie Ave. #487, Gardena, CA 90247/310-323-1021. $50 U.S 1 yr. $75 Mexico and Canada, $125 other foreign orders. Weekly newsletter that tracks inside industry news.

Paintball News
PBN Publishing, P.O. Box 1608, 24 Henniker St., Hillsboro, NH 03244/603-464-6080. $35 U.S. 1 yr. Bi-weekly newspaper covering new product reviews and industry features.

Paintball Players Bible*
American Paintball Media and Marketing, 15507 S. Normandie Ave. #487, Gardena, Ca 90247/310-323-1021. $12.95 U.S 1 yr., $19.95 foreign. Publications w. profiles of guns and accessories.

Paintball Sports (Q)
Paintball Publications, Inc., 540 Main St., Mount Kisco, NY 10549/941-241-7400. $24.75 U.S. 1 yr., $32.75 foreign. Covering the competitive paintball scene.

Performance Shooter
Belvoir Publications, Inc., 75 Holly Hill Lane, Greenwich, CT 06836-2626/203-661-6111. $45.00 (12 issues). Techniques and technolgy for improved rifle and pistol accuracy.

Petersen's HUNTING Magazine
Petersen Publishing Co., 6420 Wilshire Blvd., Los Angeles, CA 90048. $19.94 yr.; Canada $29.34 yr.; foreign countries $29.94 yr. Hunting articles for all game; test reports.

P.I. Magazine
America's Private Investigation Journal, 755 Bronx Dr., Toledo, OH 43609. Chuck Klein, firearms editor with column about handguns.

Pirsch
BLV Verlagsgesellschaft mbH, Postfach 400320, 80703 Munich, Germany/089-12704-0;Fax:089-12705-354. German text.

Point Blank
Citizens Committee for the Right to Keep and Bear Arms (sent to contributors), Liberty Park, 12500 NE 10th Pl., Bellevue, WA 98005

POINTBLANK (M)
Natl. Firearms Assn., Box 4384 Stn. C, Calgary, AB T2T 5N2, Canada. Official publication of the NFA.

The Police Marksman*
6000 E. Shirley Lane, Montgomery, AL 36117. $17.95 yr. For law enforcement personnel.

Police Times (M)
3801 Biscayne Blvd., Miami, FL 33137/305-573-0070.

Popular Mechanics
Hearst Corp., 224 W. 57th St., New York, NY 10019. $15.94 yr. Firearms, camping, outdoor oriented articles.

Safari* (M)
Safari Magazine, 4800 W. Gates Pass Rd., Tucson, AZ 85745/602-620-1220. $55.00 (6 times). The journal of big game hunting, published by Safari Club International. Also publish *Safari Times*, a monthly newspaper, included in price of $55.00 national membership.

Second Amendment Reporter
Second Amendment Foundation, James Madison Bldg., 12500 NE 10th Pl., Bellevue, WA 98005. $15.00 yr. (non-contributors).

Shooter's News
23146 Lorain Rd., Box 349, North Olmsted, OH 44070/216-979-5258;Fax:216-979-5259. $29 U.S. 1 yr., $54 2 yrs.; $52 foreign surface. A journal dedicated to precision riflery.

Shooting Industry
Publisher's Dev. Corp., 591 Camino de la Reina, Suite 200, San Diego, CA 92108. $50.00 yr. To the trade $25.00.

Shooting Sports USA
National Rifle Assn. of America, 11250 Waples Mill Road, Fairfax, VA 22030. Annual subscriptions for NRA members are $5 for classified shooters and $10 for non-classified shooters. Non-NRA member subscriptions are $15. Covering events, techniques and personalities in competitive shooting.

The Shooting Times & Country Magazine (England)†
IPC Magazines Ltd., King's Reach Tower, Stamford St, 1 London SE1 9LS, England/0171-261-6180;Fax:0171-261-7179. œ65 (approx. $98.00) yr.; œ79 yr. overseas (52 issues). Game shooting, wild fowling, hunting, game fishing and firearms articles. Britain's best selling field sports magazine.

Shooting Times
PJS Publications, News Plaza, P.O. Box 1790, Peoria, IL 61656/309-682-6626. $21.98 yr. Guns, shooting, reloading; articles on every gun activity.

The Shotgun News‡
Snell Publishing Co., Box 669, Hastings, NE 68902/800-345-6923. $29.00 yr.; foreign subscription call for rates. Sample copy $4.00. Gun ads of all kinds.

SHOT Business
Flintlock Ridge Office Center, 11 Mile Hill Rd., Newtown, CT 06470-2359/203-426-1320; FAX: 203-426-1087. For the shooting, hunting and outdoor trade retailer.

The Sixgunner (M)
Handgun Hunters International, P.O. Box 357, MAG, Bloomingdale, OH 43910

Soldier of Fortune
Subscription Dept., P.O. Box 348, Mt. Morris, IL 61054. $24.95 yr.; $34.95 Canada; $45.95 foreign.

Sporting Goods Business
Miller Freeman, Inc., One Penn Plaza, 10th Fl., New York, NY 10119-0004. Trade journal.

Sporting Goods Dealer
Two Park Ave., New York, NY 10016. $100.00 yr. Sporting goods trade journal.

Sports Afield
The Hearst Corp., 250 W. 55th St., New York, NY 10019. $13.97 yr. Tom Gresham on firearms, ammunition; Grits Gresham on shooting and Thomas McIntyre on hunting.

TACARMI
Via E. De Amicis, 25; 20123 Milano, Italy. $100.00 yr. approx. Antique and modern guns. (Italian text.)

Turkey Call* (M)
Natl. Wild Turkey Federation, Inc., P.O. Box 530, Edgefield, SC 29824. $25.00 with membership (6 issues per yr.)

Turkey & Turkey Hunting*
Krause Publications, 700 E. State St., Iola, WI 54990-0001. $12.95 (6 issue p. yr.). Magazine with leading-edge articles on all aspects of wild turkey behavior, biology and the successful ways to hunt better with that info. Learn the proper techniques to calling, the right equipment, and more.

The U.S. Handgunner* (M)
U.S. Revolver Assn., 40 Larchmont Ave., Taunton, MA 02780. $10.00 yr. General handgun and competition articles. Bi-monthly sent to members.

U.S. Airgun Magazine (Q)
2603 Rollingbrook, Benton, AR 72015/501-778-2615. Cover the sport from hunting, 10-meter, field target and collecting. Write for details.

Waffenmarkt-Intern
GFI-Verlag, Theodor-Heuss Ring 62, 50668 K"ln, Germany. Only for gunsmiths, licensed firearms dealers and their suppliers in Germany, Austria and Switzerland.

Wild Sheep (M) (Q)
Foundation for North American Wild Sheep, 720 Allen Ave., Cody, WY 82414. Official journal of the foundation.

Wisconsin Outdoor Journal
Krause Publications, 700 E. State St., Iola, WI 54990-0001. $16.95 yr. (8 issues). For Wisconsin's avid hunters and fishermen, with features from all over that state with regional reports, legislative updates, etc.

Women & Guns
P.O. Box 488, Sta. C, Buffalo, NY 14209. $24.00 yr. U.S.; $72.00 foreign (12 issues). Only magazine edited by and for women gun owners.

World War II*
Cowles History Group, 741 Miller Dr. SE, Suite D-2, Leesburg, VA 22075-8920. Annual subscriptions $19.95 U.S.; $25.95 Canada; 43.95 foreign. The title says it—WWII; good articles, ads, etc.

---

*Published bi-monthly †Published weekly ‡Published three times per month. All others are published monthly.
M=Membership requirements; write for details. Q=Published Quarterly.

ARMS ASSOCIATIONS

UNITED STATES

ALABAMA
Alabama Gun Collectors Assn.
Secretary, P.O. Box 70965, Tuscaloosa, AL 35407

ALASKA
Alaska Gun Collectors Assn., Inc.
C.W. Floyd, Pres., 5240 Little Tree, Anchorage, AK 99507

ARIZONA
Arizona Arms Assn.
Don DeBusk, President, 4837 Bryce Ave., Glendale, AZ 85301

CALIFORNIA
California Cartridge Collectors Assn.
Rick Montgomery, 1729 Christina, Stockton, CA 95204
Greater Calif. Arms & Collectors Assn.
Donald L. Bullock, 8291 Carburton St., Long Beach, CA 90808-3302
Los Angeles Gun Ctg. Collectors Assn.
F.H. Ruffra, 20810 Amie Ave., Apt. #9, Torrance, CA 90503
Stock Gun Players Assn.
6038 Appian Way, Long Beach, CA, 90803

COLORADO
Colorado Gun Collectors Assn.
L.E.(Bud) Greenwald, 2553 S. Quitman St., Denver, CO 80219/303-935-3850
Rocky Mountain Cartridge Collectors Assn.
John Roth, P.O. Box 757, Conifer, CO 80433

CONNECTICUT
Ye Connecticut Gun Guild, Inc.
Dick Fraser, P.O. Box 425, Windsor, CT 06095

FLORIDA
Unified Sportsmen of Florida
P.O. Box 6565, Tallahassee, FL 32314

GEORGIA
Georgia Arms Collectors Assn., Inc.
Michael Kindberg, President, P.O. Box 277, Alpharetta, GA 30239-0277

ILLINOIS
Mississippi Valley Gun & Cartridge Coll. Assn.
Bob Filbert, P.O. Box 61, Port Byron, IL 61275/309-523-2593
Sauk Trail Gun Collectors
Gordell M. Matson, P.O. Box 1113, Milan, IL 61264
Wabash Valley Gun Collectors Assn., Inc.
Roger L. Dorsett, 2601 Willow Rd., Urbana, IL 61801/217-384-7302

INDIANA
Indiana State Rifle & Pistol Assn.
Thos. Glancy, P.O. Box 552, Chesterton, IN 46304
Southern Indiana Gun Collectors Assn., Inc.
Sheila McClary, 309 W. Monroe St., Boonville, IN 47601/812-897-3742

IOWA
Beaver Creek Plainsmen Inc.
Steve Murphy, Secy., P.O. Box 298, Bondurant, IA 50035
Central States Gun Collectors Assn.
Avery Giles, 1104 S. 1st Ave., Marshtown, IA 50158

KANSAS
Kansas Cartridge Collectors Assn.
Bob Linder, Box 84, Plainville, KS 67663

KENTUCKY
Kentuckiana Arms Collectors Assn.
Charles Billips, President, Box 1776, Louisville, KY 40201
Kentucky Gun Collectors Assn., Inc.
Ruth Johnson, Box 64, Owensboro, KY 42302/502-729-4197

LOUISIANA
Washitaw River Renegades
Sandra Rushing, P.O. Box 256, Main St., Grayson, LA 71435

MARYLAND
Baltimore Antique Arms Assn.
Mr. Cillo, 1034 Main St., Darlington, MD 21304

MASSACHUSETTS
Bay Colony Weapons Collectors, Inc.
John Brandt, Box 111, Hingham, MA 02043
Massachusetts Arms Collectors
Bruce E. Skinner, P.O. Box 31, No. Carver, MA 02355/508-866-5259

MICHIGAN
Association for the Study and Research of .22 Caliber Rimfire Cartridges
George Kass, 4512 Nakoma Dr., Okemos, MI 48864

MINNESOTA
Sioux Empire Cartridge Collectors Assn.
Bob Cameron, 14597 Glendale Ave. SE, Prior Lake, MN 55372

MISSISSIPPI
Mississippi Gun Collectors Assn.
Jack E. Swinney, P.O. Box 16323, Hattiesburg, MS 39402

MISSOURI
Greater St. Louis Cartridge Collectors Assn.
Don MacChesney, 634 Scottsdale Rd., Kirkwood, MO 63122-1109
Mineral Belt Gun Collectors Assn.
D.F. Saunders, 1110 Cleveland Ave., Monett, MO 65708
Missouri Valley Arms Collectors Assn., Inc.
L.P Brammer II, Membership Secy., P.O. Box 33033, Kansas City, MO 64114

MONTANA
Montana Arms Collectors Assn.
Lewis E. Yearout, 308 Riverview Dr. East, Great Falls, MT 59404
Weapons Collectors Society of Montana
R.G. Schipf, Ex. Secy., 3100 Bancroft St., Missoula, MT 59801/406-728-2995

NEBRASKA
Nebraska Cartridge Collectors Club
Gary Muckel, P.O. Box 84442, Lincoln, NE 68501

NEW HAMPSHIRE
New Hampshire Arms Collectors, Inc.
James Stamatelos, Secy., P.O. Box 5, Cambridge, MA 02139

NEW JERSEY
Jersey Shore Antique Arms Collectors
Joe Sisia, P.O. Box 100, Bayville, NJ 08721-0100
New Jersey Arms Collectors Club, Inc.
Angus Laidlaw, Vice President, 230 Valley Rd., Montclair, NJ 07042/201-746-0939

NEW YORK
Iroquois Arms Collectors Assn.
Bonnie Robinson, Show Secy., P.O. Box 142, Ransomville, NY 14131/716-791-4096
Mid-State Arms Coll. & Shooters Club
Jack Ackerman, 24 S. Mountain Terr., Binghamton, NY 13903

NORTH CAROLINA
North Carolina Gun Collectors Assn.
Jerry Ledford, 3231-7th St. Dr. NE, Hickory, NC 28601

OHIO
Ohio Gun Collectors Assn.
P.O. Box 9007, Maumee, OH 43537-9007/419-897-0861;Fax:419-897-0860
The Stark Gun Collectors, Inc.
William I. Gann, 5666 Waynesburg Dr., Waynesburg, OH 44688

OKLAHOMA
Indian Territory Gun Collector's Assn.
P.O. Box 4491, Tulsa, OK 74159/918-745-9141

OREGON
Oregon Arms Collectors Assn., Inc.
Phil Bailey, P.O. Box 13000-A, Portland, OR 97213-0017/503-281-6864;off.:503-620-1024
Oregon Cartridge Collectors Assn.
Gale Stockton, 52 N.W. 2nd, Gresham, OR 97030

PENNSYLVANIA
Presque Isle Gun Collectors Assn.
James Welch, 156 E. 37 St., Erie, PA 16504

SOUTH CAROLINA
Belton Gun Club, Inc.
J.K. Phillips, 195 Phillips Dr., Belton, SC 29627
Gun Owners of South Carolina
Membership Div.: William Strozier, Secretary, P.O. Box 70, Johns Island, SC 29457-0070/803-762-3240; Fax:803-795-0711; e-mail: 76053.222@compuserve.com

SOUTH DAKOTA
Dakota Territory Gun Coll. Assn., Inc.
Curt Carter, Castlewood, SD 57223

TENNESSEE
Smoky Mountain Gun Coll. Assn., Inc.
Hugh W. Yabro, President, P.O. Box 23225, Knoxville, TN 37933
Tennessee Gun Collectors Assn., Inc.
M.H. Parks, 3556 Pleasant Valley Rd., Nashville, TN 37204-3419

TEXAS
Houston Gun Collectors Assn., Inc.
P.O. Box 741429, Houston, TX 77274-1429
Texas Cartridge Collectors Assn., Inc.
Robert Mellichamp, Memb. Contact, 907 Shirkmere, Houston, TX 77008/713-869-0558
Texas Gun Collectors Assn.
Bob Eder, Pres., P.O. Box 12067, El Paso, TX 79913/915-584-8183

WASHINGTON
Association of Cartridge Collectors on the Pacific Northwest
Robert Jardin, 14214 Meadowlark Drive KPN, Gig Harbor, WA 98329
Washington Arms Collectors, Inc.
Joyce Boss, P.O. Box 389, Renton, WA, 98057-0389/206-255-8410

WISCONSIN
Great Lakes Arms Collectors Assn., Inc.
Edward C. Warnke, 2913 Woodridge Lane, Waukesha, WI 53188
Wisconsin Gun Collectors Assn., Inc.
Lulita Zellmer, P.O. Box 181, Sussex, WI 53089

WYOMING
Wyoming Weapons Collectors
P.O. Box 284, Laramie, WY 82070/307-745-4652 or 745-9530

NATIONAL ORGANIZATIONS
American Airgun Field Target Assn.
5911 Cherokee Ave., Tampa, FL 33604
American Custom Gunmakers Guild
Jan Billeb, Exec. Director, P.O. Box 812, Burlington, IA 52601-0812/319-752-6114 (Phone or Fax)
American Defense Preparedness Assn.
Two Colonial Place, 2101 Wilson Blvd., Suite 400, Arlington, VA 22201-3061
American Paintball League
P.O. Box 3561, Johnson City, TN 37602/800-541-9169
American Pistolsmiths Guild
Alex B. Hamilton, Pres., 1449 Blue Crest Lane, San Antonio, TX 78232/210-494-3063
American Police Pistol & Rifle Assn.
3801 Biscayne Blvd., Miami, FL 33137
American Society of Arms Collectors
George E. Weatherly, P.O. Box 2567, Waxahachie, TX 75165

ARMS ASSOCIATIONS

American Tactical Shooting Assn.(A.T.S.A.)
c/o Skip Gouchenour, 2600 N. Third St., Harrisburg, PA 17110/717-233-0402;Fax:717-233-5340
Association of Firearm and Tool Mark Examiners
Lannie G. Emanuel, Secy., Southwest Institute of Forecsic Sciences, P.O. Box 35728, Dallas, TX 75235; Membership Secy., Ann D. Jones, VA Div. of Forensic Science, P.O. Box 999, Richmond, VA 23208/804-786-4706;Fax:804-371-8328
Boone & Crockett Club
250 Station Dr., Missoula, MT 59801-2753
Browning Collectors Assn.
Secretary:Scherrie L. Brennac, 2749 Keith Dr., Villa Ridge, MO 63089/314-742-0571
The Cast Bullet Assn., Inc.
Ralland J. Fortier, Membership Director, 4103 Foxcraft Dr., Traverse City, MI 49684
Citizens Committee for the Right to Keep and Bear Arms
Natl. Hq., Liberty Park, 12500 NE Tenth Pl., Bellevue, WA 98005
Colt Collectors Assn.
25000 Highland Way, Los Gatos, CA 95030
Firearms Coalition
Box 6537, Silver Spring, MD 20906/301-871-3006
Firearms Engravers Guild of America
Rex C. Pedersen, Secy., 511 N. Rath Ave., Lundington, MI 49431/616-845-7695(Phone and Fax)
Foundation for North American Wild Sheep
720 Allen Ave., Cody, WY 82414-3402
Freedom Arms Collectors Assn.
P.O. Box 160302, Miami, FL 33116-0302
Golden Eagle Collectors Assn.
Chris Showler, 11144 Slate Creek Rd., Grass Valley, CA 95945
Gun Owners of America
8001 Forbes Place, Suite 102, Springfield, VA 22151/703-321-8585
Handgun Hunters International
J.D. Jones, Director, P.O. Box 357 MAG, Bloomingdale, OH 43910
Harrington & Richardson Gun Coll. Assn.
George L. Cardet, 330 S.W. 27th Ave., Suite 603, Miami, FL 33135
High Standard Collectors' Assn.
John J. Stimson, Jr., Pres., 540 W. 92nd St., Indianapolis, IN 46260
Hopkins & Allen Arms & Memorabilia Society (HAAMS)
1309 Pamela Circle, Delphos, OH 45833
International Ammunition Association, Inc.
C.R. Punnett, Secy., 8 Hillock Lane, Chadds Ford, PA 19317/610-358-1258;Fax:610-358-1560
International Blackpowder Hunting Assn.
P.O. Box 1180, Glenrock, WY 82637/307-436-9817
IHMSA (Intl. Handgun Metallic Silhouette Assn.)
Frank Scotto, P.O. Box 5038, Meriden, CT 06451
International Handloaders Assn.
6471 Airpark Dr., Prescott, AZ 86301/520-445-7810;Fax:520-778-5124
International Paintball Field Operators Assn.
15507 S. Normandie Ave. #487, Gardena, CA 90247/310-323-1021
IPPA (International Paintball Players Assn.)
P.O. Box 26669, San Diego, CA 92196-0669/619-695-8882;Fax:619-695-6909
Jews for the Preservation of Firearms Ownership (JPFO) 501(c)(3)
2872 S. Wentworth Ave., Milwaukee, WI 53207/414-769-0760;Fax:414-483-8435
Miniature Arms Collectors/Makers Society, Ltd.
Ralph Koebbeman, Pres., 4910 Kilburn Ave., Rockford, IL 61101/815-964-2569
National Association of Buckskinners (NAB)
Territorial Dispatch, 4701 Marion St., Suite 324, Livestock Exchange Bldg., Denver, CO 80216
The National Association of Derringer Collectors
P.O. Box 20572, San Jose, CA 95160
National Assn. of Federally Licensed Firearms Dealers
Andrew Molchan, 2455 E. Sunrise, Ft. Lauderdale, FL 33304
National Association to Keep and Bear Arms
P.O. Box 78336, Seattle, WA 98178
National Automatic Pistol Collectors Assn.
Tom Knox, P.O. Box 15738, Tower Grove Station, St. Louis, MO 63163
National Firearms Assn.
P.O. Box 160038, Austin, TX 78716/403-439-1094; FAX: 403-439-4091
National Professional Paintball League (NPPL)
540 Main St., Mount Kisco, NY 10549/914-241-7400

National Reloading Manufacturers Assn.
One Centerpointe Dr., Suite 300, Lake Oswego, OR 97035
National Rifle Assn. of America
11250 Waples Mill Rd., Fairfax, VA 22030
National Shooting Sports Foundation, Inc.
Robert T. Delfay, President, Flintlock Ridge Office Center, 11 Mile @NORMAL:Hill Rd., Newtown, CT 06470-2359/203-426-1320; FAX: 203-426-1087
National Wild Turkey Federation, Inc.
P.O. Box 530, Edgefield, SC 29824
North American Hunting Club
P.O. Box 3401, Minnetonka, MN 55343
North American Paintball Referees Association (NAPRA)
584 Cestaric Dr., Milpitas, CA 95035
North-South Skirmish Assn., Inc.
Stevan F. Meserve, Exec. Secretary, 507 N. Brighton Court, Sterling, VA 20164-3919
Remington Society of America
Leon W. Wier Jr., President, 8268 Lone Feather Ln., Las Vegas, NV 89123
Rocky Mountain Elk Foundation
P.O. Box 8249, Missoula, MT 59807-8249/406-523-4500;Fax:406-523-4581
Ruger Collector's Assn., Inc.
P.O. Box 240, Greens Farms, CT 06436
Safari Club International
Philip DeLone, Executive Dir., 4800 W. Gates Pass Rd., Tucson, AZ 85745/602-620-1220
Second Amendment Foundation
James Madison Building, 12500 NE 10th Pl., Bellevue, WA 98005
Single-Action Shooting Society
1938 North Batavia St., Suite C, Orange, CA 92665/714-998-0209;Fax:714-998-1992
Smith & Wesson Collectors Assn.
George Linne, 2711 Miami St., St. Louis, MO 63118
Sporting Arms & Ammunition Manufacturers Institute (SAAMI)
Flintlock Ridge Office Center, 11 Mile Hill Rd., Newtown, CT 06470-2359/203-426-1320; FAX: 203-426-1087
The Thompson/Center Assn.
Joe Wright, President, Box 792, Northboro, MA 01532/508-845-6960
U.S. Practical Shooting Assn./IPSC
Dave Thomas, P.O. Box 811, Sedro Woolley, WA 98284/360-855-2245
U.S. Revolver Assn.
Brian J. Barer, 40 Larchmont Ave., Taunton, MA 02780/508-824-4836
U.S. Shooting Team
U.S. Olympic Shooting Center, One Olympic Plaza, Colorado Springs, CO 80909/719-578-4670
The Wildcatters
P.O. Box 170, Greenville, WI 54942
The Women's Shooting Sports Foundation (WSSF)
1505 Highway 6 South, Suite 101, Houston, TX 77077

ARGENTINA

Association Argentina de Colleccionistas de Armes y Municiones
Castilla de Correas No. 28, Succursal I B, 1401 Buenos Aires, Republica Argentina

AUSTRALIA

The Arms Collector's Guild of Queensland Inc.
Ian Skennerton, P.O. Box 433, Ashmore City 4214, Queensland, Australia
Australian Cartridge Collectors Assn., Inc.
Bob Bennett, 126 Landscape Dr., E. Doncaster 3109, Victoria, Ausrtalia
Sporting Shooters Assn. of Australia, Inc.
P.O. Box 2066, Kent Town, SA 5071, Australia

CANADA

ALBERTA

Canadian Historical Arms Society
P.O. Box 901, Edmonton, Alb., Canada T5J 2L8
National Firearms Assn.
Natl. Hq: P.O. Box 1779, Edmonton, Alb., Canada T5J 2P1

BRITISH COLUMBIA

The Historical Arms Collectors of B.C. (Canada)
Harry Moon, Pres., P.O. Box 50117, South Slope RPO, Burnaby, BC V5J 5G3, Canada/604-438-0950;Fax:604-277-3646

ONTARIO

Association of Canadian Cartridge Collectors
Monica Wright, RR 1, Millgrove, ON, LOR IVO, Canada
Tri-County Antique Arms Fair
P.O. Box 122, RR #1, North Lancaster, Ont., Canada K0C 1Z0

EUROPE

BELGIUM

European Cartridge Researchers Assn.
Graham Irving, 21 Rue Schaltin, 4900 Spa, Belgium/32.87.77.43.40;Fax:32.87.77.27.51

CZECHOSLOVAKIA

Spolecnost Pro Studium Naboju (Czech Cartridge Research Assn.)
JUDr. Jaroslav Bubak, Pod Homolko 1439, 26601 Beroun 2, Czech Republic

DENMARK

Aquila Dansk Jagtpatron Historic Forening (Danish Historical Cartridge Collectors Club)
Steen Elgaard Moler, Ulriksdalsvej 7, 4840 Nr. Alslev, Denmark 10045-53846218;Fax:004553846209

ENGLAND

Arms and Armour Society
Hon. Secretary A. Dove, P.O. Box 10232, London, 5W19 22D, England
Dutch Paintball Federation
Aceville Publ., Castle House 97 High Street, Colchester, Essex C01 1TH, England/011-44-206-564840
European Paintball Sports Foundation
c/o Aceville Publ., Castle House 97 High St., Colchester, Essex, C01 1TH, England
Historical Breechloading Smallarms Assn.
D.J. Penn M.A., Secy., Imperial War Museum, Lambeth Rd., London SE 1 6HZ, England.
Journal and newsletter are $21 a yr., including airmail.
National Rifle Assn.
(Great Britain) Bisley Camp, Brookwood, Woking Surrey GU24 OPB, England/01483.797777
United Kingdom Cartridge Club
Ian Southgate, 20 Millfield, Elmley Castle, Nr. Pershore, Worcestershire, WR10 3HR, England

FRANCE

Syndicat National de l'Arquebuserie du Commerce de l'Arme Historique
B.P. No. 3, 78110 Le Vesinet, France

GERMANY

Bund Deutscher Sportschützen e.v. (BDS)
Borsigallee 10, 53125 Bonn 1, Germany
Deutscher Schützenbund
Lahnstrasse 120, 65195 Wiesbaden, Germany

SPAIN

Asociacion Espanola de Colleccionistas de Cartuchos
Secretary, APDO. Correos No. 682, 50080 Zaragoza, Spain

SWEDEN

Scandinavian Ammunition Research Assn.
Box 107, 77622 Hedemora, Sweden

NEW ZEALAND

New Zealand Cartridge Collectors Club
Terry Castle, 70 Tiraumea Dr., Pakuranga, Auckland, New Zealand
New Zealand Deerstalkers Assn.
Michael Watt, P.O. Box 6514, Wellington, New Zealand

SOUTH AFRICA

Historical Firearms Soc. of South Africa
P.O. Box 145, 7725 Newlands, Republic of South Africa
Republic of South Africa Cartridge Collectors Assn.
Arno Klee, 20 Eugene St., Malanshof Randburg, Gauteng 2194, Republic of South Africa
S.A.A.C.A. (South African Arms and Ammunition Assn.)
P.O. Box 4065, Northway, Kwazulu-Natal 4065, Republic of South Africa
SAGA (S.A. Gunowners' Assn.)
P.O. Box 4065, Northway, Kwazulu-Natal 4065, Republic of South Africa

HANDGUNNER'S LIBRARY

*New Book

ABC's of Reloading, 5th Edition, by Dean A. Grennell, DBI Books, Inc., Northbrook, IL, 1993. 288 pp., illus. Paper covers. $19.95.
The definitive guide to every facet of cartridge and shotshell reloading.

Advanced Master Handgunning, by Charles Stephens, Paladin Press, Boulder, CO., 1994. 72 pp., illus. Paper covers. $10.00.
Secrets and surefire techniques for winning handgun competitions.

Advanced Muzzleloader's Guide, by Toby Bridges, Stoeger Publishing Co., So. Hackensack, NJ, 1985. 256 pp., illus. Paper covers. $14.95.
The complete guide to muzzle-loading rifles, pistols and shotguns—flintlock and percussion.

Air Gun Digest, 3rd Edition, by J.I. Galan, DBI Books, Inc., Northbrook, IL, 1995. 258 pp., illus. Paper covers. $18.95
Everything from A to Z on air gun history, trends and technology.

The American Cartridge, by Charles R. Suydam, Borden Publishing Co., Alhambra, CA, 1986. 184 pp., illus. $18.00.
An illustrated study of the rimfire cartridge in the United States.

American Gunsmiths, by Frank M. Sellers, The Gun Room Press, Highland Park, NJ, 1983. 349 pp. $39.95.
A comprehensive listing of the American gun maker, patentee, gunsmith and entrepreneur.

American and Imported Arms, Ammunition and Shooting Accessories, Catalog No. 18 of the Shooter's Bible, Stoeger, Inc., reprinted by Fayette Arsenal, Fayetteville, NC, 1988. 142 pp., illus. Paper covers. $10.95.
A facsimile reprint of the 1932 Stoeger's Shooter's Bible.

America's Great Gunmakers, by Wayne van Zwoll, Stoeger Publishing Co., So. Hackensack, NJ, 1992. 288 pp., illus. Paper covers. $16.95.
This book traces in great detail the evolution of guns and ammunition in America and the men who formed the companies that produced them.

Ammunition Making, by George E. Frost, National Rifle Association of America, Washington, D.C., 1990. 160 pp., illus. Paper covers. $17.95.
Reflects the perspective of "an insider" with half a century's experience in successful management of ammunition manufacturing operations.

Antique Guns, the Collector's Guide, 2nd Edition, edited by John Traister, Stoeger Publishing Co., S. Hackensack, NJ, 1994. 320 pp., illus. Paper covers. $19.95.
Covers a vast spectrum of pre-1900 firearms: those manufactured by U.S. gunmakers as well as Canadian, French, German, Belgian, Spanish and other foreign firms.

Armed and Female, by Paxton Quigley, E.P. Dutton, New York, NY, 1989. 237 pp., illus. $16.95.
The first complete book on one of the hottest subjects in the media today, the arming of the American woman.

Arms & Accoutrements of the Mounted Police 1873-1973, by Roger F. Phillips and Donald J. Klancher, Museum Restoration Service, Ont., Canada, 1982. 224 pp., illus. $49.95.
A definitive history of the revolvers, rifles, machine guns, cannons, ammunition, swords, etc. used by the NWMP, the RNWMP and the RCMP during the first 100 years of the Force.

***Arms and Armour in Antiquity and the Middle Ages,** by Charles Boutell, Stackpole Books, Mechanicsburg, PA, 1996. 352 pp., illus. $22.95.
Detailed descriptions of arms and armor, the development of tactics and the outcome of specific battles.

***Arms & Armor in the Art Institute of Chicago,** by Walter J. Karcheski, Jr., Bulfinch Press, Boston, MA, 1995. 128 pp., illus. $35.00.
Now, for the first time, the Art Institute of Chicago's arms and armor collection is presented in the visual delight of 103 color illustrations.

Arms Makers of Maryland, by Daniel D. Hartzler, George Shumway, York, PA, 1975. 200 pp., illus. $50.00.
A thorough study of the gunsmiths of Maryland who worked during the late 18th and early 19th centuries.

The Art of Engraving, by James B. Meek, F. Brownell & Son, Montezuma, IA, 1973. 196 pp., illus. $33.95.
A complete, authoritative, imaginative and detailed study in training for gun engraving. The first book of its kind—and a great one.

Artistry in Arms, The R. W. Norton Gallery, Shreveport, LA, 1970. 42 pp., illus. Paper covers. $9.95.
The art of gunsmithing and engraving.

Artistry in Arms: The Guns of Smith & Wesson, by Roy G. Jinks, Smith & Wesson, Springfield, MA, 1991. 85 pp., illus. Paper covers. $19.95.
Catalog of the Smith & Wesson International Museum Tour 1991-1995 organized by the Connecticut Valley Historical Museum and Springfield Library and Museum Association.

***Assault Weapons, 4th Edition, The Gun Digest Book of,** edited by Jack Lewis, DBI Books, Inc., Northbrook, IL. 256 pp. illus. Paper covers. $19.95.
An in-depth look at the history and use of these arms.

Astra Automatic Pistols, by Leonardo M. Antaris, FIRAC Publishing Co., Sterling, CO, 1989. 248 pp., illus. $45.00.
Charts, tables, serial ranges, etc. The definitive work on Astra pistols.

***The Ayoob Files: The Book,** by Massad Ayoob, Police Bookshelf, Concord, NH, 1995. 223 pp., illus. Paper covers. $14.95.
The best of Massad Ayoob's acclaimed series in American Handgunner magazine.

***Barnes Reloading Manual #1,** Barnes Bullets, American Fork, UT, 1995. 350 pp., illus. $24.95.
Data for more than 65 cartridges from 243 to 50 BMG.

Basic Handloading, by George C. Nonte, Jr., Outdoor Life Books, New York, NY, 1982. 192 pp., illus. Paper covers. $6.95.
How to produce high-quality ammunition using the safest, most efficient methods.

Beretta Automatic Pistols, by J.B. Wood, Stackpole Books, Harrisburg, PA, 1985. 192 pp., illus. $24.95.
Only English-language book devoted to the Beretta line. Includes all important models.

A Bibliography of American Sporting Books, compiled by John C. Phillips, James Cummins, Bookseller, New York, NY, 1991. 650 pp. Edition limited to 250 numbered copies. $75.00.
A reprinting of the very scarce 1930 edition originally published by the Boone & Crockett Club.

Black Powder Guide, 2nd Edition, by George C. Nonte, Jr., Stoeger Publishing Co., So. Hackensack, NJ, 1991. 288 pp., illus. Paper covers. $14.95.
How-to instructions for selection, repair and maintenance of muzzleloaders, making your own bullets, restoring and refinishing, shooting techniques.

Black Powder Hobby Gunsmithing, by Sam Fadala and Dale Storey, DBI Books, Inc., Northbrook, IL., 1994. 256 pp., illus. Paper covers. $18.95.
A how-to guide for gunsmithing blackpowder pistols, rifles and shotguns from two men at the top of their respective fields.

Blackpowder Loading Manual, 3rd Edition, edited by Sam Fadala, DBI Books, Inc., Northbrook, IL, 1995. 368 pp., illus. Paper covers. $19.95.
Revised and expanded edition of this landmark blackpowder loading book. Covers hundreds of loads for most of the popular blackpowder rifles, handguns and shotguns.

The Blackpowder Notebook, by Sam Fadala, Wolfe Publishing Co., Prescott, AZ, 1994. 212 pp., illus. $22.50.
For anyone interested in shooting muzzleloaders, this book will help improve scores and obtain accuracy and reliability.

Blacksmith Guide to Ruger Flat-top & Super Blackhawks, by H.W. Ross, Jr., Blacksmith Corp., Chino Valley, AZ, 1990. 96 pp., illus. Paper covers. $9.95.
A key source on the extensively collected Ruger Blackhawk revolvers.

***Blue Book of Gun Values, 17th Edition,** edited by E. P. Fjestad, Investment Rarities, Inc., Minneapolis, MN, 1996. 1301 pp., illus. Paper covers. $24.95.
Covers all new 1996 firearm prices. Gives technical data on both new and discontinued domestic and foreign commercial and military guns, modern commemoratives and major trademark antiques.

Blue Steel and Gun Leather, by John Bianchi, Beinfeld Publishing, Inc., No. Hollywood, CA, 1978. 200 pp., illus. $19.95.
A complete and comprehensive review of holster uses plus an examination of available products on today's market.

Boarders Away, Volume II: Firearms of the Age of Fighting Sail, by William Gilkerson, Andrew Mowbray, Inc. Publishers, Lincoln, RI, 1993. 331 pp., illus. $65.00.
Covers the pistols, muskets, combustibles and small cannon used aboard American and European fighting ships, 1626-1826.

British Military Firearms 1650-1850, by Howard L. Blackmore, Stackpole Books, Mechanicsburg, PA, 1994. 224 pp., illus. $50.00.
The definitive work on British military firearms.

British Small Arms Ammunition, 1864-1938, by Peter Labett, Armory Publications, Oceanside, CA, 1994. 352 pp., illus. $75.00.
The military side of the story illustrating the rifles, carbines, machine guns, revolvers and automatic pistols and their ammunition, experimental and adopted, from 577 Snider to modern times.

British Small Arms of World War 2, by Ian D. Skennerton, I.D.S.A. Books, Piqua, OH, 1988. 110 pp., 37 illus. $25.00.

The British Soldier's Firearms from Smoothbore to Rifled Arms, 1850-1864, by Dr. C.H. Roads, R&R Books, Livonia, NY, 1994. 332 pp., illus. $49.00.
A reprint of the classic text covering the development of British military hand and shoulder firearms in the crucial years between 1850 and 1864.

Browning Dates of Manufacture, compiled by George Madis, Art and Reference House, Brownsboro, TX, 1989. 48 pp. $5.00.
Gives the date codes and product codes for all models from 1824 to the present.

Browning Hi-Power Pistols, Desert Publications, Cornville, AZ, 1982. 20 pp., illus. Paper covers. $9.95.
Covers all facets of the various military and civilian models of the Browning Hi-Power pistol.

Browning Sporting Arms of Distinction 1903-1992, by Matt Eastman, Matt Eastman Publications, Fitzgerald, GA, 1995. 450 pp., illus. $49.95.
The most recognized publication on Browning sporting arms ever written; covers all models.

The Bullet Swage Manual. MDSU/I, by Ted Smith, Corbin Manufacturing and Supply Co., White City, OR, 1988. 45 pp., illus. Paper covers. $10.00.
A book that fills the need for information on bullet swaging.

Burning Powder, compiled by Major D.B. Wesson, Wolfe Publishing Company, Prescott, AZ, 1992. 110 pp. Soft cover. $10.95.
A rare booklet from 1932 for Smith & Wesson collectors.

California Gunsmiths 1846-1900, by Lawrence P. Sheldon, Far Far West Publ., Fair Oaks, CA, 1977. 289 pp., illus. $29.65.
A study of early California gunsmiths and the firearms they made.

Canadian Military Handguns 1855-1985, by Clive M. Law, Museum Restoration Service, Bloomfield, Ont. Canada, 1994. 130pp., illus. $40.00.
A long-awaited and important history for arms historians and pistol collectors.

***Cap Guns,** by James Dundas, Schiffer Publishing, Atglen, PA, 1996. 160 pp., illus. Paper covers. $29.95.
Over 600 full-color photos of cap guns and gun accessories with a current value guide.

***Cartridges of the World, 8th Edition,** by Frank Barnes, edited by M. L. McPherson, DBI Books, Inc., Northbrook, IL, 1996. 480 pp., illus. Paper covers. $24.95.
Completely revised edition of the general purpose reference work for which collectors, police, scientists and laymen reach first for answers to cartridge identification questions. Available October, 1996.

Checkering and Carving of Gun Stocks, by Monte Kennedy, Stackpole Books, Harrisburg, PA, 1962. 175 pp., illus. $34.95.
Revised, enlarged cloth-bound edition of a much sought-after, dependable work.

Civil War Pistols, by John D. McAulay, Andrew Mowbray Inc., Lincoln, RI, 1992. 166 pp., illus. $38.50.

A survey of the handguns used during the American Civil War.

A Collector's Guide to the '03 Springfield, by Bruce N. Canfield, Andrew Mowbray Inc, Lincoln, RI, 1989. 160 pp., illus. Paper covers. $22.00.

A comprehensive guide follows the '03 through its unparalleled tenure of service. Covers all of the interesting variations, modifications and accessories of this highly collectible military rifle.

Collector's Illustrated Encyclopedia of the American Revolution, by George C. Neumann and Frank J. Kravic, Rebel Publishing Co., Inc., Texarkana, TX, 1989. 286 pp., illus. $29.95.

A showcase of more than 2,300 artifacts made, worn, and used by those who fought in the War for Independence.

Colonial Frontier Guns, by T.M. Hamilton, Pioneer Press, Union City, TN, 1988. 176 pp., illus. Paper covers. $13.95.

A complete study of early flint muskets of this country.

***The Colt Armory,** by Ellsworth Grant, Man-at-Arms Bookshelf, Lincoln, RI, 1996. 232 pp., illus. $35.00.

A history of Colt's Manufacturing Company.

Colt Automatic Pistols, by Donald B. Bady, Borden Publ. Co., Alhambra, CA, 1974, 368 pp., illus. $25.00.

The rev. and enlarged ed. of a key work on a fascinating subject. Complete information on every automatic marked with Colt's name.

The Colt Double Action Revolvers: A Shop Manual, Volume 1, by Jerry Kuhnhausen, VSP Publishers, McCall, ID, 1988. 224 pp., illus. Paper covers. $24.95.

Covers D, E, and I frames.

The Colt Double Action Revolvers: A Shop Manual, Volume 2, by Jerry Kuhnhausen, VSP Publishers, McCall, ID, 1988. 156 pp., illus. Paper covers. $18.95.

Covers J, V, and AA models.

The Colt .45 Auto Pistol, compiled from U.S. War Dept. Technical Manuals, and reprinted by Desert Publications, Cornville, AZ, 1978. 80 pp., illus. Paper covers. $9.95.

Covers every facet of this famous pistol from mechanical training, manual of arms, disassembly, repair and replacement of parts.

The Colt .45 Automatic Shop Manual, by Jerry Kuhnhausen, VSP Publishers, McCall, ID, 1987. 200 pp., illus. Paper covers. $22.95.

Covers repairing, accurizing, trigger/sear work, action tuning, springs, bushings, rebarreling, and custom .45 modification.

Colt Heritage, by R.L. Wilson, Simon & Schuster, 1979. 358 pp., illus. $75.00.

The official history of Colt firearms 1836 to the present.

Colt Peacemaker British Model, by Keith Cochran, Cochran Publishing Co., Rapid City, SD, 1989. 160 pp., illus. $35.00.

Covers those revolvers Colt squeezed in while completing a large order of revolvers for the U.S. Cavalry in early 1874, to those magnificent cased target revolvers used in the pistol competitions at Bisley Commons in the 1890s.

Colt Peacemaker Encyclopedia, by Keith Cochran, Keith Cochran, Rapid City, SD, 1986. 434 pp., illus. $65.00.

A must book for the Peacemaker collector.

Colt Peacemaker Encyclopedia, Volume 2, by Keith Cochran, Cochran Publishing Co., SD, 1992. 416 pp., illus. $60.00.

Included in this volume are extensive notes on engraved, inscribed, historical and noted revolvers, as well as those revolvers used by outlaws, lawmen, movie and television stars.

Colt Percussion Accoutrements 1834-1873, by Robin Rapley, Robin Rapley, Newport Beach, CA, 1994. 432 pp., illus. Paper covers. $39.95.

The complete collector's guide to the identification of Colt percussion accoutrements; including Colt conversions and their values.

***Colt Pocket Pistols,** by Dr. John W. Brunner, Phillips Publications, Williamstown, NJ, 1996. 200 pp., illus. $50.00.

The definitive reference guide on the 25, 32 and 380 Colt automatic pistols.

Colt Revolvers and the Tower of London, by Joseph G. Rosa, Royal Armouries of the Tower of London, London, England, 1988. 72 pp., illus. Soft covers. $15.00.

Details the story of Colt in London through the early cartridge period.

Colt Revolvers and the U.S. Navy 1865-1889, by C. Kenneth Moore, Dorrance and Co., Bryn Mawr, PA, 1987. 140 pp., illus. $29.95.

The Navy's use of all Colt handguns and other revolvers during this era of change.

Colt Single Action Army Revolvers and the London Agency, by C. Kenneth Moore, Andrew Mowbray Publishers, Lincoln, RI, 1990. 144 pp., illus. $35.00.

Drawing on vast documentary sources, this work chronicles the relationship between the London Agency and the Hartford home office.

The Colt U.S. General Officers' Pistols, by Horace Greeley IV, Andrew Mowbray Inc., Lincoln, RI, 1990. 199 pp., illus. $38.00.

These unique weapons, issued as a badge of rank to General Officers in the U.S. Army from WWII onward, remain highly personal artifacts of the military leaders who carried them. Includes serial numbers and dates of issue.

The Colt Whitneyville-Walker Pistol, by Lt. Col. Robert D. Whittington, Brownlee Books, Hooks, TX, 1984. 96 pp., illus. Limited edition. $20.00.

A study of the pistol and associated characters 1846-1851.

Colt's Dates of Manufacture 1837-1978, by R.L. Wilson, published by Maurie Albert, Coburg, Australia; N.A. distributor I.D.S.A. Books, Hamilton, OH, 1983. 61 pp. $10.00.

An invaluable pocket guide to the dates of manufacture of Colt firearms up to 1978.

Colt's 100th Anniversary Firearms Manual 1836-1936: A Century of Achievement, Wolfe Publishing Co., Prescott, AZ, 1992. 100 pp., illus. Paper covers. $12.95.

Originally published by the Colt Patent Firearms Co., this booklet covers the history, manufacturing procedures and the guns of the first 100 years of the genius of Samuel Colt.

***Colt's SAA Post War Models,** by George Garton, The Gun Room Press, Highland Park, NJ, 1995. 166 pp., illus. $39.95.

Complete facts on the post-war Single Action Army revolvers. Information on calibers, production numbers and variations taken from factory records.

***Combat Handgunnery, 4th Edition,** by Chuck Taylor, DBI Books, Inc., Northbrook, IL, 1996. 256 pp., illus. Paper covers. $18.95.

This all-new edition looks at real world combat handgunnery from three different perspectives—military, police and civilian. Available, October, 1996.

Combat Pistols, by Terry Gander, Sterling Publishing Co., Inc., 1991. Paper covers. $9.95.

The world's finest and deadliest pistols are shown close-up, with detailed specifications, muzzle velocity, rate of fire, ammunition, etc.

Combat Raceguns, by J.M. Ramos, Paladin Press, Boulder, CO, 1994. 168 pp., illus. Paper covers. $25.00.

Learn how to put together precision combat raceguns with the best compensators, frames, controls, sights and custom accessories.

***Competitive Pistol Shooting,** by Dr. Laslo Antal, A&C Black, London, England, 2nd edition, 1995. 176 pp., illus. Paper covers. $24.95.

Covers the basic principles followed in each case by a well illustrated and detailed discussion of the rules, technique, and training as well as the choice and maintenance of weapons.

Competitive Shooting, by A.A. Yuryev, introduction by Gary L. Anderson, NRA Books, The National Rifle Assoc. of America, Wash., DC, 1985. 399 pp., illus. $29.95.

A unique encyclopedia of competitive rifle and pistol shooting.

***Complete Blackpowder Handbook, 3rd Edition,** by Sam Fadala, DBI Books, Inc., Northbrook, IL, 1996. 416 pp., illus. Paper covers. $21.95.

Expanded and refreshed edition of the definitive book on the subject of blackpowder. Available, September, 1996.

The Complete Book of Combat Handgunning, by Chuck Taylor, Desert Publications, Cornville, AZ, 1982. 168 pp., illus. Paper covers. $16.95.

Covers virtually every aspect of combat handgunning.

The Complete Guide to Game Care and Cookery, 3rd Edition, by Sam Fadala, DBI Books, Inc., Northbrook, IL, 1994. 320 pp., illus. Paper covers. $18.95.

Over 500 photos illustrating the care of wild game in the field and at home with a separate recipe section providing over 400 tested recipes.

Complete Guide to Guns & Shooting, by John Malloy, DBI Books, Inc., Northbrook, IL, 1995. 256 pp., illus. Paper covers. $18.95.

What every shooter and gun owner should know about firearms, ammunition, shooting techniques, safety, collecting and much more.

The Complete Guide to U.S. Infantry Weapons of World War Two, by Bruce Canfield, Andrew Mowbray, Publisher, Lincoln, RI, 1995. 303 pp., illus. $35.00.

A definitive work on the weapons used by the United States Armed Forces in WWII.

The Complete Handloader for Rifles, Handguns and Shotguns, by John Wootters, Stackpole Books, Harrisburg, PA, 1988. 214 pp., $29.95.

Loading-bench know-how.

The Complete Metal Finishing Book, by Harold Hoffman, H&P Publishers, San Angelo, TX, 1992. 364 pp., illus. Paper covers. $29.95.

Instructions for the different metal finishing operations that the normal craftsman or shop will use. Primarily firearm related.

Compliments of Col. Ruger: A Study of Factory Engraved Single Action Revolvers, by John C. Dougan, Taylor Publishing Co., El Paso, TX, 1992. 238 pp., illus. $46.50.

Clearly detailed black and white photographs and a precise text present an accurate istory of the Sturm, Ruger & Co. single-action revolver engraving project.

Confederate Revolvers, by William A. Gary, Taylor Publishing Co., Dallas, TX, 1987. 174 pp., illus. $49.95.

Comprehensive work on the rarest of Confederate weapons.

Cowboy Action Shooting, by Charly Gullett, Wolfe Publishing Co., Prescott, AZ, 1995. 400 pp., illus. Paper covers. $24.50.

The fast growing of the shooting sports is comprehensively covered in this text—the guns, loads, tactics and the fun and flavor of this Old West era competition.

Cowboy Collectibles and Western Memorabilia, by Bob Bell and Edward Vebell, Schiffer Publishing, Atglen, PA, 1992. 160 pp., illus. Paper covers. $29.95.

The exciting era of the cowboy and the wild west collectibles including rifles, pistols, gun rigs, etc.

***Cowboy and Gunfighter Collectible,** by Bill Mackin, Mountain Press Publishing Co., Missoula, MT, 1995. 178 pp., illus. Paper covers. $25.00.

A photographic encyclopedia with price guide and makers' index.

Coykendall's 2nd Sporting Collectible Price Guide, by Ralf Coykendall, Jr., Lyons & Burford Publishers, New York, NY, 1992. 223 pp., illus. Paper covers. $16.95.

The all-new second volume with new sections on knives and sporting magazines.

The Custom Government Model Pistol, by Layne Simpson, Wolfe Publishing Co., Prescott, AZ, 1994. 639 pp., illus. Paper covers. $24.50.

The book about one of the world's greatest firearms and the things pistolsmiths do to make it even greater.

The CZ-75 Family: The Ultimate Combat Handgun, by J.M. Ramos, Paladin Press, Boulder, CO, 1990. 100 pp., illus. Soft covers. $16.00.

An in-depth discussion of the early-and-late model CZ-75s, as well as the many newest additions to the Czech pistol family.

The Deringer in America, Volume 1, The Percussion Period, by R.L. Wilson and L.D. Eberhart, Andrew Mowbray Inc., Lincoln, RI, 1985. 271 pp., illus. $48.00.

A long awaited book on the American percussion deringer.

The Deringer in America, Volume 2, The Cartridge Period, by L.D. Eberhart and R.L. Wilson, Andrew Mowbray Inc., Publishers, Lincoln, RI, 1993. 284 pp., illus. $65.00.

Comprehensive coverage of cartridge deringers organized alphabetically by maker. Includes all types of deringers known by the authors to have been offered to the American market.

***Designing and Forming Custom Cartridges,** by Ken Howell, Ken Howell, Stevensville, MT, 1995. 596 pp., illus. $59.95.

Covers cartridge dimensions and includes complete introductory material on cartridge manufacture and appendices on finding loading data and equipment.

Drums A'beating Trumpets Sounding, by William H. Guthman, The Connecticut Historical Society, Westport, CT, 1993. 232 pp., illus. $75.00.

Artistically carved powder horns in the provincial manner, 1746-1781.

***The Dutch Luger (Parabellum) A Complete History,** by Bas J. Martens and Guus de Vries, Ironside International Publishers, Inc., Alexandria, VA, 1995. 268 pp., illus. $49.95.

The history of the Luger in the Netherlands. An extensive description of the Dutch pistol and trials and the different models of the Luger in the Dutch service.

The Eagle on U.S. Firearms, by John W. Jordan, Pioneer Press, Union City, TN, 1992. 140 pp., illus. Paper covers. $14.95.

Stylized eagles have been stamped on government owned or manufactured firearms in the U.S. since the beginning of our country. This book lists and illustrates these various eagles in an informative and refreshing manner.

Early Indian Trade Guns: 1625-1775, by T.M. Hamilton, Museum of the Great Plains, Lawton, OK, 1968. 34 pp., illus. Paper covers. $12.95.

Detailed descriptions of subject arms, compiled from early records and from the study of remnants found in Indian country.

Encyclopedia of Modern Firearms, Vol. 1, compiled and publ. by Bob Brownell, Montezuma, IA, 1959. 1057 pp. plus index, illus. $60.00. Dist. By Bob Brownell, Montezuma, IA 50171.

Massive accumulation of basic information of nearly all modern arms pertaining to "parts and assembly." Replete with arms photographs, exploded drawings, manufacturers' lists of parts, etc.

Encyclopædia of Ruger Rimfire Semi-Automatic Pistols: 1949-1992, by Chad Hiddleson, Krause Publications, Iola, WI, 1993. 250 pp., illus. $29.95.

Covers all physical aspects of Ruger 22-caliber pistols including important features such as boxes, grips, muzzlebrakes, instruction manuals, serial numbers, etc.

HANDGUNNER'S LIBRARY

Encyclopedia of Ruger Semi-Automatic Rimfire Pistols 1949-1992, by Chad Hiddleson, Krause Publications, Iola, WI, 1994. 304 pp., illus. $29.95.

This book is a compilation of years of research, outstanding photographs and technical data on Ruger.

English Pistols: The Armories of H.M. Tower of London Collection, by Howard L. Blackmore, Arms and Armour Press, London, England, 1985. 64 pp., illus. Soft covers. $14.95.

All the pistols described and pictured are from this famed collection.

European Firearms in Swedish Castles, by Kaa Wennberg, Bohuslaningens Boktryckeri AB, Uddevalla, Sweden, 1986. 156 pp., illus. $50.00.

The famous collection of Count Keller, the Ettersburg Castle collection, and others. English text.

Experiments of a Handgunner, by Walter Roper, Wolfe Publishing Co., Prescott, AZ, 1989. 202 pp., illus. $37.00.

A limited edition reprint. A listing of experiments with functioning parts of handguns, with targets, stocks, rests, handloading, etc.

Exploded Handgun Drawings, The Gun Digest Book of, edited by Harold A. Murtz, DBI Books, Inc., Northbrook, IL. 1992. 512 pp., illus. Paper covers. $20.95.

Exploded or isometric drawings for 494 of the most popular handguns.

The Farnam Method of Defensive Handgunning, by John S. Farnam, DTI, Inc., Seattle, WA, 1994. 191 pp., illus. Paper covers. $13.95.

A book intended to not only educate the new shooter, but also to serve as a guide and textbook for his and his instructor's training courses.

Fast and Fancy Revolver Shooting, by Ed. McGivern, Anniversary Edition, Winchester Press, Piscataway, NJ, 1984. 484 pp., illus. $18.95.

A fascinating volume, packed with handgun lore and solid information by the acknowledged dean of revolver shooters.

Fifteen Years in the Hawken Lode, by John D. Baird, The Gun Room Press, Highland Park, NJ, 1976. 120 pp., illus. $24.95.

A collection of thoughts and observations gained from many years of intensive study of the guns from the shop of the Hawken brothers.

'51 Colt Navies, by Nathan L. Swayze, The Gun Room Press, Highland Park, NJ, 1993. 243 pp., illus. $59.95.

The Model 1851 Colt Navy, its variations and markings.

Firearms and Tackle Memorabilia, by John Delph, Schiffer Publishing, Ltd., West Chester, PA, 1991. 124 pp., illus. $39.95.

A collector's guide to signs and posters, calendars, trade cards, boxes, envelopes, and other highly sought after memorabilia. With a value guide.

Firearms Assembly/Disassembly, Part I: Automatic Pistols, Revised Edition, The Gun Digest Book of, by J.B. Wood, DBI Books, Inc., Northbrook, IL, 1990. 480 pp., illus. Soft covers. $19.95.

Covers 58 popular autoloading pistols plus nearly 200 variants of those models integrated into the text and completely cross-referenced in the index.

Firearms Assembly/Disassembly Part II: Revolvers, Revised Edition, The Gun Digest Book of, by J.B. Wood, DBI Books, Inc., Northbrook, IL, 1990. 480 pp., illus. Soft covers. $19.95.

Covers 49 popular revolvers plus 130 variants. The most comprehensive and professional presentation available to either hobbyist or gunsmith.

Firearms Assembly 4: The NRA Guide to Pistols and Revolvers, NRA Books, Wash., DC, 1980. 253 pp., illus. Paper covers. $13.95.

Text and illustrations explaining the takedown of 124 pistol and revolver models, domestic and foreign.

Firearms Bluing and Browning, By R.H. Angier, Stackpole Books, Harrisburg, PA. 151 pp., illus. $18.95.

A world master gunsmith reveals his secrets of building, repairing and renewing a gun, quite literally, lock, stock and barrel. A useful, concise text on chemical coloring methods for the gunsmith and mechanic.

Firearms Disassembly—With Exploded Views, by John A. Karns & John E. Traister, Stoeger Publishing Co., S. Hackensack, NJ, 1995. 320 pp., illus. Paper covers. $19.95.

Provides the do's and don'ts of firearms disassembly. Enables owners and gunsmiths to disassemble firearms in a professional manner.

Firearms Engraving as Decorative Art, by Dr. Fredric A. Harris, Barbara R. Harris, Seattle, WA, 1989. 172 pp., illus. $115.00.

The origin of American firearms engraving motifs in the decorative art of the Middle East. Illustrated with magnificent color photographs.

Firing Back, by Clayton E. Cramer, Krause Publications, Iola, WI, 1995. 208 pp., Paper covers. $9.95.

Proposes answers and arguments to counter the popular anti-gun sentiments.

Flayderman's Guide to Antique American Firearms...and Their Values, 6th Edition, by Norm Flayderman, DBI Books, Inc., Northbrook, IL, 1994. 624 pp., illus. Paper covers. $29.95.

Updated edition of this bible of the antique gun field.

.45 ACP Super Guns, by J.M. Ramos, Paladin Press, Boulder, CO, 1991. 144 pp., illus. Paper covers. $24.00.

Modified .45 automatic pistols for competition, hunting and personal defense.

The .45, The Gun Digest Book of, by Dean A. Grennell, DBI Books, Inc., Northbrook, IL, 1989. 256 pp., illus. Paper covers. $17.95.

Definitive work on one of America's favorite calibers.

*****Frank Pachmayr: The Story of America's Master Gunsmith and his Guns,** by John Lachuk, Safari Press, Huntington Beach, CA, 1996. 254 pp., illus. First edition, limited, signed and slipcased. $85.00; Second printing trade edition. $50.00.

The colorful and historically significant biography of Frank A Pachmayr, America's own gunsmith emeritus.

French Military Weapons, 1717-1938, Major James E. Hicks, N. Flayderman & Co., Publishers, New Milford, CT, 1973. 281 pp., illus. $35.00.

Firearms, swords, bayonets, ammunition, artillery, ordnance equipment of the French army.

The French 1935 Pistols, by Eugene Medlin and Colin Doane, Eugene Medlin, El Paso, TX, 1995. 172 pp., illus. Paper covers. $25.95.

The development and identification of successive models, fakes and variants, holsters and accessories, and serial numbers by dates of production.

From the Kingdom of Lilliput: The Miniature Firearms of David Kucer, by K. Corey Keeble and **The Making of Miniatures,** by David Kucer, Museum Restoration Service, Ontario, Canada, 1994. 51 pp., illus, $25.00.

An overview of the subject of miniatures in general combined with an outline by the artist himself on the way he makes a miniature firearm.

Game Loads and Practical Ballistics for the American Hunter, by Bob Hagel, Wolfe Publishing Co., Prescott, AZ, 1992. 310 pp., illus. $27.90.

Hagel's knowledge gained as a hunter, guide and gun enthusiast is gathered in this informative text.

German Pistols and Holsters 1934-1945, Vol. 2, by Robert Whittington, Brownlee Books, Hooks, TX, 1990. 312 pp., illus. $55.00.

This volume addresses pistols only: military (Heer, Luftwaffe, Kriegsmarine & Waffen-SS), captured, commercial, police, NSDAP and government.

German Pistols and Holsters, 1934-1945, Volume 4, by Lt. Col. Robert D. Whittington, 3rd, U.S.A.R., Brownlee Books, Hooks, TX, 1991. 208 pp. $30.00.

Pistols and holsters issued in 412 selected armed forces, army and Waffen-SS units including information on personnel, other weapons and transportation.

Glock: The New Wave in Combat Handguns, by Peter Alan Kasler, Paladin Press, Boulder, CO, 1993. 304 pp., illus. $25.00.

Kasler debunks the myths that surround what is the most innovative handgun to be introduced in some time.

The Golden Age of Remington, by Robert W.D. Ball, Krause publications, Iola, WI, 1995. 208 pp., illus. $29.95.

For Remington collectors or firearms historians, this book provides a pictorial history of Remington through World War I. Includes value guide.

Good Guns Again, by Stephen Bodio, Wilderness Adventures Press, Bozeman, MT, 1994. 183 pp., illus. $29.00.

A celebration of fine sporting arms.

Great British Gunmakers: The Mantons 1782-1878, by D.H.L. Back, Historical Firearms, Norwich, England, 1994. 218 pp., illus. Limited edition of 500 copies. $175.00.

Detailed descriptions of all the firearms made by members of this famous family.

Great Combat Handguns, by Leroy Thompson and Rene Smeets, Sterling Publishing Co., New York, NY, 1993. 256 pp., illus. $29.95.

Revised and newly designed edition of the successful classic in handgun use and reference.

Great Shooters of the World, by Sam Fadala, Stoeger Publishing Co., So. Hackensack, NJ, 1991. 288 pp., illus. Paper covers. $18.95.

This book offers gun enthusiasts an overview of the men and women who have forged the history of firearms over the past 150 years.

Guerrilla Warfare Weapons, by Terry Gander, Sterling Publishing Co., Inc., 1990. 128 pp., illus. Paper covers. $9.95.

The latest and most sophisticated armaments of the modern underground fighter's armory.

Guide to Ruger Single Action Revolvers Production Dates, 1953-73, by John C. Dougan, Blacksmith Corp., Chino Valley, AZ, 1991. 22 pp., illus. Paper covers. $9.95.

A unique pocket-sized handbook providing production information for the popular Ruger single-action revolvers manufactured during the first 20 years.

Gun Collecting, by Geoffrey Boothroyd, Sportsman's Press, London, 1989. 208 pp., illus. $29.95.

The most comprehensive list of 19th century British gunmakers and gunsmiths ever published.

Gun Collector's Digest, 5th Edition, edited by Joseph J. Schroeder, DBI Books, Inc., Northbrook, IL, 1989. 224 pp., illus. Paper covers. $17.95.

The latest edition of this sought-after series.

*****Gun Digest, 1997, 51st Edition,** edited by Ken Warner, DBI Books, Inc., Northbrook, IL, 1996. 544 pp., illus. Paper covers. $23.95.

All-new edition of the world's biggest selling gun book.

Gun Digest Treasury, 7th Edition, edited by Harold A. Murtz, DBI Books, Inc., Northbrook, IL, 1994. 320 pp., illus. Paper covers. $17.95.

A collection of some of the most interesting articles which have appeared in Gun Digest over its first 45 years.

Gun Notes, by Elmer Keith, Safari Press, Huntington Beach, CA, 1995. 280 pp., illus. $30.00.

A collection of Elmer Keith's most interesting columns and feature stories that appeared in *Guns and Ammo* magazine from 1961 to the late 1970s.

Gun Talk, edited by Dave Moreton, Winchester Press, Piscataway, NJ, 1973. 256 pp., illus $9.95.

A treasury of original writing by the top gun writers and editors in America. Practical advice about every aspect of the shooting sports.

Gun Tools, Their History and Identification by James B. Shaffer, Lee A. Rutledge and R. Stephen Dorsey, Collector's Library, Eugene, OR, 1992. 375 pp., illus. $32.00.

Written history of foreign and domestic gun tools from the flintlock period to WWII.

Gun Trader's Guide, 18th Edition, published by Stoeger Publishing Co., S. Hackensack, NJ, 1995. 575 pp., illus. Paper covers. $19.95.

Complete, fully illustrated guide to identification of modern firearms along with current market values.

Gun Writers of Yesteryear, compiled by James Foral, Wolfe Publishing Co., Prescott, AZ, 1993. 449 pp. $35.00.

Here, from the pre-American rifleman days of 1898-1920, are collected some 80 articles by 34 writers from eight magazines.

The Gunfighter, Man or Myth? by Joseph G. Rosa, Oklahoma Press, Norman, OK, 1969. 229 pp., illus. (including weapons). Paper covers. $14.95.

A well-documented work on gunfights and gunfighters of the West and elsewhere. Great treat for all gunfighter buffs.

Gunmakers of London 1350-1850, by Howard L. Blackmore, George Shumway Publisher, York, PA, 1986. 222 pp., illus. $35.00.

A listing of all the known workmen of gun making in the first 500 years, plus a history of the guilds, cutlers, armourers, founders, blacksmiths, etc. 260 gunmarks are illustrated.

Gunproof Your Children/Handgun Primer, by Massad Ayoob, Police Bookshelf, Concord, NH, 1989. Paper covers. $4.95.

Two books in one. The first, keeping children safe from unauthorized guns in their hands; the second, a compact introduction to handgun safety.

Gunshot Injuries: How They Are Inflicted, Their Complications and Treatment, by Col. Louis A. La Garde, 2nd revised edition, Lancer Militaria, Mt. Ida, AR, 1991. 480 pp., illus. $34.95.

A classic work which was the standard textbook on the subject at the time of WWI.

Gunshot Wounds, by Vincent J.M. DiMaio, M.D., Elsevier Science Publishing Co., New York, NY, 1985. 331 pp., illus. $90.00.

Practical aspects of firearms, ballistics, and forensic techniques.

Gunsmith Kinks, by F.R. (Bob) Brownell, F. Brownell & Son, Montezuma, IA, 1st ed., 1969. 496 pp., well illus. $18.95.

A widely useful accumulation of shop kinks, short cuts, techniques and pertinent comments by practicing gunsmiths from all over the world.

Gunsmith Kinks 2, by Bob Brownell, F. Brownell & Son, Publishers, Montezuma, IA, 1983. 496 pp., illus. $18.95.

A collection of gunsmithing knowledge, shop kinks, new and old techniques, shortcuts and general know-how straight from those who do them best—the gunsmiths.

Gunsmith Kinks 3, edited by Frank Brownell, Brownells Inc., Montezuma, IA, 1993. 504 pp., illus. $19.95.

Tricks, knacks and "kinks" by professional gunsmiths and gun tinkerers. Hundreds of valuable ideas are given in this volume.

Gunsmithing, by Roy F. Dunlap, Stackpole Books, Harrisburg, PA, 1990. 742 pp., illus. $34.95.

A manual of firearm design, construction, alteration and remodeling. For amateur and professional gunsmiths and users of modern firearms.

Gunsmithing at Home, by John E. Traister, Stoeger Publishing Co., So. Hackensack, NJ, 1985. 256 pp., illus. Paper covers. $14.95.

Over 25 chapters of explicit information on every aspect of gunsmithing.

Gunsmithing Tips and Projects, a collection of the best articles from the *Handloader* and *Rifle* magazines, by various authors, Wolfe Publishing Co., Prescott, AZ, 1992. 443 pp., illus. Paper covers. $25.00.

Includes such subjects as shop, stocks, actions, tuning, triggers, barrels, customizing, etc.

The Gunsmith's Manual, by J.P. Stelle and Wm. B. Harrison, The Gun Room Press, Highland Park, NJ, 1982. 376 pp., illus. $19.95.

For the gunsmith in all branches of the trade.

Gunsmiths of Illinois, by Curtis L. Johnson, George Shumway Publishers, York, PA, 1995. 160 pp., illus. $50.00.

Genealogical information is provided for nearly one thousand gunsmiths. Contains hundreds of illustrations of rifles and other guns, of handmade origin, from Illinois.

The Gunsmiths of Manhattan, 1625-1900: A Checklist of Tradesmen, by Michael H. Lewis, Museum Restoration Service, Bloomfield, Ont., Canada, 1991. 40 pp., illus. Paper covers. $4.95.

This listing of more than 700 men in the arms trade in New York City prior to about the end of the 19th century will provide a guide for identification and further research.

*****Guns Illustrated 1997, 29th Edition,** edited by Harold A. Murtz, DBI Books, Inc., Northbrook, IL, 1996. 336 pp., illus. Paper covers. $20.95.

Truly the journal of Gun Buffs, this all new edition consists of articles of interest to every shooter as well as a complete catalog of all U.S. and imported firearms with latest specs and prices. Available August, 1996.

Guns, Loads, and Hunting Tips, by Bob Hagel, Wolfe Publishing Co., Prescott, AZ, 1986. 509 pp., illus. $19.95.

A large hardcover book packed with shooting, hunting and handloading wisdom.

*****The Guns of Dagenham: Lanchester, Patchett, Sterling,** by Peter Laidler and David Howroyd, Collector Grade Publications, Inc., Cobourg, Ont., Canada, 1995. 310 pp., illus. $39.95.

An in-depth history of the small arms made by the Sterling Company of Dagenham, Essex, England, from 1940 until Sterling was purchased by British Aerospace in 1989 and closed.

Guns of the First World War, Rifle, Handguns and Ammunition from the Text Book of Small Arms, 1909, edited by John Walter, Presidio Press, Novato, CA, 1991. $30.00.

Details of the Austro-Hung. Mann., French Lebels, German Mausers, U.S. Springfields, etc.

Guns of the Wild West, by George Markham, Sterling Publishing Co., New York, NY, 1993. 160 pp., illus. Paper covers. $19.95.

Firearms of the American Frontier, 1849-1917.

Guns & Shooting: A Selected Bibliography, by Ray Riling, Ray Riling Arms Books Co., Phila., PA, 1982. 434 pp., illus. Limited, numbered edition. $75.

A limited edition of this superb bibliographical work, the only modern listing of books devoted to guns and shooting.

Hand Cannons: The World's Most Powerful Handguns, by Duncan Long, Paladin Press, Boulder, CO, 1995. 208 pp., illus. Paper covers. $20.00.

Long describes and evaluates each powerful gun according to their features.

Handbook for Shooters and Reloaders, by P.O. Ackley, Salt Lake City, UT, 1970, (Vol. I), 567 pp., illus. (Vol. II), a new printing with specific new material. 495 pp., illus. $17.95 each.

Handbook of Bullet Swaging No. 7, by David R. Corbin, Corbin Manufacturing and Supply Co., White City, OR, 1986. 199 pp., illus. Paper covers. $10.00.

This handbook explains the most precise method of making quality bullets.

Handbook of Metallic Cartridge Reloading, by Edward Matunas, Winchester Press, Piscataway, NJ, 1981. 272 pp., illus. $19.95.

Up-to-date, comprehensive loading tables prepared by four major powder manufacturers.

The Handgun, by Geoffrey Boothroyd, David and Charles, North Pomfret, VT, 1989. 566 pp., illus. $60.00.

Every chapter deals with an important period in handgun history from the 14th century to the present.

Handgun Digest, 3rd Edition, edited by Chris Christian, DBI Books, Inc., Northbrook, IL, 1995. 256 pp., illus. Paper covers. $18.95.

Full coverage of all aspects of handguns and handgunning from a highly readable and knowledgeable author.

Handgun Reloading, The Gun Digest Book of, by Dean A. Grennell and Wiley M. Clapp, DBI Books, Inc., Northbrook, IL, 1987. 256 pp., illus. Paper covers. $16.95.

Detailed discussions of all aspects of reloading for handguns, from basic to complex. New loading data.

*****Handguns '97, 9th Edition,** edited by Ray Ordorica, DBI Books, Inc., Northbrook, IL, 1995. 352 pp., illus. Paper covers. $20.95.

Top handgun experts cover what's new in the world of handguns and handgunning. Available August, 1996.

*****Handloader's Digest 1997, 16th Edition,** edited by Bob Bell, DBI Books, Inc., Northbrook, IL, 1996. 480pp., illus. Paper covers. $23.95.

Top writers in the field contribute helpful information on techniques and components. Greatly expanded and fully indexed catalog of all currently available tools, accessories and components for metallic, blackpowder cartridge, shotshell reloading and swaging.

Handloader's Guide, by Stanley W. Trzoniec, Stoeger Publishing Co., So. Hackensack, NJ, 1985. 256 pp., illus. Paper covers. $14.95.

The complete step-by-step fully illustrated guide to handloading ammunition.

Handloader's Manual of Cartridge Conversions, by John J. Donnelly, Stoeger Publishing Co., So. Hackensack, NJ, 1986. Unpaginated. $49.95.

From 14 Jones to 70-150 Winchester in English and American cartridges, and from 4.85 U.K. to 15.2x28R Gevelot in metric cartridges. Over 900 cartridges described in detail.

Handloading, by Bill Davis, Jr., NRA Books, Wash., D.C., 1980. 400 pp., illus. Paper covers. $15.95.

A complete update and expansion of the NRA Handloader's Guide.

Handloading for Hunters, by Don Zutz, Winchester Press, Piscataway, NJ, 1977. 288 pp., illus. $30.00.

Precise mixes and loads for different types of game and for various hunting situations with rifle and shotgun.

Hatcher's Notebook, by S. Julian Hatcher, Stackpole Books, Harrisburg, PA, 1992. 488 pp., illus. $29.95.

A reference work for shooters, gunsmiths, ballisticians, historians, hunters and collectors.

"Hell, I Was There!," by Elmer Keith, Petersen Publishing Co., Los Angeles, CA, 1979. 308 pp., illus. $24.95.

Adventures of a Montana cowboy who gained world fame as a big game hunter.

*****Hidden in Plain Sight,** by Trey Bloodworth & Mike Raley, Professional Press, Chapel Hill, NC, 1995. Paper covers. $13.00.

A practical guide to concealed handgun carry.

High Standard: A Collector's Guide to the Hamden & Hartford Target Pistols, by Tom Dance, Andrew Mowbray, Inc., Lincoln, RI, 1991. 192 pp., illus. Paper covers. $24.00.

From Citation to Supermatic, all of the production models and specials made from 1951 to 1984 are covered according to model number or series.

High Standard Automatic Pistols 1932-1950, by Charles E. Petty, The Gunroom Press, Highland Park, NJ, 1989. 124 pp., illus. $19.95.

A definitive source of information for the collector of High Standard arms.

*****The Hi-standard Pistol Guide,** by Burr Leyson, Duckett's Sporting Books, Tempe AZ, 1995. 128 pp., illus. Paper covers. $22.00.

Complete information on selection, care and repair, ammunition, parts, and accessories.

Historic Pistols: The American Martial Flintlock 1760-1845, by Samuel E. Smith and Edwin W. Bitter, The Gun Room Press, Highland Park, NJ, 1986. 353 pp., illus. $45.00.

Covers over 70 makers and 163 models of American martial arms.

Historical Hartford Hardware, by William W. Dalrymple, Colt Collector Press, Rapid City, SD, 1976. 42 pp., illus. Paper covers. $10.00.

Historically associated Colt revolvers.

The History and Development of Small Arms Ammunition, Volume 2, by George A. Hoyem, Armory Publications, Oceanside, CA, 1991. 303 pp., illus. $60.00.

Covers the blackpowder military centerfire rifle, carbine, machine gun and volley gun ammunition used in 28 nations and dominions, together with the firearms that chambered them.

The History and Development of Small Arms Ammunition (British Sporting Rifle) Volume 3, by George A. Hoyem, Armory Publications, Oceanside, CA, 1991. 300 pp., illus. $60.00.

Concentrates on British sporting rifle cartridges that run from the 4-bore through the .600 Nitro to the .297/.230 Morris.

The History of Smith and Wesson, by Roy G. Jinks, Willowbrook Enterprises, Springfield, MA, 1988. 290 pp., illus. $27.95.

Revised 10th anniversary edition of the definite book on S&W firearms.

Hodgdon Data Manual No. 26, Hodgdon Powder Co., Shawnee Mission, KS, 1993. 797 pp. $22.95.

Includes Hercules, Winchester and Dupont powders; data on cartridge cases; loads; silhouette; shotshell; pyrodex and blackpowder; conversion factors; weight equivalents, etc.

The Home Guide to Cartridge Conversions, by Maj. George C. Nonte Jr., The Gun Room Press, Highland Park, NJ, 1976. 404 pp., illus. $24.95.

Revised and updated version of Nonte's definitive work on the alteration of cartridge cases for use in guns for which they were not intended.

Home Gunsmithing the Colt Single Action Revolvers, by Loren W. Smith, Ray Riling Arms Books, Co., Phila., PA, 1995. 119 pp., illus. $24.95.

Affords the Colt Single Action owner detailed, pertinent information on the operating and servicing of this famous and historic handgun.

Hornady Handbook of Cartridge Reloading, 4th Edition, Vol. I and II, Hornady Mfg. Co., Grand Island, NE, 1991. 1200 pp., illus. $28.50.

New edition of this famous reloading handbook. Latest loads, ballistic information, etc.

Hornady Handbook of Cartridge Reloading, Abridged Edition, Hornady Mfg. Co., Grand Island, NE, 1991. $19.95.

Ballistic data for 25 of the most popular cartridges.

Hornady Load Notes, Hornady Mfg. Co., Grand Island, NE, 1991. $4.95.

Complete load data and ballistics for a single caliber. Eight pistol 9mm-45ACP; 16 rifle, 222-45-70.

How to Become a Master Handgunner: The Mechanics of X-Count Shooting, by Charles Stephens, Paladin Press, Boulder, CO, 1993. 64 pp., illus. Paper covers. $10.00.

Offers a simple formula for success to the handgunner who strives to master the technique of shooting accurately.

How to Buy and Sell Used Guns, by John Traister, Stoeger Publishing Co., So. Hackensack, NJ, 1984. 192 pp., illus. Paper covers. $10.95.

A new guide to buying and selling guns.

Hunting for Handgunners, by Larry Kelly and J.D. Jones, DBI Books, Inc., Northbrook, IL, 1990. 256 pp., illus. Paper covers. $16.95.

Covers the entire spectrum of hunting with handguns in an amusing, easy-flowing manner that combines entertainment with solid information.

Il Grande Libro Delle Incision (Modern Engravings Real Book), by Marco E. Nobili, Editrice Il Volo, Milano, Italy, 1992. 399 pp., illus. $95.00.

The best existing expressions of engravings on guns, knives and other items. Text in English and Italian.

Illustrated Encyclopedia of Handguns, by A.B. Zhuk, Stackpole Books, Mechanicsburg, PA, 1994. 256 pp., illus. $49.95.

Identifies more than 2,000 military and commercial pistols and revolvers with details of more than 100 popular handgun cartridges.

The Illustrated Reference of Cartridge Dimensions, edited by Dave Scovill, Wolfe Publishing Co., Prescott, AZ, 1994. 343 pp., illus. Paper covers. $19.00.

A comprehensive volume with over 300 cartridges. Standard and metric dimensions have been taken from SAAMI drawings and/or fired cartridges.

Illustrations of United States Military Arms 1776-1903 and Their Inspector's Marks, compiled by Turner Kirkland, Pioneer Press, Union City, TN, 1988. 37 pp., illus. Paper covers. $4.95.

Reprinted from the 1949 Bannerman catalog. Valuable information for both the advanced and beginning collector.

Indian War Cartridge Pouches, Boxes and Carbine Boots, by R. Stephen Dorsey, Collector's Library, Eugene, OR, 1993. 156 pp., illus. Paper Covers. $25.00.

The key reference work to the cartridge pouches, boxes, carbine sockets and boots of the Indian War period 1865-1890.

Instinct Combat Shooting, by Chuck Klein, Chuck Klein, The Goose Creek, IN, 1989. 49 pp., illus. Paper covers. $12.00.

Defensive handgunning for police.

An Introduction to the Civil War Small Arms, by Earl J. Coates and Dean S. Thomas, Thomas Publishing Co., Gettysburg, PA, 1990. 96 pp., illus. Paper covers. $10.00.

The small arms carried by the individual soldier during the Civil War.

Iver Johnson's Arms & Cycle Works Handguns, 1871-1964, by W.E. "Bill" Goforth, Blacksmith Corp., Chino Valley, AZ, 1991. 160 pp., illus. Paper covers. $14.95.

Covers all of the famous Iver Johnson handguns from the early solid-frame pistols and revolvers to optional accessories, special orders and patents.

James Reid and His Catskill Knuckledusters, by Taylor Brown, Andrew Mowbray Publishers, Lincoln, RI, 1990. 288 pp., illus. $24.95.

A detailed history of James Reid, his factory in the picturesque Catskill Mountains, and the pistols which he manufactured there.

Jane's Infantry Weapons, 21st Edition, 1995-96, Jane's Information Group, Alexandria, VA, 1995. 750 pp., illus. $265.00.
Complete coverage on over 1,700 weapons and accessories from nearly 300 manufacturers in 69 countries. Completely revised and updated.

Japanese Handguns, by Frederick E. Leithe, Borden Publishing Co., Alhambra, CA, 1985. 160 pp., illus. $22.95.
An identification guide to all models and variations of Japanese handguns.

Know Your Broomhandle Mausers, by R.J. Berger, Blacksmith Corp., Southport, CT, 1985. 96 pp., illus. Paper covers. $9.95.
An interesting story on the big Mauser pistol and its variations.

Know Your Czechoslovakian Pistols, by R.J. Berger, Blacksmith Corp., Chino Valley, AZ, 1989. 96 pp., illus. Soft covers. $9.95.
A comprehensive reference which presents the fascinating story of Czech pistols.

Know Your 45 Auto Pistols—Models 1911 & A1, by E.J. Hoffschmidt, Blacksmith Corp., Southport, CT, 1974. 58 pp., illus. Paper covers. $9.95.
A concise history of the gun with a wide variety of types and copies.

Know Your Walther P.38 Pistols, by E.J. Hoffschmidt, Blacksmith Corp., Southport, CT, 1974. 77 pp., illus. Paper covers. $9.95.
Covers the Walther models Armee, M.P., H.P., P.38—history and variations.

Know Your Walther PP & PPK Pistols, by E.J. Hoffschmidt, Blacksmith Corp., Southport, CT, 1975. 87 pp., illus. Paper covers. $9.95.
A concise history of the guns with a guide to the variety and types.

The Krieghoff Parabellum, by Randall Gibson, Midland, TX, 1988. 279 pp., illus. $40.00.
A comprehensive text pertaining to the Lugers manufactured by H. Krieghoff Waffenfabrik.

Lasers and Night Vision Devices, by Duncan Long, Desert Publications, El Dorado, AZ, 1993. 150 pp., illus. Paper covers. $29.95.
A comprehensive look at the evolution of devices that allow firearms to be operated in low light conditions and at night.

Levine's Guide to Knives And Their Values, 3rd Edition, by Bernard Levine, DBI Books, Inc., Northbrook, IL, 1993. 480 pp., illus. Paper covers. $25.95
All the basic tools for identifying, valuing and collecting folding and fixed blade knives.

***Loading the Peacemaker—Colt's Model P,** by Dave Scovill, Wolfe Publishing Co., Prescott, AZ, 1995. $24.95.
A comprehensive work about the most famous revolver ever made, including the most extensive load data ever published.

***The Luger Story,** by John Walter, Stackpole Books, Mechanicsburg, PA, 1995. 256 pp., illus. $39.95.
The standard history of the world's most famous handgun.

Lugers at Random, by Charles Kenyon, Jr., Handgun Press, Glenview, IL, 1990. 420 pp., illus. $49.95.
A new printing of this classic, comprehensive reference for all Luger collectors.

Lyman Cast Bullet Handbook, 3rd Edition, edited by C. Kenneth Ramage, Lyman Publications, Middlefield, CT, 1980. 416 pp., illus. Paper covers. $19.95.
Information on more than 5000 tested cast bullet loads and 19 pages of trajectory and wind drift tables for cast bullets.

Lyman Black Powder Handbook, ed. by C. Kenneth Ramage, Lyman Products for Shooters, Middlefield, CT, 1975. 239 pp., illus. Paper covers. $14.95.
Comprehensive load information for the modern blackpowder shooter.

***Lyman Pistol & Revolver Handbook, 2nd Edition,** edited by Thomas J. Griffin, Lyman Products Co., Middlefield, CT, 1996. 287 pp., illus. Paper covers. $18.95.
The most up-to-date loading data available including the hottest new calibers, like 40 S&W, 9x21, 9mm Makarov, 9x25 Dillon and 454 Casull.

Lyman Reloading Handbook No. 47, edited by Edward A. Matunas, Lyman Publications, Middlefield, CT, 1992. 480 pp., illus. Paper covers. $23.00.
"The world's most comprehensive reloading manual." Complete "How to Reload" information. Expanded data section with all the newest rifle and pistol calibers.

Making Loading Dies and Bullet Molds, by Harold Hoffman, H&P Publishing, San Angelo, TX, 1993. 230 pp., illus. Paper covers. $24.95.
A good book for learning tool and die making.

Master Tips, by J. Winokur, Potshot Press, Pacific Palisades, CA, 1985. 96 pp., illus. Paper covers. $11.95.
Basics of practical shooting.

The Mauser Self-Loading Pistol, by Belford & Dunlap, Borden Publ. Co., Alhambra, CA. Over 200 pp., 300 illus., large format. $24.95.
The long-awaited book on the "Broom Handles," covering their inception in 1894 to the end of production. Complete and in detail: pocket pistols, Chinese and Spanish copies, etc.

***Metallic Cartridge Reloading, 3rd Edition,** by M. L. McPherson, DBI Books, Inc., Northbrook, IL., 1996. 384 pp., illus. Paper covers. $21.95.
A true reloading manual with over 10,000 loads fro all popular metallic cartridges and a wealth of invaluable technical data provided by a recognized expert.

Military Handguns of France 1858-1958, by Eugene Medlin and Jean Huon, Excalibur Publications, Latham, NY, 1994. 124 pp., illus. Paper covers. $24.95.
The first book written in English that provides students of arms with a thorough history of French military handguns.

Military Pistols of Japan, by Fred L. Honeycutt, Jr., Julin Books, Palm Beach Gardens, FL, 1991. 168 pp., illus. $34.00.
Covers every aspect of military pistol production in Japan through WWII.

Military Small Arms of the 20th Century, 6th Edition, by Ian V. Hogg, DBI Books, Inc., Northbrook, IL, 1991. 352 pp., illus. Paper covers. $20.95.
Fully revised and updated edition of the standard reference in its field.

Modern American Pistols and Revolvers, by A.C. Gould, Wolfe Publishing Co., Prescott, AZ, 1988. 222 pp., illus. $37.00.
A limited edition reprint. An account of the development of those arms as well as the manner of shooting them.

Modern Beretta Firearms, by Gene Gangarosa, Jr., Stoeger Publishing Co., S. Hackensack, NJ, 1994. 288 pp., illus. Paper covers. $16.95.
Traces all models of modern Beretta pistols, rifles, machine guns and combat shotguns.

***Modern Gun Values, 10th Edition, The Gun Digest Book of** by the editors of Gun Digest, DBI Books, Inc., Northbrook, IL, 1996. 560 pp., illus. paper covers. $21.95.
Greatly updated and expanded edition describing and valuing over 7,000 firearms manufactured between 1900 and 1995. The standard reference for valuing modern firearms.

Modern Guns Identification and Values, 10th Edition, by Steven and Russell Quertermous, Collector Books, Paducah, KY, 1994. 496 pp., illus. Paper covers. $12.95.
Over 2,500 models of rifles, handguns and shotguns from 1900 to the present are described and prices given for NRA excellent and very good.

Modern Handloading, by Maj. Geo. C. Nonte, Winchester Press, Piscataway, NJ, 1972. 416 pp., illus. $15.00.
Covers all aspects of metallic and shotshell ammunition loading, plus more loads than any book in print.

Modern Law Enforcement Weapons & Tactics, 2nd Edition, by Tom Ferguson, DBI Books, Inc., Northbrook, IL, 1991. 256 pp., illus. Paper covers. $18.95.
An in-depth look at the weapons and equipment used by law enforcement agencies of today.

Modern Practical Ballistics, by Art Pejsa, Pejsa Ballistics, Minneapolis, MN, 1990. 150 pp., illus. $24.95.
Covers all aspects of ballistics and new, simplified methods. Clear examples illustrate new, easy but very accurate formulas.

Modern Small Arms, by Ian Hogg, Book Sales, Edison, NJ, 1995. 160 pp., illus. $17.98.
Encyclopedia coverage of more than 150 of the most sought after small arms produced today—rifles, pistols, machine guns and shotguns are covered.

The Modern Technique of the Pistol, by Gregory Boyce Morrison, Gunsite Press, Paulden, AZ, 1991. 153 pp., illus. $45.00.
The theory of effective defensive use of modern handguns.

***Mossberg: More Gun for the Money,** by V. and C. Havlin, Investment Rarities, Inc., Minneapolis, MN, 1995. 304 pp., illus. Paper covers. $24.95.
The history of O. F. Mossberg and Sons, Inc.

Mortimer, the Gunmakers, 1753-1923, by H. Lee Munson, Andrew Mowbray Inc., Lincoln, RI, 1992. 320 pp., illus. $65.00.
Seen through a single, dominant, English gunmaking dynasty this fascinating study provides a window into the classical era of firearms artistry.

***Naval Percussion Locks and Primers,** by Lt. J. A. Dahlgren, Museum Restoration Service, Bloomfield, Canada, 1996. 140 pp., illus. $35.00
First published as an Ordnance Memoranda in 1853, this is the finest existing study of percussion locks and primers origin and development.

The Navy Luger, by Joachim Gortz and John Walter, Handgun Press, Glenview, IL, 1988. 128 pp., illus. $24.95.
The 9mm Pistole 1904 and the Imperial German Navy. A concise illustrated history.

***Nick Harvey's Practical Reloading Manual,** by Nick Harvey, Australian Print Group, Maryborough, Victoria, Australia, 1995. 235 pp., illus. Paper covers. $24.95.
Contains data for rifle and handgun including many popular wildcat and improved cartridges. Tools, powders, components and techniques for assembling optimum reloads with particular application to North America.

L.D. Nimschke Firearms Engraver, by R.L. Wilson, R&R Books, Livonia, NY, 1992. 108 pp., illus. $100.00.
The personal work record of one of the 19th century America's foremost engravers. Augmented by a comprehensive text, photographs of deluxe-engraved firearms, and detailed indexes.

9mm Handguns, 2nd Edition, The Gun Digest Book of, edited by Steve Comus, DBI Books, Inc., Northbrook, IL, 1993. 256 pp., illus. Paper covers. $18.95.
Covers the 9mmP cartridge and the guns that have been made for it in greater depth than any other work available.

9mm Parabellum; The History & Developement of the World's 9mm Pistols & Ammunition, by Klaus-Peter Konig and Martin Hugo, Schiffer Publishing Ltd., Atglen, PA, 1993. 304 pp., illus. $39.95.
Detailed history of 9mm weapons from Belguim, Italy, Germany, Israel, France, USA, Czechoslovakia, Hungary, Poland, Brazil, Finland and Spain.

No Second Place Winner, by Wm. H. Jordan, publ. by the author, Shreveport, LA (Box 4072), 1962. 114 pp., illus. $15.95.
Guns and gear of the peace officer, ably discussed by a U.S. Border Patrolman for over 30 years, and a first-class shooter with handgun, rifle, etc.

Nosler Reloading Manual No. 3, edited by Gail Root, Nosler Bullets, Inc., Bend, OR, 1989. 516 pp., illus. $21.95.
All-new book. New format including featured articles and cartridge introductions by well-known shooters, gun writers and editors.

The NRA Gunsmithing Guide—Updated, by Ken Raynor and Brad Fenton, National Rifle Association, Wash., DC, 1984. 336 pp., illus. Paper covers. $15.95.
Material includes chapters and articles on all facets of the gunsmithing art.

***The Official 9mm Markarov Pistol Manual,** translated into English by Major James Gebhardt, U.S. Army (Ret.), Desert Publications, El Dorado, AR, 1996. 84 pp., illus. Paper covers. $12.95.
The information found in this book will be of enormous benefit and interest to the owner or a prospective owner of one of these pistols.

The 100 Greatest Combat Pistols, by Timothy J. Mullin, Paladin Press, Boulder, CO, 1994. 409 pp., illus. Paper covers. $40.00.
Hands-on tests and evaluations of handguns from around the world.

***OSS Weapons,** by Dr. John W. Brunner, Phillips Publications, Williamstown, NJ, 1996. 224 pp., illus. $44.95.
The most definitive book ever written on the weapons and equipment used by the supersecret warriors of the Office of Strategic Services.

The P-08 Parabellum Luger Automatic Pistol, edited by J. David McFarland, Desert Publications, Cornville, AZ, 1982. 20 pp., illus. Paper covers. $10.00.
Covers every facet of the Luger, plus a listing of all known Luger models.

P-38 Automatic Pistol, by Gene Gangarosa, Jr., Stoeger Publishing Co., S. Hackensack, NJ, 1993. 272 pp., illus. Paper covers. $16.95
This book traces the origins and development of the P-38, including the momentous political forces of the World War II era that caused its near demise and, later, its rebirth.

Packing Iron, by Richard C. Rattenbury, Zon International Publishing, Millwood, NY, 1993. 216 pp., illus. $45.00.
The best book yet produced on pistol holsters and rifle scabbards. Over 300 variations of holster and scabbards are illustrated in large, clear plates.

Patents for Inventions, Class 119 (Small Arms), 1855-1930. British Patent Office, Armory Publications, Oceanside, CA, 1993. 7 volume set. $350.00.
Contains 7980 abridged patent descriptions and their sectioned line drawings, plus a 37-page alphabetical index of the patentees.

Paterson Colt Pistol Variations, by R.L. Wilson and R. Phillips, Jackson Arms Co., Dallas, TX, 1979. 250 pp., illus. $35.00.
A book about the different models and barrel lengths in the Paterson Colt story.

Pin Shooting: A Complete Guide, by Mitchell A. Ota, Wolfe Publishing Co., Prescott, AZ, 1992. 145 pp., illus. Paper covers. $14.95.
Traces the sport from its humble origins to today's thoroughly enjoyable social event, including the mammoth eight-day Second Chance Pin Shoot in Michigan.

Pistol Guide, by George C. Nonte, Jr., Stoeger Publishing Co., So. Hackensack, NJ, 1991. 280 pp., illus. Paper covers. $13.95.
Covers handling and marksmanship, care and maintenance, pistol ammunition, how to buy a used gun, military pistols, air pistols and repairs.

Pistol & Revolver Guide, 3rd Ed., by George C. Nonte, Stoeger Publ. Co., So. Hackensack, NJ, 1975. 224 pp., illus. Paper covers. $11.95.
The standard reference work on military and sporting handguns.

Pistols of the World, 3rd Edition, by Ian Hogg and John Weeks, DBI Books, Inc., Northbrook, IL, 1992. 320 pp., illus. Paper covers. $20.95.
A totally revised edition of one of the leading studies of small arms.

Pistolsmithing, The Gun Digest Book of, by Jack Mitchell, DBI Books, Inc., Northbrook, IL, 1980. 256 pp., illus. Paper covers. $16.95.
An expert's guide to the operation of each of the handgun actions with all the major functions of pistolsmithing explained.

Pistolsmithing, by George C. Nonte, Jr., Stackpole Books, Harrisburg, PA, 1974. 560 pp., illus. $29.95.
A single source reference to handgun maintenance, repair, and modification at home, unequaled in value.

The Pitman Notes on U.S. Martial Small Arms and Ammunition, 1776-1933, Volume 2, Revolvers and Automatic Pistols, by Brig. Gen. John Pitman, Thomas Publications, Gettysburg, PA, 1990. 192 pp., illus. $29.95.
A most important primary source of information on United States military small arms and ammunition.

Police Handgun Manual, by Bill Clede, Stackpole Books, Inc., Harrisburg, PA, 1985. 128 pp., illus. $18.95.
How to get street-smart survival habits.

The Powder Flask Book, by Ray Riling, R&R Books, Livonia, NY, 1993. 514 pp., illus. $70.00.
The complete book on flasks of the 19th century. Exactly scaled pictures of 1,600 flasks are illustrated.

Powerhouse Pistols—The Colt 1911 and Browning Hi-Power Source Book, by Duncan Long, Paladin Press, Boulder, CO, 1989. 152 pp., illus. Soft covers. $19.95.
The author discusses internal mechanisms, outward design, test-firing results, maintenance and accessories.

*__Practical Gunsmithing,__ by the editors of American Gunsmith, DBI Books, Inc., Northbrook, IL, 1996. 256 pp., illus. Paper covers. $19.95.
A book intended primarily for home gunsmithing, but one that will be extremely helpful to professionals as well.

Practical Shooting: Beyond Fundamentals, by Brian Enos, Zediker Publishing, Clifton, CO, 1996. 201 pp., illus. $27.95.
This prize-winning master covers the advanced techniques of competitive shooting in all its facets.

Precision Handloading, by John Withers, Stoeger Publishing Co., So. Hackensack, NJ, 1985. 224 pp., illus. Paper covers. $14.95.
An entirely new approach to handloading ammunition.

Propellant Profiles New and Expanded, 3rd Edition, Wolfe Publishing Co., Prescott, AZ, 1991. Paper covers. $16.95.

*__E. C. Prudhomme's Gun Engraving Review,__ by E. C. Prudhomme, R&R Books, Livonia, NY, 1994. 164 pp., illus. $60.00.
As a source for engravers and collectors, this book is an indispensable guide to styles and techniques of the world's foremost engravers.

E.C. Prudhomme, Master Gun Engraver, A Retrospective Exhibition: 1946-1973, intro. by John T. Amber, The R. W. Norton Art Gallery, Shreveport, LA, 1973. 32 pp., illus. Paper covers. $9.95.
Examples of master gun engravings by Jack Prudhomme.

The Rare and Valuable Antique Arms, by James E. Serven, Pioneer Press, Union City, TN, 1976. 106 pp., illus. Paper covers. $4.95.
A guide to the collector in deciding which direction his collecting should go, investment value, historic interest, mechanical ingenuity, high art or personal preference.

Reloader's Guide, 3rd Edition, by R.A. Steindler, Stoeger Publishing Co., So. Hackensack, NJ, 1984. 224 pp., illus. Paper covers. $11.95.
Complete, fully illustrated step-by-step guide to handloading ammunition.

Reloading Tools, Sights and Telescopes for Single Shot Rifles, by Gerald O. Kelver, Brighton, CO, 1982. 163 pp., illus. Paper covers. $15.00.
A listing of most of the famous makers of reloading tools, sights and telescopes with a brief description of the products they manufactured.

Report of Board on Tests of Revolvers and Automatic Pistols, From the Annual Report of the Chief of Ordnance, 1907. Reprinted by J.C. Tillinghast, Marlow, NH, 1969. 34 pp., 7 plates, paper covers. $9.95.
A comparison of handguns, including Luger, Savage, Colt, Webley-Fosbery and other makes.

Revolver Guide, by George C. Nonte, Jr., Stoeger Publishing Co., So. Hackensack, NJ, 1991. 288 pp., illus. Paper covers. $10.95.
A detailed and practical encyclopedia of the revolver, the most common handgun to be found.

Revolvers of the British Services 1854-1954, by W.H.J. Chamberlain and A.W.F. Taylerson, Museum Restoration Service, Ottawa, Canada, 1989. 80 pp., illus. $27.50.
Covers the types issued among many of the United Kingdom's naval, land or air services.

Rhode Island Arms Makers & Gunsmiths, by William O. Archibald, Andrew Mowbray, Inc., Lincoln, RI, 1990. 108 pp., illus. $16.50.
A serious and informative study of an important area of American arms making.

Ruger, edited by Joseph Roberts, Jr., the National Rifle Association of America, Washington, D.C., 1991. 109 pp. illus. Paper covers. $14.95.
The story of Bill Ruger's indelible imprint in the history of sporting firearms.

Ruger Automatic Pistols and Single Action Revolvers, by Hugo A. Lueders, edited by Don Findley, Blacksmith Corp., Chino Valley, AZ, 1993. 79 pp., illus. Paper covers. $14.95.
The definitive work on Ruger automatic pistols and single action revolvers.

Ruger Double Action Revolvers, Vol. 1, Shop Manual, by Jerry Kuhnhausen, VSP Publishers, McCall, ID, 1989. 176 pp., illus. Soft covers. $18.95.
Covers the Ruger Six series of revolvers: Security-Six, Service-Six, and Speed-Six. Includes step-by-step function checks, disassembly, inspection, repairs, rebuilding, reassembly, and custom work.

The Ruger "P" Family of Handguns, by Duncan Long, Desert Publications, El Dorado, AZ, 1993. 128 pp., illus. Paper covers. $14.95.
A full-fledged documentary on a remarkable series of Sturm Ruger handguns.

The Ruger .22 Automatic Pistol, Standard/Mark I/Mark II Series, by Duncan Long, Paladin Press, Boulder, CO, 1989. 168 pp., illus. Paper covers. $12.00.
The definitive book about the pistol that has served more than 1 million owners so well.

Sam Colt's Own Record 1847, by John Parsons, Wolfe Publishing Co., Prescott, AZ, 1992. 167 pp., illus. $24.50.
Chronologically presented, the correspondence published here completes the account of the manufacture, in 1847, of the Walker Model Colt revolver.

Scottish Firearms, by Claude Blair and Robert Woosnam-Savage, Museum Restoration Service, Bloomfield, Ont., Canada, 1995. 52 pp., illus. Paper covers. $4.95.
This revision of the first book devoted entirely to Scottish firearms is supplemented by a register of surviving Scottish long guns.

*__Scouts, Peacemakers and New Frontiers in .22 Caliber,__ by Don Wilkerson, Cherokee Publications, Kansas City, MO, 1995. 224 pp., illus. $40.00.
Covers the 48 variations and numerous subvariants of the later rimfire Single Actions.

Second to None, edited by John Culler and Chuck Wechsler, Live Oak Press, Inc., Camden, SC, 1988. 227 pp., illus. $39.95.
The most popular articles from *Sporting Classics* magazine on great sporting firearms.

The Semiautomatic Pistols in Police Service and Self Defense, by Massad Ayoob, Police Bookshelf, Concord, NH, 1990. 25 pp., illus. Soft covers. $9.95.
First quantitative, documented look at actual police experience with 9mm and 45 police service automatics.

The Sharpshooter—How to Stand and Shoot Handgun Metallic Silhouettes, by Charles Stephens, Yucca Tree Press, Las Cruces, NM, 1993. 86 pp., illus. Paper covers. $10.00.
A narration of some of the author's early experiences in silhouette shooting, plus how-to information.

Shoot a Handgun, by Dave Arnold, PVA Books, Canyon County, CA, 1983. 144 pp., illus. Paper covers. $12.95.
A complete manual of simplified handgun instruction.

Shoot to Win, by John Shaw, Blacksmith Corp., Southport, CT, 1985. 160 pp., illus. Paper covers. $15.50.
The lessons taught here are of interest and value to all handgun shooters.

*__Shooter's Bible, 1997, No. 87,__ edited by William S. Jarrett, Stoeger Publishing Co., S. Hackensack, NJ, 1995. 576 pp., illus. Paper covers.
Contains specifications, photos and retail prices of handguns, rifles, shotguns and blackpowder arms currently manufactured by major U.S. and foreign gunmakers.

Shooting, by J.H. FitzGerald, Wolfe Publishing Co., Prescott, AZ, 1993. 421 pp., illus. $29.00.
A classic book and reference for anyone interested in pistol and revolver shooting.

Sierra Handgun Manual, 3rd Edition, edited by Kenneth Ramage, Sierra Bullets, Santa Fe Springs, CA, 1990. 704 pp., illus. 3-ring binder. $19.95.
New listings for XP-100 and Contender pistols and TCU cartridges...part of a new single shot section. Covers the latest loads for 10mm Auto, 455 Super Mag, and Accurate powders.

Sig/Sauer Handguns, by Duncan Long, Desert Publications, El Dorado, AZ, 1995. 150 pp., illus. Paper covers. $16.95.
The history of Sig/Sauer handguns, including Sig, Sig-Hammerli and Sig/Sauer variants.

Simeon North: First Official Pistol Maker of the United States, by S. North and R. North, The Gun Room Press, Highland Park, NJ, 1972. 207 pp., illus. $15.95.
Reprint of the rare first edition.

Sixgun Cartridges and Loads, by Elmer Keith, The Gun Room Press, Highland Park, NJ, 1986. 151 pp., illus. $24.95.
A manual covering the selection, uses and loading of the most suitable and popular revolver cartridges. Originally published in 1936. Reprint.

Sixguns, by Elmer Keith, Wolfe Publishing Company, Prescott, AZ, 1992. 336 pp. Hardcover. $34.95.
The history, selection, repair, care, loading, and use of this historic frontiersman's friend—the one-hand firearm.

Small Arms: Pistols & Rifles, by Ian V. Hogg, Greenhill Books, London, England, 1994. 160 pp., illus. $19.95.
An in-depth description of small arms, focusing on pistols and rifles, with detailed information about all small arms used by the world's armed forces.

Smith & Wesson Handguns, by Roy McHenry and Walter Roper, Wolfe Publishing Co., Prescott, AZ, 1994. 233 pp., illus. $32.00.
The bible on Smith & Wesson handguns.

The S&W Revolver: A Shop Manual, by Jerry Kuhnhausen, VSP Publishers, McCall, ID, 1987. 152 pp., illus. Paper covers. $24.95.
Covers accurizing, trigger jobs, action tuning, rebarreling, barrel setback, forcing cone angles, polishing and rebluing.

Smith & Wesson's Automatics, by Larry Combs, Desert Publications, El Dorado, AZ, 1994. 143 pp., illus. Paper covers. $27.95.
A must for every S&W auto owner or prospective owner.

Southern Derringers of the Mississippi Valley, by Turner Kirkland, Pioneer Press, Tenn., 1971. 80 pp., illus., paper covers. $10.00.
A guide for the collector, and a much-needed study.

*__Soviet Russian Postwar Military Pistols and Cartridges,__ by Fred A. Datig, Handgun Press, Glenview, IL, 1988. 152 pp., illus. $29.95.
Thoroughly researched, this definitive sourcebook covers the development and adoption of the Makarov, Stechkin and the new PSM pistols. Also included in this source book is coverage on Russian clandestine weapons and pistol cartridges.

Soviet Russian Tokarev "TT" Pistols and Cartridges 1929-1953, by Fred Datig, Graphic Publishers, Santa Ana, CA, 1993. 168 pp., illus. $39.95.
Details of rare arms and their accessories are shown in hundreds of photos. It also contains a complete bibliography and index.

Soviet Small-Arms and ammunition, by David Bolotin, Handgun Press, Glenview, IL, 1996. 264 pp., illus. $49.95.
An authoritative and complete book on Soviet small arms.

Speer Reloading Manual Number 12, edited by members of the Speer research staff, Omark Industries, Lewiston, ID, 1987. 621 pp., illus. $18.95.
Reloading manual for rifles and pistols.

Sporting Collectibles, by Jim and Vivian Karsnitz, Schiffer Publishing Ltd., West Chester, PA, 1992. 160 pp., illus. Paper covers. $29.95.
The fascinating world of hunting related collectibles presented in an informative text.

The Sporting Craftsmen: A Complete Guide to Contemporary Makers of Custom-Built Sporting Equipment, by Art Carter, Countrysport Press, Traverse City, MI, 1994. 240 pp., illus. $49.50.
Profiles leading makers of centerfire rifles; muzzleloading rifles; bamboo fly rods; fly reels; flies; waterfowl calls; decoys; handmade knives; and traditional longbows and recurves.

*__Standard Catalog of Firearms, 6th Edition,__ compiled by Ned Schwing and Herbert Houze, Krause Publications, Iola, WI, 1996. 1,116 pp., illus. Paper covers. $29.95.
1996 pricing guide in six grades with more than 2,300 photos and over 1,100 manufacturers.

*__Standard Catalog of Smith and Wesson,__ by Jim Supica and Richard Nahas, Krause Publications, Iola, WI, 1996. 256 pp., illus. $29.95.
Clearly details hundreds of products by the legendary manufacturer. How to identify, evaluate the condition and assess the value of 752 Smith & Wesson models and variations.

*__Steel Canvas: The Art of American Arms,__ by R. L. Wilson, Random House, NY, 1995, 384 pp., illus. $65.00.
Presented here for the first time is the breathtaking panorama of America's extraordinary engravers and embellishers of arms, from the 1700s to modern times.

Stevens Pistols & Pocket Rifles, by K.L. Cope, Museum Restoration Service, Alexandria Bay, NY, 1992. 114 pp., illus. $24.50.

This is the story of the guns and the man who designed them and the company which he founded to make them.

The Street Smart Gun Book, by John Farnam, Police Bookshelf, Concord, NH, 1986. 45 pp., illus. Paper covers. $11.95.

Weapon selection, defensive shooting techniques, and gunfight-winning tactics from one of the world's leading authorities.

Stress Fire, Vol. 1: Stress Fighting for Police, by Massad Ayoob, Police Bookshelf, Concord, NH, 1984. 149 pp., illus. Paper covers. $9.95.

Gunfighting for police, advanced tactics and techniques.

Successful Pistol Shooting, by Frank and Paul Leatherdale, The Crowood Press, Ramsbury, England, 1988. 144 pp., illus. $34.95.

Easy-to-follow instructions to help you achieve better results and gain more enjoyment from both leisure and competitive shooting.

The Sumptuous Flaske, by Herbert G. Houze, Andrew Mowbray, Inc., Lincoln, RI, 1989. 158 pp., illus. Soft covers. $35.00.

Catalog of a recent show at the Buffalo Bill Historical Center bringing together some of the finest European and American powder flasks of the 16th to 19th centuries.

Survival Guns, by Mel Tappan, Desert Publications, El Dorado, AZ, 1993. 456 pp., illus. Paper covers. $21.95.

Discusses in a frank and forthright manner which handguns, rifles and shotguns to buy for personal defense and securing food, and the ones to avoid.

Survival Gunsmithing, by J.B. Wood, Desert Publications, Cornville, AZ, 1986. 92 pp., illus. Paper covers. $9.95.

A guide to repair and maintenance of the most popular rifles, shotguns and handguns.

System Mauser—2nd Edition: An Illustrated History of the 1896 Self-Loading Pistol, by John W. Breathed, Jr. and Joseph J. Schrieder, Jr., Handgun Press, Glenview, IL, 1995. Illus. $49.95.

Newly revised and enlarged edition of the definitive work on this famous German handgun.

The .380 Enfield No. 2 Revolver, by Mark Stamps and Ian Skennerton, I.D.S.A. Books, Piqua, OH, 1993. 124 pp., 80 illus. Paper covers. $19.95.

The Tactical Pistol, by Gabriel Suarez with a foreword by Jeff Cooper, Paladin Press, Boulder, CO, 1996. 216 pp., illus. Paper covers. $25.00.

Advanced gunfighting concepts and techniques.

Textbook of Automatic Pistols, by R.K. Wilson, Wolfe Publishing Co., Prescott, AZ, 1990. 349 pp., illus. $54.00.

Reprint of the 1943 classic being a treatise on the history, development and functioning of modern military self-loading pistols.

Unrepentant Sinner, by Charles Askins, Tejano Publications, San Antonio, TX, 1985. 322 pp., illus. Soft covers. $19.95.

The autobiography of Colonel Charles Askins.

U.S. Marine Corp Rifle and Pistol Marksmanship, 1935, reprinting of a government publication, Lancer Militaria, Mt. Ida, AR, 1991. 99 pp., illus. Paper covers. $11.95.

The old corps method of precision shooting.

U.S. Military Arms Dates of Manufacture from 1795, by George Madis, David Madis, Dallas, TX, 1989. 64 pp. Soft covers. $5.00.

Lists all U.S. military arms of collector interest alphabetically, covering about 250 models.

U.S. Military Small Arms 1816-1865, by Robert M. Reilly, The Gun Room Press, Highland Park, NJ, 1983. 270 pp., illus. $39.95.

Covers every known type of primary and secondary martial firearms used by Federal forces.

U.S. Naval Handguns, 1808-1911, by Fredrick R. Winter, Andrew Mowbray Publishers, Lincoln, RI, 1990. 128 pp., illus. $26.00.

The story of U.S. Naval Handguns spans an entire century—included are sections on each of the important naval handguns within the period.

Variations of the Smooth Bore H&R Handy Gun, by Eric M. Larson, Eric M. Larson, Takoma Park, MD, 1993. 63 pp., illus. Paper covers. $10.00.

A pocket guide to the identification of the variations of the H&R Handy Gun.

Walther Models PP and PPK, 1929-1945, by James L. Rankin, assisted by Gary Green, James L. Rankin, Coral Gables, FL, 1974. 142 pp., illus. $35.00.

Complete coverage on the subject as to finish, proofmarks and Nazi Party inscriptions.

Walther P-38 Pistol, by Maj. George Nonte, Desert Publications, Cornville, AZ, 1982. 100 pp., illus. Paper covers. $11.95.

Complete volume on one of the most famous handguns to come out of WWII. All models covered.

Walther Volume II, Engraved, Presentation and Standard Models, by James L. Rankin, J.L. Rankin, Coral Gables, FL, 1977. 112 pp., illus. $35.00.

The new Walther book on embellished versions and standard models. Has 88 photographs, including many color plates.

Walther, Volume III, 1908-1980, by James L. Rankin, Coral Gables, FL, 1981. 226 pp., illus. $35.00.

Covers all models of Walther handguns from 1908 to date, includes holsters, grips and magazines.

Weapons of the Highland Regiments 1740-1780, by Anthony D. Darling, Museum Restoration Service, Bloomfield, Canada, 1996. 28 pp., illus. Paper covers. $5.95.

This study deals with the formation and arming of the famous Highland regiments.

Weapons of the Waffen-SS, by Bruce Quarrie, Sterling Publishing Co., Inc., 1991. 168 pp., illus. $24.95.

An in-depth look at the weapons that made Hitler's Waffen-SS the fearsome fighting machine it was.

Webley & Scott Automatic Pistols, by Gordon Bruch, Stocker-Schmid Publishing Co., Dietikon, Switzerland, 1992. 256 pp., illus. $50.00.

The fundamental representation of the history and development of all Webley & Scott automatic pistols.

Webley Revolvers, by Gordon Bruce and Christien Reinhart, Stocker-Schmid, Zurich, Switzerland, 1988. 256 pp., illus. $69.50.

A revised edition of Dowell's "Webley Story."

Weimar and Early Lugers, by Jan C. Still, Jan C. Still, Douglas, AK, 1994. 312 pp., illus.

Volume 5 of the series *The Pistol of Germany and Here Allies in Two World Wars.*

The Whitney Firearms, by Claud Fuller, Standard Publications, Huntington, WV, 1946. 334 pp., many plates and drawings. $50.00.

An authoritative history of all Whitney arms and their maker. Highly recommended. An exclusive with Ray Riling Arms Books Co.

Why Not Load Your Own?, by Col. T. Whelen, A. S. Barnes, New York, 1957, 4th ed., rev. 237 pp., illus. $20.00.

A basic reference on handloading, describing each step, materials and equipment. Includes loads for popular cartridges.

Wildcat Cartridges, Volume I, Wolfe Publishing Company, Prescott, AZ, 1992. 125 pp. Soft cover. $16.95.

From *Handloader* magazine, the more popular and famous wildcats are profiled.

Wildcat Cartridges, Volume II, compiled from *Handloader* and *Rifle* magazine articles written by featured authors, Wolfe Publishing Co., Prescott, AZ, 1992. 971 pp., illus. Paper covers. $34.95.

This volume details rifle and handtgun cartridges from the 14-221 to the 460 Van Horn. A comprehensive work containing loading tables and commentary.

World's Deadliest Rimfire Battleguns, by J.M. Ramos, Paladin Press, Boulder, CO, 1990. 184 pp., illus. Paper covers. $14.00.

This heavily illustrated book shows international rimfire assault weapon innovations from World War II to the present.

You Can't Miss, by John Shaw and Michael Bane, John Shaw, Memphis, TN, 1983. 152 pp., illus. Paper covers. $12.95.

The secrets of a successful combat shooter; how to better defensive shooting skills.

Yours Truly, Harvey Donaldson, by Harvey Donaldson, Wolfe Publ. Co., Inc., Prescott, AZ, 1980. 288 pp., illus. $19.50.

Reprint of the famous columns by Harvey Donaldson which appeared in "Handloader" from May 1966 through December 1972.

HANDGUNS 97

DIRECTORY

OF THE

HANDGUNNER'S TRADE

PRODUCT DIRECTORY

AMMUNITION, COMMERCIAL

American Ammunition
Bergman & Williams
Black Hills Ammunition, Inc.
Blammo Ammo
Bull-X, Inc.
CBC
CCI
Cor-Bon Bullet & Ammo Co.
Daisy Mfg. Co.
Delta Frangible Ammunition, LLC
Denver Bullets, Inc.
Diana
Dynamit Nobel-RWS, Inc.
Eley Ltd.
Federal Cartridge Co.
Fiocchi of America, Inc.
Gamo
Goldcoast Reloaders, Inc.
Grand Falls Bullets, Inc.
Hansen & Co.
Hansen Cartridge Co.
Hart & Son, Inc., Robert W.
Hirtenberger Aktiengesellschaft
Hornady Mfg. Co.
ICI-America
IMI
Keng's Firearms Specialty, Inc.
Kent Cartridge Mfg. Co. Ltd.
Lapua Ltd.
M&D Munitions Ltd.
Mac-1 Distributors
Magnum Research, Inc.
MagSafe Ammo Co.

MAGTECH Recreational
    Products, Inc.
Markell, Inc.
Men—Metallwerk Elisenhuette,
    GmbH
Moreton/Fordyce Enterprises
Mullins Ammo
NECO
New England Ammunition Co.
Oklahoma Ammunition Co.
Old Western Scrounger, Inc.
Omark Industries
PMC/Eldorado Cartridge Corp.
Pony Express Reloaders
Precision Delta Corp.
Pro Load Ammunition, Inc.
Remington Arms Co., Inc.
Rocky Fork Enterprises
Rucker Dist. Inc.
RWS
Speer
Spence, George W.
Star Reloading Co., Inc.
Talon Mfg. Co., Inc.
3-D Ammunition & Bullets
USAC
Victory USA
Voere-KGH m.b.H.
Widener's Reloading & Shooting
    Supply, Inc.
Winchester Div., Olin Corp.
Zero Ammunition Co., Inc.

AMMUNITION, CUSTOM

Accuracy Unlimited (Littleton, CO)
AFSCO Ammunition
American Derringer Corp.
Arms Corporation of the Philippines
Ballistica Maximus North
Bergman & Williams
Black Hills Ammunition, Inc.
Brynin, Milton
BulletMakers Workshop, The
CBC
CHAA, Ltd.
Christman Jr., David
Country Armourer, The
Custom Tackle and Ammo
Dead Eye's Sport Center
DKT, Inc.
Elko Arms
Freedom Arms, Inc.
Gammog, Gregory B. Gally
GDL Enterprises
Glaser Safety Slug, Inc.
Grand Falls Bullets, Inc.
Granite Custom Bullets
Heidenstrom Bullets
Hirtenberger Aktiengesellschaft
Hoelscher, Virgil
Horizons Unlimited
Hornady Mfg. Co.
Jackalope Gun Shop
Jones, J.D.
Kaswer Custom, Inc.
Keeler, R.H.
Kent Cartridge Mfg. Co. Ltd.
KJM Fabritek, Inc.
Lindsley Arms Cartridge Co.

Lomont Precision Bullets
MagSafe Ammo Co.
McMurdo, Lynn
Men-Metallwerk Elisenhuette, GmbH
Moreton/Fordyce Enterprises
Mullins Ammo
Naval Ordnance Works
NECO
Old Western Scrounger, Inc.
Oklahoma Ammunition Company
Parts & Surplus
Personal Protection Systems
Precision Delta Corp.
Precision Munitions, Inc.
Precision Reloading, Inc.
Professional Hunter Supplies
Rolston, Inc., Fred W.
Sandia Die & Cartridge Co.
SOS Products Co.
Specialty Gunsmithing
Spence, George W.
Spencer's Custom Guns
SSK Industries
Star Custom Bullets
State Arms Gun Co.
Stewart's Gunsmithing
Talon Mfg. Co., Inc.
TCCI
3-D Ammunition & Bullets
Vulpes Ventures, Inc.
Weaver Arms Corp. Gun Shop
Wells Custom Gunsmith, R.A.
Worthy Products, Inc.
Yukon Arms Classic Ammunition
Zonie Bullets

AMMUNITION, FOREIGN

AFSCO Ammunition
Armscorp USA, Inc.
Beretta S.p.A., Pietro
B-West Imports, Inc.
BulletMakers Workshop, The
CBC
Century International Arms, Inc.
Dead Eye's Sport Center
Diana
DKT, Inc.
Dynamit Nobel-RWS, Inc.
Fiocchi of America, Inc.
Fisher Enterprises, Inc.
Fisher, R. Kermit
FN Herstal
Forgett Jr., Valmore J.
Gamo
Hansen & Co.
Hansen Cartridge Co.
Hornady Mfg. Co.
IMI
IMI Services USA, Inc.
Jackalope Gun Shop
JagerSport, Ltd.

K.B.I., Inc.
Keng's Firearms Specialty, Inc.
MagSafe Ammo Co.
Mandall Shooting Supplies, Inc.
Merkuria Ltd.
New England Arms Co.
Oklahoma Ammunition Co.
Old Western Scrounger, Inc.
Paragon Sales & Services, Inc.
Precision Delta Corp.
R.E.T. Enterprises
Rocky Fork Enterprises
RWS
Sentinel Arms
Stoeger Industries
Southern Ammunition Co., Inc.
Spence, George W.
Stratco, Inc.
SwaroSports, Inc.
Talon Mfg. Co., Inc.
T.F.C. S.p.A.
Vihtavuori Oy/Kaltron-Pettibone
Yukon Arms Classic Ammunition

AMMUNITION COMPONENTS—BULLETS, POWDER, PRIMERS, CASES

Acadian Ballistic Specialties
Accuracy Unlimited (Littleton, CO)
Accurate Arms Co., Inc.
Action Bullets, Inc.
Alaska Bullet Works
Alliant Techsystems
Arco Powder
Atlantic Rose, Inc.
Ballard Built
Barnes Bullets, Inc.
Beeline Custom Bullets Limited
Bell Reloading, Inc.
Belt MTN Arms
Bergman & Williams
Berry's Bullets
Bertram Bullet Co.
Black Belt Bullets
Black Hills Shooters Supply
Briese Bullet Co., Inc.
Brown Co., E. Arthur
Brownells, Inc.
BRP, Inc.
Buckskin Bullet Co.
Buffalo Arms
Buffalo Rock Shooters Supply
Bullet, Inc.
Bull-X, Inc.
Butler Enterprises
Buzztail Brass
Canyon Cartridge Corp.
Carnahan Bullets
Cascade Bullet Co., Inc.
CCI
Champion's Choice, Inc.
Cheddite France, S.A.
CheVron Bullets
C.J. Ballistics, Inc.
Clark Custom Guns, Inc.
Classic Brass
Competitor Corp., Inc.
Cor-Bon Bullet & Ammo Co.
Crawford Co., Inc., R.M.
Creative Cartridge Co.

Cummings Bullets
Curtis Gun Shop
Cutsinger Bench Rest Bullets
D&J Bullet Co. & Custom Gun
    Shop, Inc.
Diamondback Supply
DKT, Inc.
Dohring Bullets
Double A Ltd.
DuPont
Epps, Ellwood
Federal Cartridge Co.
Finch Custom Bullets
Fiocchi of America, Inc.
Forkin, Ben
Foy Custom Bullets
Freedom Arms, Inc.
Fusilier Bullets
G&C Bullet Co., Inc.
Gander Mountain, Inc.
Gehmann, Walter
GOEX, Inc.
Golden Bear Bullets
Gotz Bullets
"Gramps" Antique Cartridges
Granite Custom Bullets
Grayback Wildcats
Green Bay Bullets
Grier's Hard Cast Bullets
Gun City
Hardin Specialty Dist.
Harrison Bullets
Haselbauer Products, Jerry
Hawk Laboratories, Inc.
Heidenstrom Bullets
Hirtenberger Aktiengesellschaft
Hobson Precision Mfg. Co.
Hodgdon Powder Co., Inc.
Hornady Mfg. Co.
Huntington Die Specialties
IMI
IMI Services USA, Inc.
IMR Powder Co.

J-4, Inc.
J&D Components
J&L Superior Bullets
Jensen's Firearms Academy
Jester Bullets
JRP Custom Bullets
Ka Pu Kapili
Kasmarsik Bullets
Kaswer Custom, Inc.
Keith's Bullets
Ken's Kustom Kartridge
Keng's Firearms Specialty, Inc.
Kent Cartridge Mfg. Co. Ltd.
KJM Fabritek, Inc.
KLA Enterprises
Kodiak Custom Bullets
Lapua Ltd.
Legend Products Corp.
Liberty Shooting Supplies
Lightning Performance
  Innovations, Inc.
M&D Munitions Ltd.
Magnus Bullets
Maine Custom Bullets
Marchmon Bullets
Marple & Associates, Dick
Master Class Bullets
McMurdo, Lynn
Meister Bullets
Men-Metallwerk Elisenhuette,
  GmbH
Merkuria Ltd.
Miller Enterprises, Inc., R.P.
MI-TE Bullets
Montana Precision Swaging
Mt. Baldy Bullet Co.
Murmur Corp.
Mushroom Express Bullet Co.
Nagel's Bullets
National Bullet Co.
Naval Ordnance Works
Necromancer Industries, Inc.
Norma
North American Shooting
  Systems
North Devon Firearms Services
Northern Precision Custom
  Swaged Bullets
Nosler, Inc.
Oklahoma Ammunition Co.
Old Wagon Bullets
Old Western Scrounger, Inc.
Omark Industries
Ordnance Works, The
Page Custom Bullets
Patrick Bullets
Peerless Alloy, Inc.
Petro-Explo, Inc.
Phillippi Custom Bullets, Justin

Pinetree Bullets
Pomeroy, Robert
Powder Valley Services
Precision Components
Precision Components and Guns
Precision Delta Corp.
Precision Munitions, Inc.
Prescott Projectile Co.
Price Bullets, Patrick W.
Professional Hunter Supplies
Rainier Ballistics Corp.
Ranger Products
Red Cedar Precision Mfg.
Redwood Bullet Works
Reloading Specialties, Inc.
Radical Concepts
R.M. Precision, Inc.
Robinson H.V. Bullets
Rolston, Inc., Fred W.
Scharch Mfg., Inc.
Schmidtman Custom Ammunition
Schroeder Bullets
Scot Powder
Seebeck Assoc., R.E.
Shilen Rifles, Inc.
Shooting Components Marketing
Sierra Bullets
Silhouette, The
Specialty Gunsmithing
Speer Products
Stanley Bullets
Stark's Bullet Mfg.
Stewart's Gunsmithing
Talon Mfg. Co., Inc.
TCCI
TCSR
T.F.C. S.p.A.
Thompson Precision
3-D Ammunition & Bullets
TMI Products
True Flight Bullet Co.
USAC
Vann Custom Bullets
Vihtavuori Oy/Kaltron-Pettibone
Vincent's Shop
Western Nevada West Coast
  Bullets
Widener's Reloading & Shooting
  Supply
Williams Bullet Co., J.R.
Winchester Div., Olin Corp.
Winkle Bullets
Worthy Products, Inc.
Wyant Bullets
Wyoming Custom Bullets
Yukon Arms Classic Ammunition
Zero Ammunition Co., Inc.
Zonie Bullets

Guncraft Sports, Inc.
Hansen & Co.
Hunkeler, A.
Johns, Bill
Kelley's
Ledbetter Airguns, Riley
LeFever Arms Co., Inc.
Liberty Antique Gunworks
Lock's Philadelphia Gun
  Exchange
Log Cabin Sport Shop
Martin's Gun Shop
Mathews & Son, Inc., George E.
Mendez, John A.
Montana Outfitters
Museum of Historical Arms, Inc.
Muzzleloaders Etcetera, Inc.
Navy Arms Co.

N.C. Ordnance Co.
Pioneer Guns
Pony Express Sport Shop, Inc.
Retting, Inc., Martin B.
S&S Firearms
Sarco, Inc.
Scott Fine Guns, Inc., Thad
Semmer, Charles
Shootin' Shack, Inc.
Steves House of Guns
Stott's Creek Armory, Inc.
Strawbridge, Victor W.
Track of the Wolf, Inc.
Vic's Gun Refinishing
Vintage Arms, Inc.
Wiest, M.C.
Wood, Frank
Yearout, Lewis E.

ANTIQUE ARMS DEALERS

Ackerman & Co.
Ad Hominem
Ahlman Guns
Antique American Firearms
Antique Arms Co.
Aplan Antiques & Art, James O.
Armoury, Inc., The
Bear Mountain Gun & Tool
Bob's Tactical Indoor Shooting
  Range & Gun Shop
Boggs, Wm.
British Antiques
Buckskin Machine Works
Burgess & Son Gunsmiths, R.W.
Cabela's
Cannon's Guns
Carlson, Douglas R.
Chadick's Ltd.
Chambers Flintlocks Ltd., Jim
Chuck's Gun Shop
Classic Guns, Inc.
Cole's Gun Works

D&D Gunsmiths, Ltd.
Delhi Gun House
Dixie Gun Works, Inc.
Dixon Muzzleloading Shop, Inc.
Duffy, Charles E.
Ed's Gun House
Enguix Import-Export
Fagan & Co., William
Fish, Marshall F.
Flayderman & Co., N.
Forgett Jr., Valmore J.
Frielich Police Equipment
Fulmer's Antique Firearms, Chet
Getz Barrel Co.
Glass, Herb
Golden Age Arms Co.
Greenwald, Leon E. "Bud"
Gun Room, The
Gun Room Press, The
Gun Works, The
Guns Antique & Modern
  DBA/Charles E. Duffy

APPRAISERS—GUNS, ETC.

Accuracy Gun Shop
Ahlman Guns
Antique Arms Co.
Armoury, Inc., The
Arundel Arms & Ammunition,
  Inc., A.
Blue Book Publications, Inc.
Bob's Tactical Indoor Shooting
  Range & Gun Shop
Bustani, Leo
Butterfield & Butterfield
Camilli, Lou
Cannon's Guns
Chadick's Ltd.
Champlin Firearms, Inc.
Christie's East
Clark Custom Guns, Inc.
Clark Firearms Engraving
Classic Guns, Inc.
Clements' Custom Leathercraft,
  Chas
Cole's Gun Works
Colonial Repair
Corry, John
Costa, David
Custom Tackle and Ammo
D&D Gunsmiths, Ltd.
DGR Custom Rifles
Dixie Gun Works, Inc.
Dixon Muzzleloading Shop, Inc.
Duane's Gun Repair
Ed's Gun House
Epps, Ellwood
Eversull Co., Inc., K.
Fagan & Co., William
Fish, Marshall F.
Flayderman & Co., Inc., N.
Forgett, Valmore J., Jr.
Forty Five Ranch Enterprises
Frontier Arms Co., Inc.
Golden Age Arms Co.
Gonzalez Guns, Ramon B.
"Gramps" Antique Cartridges
Greenwald, Leon E. "Bud"
Griffin & Howe, Inc.
Groenewold, John
Gun City
Gun Shop, The
Gun Works, The
Guncraft Sports, Inc.
Hank's Gun Shop
Hansen & Co.
Hughes, Steven Dodd
Idaho Ammunition Service
Irwin, Campbell H.

Island Pond Gun Shop
Jensen's Custom Ammunition
Jonas Appraisers—Taxidermy
  Animals, Jack
Kelley's
Ledbetter Airguns, Riley
LeFever Arms Co., Inc.
Liberty Antique Gunworks
Lock's Philadelphia Gun
  Exchange
Mac's .45 Shop
Madis, George
Martin's Gun Shop
Montana Outfitters
Mowrey's Guns & Gunsmithing
Museum of Historical Arms, Inc.
Muzzleloaders Etcetera, Inc.
Navy Arms Co.
N.C. Ordnance Co.
New England Arms Co.
Nitex, Inc.
Pasadena Gun Center
Pentheny de Pentheny
Peterson Gun Shop, Inc., A.W.
Pettinger Books, Gerald
Pioneer Guns
Pony Express Sport Shop, Inc.
R.E.T. Enterprises
Retting, Inc., Martin B.
Richards, John
S&S Firearms
Safari Outfitters Ltd.
Scott Fine Guns, Inc., Thad
Shell Shack
Shootin' Shack, Inc.
Sipes Gun Shop
Sotheby's
Sportsmen's Exchange &
  Western
Starnes Gunmaker, Ken
Steger, James R.
Stott's Creek Armory, Inc.
Stratco, Inc.
Strawbridge, Victor W.
Thurston Sports, Inc.
Vic's Gun Refinishing
Walker Arms Co., Inc.
Wayne Firearms for Collectors
  and Investors, James
Wells Custom Gunsmith, R.A.
Whildin & Sons Ltd., E.H.
Wiest, M.C.
Williams Shootin' Iron Service
Wood, Frank
Yearout, Lewis E.

AUCTIONEERS—GUNS, ETC.

Butterfield & Butterfield
Christie's East
Kelley's

"Little John's" Antique Arms
Sotheby's

BOOKS (Publishers and Dealers)

American Handgunner Magazine
Armory Publications
Arms & Armour Press
Arms, Peripheral Data Systems
Arms Software
Barnes Bullets, Inc.
Blackhawk West
Blacksmith Corp.
Blacktail Mountain Books
Blue Book Publications, Inc.
Brown Co., E. Arthur
Brownell's, Inc.
Buffalo Arms
Calibre Press, Inc.
Colonial Repair
Colorado Sutlers Arsenal
Corbin, Inc.
Crit'R Call
Cumberland States Arsenal
DBI Books
Flores Publications, Inc., J.
Golden Age Arms Co.
Gun City
Gun Hunter Books
Gun List
Gun Parts Corp., The
Gun Room Press, The
Gun Works, The
Guncraft Books
Guncraft Sports, Inc.
Gunnerman Books
Guns, (Div. of D.C. Engineering, Inc.)
GUNS Magazine
H&P Publishing
Handgun Press
Harris Publications
Hawk, Inc.
Hawk Laboratories, Inc.
Heritage/VSP Gun Books
Hodgdon Powder Co., Inc.
Home Shop Machinist, The
Hornady Mfg. Co.
Hungry Horse Books
Info-Arm

Ironside International Publishers, Inc.
King & Co.
Krause Publications, Inc.
Lane Publishing
Lapua Ltd.
Lethal Force Institute
Lyman Products Corp.
Martin Bookseller, J.
MI-TE Bullets
Mountain South
New Win Publishing, Inc.
NgraveR Co., The
OK Weber, Inc.
Old Western Scrounger, Inc.
Outdoorsman's Bookstore, The
Pejsa Ballistics
Petersen Publishing Co.
Pettinger Books, Gerald
Police Bookshelf
Reloading Specialties, Inc.
R.G.-G., Inc.
Riling Arms Books Co., Ray
Rutgers Book Center
S&S Firearms
Safari Press, Inc.
Saunders Gun & Machine Shop
Shootin' Accessories, Ltd.
Sierra Bullets
S.P.G., Inc.
Stackpole Books
Stoeger Industries
Stoeger Publishing Co.
"Su-Press-On," Inc.
Thomas, Charles C.
Trafalgar Square
Trotman, Ken
Vega Tool Co.
VSP Publishers
WAMCO—New Mexico
Wiest, M.C.
Wilderness Sound Products Ltd.
Williams Gun Sight Co.
Wolfe Publishing Co.
Wolf's Western Traders

BULLET AND CASE LUBRICANTS

Blackhawk West
Brass-Tech Industries
Break-Free, Inc.
Brown Co., E. Arthur
Camp-Cap Products
CFVentures
Chem-Pak, Inc.
Cooper-Woodward
Elkhorn Bullets
E-Z-Way Systems
Forster Products
Green Bay Bullets
Guardsman Products
HEBB Resources
Hollywood Engineering
Hornady Mfg. Co.
Imperial

Le Clear Industries
Lithi Bee Bullet Lube
M&N Bullet Lube
MI-TE Bullets
NECO
Paco's
RCBS
Reardon Products
Rooster Laboratories
Shay's Gunsmithing
Small Custom Mould & Bullet Co.
S.P.G., Inc.
Tamarack Products, Inc.
Warren Muzzleloading Co., Inc.
Widener's Reloading & Shooting Supply, Inc.
Young Country Arms

BULLET SWAGE DIES AND TOOLS

Brynin, Milton
Bullet Swaging Supply, Inc.
Camdex, Inc.
Corbin, Inc.
Holland's
Hollywood Engineering

Necromancer Industries, Inc.
Niemi Engineering, W.B.
North Devon Firearms Services
Rorschach Precision Products
Sport Flite Manufacturing Co.

CARTRIDGES FOR COLLECTORS

Ad Hominem
Alpha 1 Drop Zone
Buck Stix—SOS Products Co.
Cameron's
Campbell, Dick

Cole's Gun Works
Colonial Repair
Country Armourer, The
Delhi Gun House
DGR Custom Rifles

Duane's Gun Repair
Eichelberger Bullets, Wm.
Enguix Import-Export
Epps, Ellwood
Forty Five Ranch Enterprises
Goergen's Gun Shop, Inc.
"Gramps" Antique Cartridges
Gun Parts Corp., The
Gun Room Press, The
Idaho Ammunition Service

Michael's Antiques
Montana Outfitters
Mountain Bear Rifle Works, Inc.
Pasadena Gun Center
Pioneer Guns
Samco Global Arms, Inc.
San Francisco Gun Exchange
SOS Products Co.
Ward & Van Valkenburg
Yearout, Lewis E.

CASES, CABINETS, RACKS AND SAFES—GUN

Abel Safe & File, Inc.
Alco Carrying Cases
All Rite Products, Inc.
Allen Co., Inc.
Alumna Sport by Dee Zee
American Display Co.
American Security Products Co.
Americase
Ansen Enterprises
Arkfeld Mfg. & Dist. Co., Inc.
Art Jewel Enterprises Ltd.
Big Spring Enterprises "Bore Stores"
Boyt
Brauer Bros. Mfg. Co.
Browning Arms Co.
Bucheimer, J.M.
Cannon Safe, Inc.
Clark Custom Guns, Inc.
Doskocil Mfg. Co., Inc.
Fort Knox Security Products
Frontier Safe Co.
Galati Internationl
GALCO International Ltd.
Gun Locker
Gun-Ho Sports Cases
Gun Vault, Inc.

Hall Plastics, Inc., John
Homak Mfg. Co., Inc.
Hoppe's Div.
Huey Gun Cases
Hugger Hooks Co.
Hunter Co., Inc.
Impact Case Co.
Kalispel Case Line
KK Air International
Kolpin Mfg., Inc.
Liberty Safe
Maximum Security Corp.
Morton Booth Co.
MTM Molded Products Co., Inc.
National Security Safe Co., Inc.
Outa-Site Gun Carriers
Pachmayr Ltd.
Palmer Security Products
Penguin Industries, Inc.
Protecto Plastics
Southern Security
Sun Welding Safe Co.
Surecase Co., The
WAMCO, Inc.
Wilson Case, Inc.
Woodstream
Zanotti Armor, Inc.

CHRONOGRAPHS AND PRESSURE TOOLS

Brown Co., E. Arthur
Canons Delcour
Chronotech
Competition Electronics, Inc.
Custom Chronograph, Inc.
D&H Precision Tooling
Hornady Mfg. Co.

Kent Cartridge Mfg. Co. Ltd.
Oehler Research, Inc.
P.A.C.T., Inc.
Shooting Chrony, Inc.
SKAN A.R.
Tepeco

CLEANING AND REFINISHING SUPPLIES

AC Dyna-tite Corp.
Acculube II, Inc.
Accupro Gun Care
ADCO International
American Gas & Chemical Co., Ltd.
Answer Products Co.
Atlantic Mills, Inc.
Barnes Bullets, Inc.
Belltown, Ltd.
Birchwood Casey
Blackhawk East
Blue and Gray Products, Inc.
Break-Free, Inc.
Bridgers Best
Brown Co., E. Arthur
Cape Outfitters
Chem-Pak, Inc.
Chopie Mfg., Inc.
Clenzoil Corp.
Colonial Arms, Inc.
CONKKO
Custom Products
D&H Prods. Co., Inc.
Dara-Nes, Inc.
Du-Lite Corp.
Dutchman's Firearms, Inc., The
Dykstra, Doug
E&L Mfg., Inc.
Eezox, Inc.
Ekol Leather Care
Faith Associates, Inc.

Flitz International Ltd.
Fluoramics, Inc.
Forster Products
Frontier Products Co.
G96 Products Co., Inc.
Golden Age Arms Co.
Gozon Corp., U.S.A.
Guardsman Products
Half Moon Rifle Shop
Heatbath Corp.
Hoppe's Div.
Hornady Mfg. Co.
Hydrosorbent Products
J-B Bore Cleaner
Johnston Bros.
Kellogg's Professional Products
Kleen-Bore, Inc.
LEM Gun Specialties, Inc.
Lewis Lead Remover, The
List Precision Engineering
LPS Laboratories, Inc.
Marble Arms
Micro Sight Co.
MTM Molded Products Co., Inc.
Muscle Products Corp.
Nesci Enterprises, Inc.
Old World Oil Products
Omark Industries
Outers Laboratories, Div. of Blount
Ox-Yoke Originals, Inc.
P&M Sales and Service

PRODUCT DIRECTORY

Pachmayr Ltd.
Parker Gun Finishes
Pendleton Royal
Penguin Industries, Inc.
Precision Reloading, Inc.
Prolix® Lubricants
Pro-Shot Products, Inc.
Rickard, Inc., Pete
RIG Products Co.
Rod Guide Co.
Rooster Laboratories
Rusteprufe Laboratories
Saunders Gun & Machine Shop
Shiloh Creek

Shooter's Choice
Shootin' Accessories, Ltd.
Spencer's Custom Guns
TDP Industries, Inc.
Tetra Gun Lubricants
Texas Platers Supply Co.
United States Products Co.
Venco Industries, Inc.
Warren Muzzleloading Co., Inc.
WD-40 Co.
Wick, David E.
Williams Shootin' Iron Service
Young Country Arms
Z-Coat Industrial Coatings, Inc.

COMPUTER SOFTWARE—BALLISTICS

Action Target, Inc.
AmBr Software Group Ltd.
Arms, Peripheral Data Systems
Arms Software
Ballistic Engineering &
  Software, Inc.
Ballistic Program Co., Inc., The
Barnes Bullets, Inc.
Beartooth Bullets
Bestload, Inc.
Blackwell, W.
Canons Delcour
Corbin, Inc.
Country Armourer, The
Data Tech Software Systems
Exe, Inc.

Ford, Jack
JBM Software
Jensen Bullets
J.I.T. Ltd.
JWH:Software
Kent Cartridge Mfg. Co. Ltd.
Load From A Disk
Maionchi-L.M.I.
Oehler Research, Inc.
P.A.C.T., Inc.
PC Bullet/ADC, Inc.
Pejsa Ballistics
RCBS
Sierra Bullets
Tioga Engineering Co., Inc.
Vancini, Carl

CUSTOM METALSMITHS

Adair Custom Shop, Bill
Ahlman Guns
Aldis Gunsmithing & Shooting
  Supply
Allen, Richard L.
Amrine's Gun Shop
Answer Products Co.
Arnold Arms Co., Inc.
Arundel Arms & Ammunition,
  Inc., A.
Baer Custom, Inc., Les
Bansner's Gunsmithing
  Specialties
Baron Technology
Bear Mountain Gun & Tool
Behlert Precision, Inc.
Beitzinger, George
Benchmark Guns
Bengtson Arms Co., L.
Billingsley & Brownell
BlackStar AccuMax Barrels
BlackStar Barrel Accurizing
Brace, Larry D.
Broad Creek Rifle Works
Brockmans Custom Gunsmithing
Buckhorn Gun Works
Bullberry Barrel Works, Ltd.
Campbell, Dick
Carter's Gun Shop
Checkmate Refinishing
Classic Guns, Inc.
Colonial Repair
Colorado Gunsmithing Academy
  Lamar
Craftguard
Crandall Tool & Machine Co.
Cullity Restoration, Daniel
Custom Gun Products
Custom Gunsmiths
D&D Gunsmiths, Ltd.
D&H Precision Tooling
Dietz Gun Shop & Range, Inc.
Duncan's Gunworks, Inc.
Erhardt, Dennis
Eyster Heritage Gunsmiths, Inc.,
  Ken
Fisher, Jerry A.
Forster, Larry L.
Francesca, Inc.

Frank Custom Classic Arms, Ron
Fullmer, Geo. M.
Gordie's Gun Shop
Grace, Charles E.
Graybill's Gun Shop
Green, Roger M.
Gun Shop, The
Guns
Gunsmithing Ltd.
Hallberg Gunsmith, Fritz
Hecht, Hubert J.
Heilmann, Stephen
Heppler's Machining
Highline Machine Co.
Hiptmayer, Armurier
Hiptmayer, Klaus
Hoelscher, Virgil
Holland's
Hollis Gun Shop
Horst, Alan K.
Hyper-Single, Inc.
Ivanoff, Thomas G.
J&S Heat Treat
Jeffredo Gunsight
Johnston, James
Ken's Gun Specialties
Kilham & Co.
Klein Custom Guns, Don
Kleinendorst, K.W.
Kopp, Terry K.
Lampert, Ron
LaRocca Gun Works, Inc.
Lawson Co., Harry
Lind Custom Guns, Al
List Precision Engineering
Mac's .45 Shop
Mains Enterprises, Inc.
Mazur Restoration, Pete
McCament, Jay
McFarland, Stan
Mullis Guncraft
Nettestad Gun Works
Nicholson Custom
Nitex, Inc.
Noreen, Peter H.
North Fork Custom Gunsmithing
Nu-Line Guns, Inc.
Olson, Vic
Ozark Gun Works

P&S Gun Service
Pagel Gun Works, Inc.
Parker Gun Finishes
Pasadena Gun Center
Penrod Precision
Precision Metal Finishing
Precision Specialties
Rice, Keith
Robar Co.'s, Inc., The
Rocky Mountain Arms, Inc.
Simmons Gun Repair, Inc.
Sipes Gun Shop
Skeoch, Brian R.
Smith, Art
Snapp's Gunshop
Spencer's Custom Guns
Sportsmen's Exchange &
  Western Gun Traders, Inc.
Steffens, Ron
Stiles Custom Guns
Stott's Creek Armory, Inc.
Strawbridge, Victor W.
Talmage, William G.

Taylor & Robbins
Thompson, Randall
Tom's Gun Repair
Von Minden Gunsmithing
  Services
Waldron, Herman
Weber & Markin Custom
  Gunsmiths
Welsh, Bud
Werth, T.W.
Wessinger Custom Guns &
  Engraving
West, Robert G.
Westrom, John
White Rock Tool & Die
Wiebe, Duane
Williams Gun Sight Co.
Williamson Precision
  Gunsmithing
Winter, Robert M.
Wise Guns, Dale
Wood, Frank
Zufall, Joseph F.

ENGRAVERS, ENGRAVING TOOLS

Ackerman & Co.
Adair Custom Shop, Bill
Adams, John J. & Son Engravers
Adams Jr., John J.
Ahlman Guns
Alfano, Sam
Allard, Gary
Allen, Richard L.
Allok
Altamont Co.
American Pioneer Video
Anthony and George Ltd.
Baron Technology
Barraclough, John K.
Bates Engraving, Billy
Bell Originals, Inc., Sid
Blair, Jim
Bleile, C. Roger
Boessler, Erich
Bone Engraving, Ralph
Bratcher, Dan
Brooker, Dennis
Brownell Checkering Tools, W.E.
Burgess, Byron
Churchill, Winston
Clark Firearms Engraving
Collings, Ronald
Creek Side Metal & Woodcrafters
Cullity Restoration, Daniel
Cupp, Custom Engraver, Alana
Davidson, Jere
Delorge, Ed
Desquesnes, Gerald
Dixon Muzzleloading Shop, Inc.
Dolbare, Elizabeth
Drain, Mark
Dubber, Michael W.
Dyson & Son Ltd., Peter
Engraving Artistry
Evans Engraving, Robert
Fanzoj GmbH
Firearms Engraver's Guild of
  America
Flannery Engraving Co., Jeff W.
Floatstone Mfg. Co.
Forty Five Ranch Enterprises
Fountain Products
Francolini, Leonard
Frank Custom Classic Arms, Ron
Frank Knives
French, J.R.
Gene's Custom Guns
George, Tim
Glimm, Jerome C.
Golden Age Arms Co.
Gournet, Geoffroy
Grant, Howard V.
Griffin & Howe, Inc.
GRS Corp., Glendo

Gun Room, The
Guns
Gurney, F.R.
Gwinnell, Bryson J.
Hale/Engraver, Peter
Half Moon Rifle Shop
Hands Engraving, Barry Lee
Harris Gunworks
Harris Hand Engraving, Paul A.
Harwood, Jack O.
Hendricks, Frank E.
Hiptmayer, Armurier
Hiptmayer, Heidemarie
Hiptmayer, Klaus
Horst, Alan K.
Ingle, Ralph W.
Jaeger, Inc., Paul/Dunn's
Jantz Supply
Johns Master Engraver, Bill
Kamyk Engraving Co., Steve
Kane, Edward
Kehr, Roger
Kelly, Lance
Klingler Woodcarving
Koevenig's Engraving Service
Kudlas, John M.
Lebeau-Courally
LeFever Arms Co., Inc.
Leibowitz, Leonard
Lindsay, Steve
Lister, Weldon
Little Trees Ramble
Lutz Engraving, Ron
Mains Enterprises, Inc.
Master Engravers, Inc.
McCombs, Leo
McDonald, Dennis
McKenzie, Lynton
Mele, Frank
Mittermeier, Inc., Frank
Moschetti, Mitchell R.
Mountain States Engraving
Napoleon Bonaparte, Inc.
Nelson, Gary K.
New Orleans Jewelers
  Supply Co.
NgraveR Co., The
Oker's Engraving
Old Dominion Engravers
P&S Gun Service
Pedersen, C.R.
Pedersen, Rex C.
Pilgrim Pewter, Inc.
Pilkington, Scott
Piquette, Paul R.
Potts, Wayne E.
Rabeno, Martin
Reed, Dave
Reno, Wayne

Riggs, Jim
Roberts, J.J.
Rohner, Hans
Rohner, John
Rosser, Bob
Rundell's Gun Shop
Runge, Robert P.
Sampson, Roger
Schiffman, Mike
Sherwood, George
Sinclair, W.P.
Singletary, Kent
Skaggs, R.E.
Smith, Mark A.
Smith, Ron
Smokey Valley Rifles
Theis, Terry
Thiewes, George W.

Thirion Gun Engraving, Denise
Valade Engraving, Robert
Vest, John
Viramontez, Ray
Vorhes, David
Wagoner, Vernon G.
Wallace, Terry
Warenski, Julie
Warren, Kenneth W.
Weber & Markin Custom
   Gunsmiths
Welch, Sam
Wells, Rachel
Wessinger Custom Guns &
   Engraving
Willig Custom Engraving, Claus
Wood, Mel

GUN PARTS, U.S. AND FOREIGN

Accuracy Gun Shop
Ahlman Guns
Amherst Arms
Armscorp USA, Inc.
Aro-Tek, Ltd.
Badger Shooters Supply, Inc.
Bear Mountain Gun & Tool
Bob's Gun Shop
Briese Bullet Co., Inc.
Bustani, Leo
Caspian Arms Ltd.
Century International Arms, Inc.
Clark Custom Guns, Inc.
Cole's Gun Works
Colonial Repair
Cylinder & Slide, Inc.
Delta Arms Ltd.
Dibble, Derek A.
Dilliott Gunsmithing, Inc.
Dixie Gun Works, Inc.
Duane's Gun Repair
Duffy, Charles E.
E&L Mfg., Inc.
Elliott Inc., G.W.
EMF Co., Inc.
Enguix Import-Export
Fleming Firearms
Forrest, Inc., Tom
Galati International
Goodwin, Fred
Groenewold, John
Gun Parts Corp., The
Gun Shop, The
Guns Antique & Modern
   DBA/Charles E. Duffy
Gun-Tec
High Performance International
Irwin, Campbell H.
I.S.S.
Johnson's Gunsmithing, Inc.,
   Neal G.
K&T Co.
Kimber of America, Inc.
K.K. Arms Co.
Laughridge, William R.
List Precision Engineering
Lothar Walther Precision Tool, Inc.
L.P.A. Snc
Mac's .45 Shop
Mandall Shooting Supplies, Inc.
Markell, Inc.

Martin's Gun Shop
Martz, John V.
Mathews & Son, Inc., George E.
McCann's Machine & Gun Shop
McCormick Corp., Chip
Merkuria Ltd.
Mid-America Recreation, Inc.
Morrow, Bud
Nu-Line Guns, Inc.
Pachmayr Ltd.
Parts & Surplus
Performance Specialists
Peterson Gun Shop, Inc., A.W.
P.S.M.G. Gun Co.
Quality Firearms of Idaho, Inc.
Ranch Products
Randco UK
Retting, Inc., Martin B.
Ruvel & Co., Inc.
S&S Firearms
Sabatti S.R.L.
Sarco, Inc.
Scherer
Shockley, Harold H.
Silver Ridge Gun Shop
Sipes Gun Shop
Smires, C.L.
Smith & Wesson
Southern Ammunition Co., Inc.
Southern Armory, The
Sportsmen's Exchange &
   Western Gun Traders, Inc.
Springfield, Inc.
Springfield Sporters, Inc.
Starr Trading Co., Jedediah
"Su-Press-On," Inc.
Swampfire Shop, The
Tank's Rifle Shop
Tarnhelm Supply Co., Inc.
Twin Pine Armory
USA Sporting Inc.
Vintage Arms, Inc.
Vintage Industries, Inc.
Volquartsen Custom Ltd.
Walker Arms Co., Inc.
Weaver Arms Corp. Gun Shop
Westfield Engineering
Williams Mfg. of Oregon
Winchester Sutler, Inc., The
Wise Guns, Dale
Wolff Co., W.C.

GUNS, AIR

Airrow
•Beeman Precision Airguns
•Benjamin/Sheridan Co.
Brass Eagle, Inc.
•BSA Guns Ltd.
•Crosman Airguns
Crosman Products of Canada Ltd.
•Daisy Mfg. Co.
•Diana
•Dynamit Nobel-RWS, Inc.

•FAS
•FWB
•Gamo
Gamo USA, Inc.
•Great Lakes Airguns
GZ Paintball Sports Products
Hebard Guns, Gil
•Interarms
•Marksman Products
Maryland Paintball Supply

•Pardini Armi Srl
•Precision Airgun Sales, Inc.
Precision Sales Int'l, Inc.
•RWS
Shanghai Airguns, Ltd.
SKAN A.R.
Sportsman Airguns, Inc.

•Steyr Mannlicher AG
Stone Enterprises Ltd.
•Swivel Machine Works, Inc.
Vortek Products
•Walther GmbH, Carl
•Webley and Scott Ltd.
•Weihrauch KG, Hermann

GUNS, FOREIGN—IMPORTERS (Manufacturers)

Accuracy International
   (Anschutz GmbH)
AcuSport Corporation (Anschutz
   GmbH)
Airguns-R-Us (Falcon Pneumatic
   Systems; air rifles and pistols)
•American Arms, Inc. (Fausti
   Cav. Stefano & Figlie snc;
   Franchi S.p.A.; Grulla Armes;
   Uberti, Aldo; Zabala Hermanos
   S.A.; blackpowder arms)
•Amtec 2000, Inc. (Erma Werke
   GmbH)
•Anics Firm, Inc. (Anics)
Arms United Corp. (Gamo)
Armsport, Inc. (airguns, black-
   powder arms and shotguns)
Auto-Ordnance Corp. (Techno
   Arms)
•Beeman Precision Airguns (Bee-
   man Precision Airguns; FWB;
   Webley & Scott Ltd.;
   Weihrauch KG, Hermann)
•Beretta U.S.A. Corp. (Beretta
   S.p.A., Pietro)
•Browning Arms Co. (Browning
   Arms Co.)
•Cabela's (Pedersoli, Davide &
   C.; blackpowder arms)
•Century International Arms, Inc.
   (Famas; FEG; Norinco)
Champion's Choice (Anschutz
   GmbH; Lapua; Walther
   GmbH, Carl)
•Cimarron Arms (Uberti, Aldo;
   blackpowder arms)
•CVA (blackpowder arms)
•Daisy Mfg. Co. (Daisy Mfg. Co.;
   Gamo)
•Dixie Gun Works, Inc. (Peder-
   soli, Davide & C.; Uberti, Aldo;
   blackpowder arms)
•Dynamit Nobel-RWS, Inc. (Bren-
   neke KG, Wilhelm; Diana; Gamo;
   Norma Precision AB; RWS)
•E.A.A. Corp. (Astra-Sport, S.A.;
   Benelli Armi S.p.A.; Sabatti
   S.r.l.; Tanfoglio S.r.l., Fratelli;
   Weihrauch KG, Hermann)
Eagle Imports, Inc. (Bersa S.A.)
•EMF Co., Inc. (Dakota; Hartford;
   Pedersoli, Davide & C.; San
   Marco; Uberti, Aldo; blackpow-
   der arms)
•Forgett Jr., Valmore J. (Navy
   Arms Co.; Uberti, Aldo)
Gamo USA, Inc. (Gamo)
•Glock, Inc. (Glock GmbH)
•Great Lakes Airguns (air pistols)
Groenewold, John (BSA Guns
   Ltd.; Paragon and Prometheus
   pellets; Webley & Scott Ltd.)
•Hammerli USA (Hammerli Ltd.)
Harris Gunworks (Peters Stahl
   GmbH)

•Heckler & Koch, Inc. (Benelli
   Armi S.p.A.; Heckler & Koch,
   GmbH)
Import Sports Inc. (Llama
   Gabilondo Y Cia)
•Interarms (Helwan; Howa
   Machinery Ltd.; Interarms;
   Korth; Norinco; Rossi S.A.,
   Amadeo Rua; Star Bonifacio
   Echeverria S.A.; Walther
   GmbH, Carl)
•JägerSport, Ltd. (Voere-KGH
   m.b.H.)
•J.O. Arms Inc. (KSN Industries,
   Ltd.)
•K.B.I., Inc. (Armscorp USA, Inc.;
   Baikal; FEG; K.B.I., Inc.; Sabat-
   ti S.R.L.)
•Magnum Research, Inc. (BRNO;
   CZ)
•Mandall Shooting Supplies, Inc.
   (Arizaga; Atamec-Bretton;
   Cabanas; Crucelegui, Her-
   manos; Erma Werke GmbH;
   Firearms Co. Ltd./Alpine; Ham-
   merli Ltd.; Korth; Krico Jagd-
   und Sportwaffen GmbH; Morini;
   SIG; Tanner; Ugartechea S.A.,
   Ignacio; Zanoletti, Pietro; black-
   powder arms)
•Mitchell Arms, Inc. (Mitchell
   Arms, Inc.)
•Nationwide Sports Distributors,
   Inc. (Daewoo Precision Indus-
   tries Ltd.)
•Navy Arms Co. (Navy Arms Co.;
   Pedersoli, Davide & C.; Pietta;
   Uberti, Aldo; blackpowder and
   cartridge arms)
•Nygord Precision Products
   (FAS; Morini; Pardini Armi Srl;
   Steyr; Steyr-Mannlicher AG;
   TOZ; Unique/M.A.P.F.)
•Para-Ordnance, Inc. (Para-Ord-
   nance Mfg., Inc.)
P.S.M.G. Gun Co. (Astra Sport,
   S.A.; Interarms; Star Bonifacio
   Echeverria S.A.; Walther
   GmbH, Carl)
Sarco, Inc.
Schuetzen Pistol Works (Peters
   Stahl GmbH)
•Sigarms, Inc. (Hammerli Ltd.;
   Sauer; SIG-Sauer)
Sphinx USA Inc. (Sphinx Engi-
   neering SA)
•Springfield, Inc. (Springfield, Inc.)
•Stoeger Industries (IGA; Sako
   Ltd.; Tikka; target pistols)
Stone Enterprises Ltd. (airguns)
•Taurus Firearms, Inc. (Taurus
   International Firearms)
•Uberti USA, Inc. (Uberti, Aldo;
   blackpowder arms)

GUNS, FOREIGN—MANUFACTURERS (Importers)

Anics (Anics Firm, Inc.)
•Anschutz GmbH (Accuracy
   International; AcuSport Corpo-
   ration; Champion Shooters'
   Supply; Champion's Choice;
   Gunsmithing, Inc.)
Arms Corporation of the Philippines

Armscorp USA, Inc. (K.B.I., Inc.)
•Astra Sport, S.A. (E.A.A. Corp.;
   P.S.M.G. Gun Co.)
•Beeman Precision Airguns (Bee-
   man Precision Airguns)
•Beretta S.p.A., Pietro (Beretta
   U.S.A. Corp.)

•See page 285 for Warranty Service Center Addresses

- Bernardelli S.p.A., Vincenzo Bersa S.A. (Eagle Imports, Inc.)
- BRNO (Bohemia Arms Co.; Magnum Research, Inc.)
- Browning Arms Co. (Browning Arms Co.)
- BSA Guns Ltd. (Groenewold, John)
- CVA (blackpowder arms)
- CZ (Magnum Research, Inc.)
- Daewoo Precision Industries Ltd. (Nationwide Sports Distributors, Inc.)
- Dakota (EMF Co., Inc.)
- Daisy Mfg. Co. (Daisy Mfg. Co.)
- Diana (Dynamit Nobel-RWS, Inc.)
- Erma Werke GmbH (Amtec 2000, Inc.; Mandall Shooting Supplies, Inc.)
- FAS (Nygord Precision Products)
- FEG (Century International Arms, Inc.; K.B.I., Inc.)
  Fiocchi Munizioni S.P.A. (Fiocchi of America, Inc.)
  FN Herstal
- FWB (Beeman Precision Airguns)
- Gamba S.p.A.-Societa Armi Bresciane Srl., Renato (First National Gun Bank Corp., The)
- Gamo (Arms United Corp.; Daisy Mfg. Co.; Dynamit Nobel-RWS, Inc.; Gamo USA, Inc.)
  Gaucher Armes S.A.
- Glock GmbH (Glock, Inc.)
- Hammerli Ltd. (Hammerli USA; Mandall Shooting Supplies, Inc.; Sigarms, Inc.)
  Hartford (EMF Co., Inc.)
- Heckler & Koch, GmbH (Heckler & Koch, Inc.)
- IMI
- Interarms (Interarms; P.S.M.G. Gun Co.)
- K.B.I., Inc. (K.B.I., Inc.)
- Korth (Interarms; Mandall Shooting Supplies, Inc.)
  KSN Industries, Ltd. (J.O. Arms Inc.)
- Llama Gabilondo Y Cia (Import Sports Inc.)
  Mauser Werke Oberndorf (GSI, Inc.)

- Mitchell Arms, Inc. (Mitchell Arms, Inc.)
- Morini (Mandall Shooting Supplies; Nygord Precision Products)
- Navy Arms Co. (Forgett Jr., Valmore J.; Navy Arms Co.)
- Para-Ordnance Mfg., Inc. (Para-Ordnance, Inc.)
- Pardini Armi Srl. (Nygord Precision Products)
  Peters Stahl GmbH (Harris Gunworks; Schuetzen Pistol Works)
- Rossi S.A., Amadeo Rua (Interarms)
- RWS (Dynamit Nobel-RWS, Inc.)
- SIG (Mandall Shooting Supplies, Inc.)
- SIG-Sauer (Sigarms, Inc.)
  Sphinx Engineering SA (Sphinx USA Inc.)
- Springfield, Inc. (Springfield, Inc.)
- Star Bonifacio Echeverria S.A. (Interarms; P.S.M.G. Gun Co.)
- Tanfoglio S.r.l., Fratelli (E.A.A. Corp.)
- Taurus International Firearms (Taurus Firearms, Inc.)
  Taurus S.A., Forjas
  TOZ (Nygord Precision Products)
- Uberti, Aldo (American Arms, Inc.; Cimarron Arms; Dixie Gun Works, Inc.; EMF Co., Inc.; Forgett Jr., Valmore J.; Navy Arms Co.; Taylor's & Co., Inc.; Uberti USA, Inc.)
- Unique/M.A.P.F. (Nygord Precision Products)
- Voere-KGH m.b.H. (JägerSport, Ltd.)
- Walther GmbH, Carl (Champion's Choice; Interarms; P.S.M.G. Gun Co.)
- Webley & Scott Ltd. (Beeman Precision Airguns; Groenewold, John)
- Weihrauch KG, Hermann (Beeman Precision Airguns; E.A.A. Corp.)

- Seecamp Co., Inc., L.W.
- Smith & Wesson
- Springfield, Inc.
  Stoeger Industries
- Sturm, Ruger & Co., Inc.
- Sundance Industries, Inc.
- Swivel Machine Works, Inc.
- Taurus Firearms, Inc.

- Texas Armory
- Texas Longhorn Arms, Inc.
- Thompson/Center Arms
- Ultra Light Arms, Inc.
- Wichita Arms, Inc.
- Wildey, Inc.
- Wilkinson Arms

GUNS AND GUN PARTS, REPLICA AND ANTIQUE

Ahlman Guns
Armi San Paolo
Bear Mountain Gun & Tool
Beauchamp & Son, Inc.
Bob's Gun Shop
British Antiques
Buckskin Machine Works
Buffalo Arms
Cache La Poudre Rifleworks
Century International Arms, Inc.
Chambers Flintlocks Ltd., Jim
Cogar's Gunsmithing
Cole's Gun Works
Colonial Repair
Dangler, Homer L.
Day & Sons, Inc., Leonard
Delhi Gun House
Delta Arms Ltd.
Dilliott Gunsmithing, Inc.
Dixie Gun Works, Inc.
Dixon Muzzleloading Shop, Inc.
Ed's Gun House
Flintlocks, Etc.
Forgett, Valmore J., Jr.
Galazan
Golden Age Arms Co.
Goodwin, Fred
Groenewold, John
Gun Parts Corp., The
Gun-Tec
Hunkeler, A.
Liberty Antique Gunworks
List Precision Engineering
Lock's Philadelphia Gun

Exchange
Lucas, Edw. E.
McKinney, R.P.
Meier Works
Mountain State Muzzleloading Supplies
Munsch Gunsmithing, Tommy
Museum of Historical Arms, Inc.
Neumann GmbH
Pasadena Gun Center
Peacemaker Specialists
PEM's Mfg. Co.
P.M. Enterprises, Inc.
Pony Express Sport Shop, Inc.
Precise Metalsmithing Enterprises
Quality Firearms of Idaho, Inc.
Randco UK
Retting, Inc., Martin B.
S&S Firearms
Sarco, Inc.
Scattergun Technologies, Inc.
Schuetzen Gun Co.
Silver Ridge Gun Shop
Sipes Gun Shop
South Bend Replicas, Inc.
Southern Ammunition Co., Inc.
Stott's Creek Armory, Inc.
Tennessee Valley Mfg.
Tiger-Hunt
Track of the Wolf, Inc.
Uberti USA, Inc.
Vintage Industries, Inc.
Weisz Parts

GUNS, SURPLUS—PARTS AND AMMUNITION

Ad Hominem
Armscorp USA, Inc.
Arundel Arms & Ammunition, Inc., A.
Aztec International Ltd.
Badger Shooters Supply, Inc.
Ballistica Maximus North
Bohemia Arms Co.
Bondini Paolo
Braun, M.
Century International Arms, Inc.
Chuck's Gun Shop
Cole's Gun Works
Combat Military Ordnance Ltd.
Delta Arms Ltd.
First, Inc., Jack
Fleming Firearms
Forgett, Valmore J., Jr.
Forrest, Inc., Tom
Garcia National Gun Traders, Inc.
Goodwin, Fred
Gun Parts Corp., The
Interarms
Lomont Precision Bullets
Moreton/Fordyce Enterprises

Navy Arms Co.
Nevada Pistol Academy Inc.
Oil Rod and Gun Shop
Parts & Surplus
Pasadena Gun Center
Perazone, Brian
Quality Firearms of Idaho, Inc.
Ravell Ltd.
Retting, Inc., Martin B.
Samco Global Arms, Inc.
Sarco, Inc.
Shell Shack
Shootin' Shack, Inc.
Silver Ridge Gun Shop
Sipes Gun Shop
Southern Armory, The
Sportsmen's Exchange & Western Gun Traders, Inc.
Springfield Sporters, Inc.
Stratco, Inc.
Tarnhelm Supply Co., Inc.
T.F.C. S.p.A.
Thurston Sports, Inc.
Westfield Engineering

GUNS, U.S.-MADE

A.A. Arms, Inc.
- Accu-Tek
- Airrow
- American Arms & Ordnance, Inc.
- American Arms, Inc.
- American Derringer Corp.
- AMT
  Amtec 2000, Inc.
- Auto-Ordnance Corp.
- Baer Custom, Inc., Les
  Bar-Sto Precision Machine
- Beretta U.S.A. Corp.
- Braverman, R.J.
- Brolin Arms
- Brown Co., E. Arthur
  Brown Products, Inc., Ed
- Browning Arms Co. (Parts & Service)
  Bullberry Barrel Works, Ltd.
- Calico Light Weapon Systems
- Century Gun Dist., Inc.
- Colt's Mfg. Co., Inc.
- Competitor Corp., Inc.
- Coonan Arms
- Cumberland Arms
- CVA
- Davis Industries
- Desert Industries, Inc.
- Emerging Technologies, Inc.
- Essex Arms
- Feather Industries, Inc.

- Freedom Arms, Inc.
  Gunsite Custom Shop
  Gunsite Gunsmithy
- H&R 1871, Inc.
  Harrington & Richardson
- Harris Gunworks
  Heritage Manufacturing, Inc.
- High Standard Mfg. Co., Inc.
- Hi-Point Firearms
- HJS Arms, Inc.
- Intratec
- Jennings Firearms Inc.
- Kahr Arms
- Kel-Tec CNC Industries, Inc.
- Kimber of America, Inc.
- Kimel Industries
- Knight's Mfg. Co.
- L.A.R. Mfg., Inc.
- Laseraim, Inc.
- Lorcin Engineering Co., Inc.
- Magnum Research, Inc.
- Mitchell Arms, Inc.
- MKS Supply, Inc.
- M.O.A. Corp.
- New Advantage Arms Corp.
- North American Arms, Inc.
  Nowlin Custom Mfg.
- Phoenix Arms
- Precision Small Arms
  Recoilless Technologies, Inc.
- Rocky Mountain Arms, Inc.
  Ruger

GUNSMITH SCHOOLS

Bull Mountain Rifle Co.
Colorado Gunsmithing Academy Lamar
Colorado School of Trades
Cylinder & Slide, Inc.
Lassen Community College, Gunsmithing Dept.
Laughridge, William R.

Mathews & Son, Inc., George E.
Modern Gun Repair School
Montgomery Community College
Murray State College
North American Correspondence Schools
Nowlin Custom Mfg.
NRI Gunsmith School

- **See page 285 for Warranty Service Center Addresses**

Pennsylvania Gunsmith School
Piedmont Community College
Pine Technical College
Professional Gunsmiths of
America, Inc.
Southeastern Community College

Smith & Wesson
Spencer's Custom Guns
Trinidad State Junior College
Gunsmithing Dept.
Weigand Combat Handguns, Inc.

GUNSMITH SUPPLIES, TOOLS, SERVICES

Actions by "T"
Aldis Gunsmithing & Shooting
Supply
Auto-Ordnance Corp.
Baer Custom, Inc., Les
Bar-Sto Precision Machine
Bear Mountain Gun & Tool
Belltown, Ltd.
Belt MTN Arms
Bengtson Arms Co., L.
Biesen, Al
Biesen, Roger
Bill's Gun Repair
Blue Ridge Machinery & Tools,
Inc.
Bowen Classic Arms Corp.
Break-Free, Inc.
Briley Mfg., Inc.
Brownells, Inc.
B-Square Co., Inc.
Bull Mountain Rifle Co.
Carbide Checkering Tools
Chapman Manufacturing Co.
Chem-Pak, Inc.
Choate Machine & Tool Co., Inc.
Chopie Mfg., Inc.
Chuck's Gun Shop
Clark Custom Guns, Inc.
Clenzoil Corp.
Colonial Arms, Inc.
Conetrol Scope Mounts
Craig Custom Ltd.
Cumberland Arms
Custom Checkering Service
Custom Gun Products
D&J Bullet Co. & Custom Gun
Shop, Inc.
Dakota Arms, Inc.
Dan's Whetstone Co., Inc.
Dayton Traister
Dem-Bart Checkering Tools, Inc.
Dever Co., Jack
Dremel Mfg. Co.
Du-Lite Corp.
Dutchman's Firearms, Inc., The
Echols & Co., D'Arcy
EGW Evolution Gun Works
Faith Associates, Inc.
Fisher, Jerry A.
Forgreens Tool Mfg., Inc.
Forkin, Ben
Forster, Kathy
Forster Products
Frazier Brothers Enterprises
G.B.C. Industries, Inc.
Grace Metal Products, Inc.
Greider Precision
Gunline Tools
Gun-Tec
Half Moon Rifle Shop
Hastings Barrels
Henriksen Tool Co., Inc.
High Performance International
Hoelscher, Virgil
Holland's
Ivanoff, Thomas G.
J&R Engineering
J&S Heat Treat
Jantz Supply
JBM Software
JGS Precision Tool Mfg.
Kasenit Co., Inc.
KenPatable Ent., Inc.
Kimball, Gary
Kleinendorst, K.W.

Kmount
Korzinek Riflesmith, J.
Kwik Mount Corp.
LaBounty Precision Reboring
Lea Mfg. Co.
Lee Supplies, Mark
Lee's Red Ramps
List Precision Engineering
London Guns Ltd.
Mag-Na-Port International, Inc.
Mahovsky's Metalife
Marsh, Mike
MCS, Inc.
Menck, Thomas W.
Metalife Industries
Metaloy Inc.
Michael's Antiques
Millett Sights
MMC
Morrow, Bud
Mo's Competitor Supplies
N&J Sales
NCP Products, Inc.
Nowlin Custom Mfg.
Ole Frontier Gunsmith Shop
PanaVise Products, Inc.
Passive Bullet Traps, Inc.
PEM's Mfg. Co.
Perazone, Brian
Power Custom, Inc.
Practical Tools, Inc.
Precision Metal Finishing
Precision Specialties
Prolix® Lubricants
Reardon Products
Rice, Keith
Romain's Custom Guns, Inc.
Roto Carve
Royal Arms Gunstocks
Rusteprufe Laboratories
Savage Range Systems, Inc.
Scott, McDougall & Associates
Shirley Co. Gun & Riflemakers
Ltd., J.A.
Shooter's Choice
Slug Group, Inc.
Smith Abrasives, Inc.
Starrett Co., L.S.
Sullivan, David S.
Talley, Dave
Texas Platers Supply
Time Precision, Inc.
Tom's Gun Repair
Tom's Gunshop
Trulock Tool
Turnbull Restoration, Doug
Van Gorden & Son, Inc., C.S.
Venco Industries, Inc.
Vintage Industries, Inc.
Washita Mountain Whetstone Co.
Weaver Arms Corp. Gun Shop
Weigand Combat Handguns, Inc.
Welsh, Bud
Westfield Engineering
Westrom, John
Westwind Rifles, Inc.
White Rock Tool & Die
Wilcox All-Pro Tools & Supply
Wild West Guns
Will-Burt Co.
Williams Gun Sight Co.
Williams Shootin' Iron Service
Willow Bend
Wilson's Gun Shop
Wise Guns, Dale

HANDGUN ACCESSORIES

A.A. Arms, Inc.
ADCO International
Adventurer's Outpost
Alpha Gunsmith Division
American Derringer Corp.
Armite Laboratories
Arms Corporation of the
Philippines
Aro-Tek, Ltd.
Astra Sport, S.A.
Auto-Ordnance Corp.
Baer Custom, Inc., Les
Bar-Sto Precision Machine
Baumannize Custom
Behlert Precision, Inc.
Beretta S.p.A., Pietro
Bill's Custom Cases
Black Sheep Brand
Blue and Gray Products, Inc.
Bob's Gun Shop
Bond Custom Firearms
Bowen Classic Arms Corp.
Broken Gun Ranch
Brown Products, Inc., Ed
Brownells, Inc.
Bucheimer, J.M.
Bushmaster Firearms
Bushmaster Hunting & Fishing
Butler Creek Corp.
C3 Systems
Centaur Systems, Inc.
Central Specialties Ltd.
Clark Custom Guns, Inc.
Cobra Gunskin
Craig Custom Ltd.
D&L Industries
Dade Screw Machine Products
Delhi Gun House
Dewey Mfg. Co., Inc., J.
D.J. Marketing
Doskocil Mfg. Co., Inc
E&L Mfg., Inc.
E.A.A. Corp.
Eagle International, Inc.
EGW Evolution Gun Works
Faith Associates, Inc.
FAS
Feather Industries, Inc.
Feminine Protection, Inc.
Ferris Firearms
Fleming Firearms
Frielich Police Equipment
Galati International
GALCO International Ltd.
Glock, Inc.
Greider Precision
Gremmel Enterprises
Gun Parts Corp., The
Gun-Alert
Gun-Ho Sports Cases
Harvey, Frank
Haselbauer Products, Jerry

Hebard Guns, Gil
Heinie Specialty Products
Hill Speed Leather, Ernie
H.K.S. Products
Hoppe's Div.
Hunter Co., Inc.
Jarvis, Inc.
Jeffredo Gunsight
J.P. Enterprises, Inc.
Jumbo Sports Products
KeeCo Impressions
Keller Co., The
King's Gun Works
K.K. Arms Co.
Lakewood Products, Inc.
Lee's Red Ramps
Lem Sports, Inc.
Loch Leven Industries
Lohman Mfg. Co., Inc.
Mac's .45 Shop
Mag-Na-Port International, Inc.
Magnolia Sports, Inc.
Magnum Research, Inc.
Mahony, Philip Bruce
Mandall Shooting Supplies, Inc.
Markell Inc.
McCormick Corp., Chip
MEC-Gar S.R.L.
Merkuria Ltd.
Mid-America Guns and Ammo
Minute Man High Tech Industries
Mitchell Arms, Inc.
MTM Molded Products Co., Inc.
Mustra's Custom Guns, Inc., Carl
North American Specialties
No-Sho Mfg. Co.
Ox-Yoke Originals, Inc.
PAST Sporting Goods, Inc.
Penguin Industries, Inc.
Power Custom, Inc.
Practical Tools, Inc.
Protector Mfg. Co., Inc., The
Protektor Model
Quality Parts Co.
Ram-Line, Inc.
Ranch Products
Round Edge, Inc.
RPM
Slings 'N Things, Inc.
Southwind Sanctions
TacStar Industries, Inc.
TacTell, Inc.
T.F.C. S.p.A.
TMI Products
Trijicon, Inc.
Tyler Mfg.-Dist., Melvin
Valor Corp.
Vintage Industries, Inc.
Volquartsen Custom Ltd.
Weigand Combat Handguns, Inc.
Western Design
Wilson Combat

HANDGUN GRIPS

Ahrends, Kim
Ajax Custom Grips, Inc.
Altamont Co.
American Derringer Corp.
American Gripcraft
Arms Corporation of the
Philippines
Art Jewel Enterprises Ltd.
Baer Custom, Inc., Les
Barami Corp.
Bear Hug Grips, Inc.
Bell Originals, Inc., Sid
Beretta S.p.A., Pietro
Bob's Gun Shop
Boone's Custom Ivory Grips, Inc.
Boyds' Gunstock Industries, Inc.
Brooks Tactical Systems
Brown Products, Inc., Ed

Clark Custom Guns, Inc.
Cobra Gunskin
Cole-Grip
Colonial Repair
Custom Firearms
Dayson Arms Ltd.
Desert Industries, Inc.
E.A.A. Corp.
Eagle Mfg. & Engineering
EMF Co., Inc.
Ferris Firearms
Fisher Custom Firearms
Fitz Pistol Grip Co.
Forrest, Inc., Tom
Harrison-Hurtz Enterprises, Inc.
Herrett's Stocks, Inc.
Hogue Grips
J.P. Enterprises, Inc.

PRODUCT DIRECTORY

KeeCo Impressions
Lett Custom Grips
Linebaugh Custom Sixguns & Rifle Works
Mac's .45 Shop
Mandall Shooting Supplies, Inc.
Masen Co., Inc., John
Michaels of Oregon
Mid-America Guns and Ammo
Millett Sights
Monte Kristo Pistol Grip Co.
N.C. Ordnance Co.
Newell, Robert H.
North American Specialties
Pacific Rifle Co.
Pardini Armi Srl

Pilgrim Pewter, Inc.
Radical Concepts
Rosenberg & Sons, Jack A.
Roy's Custom Grips
Savana Sports, Inc.
Sile Distributors, Inc.
Smith & Wesson
Speedfeed, Inc.
Spegel, Craig
Taurus Firearms, Inc.
Triple-K Mfg. Co., Inc.
Tyler Mfg.-Dist., Melvin
Uncle Mike's
Vintage Industries, Inc.
Volquartsen Custom Ltd.
Wilson Combat

Pathfinder Sports Leather
PWL Gunleather
Renegade
Ringler Custom Leather Co.
Rybka Custom Leather Equipment, Thad
Safariland Ltd., Inc.
Safety Speed Holster, Inc.
Savana Sports, Inc.
Schulz Industries
Second Chance Body Armor
Shoemaker & Sons, Inc., Tex
Silhouette Leathers
Smith Saddlery, Jesse W.
Southwind Sanctions
Sparks, Milt

Stalker, Inc.
Strong Holster Co.
Stuart, V. Pat
Tabler Marketing
Texas Longhorn Arms, Inc.
Top-Line USA Inc.
Torel, Inc.
Triple-K Mfg. Co., Inc.
Tyler Mfg.-Dist., Melvin
Uncle Mike's
Valor Corp.
Venus Industries
Viking Leathercraft, Inc.
Walt's Custom Leather
Whinnery, Walt
Wild Bill's Originals

HEARING PROTECTORS

Brown Co., E. Arthur
Brown Products, Inc., Ed
Browning Arms Co.
Clark Co., Inc., David
Clark Custom Guns, Inc.
Cobra Gunskin
E-A-R, Inc.
Electronic Shooters Protection, Inc.
Faith Associates, Inc.
Flents Products Co., Inc.
Gentex Corp.

Hoppe's Div.
Kesselring Gun Shop
North American Specialties
North Specialty Products
Paterson Gunsmithing
Peltor, Inc.
Penguin Industries, Inc.
R.E.T. Enterprises
Rucker Dist. Inc.
Safesport Manufacturing Co.
Silencio/Safety Direct
Willson Safety Prods. Div.

LABELS, BOXES, CARTRIDGE HOLDERS

American Sales & Kirkpatrick
Ballistic Products, Inc.
Berry's Mfg. Inc.
Brown Co., E. Arthur
Cabinet Mountain Outfitters Scents & Lures
Crane & Crane Ltd.
Del Rey Products
DeSantis Holster & Leather Goods, Inc.

Fitz Pistol Grip Co.
Flambeau Products Corp.
J&J Products Co.
Kolpin Mfg., Inc.
Lakewood Products, Inc.
Liberty Shooting Supplies
Loadmaster
Midway Arms, Inc.
MTM Molded Products Co., Inc.
Pendleton Royal

HOLSTERS AND LEATHER GOODS

A&B Industries, Inc.
Action Products, Inc.
Aker Leather Products
Alessi Holsters, Inc.
American Sales & Kirkpatrick
Arratoonian, Andy
Bagmaster Mfg., Inc.
Baker's Leather Goods, Roy
Bandcor Industries
Bang-Bang Boutique
Barami Corp.
Bear Hug Grips, Inc.
Bianchi International, Inc.
Bill's Custom Cases
Black Sheep Brand
Blocker Holsters, Inc., Ted
Brauer Bros. Mfg. Co.
Brown, H.R.
Browning Arms Co.
Bucheimer, J.M.
Bull-X, Inc.
Bushwacker Backpack & Supply Co.
Carvajal Belts & Holsters
Cathey Enterprises, Inc.
Chace Leather Products
Churchill Glove Co., James
Cimarron Arms
Clark Custom Guns, Inc.
Clements' Custom Leathercraft, Chas
Cobra Gunskin
Cobra Sport
Colonial Repair
Counter Assault
Crawford Co., Inc., R.M.
Creedmoor Sports, Inc.
Davis Leather Co., G. Wm.
Delhi Gun House
DeSantis Holster & Leather Goods, Inc.
Desert Industries, Inc.
D-Max, Inc.
Easy Pull Outlaw Products
Ekol Leather Care
El Dorado Leather
El Paso Saddlery Co.
EMF Co., Inc.
Eutaw Co., Inc., The
F&A Inc.
Faust, Inc., T.G.

Ferdinand, Inc.
Flores Publications, Inc., J.
Fobus International Ltd.
Fury Cutlery
Gage Manufacturing
GALCO International Ltd.
Glock, Inc.
GML Products, Inc.
Gould & Goodrich
Gun Leather Limited
Gunfitters, The
Gusty Winds Corp.
Hafner Creations, Inc.
HandiCrafts Unltd.
Hebard Guns, Gil
Hellweg Ltd.
Henigson & Associates, Steve
High North Products, Inc.
Hill Speed Leather, Ernie
Holster Shop, The
Horseshoe Leather Products
Hoyt Holster Co., Inc.
Hume, Don
Hunter Co., Inc.
John's Custom Leather
Joy Enterprises
Jumbo Sports Products
Kane Products, Inc.
Keller Co., The
Kirkpatrick Leather Co.
Kolpin Mfg., Inc.
Korth
Kramer Handgun Leather, Inc.
L.A.R. Mfg., Inc.
Law Concealment Systems, Inc.
Lawrence Leather Co.
Leather Arsenal
Lone Star Gunleather
Magnolia Sports, Inc.
Markell, Inc.
Michaels of Oregon Co.
Minute Man High Tech Industries
Mixson Corp.
Nelson Combat Leather, Bruce
Noble Co., Jim
No-Sho Mfg. Co.
Null Holsters Ltd., K.L.
October Country
Ojala Holsters, Arvo
Oklahoma Leather Products, Inc.
Old West Reproductions, Inc.

LOAD TESTING AND PRODUCT TESTING,
(Chronographing, Ballistic Studies)

Ballistic Research
Bartlett, Don
Bestload, Inc.
Briese Bullet Co., Inc.
Briganti & Co., A.
Buck Stix—SOS Products Co.
CFVentures
Clerke Co., J.A.
D&H Precision Tooling
Dead Eye's Sport Center
Defense Training International, Inc.
DGR Custom Rifles
DKT, Inc.
Duane's Gun Repair
Gonzalez Guns, Ramon B.
Hank's Gun Shop
Hensler, Jerry
Hoelscher, Virgil
Jackalope Gun Shop
Jensen Bullets

Jurras, L.E.
Lomont Precision Bullets
Maionchi-L.M.I.
MAST Technology
Master Class Bullets
McCann's Machine & Gun Shop
McMurdo, Lynn
Moreton/Fordyce Enterprises
Multiplex International
Oil Rod and Gun Shop
Ransom International Corp.
RPM
Rupert's Gun Shop
SOS Products Co.
Spencer's Custom Guns
Vancini, Carl
Vulpes Ventures, Inc.
Wells Custom Gunsmith, R.A.
Whildin & Sons Ltd., E.H.
White Laboratory, Inc., H.P.
X-Spand Target Systems

MUZZLE-LOADING GUNS, BARRELS AND EQUIPMENT

Accuracy Unlimited (Littleton, CO)
Adkins, Luther
Allen Manufacturing
•Anderson Manufacturing Co., Inc.
Armi San Paolo
Bauska Barrels
•Beauchamp & Son, Inc.
Beaver Lodge
Bentley, John
Birdsong & Associates, W.E.
Blackhawk West
Blue and Gray Products, Inc.
Bridgers Best
Buckskin Machine Works
Burgess & Son Gunsmiths, R.W.
Butler Creek Corp.
California Sights
•Cape Outfitters
Cash Manufacturing Co., Inc.
CenterMark
Chambers Flintlocks, Ltd., Jim
Chopie Mfg., Inc.
•Cimarron Arms
Cogar's Gunsmithing
Colonial Repair
•Colt Blackpowder Arms Co.

Cousin Bob's Mountain Products
•Cumberland Arms
•Cumberland Knife & Gun Works
•CVA
Dangler, Homer L.
Davis Co., R.E.
Day & Sons, Inc., Leonard
•Dayton Traister
deHaas Barrels
Delhi Gun House
Desert Industries, Inc.
Dewey Mfg. Co., Inc., J.
DGS, Inc.
Dyson & Son Ltd., Peter
•EMF Co., Inc.
•Euroarms of America, Inc.
Eutaw Co., Inc., The
Fautheree, Andy
Feken, Dennis
Fellowes, Ted
Fire'n Five
Flintlocks, Etc.
•Forster Products
Fort Hill Gunstocks
Frontier
Getz Barrel Co.
GOEX, Inc.
Golden Age Arms Co.

•See page 285 for Warranty Service Center Addresses

Hastings Barrels
•Hawken Shop, The
Hege Jagd-u. Sporthandels, GmbH
Hoppe's Div.
•Hornady Mfg. Co.
House of Muskets, Inc., The
Hunkeler, A.
Jamison's Forge Works
Jones Co., Dale
K&M Industries, Inc.
Kennedy Firearms
L&R Lock Co.
Legend Products Corp.
•Log Cabin Sport Shop
Lothar Walther Precision Tool, Inc.
•Lyman Products Corp.
McCann's Muzzle-Gun Works
Michaels of Oregon Co.
MMP
•Modern MuzzleLoading, Inc.
Montana Precision Swaging
Mountain State Muzzleloading Supplies
MSC Industrial Supply Co.
Mt. Alto Outdoor Products
Mushroom Express Bullet Co.
Muzzleloaders Etcetera, Inc.
Navy Arms Co.
North Star West
October Country
Oklahoma Leather Products, Inc.
Olson, Myron
Ox-Yoke Originals, Inc.
Penguin Industries, Inc.

•Pioneer Arms Co.
Radical Concepts
Rusty Duck Premium Gun Care Products
R.V.I.
S&B Industries
S&S Firearms
Selsi Co., Inc.
Shooter's Choice
•Sile Distributors
Single Shot, Inc.
Sklany, Steve
Slings 'N Things, Inc.
Southern Bloomer Mfg. Co.
Starr Trading Co., Jedediah
Stone Mountain Arms
Storey, Dale A.
Tennessee Valley Mfg.
Thompson Bullet Lube Co.
Thompson/Center Arms
•Thunder Mountain Arms
Tiger-Hunt
Track of the Wolf, Inc.
•Traditions, Inc.
Treso, Inc.
•Uberti, Aldo
Uncle Mike's
•Upper Missouri Trading Co.
Venco Industries, Inc.
Walters, John
Warren Muzzleloading Co., Inc.
Wescombe
White Owl Enterprises
Williams Gun Sight Co.
Woodworker's Supply
Young Country Arms

PISTOLSMITHS

Accuracy Gun Shop
Accuracy Unlimited (Glendale, AZ)
Ace Custom 45's, Inc.
Actions by "T"
Adair Custom Shop, Bill
Ahlman Guns
Aldis Gunsmithing & Shooting Supply
Alpha Precision, Inc.
Alpine's Precision Gunsmithing & Indoor Shooting Range
Armament Gunsmithing Co., Inc.
AWC Systems Technology
Baer Custom, Inc., Les
Bain & Davis, Inc.
Banks, Ed
Behlert Precision, Inc.
Bellm Contenders
Belt MTN Arms
Bengtson Arms Co., L.
BlackStar AccuMax Barrels
BlackStar Barrel Accurizing
Bowen Classic Arms Corp.
Campbell, Dick
Cannon's Guns
Caraville Manufacturing
Clark Custom Guns, Inc.
Colonial Repair
Colorado Gunsmithing Academy Lamar
Corkys Gun Clinic
Costa, David
Craig Custom Ltd.
Curtis Custom Shop
Custom Gunsmiths
D&L Sports
Davis Service Center, Bill
Ellicott Arms, Inc./Woods Pistolsmithing
Ferris Firearms
Fisher Custom Firearms
Forkin, Ben
Francesca, Inc.
Frank Custom Classic Arms, Ron
Frielich Police Equipment
Garthwaite, Jim

Giron, Robert E.
Gonzalez Guns, Ramon B.
Greider Precision
Gun Room Press, The
Guncraft Sports, Inc.
Guns
Gunsite Custom Shop
Gunsite Gunsmithy
Gunsite Training Center
Gunsmithing Ltd.
Hamilton, Alex B.
Hamilton, Keith
Hank's Gun Shop
Hanson's Gun Center, Dick
Hardison, Charles
Harris Gunworks
Hebard Guns, Gil
Heinie Specialty Products
High Bridge Arms, Inc.
Highline Machine Co.
Hoag, James W.
Intermountain Arms & Tackle, Inc.
Irwin, Campbell H.
Island Pond Gun Shop
Ivanoff, Thomas G.
J&S Heat Treat
Jarvis, Inc.
Jensen's Custom Ammunition
Johnston, James
Jones, J.D.
J.P. Enterprises, Inc.
Jungkind, Reeves C.
K-D, Inc.
Kaswer Custom, Inc.
Ken's Gun Specialties
Kilham & Co.
Kimball, Gary
Kopp, Terry K.
La Clinique du .45
LaFrance Specialties
LaRocca Gun Works, Inc.
Lathrop's, Inc.
Lawson, John G.
Leckie Professional Gunsmithing
Lee's Red Ramps

Linebaugh Custom Sixguns & Rifle Works
List Precision Engineering
Long, George F.
Mac's .45 Shop
Mahony, Philip Bruce
Marent, Rudolf
Martin's Gun Shop
Marvel, Alan
McCann's Machine & Gun Shop
McGowen Rifle Barrels
Middlebrooks Custom Shop
Miller Custom
Mitchell's Accuracy Shop
MJK Gunsmithing, Inc.
Mountain Bear Rifle Works, Inc.
Mullis Guncraft
Mustra's Custom Guns, Inc., Carl
Nastoff's 45 Shop, Inc., Steve
NCP Products, Inc.
North Fork Custom Gunsmithing
Novak's Inc.
Nowlin Custom Mfg.
Oglesby & Oglesby Gunmakers, Inc.
Paris, Frank J.
Pasadena Gun Center
Peacemaker Specialists
PEM's Mfg. Co.
Performance Specialists
Peterson Gun Shop, Inc., A.W.
Pierce Pistols
Plaxco, J. Michael
Precision Specialties
Randco UK

Ries, Chuck
Rim Pac Sports, Inc.
Robar Co.'s, Inc., The
Rogers Gunsmithing, Bob
Scott, McDougall & Associates
Seecamp Co., Inc., L.W.
Shooter Shop, The
Shooters Supply
Shootin' Shack, Inc.
Sight Shop, The
Singletary, Kent
Sipes Gun Shop
Springfield, Inc.
SSK Industries
Steger, James R.
Swampfire Shop, The
Swenson's 45 Shop, A.D.
300 Gunsmith Service, Inc.
Ten-Ring Precision, Inc.
Thompson, Randall
Thurston Sports, Inc.
Tom's Gun Repair
Vic's Gun Refinishing
Volquartsen Custom Ltd.
Walker Arms Co., Inc.
Walters Industries
Wardell Precision Handguns Ltd.
Weigand Combat Handguns, Inc.
Wessinger Custom Guns & Engraving
Whitestone Lumber Corp.
Wichita Arms, Inc.
Williams Gun Sight Co.
Williamson Precision Gunsmithing
Wilson Combat

REBORING AND RERIFLING

Flaig's
H&S Liner Service
Ivanoff, Thomas G.
Jackalope Gun Shop
K-D, Inc.
Kopp, Terry K.
LaBounty Precision Reboring
Matco, Inc.
Pence Precision Barrels
Redman's Rifling & Reboring
Rice, Keith

Ridgetop Sporting Goods
Shaw, Inc., E.R.
Siegrist Gun Shop
Simmons Gun Repair, Inc.
300 Gunsmith Service, Inc.
Tom's Gun Repair
Van Patten, J.W.
West, Robert G.
White Rock Tool & Die
Zufall, Joseph F.

RELOADING TOOLS AND ACCESSORIES

Action Bullets, Inc.
Advance Car Mover Co., Rowell Div.
American Products Co.
Ames Metal Products
•Ammo Load, Inc.
Anderson Manufacturing Co., Inc.
Arms Corporation of the Philippines
Atlantic Rose, Inc.
Bald Eagle Precision Machine Co.
Ballisti-Cast, Inc.
Bear Reloaders
Belltown, Ltd.
Ben's Machines
Berry's Mfg. Inc.
Birchwood Casey
Blue Ridge Machinery & Tools, Inc.
Brass-Tech Industries
Break-Free, Inc.
Briganti & Co., A.
Brobst, Jim
•Brown Co., E. Arthur
BRP, Inc. High Performance Cast Bullets
Bruno Shooters Supply
Brynin, Milton
B-Square Co., Inc.
Buck Stix—SOS Products Co.
Buffalo Arms
Bull Mountain Rifle Co.
Bullet Swaging Supply, Inc.
Bullseye Bullets
C&D Special Products
•Camdex, Inc.
Canyon Cartridge Corp.
Carbide Die & Mfg. Co., Inc.

Case Sorting System
CFVentures
•C-H Tool & Die Corp.
Chem-Pak, Inc.
CheVron Case Master
Clark Custom Guns, Inc.
Claybuster Wads & Harvester Bullets
Clymer Manufacturing Co., Inc.
Coats, Mrs. Lester
Colorado Shooter's Supply
CONKKO
Cook Engineering Service
•Corbin, Inc.
Crouse's Country Cover
Custom Products, Neil A. Jones
Davis, Don
Davis Products, Mike
D.C.C. Enterprises
Denver Bullets, Inc.
•Denver Instrument Co.
Dever Co., Jack
Dewey Mfg. Co., Inc., J.
•Dillon Precision Prods., Inc.
Dropkick
Dutchman's Firearms, Inc., The
E&L Mfg., Inc.
Eagan, Donald V.
Eezox, Inc.
Engineered Accessories
Enguix Import-Export
Essex Metals
•4-D Custom Die Co.
F&A Inc.
Federal Cartridge Co.

•**See page 285 for Warranty Service Center Addresses**

Federated-Fry
Feken, Dennis
Ferguson, Bill
First, Inc., Jack
Fitz Pistol Grip Co.
Flambeau Products Corp.
Forgett Jr., Valmore J.
Forgreens Tool Mfg., Inc.
•Forster Products
•Fremont Tool Works
Fry Metals
Fusilier Bullets
G&C Bullet Co., Inc.
GAR
Goddard, Allen
GOEX, Inc.
Gozon Corp., U.S.A.
Graphics Direct
Graves Co.
Green, Arthur S.
Greenwood Precision
Grizzly Bullets
Hanned Line, The
Hanned Precision
Harrell's Precision
Harris Enterprises
Harrison Bullets
Haydon Shooters' Supply, Russ
Heidenstrom Bullets
Hensley & Gibbs
Hirtenberger Aktiengesellschaft
Hobson Precision Mfg. Co.
Hoch Custom Bullet Moulds
Hoehn Sales, Inc.
Hoelscher, Virgil
•Hollywood Engineering
Hondo Industries
•Hornady Mfg. Co.
Howell Machine
•Huntington Die Specialties
IMI Services USA, Inc.
INTEC International, Inc.
Iosso Products
Javelina Lube Products
JGS Precision Tool Mfg.
JLK Bullets
Jonad Corp.
Jones Custom Products, Neil A.
Jones Moulds, Paul
•K&M Services
K&S Mfg. Inc.
Kapro Mfg. Co., Inc.
King & Co.
KLA Enterprises
Kleen-Bore, Inc.
Lane Bullets, Inc.
LBT
•Lee Precision, Inc.
Legend Products Corp.
Liberty Metals
Littleton, J.F.
Lomont Precision Bullets
Lortone, Inc.
Loweth, Richard
Luch Metal Merchants, Barbara
Lyman Instant Targets, Inc.
•Lyman Products Corp.
M&D Munitions Ltd.
MA Systems
•Magma Engineering Co.
MarMik Inc.
Marquart Precision Co., Inc.
Master Class Bullets
Match Prep
McKillen & Heyer, Inc.
MCRW Associates Shooting Supplies
Midway Arms, Inc.
Miller Engineering
MI-TE Bullets
MKL Service Co.
MMP
Mt. Baldy Bullet Co.
MTM Molded Products Co., Inc.
Naval Ordnance Works
Necromancer Industries, Inc.
NEI Handtools, Inc.

Niemi Engineering, W.B.
North Devon Firearms Services
Old West Bullet Moulds
•Old Western Scrounger, Inc.
Omark Industries
Paco's
Peerless Alloy, Inc.
Pend Oreille Sport Shop
Petro-Explo, Inc.
Pinetree Bullets
Plum City Ballistic Range
Policlips North America
Pomeroy, Robert
Powder Valley Services
Precision Castings & Equipment, Inc.
•Precision Reloading, Inc.
Prime Reloading
Prolix® Lubricants
Pro-Shot Products, Inc.
Protector Mfg. Co., Inc., The
Rapine Bullet Mould Mfg. Co.
Raytech
•RCBS
•Redding Reloading Equipment
R.E.I.
Reloading Specialties, Inc.
Rice, Keith
Riebe Co., W.J.
RIG Products
R.I.S. Co., Inc.
Roberts Products
Rochester Lead Works, Inc.
Rooster Laboratories
Rorschach Precision Products
Rosenthal, Brad and Sallie
SAECO
Sandia Die & Cartridge Co.
Saunders Gun & Machine Shop
Saville Iron Co.
Scharch Mfg., Inc.
Scot Powder Co. of Ohio, Inc.
Scott, Dwight
Seebeck Assoc., R.E.
Sierra Specialty Prod. Co.
Silhouette, The
Silver Eagle Machining
Simmons, Jerry
Sinclair International, Inc.
Skip's Machine
S.L.A.P. Industries
Small Custom Mould & Bullet Co.
SOS Products Co.
Spence, George W.
Spencer's Custom Guns
Sport Flite Manufacturing Co.
Sportsman Supply Co.
•Stalwart Corp.
•Star Machine Works
Stillwell, Robert
Stoney Point Products, Inc.
Talon Mfg. Co., Inc.
Tamarack Products, Inc.
Taracorp Industries
TCCI
TCSR
TDP Industries, Inc.
Tetra Gun Lubricants
Thompson Bullet Lube Co.
Timber Heirloom Products
TMI Products
TR Metals Corp.
Trammco, Inc.
Trophy Bonded Bullets, Inc.
Tru-Square Metal Prods., Inc.
TTM
Tyler Scott, Inc.
Varner's Service
Vega Tool Co.
VibraShine, Inc.
Vibra-Tek Co.
Vihtavuori Oy
Vitt/Boos
Von Minden Gunsmithing Services
Walters, John
Webster Scale Mfg. Co.
Welsh, Bud

Werner, Carl
Westfield Engineering
White Rock Tool & Die
Whitetail Design & Engineering Ltd.
Widener's Reloading &
  Shooting Supply

•William's Gun Shop, Ben
Wilson, Inc., L.E.
Wise Guns, Dale
Wolf's Western Traders
Yesteryear Armory & Supply
Young Country Arms

RESTS—BENCH, PORTABLE—AND ACCESSORIES

Accuright
Adaptive Technology
Adventure 16, Inc.
Armor Metal Products
Aspen Outdoors, Inc.
Bald Eagle Precision Machine Co.
Bartlett Engineering
Browning Arms Co.
B-Square Co., Inc.
Bull Mountain Rifle Co.
Canons Delcour
Chem-Pak, Inc.
Clift Mfg., L.R.
Clift Welding Supply
Decker Shooting Products
Desert Mountain Mfg.
F&A Inc.
Greenwood Precision
Harris Engineering, Inc.
Hidalgo, Tony
Hoelscher, Virgil
Hoppe's Div.
J&J Sales

Kolpin Mfg., Inc.
Kramer Designs
Midway Arms, Inc.
Millett Sights
MJM Manufacturing
MTM Molded Products Co., Inc.
Outdoor Connection, Inc., The
Outers Laboratories
PAST Sporting Goods, Inc.
Pease Accuracy, Bob
Penguin Industries, Inc.
Portus, Robert
Protektor Model
Ransom International Corp
Saville Iron Co.
Slug Group, Inc.
Stoney Point Products, Inc.
Thompson Target Technology
T.H.U. Enterprises, Inc.
Tonoloway Tack Drivers
Varner's Service
Wichita Arms, Inc.
Zanotti Armor, Inc.

SCOPES, MOUNTS, ACCESSORIES, OPTICAL EQUIPMENT

ADCO International
•Aimpoint, Inc.
•Aimtech Mount Systems
•Anderson Manufacturing Co., Inc.
Anschutz GmbH
Baer Custom, Inc., Les
Bushnell Sports Optics Worldwide
•Brown Co., E. Arthur
Brownells, Inc.
•Browning Arms Co.
Brunton U.S.A.
•B-Square Co., Inc.
•Burris Co., Inc.
•Bushnell
Butler Creek Corp.
Celestron International
Center Lock Scope Rings
Clark Custom Guns, Inc.
Clearview Mfg. Co., Inc.
Conetrol Scope Mounts
CRDC Laser Systems Group
Emerging Technologies, Inc.
Great Lakes Airguns
•Hammerli USA
Ironsighter Co.
Jones, J.D.
•Kowa Optimed, Inc.
Kris Mounts
Kwik Mount Corp.
Kwik-Site Co.
•L&S Technologies, Inc.
L.A.R. Mfg., Inc.
•Laser Devices, Inc.
•Laseraim
LaserMax
•Leica USA, Inc.
•Leupold & Stevens, Inc.

Mac's .45 Shop
Maxi-Mount
Michaels of Oregon Co.
Millett Sights
•Mirador Optical Corp.
•Nikon, Inc.
Parsons Optical Mfg. Co.
•Pentax Corp.
•Precision Sport Optics
•Ram-Line, Inc.
Ranch Products
•Ranging, Inc.
•Redfield, Inc.
S&K Mfg. Co.
ScopLevel
Seattle Binocular & Scope
  Repair Co.
Sightron, Inc.
•Simmons Outdoor Corp.
•Springfield, Inc.
SSK Industries
Stoeger Industries
SwaroSports, Inc.
Swarovski Optik North America Ltd.
•Swift Instruments, Inc.
Talley, Dave
•Tasco Sales, Inc.
Tele-Optics
•Thompson/Center Arms
•Trijicon, Inc.
Uncle Mike's
Volquartsen Custom Ltd.
Warne Manufacturing Co.
Weigand Combat Handguns, Inc.
Wideview Scope Mount Corp.
•Williams Gun Sight Co.
Zeiss Optical, Carl

SHOOTING/TRAINING SCHOOLS

Accuracy Gun Shop
Alpine Precision Gunsmithing &
  Indoor Shooting Range
American Small Arms Academy
Auto Arms
Bob's Tactical Indoor Shooting
  Range & Gun Shop
Chapman Academy of Practical
  Shooting
Chelsea Gun Club of New York
  City, Inc.

Clark Custom Guns, Inc.
CQB Training
Daisy Mfg. Co.
Defense Training International, Inc.
Dowtin Gunworks
Executive Protection Institute
Farnam, John
Firearm Training Center, The
Firearms Academy of Seattle
G.H. Enterprises Ltd.
Gonzalez Guns, Ramon B.

•See page 285s for Warranty Service Center Addresses

PRODUCT DIRECTORY

Gunsite Training Center
Hank's Gun Shop
I.S.S.
Jensen's Custom Ammunition
Jensen's Firearms Acadamy
J.P. Enterprises, Inc.
Lethal Force Institute
McMurdo, Lynn
Mendez, John A.
Middlebrooks Custom Shop
Modern Gun School
Nevada Pistol Academy Inc.
North American Shooting
  Systems
North Mountain Pines Training
  Center
Pacific Pistolcraft
Passive Bullet Traps, Inc.
Performance Specialists

Quigley's Personal Protection
  Strategies, Paxton
River Road Sporting Clays
Robar Co.'s, Inc., The
SAFE
Savage Range Systems, Inc.
Shooter's World
Shooting Gallery, The
Shotgun Shop, The
Smith & Wesson
Specialty Gunsmithing
Starlight Training Center, Inc.
300 Gunsmith Service, Inc.
Tactical Defense Institute
Thunder Ranch
Western Missouri Shooters
  Alliance
Yankee Gunsmith
Yavapai Firearms Academy Ltd.

SIGHTS, METALLIC

Baer Custom, Inc., Les
Bob's Gun Shop
Bo-Mar Tool & Mfg. Co.
Bowen Classic Arms Corp.
Brown Co., E. Arthur
Brown Products, Inc., Ed
C-More Systems
Heinie Specialty Products
Hesco-Meprolight
Innovative Weaponry, Inc.
Lee's Red Ramps
Lyman Products Corp.

Mac's .45 Shop
Marble Arms
Meprolight
Merit Corp.
Millett Sights
MMC
Novak's Inc.
Pachmayr Ltd.
Robar Co.'s, Inc., The
RPM
Wichita Arms, Inc.
Williams Gun Sight Co.

TARGETS AND BULLET TRAPS

Action Target, Inc.
American Target
American Whitetail Target Systems
A-Tech Corp.
Barsotti, Bruce

Beomat of America Inc.
Birchwood Casey
Blue and Gray Products, Inc.
Bull-X, Inc.
Caswell International Corp.

Champion Target Co.
Champion's Choice, Inc.
Cunningham Co., Eaton
Dapkus Co., Inc., J.G.
Datumtech Corp.
Dayson Arms Ltd.
D.C.C. Enterprises
Detroit-Armor Corp.
Diamond Mfg. Co.
Erickson's Mfg., Inc., C.W.
Freeman Animal Targets
G.H. Enterprises Ltd.
Gun Parts Corp., The
Innovision Enterprises
Jackalope Gun Shop
JWH: Software
Kennebec Journal
Kleen-Bore, Inc.
Littler Sales Co.
Lyman Instant Targets, Inc.
Lyman Products Corp.
M&D Munitions Ltd.
MSR Targets
National Target Co.

N.B.B., Inc.
North American Shooting
  Systems
Nu-Teck
Outers Laboratories, Div. of Blount
Ox-Yoke Originals, Inc.
Passive Bullet Traps, Inc.
Pease Accuracy, Bob
PlumFire Press, Inc.
Red Star Target Co.
Remington Arms Co., Inc.
River Road Sporting Clays
Rockwood Corp., Speedwell Div.
Rocky Mountain Target Co.
Savage Range Systems, Inc.
Schaefer Shooting Sports
Seligman Shooting Products
Shooters Supply
Shoot-N-C Targets
Thompson Target Technology
World of Targets
X-Spand Target Systems
Z's Metal Targets & Frames
Zriny's Metal Targets

TAXIDERMY

African Import Co.
Jonas Appraisers—Taxidermy
  Animals, Jack
Keith's Custom Taxidermy

Kulis Freeze Dry Taxidermy
Parker, Mark D.
World Trek, Inc.

TRIGGERS, RELATED EQUIPMENT

Actions by "T"
B&D Trading Co., Inc.
Baer Custom, Inc., Les
Behlert Precision, Inc.
Bob's Gun Shop
Bond Custom Firearms
Boyds' Gunstock Industries, Inc.

Clark Custom Guns, Inc.
Electronic Trigger Systems, Inc.
Galati International
J.P. Enterprises, Inc.
Master Lock Co.
Timney Mfg., Inc.
Videki

MANUFACTURERS' DIRECTORY

A

A&B Industries, Inc. (See Top-Line USA, Inc.)

A.A. Arms, Inc., 4811 Persimmont Ct., Monroe, NC 28110/704-289-5356, 800-935-1119; FAX: 704-289-5859

Abel Safe & File, Inc., 124 West Locust St., Fairbury, IL 61739/800-346-9280, 815-692-2131; FAX: 815-692-3350

AC Dyna-tite Corp., 155 Kelly St., P.O. Box 0984, Elk Grove Village, IL 60007/847-593-5566; FAX: 847-593-1304

Acadian Ballistic Specialties, P.O. Box 61, Covington, LA 70434

Acculube II, Inc., 4366 Shackleford Rd., Norcross, GA 30093-2912

Accupro Gun Care, 15512-109 Ave., Surrey, BC U3R 7E8, CANADA/604-583-7807

Accuracy Gun Shop, 7818 Wilkerson Ct., San Diego, CA 92111/619-282-8500

Accuracy International, 9115 Trooper Trail, P.O. Box 2019, Bozeman, MT 59715/406-587-7922; FAX: 406-585-9434

Accuracy Unlimited, 7479 S. DePew St., Littleton, CO 80123

Accuracy Unlimited, 16036 N. 49 Ave., Glendale, AZ 85306/602-978-9089; FAX: 602-978-9089

Accurate Arms Co., Inc., 5891 Hwy. 230 West, McEwen, TN 37101/615-729-4207, 800-416-3006; FAX 615-729-4211

Accuright, RR 2 Box 397, Sebeka, MN 56477/218-472-3383

Accu-Tek, 4525 Carter Ct., Chino, CA 91710/909-627-2404; FAX: 909-627-7817

Ace Custom 45's, Inc., 1880$^1/_2$ Upper Turtle Creek Rd., Kerrville, TX 78028/210-257-4290; FAX: 210-257-5724

Action Bullets, Inc., 1811 W. 13th Ave., Denver, CO 80204/303-595-9636; FAX: 303-595-4413

Action Products, Inc., 22 N. Mulberry St., Hagerstown, MD 21740/301-797-1414; FAX: 301-733-2073

Action Target, Inc., P.O. Box 636, Provo, UT 84603/801-377-8033; FAX: 801-377-8096

Actions by "T", Teddy Jacobson, 16315 Redwood Forest Ct., Sugar Land, TX 77478/713-277-4008

AcuSport Corporation, 1 Hunter Place, Bellefontaine, OH 43311-3001/513-593-7010; FAX: 513-592-5625

Ad Hominem, RR 3, Orillia, Ont. L3V 6H3, CANADA/705-689-5303

Adair Custom Shop, Bill, 2886 Westridge, Carrollton, TX 75006

Adams & Son Engravers, John J., 87 Acorn Rd., Dennis, MA 02638/508-385-7971

Adams Jr., John J., 87 Acorn Rd., Dennis, MA 02638/508-385-7971

Adaptive Technology, 939 Barnum Ave, Bridgeport, CT 06609/800-643-6735; FAX: 800-643-6735

ADCO International, 10 Cedar St., Unit 17, Woburn, MA 01801/617-935-1799; FAX: 617-935-1011

Adkins, Luther, 1292 E. McKay Rd., Shelbyville, IN 46176-9353/317-392-3795

Advance Car Mover Co., Rowell Div., P.O. Box 1, 240 N. Depot St., Juneau, WI 53039/414-386-4464; FAX: 414-386-4416

Adventure 16, Inc., 4620 Alvarado Canyon Rd., San Diego, CA 92120/619-283-6314

Adventurer's Outpost, P.O. Box 70, Cottonwood, AZ 86326/800-762-7471; FAX: 602-634-8781

African Import Co., 20 Braunecker Rd., Plymouth, MA 02360/508-746-8552

AFSCO Ammunition, 731 W. Third St., P.O. Box L, Owen, WI 54460/715-229-2516

Ahlman Guns, Rt. 1, Box 20, Morristown, MN 55052/507-685-4243; FAX: 507-685-4247

Ahrends, Kim, Custom Firearms, Box 203, Clarion, IA 50525/515-532-3449; FAX: 515-532-3926

Aimpoint, Inc., 580 Herndon Parkway, Suite 500, Herndon, VA 22070/703-471-6828; FAX: 703-689-0575

Aimtech Mount Systems, P.O. Box 223, 101 Inwood Acres, Thomasville, GA 31799/912-226-4313; FAX: 912-227-0222

Airguns-R-Us, 101 7th Ave., Columbia, TN 38401/615-381-4428; FAX: 615-381-1218

Airrow (See Swivel Machine Works, Inc.)

Ajax Custom Grips, Inc., 9130 Viscount Row, Dallas, TX 75247/214-630-8893; FAX: 214-630-4942

Aker Leather Products, 2248 Main St., Suite 6, Chula Vista, CA 91911/619-423-5182; FAX: 619-423-1363

Alaska Bullet Works, P.O. Box 54, Douglas, AK 99824/907-789-3834

Alco Carrying Cases, 601 W. 26th St., New York, NY 10001/212-675-5820; FAX: 212-691-5935

Aldis Gunsmithing & Shooting Supply, 502 S. Montezuma St., Prescott, AZ 86303/602-445-6723; FAX: 602-445-6763

Alessi Holsters, Inc., 2465 Niagara Falls Blvd., Amherst, NY 14228-3527/716-691-5615

Alfano, Sam, 36180 Henry Gaines Rd., Pearl River, LA 70452/504-863-3364; FAX: 504-863-7715

All Rite Products, Inc., 5752 N. Silverstone Circle, Mountain Green, UT 84050/801-876-3330; 801-876-2216

Allard, Gary, Creek Side Metal & Woodcrafters, Fishers Hill, VA 22626/703-465-3903

Allen Co., Inc., 525 Burbank St., Broomfield, CO 80020/303-469-1857, 800-876-8600; FAX: 303-466-7437

Allen Mfg., 6449 Hodgson Rd., Circle Pines, MN 55014/612-429-8231

Allen, Richard L., 339 Grove Ave., Prescott, AZ 86301/602-778-1237

Alliant Techsystems, Smokeless Powder Group, 200 Valley Rd., Suite 305, Mt. Arlington, NJ 07856/800-276-9337; FAX: 201-770-2528

Alpha 1 Drop Zone, 2121 N. Tyler, Wichita, KS 67212/316-729-0800

Alpha Gunsmith Division, 1629 Via Monserate, Fallbrook, CA 92028/619-723-9279, 619-728-2663

Alpha Precision, Inc., 2765-B Preston Rd. NE, Good Hope, GA 30641/770-267-6163

Alpine's Precision Gunsmithing & Indoor Shooting Range, 2401 Government Way, Coeur d'Alene, ID 83814/208-765-3559; FAX: 208-765-3559

Altamont Co., 901 N. Church St., P.O. Box 309, Thomasboro, IL 61878/217-643-3125, 800-626-5774; FAX: 217-643-7973

Alumna Sport by Dee Zee, 1572 NE 58th Ave., P.O. Box 3090, Des Moines, IA 50316/800-798-9899

AmBr Software Group Ltd., P.O. Box 301, Reisterstown, MD 21136-0301/410-526-4106; FAX: 410-526-7212

American Ammunition, 3545 NW 71st St., Miami FL 33147/305-835-7400; FAX: 305-694-0037

American Arms & Ordnance, Inc., P.O. Box 2691, 1303 S. College Ave., Bryan, TX 77805/409-822-4983

American Arms, Inc., 715 Armour Rd., N. Kansas City, MO 64116/816-474-3161; FAX: 816-474-1225

American Derringer Corp., 127 N. Lacy Dr., Waco, TX 76705/800-642-7817, 817-799-9111; FAX: 817-799-7935

American Display Co., 55 Cromwell St., Providence, RI 02907/401-331-2464; FAX: 401-421-1264

American Gas & Chemical Co., Ltd., 220 Pegasus Ave., Northvale, NJ 07647/201-767-7300

American Gripcraft, 3230 S. Dodge 2, Tucson, AZ 85713/602-790-1222

American Handgunner Magazine, 591 Camino de la Reina, Suite 200, San Diego, CA 92108/619-297-5350; FAX: 619-297-5353

American Pioneer Video, P.O. Box 50049, Bowling Green, KY 42102-2649/800-743-4675

American Products Co., 14729 Spring Valley Road, Morrison, IL 61270/815-772-3336; FAX: 815-772-7921

American Sales & Kirkpatrick, P.O. Box 677, Laredo, TX 78042/210-723-6893; FAX: 210-725-0672

American Security Products Company, 11925 Pacific Ave., Fontana, CA 92337/909-685-9680, 800-421-6142; FAX: 909-685-9685

American Small Arms Academy, P.O. Box 12111, Prescott, AZ 86304/602-778-5623

American Target, 1328 S. Jason St., Denver, CO 80223/303-733-0433; FAX: 303-777-0311

American Whitetail Target Systems, P.O. Box 41, 106 S. Church St., Tennyson, IN 47637/812-567-4527

Americase, P.O. Box 271, 1610 E. Main, Waxahachie, TX 75165/800-880-3629; FAX: 214-937-8373

Ames Metal Products, 4324 S. Western Blvd., Chicago, IL 60609/312-523-3230; FAX: 312-523-3854

Amherst Arms, P.O. Box 1457, Englewood, FL 34295/941-475-2020; FAX: 941-473-1212

Ammo Load, Inc., 1560 E. Edinger, Suite G, Santa Ana, CA 92705/714-558-8858; FAX: 714-569-0319

Amrine's Gun Shop, 937 La Luna, Ojai, CA 93023/805-646-2376

AMT, 6226 Santos Diaz St., Irwindale, CA 91702/818-334-6629; FAX: 818-969-5247

Amtec 2000, Inc., 84 Industrial Rowe, Gardner, MA 01440/508-632-9608; FAX: 508-632-2300

Anderson Manufacturing Co., Inc., 22602 53rd Ave. SE, Bothell, WA 98021/206-481-1858; FAX: 206-481-7839

Anics Firm, Inc., 3 Commerce Park Square, 23200 Chagrin Blvd., Suite 240, Beechwood, OH 44122/216-292-4363, 800-550-1582; FAX: 216-292-2588

Anschutz GmbH, Postfach 1128, D-89001 Ulm, Donau, GERMANY (U.S. importers—Accuracy International; AcuSport Corporation; Champion Shooters' Supply; Champion's Choice; Gunsmithing, Inc.)

Ansen Enterprises, Inc., 1506 W. 228th St., Torrance, CA 90501-5105/310-534-1837; FAX: 310-534-3162

Answer Products Co., 1519 Westbury Drive, Davison, MI 48423/810-653-2911

Anthony and George Ltd., Rt. 1, P.O. Box 45, Evington, VA 24550/804-821-8117

Antique American Firearms (See Carlson, Douglas R.)

Antique Arms Co., 1110 Cleveland Ave., Monett, MO 65708/417-235-6501

Aplan Antiques & Art, James O., HC 80, Box 793-25, Piedmont, SD 57769/605-347-5016

Arco Powder, HC-Rt. 1, P.O. Box 102, County Rd. 357, Mayo, FL 32066/904-294-3882; FAX: 904-294-1498

Arkfeld Mfg. & Dist. Co., Inc., 1230 Monroe Ave., Norfolk, NE 68702-0054/402-371-9430; 800-533-0676

Armament Gunsmithing Co., Inc., 525 Rt. 22, Hillside, NJ 07205/908-686-0960

Armi San Paolo, via Europa 172-A, I-25062 Concesio, 030-2751725 (BS) ITALY

Armite Laboratories, 1845 Randolph St., Los Angeles, CA 90001/213-587-7768; FAX: 213-587-5075

Armor Metal Products, P.O. Box 4609, Helena, MT 59604/406-442-5560

Armory Publications, P.O. Box 4206, Oceanside, CA 92052-4206/619-757-3930; FAX: 619-722-4108

Armoury, Inc., The, Rt. 202, Box 2340, New Preston, CT 06777/203-868-0001

Arms & Armour Press, Ltd., Wellington House, 125 Strand, London WC2R 0BB ENGLAND/0171-420-5555; FAX: 0171-240-7265

Arms Corporation of the Philippines, Bo. Parang Marikina, Metro Manila, PHILIPPINES/632-941-6243, 632-941-6244; FAX: 632-942-0682

Arms, Peripheral Data Systems (See Arms Software)

Arms Software, P.O. Box 1526, Lake Oswego, OR 97035/800-366-5559, 503-697-0533; FAX: 503-697-3337

Arms United Corp., 1018 Cedar St., Niles, MI 49120/616-683-6837

Armscorp USA, Inc., 4424 John Ave., Baltimore, MD 21227/410-247-6200; FAX: 410-247-6205

Armsport, Inc., 3950 NW 49th St., Miami, FL 33142/305-635-7850; FAX: 305-633-2877

Arnold Arms Co., Inc., P.O. Box 1011, Arlington, WA 98223/800-371-1011, 360-435-1011; FAX: 360-435-7304

Aro-Tek, Ltd., 206 Frontage Rd. North, Suite C, Pacific, WA 98047/206-351-2984; FAX: 206-833-4483

Arratoonian, Andy (See Horseshoe Leather Products)

Art Jewel Enterprises Ltd., Eagle Business Ctr., 460 Randy Rd., Carol Stream, IL 60188/708-260-0400

Arundel Arms & Ammunition, Inc., A., 24 Defense St., Annapolis, MD 21401/301-224-8683

Aspen Outdoors, Inc., 1059 W. Market St., York, PA 17404/717-846-0255, 800-677-4780; FAX: 717-845-7447

Astra Sport, S.A., Apartado 3, 48300 Guernica, Espagne, SPAIN/34-4-6250100; FAX: 34-4-6255186 (U.S. importer—E.A.A. Corp.; P.S.M.G. Gun Co.)

A-Tech Corp., P.O. Box 1281, Cottage Grove, OR 97424

Atlantic Mills, Inc., 1325 Washington Ave., Asbury Park, NJ 07712/800-242-7374

Atlantic Rose, Inc., P.O. Box 1305, Union, NJ 07083

Auto Arms, 738 Clearview, San Antonio, TX 78228/512-434-5450

Auto-Ordnance Corp., Williams Lane, West Hurley, NY 12491/914-679-4190; FAX: 914-679-2698

AWC Systems Technology, P.O. Box 41938, Phoenix, AZ 85080-1938/602-780-1050

Aztec International Ltd., P.O. Box 1384, Clarkesville, GA 30523/706-754-7263

B

B&D Trading Co., Inc., 3935 Fair Hill Rd., Fair Oaks, CA 95628/800-334-3790, 916-967-9366; FAX: 916-967-4873

Badger Shooters Supply, Inc., P.O. Box 397, Owen, WI 54460/800-424-9069; FAX: 715-229-2332

Baer Custom, Inc., Les, 29601 34th Ave., Hillsdale, IL 61257/309-658-2716; FAX: 309-658-2610

Bagmaster Mfg., Inc., 2731 Sutton Ave., St. Louis, MO 63143/314-781-8002; FAX: 314-781-3363

Bain & Davis, Inc., 307 E. Valley Blvd., San Gabriel, CA 91776-3522/818-573-4241, 213-283-7449

Baker's Leather Goods, Roy, P.O. Box 893, Magnolia, AR 71753/501-234-0344

Bald Eagle Precision Machine Co., 101-K Allison St., Lock Haven, PA 17745/717-748-6772; FAX: 717-748-4443

Ballard Built, P.O. Box 1443, Kingsville, TX 78364/512-592-0853

Ballistic Engineering & Software, Inc., 185 N. Park Blvd., Suite 330, Lake Orion, MI 48362/313-391-1074

Ballistic Products, Inc., 20015 75th Ave. North, Hamel, MN 55340-9456/612-494-9237; FAX: 612-494-9236

Ballistic Program Co., Inc., The, 2417 N. Patterson St., Thomasville, GA 31792/912-228-5739, 800-368-0835

Ballistic Research, 1108 W. May Ave., McHenry, IL 60050/815-385-0037

Ballistica Maximus North, 107 College Park Plaza, Johnstown, PA 15904/814-266-8380

Ballisti-Cast, Inc., Box 383, Parshall, ND 58770/701-862-3324; FAX: 701-862-3331

Bandcor Industries, Div. of Man-Sew Corp., 6108 Sherwin Dr., Port Richey, FL 34668/813-848-0432

Bang-Bang Boutique (See Holster Shop, The)

Banks, Ed, 2762 Hwy. 41 N., Ft. Valley, GA 31030/912-987-4665

Bansner's Gunsmithing Specialties, 261 East Main St. Box VH, Adamstown, PA 19501/800-368-2379; FAX: 717-484-0523

Barami Corp., 6689 Orchard Lake Rd. No. 148, West Bloomfield, MI 48322/810-738-0462; FAX: 810-855-4084

Barnes Bullets, Inc., P.O. Box 215, American Fork, UT 84003/801-756-4222, 800-574-9200; FAX: 801-756-2465; WEB: http://www.itsnet.com/home/bbullets

Baron Technology, 62 Spring Hill Rd., Trumbull, CT 06611/203-452-0515; FAX: 203-452-0663

Barraclough, John K., 55 Merit Park Dr., Gardena, CA 90247/310-324-2574

Barsotti, Bruce (See River Road Sporting Clays)

Bar-Sto Precision Machine, 73377 Sullivan Rd., P.O. Box 1838, Twentynine Palms, CA 92277/619-367-2747; FAX: 619-367-2407

Bartlett, Don, P.O. Box 55, Colbert, WA 99005/509-467-5009

Bartlett Engineering, 40 South 200 East, Smithfield, UT 84335-1645/801-563-5910; FAX: 801-563-8416

Bates Engraving, Billy, 2302 Winthrop Dr., Decatur, AL 35603/205-355-3690

Baumannize Custom, 4784 Sunrise Hwy., Bohemia, NY 11716/800-472-4387; FAX: 516-567-0001

Bauska Barrels, 105 9th Ave. W., Kalispell, MT 59901/406-752-7706

Bear Hug Grips, Inc., 17230 County Rd. 338, Buena Vista, CO 81211/800-232-7710

Bear Mountain Gun & Tool, 120 N. Plymouth, New Plymouth, ID 83655/208-278-5221; FAX: 208-278-5221

Bear Reloaders, P.O. Box 1613, Akron, OH 44309-1613/216-920-1811

Beartooth Bullets, P.O. Box 491, Dept. HLD, Dover, ID 83825-0491/208-448-1865

Beauchamp & Son, Inc., 160 Rossiter Rd., P.O. Box 181, Richmond, MA 01254/413-698-3822; FAX: 413-698-3866

Beaver Lodge (See Fellowes, Ted)

Beeline Custom Bullets Limited, P.O. Box 85, Yarmouth, Nova Scotia CANADA B5A 4B1/902-648-3494; FAX: 902-648-0253

Beeman Precision Airguns, 5454 Argosy Dr., Huntington Beach, CA 92649/714-890-4800; FAX: 714-890-4808

Behlert Precision, Inc., P.O. Box 288, 7067 Easton Rd., Pipersville, PA 18947/215-766-8681, 215-766-7301; FAX: 215-766-8681

Beitzinger, George, 116-20 Atlantic Ave., Richmond Hill, NY 11419/718-847-7661

Bell Originals, Inc., Sid, 7776 Shackham Rd., Tully, NY 13159-9333/607-842-6431

Bell Reloading, Inc., 1725 Harlin Lane Rd., Villa Rica, GA 30180

Bellm Contenders, P.O. Box 459, Cleveland, UT 84518/801-653-2530

Belltown, Ltd., 11 Camps Rd., Kent, CT 06757/860-354-5750

Belt MTN Arms, 107 10th Ave. SW, White Sulphur Springs, MT 59645/406-586-4495

Ben's Machines, 1151 S. Cedar Ridge, Duncanville, TX 75137/214-780-1807; FAX: 214-780-0316

Benchmark Guns, 12593 S. Ave. 5 East, Yuma, AZ 85365

Bengtson Arms Co., L., 6345-B E. Akron St., Mesa, AZ 85205/602-981-6375

Benjamin/Sheridan Co., Crossman, Rts. 5 and 20, E. Bloomfield, NY 14443/716-657-6161; FAX: 716-657-5405

Bentley, John, 128-D Watson Dr., Turtle Creek, PA 15145

Beomat of America Inc., 300 Railway Ave., Campbell, CA 95008/408-379-4829

Beretta S.p.A., Pietro, Via Beretta, 18-25063 Gardone V.T. (BS) ITALY/XX39/30-8341.1; FAX: XX39/30-8341.421 (U.S. importer—Beretta U.S.A. Corp.)

Beretta U.S.A. Corp., 17601 Beretta Drive, Accokeek, MD 20607/301-283-2191; FAX: 301-283-0435

Bergman & Williams, 2450 Losee Rd., Suite F, Las Vegas, NV 89030/702-642-1901; FAX: 702-642-1540

Bernardelli S.p.A., Vincenzo, 125 Via Matteotti, P.O. Box 74, Gardone V.T., Brescia ITALY, 25063/39-30-8912851-2-3; FAX: 39-30-8910249

Berry's Bullets, Div. of Berry's Mfg., Inc., 401 N. 3050 E., St. George, UT 84770-9004

Berry's Mfg., Inc., 401 North 3050 East St., St. George, UT 84770/801-634-1682; FAX: 801-634-1683

Bersa S.A., Gonzales Castillo 312, 1704 Ramos Mejia, ARGENTINA/541-656-2377; FAX: 541-656-2093 (U.S. importer—Eagle Imports, Inc.)

Bertram Bullet Co., P.O. Box 313, Seymour, Victoria 3660, AUSTRALIA/61-57-922912; FAX: 61-57-991650

Bestload, Inc., Carl Vancini, P.O. Box 4354, Stamford, CT 06907/203-978-0796; FAX: 203-978-0796

Bianchi International, Inc., 100 Calle Cortez, Temecula, CA 92590/909-676-5621; FAX: 909-676-6777

Biesen, Al, 5021 Rosewood, Spokane, WA 99208/509-328-9340

Biesen, Roger, 5021 W. Rosewood, Spokane, WA 99208/509-328-9340

Big Spring Enterprises "Bore Stores", P.O. Box 1115, Big Spring Rd., Yellville, AR 72687/501-449-5297; FAX: 501-449-4446

Bill's Custom Cases, P.O. Box 2, Dunsmuir, CA 96025/916-235-0177; FAX: 916-235-4959

Bill's Gun Repair, 1007 Burlington St., Mendota, IL 61342/815-539-5786

Billingsley & Brownell, P.O. Box 25, Dayton, WY 82836/307-655-9344

Birchwood Casey, 7900 Fuller Rd., Eden Prairie, MN 55344/800-328-6156, 612-937-7933; FAX: 612-937-7979

Birdsong & Assoc., W.E., 1435 Monterey Rd., Florence, MS 39073-9748/601-366-8270

Black Belt Bullets, Big Bore Express Ltd., 7154 W. State St., Suite 200, Boise, ID 83703

Black Hills Ammunition, Inc., P.O. Box 3090, Rapid City, SD 57709-3090/605-348-5150; FAX: 605-348-9827

Black Hills Shooters Supply, P.O. Box 4220, Rapid City, SD 57709/800-289-2506

Black Sheep Brand, 3220 W. Gentry Parkway, Tyler, TX 75702/903-592-3853; FAX: 903-592-0527

Blackhawk East, Box 2274, Loves Park, IL 61131

Blackhawk West, Box 285, Hiawatha, KS 66434

Blacksmith Corp., 830 N. Road No. 1 E., P.O. Box 1752, Chino Valley, AZ 86323/520-636-4456; FAX: 520-636-4457

BlackStar Accurizing, 11501 Brittmoore Park Drive, Houston, TX 77041/713-849-9999; FAX: 713-849-5445

BlackStar AccuMax Barrels (See BlackStar Accurizing)

BlackStar Barrel Accurizing (See BlackStar Accurizing)

Blacktail Mountain Books, 42 First Ave. W., Kalispell, MT 59901/406-257-5573

Blackwell, W. (See Load From a Disk)

Blair Engraving, J.R., P.O. Box 64, Glenrock, WY 82637/307-436-8115

Blammo Ammo, P.O. Box 1677, Seneca, SC 29679/803-882-1768

Bleile, C. Roger, 5040 Ralph Ave., Cincinnati, OH 45238/513-251-0249

Blocker Holsters, Inc., Ted, Clackamas Business Park Bld. A, 14787 S.E. 82nd Dr./Clackamas, OR 97015/503-557-7757; FAX: 503-557-3771

Blue and Gray Products, Inc. (See Ox-Yoke Originals, Inc.)

Blue Book Publications, Inc., One Appletree Square, Minneapolis, MN 55425/800-877-4867, 612-854-5229; FAX: 612-853-1486

Blue Ridge Machinery & Tools, Inc., P.O. Box 536-GD, Hurricane, WV 25526/800-872-6500; FAX: 304-562-5311

Bob's Gun Shop, P.O. Box 200, Royal, AR 71968/501-767-1970

Bob's Tactical Indoor Shooting Range & Gun Shop, 122 Lafayette Rd., Salisbury, MA 01952/508-465-5561

Boessler, Erich, Am Vogeltal 3, 97702 Munnerstadt, GERMANY/9733-9443

Boggs, Wm., 1816 Riverside Dr. C, Columbus, OH 43212/614-486-6965

Bohemia Arms Co., 17101 Los Modelos, Fountain Valley, CA 92708/619-442-7005; FAX: 619-442-7005

Bo-Mar Tool & Mfg. Co., Rt. 12, Box 405, Longview, TX 75605/903-759-4784; FAX: 903-759-9141

Bond Custom Firearms, 8954 N. Lewis Ln., Bloomington, IN 47408/812-332-4519

Bondini Paolo, Via Sorrento, 345, San Carlo di Cesena, ITALY I-47020/0547 663 240; FAX: 0547 663 780

Bone Engraving, Ralph, 718 N. Atlanta, Owasso, OK 74055/918-272-9745

Boone's Custom Ivory Grips, Inc., 562 Coyote Rd., Brinnon, WA 98320/206-796-4330

Bowen Classic Arms Corp., P.O. Box 67, Louisville, TN 37777/615-984-3583

Boyds' Gunstock Industries, Inc., 3rd & Main, P.O. Box 305, Geddes, SD 57342/605-337-2125; FAX: 605-337-3363

Boyt, 509 Hamilton, P.O. Drawer 668, Iowa Falls, IA 50126/515-648-4626; FAX: 515-648-2385

Brace, Larry D., 771 Blackfoot Ave., Eugene, OR 97404/503-688-1278

Brass Eagle, Inc., 7050A Bramalea Rd., Unit 19, Mississauga, Ont. L4Z 1C7, CANADA/416-848-4844

Brass-Tech Industries, P.O. Box 521-v, Wharton, NJ 07885/201-366-8540

Bratcher, Dan, 311 Belle Air Pl., Carthage, MO 64836/417-358-1518

Brauer Bros. Mfg. Co., 2020 Delman Blvd., St. Louis, MO 63103/314-231-2864; FAX: 314-249-4952

Braun, M., 32, rue Notre-Dame, 2440 LUXEMBURG

Braverman Corp., R.J., 88 Parade Rd., Meridith, NH 03293/800-736-4867

Break-Free, Inc., P.O. Box 25020, Santa Ana, CA 92799/714-953-1900; FAX: 714-953-0402

Bridgers Best, P.O. Box 1410, Berthoud, CO 80513

Briese Bullet Co., Inc., RR1, Box 108, Tappen, ND 58487/701-327-4578; FAX: 701-327-4579

Briganti & Co., A., 475 Rt. 32, Highland Mills, NY 10930/914-928-9573

Briley Mfg., Inc., 1230 Lumpkin, Houston, TX 77043/800-331-5718, 713-932-6995; FAX: 713-932-1043

British Antiques, P.O. Box 7, Latham, NY 12110/518-783-0773

BRNO (See U.S. importers—Bohemia Arms Co.; Magnum Research, Inc.)

Broad Creek Rifle Works, 120 Horsey Ave., Laurel, DE 19956/302-875-5446

Brobst, Jim, 299 Poplar St., Hamburg, PA 19526/215-562-2103

Brockman's Custom Gunsmithing, P.O. Box 357, Gooding, ID 83330/208-934-5050

Broken Gun Ranch, 10739 126 Rd., Spearville, KS 67876/316-385-2587; FAX: 316-385-2597

Brolin Arms, 2755 Thompson Creek Rd., Pomona, CA 91767/909-392-2352; FAX: 909-392-2354

Brooker, Dennis, Rt. 1, Box 12A, Derby, IA 50068/515-533-2103

Brooks Tactical Systems, 279-A Shorewood Ct., Fox Island, WA 98333/800-410-4747; FAX: 206-572-6797

Brown Co., E. Arthur, 3404 Pawnee Dr., Alexandria, MN 56308/612-762-8847

Brown, H.R. (See Silhouette Leathers)

Brown Products, Inc., Ed, Rt. 2, Box 492, Perry, MO 63462/573-565-3261; FAX: 573-565-2791

Brownell Checkering Tools, W.E., 9390 Twin Mountain Circle, San Diego, CA 92126/619-695-2479; FAX: 619-695-2479

Brownells, Inc., 200 S. Front St., Montezuma, IA 50171/515-623-5401; FAX: 515-623-3896

Browning Arms Co. (Gen. Offices), One Browning Place, Morgan, UT 84050/801-876-2711; FAX: 801-876-3331

Browning Arms Co. (Parts & Service), 3005 Arnold Tenbrook Rd., Arnold, MO 63010-9406/314-287-6800; FAX: 314-287-9751

BRP, Inc. High Performance Cast Bullets, 1210 Alexander Rd., Colorado Springs, CO 80909/719-633-0658

Bruno Shooters Supply, 111 N. Wyoming St., Hazleton, PA 18201/717-455-2281; FAX: 717-455-2211

Brunton U.S.A., 620 E. Monroe Ave., Riverton, WY 82501/307-856-6559; FAX: 307-856-1840

Brynin, Milton, P.O. Box 383, Yonkers, NY 10710/914-779-4333

BSA Guns Ltd., Armoury Rd. Small Heath, Birmingham, ENGLAND B11 2PX/011-021-772-8543; FAX: 011-021-773-0845

B-Square Company, Inc., P.O. Box 11281, 2708 St. Louis Ave., Ft. Worth, TX 76110/817-923-0964, 800-433-2909; FAX: 817-926-7012

Bucheimer, J.M., Jumbo Sports Products, 721 N. 20th St., St. Louis, MO 63103/314-241-1020

Buck Stix—SOS Products Co., Box 3, Neenah, WI 54956

Buckhorn Gun Works, 8109 Woodland Dr., Black Hawk, SD 57718/605-787-6472

Buckskin Bullet Co., P.O. Box 1893, Cedar City, UT 84721/801-586-3286

Buffalo Arms, 123 S. Third, Suite 6, Sandpoint, ID 83864/208-263-6953; FAX: 208-265-2096

Bull Mountain Rifle Co., 6327 Golden West Terrace, Billings, MT 59106/406-656-0778

Bullberry Barrel Works, Ltd., 2430 W. Bullberry Ln. 67-5, Hurricane, UT 84737/801-635-9866

Bullet, Inc., 3745 Hiram Alworth Rd., Dallas, GA 30132

Bullet Swaging Supply, Inc., P.O. Box 1056, 303 McMillan Rd, West Monroe, LA 71291/318-387-7257; FAX: 318-387-7779

BulletMakers Workshop, The, RFD 1 Box 1755, Brooks, ME 04921

Bullseye Bullets, 1610 State Road 60, No. 12, Valrico, FL 33594/813-654-6563

Bull-X, Inc., 520 N. Main, Farmer City, IL 61842/309-928-2574, 800-248-3845 orders only; FAX: 309-928-2130

Burgess, Byron, P.O. Box 6853, Los Osos, CA 93412/805-528-1005

Burgess & Son Gunsmiths, R.W., P.O. Box 3364, Warner Robins, GA 31099/912-328-7487

Burris Co., Inc., P.O. Box 1747, 331 E. 8th St., Greeley, CO 80631/970-356-1670; FAX: 970-356-8702

Bushmaster Firearms (See Quality Parts Co./Bushmaster Firearms)

Bushmaster Hunting & Fishing, 451 Alliance Ave., Toronto, Ont. M6N 2J1 CANADA/416-763-4040; FAX: 416-763-0623

Bushnell (See Bausch & Lomb)

Bushwacker Backpack & Supply Co. (See Counter Assault)

Bustani, Leo, P.O. Box 8125, W. Palm Beach, FL 33407/305-622-2710

Butler Creek Corporation, 290 Arden Dr., Belgrade, MT 59714/800-423-8327, 406-388-1356; FAX: 406-388-7204

Butler Enterprises, 834 Oberting Rd., Lawrenceburg, IN 47025/812-537-3584

Butterfield & Butterfield, 220 San Bruno Ave., San Francisco, CA 94103/415-861-7500

Buzztail Brass (See Grayback Wildcats)

B-West Imports, Inc., 2425 N. Huachuca Dr., Tucson, AZ 85745-1201/602-628-1990; FAX: 602-628-3602

C

C3 Systems, 678 Killingly St., Johnston, RI 02919

C&D Special Products (See Claybuster Wads & Harvester Bullets)

Cabela's, 812-13th Ave., Sidney, NE 69160/308-254-6644; FAX: 308-254-6669

Cabinet Mtn. Outfitters Scents & Lures, P.O. Box 766, Plains, MT 59859/406-826-3970

Cache La Poudre Rifleworks, 140 N. College, Ft. Collins, CO 80524/303-482-6913

Calibre Press, Inc., 666 Dundee Rd., Suite 1607, Northbrook, IL 60062-2760/800-323-0037; FAX: 708-498-6869

Calico Light Weapon Systems, 405 E. 19th St., Bakersfield, CA 93305/805-323-1327; FAX: 805-323-7844

California Sights (See Fautheree, Andy)

Camdex, Inc., 2330 Alger, Troy, MI 48083/810-528-2300; FAX: 810-528-0989

Cameron's, 16690 W. 11th Ave., Golden, CO 80401/303-279-7365; FAX: 303-628-5413

Camilli, Lou, 4700 Oahu Dr. NE, Albuquerque, NM 87111/505-293-5259

Campbell, Dick, 20,000 Silver Ranch Rd., Conifer, CO 80433/303-697-0150

Camp-Cap Products, P.O. Box 173, Chesterfield, MO 63006/314-532-4340; FAX: 314-532-4340

Cannon's Guns, Box 1036, 320 Main St., Polson, MT 59860/406-887-2048

Cannon Safe, Inc., 9358 Stephens St., Pico Rivera, CA 90660/310-692-0636, 800-242-1055; FAX: 310-692-7252

Canons Delcour, Rue J.B. Cools, B-4040 Herstal, BELGIUM 32.(0)41.40.61.40; FAX: 32(0)412.40.22.88

Canyon Cartridge Corp., P.O. Box 152, Albertson, NY 11507/FAX: 516-294-8946

Cape Outfitters, 599 County Rd. 206, Cape Girardeau, MO 63701/314-335-4103; FAX: 314-335-1555

Caraville Manufacturing, P.O. Box 4545, Thousand Oaks, CA 91359/805-499-1234

Carbide Checkering Tools (See J&R Engineering)

Carbide Die & Mfg. Co., Inc., 15615 E. Arrow Hwy., Irwindale, CA 91706/818-337-2518

Carlson, Douglas R., Antique American Firearms, P.O. Box 71035, Dept. GD, Des Moines, IA 50325/515-224-6552

Carnahan Bullets, 17645 110th Ave. SE, Renton, WA 98055

Carter's Gun Shop, 225 G St., Penrose, CO 81240/719-372-6240

Carvajal Belts & Holsters, 422 Chestnut, San Antonio, TX 78202/210-222-1634

Cascade Bullet Co., Inc., 2355 South 6th St., Klamath Falls, OR 97601/503-884-9316

Case & Sons Cutlery Co., W.R., Owens Way, Bradford, PA 16701/814-368-4123, 800-523-6350; FAX: 814-768-5369

Cash Mfg. Co., Inc., P.O. Box 130, 201 S. Klein Dr., Waunakee, WI 53597-0130/608-849-5664; FAX: 608-849-5664

Caspian Arms Ltd., 14 North Main St., Hardwick, VT 05843/802-472-6454; FAX: 802-472-6709

Caswell International Corp., 1221 Marshall St. NE, Minneapolis, MN 55413-1055/612-379-2000; FAX: 612-379-2367

Cathey Enterprises, Inc., P.O. Box 2202, Brownwood, TX 76804/915-643-2553; FAX: 915-643-3653

CBC, Avenida Humberto de Campos, 3220, 09400-000 Ribeirao Pires-SP-BRAZIL/55-11-742-7500; FAX: 55-11-459-7385

CCI, Div. of Blount, Inc., Sporting Equipment Div., 2299 Snake River Ave.,, P.O. Box 856/Lewiston, ID 83501/800-627-3640, 208-746-2351; FAX: 208-746-2915

Celestron International, P.O. Box 3578, 2835 Columbia St., Torrance, CA 90503/310-328-9560; FAX: 310-212-5835

Centaur Systems, Inc., 1602 Foothill Rd., Kalispell, MT 59901/406-755-8609; FAX: 406-755-8609

Center Lock Scope Rings, 9901 France Ct., Lakeville, MN 55044/612-461-2114

CenterMark, P.O. Box 4066, Parnassus Station, New Kensington, PA 15068/412-335-1319

Central Specialties Ltd., 1122 Silver Lake Road, Cary, IL 60013/708-639-3900; FAX: 708-639-3972

Century Gun Dist., Inc., 1467 Jason Rd., Greenfield, IN 46140/317-462-4524

Century International Arms, Inc., P.O. Box 714, St. Albans, VT 05478-0714/802-527-1252; FAX: 802-527-0470; WEB: http://www.generation.net/~century

CFVentures, 509 Harvey Dr., Bloomington, IN 47403-1715

C-H Tool & Die Corp. (See 4-D Custom Die Co.)

CHAA, Ltd., P.O. Box 565, Howell, MI 48844/800-677-8737; FAX: 313-894-6930

Chace Leather Products, 507 Alden St., Fall River, MA 02722/508-678-7556; FAX: 508-675-9666

Chadick's Ltd., P.O. Box 100, Terrell, TX 75160/214-563-7577

Chambers Flintlocks Ltd., Jim, Rt. 1, Box 513-A, Candler, NC 28715/704-667-8361

Champion Target Co., 232 Industrial Parkway, Richmond, IN 47374/800-441-4971

Champion's Choice, Inc., 201 International Blvd., LaVergne, TN 37086/615-793-4066; FAX: 615-793-4070

Champlin Firearms, Inc., P.O. Box 3191, Woodring Airport, Enid, OK 73701/405-237-7388; FAX: 405-242-6922

Chapman Academy of Practical Shooting, 4350 Academy Rd., Hallsville, MO 65255/573-696-5544, 573-696-2266

Chapman Manufacturing Co., 471 New Haven Rd., P.O. Box 250, Durham, CT 06422/203-349-9228; FAX: 203-349-0084

Checkmate Refinishing, 370 Champion Dr., Brooksville, FL 34601/904-799-5774

Cheddite France, S.A., 99, Route de Lyon, F-26500 Bourg-les-Valence, FRANCE/33-75-56-4545; FAX: 33-75-56-3587

Chelsea Gun Club of New York City, Inc., 237 Ovington Ave., Apt. D53, Brooklyn, NY 11209/718-836-9422, 718-833-2704

Chem-Pak, Inc., 11 Oates Ave., P.O. Box 1685, Winchester, VA 22604/800-336-9828, 703-667-1341; FAX: 703-722-3993

CheVron Bullets, RR1, Ottawa, IL 61350/815-433-2471

CheVron Case Master (See CheVron Bullets)

Choate Machine & Tool Co., Inc., P.O. Box 218, 116 Lovers Ln., Bald Knob, AR 72010/501-724-6193, 800-972-6390; FAX: 501-724-5873

Chopie Mfg., Inc., 700 Copeland Ave., LaCrosse, WI 54603/608-784-0926

Christie's East, 219 E. 67th St., New York, NY 10021/212-606-0400

Christman Jr., David, 937 Lee Hedrick Rd., Colville, WA 99114/509-684-5686 days; 509-684-3314 evenings

Chronotech, 1655 Siamet Rd. Unit 6, Mississauga, Ont. L4W 1Z4 CANADA/905-625-5200; FAX: 905-625-5190

Chuck's Gun Shop, P.O. Box 597, Waldo, FL 32694/904-468-2264

Churchill, Winston, Twenty Mile Stream Rd., RFD P.O. Box 29B, Proctorsville, VT 05153/802-226-7772

Churchill Glove Co., James, P.O. Box 298, Centralia, WA 98531

Cimarron Arms, P.O. Box 906, Fredericksburg, TX 78624-0906/210-997-9090; FAX: 210-997-0802

C.J. Ballistics, Inc., P.O. Box 132, Acme, WA 98220/206-595-5001

Clark Co., Inc., David, P.O. Box 15054, Worcester, MA 01615-0054/508-756-6216; FAX: 508-753-5827

Clark Custom Guns, Inc., 336 Shootout Lane, Princeton, LA 71067/318-949-9884; FAX: 318-949-9829

Clark Firearms Engraving, P.O. Box 80746, San Marino, CA 91118/818-287-1652

Classic Brass, 14 Grove St., Plympton, MA 02367/FAX: 617-585-5673

Classic Guns, Inc., Frank S. Wood, 3230 Medlock Bridge Rd., Suite 110, Norcross, GA 30092/404-242-7944

Claybuster Wads & Harvester Bullets, 309 Sequoya Dr., Hopkinsville, KY 42240/800-922-6287, 800-284-1746, 502-885-8088; FAX: 502-885-1951

Clearview Mfg. Co., Inc., 413 S. Oakley St., Fordyce, AR 71742/501-352-8557; FAX: 501-352-8557

Clements' Custom Leathercraft, Chas, 1741 Dallas St., Aurora, CO 80010-2018/303-364-0403

Clenzoil Corp., P.O. Box 80226, Sta. C, Canton, OH 44708-0226/330-833-9758; FAX: 330-833-4724

Clerke Co., J.A., P.O. Box 627, Pearblossom, CA 93553-0627/805-945-0713

Clift Mfg., L.R., 3821 Hammonton Rd., Marysville, CA 95901/916-755-3390; FAX: 916-755-3393

Clift Welding Supply & Cases, 1332-A Colusa Hwy., Yuba City, CA 95993/916-755-3390; FAX: 916-755-3393

Clymer Manufacturing Co., Inc., 1645 W. Hamlin Rd., Rochester Hills, MI 48309-1530/810-853-5555, 810-853-5627; FAX: 810-853-1530

C-More Systems, P.O. Box 1750, 7553 Gary Rd., Manassas, VA 22110/703-361-2663; FAX: 703-361-5881

Coats, Mrs. Lester, 300 Luman Rd., Space 125, Phoenix, OR 97535/503-535-1611

Cobra Gunskin, 133-30 32nd Ave., Flushing, NY 11354/718-762-8181; FAX: 718-762-0890

Cobra Sport s.r.l., Via Caduti Nei Lager No. 1, 56020 San Romano, Montopoli v/Arno (Pi), ITALY/0039-571-450490; FAX: 0039-571-450492

Cogar's Gunsmithing, P.O. Box 755, Houghton Lake, MI 48629/517-422-4591

Cole's Gun Works, Old Bank Building, Rt. 4, Box 250, Moyock, NC 27958/919-435-2345

Cole-Grip, 16135 Cohasset St., Van Nuys, CA 91406/818-782-4424

Collings, Ronald, 1006 Cielta Linda, Vista, CA 92083

Colonial Arms, Inc., P.O. Box 636, Selma, AL 36702-0636/334-872-9455; FAX: 334-872-9540

Colonial Repair, P.O. Box 372, Hyde Park, MA 02136-9998/617-469-4951

Colorado Gunsmithing Academy Lamar, 27533 Highway 287 South, Lamar, CO 81052/719-336-4099

Colorado School of Trades, 1575 Hoyt St., Lakewood, CO 80215/800-234-4594; FAX: 303-233-4723

Colorado Shooter's Supply, 1163 W. Paradise Way, Fruita, CO 81521/303-858-9191

Colorado Sutlers Arsenal (See Cumberland States Arsenal)

Colt Blackpowder Arms Co., 5 Centre Market Place, New York, NY 10013/212-925-2159; FAX: 212-966-4986

Colt's Mfg. Co., Inc., P.O. Box 1868, Hartford, CT 06144-1868/800-962-COLT, 203-236-6311; FAX: 203-244-1449

Combat Military Ordnance Ltd., 3900 Hopkins St., Savannah, GA 31405/912-238-1900; FAX: 912-236-7570

Competition Electronics, Inc., 3469 Precision Dr., Rockford, IL 61109/815-874-8001; FAX: 815-874-8181

Competitor Corp., Inc., Appleton Business Center, 30 Tricnit Road, Unit 16, New Ipswich, NH 03071-0508/603-878-3891; FAX: 603-878-3950

Conetrol Scope Mounts, 10225 Hwy. 123 S., Seguin, TX 78155/210-379-3030, 800-CONETROL; FAX: 210-379-3030

CONKKO, P.O. Box 40, Broomall, PA 19008/215-356-0711

Cook Engineering Service, 891 Highbury Rd., Vermont VICT 3133 AUSTRALIA

Coonan Arms (JS Worldwide DBA), 1745 Hwy. 36 E., Maplewood, MN 55109/612-777-3156; FAX: 612-777-3683

Cooper-Woodward, 3800 Pelican Rd., Helena, MT 59601/406-458-3800

Corbin, Inc., 600 Industrial Circle, P.O. Box 2659, White City, OR 97503/541-826-5211; FAX: 541-826-8669

Cor-Bon Bullet & Ammo Co., 1311 Industry Rd., Sturgis, SD 57785/800-626-7266; FAX: 800-923-2666

Corkys Gun Clinic, 4401 Hot Springs Dr., Greeley, CO 80634-9226/970-330-0516

Corry, John, 861 Princeton Ct., Neshanic Station, NJ 08853/908-369-8019

Costa, David, Island Pond Gun Shop, P.O. Box 428, Cross St., Island Pond, VT 05846/802-723-4546

Counter Assault, Box 4721, Missoula, MT 59806/406-728-6241; FAX: 406-728-8800

Country Armourer, The, P.O. Box .308, Ashby, MA 01431-0308/508-827-6797; FAX: 508-827-4845

Cousin Bob's Mountain Products, 7119 Ohio River Blvd., Ben Avon, PA 15202/412-766-5114; FAX: 412-766-5114

CQB Training, P.O. Box 1739, Manchester, MO 63011

Craftguard, 3624 Logan Ave., Waterloo, IA 50703/319-232-2959; FAX: 319-234-0804

Craig Custom Ltd., Research & Development, 629 E. 10th, Hutchinson, KS 67501/316-669-0601

Crandall Tool & Machine Co., 19163 21 Mile Rd., Tustin, MI 49688/616-829-4430

Crane & Crane Ltd., 105 N. Edison Way 6, Reno, NV 89502-2355/702-856-1516; FAX: 702-856-1616

Crawford Co., Inc., R.M., P.O. Box 277, Everett, PA 15537/814-652-6536; FAX: 814-652-9526

CRDC Laser Systems Group, 3972 Barranca Parkway, Ste. J-484, Irvine, CA 92714/714-586-1295; FAX: 714-831-4823

Creative Cartridge Co., 56 Morgan Rd., Canton, CT 06019/203-693-2529

Creedmoor Sports, Inc., P.O. Box 1040, Oceanside, CA 92051/619-757-5529

Creek Side Metal & Woodcrafters (See Allard, Gary)

Crit'R Call, Box 999G, La Porte, CO 80535/970-484-2768; FAX: 970-484-0807

Crosman Airguns, Rts. 5 and 20, E. Bloomfield, NY 14443/716-657-6161; FAX: 716-657-5405

Crosman Products of Canada Ltd., 1173 N. Service Rd. West, Oakville, Ontario, L6M 2V9 CANADA/905-827-1822

Crouse's Country Cover, P.O. Box 160, Storrs, CT 06268/860-423-8736

Cullity Restoration, Daniel, 209 Old County Rd., East Sandwich, MA 02537/508-888-1147

Cumberland Arms, 514 Shafer Road, Manchester, TN 37355/800-797-8414

Cumberland Knife & Gun Works, 5661 Bragg Blvd., Fayetteville, NC 28303/919-867-0009

Cumberland States Arsenal, 1124 Palmyra Road, Clarksville, TN 37040

Cummings Bullets, 1417 Esperanza Way, Escondido, CA 92027

Cunningham Co., Eaton, 607 Superior St., Kansas City, MO 64106/816-842-2600

Cupp, Alana, Custom Engraver, P.O. Box 207, Annabella, UT 84711/801-896-4834

Curtis Custom Shop, RR1, Box 193A, Wallingford, KY 41093/703-659-4265

Curtis Gun Shop, Dept. ST, 119 W. College, Bozeman, MT 59715/406-587-4934

Custom Checkering Service, Kathy Forster, 2124 SE Yamhill St., Portland, OR 97214/503-236-5874

Custom Chronograph, Inc., 5305 Reese Hill Rd., Sumas, WA 98295/360-988-7801

Custom Firearms (See Ahrends, Kim)

Custom Gun Products, 5021 W. Rosewood, Spokane, WA 99208/509-328-9340

Custom Gunsmiths, 4303 Friar Lane, Colorado Springs, CO 80907/719-599-3366

Custom Products (See Jones Custom Products, Neil A.)

Custom Tackle and Ammo, P.O. Box 1886, Farmington, NM 87499/505-632-3539

Cutsinger Bench Rest Bullets, RR 8, Box 161-A, Shelbyville, IN 46176/317-729-5360

CVA, 5988 Peachtree Corners East, Norcross, GA 30071/800-251-9412; FAX: 404-242-8546

Cylinder & Slide, Inc., William R. Laughridge, 245 E. 4th St., Fremont, NE 68025/402-721-4277; FAX: 402-721-0263

CZ (See U.S. importer—Magnum Research, Inc.)

D

D&D Gunsmiths, Ltd., 363 E. Elmwood, Troy, MI 48083/810-583-1512; FAX: 810-583-1524

D&H Precision Tooling, 7522 Barnard Mill Rd., Ringwood, IL 60072/815-653-4011

D&H Prods. Co., Inc., 465 Denny Rd., Valencia, PA 16059/412-898-2840, 800-776-0281; FAX: 412-898-2013

D&J Bullet Co. & Custom Gun Shop, Inc., 426 Ferry St., Russell, KY 41169/606-836-2663; FAX: 606-836-2663

D&L Industries (See D.J. Marketing)

D&L Sports, P.O. Box 651, Gillette, WY 82717/307-686-4008

Dade Screw Machine Products, 2319 NW 7th Ave., Miami, FL 33127/305-573-5050

Daewoo Precision Industries Ltd., 34-3 Yeoeuido-Dong, Yeongdeungoo-GU, 15th, Fl./Seoul, KOREA (U.S. importer—Nationwide Sports Distributors)

Daisy Mfg. Co., P.O. Box 220, Rogers, AR 72757/501-636-1200; FAX: 501-636-1601

Dakota Arms, Inc., HC 55, Box 326, Sturgis, SD 57785/605-347-4686; FAX: 605-347-4459

Dan's Whetstone Co., Inc., 130 Timbs Place, Hot Springs, AR 71913/501-767-1616; FAX: 501-767-9598

Dangler, Homer L., Box 254, Addison, MI 49220/517-547-6745

Dapkus Co., Inc., J.G., Commerce Circle, P.O. Box 293, Durham, CT 06422

Dara-Nes, Inc. (See Nesci Enterprises, Inc.)

Data Tech Software Systems, 19312 East Eldorado Drive, Aurora, CO 80013

Datumtech Corp., 2275 Wehrle Dr., Buffalo, NY 14221

Davidson, Jere, Rt. 1, Box 132, Rustburg, VA 24588/804-821-3637

Davis, Don, 1619 Heights, Katy, TX 77493/713-391-3090

Davis Co., R.E., 3450 Pleasantville NE, Pleasantville, OH 43148/614-654-9990

Davis Industries, 15150 Sierra Bonita Ln., Chino, CA 91710/909-597-4726; FAX: 909-393-9771

Davis Leather Co., G. Wm., 3990 Valley Blvd., Unit D, Walnut, CA 91789/909-598-5620

Davis Products, Mike, 643 Loop Dr., Moses Lake, WA 98837/509-765-6178, 509-766-7281 orders only

Davis Service Center, Bill, 7221 Florin Mall Dr., Sacramento, CA 95823/916-393-4867

Day & Sons, Inc., Leonard, P.O. Box 122, Flagg Hill Rd., Heath, MA 01346/413-337-8369

Dayson Arms Ltd., P.O. Box 532, Vincennes, IN 47591/812-882-8680; FAX: 812-882-8446

Dayton Traister, 4778 N. Monkey Hill Rd., P.O. Box 593, Oak Harbor, WA 98277/206-679-4657; FAX:206-675-1114

DBI Books, Division of Krause Publications, 4092 Commercial Ave., Northbrook, IL 60062/847-272-6310; FAX: 847-272-2051; For consumer orders, see Krause Publications

D.C.C. Enterprises, 259 Wynburn Ave., Athens, GA 30601

Dead Eye's Sport Center, RD 1, Box 147B, Shickshinny, PA 18655/717-256-7432

Decker Shooting Products, 1729 Laguna Ave., Schofield, WI 54476/715-359-5873

Defense Training International, Inc., 749 S. Lemay, Ste. A3-337, Ft. Collins, CO 80524/303-482-2520; FAX: 303-482-0548

deHaas Barrels, RR 3, Box 77, Ridgeway, MO 64481/816-872-6308

Del Rey Products, P.O. Box 91561, Los Angeles, CA 90009/213-823-0494

Delhi Gun House, 1374 Kashmere Gate, Delhi, INDIA 110 006/(011)237375 239116; FAX: 91-11-2917344

Delorge, Ed, 2231 Hwy. 308, Thibodaux, LA 70301/504-447-1633

Delta Arms Ltd., P.O. Box 1000, Delta, VT 84624-1000

Delta Frangible Ammunition, LLC, 1111 Jefferson Davis Hwy., Suite 508, Arlington, VA 22202/703-416-4928; FAX: 703-416-4934

Dem-Bart Checkering Tools, Inc., 6807 Bickford Ave., Old Hwy. 2, Snohomish, WA 98290/360-568-7356; FAX: 360-568-1798

Denver Bullets, Inc., 1811 W. 13th Ave., Denver, CO 80204/303-893-3146; FAX: 303-893-9161

Denver Instrument Co., 6542 Fig St., Arvada, CO 80004/800-321-1135, 303-431-7255; FAX: 303-423-4831

DeSantis Holster & Leather Goods, Inc., P.O. Box 2039, 149 Denton Ave., New Hyde Park, NY 11040-0701/516-354-8000; FAX: 516-354-7501

Desert Industries, Inc., P.O. Box 93443, Las Vegas, NV 89193-3443/702-597-1066; FAX: 702-871-9452

Desert Mountain Mfg., P.O. Box 2767, Columbia Falls, MT 59912/800-477-0762, 406-892-7772; FAX: 406-892-7772

Desquesnes, Gerald (See Napoleon Bonaparte, Inc.)

Detroit-Armor Corp., 720 Industrial Dr. No. 112, Cary, IL 60013/708-639-7666; FAX: 708-639-7694

Dever Co., Jack, 8590 NW 90, Oklahoma City, OK 73132/405-721-6393

Dewey Mfg. Co., Inc., J., P.O. Box 2014, Southbury, CT 06488/203-264-3064; FAX: 203-262-6907

DGR Custom Rifles, RR1, Box 8A, Tappen, ND 58487/701-327-8135

DGS, Inc., Dale A. Storey, 1117 E. 12th, Casper, WY 82601/307-237-2414

Diamond Mfg. Co., P.O. Box 174, Wyoming, PA 18644/800-233-9601

Diamondback Supply, 2431 Juan Tabo, Suite 163, Albuquerque, NM 87112/505-237-0068

Diana (See U.S. importer—Dynamit Nobel-RWS, Inc.)

Dibble, Derek A., 555 John Downey Dr., New Britain, CT 06051/203-224-2630

Dietz Gun Shop & Range, Inc., 421 Range Rd., New Braunfels, TX 78132/210-885-4662

Dilliott Gunsmithing, Inc., 657 Scarlett Rd., Dandridge, TN 37725/615-397-9204

Dillon Precision Products, Inc., 8009 East Dillon's Way, Scottsdale, AZ 85260/602-948-8009, 800-762-3845; FAX: 602-998-2786

Dixie Gun Works, Inc., Hwy. 51 South, Union City, TN 38261/901-885-0561, order 800-238-6785; FAX: 901-885-0440

Dixon Muzzleloading Shop, Inc., RD 1, Box 175, Kempton, PA 19529/610-756-6271

D.J. Marketing, 10602 Horton Ave., Downey, CA 90241/310-806-0891; FAX: 310-806-6231

DKT, Inc., 14623 Vera Drive, Union, MI 49130-9744/616-641-7120; FAX: 616-641-2015

D-Max, Inc., RR1, Box 473, Bagley, MN 56621/218-785-2278

Dohring Bullets, 100 W. 8 Mile Rd., Ferndale, MI 48220

Dolbare, Elizabeth, P.O. Box 222, Sunburst, MT 59482-0222

Doskocil Mfg. Co., Inc., P.O. Box 1246, 4209 Barnett, Arlington, TX 76017/817-467-5116; FAX: 817-472-9810

Double A Ltd., Dept. ST, Box 11306, Minneapolis, MN 55411

Dowtin Gunworks, Rt. 4, Box 930A, Flagstaff, AZ 86001/602-779-1898

Drain, Mark, SE 3211 Kamilche Point Rd., Shelton, WA 98584/206-426-5452

Dremel Mfg. Co., 4915-21st St., Racine, WI 53406

Dropkick, 1460 Washington Blvd., Williamsport, PA 17701/717-326-5161; FAX: 717-326-4950

Duane's Gun Repair (See DGR Custom Rifles)

Dubber, Michael W., P.O. Box 312, Evansville, IN 47702/812-424-9000; FAX: 812-424-6551

Duffy (See Guns Antique & Modern DBA/Charles E. Duffy)

Du-Lite Corp., Charles E., 171 River Rd., Middletown, CT 06457/203-347-2505; FAX: 203-347-9404

Duncan's Gun Works, Inc., 1619 Grand Ave., San Marcos, CA 92069/619-727-0515

DuPont (See IMR Powder Co.)

Dutchman's Firearms, Inc., The, 4143 Taylor Blvd., Louisville, KY 40215/502-366-0555

Dykstra, Doug, 411 N. Darling, Fremont, MI 49412/616-924-3950

Dynamit Nobel-RWS, Inc., 81 Ruckman Rd., Closter, NJ 07624/201-767-7971; FAX: 201-767-1589

Dyson & Son Ltd., Peter, 29-31 Church St., Honley Huddersfield, W. Yorkshire HD7 2AH, ENGLAND/44-1484-661062; FAX: 44-1484-663709

E

E&L Mfg., Inc., 4177 Riddle by Pass Rd., Riddle, OR 97469/541-874-2137; FAX: 541-874-3107

E.A.A. Corp., P.O. Box 1299, Sharpes, FL 32959/407-639-4842, 800-536-4442; FAX: 407-639-7006

Eagan, Donald V., P.O. Box 196, Benton, PA 17814/717-925-6134

Eagle Imports, Inc., 1750 Brielle Ave., Unit B1, Wanamassa, NJ 07712/908-493-0333; FAX: 908-493-0301

Eagle International, Inc., 5195 W. 58th Ave., Suite 300, Arvada, CO 80002/303-426-8100; FAX: 303-426-5475

Eagle Mfg. & Engineering, 2648 Keen Dr., San Diego, CA 92139/619-479-4402; FAX: 619-472-5585

E-A-R, Inc., Div. of Cabot Safety Corp., 5457 W. 79th St., Indianapolis, IN 46268/800-327-3431; FAX: 800-488-8007

Easy Pull Outlaw Products, 316 1st St. East, Polson, MT 59860/406-883-6822

Echols & Co., D'Arcy, 164 W. 580 S., Providence, UT 84332/801-753-2367

Ed's Gun House, Rt. 1, Box 62, Minnesota City, MN 55959/507-689-2925

Eezox, Inc., P.O. Box 772, Waterford, CT 06385-0772/860-447-8282, 800-462-3331; FAX: 860-447-3484

EGW Evolution Gun Works, 4050 B-8 Skyron Dr., Doylestown, PA 18901/215-348-9892; FAX: 215-348-1056

Eichelberger Bullets, Wm., 158 Crossfield Rd., King of Prussia, PA 19406

Ekol Leather Care, P.O. Box 2652, West Lafayette, IN 47906/317-463-2250; FAX: 317-463-7004

El Dorado Leather, P.O. Box 2603, Tucson, AZ 85702/520-586-4791; FAX: 520-586-4791

El Paso Saddlery Co., P.O. Box 27194, El Paso, TX 79926/915-544-2233; FAX: 915-544-2535

Electronic Shooters Protection, Inc., 11997 West 85th Place, Arvada, CO 80005/303-456-8964; 800-797-7791

Electronic Trigger Systems, Inc., P.O. Box 13, 230 Main St. S., Hector, MN 55342/612-848-2760

Eley Ltd., P.O. Box 705, Witton, Birmingham, B6 7UT, ENGLAND/021-356-8899; FAX: 021-331-4173

Elkhorn Bullets, P.O. Box 5293, Central Point, OR 97502/541-826-7440

Elko Arms, Dr. L. Kortz, 28 rue Ecole Moderne, B-7060 Soignies, BELGIUM/(32)67-33-29-34

Ellicott Arms, Inc./Woods Pistolsmithing, 3840 Dahlgren Ct., Ellicott City, MD 21042/410-465-7979

Elliott Inc., G.W., 514 Burnside Ave., East Hartford, CT 06108/203-289-5741; FAX: 203-289-3137

Emerging Technologies, Inc. (See Laseraim Technologies, Inc.)

EMF Co., Inc., 1900 E. Warner Ave. Suite 1-D, Santa Ana, CA 92705/714-261-6611; FAX: 714-756-0133

Engineered Accessories, 1307 W. Wabash Ave., Effingham, IL 62401/217-347-7700; FAX: 217-347-7737

Engraving Artistry, 36 Alto Rd., RFD 2, Burlington, CT 06013/203-673-6837

Enguix Import-Export, Alpujarras 58, Alzira, Valencia, SPAIN 46600/(96) 241 43 95; FAX: (96) (241 43 95) 240 21 53

Epps, Ellwood (See "Gramps" Antique Cartridges)

Erhardt, Dennis, 3280 Green Meadow Dr., Helena, MT 59601/406-442-4533

Erickson's Mfg., C.W., Inc., 530 Garrison Ave. N.E., P.O. Box 522, Buffalo, MN 55313/612-682-3665; FAX: 612-682-4328

Erma Werke GmbH, Johan Ziegler St., 13/15/FeldiglSt., D-8060 Dachau, GERMANY (U.S. importers—Amtec 2000, Inc.; Mandall Shooting Supplies, Inc.)

Essex Arms, P.O. Box 345, Island Pond, VT 05846/802-723-4313

Essex Metals, 1000 Brighton St., Union, NJ 07083/800-282-8369

Euroarms of America, Inc., P.O. Box 3277, Winchester, VA 22604/540-662-1863; FAX: 540-662-4464

Eutaw Co., Inc., The, P.O. Box 608, U.S. Hwy. 176 West, Holly Hill, SC 29059/803-496-3341

Evans Engraving, Robert, 332 Vine St., Oregon City, OR 97045/503-656-5693

Eversull Co., Inc., K., 1 Tracemont, Boyce, LA 71409/318-793-8728; FAX: 318-793-5483

Exe, Inc., 18830 Partridge Circle, Eden Prairie, MN 55346/612-944-7662

Executive Protection Institute, Rt. 2, Box 3645, Berryville, VA 22611/540-955-1128

Eyster Heritage Gunsmiths, Inc., Ken, 6441 Bishop Rd., Centerburg, OH 43011/614-625-6131

E-Z-Way Systems, P.O. Box 4310, Newark, OH 43058-4310/614-345-6645, 800-848-2072; FAX: 614-345-6600

F

F&A Inc., 50 Elm St., Richfield Springs, NY 13439/315-858-1470; FAX: 315-858-2969

Fagan & Co., William, 22952 15 Mile Rd., Clinton Township, MI 48035/313-465-4637; FAX: 313-792-6996

Faith Associates, Inc., 1139 S. Greenville Hwy., Hendersonville, NC 28792/704-692-1916; FAX: 704-697-6827

Fanzoj GmbH, Griesgasse 1, 9170 Ferlach, AUSTRIA 9170/(43) 04227-2283; FAX: (43) 04227-2867

FAS, Via E. Fermi, 8, 20019 Settimo Milanese, Milano, ITALY/02-3285846; FAX: 02-33500196 (U.S. importer—Nygord Precision Products)

Faust, Inc., T.G., 544 Minor St., Reading, PA 19602/610-375-8549; FAX: 610-375-4488

Fautheree, Andy, P.O. Box 4607, Pagosa Springs, CO 81157/303-731-5003

Feather Industries, Inc., 37600 Liberty Dr., Trinidad, CO 81082/719-846-2699; FAX: 719-846-2644

Federal Cartridge Co., 900 Ehlen Dr., Anoka, MN 55303/612-323-2300; FAX: 612-323-2506

Federated-Fry (See Fry Metals)

FEG, Budapest, Soroksariut 158, H-1095 HUNGARY (U.S. importers—Century International Arms, Inc.; K.B.I., Inc.)

Feken, Dennis, Rt. 2 Box 124, Perry, OK 73077/405-336-5611

Fellowes, Ted, Beaver Lodge, 9245 16th Ave. SW, Seattle, WA 98106/206-763-1698

Feminine Protection, Inc., 10514 Shady Trail, Dallas, TX 75220/214-351-4500; FAX: 214-352-4686

Ferdinand, Inc., P.O. Box 5, 201 Main St., Harrison, ID 83833/208-689-3012, 800-522-6010 (U.S.A.), 800-258-5266 (Canada); FAX: 208-689-3142

Ferguson, Bill, P.O. Box 1238, Sierra Vista, AZ 85636/520-458-5321; FAX: 520-458-9125

Ferris Firearms, 30115 U.S. Hwy. 281 North, Suite 158, Bulverde, TX 78163/210-980-4811

Finch Custom Bullets, 40204 La Rochelle, Prairieville, LA 70769

Fiocchi Munizioni s.p.a. (See U.S. importer—Fiocchi of America, Inc.)

Fiocchi of America, Inc., 5030 Fremont Rd., Ozark, MO 65721/417-725-4118, 800-721-2666; FAX: 417-725-1039

Firearm Training Center, The, 9555 Blandville Rd., West Paducah, KY 42086/502-554-5886

Firearms Academy of Seattle, P.O. Box 2814, Kirkland, WA 98083/206-820-4853

Firearms Engraver's Guild of America, 332 Vine St., Oregon City, OR 97045/503-656-5693

Fire'n Five, P.O. Box 11 Granite Rt., Sumpter, OR 97877

First, Inc., Jack, 1201 Turbine Dr., Rapid City, SD 57701/605-343-9544; FAX: 605-343-9420

Fish, Marshall F., Rt. 22 N., P.O. Box 2439, Westport, NY 12993/518-962-4897

Fisher, Jerry A., 553 Crane Mt. Rd., Big Fork, MT 59911/406-837-2722

Fisher Custom Firearms, 2199 S. Kittredge Way, Aurora, CO 80013/303-755-3710

Fisher Enterprises, Inc., 1071 4th Ave. S., Suite 303, Edmonds, WA 98020-4143/206-771-5382

Fisher, R. Kermit (See Fisher Enterprises, Inc.)

Fitz Pistol Grip Co., P.O. Box 610, Douglas City, CA 96024/916-778-0240

Flaig's, 2200 Evergreen Rd., Millvale, PA 15209/412-821-1717

Flambeau Products Corp., 15981 Valplast Rd., Middlefield, OH 44062/216-632-1631; FAX: 216-632-1581

Flannery Engraving Co., Jeff W., 11034 Riddles Run Rd., Union, KY 41091/606-384-3127

Flayderman & Co., N., Inc., P.O. Box 2446, Ft. Lauderdale, FL 33303/305-761-8855

Fleming Firearms, 7720 E 126th St. N, Collinsville, OK 74021-7016/918-665-3624

Flents Products Co., Inc., P.O. Box 2109, Norwalk, CT 06852/203-866-2581; FAX: 203-854-9322

Flintlocks, Etc. (See Beauchamp & Son, Inc.)

Flitz International Ltd., 821 Mohr Ave., Waterford, WI 53185/414-534-5898; FAX: 414-534-2991

Floatstone Mfg. Co., 106 Powder Mill Rd., P.O. Box 765, Canton, CT 06019/203-693-1977

Flores Publications, Inc., J., P.O. Box 830131, Miami, FL 33283/305-559-4652

Fluoramics, Inc., 18 Industrial Ave., Mahwah, NJ 07430/800-922-0075, 201-825-7035

FN Herstal, Voie de Liege 33, Herstal 4040, BELGIUM/(32)41.40.82.83; FAX: (32)41.40.86.79

Fobus International Ltd., Kfar Hess, ISRAEL 40692/972-9-911716; FAX: 972-9-911716

Ford, Jack, 1430 Elkwood, Missouri City, TX 77489/713-499-9984

Forgett Jr., Valmore J., 689 Bergen Blvd., Ridgefield, NJ 07657/201-945-2500; FAX: 201-945-6859

Forgreens Tool Mfg., Inc., P.O. Box 990, 723 Austin St., Robert Lee, TX 76945/915-453-2800

Forkin, Ben (See Belt MTN Arms)

Forrest, Inc., Tom, P.O. Box 326, Lakeside, CA 92040/619-561-5800; FAX: 619-561-0227

Forster, Kathy (See Custom Checkering Service)

Forster, Larry L., P.O. Box 212, 220 First St. NE, Gwinner, ND 58040-0212/701-678-2475

Forster Products, 82 E. Lanark Ave., Lanark, IL 61046/815-493-6360; FAX: 815-493-2371

Fort Hill Gunstocks, 12807 Fort Hill Rd., Hillsboro, OH 45133/513-466-2763

Fort Knox Security Products, 1051 N. Industrial Park Rd., Orem, UT 84057/801-224-7233, 800-821-5216; FAX: 801-226-5493

Forty Five Ranch Enterprises, Box 1080, Miami, OK 74355-1080/918-542-5875

Fountain Products, 492 Prospect Ave., West Springfield, MA 01089/413-781-4651; FAX: 413-733-8217

4-D Custom Die Co., 711 N. Sandusky St., P.O. Box 889, Mt. Vernon, OH 43050-0889/614-397-7214; FAX: 614-397-6600

Foy Custom Bullets, 104 Wells Ave., Daleville, AL 36322

Francesca, Inc., 3115 Old Ranch Rd., San Antonio, TX 78217/512-826-2584; FAX: 512-826-8211

Francolini, Leonard, 106 Powder Mill Rd., P.O. Box 765, Canton, CT 06019/203-693-1977

Frank Custom Classic Arms, Ron, 7131 Richland Rd., Ft. Worth, TX 76118/817-284-9300; FAX: 817-284-9300

Frank Knives, Box 984, Whitefish, MT 59937/406-862-2681; FAX: 406-862-2681

Frazier Brothers Enterprises, 1118 N. Main St., Franklin, IN 46131/317-736-4000; FAX: 317-736-4000

Freedom Arms, Inc., P.O. Box 1776, Freedom, WY 83120/307-883-2468, 800-833-4432 (orders only); FAX: 307-883-2005

Freeman Animal Targets, 5519 East County Road, 100 South, Plainsfield, IN 46168/317-487-9482; FAX: 317-487-9671

Fremont Tool Works, 1214 Prairie, Ford, KS 67842/316-369-2327

French, J.R., 1712 Creek Ridge Ct., Irving, TX 75060/214-254-2654

Frielich Police Equipment, 211 East 21st St., New York, NY 10010/212-254-3045

Frontier, 2910 San Bernardo, Laredo, TX 78040/210-723-5409; FAX: 210-723-1774

Frontier Arms Co., Inc., 401 W. Rio Santa Cruz, Green Valley, AZ 85614-3932

Frontier Products Co., 164 E. Longview Ave., Columbus, OH 43202/614-262-9357

Frontier Safe Co., 3201 S. Clinton St., Fort Wayne, IN 46806/219-744-7233; FAX: 219-744-6678

Fry Metals, 4100 6th Ave., Altoona, PA 16602/814-946-1611

Fullmer, Geo. M., 2499 Mavis St., Oakland, CA 94601/510-533-4193

Fulmer's Antique Firearms, Chet, P.O. Box 792, Rt. 2 Buffalo Lake, Detroit Lakes, MN 56501/218-847-7712

Fury Cutlery, 801 Broad Ave., Ridgefield, NJ 07657/201-943-5920; FAX: 201-943-1579

Fusilier Bullets, 10010 N. 6000 W., Highland, UT 84003/801-756-6813

FWB, Neckarstrasse 43, 78727 Oberndorf a. N., GERMANY/07423-814-0; FAX: 07423-814-89 (U.S. importer—Beeman Precision Airguns)

G

G96 Products Co., Inc., River St. Station, P.O. Box 1684, Paterson, NJ 07544/201-684-4050; FAX: 201-684-3848

G&C Bullet Co., Inc., 8835 Thornton Rd., Stockton, CA 95209/209-477-6479; FAX: 209-477-2813

Gage Manufacturing, 663 W. 7th St., San Pedro, CA 90731

Galati International, P.O. Box 326, Catawissa, MO 63015/314-257-4837; FAX: 314-257-2268

Galazan, P.O. Box 1692, New Britain, CT 06051-1692/203-225-6581; FAX: 203-832-8707

GALCO International Ltd., 2019 W. Quail Ave., Phoenix, AZ 85027/602-258-8295, 800-874-2526; FAX: 602-582-6854

Gamba-Societa Armi Bresciane Srl., Renato, Via Artigiani, 93, 25063 Gardone Val Trompia (BS), ITALY/30-8911640; FAX: 30-8911648 (U.S. importer—The First National Gun Bank Corp.)

Gammog, Gregory B. Gally, 14608 Old Gunpowder Rd., Laurel, MD 20707-3131/301-725-3838

Gamo (See U.S. importers—Daisy Mfg. Co.; Dynamit Nobel-RWS, Inc.)

Gamo USA, Inc., 3721 S.W. 47th Ave., Suite 304, Ft. Lauderdale, FL 33314

Gander Mountain, Inc., P.O. Box 128, Hwy. "W", Wilmot, WI 53192/414-862-2331,Ext. 6425

GAR, 590 McBride Avenue, West Paterson, NJ 07424/201-754-1114; FAX: 201-742-2897

Garcia National Gun Traders, Inc., 225 SW 22nd Ave., Miami, FL 33135/305-642-2355

Garthwaite, Jim, Rt. 2, Box 310, Watsontown, PA 17777/717-538-1566

Gaucher Armes, S.A., 46, rue Desjoyaux, 42000 Saint-Etienne, FRANCE/77 33 38 92; FAX: 77 61 95 72

G.B.C. Industries, Inc., P.O. Box 1602, Spring, TX 77373/713-350-9690; FAX: 713-350-0601

GDL Enterprises, 409 Le Gardeur, Slidell, LA 70460/504-649-0693

Gehmann, Walter (See Huntington Die Specialties)

Gene's Custom Guns, P.O. Box 10534, White Bear Lake, MN 55110/612-429-5105

Gentex Corp., 5 Tinkham Ave., Derry, NH 03038/603-434-0311; FAX: 603-434-3002

George, Tim, Rt. 1, P.O. Box 45, Evington, VA 24550/804-821-8117

Getz Barrel Co., P.O. Box 88, Beavertown, PA 17813/717-658-7263

GFR Corp., P.O. Box 1439, New London, NH 03257-1439

G.G. & G., 3602 E. 42nd Stravenue, Tucson, AZ 85713/520-748-7167; FAX: 520-748-7583

G.H. Enterprises Ltd., Bag 10, Okotoks, Alberta T0L 1T0 CANADA/403-938-6070

Giron, Robert E., 1328 Pocono St., Pittsburgh, PA 15218/412-731-6041

Glaser Safety Slug, Inc., P.O. Box 8223, Foster City, CA 94404-8223/800-221-3489, 415-345-7677; FAX: 415-345-8217

Glass, Herb, P.O. Box 25, Bullville, NY 10915/914-361-3021

Glimm, Jerome C., 19 S. Maryland, Conrad, MT 59425/406-278-3574

Glock GmbH, P.O. Box 50, A-2232 Deutsch Wagram, AUSTRIA (U.S. importer—Glock, Inc.)

Glock, Inc., P.O. Box 369, Smyrna, GA 30081/770-432-1202; FAX: 770-433-8719

GML Products, Inc., 394 Laredo Dr., Birmingham, AL 35226/205-979-4867

Goddard, Allen, 716 Medford Ave., Hayward, CA 94541/510-276-6830

Goergen's Gun Shop, Inc., Rt. 2, Box 182BB, Austin, MN 55912/507-433-9280

GOEX, Inc., 1002 Springbrook Ave., Moosic, PA 18507/717-457-6724; FAX: 717-457-1130

Goldcoast Reloaders, Inc., 2421 NE 4th Ave., Pompano Beach, FL 33064/305-783-4849

Golden Age Arms Co., 115 E. High St., Ashley, OH 43003/614-747-2488

Golden Bear Bullets, 3065 Fairfax Ave., San Jose, CA 95148/408-238-9515

Gonzalez Guns, Ramon B., P.O. Box 370, Monticello, NY 12701/914-794-4515

Goodwin, Fred, Silver Ridge Gun Shop, Sherman Mills, ME 04776/207-365-4451

Gordie's Gun Shop, 1401 Fulton St., Streator, IL 61364/815-672-7202

Gotz Bullets, 7313 Rogers St., Rockford, IL 61111

Gould & Goodrich, P.O. Box 1479, Lillington, NC 27546/910-893-2071; FAX: 910-893-4742

Gournet, Geoffroy, 820 Paxinosa Ave., Easton, PA 18042/215-559-0710

Gozon Corp., U.S.A., P.O. Box 6278, Folson, CA 95763/916-983-2026; FAX: 916-983-9500

Grace, Charles E., 6943 85.5 Rd., Trinchera, CO 81081/719-846-9435

Grace Metal Products, Inc., P.O. Box 67, Elk Rapids, MI 49629/616-264-8133

"Gramps" Antique Cartridges, Box 341, Washago, Ont. L0K 2B0 CANADA/705-689-5348

Grand Falls Bullets, Inc., P.O. Box 720, 803 Arnold Wallen Way, Stockton, MO 65785/816-229-0112

Granite Custom Bullets, Box 190, Philipsburg, MT 59858/406-859-3245

Grant, Howard V., Hiawatha 15, Woodruff, WI 54568/715-356-7146

Graphics Direct, P.O. Box 372421, Reseda, CA 91337-2421/818-344-9002

Graves Co., 1800 Andrews Ave., Pompano Beach, FL 33069/800-327-9103; FAX: 305-960-0301

Grayback Wildcats, 5306 Bryant Ave., Klamath Falls, OR 97603/541-884-1072

Graybill's Gun Shop, 1035 Ironville Pike, Columbia, PA 17512/717-684-2739

Great Lakes Airguns, 6175 S. Park Ave., Hamburg, NY 14075/716-648-6666; FAX: 716-648-5279

Green, Arthur S., 485 S. Robertson Blvd., Beverly Hills, CA 90211/310-274-1283

Green Bay Bullets, 1638 Hazelwood Dr., Sobieski, WI 54171/414-826-7760

Green, Roger M., P.O. Box 984, 435 E. Birch, Glenrock, WY 82637/307-436-9804

Greenwald, Leon E. "Bud", 2553 S. Quitman St., Denver, CO 80219/303-935-3850

Greenwood Precision, P.O. Box 468, Nixa, MO 65714-0468/417-725-2330

Greider Precision, 431 Santa Marina Ct., Escondido, CA 92029/619-480-8892

Gremmel Enterprises, 2111 Carriage Drive, Eugene, OR 97408-7537/541-302-3000

Grier's Hard Cast Bullets, 1107 11th St., LaGrande, OR 97850/503-963-8796

Griffin & Howe, Inc., 33 Claremont Rd., Bernardsville, NJ 07924/908-766-2287; FAX: 908-766-1068

Griffin & Howe, Inc., 36 W. 44th St., Suite 1011, New York, NY 10036/212-921-0980

Grizzly Bullets, 322 Green Mountain Rd., Trout Creek, MT 59874/406-847-2627

Groenewold, John, P.O. Box 830, Mundelein, IL 60060/708-566-2365

GRS Corp., Glendo, P.O. Box 1153, 900 Overlander St., Emporia, KS 66801/316-343-1084, 800-835-3519

Guardsman Products, 411 N. Darling, Fremont, MI 49412/616-924-3950

Gun-Alert, 1010 N. Maclay Ave., San Fernando, CA 91340/818-365-0864; FAX: 818-365-1308

Gun City, 212 W. Main Ave., Bismarck, ND 58501/701-223-2304

Gun-Ho Sports Cases, 110 E. 10th St., St. Paul, MN 55101/612-224-9491

Gun Hunter Books, Div. of Gun Hunter Trading Co., 5075 Heisig St., Beaumont, TX 77705/409-835-3006

Gun Leather Limited, 116 Lipscomb, Ft. Worth, TX 76104/817-334-0225; 800-247-0609

Gun List (See Krause Publications, Inc.)

Gun Locker, Div. of Airmold, W.R. Grace & Co.-Conn., Becker Farms Ind. Park,, P.O. Box 610/Roanoke Rapids, NC 27870/800-344-5716; FAX: 919-536-2201

Gun Parts Corp., The, 226 Williams Lane, West Hurley, NY 12491/914-679-2417; FAX: 914-679-5849

Gun Room, The, 1121 Burlington, Muncie, IN 47302/317-282-9073; FAX: 317-282-5270

Gun Room Press, The, 127 Raritan Ave., Highland Park, NJ 08904/908-545-4344; FAX: 908-545-6686

Gun Shop, The, 5550 S. 900 East, Salt Lake City, UT 84117/801-263-3633

Gun Shop, The, 62778 Spring Creek Rd., Montrose, CO 81401

Gun-Tec, P.O. Box 8125, W. Palm Beach, FL 33407

Gun Works, The, 247 S. 2nd, Springfield, OR 97477/541-741-4118; FAX: 541-988-1097

Guncraft Books (See Guncraft Sports, Inc.)

Guncraft Sports, Inc., 10737 Dutchtown Rd., Knoxville, TN 37932/423-966-4545; FAX: 423-966-4500

Gunfitters, The, P.O. 426, Cambridge, WI 53523-0426/608-764-8128

Gunline Tools, 2950 Saturn St., Suite O, Brea, CA 92621/714-993-5100; FAX: 714-572-4128

Gunnerman Books, P.O. Box 214292, Auburn Hills, MI 48321/810-879-2779

Guns, 81 E. Streetsboro St., Hudson, OH 44236/216-650-4563

Guns Antique & Modern DBA/Charles E. Duffy, Williams Lane, West Hurley, NY 12491/914-679-2997

Guns, Div. of D.C. Engineering, Inc., 8633 Southfield Fwy., Detroit, MI 48228/313-271-7111, 800-886-7623 (orders only); FAX: 313-271-7112

GUNS Magazine, 591 Camino de la Reina, Suite 200, San Diego, CA 92108/619-297-5350; FAX: 619-297-5353

Gunsite Custom Shop, P.O. Box 451, Paulden, AZ 86334/520-636-4104; FAX: 520-636-1236

Gunsite Gunsmithy (See Gunsite Custom Shop)

Gunsite Training Center, P.O. Box 700, Paulden, AZ 86334/520-636-4565; FAX: 520-636-1236

Gunsmithing Ltd., 57 Unquowa Rd., Fairfield, CT 06430/203-254-0436; FAX: 203-254-1535

Gurney, F.R., Box 13, Sooke, BC V0S 1N0 CANADA/604-642-5282; FAX: 604-642-7859

Gusty Winds Corp., 2950 Bear St., Suite 120, Costa Mesa, CA 92626/714-536-3587

Gwinnell, Bryson J., P.O. Box 248C, Maple Hill Rd., Rochester, VT 05767/802-767-3664

GZ Paintball Sports Products (See GFR Corp.)

H

H&P Publishing, 7174 Hoffman Rd., San Angelo, TX 76905/915-655-5953

H&R 1871, Inc., 60 Industrial Rowe, Gardner, MA 01440/508-632-9393; FAX: 508-632-2300

H&S Liner Service, 515 E. 8th, Odessa, TX 79761/915-332-1021

Hafner Creations, Inc., P.O. Box 1987, Lake City, FL 32055/904-755-6481; FAX: 904-755-6595

Hale/Engraver, Peter, 800 E. Canyon Rd., Spanish Fork, UT 84660/801-798-8215

Half Moon Rifle Shop, 490 Halfmoon Rd., Columbia Falls, MT 59912/406-892-4409

Hall Plastics, Inc., John, P.O. Box 1526, Alvin, TX 77512/713-489-8709

Hallberg Gunsmith, Fritz, 33 S. Main, Payette, ID 83661/208-642-7157; FAX: 208-642-9643

Hamilton, Alex B. (See Ten-Ring Precision, Inc.)

Hamilton, Keith, P.O. Box 871, Gridley, CA 95948/916-846-2316

Hammerli USA, 19296 Oak Grove Circle, Groveland, CA 95321/209-962-5311; FAX: 209-962-5931

Hammerli Ltd., Seonerstrasse 37, CH-5600 Lenzburg, SWITZERLAND/064-50 11 44; FAX: 064-51 38 27 (U.S. importer—Hammerli USA)

Handgun Press, P.O. Box 406, Glenview, IL 60025/847-657-6500; FAX: 847-724-8831

HandiCrafts Unltd. (See Clements' Custom Leathercraft, Chas)

Hands Engraving, Barry Lee, 26192 E. Shore Route, Bigfork, MT 59911/406-837-0035

Hank's Gun Shop, Box 370, 50 West 100 South, Monroe, UT 84754/801-527-4456

Hanned Line, The, P.O. Box 2387, Cupertino, CA 95015-2387

Hanned Precision (See Hanned Line, The)

Hansen & Co. (See Hansen Cartridge Co.)

Hansen Cartridge Co., 244-246 Old Post Rd., Southport, CT 06490/203-259-6222, 203-259-7337; FAX: 203-254-3832

Hanson's Gun Center, Dick, 233 Everett Dr., Colorado Springs, CO 80911

Hardin Specialty Dist., P.O. Box 338, Radcliff, KY 40159-0338/502-351-6649

Hardison, Charles, P.O. Box 356, 200 W. Baseline Rd., Lafayette, CO 80026-0356/303-666-5171

Harrell's Precision, 5756 Hickory Dr., Salem, VA 24133/703-380-2683

Harrington & Richardson (See H&R 1871, Inc.)

Harris Engineering, Inc., Rt. 1, Barlow, KY 42024/502-334-3633; FAX: 502-334-3000

Harris Enterprises, P.O. Box 105, Bly, OR 97622/503-353-2625

Harris Gunworks, 3840 N. 28th Ave., Phoenix, AZ 85017-4733/602-230-1414; FAX: 602-230-1422

Harris Hand Engraving, Paul A., 10630 Janet Lee, San Antonio, TX 78230/512-391-5121

Harris Publications, 1115 Broadway, New York, NY 10010/212-807-7100; FAX: 212-627-4678

Harrison Bullets, 6437 E. Hobart St., Mesa, AZ 85205

Harrison-Hurtz Enterprises, Inc., P.O. Box 268, RR1, Wymore, NE 68466/402-645-3378; FAX: 402-645-3606

Hart & Son, Inc., Robert W., 401 Montgomery St., Nescopeck, PA 18635/717-752-3655, 800-368-3656; FAX: 717-752-1088

Hartford (See U.S. importer— EMF Co., Inc.)

Harvey, Frank, 218 Nightfall, Terrace, NV 89015/702-558-6998

Harwood, Jack O., 1191 S. Pendlebury Lane, Blackfoot, ID 83221/208-785-5368

Haselbauer Products, Jerry, P.O. Box 27629, Tucson, AZ 85726/602-792-1075

Hastings Barrels, 320 Court St., Clay Center, KS 67432/913-632-3169; FAX: 913-632-6554

Hawk, Inc., 849 Hawks Bridge Rd., Salem, NJ 08079/609-299-2700; FAX: 609-299-2800

Hawk Laboratories, Inc. (See Hawk, Inc.)

Hawken Shop, The (See Dayton Traister)

Haydon Shooters' Supply, Russ, 15018 Goodrich Dr. NW, Gig Harbor, WA 98329/206-857-7557

Heatbath Corp., P.O. Box 2978, Springfield, MA 01101/413-543-3381

Hebard Guns, Gil, 125-129 Public Square, Knoxville, IL 61448

HEBB Resources, P.O. Box 999, Mead, WA 99021-09996/509-466-1292

Hecht, Hubert J., Waffen-Hecht, P.O. Box 2635, Fair Oaks, CA 95628/916-966-1020

Heckler & Koch GmbH, P.O. Box 1329, 78722 Oberndorf, Neckar, GERMANY/49-7423179-0; FAX: 49-7423179-2406 (U.S. importer—Heckler & Koch, Inc.)

Heckler & Koch, Inc., 21480 Pacific Blvd., Sterling, VA 20166-8903/703-450-1900; FAX: 703-450-8160

Hege Jagd-u. Sporthandels, GmbH, P.O. Box 101461, W-7770 Ueberlingen a. Bodensee, GERMANY

Heidenstrom Bullets, Urds GT 1 Heroya, 3900 Porsgrunn, NORWAY

Heilmann, Stephen, P.O. Box 657, Grass Valley, CA 95945/916-272-8758

Heinie Specialty Products, 301 Oak St., Quincy, IL 62301-2500/309-543-4535; FAX: 309-543-2521

Hellweg Ltd., 40356 Oak Park Way, Suite H, Oakhurst, CA 93644/209-683-3030; FAX: 209-683-3422

Hendricks, Frank E., Master Engravers, Inc., HC03, Box 434, Dripping Springs, TX 78620/512-858-7828

Henigson & Associates, Steve, 2049 Kerwood Ave., Los Angeles, CA 90025/213-305-8288

Henriksen Tool Co., Inc., 8515 Wagner Creek Rd., Talent, OR 97540/541-535-2309

Hensler, Jerry, 6614 Country Field, San Antonio, TX 78240/210-690-7491

Hensley & Gibbs, Box 10, Murphy, OR 97533/541-862-2341

Heppler's Machining, 2240 Calle Del Mundo, Santa Clara, CA 95054/408-748-9166; FAX: 408-988-7711

Heritage Manufacturing, Inc., 4600 NW 135th St., Opa Locka, FL 33054/305-685-5966; FAX: 305-687-6721

Heritage/VSP Gun Books, P.O. Box 887, McCall, ID 83638/208-634-4104; FAX: 208-634-3101

Herrett's Stocks, Inc., P.O. Box 741, Twin Falls, ID 83303/208-733-1498

Hesco-Meprolight, 2139 Greenville Rd., LaGrange, GA 30240/706-884-7967; FAX: 706-882-4683

Hi-Point Firearms, 5990 Philadelphia Dr., Dayton, OH 45415/513-275-4991; FAX: 513-522-8330

Hidalgo, Tony, 12701 SW 9th Pl., Davie, FL 33325/305-476-7645

High Bridge Arms, Inc., 3185 Mission St., San Francisco, CA 94110/415-282-8358

High North Products, Inc., P.O. Box 2, Antigo, WI 54409/715-627-2331

High Performance International, 5734 W. Florist Ave., Milwaukee, WI 53218/414-466-9040

High Standard Mfg. Co., Inc., 4601 S. Pinemont, 148-B, Houston, TX 77041/713-462-4200; FAX: 713-462-6437

Highline Machine Co., 654 Lela Place, Grand Junction, CO 81504/970-434-4971

Hill Speed Leather, Ernie, 4507 N. 195th Ave., Litchfield Park, AZ 85340/602-853-9222; FAX: 602-853-9235

Hiptmayer, Armurier, RR 112 750, P.O. Box 136, Eastman, Quebec J0E 1P0, CANADA/514-297-2492

Hiptmayer, Heidemarie, RR 112 750, P.O. Box 136, Eastman, Quebec J0E 1PO, CANADA/514-297-2492

Hiptmayer, Klaus, RR 112 750, P.O. Box 136, Eastman, Quebec J0E 1P0, CANADA/514-297-2492

Hirtenberger Aktiengesellschaft, Leobersdorferstrasse 31, A-2552 Hirtenberg, AUSTRIA/43(0)2256 81184; FAX: 43(0)2256 81807

HJS Arms, Inc., P.O. Box 3711, Brownsville, TX 78523-3711/800-453-2767, 210-542-2767

H.K.S. Products, 7841 Founion Dr., Florence, KY 41042/606-342-7841, 800-354-9814; FAX: 606-342-5865

Hoag, James W., 8523 Canoga Ave., Suite C, Canoga Park, CA 91304/818-998-1510

Hobson Precision Mfg. Co., Rt. 1, Box 220-C, Brent, AL 35034/205-926-4662

Hoch Custom Bullet Moulds (See Colorado Shooter's Supply)

Hodgdon Powder Co., Inc., P.O. Box 2932, 6231 Robinson, Shawnee Mission, KS 66202/913-362-9455; FAX: 913-362-1307; WEB: http://www.unicom.net/hpc

Hoehn Sales, Inc., 75 Greensburg Ct., St. Charles, MO 63304/314-441-4231

Hoelscher, Virgil, 11047 Pope Ave., Lynwood, CA 90262/310-631-8545

Hogue Grips, P.O. Box 1138, Paso Robles, CA 93447/800-438-4747, 805-239-1440; FAX: 805-239-2553

Holland's, Box 69, Powers, OR 97466/503-439-5155; FAX: 503-439-5155

Hollis Gun Shop, 917 Rex St., Carlsbad, NM 88220/505-885-3782

Hollywood Engineering, 10642 Arminta St., Sun Valley, CA 91352/818-842-8376

Holster Shop, The, 720 N. Flagler Dr., Ft. Lauderdale, FL 33304/305-463-7910; FAX: 305-761-1483

Homak Mfg. Co., Inc., 3800 W. 45th St., Chicago, IL 60632/312-523-3100; FAX: 312-523-9455

Home Shop Machinist, The, Village Press Publications, P.O. Box 1810, Traverse City, MI 49685/800-447-7367; FAX: 616-946-3289

Hondo Ind., 510 S. 52nd St.,I04, Tempe, AZ 85281

Hoppe's Div., Penguin Industries, Inc., Airport Industrial Mall, Coatesville, PA 19320/610-384-6000

Horizons Unlimited, P.O. Box 426, Warm Springs, GA 31830/706-655-3603; FAX: 706-655-3603

Hornady Mfg. Co., P.O. Box 1848, Grand Island, NE 68802/800-338-3220, 308-382-1390; FAX: 308-382-5761

Horseshoe Leather Products, Andy Arratoonian, The Cottage Sharow, Ripon HG4 5BP ENGLAND/44-1765-605858

Horst, Alan K., 3221 2nd Ave. N., Great Falls, MT 59401/406-454-1831

House of Muskets, Inc., The, P.O. Box 4640, Pagosa Springs, CO 81157/303-731-2295

Howell Machine, 815 1/2 D St., Lewiston, ID 83501/208-743-7418

Hoyt Holster Co., Inc., P.O. Box 69, Coupeville, WA 98239-0069/360-678-6640; FAX: 360-678-6549

Huey Gun Cases, P.O. Box 22456, Kansas City, MO 64113/816-444-1637; FAX: 816-444-1637

Hugger Hooks Co., 3900 Easley Way, Golden, CO 80403/303-279-0600

Hughes, Steven Dodd, P.O. Box 545, Livingston, MT 59047/406-222-9377

Hume, Don, P.O. Box 351, Miami, OK 74355/918-542-6604; FAX: 918-542-4340

Hungry Horse Books, 4605 Hwy. 93 South, Whitefish, MT 59937/406-862-7997

Hunkeler, A. (See Buckskin Machine Works)

Hunter Co., Inc., 3300 W. 71st Ave., Westminster, CO 80030/303-427-4626; FAX: 303-428-3980

Huntington Die Specialties, 601 Oro Dam Blvd., Oroville, CA 95965/916-534-1210; FAX: 916-534-1212

Hydrosorbent Products, P.O. Box 437, Ashley Falls, MA 01222/413-229-2967; FAX: 413-229-8743

Hyper-Single, Inc., 520 E. Beaver, Jenks, OK 74037/918-299-2391

I

ICI-America, P.O. Box 751, Wilmington, DE 19897/302-575-3000

Idaho Ammunition Service, 2816 Mayfair Dr., Lewiston, ID 83501/208-743-0270; FAX: 208-743-4930

IMI, P.O. Box 1044, Ramat Hasharon 47100, ISRAEL/972-3-5485222

IMI Services USA, Inc., 2 Wisconsin Circle, Suite 420, Chevy Chase, MD 20815/301-215-4800; FAX: 301-657-1446

Impact Case Co., P.O. Box 9912, Spokane, WA 99209-0912/800-262-3322, 509-467-3303; FAX: 509-326-5436

Imperial (See E-Z-Way Systems)

Import Sports Inc., 1750 Brielle Ave., Unit B1, Wanamassa, NJ 07712/908-493-0302; FAX: 908-493-0301

IMR Powder Co., 1080 Military Turnpike, Suite 2, Plattsburgh, NY 12901/518-563-2253; FAX: 518-563-6916

Info-Arm, P.O. Box 1262, Champlain, NY 12919

Ingle, Ralph W., 4 Missing Link, Rossville, GA 30741/404-866-5589

Innovative Weaponry, Inc., 337 Eubank NE, Albuquerque, NM 87123/800-334-3573, 505-296-4645; FAX: 505-271-2633

Innovision Enterprises, 728 Skinner Dr., Kalamazoo, MI 49001/616-382-1681; FAX: 616-382-1830

INTEC International, Inc., P.O. Box 5708, Scottsdale, AZ 85261/602-483-1708

Interarms, 10 Prince St., Alexandria, VA 22314/703-548-1400; FAX: 703-549-7826

Intermountain Arms & Tackle, Inc., 1375 E. Fairview Ave., Meridian, ID 83642-1816/208-888-4911; FAX: 208-888-4381

Intratec, 12405 SW 130th St., Miami, FL 33186/305-232-1821; FAX: 305-253-7207

Iosso Products, 1485 Lively Blvd., Elk Grove Village, IL 60007/708-437-8400; FAX: 708-437-8478

Ironside International Publishers, Inc., P.O. Box 55, 800 Slaters Lane, Alexandria, VA 22313/703-684-6111; FAX: 703-683-5486

Ironsighter Co., P.O. Box 85070, Westland, MI 48185/313-326-8731; FAX: 313-326-3378

Irwin, Campbell H., 140 Hartland Blvd., East Hartland, CT 06027/203-653-3901

Island Pond Gun Shop (See Costa, David)

I.S.S., P.O. Box 185234, Ft. Worth, TX 76181/817-595-2090

Ivanoff, Thomas G. (See Tom's Gun Repair)

J

J-4, Inc., 1700 Via Burton, Anaheim, CA 92806/714-254-8315; FAX: 714-956-4421

J&D Components, 75 East 350 North, Orem, UT 84057-4719/801-225-7007

J&J Products, Inc., 9240 Whitmore, El Monte, CA 91731/818-571-5228, 800-927-8361; FAX: 818-571-8704

J&J Sales, 1501 21st Ave. S., Great Falls, MT 59405/406-453-7549

J&L Superior Bullets (See Huntington Die Specialties)

J&R Engineering, P.O. Box 77, 200 Lyons Hill Rd., Athol, MA 01331/508-249-9241

J&S Heat Treat, 803 S. 16th St., Blue Springs, MO 64015/816-229-2149; FAX: 816-228-1135

Jackalope Gun Shop, 1048 S. 5th St., Douglas, WY 82633/307-358-3441

Jaeger, Paul, Inc./Dunn's, P.O. Box 449, 1 Madison Ave., Grand Junction, TN 38039/901-764-6909; FAX: 901-764-6503

JagerSport, Ltd., One Wholesale Way, Cranston, RI 02920/800-962-4867, 401-944-9682; FAX: 401-946-2587

Jamison's Forge Works, 4527 Rd. 6.5 NE, Moses Lake, WA 98837/509-762-2659

Jantz Supply, P.O. Box 584-GD, Davis, OK 73030-0584/405-369-2316; FAX: 405-369-3082

Jarvis, Inc., 1123 Cherry Orchard Lane, Hamilton, MT 59840/406-961-4392

Javelina Lube Products, P.O. Box 337, San Bernardino, CA 92402/714-882-5847; FAX: 714-434-6937

J-B Bore Cleaner, 299 Poplar St., Hamburg, PA 19526/610-562-2103

JBM, P.O. Box 3648, University Park, NM 88003

Jeffredo Gunsight, P.O. Box 669, San Marcos, CA 92079/619-728-2695

Jennings Firearms, Inc., 17692 Cowan, Irvine, CA 92714/714-252-7621; FAX: 714-252-7626

Jensen Bullets, 86 North, 400 West, Blackfoot, ID 83221/208-785-5590

Jensen's Custom Ammunition, 5146 E. Pima, Tucson, AZ 85712/602-325-3346; FAX: 602-322-5704

Jensen's Firearms Academy, 1280 W. Prince, Tucson, AZ 85705/602-293-8516

Jester Bullets, Rt. 1 Box 27, Orienta, OK 73737

JGS Precision Tool Mfg., 1141 S. Summer Rd., Coos Bay, OR 97420/503-267-4331; FAX:503-267-5996

J.I.T., Ltd., P.O. Box 230, Freedom, WY 83120/708-494-0937

JLK Bullets, 414 Turner Rd., Dover, AR 72837/501-331-4194

J.O. Arms Inc., 5709 Hartsdale, Houston, TX 77036/713-789-0745; FAX: 713-789-7513

John's Custom Leather, 523 S. Liberty St., Blairsville, PA 15717/412-459-6802

Johns Master Engraver, Bill, RR 4, Box 220, Fredericksburg, TX 78624-9545/210-997-6795

Johnson's Gunsmithing, Inc., Neal, 208 W. Buchanan St., Suite B, Colorado Springs, CO 80907/800-284-8671 (orders), 719-632-3795; FAX: 719-632-3493

Johnston Bros., 1889 Rt. 9, Unit 22, Toms River, NJ 08755/800-257-2595; FAX: 800-257-2534

Johnston, James (See North Fork Custom Gunsmithing)

Jonad Corp., 2091 Lakeland Ave., Lakewood, OH 44107/216-226-3161

Jonas Appraisals & Taxidermy, Jack, 1675 S. Birch, Suite 506, Denver, CO 80222/303-757-7347; FAX: 303-639-9655

Jones Co., Dale, 680 Hoffman Draw, Kila, MT 59920/406-755-4684

Jones Custom Products, Neil A., 17217 Brookhouser Road, Saegertown, PA 16433/814-763-2769; FAX: 814-763-4228

Jones Moulds, Paul, 4901 Telegraph Rd., Los Angeles, CA 90022/213-262-1510

Jones, J.D. (See SSK Industries)

Joy Enterprises (See Fury Cutlery)

J.P. Enterprises, Inc., P.O. Box 26324, Shoreview, MN 55126/612-486-9064; FAX: 612-482-0970

JRP Custom Bullets, RR2-2233 Carlton Rd., Whitehall, NY 12887/802-438-5548 (p.m.), 518-282-0084 (a.m.)

Jumbo Sports Products (See Bucheimer, J.M.)

Jungkind, Reeves C., 5001 Buckskin Pass, Austin, TX 78745-2841/512-442-1094

Jurras, L.E., P.O. Box 680, Washington, IN 47501/812-254-7698

JWH: Software, 6947 Haggerty Rd., Hillsboro, OH 45133/513-393-2402

K

K&M Industries, Inc., Box 66, 510 S. Main, Troy, ID 83871/208-835-2281; FAX: 208-835-5211

K&M Services, 5430 Salmon Run Rd., Dover, PA 17315/717-764-1461

K&S Mfg., 2611 Hwy. 40 East, Inglis, FL 34449/904-447-3571

K&T Co., Div. of T&S Industries, Inc., 1027 Skyview Dr., W. Carrollton, OH 45449/513-859-8414

Kahr Arms, P.O. Box 220, 630 Route 303, Blauvelt, NY 10913/914-353-5996; FAX: 914-353-7833

Kalispel Case Line, P.O. Box 267, Cusick, WA 99119/509-445-1121

Kamyk Engraving Co., Steve, 9 Grandview Dr., Westfield, MA 01085-1810/413-568-0457

Kane, Edward, P.O. Box 385, Ukiah, CA 95482/707-462-2937

Kane Products, Inc., 5572 Brecksville Rd., Cleveland, OH 44131/216-524-9962

Ka Pu Kapili, P.O. Box 745, Honokaa, HI 96727/808-776-1644; FAX: 808-776-1731

Kapro Mfg. Co., Inc. (See R.E.I.)

Kasenit Co., Inc., 13 Park Ave., Highland Mills, NY 10930/914-928-9595; FAX: 914-928-7292

Kasmarsik Bullets, 152 Crstler Rd., Chehalis, WA 98532

Kaswer Custom, Inc., 13 Surrey Drive, Brookfield, CT 06804/203-775-0564; FAX: 203-775-6872

K.B.I., Inc., P.O. Box 5440, Harrisburg, PA 17110-0440/717-540-8518; FAX: 717-540-8567

K-D, Inc., Box 459, 585 N. Hwy. 155, Cleveland, UT 84518/801-653-2530

KeeCo Impressions, Inc., 346 Wood Ave., North Brunswick, NJ 08902/800-468-0546

Keeler, R.H., 817 "N" St., Port Angeles, WA 98362/206-457-4702

Kehr, Roger, 2131 Agate Ct. SE, Lacy, WA 98503/360-456-0831

Keith's Bullets, 942 Twisted Oak, Algonquin, IL 60102/708-658-3520

Keith's Custom Taxidermy, 2241 Forest Ave., Rolling Meadows, IL 60008/847-255-7059

Keller Co., The, 4215 McEwen Rd., Dallas, TX 75244/214-770-8585

Kelley's, P.O. Box 125, Woburn, MA 01801/617-935-3389

Kellogg's Professional Products, 325 Pearl St., Sandusky, OH 44870/419-625-6551; FAX: 419-625-6167

Kelly, Lance, 1723 Willow Oak Dr., Edgewater, FL 32132/904-423-4933

Kel-Tec CNC Industries, Inc., P.O. Box 3427, Cocoa, FL 32924/407-631-0068; FAX: 407-631-1169

Ken's Gun Specialties, Rt. 1, Box 147, Lakeview, AR 72642/501-431-5606

Ken's Kustom Kartridges, 331 Jacobs Rd., Hubbard, OH 44425/216-534-4595

Keng's Firearms Specialty, Inc., P.O. Box 44405, 875 Wharton Dr. SW, Atlanta, GA 30336/404-691-7611: FAX: 404-505-8445

Kennebec Journal, 274 Western Ave., Augusta, ME 04330/207-622-6288

Kennedy Firearms, 10 N. Market St., Muncy, PA 17756/717-546-6695

KenPatable Ent., Inc., P.O. Box 19422, Louisville, KY 40259/502-239-5447

Kent Cartridge Mfg. Co. Ltd., Unit 16, Branbridges Industrial Estate, East, Peckham/Tonbridge, Kent, TN12 5HF ENGLAND/622-872255; FAX: 622-872645

Kesselring Gun Shop, 400 Hwy. 99 North, Burlington, WA 98233/206-724-3113; FAX: 206-724-7003

Kilham & Co., Main St., P.O. Box 37, Lyme, NH 03768/603-795-4112

Kimball, Gary, 1526 N. Circle Dr., Colorado Springs, CO 80909/719-634-1274

Kimber of America, Inc., 9039 SE Jannsen Rd., Clackamas, OR 97015/503-656-1704, 800-880-2418; FAX: 503-656-5357

Kimel Industries (See A.A. Arms, Inc.)

King & Co., P.O. Box 1242, Bloomington, IL 61702/309-473-3964

King's Gun Works, 1837 W. Glenoaks Blvd., Glendale, CA 91201/818-956-6010; FAX: 818-548-8606

Kirkpatrick Leather Co., 1910 San Bernardo, Laredo, TX 78040/210-723-6631; FAX: 210-725-0672

KJM Fabritek, Inc., P.O. Box 162, Marietta, GA 30061/404-426-8251

KK Air International (See Impact Case Co.)

K.K. Arms Co., Star Route Box 671, Kerrville, TX 78028/210-257-4718; FAX: 210-257-4891

KLA Enterprises, P.O. Box 2028, Eaton Park, FL 33840/941-682-2829; FAX: 941-682-2829

Kleen-Bore, Inc., 16 Industrial Pkwy., Easthampton, MA 01027/413-527-0300; FAX: 413-527-2522

Klein Custom Guns, Don, 433 Murray Park Dr., Ripon, WI 54971/414-748-2931

Kleinendorst, K.W., RR 1, Box 1500, Hop Bottom, PA 18824/717-289-4687

Klingler Woodcarving, P.O. Box 141, Thistle Hill, Cabot, VT 05647/802-426-3811

Kmount, P.O. Box 19422, Louisville, KY 40259/502-239-5447

Knight's Mfg. Co., 7750 9th St. SW, Vero Beach, FL 32968/407-562-5697; FAX: 407-569-2955

Kodiak Custom Bullets, 8261 Henry Circle, Anchorage, AK 99507/907-349-2282

Koevenig's Engraving Service, Box 55 Rabbit Gulch, Hill City, SD 57745

Kolpin Mfg., Inc., P.O. Box 107, 205 Depot St., Fox Lake, WI 53933/414-928-3118; FAX: 414-928-3687

Kopp, Terry K., Route 1, Box 224F, Lexington, MO 64067/816-259-2636

Korth, Robert-Bosch-Str. 4, P.O. Box 1320, 23909 Ratzeburg, GERMANY/451-4991497; FAX: 451-4993230 (U.S. importer—Interarms; Mandall Shooting Supplies, Inc.)

Korzinek Riflesmith, J., RD 2, Box 73D, Canton, PA 17724/717-673-8512

Kowa Optimed, Inc., 20001 S. Vermont Ave., Torrance, CA 90502/310-327-1913; FAX: 310-327-4177

Kramer Designs, 36 Chokecherry Ln., Clancy, MT 59634/406-933-8658; FAX: 406-933-8658

Kramer Handgun Leather, P.O. Box 112154, Tacoma, WA 98411/206-564-6652; FAX: 206-564-1214

Krause Publications, Inc., 700 E. State St., Iola, WI 54990/715-445-2214; FAX: 715-445-4087; Consumer orders only 800-258-0929

Kris Mounts, 108 Lehigh St., Johnstown, PA 15905/814-539-9751

KSN Industries, Ltd. (See U.S. importer—J.O. Arms Inc.)

Kudlas, John M., 622 14th St. SE, Rochester, MN 55904/507-288-5579

Kulis Freeze Dry Taxidermy, 725 Broadway Ave., Bedford, OH 44146/216-232-8352; FAX: 216-232-7305

Kwik Mount Corp., P.O. Box 19422, Louisville, KY 40259/502-239-5447

Kwik-Site Co., 5555 Treadwell, Wayne, MI 48184/313-326-1500; FAX: 313-326-4120

L

L&R Lock Co., 1137 Pocalla Rd., Sumter, SC 29150/803-775-6127

L&S Technologies, Inc. (See Aimtech Mount Systems)

La Clinique du .45, 1432 Rougemont, Chambly, Quebec, J3L 2L8 CANADA/514-658-1144

LaBounty Precision Reboring, P.O. Box 186, 7968 Silver Lk. Rd., Maple Falls, WA 98266/360-599-2047

LaFrance Specialties, P.O. Box 178211, San Diego, CA 92177-8211/619-293-3373

Lakewood Products, Inc., 275 June St., P.O. Box 230, Berlin, WI 54923/800-US-BUILT; FAX: 414-361-5058

Lampert, Ron, Rt. 1, Box 177, Guthrie, MN 56461/218-854-7345

Lane Bullets, Inc., 1011 S. 10th St., Kansas City, KS 66105/913-621-6113, 800-444-7468

Lane Publishing, P.O. Box 459, Lake Hamilton, AR 71951/501-525-7514; FAX: 501-525-7519

Lapua Ltd., P.O. Box 5, Lapua, FINLAND SF-62101/64-310111; FAX: 64-4388991 (U.S. importers—Champion's Choice; Keng's Firearms Specialty, Inc.

L.A.R. Mfg., Inc., 4133 W. Farm Rd., West Jordan, UT 84088/801-280-3505; FAX: 801-280-1972

LaRocca Gun Works, Inc., 51 Union Place, Worcester, MA 01608/508-754-2887; FAX: 508-754-2887

Laser Devices, Inc., 2 Harris Ct. A4, Monterey, CA 93940/408-373-0701, 800-235-2162; FAX: 408-373-0903

Laseraim, Inc. (See Emerging Technologies, Inc.)

LaserMax, 3495 Winton Place, Bldg. B, Rochester, NY 14623/716-272-5420; FAX: 716-272-5427

Lassen Community College, Gunsmithing Dept., P.O. Box 3000, Hwy. 139, Susanville, CA 96130/916-251-8809 ext. 109 or 200; FAX: 916-257-8964

Lathrop's, Inc., 5146 E. Pima, Tucson, AZ 85712/520-881-0266, 800-875-4867; FAX: 520-322-5704

Laughridge, William R. (See Cylinder & Slide, Inc.)

Law Concealment Systems, Inc., P.O. Box 3952, Wilmington, NC 28406/919-791-6656, 800-373-0116 orders

Lawrence Leather Co., P.O. Box 1479, Lillington, NC 27546/910-893-2071; FAX: 910-893-4742

Lawson Co., Harry, 3328 N. Richey Blvd., Tucson, AZ 85716/520-326-1117

Lawson, John G. (See Sight Shop, The)

LBT, HCR 62, Box 145, Moyie Springs, ID 83845/208-267-3588

Le Clear Industries (See E-Z-Way Systems)

Lea Mfg. Co., 237 E. Aurora St., Waterbury, CT 06720/203-753-5116

Leather Arsenal, 27549 Middleton Rd., Middleton, ID 83644/208-585-6212

Lebeau-Courally, Rue St. Gilles, 386, 4000 Liege, BELGIUM/041-52-48-43; FAX: 32-041-52-20-08 (U.S. importer—New England Arms Co.)

Leckie Professional Gunsmithing, 546 Quarry Rd., Ottsville, PA 18942/215-847-8594

Ledbetter Airguns, Riley, 1804 E. Sprague St., Winston Salem, NC 27107-3521/919-784-0676

Lee Precision, Inc., 4275 Hwy. U, Hartford, WI 53027/414-673-3075

Lee's Red Ramps, 4 Kristine Ln., Silver City, NM 88061/505-538-8529

LeFever Arms Co., Inc., 6234 Stokes, Lee Center Rd., Lee Center, NY 13363/315-337-6722; FAX: 315-337-1543

Legend Products Corp., 1555 E. Flamingo Rd., Suite 404, Las Vegas, NV 89119/702-228-1808, 702-796-5778; FAX: 702-228-7484

Leibowitz, Leonard, 1205 Murrayhill Ave., Pittsburgh, PA 15217/412-361-5455

Leica USA, Inc., 156 Ludlow Ave., Northvale, NJ 07647/201-767-7500; FAX: 201-767-8666

L.E.M. Gun Specialties, Inc., The Lewis Lead Remover, P.O. Box 2855, Peachtree City, GA 30269-2024/770-487-0556

Lem Sports, Inc., P.O. Box 2107, Aurora, IL 60506/815-286-7421, 800-688-8801 (orders only)

Lethal Force Institute, P.O. Box 122, Concord, MA 03302/603-226-1484; FAX: 603-226-3554

Lett Custom Grips, 672 Currier Rd., Hopkinton, NH 03229-2652

Leupold & Stevens, Inc., P.O. Box 688, Beaverton, OR 97075/503-646-9171; FAX: 503-526-1455

Lewis Lead Remover, The (See LEM Gun Specialties, Inc.)

Liberty Antique Gunworks, 19 Key St., P.O. Box 183, Eastport, ME 04631/207-853-4116

Liberty Metals, 2233 East 16th St., Los Angeles, CA 90021/213-581-9171; FAX: 213-581-9351

Liberty Safe, 1060 N. Spring Creek Pl., Springville, UT 84663/800-247-5625; FAX: 801-489-6409

Liberty Shooting Supplies, P.O. Box 357, Hillsboro, OR 97123/503-640-5518

Lightning Performance Innovations, Inc., RD1 Box 555, Mohawk, NY 13407/315-866-8819, 800-242-5873; FAX: 315-866-8819

Lind Custom Guns, Al, 7821 76th Ave. SW, Tacoma, WA 98498/206-584-6361

Lindsay, Steve, RR 2 Cedar Hills, Kearney, NE 68847/308-236-7885

Lindsley Arms Cartridge Co., P.O. Box 757, 20 College Hill Rd., Henniker, NH 03242/603-428-3127

Linebaugh Custom Sixguns, Route 2, Box 100, Maryville, MO 64468/816-562-3031

List Precision Engineering, Unit 1, Ingley Works, 13 River Road, Barking, Essex 1G11 0HE ENGLAND/011-081-594-1686

Lister, Weldon, Route 1, P.O. Box 1517, Boerne, TX 78006/210-755-2210

Lithi Bee Bullet Lube, 1885 Dyson St., Muskegon, MI 49442/616-726-3400

"Little John's" Antique Arms, 1740 W. Laveta, Orange, CA 92668

Little Trees Ramble (See Scott Pilkington, Little Trees Ramble)

Littler Sales Co., 20815 W. Chicago, Detroit, MI 48228/313-273-6889; FAX: 313-273-1099

Littleton, J.F., 275 Pinedale Ave., Oroville, CA 95966/916-533-6084

Llama Gabilondo Y Cia, Apartado 290, E-01080, Victoria, SPAIN (U.S. importer—Import Sports, Inc.)

Load From A Disk, 9826 Sagedale, Houston, TX 77089/713-484-0935

Loadmaster, P.O. Box 1209, Warminster, Wilts. BA12 9XJ ENGLAND/01044 1985 218544; FAX: 01044 1985 214111

Loch Leven Industries, P.O. Box 2751, Santa Rosa, CA 95405/707-573-8735; FAX: 707-573-0369

Lock's Philadelphia Gun Exchange, 6700 Rowland Ave., Philadelphia, PA 19149/215-332-6225; FAX: 215-332-4800

Log Cabin Sport Shop, 8010 Lafayette Rd., Lodi, OH 44254/216-948-1082

Lomont Precision Bullets, RR 1, P.O. Box 34, Salmon, ID 83467/208-756-6819; FAX: 208-756-6824

London Guns Ltd., Box 3750, Santa Barbara, CA 93130/805-683-4141; FAX: 805-683-1712

Lone Star Gunleather, 1301 Brushy Bend Dr., Round Rock, TX 78681/512-255-1805

Long, George F., 1500 Rogue River Hwy., Ste. F, Grants Pass, OR 97527/541-476-7552

Lorcin Engineering Co., Inc., 10427 San Sevaine Way, Ste. A, Mira Loma, CA 91752/909-360-1406; FAX: 909-360-0623

Lortone, Inc., 2856 NW Market St., Seattle, WA 98107/206-789-3100

Lothar Walther Precision Tool, Inc., 2190 Coffee Rd., Lithonia, GA 30058/770-482-4253; Fax: 770-482-9344

Loweth, Richard, 29 Hedgegrow Lane, Kirby Muxloe, Leics. LE9 9BN ENGLAND

L.P.A. Snc, Via Alfieri 26, Gardone V.T., Brescia, ITALY 25063/30-891-14-81; FAX: 30-891-09-51

LPS Laboratories, Inc., 4647 Hugh Howell Rd., P.O. Box 3050, Tucker, GA 30084/404-934-7800

Lucas, Edward E., 32 Garfield Ave., East Brunswick, NJ 08816/201-251-5526

Luch Metal Merchants, Barbara, 48861 West Rd., Wixon, MI 48393/800-876-5337

Lutz Engraving, Ron, E. 1998 Smokey Valley Rd., Scandinavia, WI 54977/715-467-2674

Lyman Instant Targets, Inc. (See Lyman Products Corp.)

Lyman Products Corporation, 475 Smith Street, Middletown, CT 06457-1541/860-632-2020, 800-22-LYMAN; FAX: 860-632-1699

M

M&D Munitions Ltd., 127 Verdi St., Farmingdale, NY 11735/800-878-2788, 516-752-1038; FAX: 516-752-1905

M&N Bullet Lube, P.O. Box 495, 151 NE Jefferson St., Madras, OR 97741/503-255-3750

MA Systems, P.O. Box 1143, Chouteau, OK 74337/918-479-6378

Mac-1 Distributors, 13974 Van Ness Ave., Gardena, CA 90249/310-327-3582

Mac's .45 Shop, P.O. Box 2028, Seal Beach, CA 90740/310-438-5046

Madis, George, P.O. Box 545, Brownsboro, TX 75756

Mag-Na-Port International, Inc., 41302 Executive Dr., Harrison Twp., MI 48045-1306/810-469-6727; FAX: 810-469-0425

Magma Engineering Co., P.O. Box 161, 20955 E. Ocotillo Rd., Queen Creek, AZ 85242/602-987-9008; FAX: 602-987-0148

Magnolia Sports, Inc., 211 W. Main, Magnolia, AR 71753/501-234-8410, 800-530-7816; FAX: 501-234-8117

Magnum Research, Inc., 7110 University Ave. NE, Minneapolis, MN 55432/800-772-6168, 612-574-1868; FAX: 612-574-0109

Magnus Bullets, P.O. Box 239, Toney, AL 35773/205-828-5089; FAX: 205-828-7756

MagSafe Ammo Co., 2725 Friendly Grove Rd NE, Olympia, WA 98506/360-357-6383; FAX: 360-705-4715

MAGTECH Recreational Products, Inc., 5030 Paradise Rd., Suite A104, Las Vegas, NV 89119/702-736-2043; FAX: 702-736-2140

Mahony, Philip Bruce, 67 White Hollow Rd., Lime Rock, CT 06039-2418/203-435-9341

Mahovsky's Metalife, R.D. 1, Box 149a Eureka Road, Grand Valley, PA 16420/814-436-7747

Maine Custom Bullets, RFD 1, Box 1755, Brooks, ME 04921

Mains Enterprises, Inc., 3111 S. Valley View Blvd., Suite B120, Las Vegas, NV 89102-7790/702-876-6278; FAX: 702-876-1269

Maionchi-L.M.I., Via Di Coselli-Zona Industriale Di Guamo, Lucca, ITALY 55060/011 39-583 94291

Mandall Shooting Supplies, Inc., 3616 N. Scottsdale Rd., Scottsdale, AZ 85252/602-945-2553; FAX: 602-949-0734

Marble Arms, P.O. Box 111, Gladstone, MI 49837/906-428-3710; FAX: 906-428-3711

Marchmon Bullets, 8191 Woodland Shore Dr., Brighton, MI 48116

Marent, Rudolf, 9711 Tiltree St., Houston, TX 77075/713-946-7028

Markell, Inc., 422 Larkfield Center 235, Santa Rosa, CA 95403/707-573-0792; FAX: 707-573-9867

Marksman Products, 5482 Argosy Dr., Huntington Beach, CA 92649/714-898-7535, 800-822-8005; FAX: 714-891-0782

Marmik Inc., 2116 S. Woodland Ave., Michigan City, IN 46361-7508/219-872-7231

Marple & Associates, Dick, 21 Dartmouth St., Hooksett, NH 03106/603-627-1837; FAX: 603-627-1837

Marquart Precision Co., Inc., Rear 136 Grove Ave., Box 1740, Prescott, AZ 86302/602-445-5646

Marsh, Mike, Croft Cottage, Main St., Elton, Derbyshire DE4 2BY, ENGLAND/01629 650 669

Martin Bookseller, J., P.O. Drawer AP, Beckley, WV 25802/304-255-4073; FAX: 304-255-4077

Martin's Gun Shop, 937 S. Sheridan Blvd., Lakewood, CO 80226/303-922-2184

Martz, John V., 8060 Lakeview Lane, Lincoln, CA 95648/916-645-2250

Marvel, Alan, 3922 Madonna Rd., Jarretsville, MD 21084/301-557-6545

Maryland Paintball Supply, 8507 Harford Rd., Parkville, MD 21234/410-882-5607

Masen Co., Inc., John, 1305 Jelmak, Grand Prairie, TX 75050/817-430-8732; FAX: 817-430-1715

MAST Technology, 4350 S. Arville, Suite 3, Las Vegas, NV 89103/702-362-5043; FAX: 702-362-9554

Master Class Bullets, 4209-D West 6th, Eugene, OR 97402/503-687-1263, 800-883-1263

Master Engravers, Inc. (See Hendricks, Frank E.)

Master Lock Co., 2600 N. 32nd St., Milwaukee, WI 53245/414-444-2800

Match Prep, P.O. Box 155, Tehachapi, CA 93581/805-822-5383

Matco, Inc., 1003-2nd St., N. Manchester, IN 46962/219-982-8282

Mathews & Son, Inc., George E., 10224 S. Paramount Blvd., Downey, CA 90241/310-862-6719; FAX: 310-862-6719

Mauser Werke Oberndorf Waffensysteme GmbH, Postfach 1349, 78722 Oberndorf/N. GERMANY (U.S. importer—GSI, Inc.)

Maxi-Mount, P.O. Box 291, Willoughby Hills, OH 44094-0291/216-944-9456; FAX: 216-944-9456

Maximum Security Corp., 32841 Calle Perfecto, San Juan Capistrano, CA 92675/714-493-3684; FAX: 714-496-7733

Mazur Restoration, Pete, 13083 Drummer Way, Grass Valley, CA 95949/916-268-2412

McCament, Jay, 1730-134th St. Ct. S., Tacoma, WA 98444/206-531-8832

McCann's Machine & Gun Shop, P.O. Box 641, Spanaway, WA 98387/206-537-6919; FAX: 206-537-6993

McCann's Muzzle-Gun Works, 14 Walton Dr., New Hope, PA 18938/215-862-2728

McCombs, Leo, 1862 White Cemetery Rd., Patriot, OH 45658/614-256-1714

McCormick Corp., Chip, 1825 Fortview Rd., Ste. 115, Austin, TX 78704/800-328-CHIP, 512-462-0004; FAX: 512-462-0009

McDonald, Dennis, 8359 Brady St., Peosta, IA 52068/319-556-7940

McFarland, Stan, 2221 Idella Ct., Grand Junction, CO 81505/303-243-4704

McGowen Rifle Barrels, 5961 Spruce Lane, St. Anne, IL 60964/815-937-9816; FAX: 815-937-4024

McKenzie, Lynton, 6940 N. Alvernon Way, Tucson, AZ 85718/520-299-5090

McKillen & Heyer, Inc., 35535 Euclid Ave. Suite 11, Willoughby, OH 44094/216-942-2044

McKinney, R.P. (See Schuetzen Gun Co.)

McMurdo, Lynn (See Specialty Gunsmithing)

MCRW Associates Shooting Supplies, R.R. 1 Box 1425, Sweet Valley, PA 18656/717-864-3967; FAX: 717-864-2669

MCS, Inc., 34 Delmar Dr., Brookfield, CT 06804/203-775-1013; FAX: 203-775-9462

MEC-Gar S.R.L., Via Madonnina 64, Gardone V.T., Brescia, ITALY 25063/39-30-8912687; FAX: 39-30-8910065 (U.S. importer—MEC-Gar U.S.A., Inc.)

Meier Works, P.O. Box 423, Tijeras, NM 87059/505-281-3783

Meister Bullets (See Gander Mountain)

Mele, Frank, 201 S. Wellow Ave., Cookeville, TN 38501/615-526-4860

Men-Metallwerk Elisenhuette, GmbH, P.O. Box 1263, D-56372 Nassau/Lahn, GERMANY/2604-7819

Menck, Thomas W., 5703 S. 77th St., Ralston, NE 68127-4201

Mendez, John A., P.O. Box 620984, Orlando, FL 32862/407-282-2178

Meprolight (See Hesco-Meprolight)

Mercer Custom Stocks, R.M., 216 S. Whitewater Ave., Jefferson, WI 53549/414-674-5130

Merit Corporation, Box 9044, Schenectady, NY 12309/518-346-1420

Merkuria Ltd., Argentinska 38, 17005 Praha 7, CZECH REPUBLIC/422-875117; FAX: 422-809152

Metalife Industries (See Mahovsky's Metalife)

Metaloy Inc., Rt. 5, Box 595, Berryville, AR 72616/501-545-3611

Michael's Antiques, Box 591, Waldoboro, ME 04572

Michaels of Oregon Co., P.O. Box 13010, Portland, OR 97213/503-255-6890; FAX: 503-255-0746

Micro Sight Co., 242 Harbor Blvd., Belmont, CA 94002/415-591-0769; FAX: 415-591-7531

Mid-America Guns and Ammo, 1205 W. Jefferson, Suite E, Effingham, IL 62401/800-820-5177

Mid-America Recreation, Inc., 1328 5th Ave., Moline, IL 61265/309-764-5089; FAX: 309-764-2722

Middlebrooks Custom Shop, 7366 Colonial Trail East, Surry, VA 23883/804-357-0881; FAX: 804-365-0442

Midway Arms, Inc., 5875 W. Van Horn Tavern Rd., Columbia, MO 65203/800-243-3220, 314-445-6363; FAX: 314-446-1018

Miller Co., David, 3131 E. Greenlee Rd., Tucson, AZ 85716/602-326-3117

Miller Custom, 210 E. Julia, Clinton, IL 61727/217-935-9362

Miller Enterprises, Inc., R.P., 1557 E. Main St., P.O. Box 234, Brownsburg, IN 46112/317-852-8187

Millett Sights, 16131 Gothard St., Huntington Beach, CA 92647/714-842-5575, 800-645-5388; FAX: 714-843-5707

Minute Man High Tech Industries, 10611 Canyon Rd. E., Suite 151, Puyallup, WA 98373/800-233-2734

Mirador Optical Corp., P.O. Box 11614, Marina Del Rey, CA 90295-7614/310-821-5587; FAX: 310-305-0386

Mitchell Arms, Inc., 3433-B. W. Harvard St., Santa Ana, CA 92704/714-957-5711; FAX: 714-957-5732

Mitchell's Accuracy Shop, 68 Greenridge Dr., Stafford, VA 22554/703-659-0165

MI-TE Bullets, R.R. 1 Box 230, Ellsworth, KS 67439/913-472-4575

Mittermeier, Inc., Frank, P.O. Box 2G, 3577 E. Tremont Ave., Bronx, NY 10465/718-828-3843

Mixson Corp., 7435 W. 19th Ct., Hialeah, FL 33014/305-821-5190, 800-327-0078; FAX: 305-558-9318

MJK Gunsmithing, Inc., 417 N. Huber Ct., E. Wenatchee, WA 98802/509-884-7683

MJM Mfg., 3283 Rocky Water Ln. Suite B, San Jose, CA 95148/408-270-4207

MKL Service Co., 610 S. Troy St., P.O. Box D, Royal Oak, MI 48068/810-548-5453

MKS Supply, Inc. (See Hi-Point Firearms)

MMP, Rt. 6, Box 384, Harrison, AR 72601/501-741-5019; FAX: 501-741-3104

M.O.A. Corp., 2451 Old Camden Pike, Eaton, OH 45320/513-456-3669

Modern Gun Repair School, P.O. Box 92577, Southlake, TX 76092/800-493-4114; FAX: 800-556-5112

Modern Gun School, 500 N. Kimball, Suite 105, Southlake, TX 76092/800-774-5112

Modern MuzzleLoading, Inc., 234 Airport Rd., P.O. Box 130, Centerville, IA 52544/515-856-2626; FAX: 515-856-2628

Montana Outfitters, Lewis E. Yearout, 308 Riverview Dr. E., Great Falls, MT 59404/406-761-0859

Montana Precision Swaging, P.O. Box 4746, Butte, MT 59702/406-782-7502

Monte Kristo Pistol Grip Co., P.O. Box 85, Whiskeytown, CA 96095/916-778-0240

Montgomery Community College, P.O. Box 787-GD, Troy, NC 27371/910-572-3691, 800-839-6222

Moreton/Fordyce Enterprises, P.O. Box 940, Saylorsburg, PA 18353/717-992-5742; FAX: 717-992-8775

Morini (See U.S. importers—Mandall Shooting Supplies, Inc.; Nygord Precision Products)

Morrow, Bud, 11 Hillside Lane, Sheridan, WY 82801-9729/307-674-8360

Morton Booth Co., P.O. Box 123, Joplin, MO 64802/417-673-1962; FAX: 417-673-3642

Mo's Competitor Supplies (See MCS, Inc.)

Moschetti, Mitchell R., P.O. Box 27065, Denver, CO 80227

Mountain Bear Rifle Works, Inc., 100 B Ruritan Rd., Sterling, VA 20164/703-430-0420; FAX: 703-430-7068

Mountain South, P.O. Box 381, Barnwell, SC 29812/FAX: 803-259-3227

Mountain State Muzzleloading Supplies, Box 154-1, Rt. 2, Williamstown, WV 26187/304-375-7842; FAX: 304-375-3737

Mountain States Engraving, Kenneth W. Warren, P.O. Box 2842, Wenatchee, WA 98802/509-663-6123

Mowrey's Guns & Gunsmithing, RR1, Box 82, Canajoharie, NY 13317/518-673-3483

MSC Industrial Supply Co., 151 Sunnyside Blvd., Plainview, NY 11803-9915/516-349-0330

MSR Targets, P.O. Box 1042, West Covina, CA 91793/818-331-7840

Mt. Alto Outdoor Products, Rt. 735, Howardsville, VA 24562

Mt. Baldy Bullet Co., 12981 Old Hill City Rd., Keystone, SD 57751-6623/605-666-4725

MTM Molded Products Co., Inc., 3370 Obco Ct., Dayton, OH 45414/513-890-7461; FAX: 513-890-1747

Mullins Ammo, Rt. 2, Box 304K, Clintwood, VA 24228/703-926-6772

Mullis Guncraft, 3523 Lawyers Road E., Monroe, NC 28110/704-283-6683

Multiplex International, 26 S. Main St., Concord, NH 03301/FAX: 603-796-2223

Munsch Gunsmithing, Tommy, Rt. 2, P.O. Box 248, Little Falls, MN 56345/612-632-6695

Murmur Corp., 2823 N. Westmoreland Ave., Dallas, TX 75222/214-630-5400

Murray State College, 100 Faculty Dr., Tishomingo, OK 73460/405-371-2371 ext. 238, 800-342-0698

Muscle Products Corp., 112 Fennell Dr., Butler, PA 16001/800-227-7049, 412-283-0567; FAX: 412-283-8310

Museum of Historical Arms Inc., 2750 Coral Way, Suite 204, Miami, FL 33145/305-444-9199

Mushroom Express Bullet Co., 601 W. 6th St., Greenfield, IN 46140-1728/317-462-6332

Mustra's Custom Guns, Inc., Carl, 1002 Pennsylvania Ave., Palm Harbor, FL 34683/813-785-1403

Muzzleloaders Etcetera, Inc., 9901 Lyndale Ave. S., Bloomington, MN 55420/612-884-1161

N

N&J Sales, Lime Kiln Rd., Northford, CT 06472/203-484-0247

Nagel's Bullets, 9 Wilburn, Baytown, TX 77520

Napoleon Bonaparte, Inc., Gerald Desquesnes, 640 Harrison St., Santa Clara, CA 95050

Nastoff's 45 Shop, Inc., Steve, 12288 Mahoning Ave., P.O. Box 446, North Jackson, OH 44451/216-538-2977

National Bullet Co., 1585 E. 361 St., Eastlake, OH 44095/216-951-1854; FAX: 216-951-7761

National Security Safe Co., Inc., P.O. Box 39, 620 S. 380 E., American Fork, UT 84003/801-756-7706, 800-544-3829; FAX: 801-756-8043

National Target Co., 4690 Wyaconda Rd., Rockville, MD 20852/800-827-7060, 301-770-7060; FAX: 301-770-7892

Nationwide Sports Distributors, Inc., 70 James Way, Southampton, PA 18966/215-322-2050, 800-355-3006; FAX: 702-358-2093

Naval Ordnance Works, Rt. 2, Box 919, Sheperdstown, WV 25443/304-876-0998

Navy Arms Co., 689 Bergen Blvd., Ridgefield, NJ 07657/201-945-2500; FAX: 201-945-6859

N.B.B., Inc., 24 Elliot Rd., Sterling, MA 01564/508-422-7538, 800-942-9444

N.C. Ordnance Co., P.O. Box 3254, Wilson, NC 27895/919-237-2440; FAX: 919-243-0927

NCP Products, Inc., 3500 12th St. N.W., Canton, OH 44708/330-456-5130: FAX: 330-456-5234

NECO, 1316-67th St., Emeryville, CA 94608/510-450-0420; FAX: 510-450-0421

Necromancer Industries, Inc., 14 Communications Way, West Newton, PA 15089/412-872-8722

NEI Handtools, Inc., 51583 Columbia River Hwy., Scappoose, OR 97056/503-543-6776; FAX: 503-543-6799; E-MAIL: neiht@mcimail.com

Nelson Combat Leather, Bruce, P.O. Box 8691 CRB, Tucson, AZ 85738

Nelson, Gary K., 975 Terrace Dr., Oakdale, CA 95361/209-847-4590

Nesci Enterprises, Inc., P.O. Box 119, Summit St., East Hampton, CT 06424/860-267-2588; FAX: 860-267-2589

Nettestad Gun Works, RR 1, Box 160, Pelican Rapids, MN 56572/218-863-4301

Neumann GmbH, Am Galgenberg 6, 90575 Langenzenn, GERMANY/09101/8258; FAX: 09101/6356

Nevada Pistol Academy Inc., 4610 Blue Diamond Rd., Las Vegas, NV 89139/702-897-1100

New Advantage Arms Corp., 2843 N. Alvernon Way, Tucson, AZ 85712/602-881-7444; FAX: 602-323-0949

New England Ammunition Co., 1771 Post Rd. East, Suite 223, Westport, CT 06880/203-254-8048

New England Arms Co., Box 278, Lawrence Lane, Kittery Point, ME 03905/207-439-0593; FAX: 207-439-6726

New Orleans Jewelers Supply Co., 206 Charters St., New Orleans, LA 70130/504-523-3839; FAX: 504-523-3836

New Win Publishing, Inc., Box 5159, Clinton, NJ 08809/201-735-9701; FAX: 201-735-9703

Newell, Robert H., 55 Coyote, Los Alamos, NM 87544/505-662-7135

NgraveR Co., The, 67 Wawecus Hill Rd., Bozrah, CT 06334/203-823-1533

Nicholson Custom, Rt. 1, Box 176-3, Sedalia, MO 65301/816-826-8746

Niemi Engineering, W.B., Box 126 Center Road, Greensboro, VT 05841/802-533-7180 days, 802-533-7141 evenings

Nikon, Inc., 1300 Walt Whitman Rd., Melville, NY 11747/516-547-8623; FAX: 516-547-0309

Nitex, Inc., P.O. Box 1706, Uvalde, TX 78801/210-278-8843

Noble Co., Jim, 1305 Columbia St., Vancouver, WA 98660/206-695-1309

Noreen, Peter H., 5075 Buena Vista Dr., Belgrade, MT 59714/406-586-7383

Norma Precision AB (See U.S. importers—Dynamit Nobel-RWS Inc.; Paul Co. Inc., The)

North American Arms, Inc., 2150 South 950 East, Provo, UT 84606-6285/800-821-5783, 801-374-9990; FAX: 801-374-9998

North American Correspondence Schools, The Gun Pro School, Oak & Pawney St., Scranton, PA 18515/717-342-7701

North American Shooting Systems, P.O. Box 306, Osoyoos, B.C. V0H 1V0 CANADA/604-495-3131; FAX: 604-495-2816

North American Specialties, P.O. Box 189, Baker City, OR 97814/503-523-6954

North Devon Firearms Services, 3 North St., Braunton, EX33 1AJ ENGLAND/01271 813624; FAX: 01271 813624

North Fork Custom Gunsmithing, James Johnston, 428 Del Rio Rd., Roseburg, OR 97470/503-673-4467

North Mountain Pine Training Center (See Executive Protection Institute)

North Specialty Products, 2664-B Saturn St., Brea, CA 92621/714-524-1665

North Star West, P.O. Box 488, Glencoe, CA 95232/209-293-7010

Northern Precision Custom Swaged Bullets, 329 S. James St., Carthage, NY 13619/315-493-1711

No-Sho Mfg. Co., 10727 Glenfield Ct., Houston, TX 77096/713-723-5332

Nosler, Inc., P.O. Box 671, Bend, OR 97709/800-285-3701, 503-382-3921; FAX: 503-388-4667

Novak's, Inc., 1206½ 30th St., P.O. Box 4045, Parkersburg, WV 26101/304-485-9295; FAX: 304-428-6722

Nowlin Custom Mfg., Rt. 1, Box 308, Claremore, OK 74017/918-342-0689; FAX: 918-342-0624

NRI Gunsmith School, 4401 Connecticut Ave. NW, Washington, D.C. 20008

Nu-Line Guns, Inc., 1053 Caulks Hill Rd., Harvester, MO 63304/314-441-4500, 314-447-4501; FAX: 314-447-5018

Null Holsters Ltd., K.L., 161 School St. NW, Hill City Station, Resaca, GA 30735/706-625-5643; FAX: 706-625-9392

Nu-Teck, 30 Industrial Park Rd., Box 37, Centerbrook, CT 06409/203-767-3573; FAX: 203-767-9137

Nygord Precision Products, P.O. Box 12578, Prescott, AZ 86304/520-717-2315; FAX: 520-717-2198

O

October Country, P.O. Box 969, Dept. GD, Hayden, ID 83835/208-772-2068; FAX: 208-772-9230

Oehler Research, Inc., P.O. Box 9135, Austin, TX 78766/512-327-6900, 800-531-5125; FAX: 512-327-6903

Oglesby & Oglesby Gunmakers, Inc., RR 5, Springfield, IL 62707/217-487-7100

Oil Rod and Gun Shop, 69 Oak St., East Douglas, MA 01516/508-476-3687

Ojala Holsters, Arvo, P.O. Box 98, N. Hollywood, CA 91603/503-669-1404

Oker's Engraving, 365 Bell Rd., P.O. Box 126, Shawnee, CO 80475/303-838-6042

Oklahoma Ammunition Co., 4310 W. Rogers Blvd., Skiatook, OK 74070/918-396-3187; FAX: 918-396-4270

Oklahoma Leather Products, Inc., 500 26th NW, Miami, OK 74354/918-542-6651; FAX: 918-542-6653

OK Weber, Inc., P.O. Box 7485, Eugene, OR 97401/541-747-0458; FAX: 541-747-5927

Old Dominion Engravers, 100 Progress Drive, Lynchburg, VA 24502/804-237-4450

Old Wagon Bullets, 32 Old Wagon Rd., Wilton, CT 06897

Old West Bullet Moulds, P.O. Box 519, Flora Vista, NM 87415/505-334-6970

Old West Reproductions, Inc., 446 Florence S. Loop, Florence, MT 59833/406-273-2615

Old Western Scrounger, Inc., 12924 Hwy. A-l2, Montague, CA 96064/916-459-5445; FAX: 916-459-3944

Old World Oil Products, 3827 Queen Ave. N., Minneapolis, MN 55412/612-522-5037

Ole Frontier Gunsmith Shop, 2617 Hwy. 29 S., Cantonment, FL 32533/904-477-8074

Olson, Myron, 989 W. Kemp, Watertown, SD 57201/605-886-9787

Olson, Vic, 5002 Countryside Dr., Imperial, MO 63052/314-296-8086

Omark Industries, Div. of Blount, Inc., 2299 Snake River Ave., P.O. Box 856, Lewiston, ID 83501/800-627-3640, 208-746-2351

Ordnance Works, The, 2969 Pidgeon Point Road, Eureka, CA 95501/707-443-3252

Outa-Site Gun Carriers, 219 Market St., Laredo, TX 78040/210-722-4678, 800-880-9715; FAX: 210-726-4858

Outdoor Connection, Inc., The, 201 Cotton Dr., P.O. Box 7751, Waco, TX 76714-7751/800-533-6076; 817-772-5575; FAX: 817-776-3553

Outdoorsman's Bookstore, The, Llangorse, Brecon, Powys LD3 7UE, U.K./44-1874-658-660; FAX: 44-1874-658-650

Outers Laboratories, Div. of Blount, Inc., Sporting Equipment Div., Route 2,, P.O. Box 39/Onalaska, WI 54650/608-781-5800; FAX: 608-781-0368

Ox-Yoke Originals, Inc., 34 Main St., Milo, ME 04463/800-231-8313, 207-943-7351; FAX: 207-943-2416

Ozark Gun Works, 11830 Cemetery Rd., Rogers, AR 72756/501-631-6944; FAX: 501-631-6944

P

P&M Sales and Service, 5724 Gainsborough Pl., Oak Forest, IL 60452/708-687-7149

P&S Gun Service, 2138 Old Shepardsville Rd., Louisville, KY 40218/502-456-9346

Pachmayr, Ltd., 1875 S. Mountain Ave., Monrovia, CA 91016/818-357-7771, 800-423-9704; FAX: 818-358-7251

Pacific Pistolcraft, 1810 E. Columbia Ave., Tacoma, WA 98404/206-474-5465

Pacific Rifle Co., 1040-D Industrial Parkway, Newberg, OR 97132/503-538-7437

Paco's (See Small Custom Mould & Bullet Co.)

P.A.C.T., Inc., P.O. Box 531525, Grand Prairie, TX 75053/214-641-0049

Page Custom Bullets, P.O. Box 25, Port Moresby Papua, NEW GUINEA

Pagel Gun Works, Inc., 1407 4th St. NW, Grand Rapids, MN 55744/218-326-3003

Palmer Security Products, 2930 N. Campbell Ave., Chicago, IL 60618/800-788-7725; FAX: 312-267-8080

PanaVise Products, Inc., 1485 Southern Way, Sparks, NV 89431/702-353-2900; FAX: 702-353-2929

Para-Ordnance Mfg., Inc., 980 Tapscott Rd., Scarborough, Ont. M1X 1E7, CANADA/416-297-7855; FAX: 416-297-1289 (U.S. importer—Para-Ordnance, Inc.)

Para-Ordnance, Inc., 1919 NE 45th St., Ft. Lauderdale, FL 33308

Paragon Sales & Services, Inc., P.O. Box 2022, Joliet, IL 60434/815-725-9212; FAX: 815-725-8974

Pardini Armi Srl, Via Italica 154, 55043 Lido Di Camaiore Lu, ITALY/584-90121; FAX: 584-90122 (U.S. importers—Nygord Precision Products)

Paris, Frank J., 17417 Pershing St., Livonia, MI 48152-3822

Parker Gun Finishes, 9337 Smokey Row Rd., Strawberry Plains, TN 37871/423-933-3286

Parker, Mark D., 1240 Florida Ave. 7, Longmont, CO 80501/303-772-0214

Parsons Optical Mfg. Co., P.O. Box 192, Ross, OH 45061/513-867-0820; FAX: 513-867-8380

Parts & Surplus, P.O. Box 22074, Memphis, TN 38122/901-683-4007

Pasadena Gun Center, 206 E. Shaw, Pasadena, TX 77506/713-472-0417; FAX: 713-472-1322

Passive Bullet Traps, Inc. (See Savage Range Systems, Inc.)

PAST Sporting Goods, Inc., P.O. Box 1035, Columbia, MO 65205/314-445-9200; FAX: 314-446-6606

Paterson Gunsmithing, 438 Main St., Paterson, NJ 07502/201-345-4100

Pathfinder Sports Leather, 2920 E. Chambers St., Phoenix, AZ 85040/602-276-0016

Patrick Bullets, P.O. Box 172, Warwick QSLD 4370 AUSTRALIA

PC Bullet/ADC, Inc., 52700 NE First, Scappoose, OR 97056-3212/503-543-5088; FAX: 503-543-5990

Peacemaker Specialists, P.O. Box 157, Whitmore, CA 96096/916-472-3438

Pease Accuracy, Bob, P.O. Box 310787, New Braunfels, TX 78131/210-625-1342

Pedersen, C.R., 2717 S. Pere Marquette Hwy., Ludington, MI 49431/616-843-2061

Pedersen, Rex C., 2717 S. Pere Marquette Hwy., Ludington, MI 49431/616-843-2061

Peerless Alloy, Inc., 1445 Osage St., Denver, CO 80204-2439/303-825-6394, 800-253-1278

Pejsa Ballistics, 2120 Kenwood Pkwy., Minneapolis, MN 55405/612-374-3337; FAX: 612-374-3337

Peltor, Inc., 41 Commercial Way, E. Providence, RI 02914/401-438-4800; FAX: 401-434-1708

PEM's Mfg. Co., 5063 Waterloo Rd., Atwater, OH 44201/216-947-3721

Pence Precision Barrels, 7567 E. 900 S., S. Whitley, IN 46787/219-839-4745

Pend Oreille Sport Shop, 3100 Hwy. 200 East, Sandpoint, ID 83864/208-263-2412

Pendleton Royal, c/o Swingler Buckland Ltd., 4/7 Highgate St., Birmingham, ENGLAND B12 0XS/44 121 440 3060, 44 121 446 5898; FAX: 44 121 446 4165

Penguin Industries, Inc., Airport Industrial Mall, Coatesville, PA 19320/610-384-6000; FAX: 610-857-5980

Pennsylvania Gunsmith School, 812 Ohio River Blvd., Avalon, Pittsburgh, PA 15202/412-766-1812

Penrod Precision, 312 College Ave., P.O. Box 307, N. Manchester, IN 46962/219-982-8385

Pentax Corp., 35 Inverness Dr. E., Englewood, CO 80112/303-799-8000; FAX: 303-790-1131

Pentheny de Pentheny, 2352 Baggett Ct., Santa Rosa, CA 95401/707-573-1390; FAX: 707-573-1390

Perazone-Gunsmith, Brian, P.O. Box 275GD, Cold Spring Rd., Roxbury, NY 12474/607-326-4088; FAX: 607-326-3140

Performance Specialists, 308 Eanes School Rd., Austin, TX 78746/512-327-0119

Personal Protection Systems, RD 5, Box 5027-A, Moscow, PA 18444/717-842-1766

Peters Stahl GmbH, Stettiner Strasse 42, D-33106 Paderborn, GERMANY/05251-750025; FAX: 05251-75611 (U.S. importers—Harris Gunworks; Olympic Arms)

Petersen Publishing Co., 6420 Wilshire Blvd., Los Angeles, CA 90048/213-782-2000; FAX: 213-782-2867

Petro-Explo, Inc., 7650 U.S. Hwy. 287, Suite 100, Arlington, TX 76017/817-478-8888

Pettinger Books, Gerald, Rt. 2, Box 125, Russell, IA 50238/515-535-2239

Phillippi Custom Bullets, Justin, P.O. Box 773, Ligonier, PA 15658/412-238-9671

Phoenix Arms, 1420 S. Archibald Ave., Ontario, CA 91761/909-947-4843; FAX: 909-947-6798

Piedmont Community College, P.O. Box 1197, Roxboro, NC 27573/910-599-1181

Pierce Pistols, 2326 E. Hwy. 34, Newnan, GA 30263/404-253-8192

Pilgrim Pewter, Inc. (See Bell Originals Inc., Sid)

Pilkington, Scott, Little Trees Ramble, P.O. Box 97, Monteagle, TN 37356/615-924-3475; FAX: 615-924-3489

Pine Technical College, 1100 4th St., Pine City, MN 55063/800-521-7463; FAX: 612-629-6766

Pinetree Bullets, 133 Skeena St., Kitimat BC, CANADA V8C 1Z1/604-632-3768; FAX: 604-632-3768

Pioneer Arms Co., 355 Lawrence Rd., Broomall, PA 19008/215-356-5203

Pioneer Guns, 5228 Montgomery Rd., Norwood, OH 45212/513-631-4871

Piquette, Paul R., 80 Bradford Dr., Feeding Hills, MA 01030/413-781-8300, Ext. 682

Plaxco, J. Michael, Rt. 1, P.O. Box 203, Roland, AR 72135/501-868-9787

Plum City Ballistic Range, N2162 80th St., Plum City, WI 54761-8622/715-647-2539

PlumFire Press, Inc., 30-A Grove Ave., Patchogue, NY 11772-4112/800-695-7246; FAX:516-758-4071

PMC/Eldorado Cartridge Corp., P.O. Box 62508, 12801 U.S. Hwy. 95 S., Boulder City, NV 89005/702-294-0025; FAX: 702-294-0121

P.M. Enterprises, Inc., 146 Curtis Hill Rd., Chehalis, WA 98532/206-748-3743; FAX: 206-748-1802

Police Bookshelf, P.O. Box 122, Concord, NH 03301/603-224-6814; FAX: 603-226-3554

Policlips North America, 59 Douglas Crescent, Toronto, Ont. CANADA M4W 2E6/800-229-5089, 416-924-0383; FAX: 416-924-4375

Pomeroy, Robert, RR1, Box 50, E. Corinth, ME 04427/207-285-7721

Pony Express Reloaders, 608 E. Co. Rd. D, Suite 3, St. Paul, MN 55117/612-483-9406; FAX: 612-483-9884

Pony Express Sport Shop, Inc., 16606 Schoenborn St., North Hills, CA 91343/818-895-1231

Portus, Robert, 130 Ferry Rd., Grants Pass, OR 97526/503-476-4919

Potts, Wayne E., 912 Poplar St., Denver, CO 80220/303-355-5462

Powder Valley Services, Rt. 1, Box 100, Dexter, KS 67038/316-876-5418

Power Custom, Inc., RR 2, P.O. Box 756AB, Gravois Mills, MO 65037/314-372-5684

Practical Tools, Inc., Div. Behlert Precision, 7067 Easton Rd., P.O. Box 133, Pipersville, PA 18947/215-766-7301; FAX: 215-766-8681

Precise Metalsmithing Enterprises, 146 Curtis Hill Rd., Chehalis, WA 98532/206-748-3743; FAX: 206-748-8102

Precision Airgun Sales, Inc., 5139 Warrensville Center Rd., Maple Hts., OH 44137-1906/216-587-5005

Precision Castings & Equipment, Inc., P.O. Box 326, Jasper, IN 47547-0135/812-634-9167

Precision Components, 3177 Sunrise Lake, Milford, PA 18337/717-686-4414

Precision Components and Guns, Rt. 55, P.O. Box 337, Pawling, NY 12564/914-855-3040

Precision Delta Corp., P.O. Box 128, Ruleville, MS 38771/601-756-2810; FAX: 601-756-2590

Precision Metal Finishing, John Westrom, P.O. Box 3186, Des Moines, IA 50316/515-288-8680; FAX: 515-244-3925

Precision Munitions, Inc., P.O. Box 326, Jasper, IN 47547

Precision Reloading, Inc., P.O. Box 122, Stafford Springs, CT 06076/860-684-7979; FAX: 860-684-6788

Precision Sales International, Inc., P.O. Box 1776, Westfield, MA 01086/413-562-5055; FAX: 413-562-5056

Precision Small Arms, 9777 Wilshire Blvd., Suite 1005, Beverly Hills, CA 90212/310-859-4867; FAX: 310-859-2868

Precision Specialties, 131 Hendom Dr., Feeding Hills, MA 01030/413-786-3365; FAX: 413-786-3365

Precision Sport Optics, 15571 Producer Lane, Unit G, Huntington Beach, CA 92649/714-891-1309; FAX: 714-892-6920

Prescott Projectile Co., 1808 Meadowbrook Road, Prescott, AZ 86303

Price Bullets, Patrick W., 16520 Worthley Drive, San Lorenzo, CA 94580/510-278-1547

Prime Reloading, 30 Chiswick End, Meldreth, Royston SG8 6LZ UK/0763-260636

Pro Load Ammunition, Inc., 5180 E. Seltice Way, Post Falls, ID 83854/208-773-9444; FAX: 208-773-9441

Pro-Shot Products, Inc., P.O. Box 763, Taylorville, IL 62568/217-824-9133; FAX: 217-824-8861

Professional Gunsmiths of America, Inc., Route 1, Box 224F, Lexington, MO 64067/816-259-2636

Professional Hunter Supplies (See Star Custom Bullets)

Prolix® Lubricants, P.O. Box 1348, Victorville, CA 92393/800-248-LUBE, 619-243-3129; FAX: 619-241-0148

Protecto Plastics, Div. of Penguin Ind., Airport Industrial Mall, Coatesville, PA 19320/215-384-6000

Protector Mfg. Co., Inc., The, 443 Ashwood Place, Boca Raton, FL 33431/407-394-6011

Protektor Model, 1-11 Bridge St., Galeton, PA 16922/814-435-2442

P.S.M.G. Gun Co., 10 Park Ave., Arlington, MA 02174/617-646-8845; FAX: 617-646-2133

PWL Gunleather, P.O. Box 450432, Atlanta, GA 31145/404-822-1640; FAX: 404-822-1704

Q

Quality Firearms of Idaho, Inc., 114 13th Ave. S., Nampa, ID 83651/208-466-1631

Quality Parts Co./Bushmaster Firearms, 999 Roosevelt Trail, Bldg. 3, Windham, ME 04062/800-998-7928, 207-892-2005; FAX: 207-892-8068

Quigley's Personal Protection Strategies, Paxton, 9903 Santa Monica Blvd.,, 300/Beverly Hills, CA 90212/310-281-1762

R

Rabeno, Martin, 92 Spook Hole Rd., Ellenville, NY 12428/914-647-4567

Radical Concepts, P.O. Box 1473, Lake Grove, OR 97035/503-538-7437

Rainier Ballistics Corp., 4500 15th St. East, Tacoma, WA 98424/800-638-8722, 206-922-7589; FAX: 206-922-7854

Ram-Line, Inc., 545 Thirty-One Rd., Grand Junction, CO 81504/303-434-4500; FAX: 303-434-4004

Ranch Products, P.O. Box 145, Malinta, OH 43535/313-277-3118; FAX: 313-565-8536

Randco UK, 286 Gipsy Rd., Welling, Kent DA16 1JJ, ENGLAND/44 81 303 4118

Ranger Products, 2623 Grand Blvd., Suite 209, Holiday, FL 34609/813-942-4652, 800-407-7007; FAX: 813-942-6221

Ranging, Inc., Routes 5 & 20, East Bloomfield, NY 14443/716-657-6161; FAX: 716-657-5405

Ransom International Corp., P.O. Box 3845, 1040-A Sandretto Dr., Prescott, AZ 86302/520-778-7899; FAX: 520-778-7993; E-MAIL: ransom@primenet.com; WEB: http://www.primenet.com/~ransom

Rapine Bullet Mould Mfg. Co., 9503 Landis Lane, East Greenville, PA 18041/215-679-5413; FAX: 215-679-9795

Ravell Ltd., 289 Diputacion St., 08009, Barcelona SPAIN/34(3) 4874486; FAX: 34(3) 4881394

Raytech, Div. of Lyman Products Corp., 475 Smith Street, Middletown, CT 06457-1541/860-632-2020; FAX: 860-632-1699

RCBS, Div. of Blount, Inc., Sporting Equipment Div., 605 Oro Dam Blvd., Oroville, CA 95965/800-533-5000, 916-533-5191; FAX: 916-533-1647

Reardon Products, P.O. Box 126, Morrison, IL 61270/815-772-3155

Recoilless Technologies, Inc., 3432 W. Wilshire Dr., Suite 11, Phoenix, AZ 85009/602-278-8903; FAX: 602-272-5946

Red Cedar Precision Mfg., W. 485 Spruce Dr., Brodhead, WI 53520/608-897-8416

Red Star Target Co., P.O. Box 275, Babb, MT 59411-0275/800-679-2917; FAX: 800-679-2918

Redding Reloading Equipment, 1097 Starr Rd., Cortland, NY 13045/607-753-3331; FAX: 607-756-8445

Redfield, Inc., 5800 E. Jewell Ave., Denver, CO 80224-2303/303-757-6411; FAX: 303-756-2338

Redman's Rifling & Reboring, 189 Nichols Rd., Omak, WA 98841/509-826-5512

Redwood Bullet Works, 3559 Bay Rd., Redwood City, CA 94063/415-367-6741

Reed, Dave, Rt. 1, Box 374, Minnesota City, MN 55959/507-689-2944

R.E.I., P.O. Box 88, Tallevast, FL 34270/813-755-0085

Reloading Specialties, Inc., Box 1130, Pine Island, MN 55463/507-356-8500; FAX: 507-356-8800

Remington Arms Co., Inc., P.O. Box 700, 870 Remington Drive, Madison, NC 27025-0700/800-243-9700

Renegade, P.O. Box 31546, Phoenix, AZ 85046/602-482-6777; FAX: 602-482-1952

Reno, Wayne, 2808 Stagestop Rd., Jefferson, CO 80456/719-836-3452

R.E.T. Enterprises, 2608 S. Chestnut, Broken Arrow, OK 74012/918-251-GUNS; FAX: 918-251-0587

Retting, Inc., Martin B., 11029 Washington, Culver City, CA 90232/213-837-2412

R.G.-G., Inc., P.O. Box 1261, Conifer, CO 80433-1261/303-697-4154; FAX: 303-697-4154

Rice, Keith (See White Rock Tool & Die)

Richards, John, Richards Classic Oil Finish, Rt. 2, Box 325, Bedford, KY 40006/502-255-7222

Rickard, Inc., Pete, RD 1, Box 292, Cobleskill, NY 12043/800-282-5663; FAX: 518-234-2454

Ridgetop Sporting Goods, P.O. Box 306, 42907 Hilligoss Ln. East, Eatonville, WA 98328/360-832-6422; FAX: 360-832-6422

Riebe Co., W.J., 3434 Tucker Rd., Boise, ID 83703

Ries, Chuck, 415 Ridgecrest Dr., Grants Pass, OR 97527/503-476-5623

RIG Products, 87 Coney Island Dr., Sparks, NV 89431-6334/702-331-5666; FAX: 702-331-5669

Riggs, Jim, 206 Azalea, Boerne, TX 78006/210-249-8567

Riling Arms Books Co., Ray, 6844 Gorsten St., P.O. Box 18925, Philadelphia, PA 19119/215-438-2456; FAX: 215-438-5395

Rim Pac Sports, Inc., 1034 N. Soldano Ave., Azusa, CA 91702-2135

Ringler Custom Leather Co., 31 Shining Mtn. Rd., Powell, WY 82435/307-645-3255

R.I.S. Co., Inc., 718 Timberlake Circle, Richardson, TX 75080/214-235-0933

River Road Sporting Clays, Bruce Barsotti, P.O. Box 3016, Gonzales, CA 93926/408-675-2473

R.M. Precision, Inc., Attn. Greg F. Smith Marketing, P.O. Box 210, LaVerkin, UT 84745/801-635-4656; FAX: 801-635-4430

Robar Co.'s, Inc., The, 21438 N. 7th Ave., Suite B, Phoenix, AZ 85027/602-581-2648; FAX: 602-582-0059

Roberts/Engraver, J.J., 7808 Lake Dr., Manassas, VA 22111/703-330-0448

Roberts Products, 25328 SE Iss. Beaver Lk. Rd., Issaquah, WA 98029/206-392-8172

Robinson H.V. Bullets, 3145 Church St., Zachary, LA 70791/504-654-4029

Rochester Lead Works, 76 Anderson Ave., Rochester, NY 14607/716-442-8500; FAX: 716-442-4712

Rockwood Corp., Speedwell Division, 136 Lincoln Blvd., Middlesex, NJ 08846/908-560-7171, 800-243-8274; FAX: 980-560-7475

Rocky Fork Enterprises, P.O. Box 427, 878 Battle Rd., Nolensville, TN 37135/615-941-1307

Rocky Mountain Arms, Inc., 600 S. Sunset, Unit C, Longmont, CO 80501/303-768-8522; FAX: 303-678-8766

Rocky Mountain Target Co., 3 Aloe Way, Leesburg, FL 34788/904-365-9598

Rod Guide Co., Box 1149, Forsyth, MO 65653/800-952-2774

Rogers Gunsmithing, Bob, P.O. Box 305, 344 S. Walnut St., Franklin Grove, IL 61031/815-456-2685; FAX: 815-288-7142

Rohner, Hans, 1148 Twin Sisters Ranch Rd., Nederland, CO 80466-9600

Rohner, John, 710 Sunshine Canyon, Boulder, CO 80302/303-444-3841

Rolston, Inc., Fred W., 210 E. Cummins St., Tecumseh, MI 49286/517-423-6002, 800-314-9061 (orders only); FAX: 517-423-6002

Romain's Custom Guns, Inc., RD 1, Whetstone Rd., Brockport, PA 15823/814-265-1948

Rooster Laboratories, P.O. Box 412514, Kansas City, MO 64141/816-474-1622; FAX: 816-474-1307

Rorschach Precision Products, P.O. Box 151613, Irving, TX 75015/214-790-3487

Rosenberg & Sons, Jack A., 12229 Cox Ln., Dallas, TX 75234/214-241-6302

Rosenthal, Brad and Sallie, 19303 Ossenfort Ct., St. Louis, MO 63038/314-273-5159; FAX: 314-273-5149

Rosser, Bob, 1824 29th Ave., Suite 24, Birmingham, AL 35209/205-870-4422

Rossi S.A., Amadeo, Rua: Amadeo Rossi, 143, Sao Leopoldo, RS, BRAZIL 93030-220/051-592-5566 (U.S. importer—Interarms)

Roto Carve, 2754 Garden Ave., Janesville, IA 50647

Round Edge, Inc., P.O. Box 723, Lansdale, PA 19446/215-361-0859

Royal Arms Gunstocks, 919 8th Ave. NW, Great Falls, MT 59404/406-453-1149

Roy's Custom Grips, Rt. 3, Box 174-E, Lynchburg, VA 24504/804-993-3470

RPM, 15481 N. Twin Lakes Dr., Tucson, AZ 85737/602-825-1233; FAX: 602-825-3333

Rucker Dist. Inc., P.O. Box 479, Terrell, TX 75160/214-563-2094

Ruger (See Sturm, Ruger & Co., Inc.)

Rundell's Gun Shop, 6198 Frances Rd., Clio, MI 48420/313-687-0559

Runge, Robert P., 94 Grove St., Ilion, NY 13357/315-894-3036

Rusteprufe Laboratories, 1319 Jefferson Ave., Sparta, WI 54656/608-269-4144

Rusty Duck Premium Gun Care Products, 7785 Foundation Dr., Suite 6, Florence, KY 41042/606-342-5553; FAX: 606-342-5556

Rutgers Book Center, 127 Raritan Ave., Highland Park, NJ 08904/908-545-4344; FAX: 908-545-6686

Ruvel & Co., Inc., 4128-30 W. Belmont Ave., Chicago, IL 60641/312-286-9494; FAX: 312-286-9323

R.V.I. (See Fire'n Five)

RWS (See U.S. importer—Dynamit Nobel-RWS, Inc.)

Rybka Custom Leather Equipment, Thad, 134 Havilah Hill, Odenville, AL 35120

S

S&B Industries, 11238 McKinley Rd., Montrose, MI 48457/810-639-5491

S&K Manufacturing Co., P.O. Box 247, Pittsfield, PA 16340/814-563-7808; FAX: 814-563-7808

S&S Firearms, 74-11 Myrtle Ave., Glendale, NY 11385/718-497-1100; FAX: 718-497-1105

Sabatti S.R.L., via Alessandro Volta 90, 25063 Gardone V.T., Brescia, ITALY/030-8912207-831312; FAX: 030-8912059 (U.S. importer—E.A.A. Corp.; K.B.I., Inc.)

SAECO (See Redding Reloading Equipment)

Safari Outfitters Ltd., 71 Ethan Allan Hwy., Ridgefield, CT 06877/203-544-9505

Safari Press, Inc., 15621 Chemical Lane B, Huntington Beach, CA 92649/714-894-9080; FAX: 714-894-4949

Safariland Ltd., Inc., 3120 E. Mission Blvd., P.O. Box 51478, Ontario, CA 91761/909-923-7300; FAX: 909-923-7400

SAFE, P.O. Box 864, Post Falls, ID 83854/208-773-3624

Safesport Manufacturing Co., 1100 W. 45th Ave., Denver, CO 80211/303-433-6506, 800-433-6506; FAX: 303-433-4112

Safety Speed Holster, Inc., 910 S. Vail Ave., Montebello, CA 90640/213-723-4140; FAX: 213-726-6973

Samco Global Arms, Inc., 6995 NW 43rd St., Miami, FL 33166/305-593-9782

Sampson, Roger, 430 N. Grove, Mora, MN 55051/320-679-4868

San Francisco Gun Exchange, 124 Second St., San Francisco, CA 94105/415-982-6097

Sandia Die & Cartridge Co., 37 Atancacio Rd. NE, Albuquerque, NM 87123/505-298-5729

Sarco, Inc., 323 Union St., Stirling, NJ 07980/908-647-3800

Saunders Gun & Machine Shop, R.R. 2, Delhi Road, Manchester, IA 52057

Savage Range Systems, Inc., 100 Springdale RD., Westfield, MA 01085/413-568-7001; FAX: 413-562-1152

Savana Sports, Inc., 5763 Ferrier St., Montreal, Quebec, CANADA H4P 1N3/514-739-1753; FAX: 514-739-1755

Saville Iron Co. (See Greenwood Precision)

Scattergun Technologies Inc., 620 8th Ave. S., Nashville, TN 37203/616-254-1441; FAX: 616-254-1449; WEB: http://www.scattergun.com

Schaefer Shooting Sports, 1923 Grand Ave., Baldwin, NY 11510/516-379-4900; FAX: 516-379-6701

Scharch Mfg., Inc., 10325 Co. Rd. 120, Unit C, Salida, CO 81201/719-539-7242, 800-836-4683; FAX: 719-539-3021

Scherer, Box 250, Ewing, VA 24240/615-733-2615; FAX: 615-733-2073

Schiffman, Mike, 8233 S. Crystal Springs, McCammon, ID 83250/208-254-9114

Schmidtman Custom Ammunition, 6 Gilbert Court, Cotati, CA 94931

Schroeder Bullets, 1421 Thermal Ave., San Diego, CA 92154/619-423-3523

Schuetzen Gun Co., P.O. Box 272113, Fort Collins, CO 80527/970-223-3678

Schuetzen Pistol Works, 620-626 Old Pacific Hwy. SE, Olympia, WA 98513/360-459-3471; FAX: 360-491-3447

Schulz Industries, 16247 Minnesota Ave., Paramount, CA 90723/213-439-5903

ScopLevel, 151 Lindbergh Ave., Suite C, Livermore, CA 94550/510-449-5052; FAX: 510-373-0861

Scot Powder Co. of Ohio, Inc., Box GD96, Only, TN 37140/615-729-4207, 800-416-3006; FAX: 615-729-4217

Scott, Dwight, 23089 Englehardt St., Clair Shores, MI 48080/313-779-4735

Scott Fine Guns, Inc., Thad, P.O. Box 412, Indianola, MS 38751/601-887-5929

Scott, McDougall & Associates, 7950 Redwood Dr., Cotati, CA 94931/707-546-2264; FAX: 707-795-1911

Seattle Binocular & Scope Repair Co., P.O. Box 46094, Seattle, WA 98146/206-932-3733

Second Chance Body Armor, P.O. Box 578, Central Lake, MI 49622/616-544-5721; FAX: 616-544-9824

Seebeck Assoc., R.E., P.O. Box 59752, Dallas, TX 75229

Seligman Shooting Products, Box 133, Seligman, AZ 86337/602-422-3607

Selsi Co., Inc., P.O. Box 10, Midland Park, NJ 07432-0010/201-935-0388; FAX: 201-935-5851

Semmer, Charles, 7885 Cyd Dr., Denver, CO 80221/303-429-6947

Sentinel Arms, P.O. Box 57, Detroit, MI 48231/313-331-1951; FAX: 313-331-1456

Shanghai Airguns, Ltd. (See U.S. importer—Sportsman Airguns, Inc.)

Shaw, Inc., E.R. (See Small Arms Mfg. Co.)

Shay's Gunsmithing, 931 Marvin Ave., Lebanon, PA 17042

Shell Shack, 113 E. Main, Laurel, MT 59044/406-628-8986

Sherwood, George, 46 N. River Dr., Roseburg, OR 97470/541-672-3159

Shilen Rifles, Inc., P.O. Box 1300, 205 Metro Park Blvd., Ennis, TX 75119/214-875-5318; FAX: 214-875-5402

Shiloh Creek, Box 357, Cottleville, MO 63338/314-447-2900; FAX: 314-447-2900

Shirley Co. Gun & Riflemakers Ltd., J.A., P.O. Box 368, High Wycombe, Bucks. HP13 6YN, ENGLAND/0494-446883; FAX: 0494-463685

Shockley, Harold H., 204 E. Farmington Rd., Hanna City, IL 61536/309-565-4524

Shoemaker & Sons, Inc., Tex, 714 W. Cienega Ave., San Dimas, CA 91773/909-592-2071; FAX: 909-592-2378

Shooter Shop, The, 221 N. Main, Butte, MT 59701/406-723-3842

Shooter's Choice, 16770 Hilltop Park Place, Chagrin Falls, OH 44023/216-543-8808; FAX: 216-543-8811

Shooter's World, 3828 N. 28th Ave., Phoenix, AZ 85017/602-266-0170

Shooters Supply, 1120 Tieton Dr., Yakima, WA 98902/509-452-1181

Shootin' Accessories, Ltd., P.O. Box 6810, Auburn, CA 95604/916-889-2220

Shootin' Shack, Inc., 1065 Silver Beach Rd., Riviera Beach, FL 33403/407-842-0990

Shooting Chrony Inc., 3269 Niagara Falls Blvd., N. Tonawanda, NY 14120/905-276-6292; FAX: 905-276-6295

Shooting Components Marketing, P.O. Box 1069, Englewood, CO 80150/303-987-2543; FAX: 303-989-3508

Shooting Gallery, The, 8070 Southern Blvd., Boardman, OH 44512/216-726-7788

Shoot-N-C Targets (See Birchwood Casey)

Shotgun Shop, The, 14145 Proctor Ave., Suite 3, Industry, CA 91746/818-855-2737; FAX: 818-855-2735

Siegrist Gun Shop, 8754 Turtle Road, Whittemore, MI 48770

Sierra Bullets, 1400 W. Henry St., Sedalia, MO 65301/816-827-6300; FAX: 816-827-6300; WEB: http://www.sierrabullets.com

Sierra Specialty Prod. Co., 1344 Oakhurst Ave., Los Altos, CA 94024/FAX: 415-965-1536

SIG, CH-8212 Neuhausen, SWITZERLAND (U.S. importer—Mandall Shooting Supplies, Inc.)

SIG-Sauer (See U.S. importer—Sigarms, Inc.)

Sigarms, Inc., Corporate Park, Industrial Drive, Exeter, NH 03833/603-772-2302; FAX: 603-772-9082

Sight Shop, The, John G. Lawson, 1802 E. Columbia Ave., Tacoma, WA 98404/206-474-5465

Sightron, Inc., Rt. 1, Box 293, Franklinton, NC 27525/919-494-5040; FAX: 919-494-2612

Sile Distributors, Inc., 7 Centre Market Pl., New York, NY 10013/212-925-4111; FAX: 212-925-3149

Silencio/Safety Direct, 56 Coney Island Dr., Sparks, NV 89431/800-648-1812, 702-354-4451; FAX: 702-359-1074

Silhouette Leathers, P.O. Box 1161, Gunnison, CO 81230/303-641-6639

Silhouette, The, P.O. Box 1509, Idaho Falls, ID 83403

Silver Eagle Machining, 18007 N. 69th Ave., Glendale, AZ 85308

Silver Ridge Gun Shop (See Goodwin, Fred)

Simmons, Jerry, 715 Middlebury St., Goshen, IN 46526/219-533-8546

Simmons Gun Repair, Inc., 700 S. Rogers Rd., Olathe, KS 66062/913-782-3131; FAX: 913-782-4189

Simmons Outdoor Corp., 2120 Kilarney Way, Tallahassee, FL 32308/904-878-5100; FAX: 904-878-0300

Sinclair International, Inc., 2330 Wayne Haven St., Fort Wayne, IN 46803/219-493-1858; FAX: 219-493-2530

Sinclair, W.P., Box 1209, Warminster, Wiltshire BA12 9XJ, ENGLAND/01044-1985-218544; FAX: 01044-1985-214111

Single Shot, Inc. (See Montana Armory, Inc.)

Singletary, Kent, 2915 W. Ross, Phoenix, AZ 85027/602-582-4900

Sipes Gun Shop, 7415 Asher Ave., Little Rock, AR 72204/501-565-8480

Skaggs, R.E., P.O. Box 555, Hamilton, IN 46742/219-488-3755

SKAN A.R., 4 St. Catherines Road, Long Melford, Suffolk, CO10 9JU ENGLAND/011-0787-312942

Skeoch, Brian R., P.O. Box 279, Glenrock, WY 82637/307-436-9655; FAX: 307-436-9034

Skip's Machine, 364 29 Road, Grand Junction, CO 81501/303-245-5417

Sklany, Steve, 566 Birch Grove Dr., Kalispell, MT 59901/406-755-4257

S.L.A.P. Industries, P.O. Box 1121, Parklands 2121, SOUTH AFRICA/27-11-788-0030; FAX: 27-11-788-0030

Slings 'N Things, Inc., 8909 Bedford Circle, Suite 11, Omaha, NE 68134/402-571-6954; FAX: 402-571-7082

Slug Group, Inc., P.O. Box 376, New Paris, PA 15554/814-839-4517; FAX: 814-839-2601

Small Custom Mould & Bullet Co., Box 17211, Tucson, AZ 85731

Smires, C.L., 28269 Old Schoolhouse Rd., Columbus, NJ 08022/609-298-3158

Smith & Wesson, 2100 Roosevelt Ave., Springfield, MA 01102/413-781-8300; FAX: 413-731-8980

Smith, Art, 230 Main St. S., Hector, MN 55342/612-848-2760; FAX: 612-848-2760

Smith, Mark A., P.O. Box 182, Sinclair, WY 82334/307-324-7929

Smith, Ron, 5869 Straley, Ft. Worth, TX 76114/817-732-6768

Smith Abrasives, Inc., 1700 Sleepy Valley Rd., P.O. Box 5095, Hot Springs, AR 71902-5095/501-321-2244; FAX: 501-321-9232

Smith Saddlery, Jesse W., 3601 E. Boone Ave., Spokane, WA 99202-4501/509-325-0622

MANUFACTURERS' DIRECTORY

Smokey Valley Rifles (See Lutz Engraving, Ron E.)

Snapp's Gunshop, 6911 E. Washington Rd., Clare, MI 48617/517-386-9226

SOS Products Co. (See Buck Stix—SOS Products Co.)

Sotheby's, 1334 York Ave. at 72nd St., New York, NY 10021/212-606-7260

South Bend Replicas, Inc., 61650 Oak Rd., South Bend, IN 46614/219-289-4500

Southeastern Community College, 1015 S. Gear Ave., West Burlington, IA 52655/319-752-2731

Southern Ammunition Co., Inc., 4232 Meadow St., Loris, SC 29569-3124/803-756-3262; FAX: 803-756-3583

Southern Armory, The, Rt. 2, Box 134, Woodlawn, VA 24381/703-238-1343; FAX: 703-238-1453

Southern Bloomer Mfg. Co., P.O. Box 1621, Bristol, TN 37620/615-878-6660; FAX: 615-878-8761

Southern Security, 1700 Oak Hills Dr., Kingston, TN 37763/423-376-6297; 800-251-9992

Southwind Sanctions, P.O. Box 445, Aledo, TX 76008/817-441-8917

Sparks, Milt, 605 E. 44th St. No. 2, Boise, ID 83714-4800

Specialty Gunsmithing, Lynn McMurdo, P.O. Box 404, Afton, WY 83110/307-886-5535

Speedfeed, Inc., 3820 Industrial Way, Suite N, Benicia, CA 94510/707-746-1221; FAX: 707-746-1888

Speer Products, Div. of Blount, Inc., Sporting Equipment Div., P.O. Box 856, Lewiston, ID 83501/208-746-2351; FAX: 208-746-2915

Spegel, Craig, P.O. Box 3108, Bay City, OR 97107/503-377-2697

Spence, George W., 115 Locust St., Steele, MO 63877/314-695-4926

Spencer's Custom Guns, Rt. 1, Box 546, Scottsville, VA 24590/804-293-6836

S.P.G., Inc., P.O. Box 761-H, Livingston, MT 59047/406-222-8416; FAX: 406-222-8416

Sphinx Engineering SA, Ch. des Grandes-Vies 2, CH-2900 Porrentruy, SWITZERLAND/41 66 66 73 81; FAX: 41 66 66 30 90 (U.S. importer—Sphinx USA Inc.)

Sphinx USA Inc., 998 N. Colony, Meriden, CT 06450/203-238-1399; FAX: 203-238-1375

Sport Flite Manufacturing Co., P.O. Box 1082, Bloomfield Hills, MI 48303/810-647-3747

Sportsman Airguns, Inc., 17712 Carmenita Rd., Cerritos, CA 90703-8639/800-424-7486

Sportsman Supply Co., 714 East Eastwood, P.O. Box 650, Marshall, MO 65340/816-886-9393

Sportsmen's Exchange & Western Gun Traders, Inc., 560 S. "C" St., Oxnard, CA 93030/805-483-1917

Springfield, Inc., 420 W. Main St., Geneseo, IL 61254/309-944-5631; FAX: 309-944-3676

Springfield Sporters, Inc., RD 1, Penn Run, PA 15765/412-254-2626; FAX: 412-254-9173

SSK Industries, 721 Woodvue Lane, Wintersville, OH 43952/614-264-0176; FAX: 614-264-2257

Stackpole Books, 5067 Ritter Rd., Mechanicsburg, PA 17055-6921/717-234-5041; FAX: 717-234-1359

Stalker, Inc., P.O. Box 21, Fishermans Wharf Rd., Malakoff, TX 75148/903-489-1010

Stalwart Corporation, 76 Imperial, Unit A, Evanston, WY 82930/307-789-7687; FAX: 307-789-7688

Stanley Bullets, 2085 Heatheridge Ln., Reno, NV 89509

Star Bonifacio Echeverria S.A., Torrekva 3, Eibar, SPAIN 20600/43-107340; FAX: 43-101524 (U.S. importer—Interarms; P.S.M.G. Gun Co.)

Star Custom Bullets, P.O. Box 608, 468 Main St., Ferndale, CA 95536/707-786-9140; FAX: 707-786-9117

Star Machine Works, 418 10th Ave., San Diego, CA 92101/619-232-3216

Star Reloading Co., Inc., 5520 Rock Hampton Ct., Indianapolis, IN 46268/317-872-5840

Stark's Bullet Mfg., 2580 Monroe St., Eugene, OR 97405

Starlight Training Center, Inc., Rt. 1, P.O. Box 88, Bronaugh, MO 64728/417-843-3555

Starnes Gunmaker, Ken, 32900 SW Laurelview Rd., Hillsboro, OR 97123/503-628-0705; FAX: 503-628-6005

Starr Trading Co., Jedediah, P.O. Box 2007, Farmington Hills, MI 48333/810-683-4343; FAX: 810-683-3282

Starrett Co., L.S., 121 Crescent St., Athol, MA 01331/617-249-3551

State Arms Gun Co., 815 S. Division St., Waunakee, WI 53597/608-849-5800

Steffens, Ron, 18396 Mariposa Creek Rd., Willits, CA 95490/707-485-0873

Steger, James R., 1131 Dorsey Pl., Plainfield, NJ 07062

Steves House of Guns, Rt. 1, Minnesota City, MN 55959/507-689-2573

Stewart's Gunsmithing, P.O. Box 5854, Pietersburg North 0750, Transvaal, SOUTH AFRICA/01521-89401

Steyr Mannlicher AG, Mannlicherstrasse 1, P.O.B. 1000, A-4400 Steyr, AUSTRIA/0043-7252-896-0; FAX: 0043-7252-68621 (U.S. importer—GSI, Inc.; Nygord Precision Products)

Stiles Custom Guns, RD3, Box 1605, Homer City, PA 15748/412-479-9945, 412-479-8666

Stillwell, Robert, 421 Judith Ann Dr., Schertz, TX 78154

Stoeger Industries, 5 Mansard Ct., Wayne, NJ 07470/201-872-9500, 800-631-0722; FAX: 201-872-2230

Stoeger Publishing Co. (See Stoeger Industries)

Stone Enterprises Ltd., Rt. 609, P.O. Box 335, Wicomico Church, VA 22579/804-580-5114; FAX: 804-580-8421

Stone Mountain Arms, 5988 Peachtree Corners E., Norcross, GA 30071/800-251-9412

Stoney Point Products, Inc., P.O. Box 234, 1815 North Spring Street, New Ulm, MN 56073-0234/507-354-3360; FAX: 507-354-7236

Storey, Dale A. (See DGS, Inc.)

Stott's Creek Armory, Inc., RR1, Box 70, Morgantown, IN 46160/317-878-5489

Stratco, Inc., P.O. Box 2270, Kalispell, MT 59901/406-755-1221; FAX: 406-755-1226

Strawbridge, Victor W., 6 Pineview Dr., Dover, NH 03820/603-742-0013

Strong Holster Co., 39 Grove St., Gloucester, MA 01930/508-281-3300; FAX: 508-281-6321

Stuart, V. Pat, Rt.1, Box 447-S, Greenville, VA 24440/804-556-3845

Sturm, Ruger & Co., Inc., Lacey Place, Southport, CT 06490/203-259-4537; FAX: 203-259-2167

"Su-Press-On," Inc., P.O. Box 09161, Detroit, MI 48209/313-842-4222 7:30-11p.m. Mon-Thurs.

Sullivan, David S. (See Westwind Rifles, Inc.)

Sundance Industries, Inc., 25163 W. Avenue Stanford, Valencia, CA 91355/805-257-4807

Sun Welding Safe Co., 290 Easy St. No.3, Simi Valley, CA 93065/805-584-6678, 800-729-SAFE; FAX: 805-584-6169

Surecase Co., The, 233 Wilshire Blvd., Ste. 900, Santa Monica, CA 90401/800-92ARMLOC

Swampfire Shop, The (See Peterson Gun Shop, Inc., A.W.)

SwaroSports, Inc. (See JagerSport, Ltd.)

Swarovski Optik North America Ltd., One Wholesale Way, Cranston, RI 02920/401-942-3380, 800-426-3089; FAX: 401-946-2587

Swenson's 45 Shop, A.D., P.O. Box 606, Fallbrook, CA 92028

Swift Instruments, Inc., 952 Dorchester Ave., Boston, MA 02125/617-436-2960, 800-446-1116; FAX: 617-436-3232

Swivel Machine Works, Inc., 11 Monitor Hill Rd., Newtown, CT 06470/203-270-6343; FAX: 203-874-9212

T

3-D Ammunition & Bullets, 112 W. Plum St., P.O. Box J, Doniphan, NE 68832/402-845-2285, 800-255-6712; FAX: 402-845-6546

300 Gunsmith Service, Inc., at Cherry Creek State Park Shooting Center,, 12500 E. Belleview Ave./Englewood, CO 80111/303-690-3300

Tabler Marketing, 2554 Lincoln Blvd., Suite 555, Marina Del Rey, CA 90291/818-755-4565; FAX: 818-755-0972

TacStar Industries, Inc., 218 Justin Drive, P.O. Box 70, Cottonwood, AZ 86326/602-639-0072; FAX: 602-634-8781

TacTell, Inc., P.O. Box 5654, Maryville, TN 37802/615-982-7855; FAX: 615-558-8294

Tactical Defense Institute, 574 Miami Bluff Ct., Loveland, OH 45140/513-677-8229

Talley, Dave, P.O. Box 821, Glenrock, WY 82637/307-436-8724, 307-436-9315

Talmage, William G., 10208 N. County Rd. 425 W., Brazil, IN 47834/812-442-0804

Talon Mfg. Co., Inc., 575 Bevans Industrial Ln., Paw Paw, WV 25434/304-947-7440; FAX: 304-947-7447

Tamarack Products, Inc., P.O. Box 625, Wauconda, IL 60084/708-526-9333; FAX: 708-526-9353

Tanfoglio S.r.l., Fratelli, via Valtrompia 39, 41, 25068 Gardone V.T., Brescia, ITALY/30-8910361; FAX: 30-8910183 (U.S. importer—E.A.A. Corp.)

Tank's Rifle Shop, P.O. Box 474, Fremont, NE 68025/402-727-1317; FAX: 402-721-2573

Taracorp Industries, Inc., 1200 Sixteenth St., Granite City, IL 62040/618-451-4400

Tarnhelm Supply Co., Inc., 431 High St., Boscawen, NH 03303/603-796-2551; FAX: 603-796-2918

Tasco Sales, Inc., 7600 NW 26th St., Miami, FL 33156/305-591-3670; FAX: 305-592-5895

Taurus Firearms, Inc., 16175 NW 49th Ave., Miami, FL 33014/305-624-1115; FAX: 305-623-7506

Taurus International Firearms (See U.S. importer—Taurus Firearms, Inc.)

Taurus S.A., Forjas, Avenida Do Forte 511, Porto Alegre, RS BRAZIL 91360/55-51-347-4050; FAX: 55-51-347-3065

Taylor & Robbins, P.O. Box 164, Rixford, PA 16745/814-966-3233

TCCI, P.O. Box 302, Phoenix, AZ 85001/602-237-3823; FAX: 602-237-3858

TCSR, 3998 Hoffman Rd., White Bear Lake, MN 55110-4626/800-328-5323; FAX: 612-429-0526

TDP Industries, Inc., 606 Airport Blvd., Doylestown, PA 18901/215-345-8687; FAX: 215-345-6057

Tele-Optics, 5514 W. Lawrence Ave., Chicago, IL 60630/312-283-7757; FAX: 312-283-7757

Ten-Ring Precision, Inc., Alex B. Hamilton, 1449 Blue Crest Lane, San Antonio, TX 78232/210-494-3063; FAX: 210-494-3066

Tennessee Valley Mfg., P.O. Box 1175, Corinth, MS 38834/601-286-5014

Tepeco, P.O. Box 342, Friendswood, TX 77546/713-482-2702

Tetra Gun Lubricants, 1812 Margaret Ave., Annapolis, MD 21401/410-268-6451; FAX: 410-268-8377

Texas Armory, P.O. Box 154906, Waco, TX 76715/817-867-6972

Texas Longhorn Arms, Inc., 5959 W. Loop South, Suite 424, Bellaire, TX 77401/713-660-6323; FAX: 713-660-0493

Texas Platers Supply Co., 2453 W. Five Mile Parkway, Dallas, TX 75233/214-330-7168

T.F.C. S.p.A., Via G. Marconi 118, B, Villa Carcina, Brescia 25069, ITALY/030-881271; FAX: 030-881826

Theis, Terry, P.O. Box 535, Fredericksburg, TX 78624/210-997-6778

Thiewes, George W., 14329 W. Parada Dr., Sun City West, AZ 85375

Thirion Gun Engraving, Denise, P.O. Box 408, Graton, CA 95444/707-829-1876

Thomas, Charles C., 2600 S. First St., Springfield, IL 62794/217-789-8980; FAX: 217-789-9130

Thompson, Randall (See Highline Machine Co.)

Thompson Bullet Lube Co., P.O. Box 472343, Garland, TX 75047-2343/214-271-8063; FAX: 214-840-6743

Thompson/Center Arms, P.O. Box 5002, Rochester, NH 03866/603-332-2394; FAX: 603-332-5133

Thompson Precision, 110 Mary St., P.O. Box 251, Warren, IL 61087/815-745-3625

Thompson Target Technology, 618 Roslyn Ave., SW, Canton, OH 44710/216-453-7707; FAX: 216-478-4723

T.H.U. Enterprises, Inc., P.O. Box 418, Lederach, PA 19450/215-256-1665; FAX: 215-256-9718

Thunder Mountain Arms, P.O. Box 593, Oak Harbor, WA 98277/206-679-4657; FAX: 206-675-1114

Thunder Ranch, HCR 1 Box 53, Mountain Home, TX 78058/210-640-3138; FAX: 210-640-3183

Thunderbird Cartridge Co., Inc. (See TCCI)

Thurston Sports, Inc., RD 3 Donovan Rd., Auburn, NY 13021/315-253-0966

Tiger-Hunt, Box 379, Beaverdale, PA 15921/814-472-5161

Timber Heirloom Products, 618 Roslyn Ave. SW, Canton, OH 44710/216-453-7707; FAX: 216-478-4723

Time Precision, Inc., 640 Federal Rd., Brookfield, CT 06804/203-775-8343

Timney Mfg., Inc., 3065 W. Fairmont Ave., Phoenix, AZ 85017/602-274-2999; FAX: 602-241-0361

Tioga Engineering Co., Inc., P.O. Box 913, 13 Cone St., Wellsboro, PA 16901/717-724-3533, 717-662-3347

TMI Products (See Haselbauer Products, Jerry)

Tom's Gun Repair, Thomas G. Ivanoff, 76-6 Rt. Southfork Rd., Cody, WY 82414/307-587-6949

Tom's Gunshop, 3601 Central Ave., Hot Springs, AR 71913/501-624-3856

Tonoloway Tack Drives, HCR 81, Box 100, Needmore, PA 17238

Top-Line USA, Inc., 7920-28 Hamilton Ave., Cincinnati, OH 45231/513-522-2992, 800-346-6699; FAX: 513-522-0916

Torel, Inc., 1708 N. South St., P.O. Box 592, Yoakum, TX 77995/512-293-2341; FAX: 512-293-3413

Totally Dependable Products (See TDP Industries, Inc.)

TOZ (See U.S. importer—Nygord Precision Products)

TR Metals Corp., 1 Pavilion Ave., Riverside, NJ 08075/609-461-9000; FAX: 609-764-6340

Track of the Wolf, Inc., P.O. Box 6, Osseo, MN 55369-0006/612-424-2500; FAX: 612-424-9860

Traditions, Inc., P.O. Box 776, 1375 Boston Post Rd., Old Saybrook, CT 06475/860-388-4656; FAX: 860-388-4657

Trafalgar Square, P.O. Box 257, N. Pomfret, VT 05053/802-457-1911

Trammco, 839 Gold Run Rd., Boulder, CO 80302

Treso, Inc., P.O. Box 4640, Pagosa Springs, CO 81157/303-731-2295

Trijicon, Inc., 49385 Shafer Ave., P.O. Box 930059, Wixom, MI 48393-0059/810-960-7700; FAX: 810-960-7725

Trinidad State Junior College, Gunsmithing Dept., 600 Prospect St., Trinidad, CO 81082/719-846-5631; FAX: 719-846-5667

Triple-K Mfg. Co., Inc., 2222 Commercial St., San Diego, CA 92113/619-232-2066; FAX: 619-232-7675

Trophy Bonded Bullets, Inc., 900 S. Loop W., Suite 190, Houston, TX 77054/713-645-4499; FAX: 713-741-6393

Trotman, Ken, 135 Ditton Walk, Unit 11, Cambridge CB5 8PY, ENGLAND/01223-211030; FAX: 01223-212317

Tru-Square Metal Prods., Inc., 640 First St. SW, P.O. Box 585, Auburn, WA 98071/206-833-2310; FAX: 206-833-2349

True Flight Bullet Co., 5581 Roosevelt St., Whitehall, PA 18052/610-262-7630; FAX: 610-262-7806

Trulock Tool, Broad St., Whigham, GA 31797/912-762-4678

TTM, 1550 Solomon Rd., Santa Maria, CA 93455/805-934-1281

Turnbull Restoration, Inc., Doug, 6426 County Rd. 30, P.O. Box 471, Bloomfield, NY 14469/716-657-6338; WEB: http://gun-shop.com/dougt.htm

Twin Pine Armory, P.O. Box 58, Hwy. 6, Adna, WA 98522/360-748-4590; FAX: 360-748-1802

Tyler Mfg.-Dist., Melvin, 1326 W. Britton Rd., Oklahoma City, OK 73114/405-842-8044, 800-654-8415

Tyler Scott, Inc., 313 Rugby Ave., Terrace Park, OH 45174/513-831-7603; FAX: 513-831-7417

U

Uberti USA, Inc., P.O. Box 469, Lakeville, CT 06039/860-435-8068; FAX: 860-435-8146

Uberti, Aldo, Casella Postale 43, I-25063 Gardone V.T., ITALY (U.S. importers—American Arms, Inc.; Cimarron Arms; Dixie Gun Works; EMF Co., Inc.; Forgett Jr., Valmore J.; Navy Arms Co; Taylor's & Co., Inc.; Uberti USA, Inc.)

Ultra Light Arms, Inc., P.O. Box 1270, 214 Price St., Granville, WV 26505/304-599-5687; FAX: 304-599-5687

Uncle Mike's (See Michaels of Oregon Co.)

Unique/M.A.P.F., 10, Les Allees, 64700 Hendaye, FRANCE 64700/33-59 20 71 93 (U.S. importer—Nygord Precision Products)

United States Products Co., 518 Melwood Ave., Pittsburgh, PA 15213/412-621-2130

Upper Missouri Trading Co., 304 Harold St., Crofton, NE 68730/402-388-4844

USAC, 4500-15th St. East, Tacoma, WA 98424/206-922-7589

USA Sporting Inc., 1330 N. Glassell, Unit M, Orange, CA 92667/714-538-3109, 800-538-3109; FAX: 714-538-1334

V

Valade Engraving, Robert, 931 3rd Ave., Seaside, OR 97138/503-738-7672

Valor Corp., 5555 NW 36th Ave., Miami, FL 33142/305-633-0127; FAX: 305-634-4536

Van Gorden & Son, Inc., C.S., 1815 Main St., Bloomer, WI 54724/715-568-2612

Van Patten, J.W., P.O. Box 145, Foster Hill, Milford, PA 18337/717-296-7069

Vancini, Carl (See Bestload, Inc.)

Vann Custom Bullets, 330 Grandview Ave., Novato, CA 94947

Varner's Service, 102 Shaffer Rd., Antwerp, OH 45813/419-258-8631

Vega Tool Co., c/o T.R. Ross, 4865 Tanglewood Ct., Boulder, CO 80301/303-530-0174

Venco Industries, Inc. (See Shooter's Choice)

Venus Industries, P.O. Box 246, Sialkot-1, PAKISTAN/FAX: 92 432 85579

Vest, John, P.O. Box 1552, Susanville, CA 96130/916-257-7228

VibraShine, Inc., P.O. Box 577, Taylorsville, MS 39168/601-785-9854; FAX: 601-785-9874

Vibra-Tek Co., 1844 Arroya Rd., Colorado Springs, CO 80906/719-634-8611; FAX: 719-634-6886

Vic's Gun Refinishing, 6 Pineview Dr., Dover, NH 03820-6422/603-742-0013

Victory USA, P.O. Box 1021, Pine Bush, NY 12566/914-744-2060; FAX: 914-744-5181

Vihtavuori Oy, FIN-41330 Vihtavuori, FINLAND/358-41-3779211; FAX: 358-41-3771643

Vihtavuori Oy/Kaltron-Pettibone, 1241 Ellis St., Bensenville, IL 60106/708-350-1116; FAX: 708-350-1606

Viking Leathercraft, Inc., 1579A Jayken Way, Chula Vista, CA 91911/800-262-6666; FAX: 619-429-8268

Vincent's Shop, 210 Antoinette, Fairbanks, AK 99701

Vintage Arms, Inc., 6003 Saddle Horse, Fairfax, VA 22030/703-968-0779; FAX: 703-968-0780

Vintage Industries, Inc., 781 Big Tree Dr., Longwood, FL 32750/407-831-8949; FAX: 407-831-5346

Viramontez, Ray, 601 Springfield Dr., Albany, GA 31707/912-432-9683

Vitt/Boos, 2178 Nichols Ave., Stratford, CT 06497/203-375-6859

Voere-KGH m.b.H., P.O. Box 416, A-6333 Kufstein, Tirol, AUSTRIA/0043-5372-62547; FAX: 0043-5372-65752 (U.S. importers—JagerSport, Ltd.)

Volquartsen Custom Ltd., 24276 240th Street, P.O. Box 271, Carroll, IA 51401/712-792-4238; FAX: 712-792-2542; E-MAIL: vcl@netins.net

Von Minden Gunsmithing Services, 2403 SW 39 Terrace, Cape Coral, FL 33914/813-542-8946

Vorhes, David, 3042 Beecham St., Napa, CA 94558/707-226-9116

Vortek Products, Inc., P.O. Box 871181, Canton, MI 48187-6181/313-397-5656; FAX:313-397-5656

VSP Publishers (See Heritage/VSP Gun Books)

Vulpes Ventures, Inc., Fox Cartridge Division, P.O. Box 1363, Bolingbrook, IL 60440-7363/708-759-1229

W

Wagoner, Vernon G., 2325 E. Encanto, Mesa, AZ 85213/602-835-1307

Waldron, Herman, Box 475, 80 N. 17th St., Pomeroy, WA 99347/509-843-1404

Walker Arms Co., Inc., 499 County Rd. 820, Selma, AL 36701/334-872-6231

Wallace, Terry, 385 San Marino, Vallejo, CA 94589/707-642-7041

Walt's Custom Leather, Walt Whinnery, 1947 Meadow Creek Dr., Louisville, KY 40218/502-458-4361

Walters Industries, 6226 Park Lane, Dallas, TX 75225/214-691-6973

Walters, John, 500 N. Avery Dr., Moore, OK 73160/405-799-0376

Walther GmbH, Carl, B.P. 4325, D-89033 Ulm, GERMANY (U.S. importer—Champion's Choice; Interarms; P.S.M.G. Gun Co.)

WAMCO, Inc., Mingo Loop, P.O. Box 337, Oquossoc, ME 04964-0337/207-864-3344

WAMCO—New Mexico, P.O. Box 205, Peralta, NM 87042-0205/505-869-0826

Ward & Van Valkenburg, 114 32nd Ave. N., Fargo, ND 58102/701-232-2351

Wardell Precision Handguns Ltd., 48851 N. Fig Springs Rd., New River, AZ 85027-8513/602-465-7995

Warenski, Julie, 590 E. 500 N., Richfield, UT 84701/801-896-5319; FAX: 801-896-5319

Warne Manufacturing Co., 9039 SE Jannsen Rd., Clackamas, OR 97015/503-657-5590, 800-683-5590; FAX: 503-657-5695

Warren Muzzleloading Co., Inc., Hwy. 21 North, P.O. Box 100, Ozone, AR 72854/501-292-3268

Warren, Kenneth W. (See Mountain States Engraving)

Washita Mountain Whetstone Co., P.O. Box 378, Lake Hamilton, AR 71951/501-525-3914

Wayne Firearms for Collectors and Investors, James, 2608 N. Laurent, Victoria, TX 77901/512-578-1258; FAX: 512-578-3559

WD-40 Co., 1061 Cudahy Pl., San Diego, CA 92110/619-275-1400; FAX: 619-275-5823

Weaver Arms Corp. Gun Shop, RR 3, P.O. Box 266, Bloomfield, MO 63825-9528

Weber & Markin Custom Gunsmiths, 4-1691 Powick Rd., Kelowna, B.C. CANADA V1X 4L1/604-762-7575; FAX: 604-861-3655

Webley and Scott Ltd., Frankley Industrial Park, Tay Rd., Rubery, Rednal, Birmingham B45 0PA, ENGLAND/011-021-453-1864; FAX: 021-457-7846 (U.S. importer—Beeman Precision Airguns; Groenewold, John)

Webster Scale Mfg. Co., P.O. Box 188, Sebring, FL 33870/813-385-6362

Weigand Combat Handguns, Inc., P.O. Box 239, Crestwood Industrial Park, Mountain Top, PA 18707/717-474-9804; FAX: 717-474-9987

Weihrauch KG, Hermann, Industriestrasse 11, 8744 Mellrichstadt, GERMANY/09776-497-498 (U.S. importers—Beeman Precision Airguns; E.A.A. Corp.)

Weisz Parts, P.O. Box 20038, Columbus, OH 43220-0038/614-45-70-500; FAX: 614-846-8585

Welch, Sam, CVSR 2110, Moab, UT 84532/801-259-8131

Wells Custom Gunsmith, R.A., 3452 1st Ave., Racine, WI 53402/414-639-5223

Wells, Rachel, 110 N. Summit St., Prescott, AZ 86301/520-445-3655

Welsh, Bud, 80 New Road, E. Amherst, NY 14051/716-688-6344

Werner, Carl, P.O. Box 492, Littleton, CO 80160

Werth, T.W., 1203 Woodlawn Rd., Lincoln, IL 62656/217-732-1300

Wescombe, P.O. Box 488, Glencoe, CA 95232/209-293-7010

Wessinger Custom Guns & Engraving, 268 Limestone Rd., Chapin, SC 29036/803-345-5677

West, Robert G., 3973 Pam St., Eugene, OR 97402/541-344-3700

Western Design (See Alpha Gunsmith Division)

Western Missouri Shooters Alliance, P.O. Box 11144, Kansas City, MO 64119/816-597-3950; FAX: 816-229-7350

Western Nevada West Coast Bullets, 2307 W. Washington St., Carson City, NV 89703/702-246-3941; FAX: 702-246-0836

Westfield Engineering, 6823 Watcher St., Commerce, CA 90040/FAX: 213-928-8270

Westrom, John (See Precision Metal Finishing)

Westwind Rifles, Inc., David S. Sullivan, P.O. Box 261, 640 Briggs St., Erie, CO 80516/303-828-3823

Whildin & Sons Ltd., E.H., RR2, Box 119, Tamaqua, PA 18252/717-668-6743; FAX: 717-668-6745

Whinnery, Walt (See Walt's Custom Leather)

White Laboratory, Inc., H.P., 3114 Scarboro Rd., Street, MD 21154/410-838-6550; FAX: 410-838-2802

White Owl Enterprises, 2583 Flag Rd., Abilene, KS 67410/913-263-2613; FAX: 913-263-2613

White Rock Tool & Die, 6400 N. Brighton Ave., Kansas City, MO 64119/816-454-0478

White Shooting Systems, Inc., 25 E. Hwy. 40, Box 330-12, Roosevelt, UT 84066/801-722-3085, 800-213-1315; FAX: 801-722-3054

Whitehead, James D., 204 Cappucino Way, Sacramento, CA 95838

Whitestone Lumber Corp., 148-02 14th Ave., Whitestone, NY 11357/718-746-4400; FAX: 718-767-1748

Whitetail Design & Engineering Ltd., 9421 E. Mannsiding Rd., Clare, MI 48617/517-386-3932

Wichita Arms, Inc., 923 E. Gilbert, P.O. Box 11371, Wichita, KS 67211/316-265-0661; FAX: 316-265-0760

Wick, David E., 1504 Michigan Ave., Columbus, IN 47201/812-376-6960

Widener's Reloading & Shooting Supply, Inc., P.O. Box 3009 CRS, Johnson City, TN 37602/615-282-6786; FAX: 615-282-6651

Wideview Scope Mount Corp., 13535 S. Hwy. 16, Rapid City, SD 57701/605-341-3220; FAX: 605-341-9142

Wiebe, Duane, 33604 Palm Dr., Burlington, WI 53105-9260

Wilcox All-Pro Tools & Supply, 4880 147th St., Montezuma, IA 50171/515-623-3138; FAX: 515-623-3104

Wild Bill's Originals, P.O. Box 13037, Burton, WA 98013/206-463-5738

Wild West Guns, 7521 Old Seward Hwy, Unit A, Anchorage, AK 99518/907-344-4500; FAX: 907-344-4005

Wilderness Sound Products Ltd., 4015 Main St. A, Springfield, OR 97478/503-741-0263, 800-437-0006; FAX: 503-741-7648

Wildey, Inc., P.O. Box 475, Brookfield, CT 06804/203-355-9000; FAX: 203-354-7759

Wilkinson Arms, 26884 Pearl Rd., Parma, ID 83660/208-722-6771; FAX: 208-722-5197

Will-Burt Co., 169 S. Main, Orrville, OH 44667

William's Gun Shop, Ben, 1151 S. Cedar Ridge, Duncanville, TX 75137/214-780-1807

Williams Bullet Co., J.R., 2008 Tucker Rd., Perry, GA 31069/912-987-0274

Williams Gun Sight Co., 7389 Lapeer Rd., Box 329, Davison, MI 48423/810-653-2131, 800-530-9028; FAX: 810-658-2140

Williams Mfg. of Oregon, 110 East B St., Drain, OR 97435/541-836-7461; FAX: 541-836-7245

Williams Shootin' Iron Service, The Lynx-Line, 8857 Bennett Hill Rd., Central Lake, MI 49622/616-544-6615

Williamson Precision Gunsmithing, 117 W. Pipeline, Hurst, TX 76053/817-285-0064

Willig Custom Engraving, Claus, D-97422 Schweinfurt, Siedlerweg 17, GERMANY/01149-9721-41446; FAX: 01149-9721-44413

Willow Bend, P.O. Box 203, Chelmsford, MA 01824/508-256-8508; FAX: 508-256-8508

Willson Safety Prods. Div., P.O. Box 622, Reading, PA 19603-0622/610-376-6161; FAX: 610-371-7725

Wilson Case, Inc., P.O. Box 1106, Hastings, NE 68902-1106/800-322-5493; FAX: 402-463-5276

Wilson, Inc., L.E., Box 324, 404 Pioneer Ave., Cashmere, WA 98815/509-782-1328

Wilson Combat, Box 578, Rt. 3, Berryville, AR 72616/501-545-3618; FAX: 501-545-3310

Wilson's Gun Shop (See Wilson Combat)

Winchester Div., Olin Corp., 427 N. Shamrock, E. Alton, IL 62024/618-258-3566; FAX: 618-258-3599

Winchester Sutler, Inc., The, 270 Shadow Brook Lane, Winchester, VA 22603/540-888-3595; FAX: 540-888-4632

Winkle Bullets, R.R. 1 Box 316, Heyworth, IL 61745

Winter, Robert M., P.O. Box 484, Menno, SD 57045/605-387-5322

Wise Guns, Dale, 333 W. Olmos Dr., San Antonio, TX 78212/210-828-3388

Wolf's Western Traders, 40 E. Works, No. 3F, Sheridan, WY 82801/307-674-5352

Wolff Co., W.C., P.O. Box 458, Newtown Square, PA 19073/610-359-9600, 800-545-0077

Wood, Frank (See Classic Guns, Inc.)

Wood, Mel, P.O. Box 1255, Sierra Vista, AZ 85636/602-455-5541

Woodstream, P.O. Box 327, Lititz, PA 17543/717-626-2125; FAX: 717-626-1912

Woodworker's Supply, 1108 North Glenn Rd., Casper, WY 82601/307-237-5354

World of Targets (See Birchwood Casey)

World Trek, Inc., 7170 Turkey Creek Rd., Pueblo, CO 81007-1046/719-546-2121; FAX: 719-543-6886

Worthy Products, Inc., RR 1, P.O. Box 213, Martville, NY 13111/315-324-5298

Wyant Bullets, Gen. Del., Swan Lake, MT 59911

Wyoming Custom Bullets, 1626 21st St., Cody, WY 82414

X, Y

X-Spand Target Systems, 26-10th St. SE, Medicine Hat, AB T1A 1P7 CANADA/403-526-7997; FAX: 403-528-2362

Yankee Gunsmith, 2901 Deer Flat Dr., Copperas Cove, TX 76522/817-547-8433

Yavapai Firearms Academy Ltd., P.O. Box 27290, Prescott Valley, AZ 86312/520-772-8262

Yearout, Lewis E. (See Montana Outfitters)

Yesteryear Armory & Supply, P.O. Box 408, Carthage, TN 37030

Young Country Arms, P.O. Box 3615, Simi Valley, CA 93093

Yukon Arms Classic Ammunition, 1916 Brooks, P.O. Box 223, Missoula, MT 59801/406-543-9614

Z

Z's Metal Targets & Frames, P.O. Box 78, South Newbury, NH 03255/603-938-2826

Zanotti Armor, Inc., 123 W. Lone Tree Rd., Cedar Falls, IA 50613/319-232-9650

Z-Coat Industrial Coatings, Inc., 3375 U.S. Hwy. 98 S. No. A, Lakeland, FL 33803-8365/813-665-1734

Zeiss Optical, Carl, 1015 Commerce St., Petersburg, VA 23803/804-861-0033, 800-388-2984; FAX: 804-733-4024

Zero Ammunition Co., Inc., 1601 22nd St. SE, P.O. Box 1188, Cullman, AL 35056-1188/800-545-9376; FAX: 205-739-4683

Zonie Bullets, 790 N. Lake Havasu Ave., Suite 26, Lake Havasu City, AZ 86403/520-680-6303; FAX: 520-680-6201

Zriny's Metal Targets (See Z's Metal Targets & Frames)

Zufall, Joseph F., P.O. Box 304, Golden, CO 80402-0304

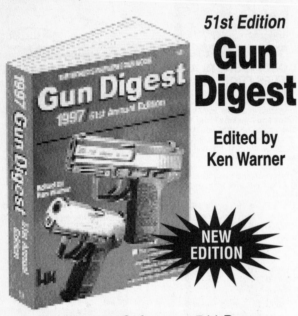